MACMILLAN ENCYCLOPEDIA of DEATH AND DYING

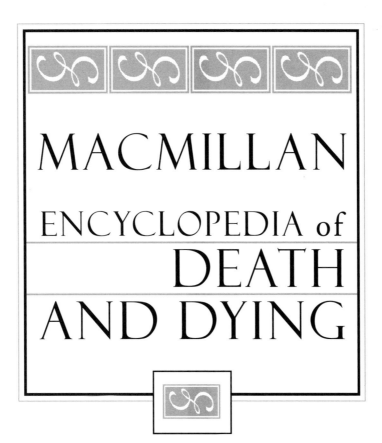

MACMILLAN ENCYCLOPEDIA of DEATH AND DYING

VOLUME 2

L-Z

ROBERT KASTENBAUM
Editor in Chief

MACMILLAN
REFERENCE
USA™

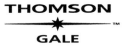

THOMSON
GALE

New York • Detroit • San Diego • San Francisco • Cleveland • New Haven, Conn. • Waterville, Maine • London • Munich

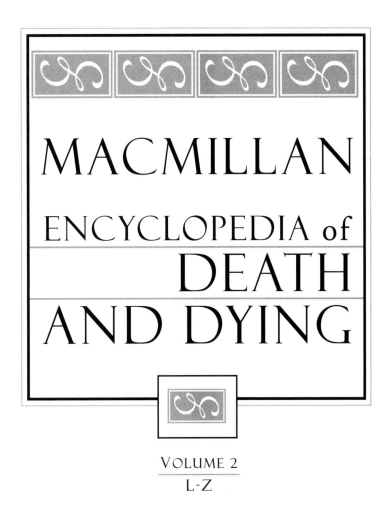

THOMSON
GALE™

Macmillan Encyclopedia of Death and Dying

Robert Kastenbaum

For more information, contact
Macmillan Reference USA
300 Park Avenue South, 9th Floor
New York, NY 10010
Or you can visit our Internet site at
http://www.gale.com

LIBRARY OF CONGRESS CATALOGING-IN-PUBLICATION DATA

Macmillan encyclopedia of death and dying / edited by Robert Kastenbaum.
p. cm.
Includes bibliographical references and index.
ISBN 0-02-865689-X (set : alk. paper) — ISBN 0-02-865690-3 (v. 1 : alk. paper) — ISBN 0-02-865691-1 (v. 2 : alk. paper)
1. Thanatology. 2. Death—Cross-cultural studies.
I. Kastenbaum, Robert.

HQ1073 .M33 2002
306.9—dc21
2002005809

Printed in the United States of America
10 9 8 7 6 5 4 3 2 1

L

Last Words

Last words have long been a subject of fascination for several reasons. The person about to die is sometimes regarded as having special access to the mysteries of death and afterlife, as well as to spirit visitors such as angels or ancestors. There have been many observations of people close to death apparently seeing and talking with a visitor invisible to others. Often, though, the last words in these interactions are not audible or intelligible to others.

The last words of the influential philosopher Georg Hegel (1770–1831) were eagerly awaited because he was regarded as one of the people most likely to have penetrating insights to offer. Hegel proved a disappointment in that regard. Instead of addressing cosmic issues, he complained about the fact that so few people really understood his writings and even fewer understood him as an individual. The expectation that last words will provide insight and enlightenment seems to be more frequently fulfilled in literature, drama, and cinema than in real-life circumstances.

Another common belief is that the dying person will speak the truth about difficult matters either because there is nothing to lose by doing so or because these disclosures will dissolve a burden of stress and guilt. An example is the Ku Klux Klan member who confessed on his deathbed that he had been responsible for church bombings that took place almost forty years prior to his death.

A related expectation is that people on the verge of death will either affirm or alter their guiding beliefs and values. American patriot Nathan Hale's words, "I regret that I have but one life to give for my country" as he awaited execution by the British for espionage, is a well-known example of affirmation. Reports of atheists or agnostics embracing religious faith in their last hours are examples of exchanging one set of beliefs for another on their deathbed. Many of the conversion reports have been fallacious. Naturalist Charles Darwin, for example, was rumored to have disavowed his theory of evolution in favor of traditional religious faith. This widely disseminated report served the interests of those who opposed the penetration of science into religious belief. It was soon discovered, however, that the "witness" had never seen Darwin on his deathbed or at any time near the end of his life.

Still another belief is that people will die "in charader," saying words that do not necessarily have universal significance but that are consistent with their individual personalities. For example, an adult daughter recalls that she tucked her dying father into bed and kissed him on the forehead before leaving the room. While performing these simple actions she was reminded of how her father had so often done the same for her in childhood: "I was embarrassed when I heard myself say, 'Sleep tight,' but he smiled and said, 'Don't let the bedbugs bite!'" Those were the last words anybody heard from him. The daughter's interpretation was that her father was being himself and saying his farewell in a way that affirmed the lifelong bonds of love between them.

A person's last words may also be treasured by family and friends even if there is nothing remarkable in their substance—these words will be remembered because they were the last. An eighteenth century French socialite's last words differed from the aged father's but were consistent with her personality. Madame Martel de Fontaine had long celebrated the pleasures of romantic love. She declared to her bedside companions, "My consolation at this hour: I am sure that somewhere in the world, someone is making love."

Diversity of Last Words

Diversity of last words is illustrated by the statements given above. Within this diversity, however, there are many examples of people trying to come to terms with their hopes, fears, and doubts at the last moment. Madame Martel de Fontaine celebrated the pleasures of romantic love that would continue to flourish although no longer for her. Today this would be considered a form of symbolic immortality that might serve to moderate the sorrow of separating from one's life on the earth. Voltaire, one of Madame de Fontaine's intimate friends, was on his deathbed in 1778 when flames flared up from the nearby oil lamp. Responding with his quick wit, the famed author and dramatist exclaimed, "What—the flames already?" Not a religious person, Voltaire deftly acknowledged the possibility of damnation while at the same time offering himself the saving grace of humor.

Increase Mather and his son Cotton were among the most illustrious people of Colonial New England. The father's passionate sermons affirmed Christian faith and inspired his congregation through difficult times. He was a pillar of strength and belief. When death was close, however, Mather did not express the same joyful anticipation he had demonstrated in the pulpit. Cotton saw his father suffer in "*Fear and Trembling,* lest he be *Deceived at the Last*" (Standard 1977, pp. 79–80). He was assailed by doubts: Despite all his good intentions and good works, perhaps he had allowed himself somehow to be deceived by the devil and was therefore on the verge of damnation rather than salvation. Mather's anxious final words seem to be at odds with his many public statements, but he doubted only his own personal fate, not his basic Christian faith. "Soul searching" is a familiar phrase that is especially apt for people who are keenly aware of their impending death and have issues of faith and doubt, and hope and fear, to resolve.

Most discussions of last words assume a mental state of clarity near the time of death. Dutch Schultz was one of the most vicious gangsters during the years when bootlegging liquor was a highly profitable criminal enterprise—even other professional gangsters considered him to be excessively wild and dangerous. Dying of bullet wounds, Schultz did not relate directly to his impending death but instead relived a variety of scenes in which he acted out bits of his everyday personality. His last words reflected this mental fragmentation: "Shut up, you got a big mouth! Henry, Max, come over here . . . French Canadian bean soup . . . I want to pay. Let them leave me alone." Schultz might have been struggling for resolution in his final moments, but the stresses and dysfunctions associated with the dying process can prevent the expression of coherent thoughts.

The distinction between coherent and incoherent statements is sometimes blurred, however. A person close to death might speak in a coded or symbolic manner, when meaning remains a matter of conjecture. One woman, for example, spoke of her cruise to Bermuda: "I have the tickets here some place, the tickets." She had been aware of her impending death, but also had occasionally surprised visitors with her talk of going on a long cruise. Were her last words confused, evasive—or a subtle way of speaking about her departure? An aged resident in a long-term care facility suddenly wanted to tell everybody about the need to dig an eighth grave. He died unexpectedly and only later was it discovered that he had been the only survivor among eight siblings. His seemingly confused statement now seemed to represent a sense of returning to the family circle and completing their stay on the earth.

The Importance of Last Words

The perceived significance of last words depends as much on cultural expectations as it does on individual circumstances. The final moment may be seen as that instant in which life and death both exercise their claims and, therefore, a parting message can have unique value. There is a tradition within Buddhist and Hindu belief systems in which a person approaching death is expected to offer a meaningful farewell statement. This tradition has been especially compelling for Zen masters whose students and friends await the final words of wisdom. For more than a thousand years it has been customary that Zen masters spontaneously compose and recite a poem with their last breath. These brief poems are seldom pious or sentimental, nor do they promise a heavenly reward. Most often these poems reflect on dying as part of nature's mysterious transformations. It is not unusual for the parting message to be flavored with tart humor and cautions against taking any system of belief too seriously. The idea of acceptance—both of life and death—is frequently paramount. For example, Zen scholar Sushila Blackman tells of a Zen master who was sitting in meditation with his students when he immediately said:

> I am at one with this and only this.
> You, my disciples,
> Uphold it firmly.
> Now I can breathe my last.
> And he did.
> *(Blackman 1997, p. 93)*

In Western culture the most fervent attention to last words has occurred within the tradition of deathbed salvation scenes. Here was the final opportunity to repent sins and affirm faith. It was a frightening prospect to die without the opportunity to give confession. By the same token, priests felt they had to make every possible effort to be with the dying person, even if it were a heretic, criminal, or inarticulate wretch. Governmental authorities also took this obligation seriously. In eighteenth century France, for example, physicians were required by law to see that a confessor was summoned when the patient was near death.

Although concern for the fate of the dying person's soul was paramount, there were other reasons for encouraging a dialogue. Perhaps the dying person had wronged somebody years ago and now could express regrets and ask for forgiveness. Similarly, perhaps the dying person could let go of his or her own anger and forgive somebody for a past injustice or disappointment.

Last words have also proved significant outside of religious considerations. Some people have waited until the last moment to reveal where the hidden financial assets can be found. Many others have shared personal memories with family or intimate friends. With his frail breath, an aged and emaciated man sang a favorite song along with his wife, strong enough only to mouth the words. A woman, exhausted after coping with her long illness, ordered her faithful niece to return to her own family: "They need you, too. Your life is with your own children." She lived another few days but had nothing more to say.

The opportunity for saying "goodbye" in one way or another is not available to all dying people. Making such communications difficult or impossible are circumstances such as social isolation, where the dying person is alone or seen only occasionally and by people who are not inclined to listen. Other situations that can make "goodbye" difficult include the individual's own communicational and/or cognitive deficits; pain that absorbs energy and attention, undermining the opportunity to interact; devices that interfere with communication (e.g., intubation); or an individual's drug-induced stupor or confusion.

These barriers to end-of-life communication are sometimes the result of inadequate management procedures (i.e., over or under medication or hospital staff who are not given enough time to be with their patients). There are no reliable data on the number of people who have a companion at the time of death and, therefore, somebody who might listen to the last words.

It is clear that last words can be of great importance to the person whose life will soon end. Suicide notes, for example, are often the final communication from a despondent and desperate person. Soldiers in Hitler's Sixth Army, abandoned deep in Russia and under punishing attack, knew that they were going to die soon as they wrote their *Last Letters From Stalingrad* (1961). These were messages of consolation to the wives, children, and parents whom they knew they would never see again. Both Confederate and Union soldiers in the U.S. Civil War also thought carefully about what they wrote in letters, as any could be their last.

Interest in last words can have positive and negative implications—positive because it might encourage continued contact with dying people, and negative because of an overemphasis on the final communication rather than sharing in the entire process.

See also: COMMUNICATION WITH THE DYING; GOOD DEATH, THE; IMMORTALITY, SYMBOLIC; IVAN ILYCH; MOMENT OF DEATH; SOCRATES

Bibliography

Blackman, Sushila, ed. *Graceful Exits: How Great Beings Die: Death Strories of Tibetan, Hindu, and Zen Masters.* New York: Weatherhill, 1997.

Boller, Paul F., Jr., and John George. *They Never Said It.* New York: Oxford University Press, 1989.

Enright, D. J., ed. *The Oxford Book of Death.* New York: Oxford University Press, 1987.

Kastenbaum, Robert. "Last Words." *The Monist: An International Quarterly Journal of General Philosophical Inquiry* 76 (1993):270–290.

Lockyer, Herbert. *Last Words of Saints and Sinners.* Grand Rapids, MI: Kregel, 1969.

Marshall, S. L. A., ed. *Last Letters from Stalingrad.* New York: The New American Library, 1961.

McManners, John. *Death and the Enlightenment.* New York: Oxford University Press, 1981.

Stannard, David E. *The Puritan Way of Death.* New York: Oxford University Press, 1977.

ROBERT KASTENBAUM

LAWN GARDEN CEMETERIES

In contrast to the graveyards that immigrants to North America initially created, the picturesque gardens early and mid-nineteenth century Americans fashioned provided a remarkable set of sites where citizens of means could bury their friends and find respite from the rush of daily life in a parklike setting. Yet, these rural cemeteries also quickly proved to be extremely expensive places for the dead and the living. As a consequence, not long after the opening of America's first rural cemetery in 1831, we find the materialization of a rather different kind of gravescape that sought to address the rising expenses of death and reflects an altogether different sensibility. Tracing the development of this new cemeterial environment thus reveals not only the outlines of a new cemeterial form, but also the appearance of a new way of looking at life and death.

Beginnings

Although signs of a new cemeterial sensibility began to appear in the United States as early as the middle of the nineteenth century, the development of a gravescape that fully reflected that sensibility came largely through the efforts of Adolph Strauch, the superintendent of Cincinnati's Spring Grove Cemetery. Just ten years earlier Spring Grove had been created as part of the wave of rural cemeteries that swept across America, but Americans of modest means quickly fostered the need for a less ornate, more frugal place for their loved ones. Originally, the plan to redesign Spring Grove appears to have been directed primarily at removing the ironwork and coping that even rural cemetery owners often described in derogatory terms. But in 1855 Strauch took the plan several steps beyond reformers' expectations.

After removing the copings and ironwork that defined individual plots, Strauch also eliminated burial mounds, hedges, stone fences, numerous trees, tombs, and gravestones, which growing numbers of citizens thought unnecessarily "break up the surface of the ground, cut it into unsymmetrical sections, destroy the effect of slopes and levels, and chop up what should be the broad and noble features of one great picture into a confused and crowded multitude of what seem like petty yards or pens" (Morris 1997, pp. 145–146). By redesigning through negation Strauch had reconceptualized places of the dead, which transformed the cemetery into a landscape "more spacious and parklike. It ceased to be a motley collection of every style, each enclosed in its own well-defined space, and became instead an integrated composition of lawn and clusters of trees" (Jackson 1972, pp. 70–71).

"Esthetic control"—the elimination of diversity in favor of homogeneity—came most distinctly in the form of rigid rules that the owners of Spring Grove Cemetery instituted to prohibit lot owners from altering their lots. Lot owners could still purchase a single monument to be erected in the center of each lot. But because the lots had been arranged symmetrically to make the most efficient use of the land and to simplify maintenance, the cemetery's owners maintained that small, ground-level markers were more than sufficient to say what needed to be said. Spring Grove's owners also encouraged lot owners to plant a single tree instead

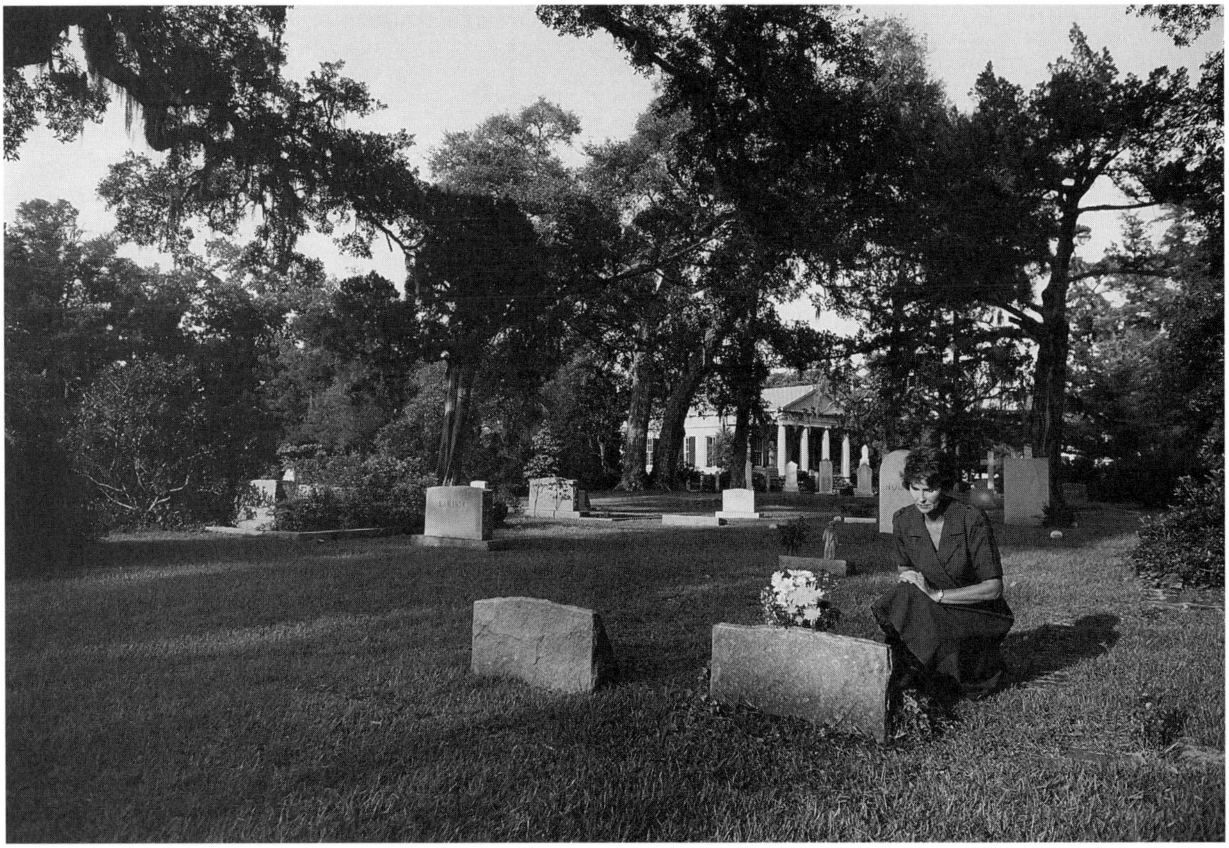

As one contemporary proponent of lawn cemeteries has remarked, Adolph Strauch "created what is known as the lawn cemetery; one in which the size and design and placement of the memorials are subject to esthetic control, and where all extraneous ornaments—railings, plantings, cemetery furniture—are forbidden in order to preserve an open and harmonious environment." PATRICK BENNETT/CORBIS

of erecting a memorial, and disallowed flower-beds and a host of other individualized efforts that had become hallmarks of rural cemeteries.

A New Kind of Death

Strauch's reconceptualization through redesign was a radical departure from the values of and sentiments expressed by cemeterial designs not only in the United States, but more globally, as advantages. First, it provided visitors with an open vista, unobstructed by fences, memorials, and trees, where signs of death and the dead find no quarter and where, at least ostensibly, an individual's societal station or place finds little expression. Second, it allowed cemetery superintendents to make the most efficient use of the land in the cemetery, thereby advancing the view that "individual rights must be subordinated to this general plan." "Civilization," according to Matthew Brazil, one of the lawn cemetery's early proponents, "consists in subordinating the will of the individual to the comfort and well-being of all" (Farrell 1980, p. 118). Third, by eliminating fences, hedges, trees, and other things associated with the rural cemetery, and by requiring markers to be small enough to be level or nearly level with the ground, proponents were able to eliminate nearly all things they associated with church graveyards and rural cemeteries. Together, as Sidney Hare, another early champion of this gravescape, remarked, these "improvements" allowed citizens to eliminate, albeit gradually, "all things that suggest death, sorrow, or pain" (Farrell 1980, p. 120).

Perhaps the strongest advantage to which proponents of this design could point, however, was that their new cemeterial form considerably lowered the cost of burial. When Mount Auburn, America's first rural cemetery, opened for public burials, for example a single lot of 300 square feet cost $60. By the time Adolph Strauch finished redesigning Spring Grove Cemetery in 1855, the price of a lot at Mount Auburn had increased to $150, and by 1883 lot prices ranged from $225 for an "unexceptional lot" to $750 for "choice lots" (Morris 1997, pp. 147–148). Add to this the cost of an elaborate memorial, creating a burial mound, landscaping the lot, an iron or stone enclosure, as well as the cost of the funeral, and the total was well beyond the modest means of most citizens.

By contrast, as late as 1875 the lot prices at Spring Grove ranged only from thirty to fifty cents per square foot—in equivalent terms, from $90 to $150 for a lot of 300 square feet. And, having eliminated elaborate memorials, grave mounds, enclosures of any kind, and the various other things that make burial in the rural cemetery extraordinarily expensive, survivors encountered few costs to add to the price of the funeral itself. As one vocal lawn cemetery advocate, F. B. Perkins, proudly told his readers in 1871, "it is a curious illustration of the power of habit over right reason, to see wealthy proprietors sinking a heavy granite coping around a lot, expending perhaps $2,500 or $3,000 for the sake of making the place look like a magnified city 'area,' and when placing a monument within it at a cost of say $2,000 more." A growing number of Americans were moving rapidly to the conclusion that the "mere statement of the contrast shows how incomparably superior in solemnity and impressiveness is the landscape lawn plan" (Morris 1997, p. 148).

Lawn cemeteries did not take the public mind by storm, as did the rural cemetery, but they did increase in number nearly as swiftly as rural cemeteries had; and in the years following the U.S. Civil War they became the most commonly created gravescape—a clear measure of the influence advocates of this gravescape were beginning to have at the national level. Instead of presenting viewers with markers to remind them of their need to prepare for death or with elaborate memorials nestled in sylvan scenes, as earlier gravescapes had sought to do, the modern lawn cemetery presents viewers with "a landscape more spacious and park-like" (Jackson 1972, p. 70) and with memorials that suggest very little in the way of artistic skill, particularity, or death.

Typically, when memorials consonant with this gravescape appear in other gravescapes, the lack of cemeterial restrictions result in memorials that are overtly expressive of sentiments compatible with the lawn cemetery's values. True to the mandates of the Strauch's design, however, cemeterial rules and regulations in lawn cemeteries require markers to be small and, in the vast majority of instances, flush with the ground. The size and position of the markers thus ensure not only that lot owners will be able to erect memorials in an environment that is clearly indicative of their values, but also that anyone who wishes to bury their friends and loved ones in this gravescape will have exceedingly little opportunity to alter or contradict the scene with incompatible sentiments.

In developing this gravescape cemetery, superintendents and owners successfully eliminated not only those things that rural cemetery owners acknowledged were excesses, but also those things lawn cemetery patrons regarded as excessive—especially efforts to particularize the gravescape, individual lots, or markers. Rather than allowing lot owners latitude to "beautify" the cemetery, cemetery owners and superintendents assumed all responsibility for cemeterial aesthetics. As a consequence, those few "works of art" that do appear in lawn cemeteries are selected and situated by others so that the will of the few may be subordinated to the comfort and well being of the many.

See also: CEMETERIES AND CEMETERY REFORM; CEMETERIES, WAR; FUNERAL INDUSTRY

Bibliography

Bergman, Edward F. *Woodlawn Remembers: Cemetery of American History.* Utica, NY: North Country Books, 1988.

Bigelow, Jacob. *A History of the Cemetery of Mount Auburn.* Boston: Munroe & Brothers, 1859.

Farmar, Alfred. "The Modern Cemetery: The Perpetual Care Lawn Plan." *Overland Monthly* 29 (1897):440–447.

Farrell, James J. *Inventing the American Way of Death.* Philadelphia: Temple University Press, 1980.

Jackson, John Brinckerhoff. *American Space: The Centennial Years, 1865–1876.* New York: W. W. Norton, 1972.

Morris, Richard. *Sinners, Lovers, and Heroes: An Essay on Memorializing in Three American Cultures.* Albany: SUNY Press, 1997.

Oring, Elliott. "Forest Lawn and the Iconography of American Death." *Southwest Folklore* 6 (1982):62–72.

Weed, Edward Evarts. *Modern Park Cemeteries.* Chicago: R. J. Haight, 1912.

RICHARD MORRIS

LAZARUS

Lazarus (in Greek, *Lazaros* or *Eleazaros,* meaning "God hath helped") is the name of a person in the New Testament of the Bible who was resurrected in one of Jesus' most spectacular miracles and certainly the most poignant one. According solely to the Gospel of John (John 11–12), when their brother Lazarus fell deathly ill, Mary and Martha of Bethany send for their friend Jesus. Four days later, upon his arrival, Jesus finds that Lazarus has already died. Weeping, the sisters insist that had Jesus been there, their brother would not have died. Jesus goes to the tomb where Lazarus is buried and weeps. Then he asks that the stone of the tomb be removed and cries: "Lazarus, come out!" The dead man comes out and is freed from his burial cloth. Soon thereafter, on the Saturday before Palm Sunday, Lazarus takes part in the banquet that Simon the Leper gives for Jesus in Bethany (John 12:1–11). No other mention of Lazarus is made in the Gospels. According to a tradition in the Orthodox Church, however, Lazarus later became Bishop of Cyprus.

Although enigmatic (experts do not know much of him before or after his resurrection), the figure of Lazarus is of paramount importance in Christianity. This miracle definitely established the "divinity" of Christ (only a God or a son of God could resurrect someone), which later is confirmed by Christ's own resurrection. Lazarus has since become a metaphor not only for resurrection but also for rebirth, recovery (e.g., the Lazarus Data Recovery company), and rehabilitation.

See also: JESUS; NECROMANCY; REINCARNATION

Bibliography

Broderick, Robert C., ed. *Catholic Encyclopedia.* Nashville: Thomas Nelson Incorporated, 1987.

JEAN-YVES BOUCHER

LESSONS FROM THE DYING

The major lesson for the living to learn from people facing the end of life is how growth can come through loss. Those who open up to these crises have much to teach.

People living with a life-threatening illness can encourage others to recognize their own priorities; to care about how they relate to others; to use time wisely; to say the simple words of apology and thanks and goodbye; to be honest about anger, protest, and negative feelings; and to recognize the releasing and positive elements of these feelings. Relationships may be healed, anger and resentments laid aside, and sources of meaning discovered together with a new sense of self. Those who are dying can teach others to hold on to hope and to cherish relaxation and creativity.

How do people learn these lessons? They will not do so unless they come close to those who are at the end of life. They will not do so unless they open themselves to true communication, not withdrawing behind often inappropriate activity. People learn when they involve themselves in competent and compassionate practice. They also learn by listening to the stories.

Perhaps the best lessons to be learned are from the patient whose last weeks of life in early 1948 proved to be the inspiration for the modern hospice and palliative care movement. David Tasma, a Polish Jew, died at the age of forty of malignant disease. He left a demanding heritage but full of potential for those who were to take up the challenge of his requests. His small legacy gave a start for St. Christopher's Hospice. In few powerful words, "I'll be a window in your home," he gave what became the founding principles of hospice. Reflection on this phrase grew into a commitment to openness, not only to all who would come for care but among those who would welcome them; openness to the outside and those who would come to learn; and, finally, openness to all future challenges.

Tasma challenged future learning and scientific study with his plea, "I only want what is in your mind and in your heart." Hearing David's appeal for comfort led researcher Cicely Saunders's mind and heart to learn about pain. A surgeon challenged her, "Go and read medicine. It is the doctors who desert the dying and there is so much more to be learned about pain. You'll only be frustrated if you don't do it properly and the doctors won't listen to you."

After medical training, and over the next seven years (1958–1965), Saunders studied hundreds of patients with end-stage malignant disease. Saunders recorded on tape their expressions of "total pain" with physical, emotional, social, and spiritual elements that make up the whole experience of overwhelming sensation. Their descriptions of such suffering and subsequent relief led to a researchable hypotheses: Regular, oral medication with opioids matched to individual need, constantly reviewed and supplemented with the control of other symptoms, would avoid both increasing doses of medication and drug dependence. Patients given space by freedom from the threat or presence of pain showed how fully they could use the chance to live the end of their lives with character and dignity.

This basic method, learning about pain from people in pain, is now being used around the world. There has been worldwide spread of effective and culturally sensitive ways to meet the needs caused by pain. The work has brought comfort and strength to countless numbers of those facing bereavement and the continual challenge of living on after profound loss. This lesson from those with terminal illness enhanced the humanistic aspect of the practice of medicine as well.

In *Experiment Perilous,* the sociologist Renée Fox illustrates the same theme of learning. She described how a group of doctors, researching the early use of steroids in a ward of mostly young men with various life-threatening conditions, came to terms with uncertainty. During the months of her study, Fox observed that in many ways the patients were the leading players. Like the doctors in this new field, they struggled with uncertainties, and their various ways of coping were remarkably similar. Working as a team led to positive outcomes on both sides.

These lessons illuminate living with and after loss. Worldwide, workers in bereavement support resonate to the same theme. They are not merely dealing with a long defeat of living, but are witnesses to a positive achievement of dying.

Another lesson is in the common theme of human dignity enhanced by the assurance of worth. This philosophy is summed up in the words, "You matter because you are you and you matter to the last moment of your life. We will do all we can not only to help you die peacefully, but to live until you die" (Saunders 1976, pp. 1003-1005). The message of Mother Teresa, the Buddhist hospices of Taiwan, and the palliative care teams of New York are one and the same as this, though their practice and resources are widely different. The end of life can be desperately unfair as health fades, relationships sour or are broken, and parting can be agonizing. Yet if there is honesty about the negative feelings and reactions, there can be a positive outcome.

Paula, a cancer patient still too young to be facing death, suddenly asked a night nurse what she believed was to come. On receiving a simple answer of faith, Paula said, "I can't say I believe now, not like that. Would it be all right if I just said I hoped?" As this was affirmed, she handed over the false eyelashes she had worn day and night, saying, "You can put them away. I won't need them anymore." The spiritual needs of the dying are not merely appropriate rituals of their religion but far wider, as relevant to atheists as to believers. Practical care needs can be met in an atmosphere that helps the dying find sources of meaning, search and question, be listened to with respect and, if asked, be answered with honesty, even when the answer can only be "I don't know."

A few patients maintain denial to the end. They heroically refuse to face defeat. But most of the dying exhibit how honesty is more creative than deception in human dealings with one another. A man having been told the truth of his approaching death said to his doctor, "Was it hard for you to tell me that?" And then, "Thank you, it is hard to be told but it is hard to tell too." It should be hard; the lesson here is that people must care what they do with their words. Words can hurt or heal; they can open or close exchange and development. People should care how the recipients of their words are affected by their delivery, whether the moment or manner was right. Nor must people forget that others need "time off" from difficult words and truths, which is not the same as denial. Discovering new talents, being creative, and celebrating are important elements in life's ending, as well as throughout it.

The important lesson is surely to recognize priorities and give them true space in one's thinking.

As the dying lose so much, the living see how people matter more than "things." Expressed in many ways, the search for self is a reminder of what will remain. As the English poet D. H. Lawrence wrote:

> There is nothing to save, now all is lost,
> But a tiny core of stillness in the heart
> Like the eye of a violet.
> *(Lawrence 1959, p. 117)*

People need to look at what really matters, what they will look to as they respond to the urge to move fast in the final crises. For many, it is still in the beliefs that have lasted throughout a lifetime. Many, too, have no religious language but turn to symbol or metaphor. They can be helped to find their own way by sensitive pastoral counseling. As one patient, finally managing the essential step of letting go, said to a sensitive nurse, "My hope is that it will lead me into peaceful waters, sailing on a calm sea. I have expended so much anger in the past and have longed to get rid of it. It seems that this tragedy has taken me on that path at last."

For the professional, the anger that is part of compassion can be a force for change. The movement for hospice and palliative care has spread around the world as a protest against pain and isolation in confidence that every person matters and that there is a better way.

The dying teach professional caregivers that all people need to be accepted. Every person needs to give as well as receive attention, concern, or love. The professional who is prepared to come close will see how ordinary people overcome adversity and make it the means for growth. There is no hierarchy among such achievements. Who is to say who has done best? Is it the young woman who fills a day center with creativity and a feeling of discovery for weeks on end, never showing how much it costs her? Or is it the old reprobate who manages to stop grumbling for his last few days? There is no place for idealizing each other or for denying that ill-led lives may also end badly.

Coming close to those who are at the end of life and opening up to true communication leads to learning and rewards. The dying teach their caregivers to look at their own needs and the priorities of life—and to never forget that time off and recreation are essential to continuing this particularly taxing work. Hope can rise up in the most adverse circumstances. It is not what death does to the deceased that their loved ones remember, but rather how the dying challenged those living to look at their thoughts about death and respond to life's challenges.

See also: GOOD DEATH, THE; HOSPICE OPTION; SAUNDERS, CICELY

Bibliography

Fox, Renée. *Experiment Perilous.* Glencoe, IL: The Free Press, 1959.

Hammarskjold, Dag. *Markings.* London: Faber and Faber, 1964.

Hinton, James. *Dying.* Middlesex, England: Penguin Books, 1967.

Lawrence, D. H. *Selected Poems.* New York: Viking Press, 1959.

Saunders, Cicely. "Care of the Dying: The Problem of Euthanasia." *Nursing Times* 72, no. 26 (1976):1003–1005.

Saunders, Cicely. *The Care of the Dying.* London: Macmillan, 1959.

Tolstoy, Leo. *The Death of Ivan Illych.* 1886. Reprint, Oxford: Oxford University Press, 1959.

CICELY SAUNDERS

LIFE EVENTS

The product of stress and coping research is the concept of a life event which refers to changes in an individual's life that are likely to have an impact on subsequent behavior. Such major changes can be either negative, such as death of a close family member, or positive, such as marriage. In addition to important life events, there are small life events—"hassles" or "uplifts." For example a hassle might be having too many things to do; an uplift might be meeting a good friend.

A person's life events have been measured frequently by using lists of events that the person has to check. Methodological problems (e.g., unwillingness to report very private problems) have prompted the development of clinical interviews.

Models

Life events have been incorporated into theoretical models designed to explain coping. A well-known example is a model of coping formulated by the stress researcher R. S. Lazarus, which emphasizes the cognitive evaluation of the event. This evaluation includes the personal relevance of the event, its potential to affect well-being (primary appraisal), and the evaluation of the options one can use for coping (secondary appraisal). A means of analyzing coping processes, this evaluation leads to either favorable or unfavorable resolution (or no resolution) and, possibly, to reappraisal, when there is a change in circumstances. The model was applied to a variety of stressors, including bereavement.

Life Events in a Life Span Perspective

Lazarus's approach was also used to develop a life span. Such a model considers life events in their life-stage or sociohistorical context. Death of a spouse, for example, may have a devastating effect at age thirty-five than at eighty-five. The change in the meaning of a life event, according to its position in the life span, has prompted the gerontologist B. L. Neugarten to distinguish between "on time" and "off time" events.

The life span perspective has encouraged a consideration of life events within the general concept of a life story. Individuals create comprehensive life stories. The life story is recreated and revised in an effort to provide life "with a sense of unity and purpose" (McAdams 1992, p. 344). According to the life-span psychologist D. P. McAdams, particular life events—"nuclear episodes"—show either continuity or change over time. In addition to their conceptualization within a life story, life events can be considered in relation to one's identity. Thus, life-span psychologist S. K. Whitbourne describes experienced events as being either assimilated into one's identity or accommodated by changing to fit the event. An individual who uses assimilation frequently might deny the significance of an age-related sign or a life-threatening disorder. An "accommodative" type, on the other hand, might overreact to such signs, perceiving himself or herself as an old person.

Death As a Life Event

Is death a life event? Obviously any biography of a deceased person would include death along with other events. The death of a person can also be a life event in another person's life, as in the case of death of a close relative. It is less clear whether one's own death is a life event. For example, while one's own death indicates a major change in life, one cannot cope with this change if we consider death to be the disappearance of the subject (of course one can still try to cope with his or her own dying).

The German philosopher Martin Heidegger (1889–1976), in his famous analysis of death in *Being and Time,* originally published in 1927, indicates that death is not an event but rather an existential phenomenon. For the subject, death exists at all times as a possibility, the possibility of the subject's inexistence. While the individual does not have to deal with his or her death as a lived life event, he or she still has to deal with it as a matter of concern for oneself. For Heidegger the relationship to death is founded in the general structure of the human being (*Dasein*) as a being that is concerned about itself. Heidegger calls this basic state of the being care and writes, "With regards to its ontological possibilities, dying is grounded in care" (p. 233). Heidegger saw death as a possibility of being that provides both individuality (no one can die in my place) and wholeness (my life exists as a totality only upon my dying). Therefore, the right attitude toward death is one of anticipation.

Among the major critics of Heidegger's construction of death, French philosopher Jean-Paul Sartre argued powerfully that death, far from giving meaning to life, deprives life of meaning. Therefore, according to Sartre, one cannot "await" his or her death. In fact, because meaning can exist only insofar as there is a future toward which one can project oneself, death deprives such an anticipation of its very meaning.

Such analyses raise the following question: Is there a correct description of "my death"? It is indeed possible to argue that no description is correct and that we are free to construct death as part of the process of creating a life story. In any case, it is likely that the way one constructs death will affect an individual's emotional attitudes toward it and toward life.

Avoiding Death

Negatively constructing death may increase the need to use protective defenses; for example, one simply might want to avoid thinking about the event. Denial as a defense mechanism might be particularly suitable when facing the end of one's life, either because of illness or because of the actions of other people (e.g., prisoners in concentration camps). In less extreme situations, individuals are likely to use more subtle forms of denial. In *The Denial of Death* (1973), anthropologist Ernest Becker discusses ways to avoid coming to grips with the reality of one's mortality by integrating in a cultural system. Both Becker and terror-management theorists see self-esteem as an important psychological part of the "buffering mechanism." In essence, one who feels good about fulfilling a role in society thinks of herself as valuable and, perhaps, immortal.

Acceptance of Death

People differ in the way they construct death. Those who view death as threatening tend to distance themselves from it. On the other hand, death can be constructed as in a way that reflects acceptance. A distinction can be made between three types of acceptance. Escape acceptance sees death as a better alternative to a very low quality life; neutral acceptance sees death as integral to life; and approach acceptance sees death as the gate to a happy afterlife. The acceptance of death among older people prompted Wong to include a spiritual dimension of meaning (involving death acceptance) in a definition of successful aging.

A congruent notion, the socioemotional selectivity theory, attempts to define perceptual changes that accompany a growing awareness of the finite nature of time, most notably paying increased attention to meaning of things, quality of relationships, positive aspects of existence, and the importance of goals. People develop a sense of appreciation of a finite life as opposed to a sense of entitlement to an infinite one. These ideas are germane to a large literature suggesting that confrontation of death and finitude may promote a sense of urgency and help one to live more fully.

Meaning Reconstruction in Grief

As pointed out by death and grief researcher Robert Neimeyer, "Meaning reconstruction in response to a loss is the central process in grieving." A central task for a theory of bereavement is therefore to specify how loss affects meaning and the restoration of meaning. For example, it is possible to distinguish between two types of meaning: meaning as making sense of the loss, and meaning as finding some benefits in the aftermath of the loss. The first might relate to the task of rebuilding a threatened worldview while the second focuses on the self.

The potential success of meaning reconstruction is evident in the frequency with which positive emotions follow a great loss. The reconstruction of meaning may bring about a reappraisal of bereavement. To account for such a reconstruction, Folkman revised the original Lazarus-Folkman model by adding meaning-based coping processes that are distinct from the ones that regulate distress and that promote positive emotions.

Conclusion

In the early twenty-first century, while substantial numbers of people die early, death occurs mostly in old age in developed countries. Nevertheless, both one's own death and the death of a person close to him or her, even when expected, can seriously affect his or her system of beliefs and sense of meaning. Acceptance of death requires the active construction of meaning throughout the life span.

See also: ANXIETY AND FEAR; BECKER, ERNEST; PSYCHOLOGY

Bibliography

Aspinwall, L. G., and S. E. Taylor. "A Stitch in Time: Self-Regulation and Proactive Coping." *Psychological Bulletin* 121 (1997):417–436.

Becker, Ernest. *The Denial of Death*. New York: Free Press, 1973.

Carstensen, L. L., D. M. Isaacowitz, and S. T. Charles. "Taking Time Seriously: A Theory of Socioemotional Selectivity." *American Psychologist* 54 (1999):165–181.

Frankl, Viktor E. *Psychotherapy and Existentialism*. New York: Simon & Schuster, 1967.

Greenberg, J., T. Pyszczynski, and S. Solomon. "The Causes and Consequences of the Need for Self-Esteem: A Terror Management Analysis." In R. F. Baumeister ed., *Public Self and Private Self*. New York: Springer, 1986.

Heidegger, Martin. *Being and Time,* translated by Joan Stambaugh. Albany: SUNY Press, 1996

Hultsch, D. F., and J. K. Plemons. "Life Events and Life-Span Development." In P. B. Baltes and O. G. Brim Jr. eds., *Life-Span Development and Behavior,* Vol. 2. New York: Academic Press, 1979.

Janoff-Bullman, R., and C. Timko. "Coping with Traumatic Life Events." In C. R. Snyder and C. E. Ford eds., *Coping with Negative Life Events*. New York: Plenum Press, 1987.

Kelly, G. A. *The Psychology of Personal Constructs*. New York: Norton, 1955.

Lazarus, R. S., and S. Folkman. *Stress, Appraisal, and Coping*. New York: Springer, 1984.

McAdams, D. P. "Unity and Purpose in Human Lives: The Emergence of Identity As a Life Story." In R. A. Zucker, A. I Rabin, J. Aronoff, and S. J. Frank eds., *Personality Structure in the Life Course*. New York: Springer, 1992.

Neimeyer, Robert A., ed. *Meaning Reconstruction & the Experience of Loss*. Washington, DC: American Psychological Association, 2001.

Neimeyer, Robert A. ed. *Death Anxiety Handbook*. Washington, DC: Taylor & Francis, 1994.

Neugarten, B. L. *Personality in Middle and Late Life*, 2nd edition. New York: Atherton Press, 1968.

Sartre, Jean-Paul. *Being and Nothingness: An Essay on Phenomenological Ontology*, translated by Hazel E. Barnes. New York: Philosophical Library, 1956.

Stroebe, Margaret S., R. O. Hansson, Wolfgang Stroebe, and Henk Schut eds. *Handbook of Bereavement Research*. Washington, DC: American Psychological Association, 2001.

Whitbourne, S. K. "Personality Development in Adulthood and Old Age: Relationships among Identity Style, Health, and Well-Being." In K. W. Schaie and C. Eisdorfer eds., *Annual Review of Gerontology and Geriatrics*, Vol. 7. New York: Springer, 1987.

Wong, P. T. P. "Meaning of Life and Meaning of Death in Successful Aging." In Adrian Tomer ed., *Death Attitudes and the Older Adult*. Philadelphia: Taylor & Francis, 2000.

ADRIAN TOMER

LIFE EXPECTANCY

Life expectancy refers to the number of years that people in a given country or population can expect to live. Conceptually, life expectancy and longevity are identical; the difference between them lies in measurement issues. Life expectancy is calculated in a very precise manner, using what social scientists call "life table analysis." Longevity is not associated with any particular statistical technique. Both life expectancy and longevity are distinct from life span, which refers to the number of years that humans could live under ideal conditions. While life expectancy is based on existing data, life span is speculative. Partly because of its speculative nature, there is considerable debate about the possible length of the human life span. Some social scientists argue that Western populations are approaching a biologically fixed maximum, or finite life span, probably in the range of 85 to 100 years. Others believe that the human life span can be extended by many more years, due to advances in molecular medicine or dietary improvements, for example. An intermediate position is taken by other researchers, who suggest that there is no rigid limit to the human life span and as-yet-unforeseen biomedical technological breakthroughs could gradually increase life span.

A considerable amount of research, based on the foundational assumption of a finite human life span, has focussed on the concept of dependency-free life expectancy (also called dependence-free life expectancy, healthy life expectancy, active life expectancy, disability-free life expectancy, and functional life expectancy). These varying terms refer to the number of years that people in a given population can expect to live in reasonably good health, with no or only minor disabling health conditions. Most of the research on dependency-free life expectancy tests, in varying ways, the validity of the compression of morbidity hypothesis, originally formulated by the researcher James F. Fries in 1983. This hypothesis states that, at least among Western populations, proportionately more people are able to postpone the age of onset of chronic disability; hence, the period of time between onset of becoming seriously ill or disabled and dying is shortening or compressing. Research findings on morbidity compression are variously supportive, negative, and mixed.

The Measurement of Life Expectancy

Life expectancy is a summary measure of mortality in a population. Statistics on life expectancy are derived from a mathematical model known as a life table. Life tables create a hypothetical cohort (or group) of 100,000 persons (usually of males and females separately) and subject it to the age-sex-specific mortality rates (the number of deaths per

1,000 or 10,000 or 100,000 persons of a given age and sex) observed in a given population. In doing this, researchers can trace how the 100,000 hypothetical persons (called a synthetic cohort) would shrink in numbers due to deaths as they age. The average age at which these persons are likely to have died is the life expectancy at birth. Life tables also provide data on life expectancy at other ages; the most commonly used statistic other than life expectancy at birth is life expectancy at age sixty-five, that is, the number of remaining years of life that persons aged sixty-five can expect to live.

Life expectancy statistics are very useful as summary measures of mortality, and they have an intuitive appeal that other measures of mortality, such as rates, lack. However, it is important to interpret data on life expectancy correctly. If it reported that life expectancy at birth in a given population is 75 years in 2000, this does not mean that all members of the population can expect to live to the age of 75. Rather, it means that babies born in that population in 2000 would have a life expectancy at birth of 75 years, if they live their lives subject to the age-specific mortality rates of the entire population in 2000. This is not likely; as they age, age-specific mortality rates will almost certainly change in some ways. Also, older people in that population will have lived their life up to the year 2000 under a different set of age-specific mortality rates. Thus, it is important to be aware of the hypothetical nature of life expectancy statistics.

Life tables require accurate data on deaths (by age and sex) and on the population (by age and sex); many countries lack that basic data and their life expectancy statistics are estimates only. However, age-specific mortality tends to be very predictable; thus, if the overall level of mortality in a population is known, it is possible to construct quite reasonable estimates of life expectancy using what are called model life tables.

Life Expectancy at Birth, Circa 2001

Life expectancy at birth for the world's population at the turn of the twenty-first century was 67 years, with females having a four-year advantage (69 years) over males (65 years); see Table 1. As expected, developed countries experience substantially higher life expectancy than less developed countries—75 years and 64 years, respectively.

TABLE 1

Life expectancy at birth by world region, 2001

Area	Total	Males	Females
World	67	65	69
Developed countries	75	72	79
Less developed countries	64	63	66
Africa	54	52	55
Asia	67	65	68
Asia (excluding China)	64	63	66
Latin America (and Caribbean)	71	68	74
Europe	74	70	78
North America (U.S. and Canada)	77	74	80

SOURCE: Population Reference Bureau. *2001 World Population Data Sheet.* Washington, DC: Population Reference Bureau, 2001.

Also, the gender difference in life expectancy that favors females is larger in the developed countries (seven years) than in the less developed parts of the world (three years). Regionally, North America (the United States and Canada) has the highest life expectancy overall, and for males and females separately. It might be expected that Europe would have this distinction and, indeed, there are a number of European countries with life expectancies higher than in North America; for example, the Scandinavian countries and the nations of Western Europe. However, the European average is pulled down by Russia; in 2001, this large country of 144 million people has a male life expectancy at birth of only 59 years and a female life expectancy at birth of 72 years. Male life expectancy in Russia declined over the last decades of the twentieth century, and shows no indication of improvement. A considerable amount of research has focused on the trend of increasing mortality (and concomitant decreasing life expectancy) among Russian men, pointing to a number of contributing factors: increased poverty since the fall of communism, which leads to malnutrition, especially among older people, and increases susceptibility to infectious diseases; unhealthy lifestyle behaviors, including heavy drinking and smoking, sedentary living, and high-fat diets; psychological stress, combined with heavy alcohol consumption, leading to suicide; and a deteriorating health care system.

With the exception of Russia (and Eastern Europe more generally), life expectancy at birth does not vary much within European and North American populations. However, the less developed countries have considerably more range in mortality, as measured by life expectancy at birth. This can be seen in Table 1, which shows a range in life expectancy at birth among females from 55 in Africa to 74 in Latin America. It is clear that Africa lags behind the rest of the world in achieving improvements in life expectancy. However, even within Africa, large differences in life expectancy exist. Life expectancy at birth (both sexes combined) statistics range from the low seventies (in Mauritius (71), Tunisia (72) and Libya (75)) to the low forties (in Swaziland and Zimbabwe (both 40), Niger and Botswana (both 41)) with one country—Rwanda—having an estimated life expectancy at birth of only 39 years.

Life Expectancy at Birth in African Countries: The Role of HIV/AIDS

The HIV/AIDS (human immunodeficiency virus/acquired immunodeficiency syndrome) epidemic has, thus far, hit hardest in parts of Africa, especially sub-Saharan Africa, which contains approximately 70 percent of the world's population with HIV/AIDS. Many of the African countries with the lowest life expectancies have the highest rates of HIV/AIDS infection. However, this is not always the case; for example, Niger and Rwanda, mentioned above as countries with very low life expectancies, do not have high rates of HIV/AIDS in their populations. Thus, AIDS cannot solely account for low life expectancy in Africa; social and political upheaval, poverty, and the high risk of death due to other infectious (and parasitic) diseases cannot be discounted in the African case. Nevertheless, HIV/AIDS does have a devastating impact on life expectancy in many places in Africa. The United Nations projects that by 2050 the effect of the AIDS epidemic will be to keep life expectancy at birth low in many sub-Saharan African countries, perhaps even lower than that experienced in the latter part of the twentieth century. Figure 1 shows two projected life expectancy at birth statistics for seven sub-Saharan African countries, one based on the assumption that HIV/AIDS continues to claim lives prematurely, and the other based on the optimistic assumption that HIV/AIDS was to disappear immediately. The effect of HIV/AIDS is to keep life expectancy in 2050 at levels well under 50; in the absence of the pandemic, life expectancy at birth would improve to the 65 to 70 year range. The projections based on the continuation of HIV/AIDS mark a sad departure for the demographers who make them. Until the 1990s, projections were based on a taken-for-granted assumption that life expectancy would gradually improve. And, for the most part, subsequent mortality trends backed up that assumption.

Trends in Life Expectancy at Birth in Developed Countries

In the developed countries, the fragmentary data that are available suggest that life expectancy at birth was around 35 to 40 years in the mid-1700s, that it rose to about 45 to 50 by the mid-1800s, and that rapid improvements began at the end of the nineteenth century, so that by the middle of the twentieth century it was approximately 66 to 67 years. Since 1950 gains in life expectancy have been smaller, approximately eight more years have been added (see Table 2).

The major factors accounting for increasing life expectancy, especially in the period of rapid improvement, were better nutrition and hygiene practices (both private and public), as well as enhanced knowledge of public health measures. These advances were particularly important in lowering infant mortality; when mortality is not controlled, the risk of death is high among infants and young children (and their mothers), and the major cause of death is infectious diseases (which are better fought off by well-fed infants and children). Being that a large proportion of deaths occurs to infants and young children, their improved longevity plays a key role in increasing life expectancy at birth. The period from the late 1800s to 1950 in the West, then, saw significant improvement in the mortality of infants and children (and their mothers); it was reductions in their mortality that led to the largest increases in life expectancy ever experienced in developed countries. It is noteworthy that medical advances, save for smallpox vaccination, played a relatively small role in reducing infant and childhood mortality and increasing life expectancy.

Since the middle of the twentieth century, gains in life expectancy have been due more to

FIGURE 1

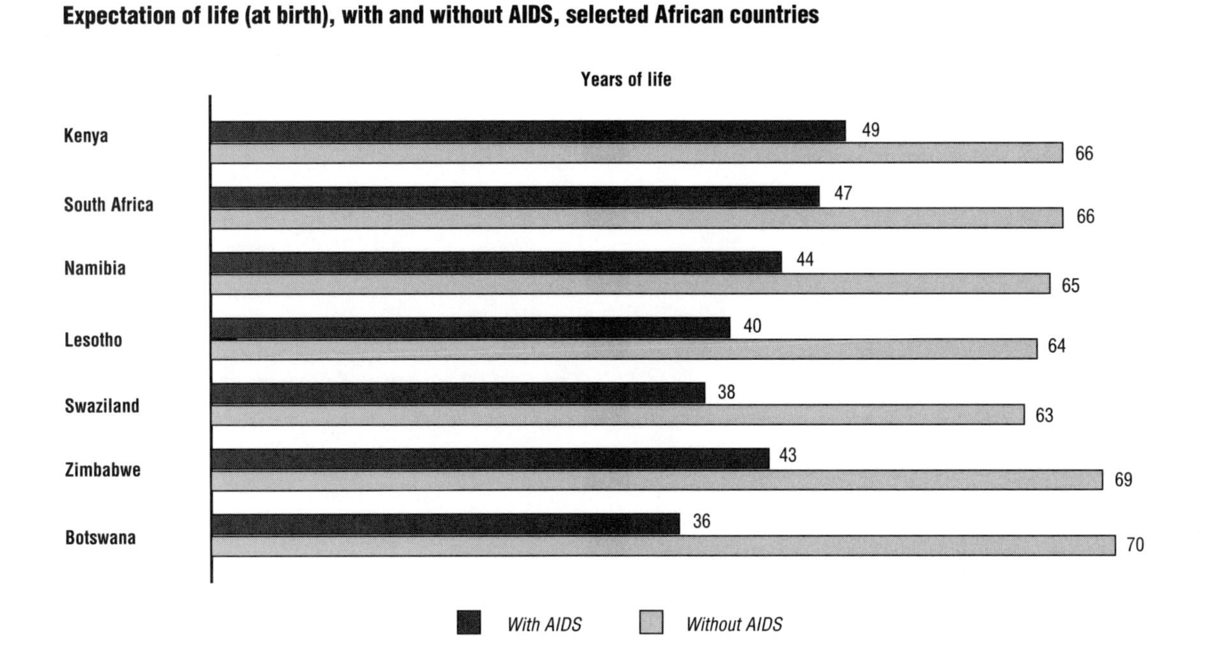

SOURCE: United Nations. *World Population Prospects: The 2000 Revision*. New York: United Nations, 2001.

medical factors that have reduced mortality among older persons. These reductions are harder to achieve than decreases in infant mortality; hence, improvements in life expectancy at birth have slowed down. However, reductions in deaths due to cardiovascular disease, cancer (at least for some kinds), and cerebrovascular disease (strokes)—the three major takers-of-life in developed countries—as well as in other types of chronic and degenerative disease have gradually taken place, and life expectancy continues to improve. Nevertheless, looking at the twentieth century as a whole, reductions in mortality among younger persons played the major role in increasing life expectancy at birth; for example, 58 percent of the gain in American life expectancy over the century was due to mortality reductions among persons aged under 20 and a further 17 percent can be accounted for by reductions among the age group 20 to 39.

TABLE 2

Life expectancy at birth by world region, 1950–2000

Area	Years					
	1950 –1955	1960 –1965	1970 –1975	1980 –1985	1990 –1995	1995 –2000
World	46	52	58	61	64	66
Developed Countries	67	70	71	73	74	74
Less Developed Countries	41	48	55	59	62	64
Africa	38	42	46	49	53	54
Asia	41	48	56	60	65	66
Latin America (and Caribbean)	51	57	61	65	69	70
Europe	66	70	71	72	73	73
North America (U.S. and Canada)	69	70	72	75	76	77

SOURCE: Yaukey, David, and Douglas L. Anderton. *Demography: The Study of Human Population*. Prospect Heights, IL: Waveland, 2001.

Trends in Life Expectancy in Less Developed Countries

Very little improvement in life expectancy at birth had occurred in the third world by the middle of the twentieth century. Unlike the developed countries, which had a life expectancy at birth of 67 years at that time, the third world's life expectancy approximated 41 years—a difference of 26 years. However, after the end of World War II, life expectancy in the developing countries began to increase very rapidly. For example, between 1950 and 1970, life expectancy at birth improved by 14 years (see Table 2). Mortality decline was faster than in the West during its period of most rapid decline, and it was much faster than in the West over the second half of the twentieth century. By the end of the century, the 26-year difference had been reduced to 10 years (although Africa lags behind the rest of the developing world).

The rapid improvement in life expectancy at birth in the third world occurred for different reasons than in the West. In the West, mortality declined paralleled socioeconomic development. In contrast, in the developing countries, mortality reductions were, in large part, due to the borrowing of Western death-control technology and public health measures. This in part was the result of the post-cold-war that saw the United States and other Western countries assist nonaligned countries with public health and mortality control in order to win their political allegiance. Whatever the political motives, the result was very successful. As in the West, life expectancy at birth was initially improved by controlling the infectious diseases to which infants and children are particularly susceptible and was accomplished by improvements in diet, sanitation, and public health. In addition, the third world was able to benefit from Western technology, such as pesticides, which played a major role in killing the mosquitoes that cause malaria, a leading cause of death in many countries. This exogenously caused reduction in mortality led to very rapid rates of population growth in most third world countries, creating what became known as the "population bomb." It also left these poor countries without a basic health (and public health) infrastructure, making them vulnerable to the effects of cutbacks in aid from foreign (Western) governments and foundations. It is in such a context that many third world countries (especially in sub-Saharan Africa but also in Southeast Asia and the Caribbean) are attempting to deal with the HIV/AIDS crisis, as well as a number of infectious diseases that were believed to have been conquered but have resurfaced through mutations.

It is difficult to predict if life expectancy differences at birth between the more and less developed countries will continue to converge. On the one hand, further increases in life expectancy in the West will be slow, resulting from improvements in the treatment and management of chronic diseases among older people. Theoretically, it would be expected that the third world could, thus, continue to catch up with West. However, new infectious diseases such as HIVS/AIDS and the re-emergence of "old" infectious diseases, sometimes in more virulent or antibiotic resistant forms, are attacking many third world countries that lack the resources to cope.

Differentials in Life Expectancy at Birth

Within populations, differences in life expectancy exist; that is, with regard to gender. Females tend to outlive males in all populations, and have lower mortality rates at all ages, starting from infancy. However, the degree to which females outlive males varies; as seen in Table 1, the difference is around three years in the less developed countries and approximately seven years in developed countries.

Another difference in life expectancy lies in social class, as assessed through occupation, income, or education. This research tends to deal with life expectancy among adults, rather than at birth. The earliest work on occupational differences was done in England using 1951 data; in 1969 the researcher Bernard Benjamin, grouping occupations into five classes, found that mortality was 18 percent higher than average in the lowest class, and 2 percent lower than average in the highest class. In the United States in 1973, Evelyn Kitagawa and Philip Hauser, using 1960 data, found that both higher education and higher income were independently associated with longer life expectancy, that is, having both high income and high education was more advantageous than just having one or the other. This was later replicated by researchers in 1993, with the additional finding that the socioeconomic difference was widening over time.

Data on social class differences in life expectancy are difficult to obtain, even in highly developed countries. A 1999 study by Tapani Valkonen contains exceptionally good data on occupational differences in life expectancy in Finland. Figure 2 shows life expectancy at age 35 for four classes of workers, by gender, for the period of 1971 to 1996. While this figure indicates that life expectancy differences by occupation show a female advantage for all occupations and that male longevity differentials are much bigger than female ones, the most important information conveyed for the purposes here is that the occupational gap in

FIGURE 2

Life expectancy at the age of 35 by occupation class, men and women, Finland 1971–1995

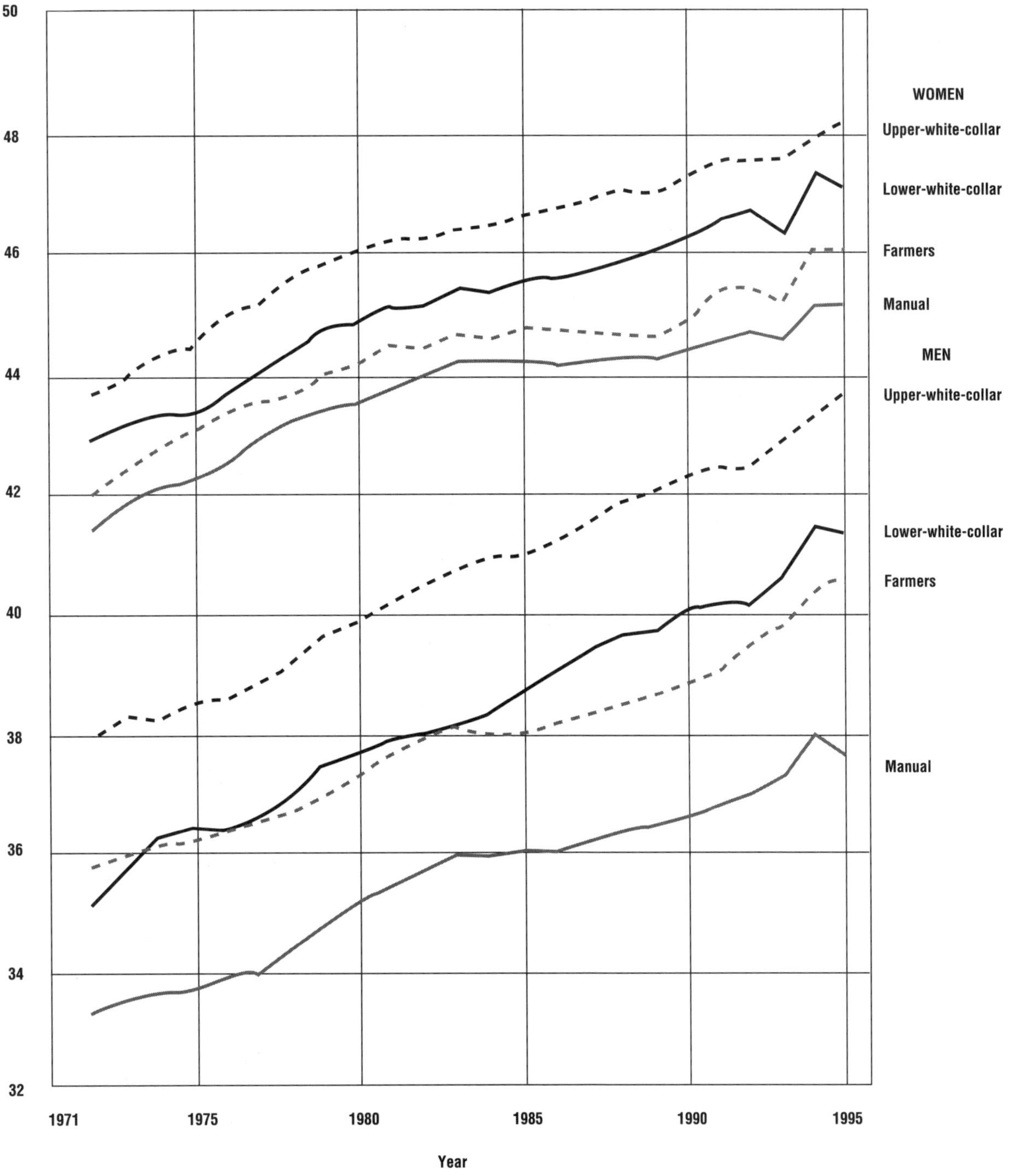

SOURCE: Valkonen, Tapani. "The Widening Differentials in Adult Mortality by Socio-Economic Status and Their Causes." In *Health and Mortality Issues of Global Concern*. New York: United Nations, 1991.

life expectancy increased over the period. This finding concurs with that for the United States.

It is not clear why socioeconomic differences in adult life expectancy are growing in Western populations. The major cause of death responsible for the widening differential is cardiovascular disease; persons of higher social classes have experienced much larger declines in death due to cardiovascular disease than persons of lower classes. It is possible that the widening is only temporary, the result of earlier declines in cardiovascular mortality among higher socioeconomic groups. Or, it may be that the widening reflects increasing polarization in health status and living conditions within Western populations. It does not appear that differences in access to health care are responsible, seeing as the trend appears in countries that both have and do not have national medical/health insurance.

Another difference in life expectancy relates to race/ethnicity. For example, in the United States, the expectation of life at birth for whites is six years higher than for African Americans. However, the difference in life expectancy at age sixty-five is less than two years. The narrowing gap with age suggests that mortality associated with younger age groups is an important factor; this inference is reinforced by high rates of homicide among African Americans, especially young males. Ethnic differences in mortality are not unique to the United States. Among countries with reliable data, it is known that the Parsis in India and the Jews in Israel have lower mortality than other ethnic groups; they share, along with whites in the United States, a place of privilege in the socioeconomic order.

See also: AIDS; CAUSES OF DEATH; PUBLIC HEALTH

Bibliography

Benjamin, Bernard. *Demographic Analysis.* New York: Praeger, 1969.

Brooks, Jeffrey D. "Living Longer and Improving Health: An Obtainable Goal in Promoting Aging Well." *American Behavioral Scientist* 39 (1996):272–287.

Coale, Ansley J., Paul Demeny, and Barbara Vaughan. *Regional Model Life Tables and Stable Populations.* New York: Academic Press, 1983.

Cockerham, William C. "The Social Determinants of the Decline in Life Expectancy in Russia and Eastern Europe: A Lifestyle Explanation." *Journal of Health and Social Behavior* 38 (1997):117–130.

Crimmins, Eileen M. "Are Americans Healthier As Well As Longer-Lived?" *Journal of Insurance Medicine* 22 (1990):89–92.

Ehrich, Paul R. *The Population Bomb.* New York: Ballantine, 1969.

Fries, James F. "Compression of Morbidity: Life Span, Disability, and Health Care Costs." In Bruno J. Vellas, Jean-Louis Albarede, and P. J. Garry eds., *Facts and Research in Gerontology,* Vol. 7. New York: Springer, 1993.

Fries, James F. "Compression of Morbidity." *Milbank Memorial Fund Quarterly* 61 (1983):397–419.

Guyer, Bernard, et al. "Annual Summary of Vital Statistics: Trends in the Health of Americans during the 20th Century." *Pediatrics* 106 (2000):1307–1318.

Hayward, Mark D., et al. "Cause of Death and Active Life Expectancy in the Older Population of the United States." *Journal of Aging and Health* 10 (1998):192–213.

Kaplan, George A. "Epidemiologic Observations on the Compression of Morbidity: Evidence from the Alameda County Study." *Journal of Aging and Health* 3 (1991):155–171.

Kitagawa, Evelyn M., and Philip M. Hauser. *Differential Mortality in the United States: A Study in Socio-Economic Epidemiology.* Cambridge, MA: Harvard University Press, 1973.

Manton, Kenneth G., and Kenneth C. Land. "Active Life Expectancy Estimates for the U.S. Elderly Population: A Multidimensional Continuous Mixture Model of Functional Change Applied to Completed Cohorts, 1982–1996." *Demography* 37 (2000):253–265.

Manton, Kenneth G., Eric Stallard, and Larry Corder. "The Limits of Longevity and Their Implications for Health and Mortality in Developed Countries." In *Health and Mortality Issues of Global Concern.* New York: United Nations, 1999.

Matoso, Gary. "Russian Roulette." *Modern Maturity* 37, no. 5 (1994):22–28.

McKeown, Thomas. *The Modern Rise of Population.* London: Edward Arnold, 1976.

National Center for Health Statistics. *Health, United States, 2000.* Hyattsville, MD: Author, 2000.

National Institute on Aging. *In Search of the Secrets of Aging.* Bethesda, MD: National Institutes of Health, 1996.

Pappas, Gregory, et al. "The Increasing Disparity in Mortality between Socioeconomic Groups in the United

States, 1960 and 1986." *New England Journal of Medicine* 329 (1993):103–109.

Population Reference Bureau. *2001 World Population Data Sheet.* Washington, DC: Author, 2001.

Rudberg, Mark A., and Christine K. Cassel. "Are Death and Disability in Old Age Preventable?" In Bruno J. Vellas, Jean-Louis Albarede, and P. J. Garry eds., *Facts and Research in Gerontology,* Vol. 7. New York: Springer, 1993.

Schwartz, William B. *Life without Disease: The Pursuit of Medical Utopia.* Berkeley: University of California Press, 1998.

Shkolnikov, Vladimir, et al. "Causes of the Russian Mortality Crisis: Evidence and Interpretation." *World Development* 26 (1998):1995–2011.

United Nations. *World Population Prospects: The 2000 Revision.* New York: Author, 2001.

Valkonen, Tapani. "The Widening Differentials in Adult Mortality by Socio-Economic Status and Their Causes." In *Health and Mortality Issues of Global Concern.* New York: United Nations, 1991.

Verbrugge, Lois M. "Longer Life but Worsening Health? Trends in Health and Mortality of Middle-Aged and Older Persons." *Milbank Memorial Fund Quarterly* 62 (1984):475–519.

Walford, Roy L. *Maximum Life Span.* New York: Norton, 1983.

Yaukey, David, and Douglas L. Anderton. *Demography: The Study of Human Population.* Prospect Heights, IL: Waveland, 2001.

ELLEN M. GEE

LIFE SUPPORT SYSTEM

The phrase "life support" refers to the medications and equipment used to keep people alive in medical situations. These people have one or more failing organs or organ systems, and would not be able to survive without assistance. The organs and organ systems that often fail and require life support are breathing (respiratory system); heart and blood pressure (cardiovascular system); kidney (renal system); and intestines (gastrointestinal system). The brain and spinal cord (central nervous system) may also fail, but in this case life support is directed at keeping the other body systems functioning so that the nervous system has time to return to a state where it can again support the other body functions. The most common types of life support are for the respiratory, cardiovascular, renal, and gastrointestinal systems.

Respiratory System

Oxygen is the basic method for improving the function of lungs. When the lungs do not function properly because they cannot transmit the oxygen across the lung to the blood, or internal temporary (asthma) or permanent (emphysema) changes make the lungs work inefficiently, adding oxygen may often overcome the defect. The problem usually resides in the lungs, but is sometimes in the blood's oxygen carrying capacity, such as in some poisonings.

In the case of severe illnesses or injuries, oxygen alone may not be sufficient. Often the mechanical problem is so severe that, to keep the person alive, a machine must assume the work of breathing. While patients in these situations may temporarily be sustained when a health care professional forces air into their lungs using a bag-valve mask, they will nearly always need a tube placed into their trachea (endotracheal tube) before they are placed on a ventilator. The clear polyvinyl endotracheal tubes can be placed through the mouth in most cases or the nose. Shorter tracheostomy tubes serve the same purpose and are placed surgically, through incisions in the front of the neck. Both can be initially connected to bags that are squeezed to help the patient breath. Patients are then placed on ventilators.

Ventilators are machines that push oxygenated, humidified, and warmed air into the lungs. These sophisticated machines monitor, among other things, the amount of oxygenated air flowing into the patient with each breath, the pressure needed to deliver that amount of air, and the resistance in the patient's lungs. Patients nearly always need medications to help them tolerate being on a ventilator. These include drugs that induce reversible paralysis, sedatives, and, when necessary, analgesics.

Special ventilators are sometimes used for children, and premature neonates now receive surfactant, which are medications that reduce alveolar surface tension, to help their lungs remain open while they develop. Adults with life-threatening spasms in their airways receive medications to reverse or prevent them.

When a lung collapses, or when blood or fluid fills a patient's chest outside the lung (pleural space) so that breathing becomes difficult, clinicians place a tube (chest or thoracostomy tube) through the chest wall to drain the fluid or air and to re-expand the lung.

Cardiovascular System

The most common method to support patients with life-threatening abnormalities of the heart or blood vessels (cardiovascular system) is with medications. These include the vasopressorsused to raise the blood pressure and antiarrhythmics used to slow, increase, or normalize the heart's rhythm. Other medications used to stabilize the cardiovascular system in life-threatening situations include antihypertensives, used to lower severely high blood pressure when organs are suffering severe damage, such as during a stroke or heart attack, and diuretics to drain excess fluid from the body so that the heart has less work to do.

The heart can be mechanically assisted to function normally. Patients with life-threatening heart rhythms can be cardioverted (shocked with electricity) back into a normal rhythm. Sometimes a temporary cardiac pacemaker must be placed when the heart's electrical system fails. Patients may also be placed on either a partial or complete mechanical system to support the heart. One of several partial systems, the Left Ventricular Assist Device, is passed through a groin artery to temporarily assume some of the heart's work until it can regain its ability to function independently. Patients sometimes go on a heart-lung bypass machine (aside from surgery) in order to maintain their heart while they are treated. Some centers also use artificial hearts, usually to maintain patients until they can receive a permanent heart transplant.

If sufficient fluid collects around the heart, it can decrease the heart's ability to function. In those cases, clinicians must perform pericardiocentesis, drawing fluid off so the heart again functions. If the heart stops, clinicians perform cardiopulmonary massage or open-chest cardiac massage in an attempt to restore an effective cardiac rhythm.

Renal System

The renal system (kidneys, ureters, and bladder) can fail acutely, causing a threat to life. Many of these patients can only be kept alive through using an artificial kidney system, known as dialysis. In some cases, this may only be used for a short time; for many patients, they spend the rest of their lives—or until they receive a kidney transplant—on this artificial blood-cleansing system. Patients can use either peritoneal dialysis or hemodialysis. Peritoneal dialysis involves instilling into and withdrawing from the abdomen liters of special dialysate (water with a careful mixture of chemicals) each day. Hemodialysis, usually performed three times a week at special centers, uses a shunt, usually in an extremity, to connect the patient to a hemodialysis machine.

Gastrointestinal System

Many patients on life support cannot take in enough calories to sustain themselves, even if they can eat. They receive artificial nutrition and hydration, essentially medically instilled supplements, to keep them alive. These may be given through nasogastric tubes for a limited period of time. Many receive this therapy through central lines (long catheters passing into the larger veins), gastrostomyn tubes, or similar surgically placed devices.

Other Types of Life Support

Life support may also include blood and blood product transfusions and many types of drugs. Many patients receive insulin, sometimes as insulin drips, if they are in diabetic crisis. Other patients, especially those with cancers affecting their spinal cord or bone marrow, may receive emergency anticancer drugs or radiation therapy.

Futility and Trials of Therapy

Clinicians may use life support appropriately or inappropriately. The most common appropriate use is to maintain patients long enough so that the individuals' organ systems return to a life-sustaining level of function. In some cases, such as patients with degenerative neurological diseases (i.e., amyotrophic lateral sclerosis, commonly

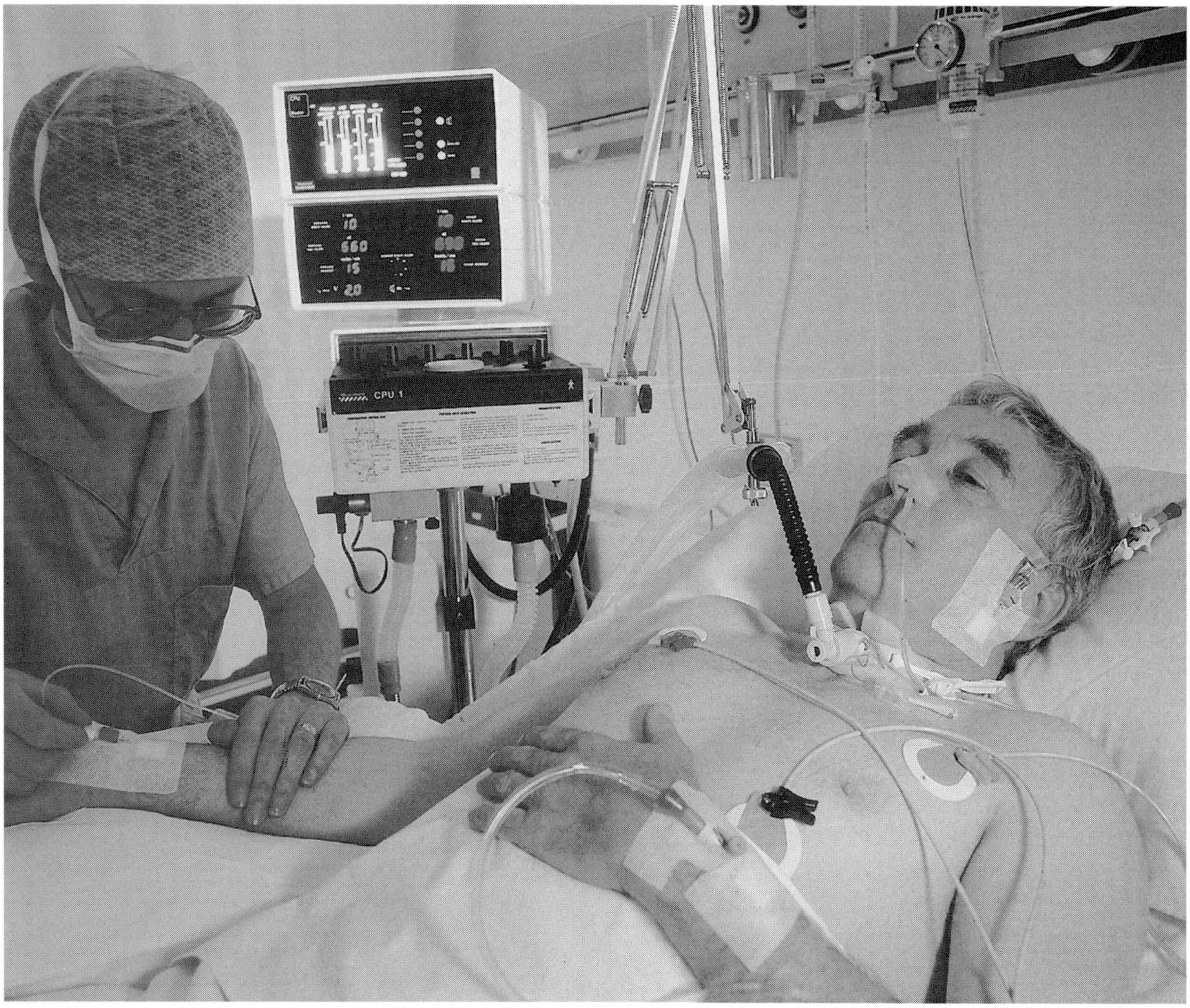

An intensive-care patient is aided by several of the many life support systems available. PHOTO RESEARCHERS

called Lou Gehrig's Disease) or kidney failure, support for a failing organ may become chronic. In the former case, patients may elect to be placed on ventilators to support their breathing, while in the latter they usually receive dialysis.

Life support is often used inappropriately to maintain patients beyond the point at which it is clear that they have no chance of recovery, sometimes called "futile treatment." Such patients often have failure in multiple organ systems and one or more severe underlying diseases. Futile and medically inappropriate interventions may violate both the ethical and medical precepts generally accepted by patients, families, and physicians. Most of those who receive such futile treatment are elderly, although futile treatment seems to be more common among the much smaller number of young people dying in hospitals. As shown by Rivera and colleagues, families are responsible for continuing futile treatment in the majority of cases, although it is sometimes accompanied by family dissent over the right course of action. Physicians continue futile treatment in only about one-third of such cases, sometimes because of liability fears. Unreasonable expectations for improvement were the most common underlying factor. Bioethics consultations can often resolve issues of unwanted or non-beneficial medical treatments.

To be on life support the patient must still be alive. However, these systems may be used to maintain the body of an individual who has been declared dead by brain criteria (brain dead) until critical organs, such as the heart, lungs, liver, kidneys, and pancreas, can be recovered in the operating room. Occasionally these systems are also continued for such a patient until families arrive or until they have come to terms with the death. In these cases, however, they are simply called support rather than life support.

When patients are recovering and as long as they or their surrogate decision makers want medical treatments, continuing life support is appropriate. When it becomes unclear whether the treatment will be of benefit, it is often appropriate for the family (or patient) and the clinician to use a time-limited trial of therapy. This is a decision to use life support for a specific period of time; if there is no improvement at that point, everyone agrees that the support will be stopped.

See also: ADVANCE DIRECTIVES; CRUZAN, NANCY; PERSISTENT VEGETATIVE STATE; QUINLAN, KAREN ANN; RESUSCITATION; SUICIDE TYPES: PHYSICIAN-ASSISTED SUICIDE

Bibliography

Iserson, Kenneth V. *Death to Dust: What Happens to Dead Bodies?* 2nd edition. Tucson, AZ: Galen Press, 2001.

Iserson, Kenneth V. *Grave Words: Notifying Survivors about Sudden, Unexpected Deaths*. Tucson, AZ: Galen Press, 1999.

Rivera, Seth, Dong Kim, Shelley Garone, Leon Morgenstern, and Zab Mohsenifar. "Motivating Factors in Futile Clinical Interventions." *Chest* 119 (2001):1944–1947.

KENNETH V. ISERSON

LINCOLN IN THE NATIONAL MEMORY

At 10:30 P.M. on April 14, 1865, while Major Henry Reed Rathbone, Clara Harris, Mary Todd Lincoln, and Abraham Lincoln watched the third act of *Our American Cousin* from the state box in John Ford's theater, twenty-six-year-old John Wilkes Booth entered the box, aimed his derringer, and discharged a shot that struck the left side of the president's head. Nearly three weeks later, following a series of dramatic funeral pageants stretching from Washington, D.C., to Springfield, Illinois, Lincoln's body was laid to rest and his place in national memory began in earnest.

An Immediate Context

Some may find it difficult to imagine that Lincoln's contemporaries would not have responded to his death with as much pomp and circumstance and devotion as they could command. Because Lincoln has become such an integral part of the nation's image, and because citizens have witnessed similar tributes during the intervening years, the pageantry and emotionality occasioned by his death, somehow may appear appropriate, inevitable, and, therefore, perhaps rather unremarkable. But this vantage point overlooks an immediate context that makes both contemporaneous responses to his death and his current status as one of the nation's most beloved and legendary presidents entirely remarkable.

In the best of times before his death Lincoln was only a moderately popular president. At other times "Lincoln was the object of far more hatred than love" (Hanchett 1983, p. 7). In the election of 1860 Lincoln received only 39 percent of the popular vote—the second lowest percentage of anyone ever elected to the presidency. Lincoln not only failed to carry a single slave state in this election, he also received only 26,388 of the 2.5 million votes cast in the slave states. Nor did he fare well in the urban North. As the historian David Potter has noted, "Whereas the North as a whole gave him 55 percent of its votes, in seven of the eleven cities with populations of 50,000 or more, he failed to get a majority" (Potter 1976, p. 443). Further, although Lincoln received 180 of the 303 electoral votes, which gave him 27 more than he needed to win the election, his margin of victory very likely was more a result of good strategists and the support of his Secretary of State William Seward, than of Lincoln's popularity. This is particularly telling in light of the fact that the electoral college inflates the margin of victory.

In the election of 1864 Lincoln received 55 percent of the popular vote and 212 of the 233 electoral votes, which seems to imply that his popularity increased significantly during his first term in office. However, several points strongly suggest the opposite. Given the generally accepted belief that changing leaders in the middle of an all-consuming war invites catastrophe, for example,

55 percent of the popular vote and 212 of the electoral votes hardly seem resounding expressions of confidence or popularity. Moreover, the population of the United States increased by more than 4 million between 1860 and 1864; there were several more potential voters in 1864 than there had been in 1860; the states that had seceded did not participate in the election of 1864; and Lincoln actually received nearly 700,00 fewer votes in 1864 than he had received in 1860—all of which adds an interesting dimension to Lincoln's contemporary status.

Even more telling indicators of Lincoln's status in the eyes of many of his contemporaries are the attacks people so frequently and openly made against his character, the constant threats to his life, and the glaring references, even in eulogies, to his flaws. Both North and South "newspapers were filled with suggestions for violence against the president" (Turner 1982, p. 69). In addition, "threatening letters arrived [at the White House] continuously and in large numbers" (Hanchett 1983, p. 23). It is difficult to know whether these constant threats would have been acted out or whether persistent rumors of organized efforts to kidnap or assassinate Lincoln had any firm basis in reality. One assassination effort obviously did come to fruition, and even then criticisms of Lincoln did not cease.

When an individual dies, as Sigmund Freud pointed out, the living typically "suspend criticism of [them], overlook [their] possible misdoings, issue the command: *De mortus nil nisi bene,* and regard it as justifiable to set forth in the funeral oration and upon the tombstone only that which is most favourable to [their] memory" (Freud 1953, p. 16). Most citizens appear to have abided by that dictum; or, at least, most manifested some degree of restraint subsequent to Lincoln's death. Many others did not.

None of this is to suggest that Lincoln was hugely unpopular, that a majority of citizens disliked him or disapproved of his policies or politics, or that the often frustrated rhetoric of his contemporaries was somehow inaccurate. To be sure, Lincoln's election to the presidency was not especially well received, even in the northern states. Throughout most of his first term in office both he and his policies frequently were objects of ridicule and derision in British and French presses, and southerners loathed him openly and incessantly. With each step Lincoln seemingly both alienated and attracted supporters. Then, the Union army's capture of Atlanta on September 2, 1864, barely two months before the presidential election, buoyed Northern hopes and virtually assured Lincoln's reelection. Yet, even Lee's surrender to General Grant five months later (April 9, 1865) produced mixed results, with Northerners celebrating "Lincoln's victory" and with Southerners vigorously pursuing a rhetorical campaign against "Lincoln's tyranny" that would continue well into the next century. Threats to his life were constant, violence and subterfuge were ever present, and some people publicly hoped for his death while others had been fearfully anticipating his assassination; therefore, Lincoln's contemporaries were shocked but not entirely surprised when they learned of his death.

Against this backdrop one of the qualities that most impressed and perplexed citizens was the unprecedented character of Lincoln's death. Perhaps because human beings are "fated to puzzle out what it actually means to feel 'right,'" as cultural anthropologist Ernest Becker so aptly put it, Lincoln's contemporaries diligently sought some historical precedent, some point of reference that would place the assassination of an American president in proper perspective (Becker 1975, p. 104). Yet even those who focused on what they thought might be historically or emotionally similar incidents eventually concluded that Lincoln's death and its consequences were simply unprecedented.

The Lincoln Myth and Beyond

The assassination of Abraham Lincoln is a unique case. Despite his status in both past and present day, Lincoln is an individual whose contemporaries continued to criticize and deride him even after his death. Many of those same contemporaries memorialized his death and life as if he had been an intimate member of their family, sparing neither expense nor effort. A partial explanation for this disparity is that the death of a significant individual, even under the least objectionable conditions, necessarily places the living squarely at the center of a nexus of disorganized emotions.

In such an exceptional case, of course, it would be entirely too simplistic to imagine that Lincoln's contemporaries responded to his death as

A drawing of President Lincoln's funeral procession through New York illustrates one of a series of dramatic funeral pageants that lasted three weeks and stretched from Washington, D.C., to Springfield, Illinois. PUBLIC DOMAIN

they did solely out of fear for the status and stability of their social roles—or, for that matter, out of sheer admiration for Lincoln. It would be too simplistic for them to respond out of political considerations necessarily drawn into focus by the fact of and circumstances surrounding his death, or out of guilt that he had been placed in such an impossible position. Responses out of shame that so many had openly and persistently hoped and prayed for his death, or out of remorse that he had been constantly the object of threats and ridicule and derision, would alone be overtly simple. Even responses out of shock for the unprecedented manner of his death, or out of the possibility that his death would provide an opportunity for cultural transformation seem improbable. Much more likely, all of these forces and more were at work within Lincoln's contemporaries, who were bound together in their extraordinary efforts to commemorate his death not by any singular emotion or motive, but by a set of intense discomforts that derived from a number of sources and that impelled the living to go to extremes to attach their emotions to something concrete.

"While we don't know exactly how the mind works in relation to emotion, how deeply words go when dealing with reality or repressions," Becker wrote, we do know that the death of an intimate occasions rhetoric, the meaningful articulation of symbols, through which "one tries to deny oblivion and to extend oneself beyond death in symbolic ways" (p. 104). In the liminal moments surrounding the death of a significant individual, those symbols finely articulate the ethos and world view that make life and death meaningful and that define how one *ought* to feel and how one can best deal with the way one actually feels.

On the other hand, even given intense discomforts at a variety of levels, it is implausible that the rhetorical and cultural efforts of Lincoln's contemporaries immediately and permanently created the images of Lincoln that now occupy places of honor and reverence in the nation's "collective memory."

Immediate responses to Lincoln's assassination and corresponding opinions of his character varied much too dramatically to have crystallized immediately and permanently into an untarnished hero-image. Indeed, the first and most obvious tribute to the nation's sixteenth president, the Lincoln National Monument in Springfield, Illinois, was dedicated on October 15, 1874. Yet the full weight of the nation's apotheosis of Lincoln did not wholly emerge until Memorial Day of 1922 when the Lincoln Memorial was dedicated in Washington, D.C. Equally important, even if those responses and opinions had been singular, creating a seemingly permanent element of the symbolic code that constitutes collective memory requires time as well as intensity. How, then, did Lincoln come to occupy such a special place in collective memory?

Part of the answer, as Merrill Peterson's *Lincoln in American Memory* (1994) demonstrates, is that a myriad of citizens, working from different assumptions and different motives, have sought to appropriate—and often have successfully appropriated—Lincoln's image over time. And it is through such efforts that Lincoln has continually "belonged to the nation's cultural heritage as well as to its civil history" (Peterson 1994, p. 375). This helps explain why the same three conflicting images that dominated contemporaneous rhetoric about Lincoln later became the three dominant elements of the Lincoln myth—namely, "the rail-splitter," the man who journeyed "from a log cabin to the White House," and "the American Christ/ Moses" (Warner 1959, pp. 270–289).

Different people memorialize, embrace, and seek to codify through public memory their different images of the memorable not merely because of temporal or spatial or physiological divergences, but because different cultures with different worldviews and ethoi require different images of and from their members. That there is a Lincoln myth at all undoubtedly owes much to circumstances; "reality," however mutable, lives within the possibilities of what is given and of what is conceivable in the midst of what is given. Would the memorial responses to his assassination been different had he not signed the Emancipation Proclamation? What would had been the response if many of his contemporaries had not needed to believe that he publicly and personally identified himself as a religious individual? What if he had not been president during such an enormous civil crisis that marked an unmistakable moment of cultural transformation? In short, had the circumstances surrounding Lincoln's life and death been substantively other than they were or other than what his contemporaries believed them to be, the memorial responses to his assassination would have been other than they were.

Yet, the struggle to recreate Lincoln reveals a great deal more than the distant sentimentality of nineteenth-century citizens, of some distant past that is only marginally related to the present. Indeed, Lincoln's place in national memory reveals an ongoing ideological conflict through which various groups continuously have sought to lay claim to the nation's hegemony and public memory. And that, fundamentally, is why his image remains so integral to the nation's memory.

See also: ASSASSINATION; BECKER, ERNEST; CELEBRITY DEATHS; CIVIL WAR, U.S.; FREUD, SIGMUND; IMMORTALITY, SYMBOLIC; MARTYRS; ROYALTY, BRITISH; WASHINGTON, GEORGE

Bibliography

Becker, Ernest. *The Denial of Death*. New York: Free Press, 1975.

Bodnar, John. *Remaking America: Public Memory, Commemoration, and Patriotism in the Twentieth Century*. Princeton, NJ: Princeton University Press, 1992.

Cole, Donald B. *Handbook of American History*. New York: Harcourt Brace Javonovich, 1986.

Freud, Sigmund. "Thoughts for the Times on War and Death." In J. Rickman ed., *Civilization, War and Death*. London: Hogarth, 1953.

Hanchett, William. *The Lincoln Murder Conspiracies*. Chicago: University of Illinois Press, 1983.

Holmes, Frederick Lionel. *Abraham Lincoln Traveled This Way*. Boston: Page & Co., 1930.

Morris, Richard. *Sinners, Lovers, and Heroes: An Essay on Memorializing in Three American Cultures*. Albany: State University of New York Press, 1997.

Peterson, Merrill. *Lincoln in American Memory*. New York: Oxford University Press, 1994.

Potter, David M. *The Impending Crisis, 1848–1861*. New York: Harper and Row, 1976.

Turner, Thomas Reed. *Beware the People Weeping: Public Opinion and the Assassination of Abraham Lincoln*. Baton Rouge: Louisiana State University Press, 1982.

Warner, W. Lloyd. *The Living and the Dead: A Study of the Symbolic Life of Americans*. New Haven, CT: Yale University Press, 1959.

RICHARD MORRIS

LITERATURE FOR ADULTS

As scholars often note, human beings can never accurately report on the experience of death, they can only imagine it. Thus it should come as no surprise that death has played such a significant role in literature, where humans use the imagination to reflect, shape, and understand their world. The scholars Elizabeth Bronfen and Sarah Webster Goodwin explain that "much of what we call culture comes together around the collective response to death" (Bronfen and Goodwin 1993, p. 3), and Garret Stewart insists that "death marks the impossible limit of representation, while at the same time, death is an inevitability of representation" (p. 51). In literature, then, death functions as an inevitable cultural exploration of what it means to be mortal. While some scholars and philosophers would insist that humans strive to deny death, especially in the twentieth century, literature reflects a constant process of trying to understand death and all its implications.

Western literature incorporates a number of conceits that are specifically associated with death. These include conceptions of the afterlife, representations of love and death, death-specific literary forms like the elegy, and staple narrative images like the deathbed scene. But in order to appreciate such conceits, one first needs to understand the way literature has reflected changing cultural responses to death and dying.

"Death in Literature" As Cultural History

Most scholars agree that in classical literature and until the Middle Ages death was represented as a natural and expected part of life. The Greeks tended to avoid details about death in their literature, in part because they simply accepted death as part of the human experience, and in part because they wanted to emphasize life. The Greeks did, however, depict death in war, demonstrating their belief in heroic, noble death, and they did emphasize the delights of the next world, and thus the afterlife became more of a focus in their literature than death itself. The sociologist Philippe Ariès has termed this era's dominant philosophy about death the "Tamed Death," a death that, as in *Le Chanson de Roland,* (twelfth century) was usually forewarned and generally accepted. Closer to the Middle Ages death portrayals increasingly took place in bed and with family and friends nearby—a set of rituals that has remained quite enduring.

The literature of the Middle Ages also began to reflect a profound shift in attitudes and beliefs about death, primarily by associating judgment with death. Christianity's influence on literature resulted in works showing death as a punishment for one's sins, and thus one's death became the crucial event in human experience. Works like *The Pricke of Conscience* (fourteenth century) described the importance and the horrors of death. The literature of this period also focused on the significance of Christ's death and his wounds, depicted the Danse Macabre, or dance of death, and emphasized bodily decay and images of the skeleton.

This focus on the body carried into the Renaissance where the performance of death, especially on stage, was tremendously emotional. Death was often conceived as it affected the body, and represented in a histrionic fashion, foregrounding time as a natural enemy. Love and death became opposing forces: love the motivation for working against time, and death the inevitable result of time's progress. Suicide became an ironic affirmation of love and of values that could transcend death. William Shakespeare's tragedies exemplify these ideas about death, as do carpe diem poems like "The Flea" (1633) and "The Sun Rising" (1633) by John Donne and "To His Coy Mistress" (1681) by Andrew Marvell.

The late eighteenth and early nineteenth centuries saw major shifts in representations of death, due in part to the growing conflict between religion and science. Ariès asserts that the late eighteenth century offered more visions of both beautiful death and eroticized death. On the one hand, popular novels like Hannah Foster's *The Coquette* (1797) depict the unwed heroine's death in childbirth as a didactic message extolling the evils of untamed sexuality. On the other hand, literature indulged in an erotics of dying—especially by incorporating emotional deathbed scenes, Little

Eva's from Harriet Beecher Stowe's *Uncle Tom's Cabin,* (1852) being perhaps the most famous. The scholar Michael Wheeler, however, notes that while such scenes might have been erotically charged, they also represented a space of comfort and of quite literal rest, transformed into eternal rest. The late nineteenth century developed the *Victorian Cult of Death,* a term used to signify the period's almost obsessive fascination with the subject.

Ironically, most scholars argue that the twentieth century ushered in a culture that strove to distance and to deny death. The literature both does and does not bear this out. Given that the century was filled with war, the threat of nuclear annihilation, and acts of genocide, the literature often reflects a preoccupation with death. At the same time, the literature reveals a developing lack of faith in religion, in science, and in institutions, all things that have helped people understand death. Wallace Stevens's famous conceit "death is the mother of beauty" from the poem "Sunday Morning," (1915) suggests that death may lead humans to create art and life; but such a notion eventually confronted a world where nuclear war threatened not merely the individual or collective life but all that humanity might create. The scholar Lawrence Langer characterizes death in modern literature as inappropriate, absurd, random, unnecessary—yet very much present. The question became, How does one negotiate a world and culture in which such death exists? Many twentieth-century texts attempted to answer that question, and the efforts continue in the present.

The history of death in literature reveals a culture that has evolved from one that accepted death as a natural part of life, to one that invested it with primary religious significance, to one that almost fetishized death, to one that tried to deny it for its now apparent irrationality. Literature suggests that as death has become increasingly less "natural" and concomitantly less meaningful, people have had to find new ways to negotiate it.

Major Literary Conceits

There are a number of standard conceits that one can identify in literature dealing with death, and not surprisingly many of these reflect the time and values in which the literature was produced. Thus, in a time when Western culture saw death as a punishment for earthly sin, the literature often focused on the body and its decomposition, and the image of the skeleton became prominent. And when Western culture was in the midst of the Victorian Cult of the Dead, its fascination with death elevated to an almost erotic level, the literature indulged in elaborate deathbed scenes, foregrounding the emotional impact of death for those surrounding the dying individual, at times emphasizing the relation between carnality and death, but also using the bed as a symbol of both beginning and ending—a place of birth and of one's final earthly rest. However, there are a number of other significant conceits.

The afterlife. In literature, the depiction of the afterlife foregrounds death's role and its significance for the individual and the culture. The most common depictions of the afterlife are versions of heaven and hell. Trips to and from the underworld abound, as the classical conception of Hades directly or indirectly recurs in much later works. It is notable, for example, that in James Joyce's *Ulysses* (1922) the "Hades" chapter centers on a funeral, or that in Allen Ginsberg's "A Supermarket in California" (1956) the persona depicts Walt Whitman crossing over into Hades, a presumably better ending than what Whitman would find if he lived in contemporary society. Images of heaven range from a place of peace and glory for figures like John Bunyan's Christian in *Pilgrim's Progress* (1678) to a sedentary and static space in which angels desperately await the return of a departed God in Tony Kushner's *Angels in America* (1992). At the same time, since the nineteenth century literature has often questioned the viability of an afterlife, implying that the natural processes of death and decay may be all that occur. Or, as in some Emily Dickinson poems, the afterlife may mean little more than remaining buried in a tomb, contemplating the life one has just passed, a sensibility that anticipated the later existentialist vision of the afterlife in works like Jean-Paul Sartre's *No Exit* (1944).

Antidotes to death—love, beauty, the imagination. Given the inevitability of human mortality, literature often depicts the effort to challenge death and its apparent omnipotence. Literature has long represented love as a challenge to death, whether in the carpe diem poems and romances of the Renaissance, in the Gothic romances of the nineteenth century (where love faced a constant battle with death), or even in the late nineteenth century where, as the scholar Rudolph Binion notes, the idea that spiritual love remained after death reappeared in literature and culture. At the same time, artists have depicted the imagination and the creation of beauty as a stay against death and the ravages of time. John Keats's "Ode to a Grecian Urn," (1819) for example, symbolizes art's ability to defy death. And even twentieth-century writers like Stevens, William Butler Yeats, and T. S. Eliot, who faced a world of death on a global scale, looked to the imagination, to beauty and to the literary arts, as a way to forge ahead despite a sense of impending apocalypse. Twentieth-century literature increasingly questioned whether any of these "antidotes" to death would suffice, however, especially as culture used its imagination to develop new and more global methods of creating death.

The elegy. The elegy, or song for the dead, is a longstanding poetic form used not only to honor the dead, but to explore human efforts to comprehend death. John Milton's *Lycidas* (1637) is an ideal example. Milton's poem mourns the death of his friend Edward King. At the same time, it explores what it suggests that death can take such a young artist. The poem reflects Milton's own anxiety about being a young poet who had taken time to learn and to experience life. The poem thus signifies Milton's fear that his time may have been wasted because he too could be cut down in his prime before he can create the art that will be his legacy. Thus, again one can see how a literary form not only depicts death or responds to it, but also explores death's significance while conveying the prevailing ideas about death for that culture—in this case, that time is life's enemy.

Crisis of faith. Beginning as early as the late eighteenth century and developing exponentially up to and throughout the twentieth century, literary representations of death began reflecting a crisis of faith, initially of faith in God or religion, but eventually of faith in science, in government, and in society at large. Again, Stevens's "Sunday Morning" serves as a useful example. While the poem asserts that death is the mother of beauty, inspiring one to create, it also suggests that the contemporary culture can only see Christ's death as human—the tomb in Palestine holds his body; there was no resurrection; and there is no paradise. Existentialism would go so far as to suggest that one's death seals off and defines the significance and meaning of one's life. At the same time, twentieth-century writers like Thomas Pynchon characterize America as a culture headed toward an entropic ending, society and culture winding down in a kind of cultural death. Robert Lowell's "For the Union Dead" (1959) and Randall Jarrell's "The Death of the Ball Turret Gunner" (1945) depict society's callous treatment of the living and of those who have died to protect the living. Death became especially meaningless when governments and other institutions were involved. And, of course, scientific progress more often than not led to death, whether via the automobile in F. Scott Fitzgerald's *The Great Gatsby* (1925) and E. L. Doctorow's *Ragtime* (1974). In both, the development of this new technology directly or indirectly leads to the death of major characters—or via the war machines and diverse weaponry depicted in numerous works of this century.

War. From classical literature to the present, war has been a staple subject. For most of literary history death in war was represented as noble and heroic. Again, however, since the mid–nineteenth century, literature has seriously challenged this idea, often by depicting death in war as senseless and brutal or by suggesting that such belief is culturally necessary; that is, Western cultures can only send its young men to war if it believes that such death carries nobility. Consistently, however, representations of death in war reflect both our human ability to rise, to defend and to prevail as well as the ability to commit inhumane atrocities. Death in war literature remains one of the most compelling ways in which artists use death to speak to readers about their values.

The undead. Whether one considers the ghost of Hamlet's father returning to speak the name of his murderer in Shakespeare's play (1603), or Victor Frankenstein's creature in Mary Shelley's novel (1818), or Bram Stoker's vampire (1897), or Sethe's dead daughter returned to life in Toni Morrison's *Beloved,* (1987) literature reveals a fascination with the dead who have in some way returned to the living. The monstrous undead serve a crucial role in literature's engagement with death. On the one hand, these figures foreground a cultural anxiety about maintaining clear boundaries—living and dead should remain separate, and when humans cross that boundary, they produce something monstrous. But there are often deeper implications. Stoker's Dracula, for example, embodies the

Victorian anxiety about the individual's underlying sexuality and desires. Dracula inverts the living: he penetrates his victims to take life rather than to create life. But he also elicits from his victims' desires that must otherwise be suppressed within Victorian culture. Similarly, Victor Frankenstein's monstrous creature serves as a living, breathing testament to what happens if one strives to play God, and it remains an enduring symbol, reminding readers of the ethical implications resulting from unchecked scientific progress. And the ghost who returns to name its murderer or to remind others of its unfair demise foregrounds the way people are haunted by the sins of their past. In other words, the dead often remain alive in people's collective memory. Beloved, arguably the resurrected daughter who Sethe killed to keep from slavery, clearly signifies the way the history of slavery, and its creation of a life worse than death, both must, and cannot help but, be remembered.

Death is everywhere in literature, in large part because it is a force that individually and collectively people must negotiate. In fact, it is so pervasive in literature that any attempt to provide an overview is inevitably incomplete. However, literature clearly reflects humanity's struggle to understand death, to explore the implications of death for the living, and to use death as a way of questioning the value of life, society, and art.

See also: ARIÈS, PHILIPPE; BECKER, ERNEST; DANSE MACABRE; IVAN ILYCH; LITERATURE FOR CHILDREN; SHAKESPEARE, WILLIAM; VAMPIRES

Bibliography

Andrews, Michael. *This Action of Our Death: The Performance of Death in English Renaissance Drama.* Newark: University of Delaware Press, 1989.

Ariès Philippe. *The Hour of Our Death,* translated by Helen Weaver. New York: Oxford University Press, 1981.

Ariès, Philippe. *Western Attitudes toward Death from the Middle Ages to the Present,* translated by Patricia M. Ranum. Baltimore, MD: Johns Hopkins University Press, 1972.

Becker, Ernest. *The Denial of Death.* New York: Free Press, 1973.

Binion, Rudolph. *Love beyond Death: The Anatomy of a Myth in the Arts.* New York: New York University Press, 1993.

Bronfen, Elizabeth, and Sarah Webster Goodwin. "Introduction." In Elizabeth Bronfen and Sarah Webster Goodwin eds., *Death and Representation.* Baltimore, MD: Johns Hopkins University Press, 1993.

Langer, Lawrence. *The Age of Atrocity: Death in Modern Literature.* Boston: Beacon Press, 1978.

Segal, Charles. "Euripides' *Alcestis*: How to Die a Normal Death in Greek Tragedy." In Elizabeth Bronfen and Sarah Webster Goodwin eds., *Death and Representation.* Baltimore, MD: Johns Hopkins University Press, 1993.

Spencer, Theodore. *Death and Elizabethan Tragedy: A Study of Convention and Opinion in the Elizabethan Drama.* New York: Pageant Books, 1960.

Stewart, Garrett. "A Valediction for Bidding Mourning: Death and the Narratee in Bronte's *Villette.*" In Elizabeth Bronfen and Sarah Webster Goodwin eds., *Death and Representation.* Baltimore. MD: Johns Hopkins University Press, 1993.

Stilling, Roger. *Love and Death in Renaissance Tragedy.* Baton Rouge: Louisiana State University Press, 1976.

Wheeler, Michael. *Death and the Future Life in Victorian Literature and Theology.* Cambridge: Cambridge University Press, 1990.

ANDREW J. SCHOPP

LITERATURE FOR CHILDREN

A historical overview of children's literature, especially fairy tales, reflects society's attitudes toward children and death. Most readers are unaware that every fairy tale has its own history, and many of them originated in the seventeenth century as oral, adult entertainment. Many featured coarse humor and sensational events. As these tales were transcribed and developed specifically for children, they were modified to contain incidents and behavior that reflected the customs of the place and period in which they were told. They contained material intended to provide moral guidance, and in the earliest versions of children's stories death was prominent because of its ubiquity and drama. Over the centuries there has been significant transformation of fairy tales, storybooks, and schoolbooks (basal readers). In the early twentieth century until the 1970s, topics considered disturbing to children, including death, were toned down and removed. Although late twentieth-century works began to reverse this trend, many children today are insulated from discussions of death in their literature.

The Evolution of Children's Literature

Schoolbooks were developed primarily to educate, teach morality, and assist in children's socialization. Books for children's education preceded the development of children's literature for pleasure. Charles Perrault and Wilhelm and Jacob Grimm wrote tales to caution children about the perils and consequences of inappropriate behavior.

Literature intended specifically for children did not develop until the mid-seventeenth century. Prior to that time children were perceived as miniature adults or as less than human, as typified by Michel de Montaigne, the sixteenth-century French humanist and essayist. In *Off with Their Heads!* (1992), Maria Tatar, a professor of Germanic languages and literature at Harvard University, notes that early children's literature had an unusually cruel and coercive streak. Early books were often written to frighten children into behaving as parents wished. Two approaches predominated: cautionary tales and exemplary tales. In cautionary tales the protagonist was either killed or made perpetually miserable for having disobeyed. Stories of exemplary behavior also had a strange way of ending at the deathbeds of their protagonists.

John Amos Comenius's 1658 Latin schoolbook *A World of Things Obvious to the Senses Drawn in Pictures* was the first picture book for children and the first to recognize that children needed their own literature. In 1744 John Newbery wrote *A Little Pretty Pocket Book* for children. Although other books for children had been published earlier, this book is credited as the start of English children's literature because this book was meant to entertain rather than educate. Newbery is recognized as the first serious publisher of children's literature.

Between the 1920s and the 1970s incidents of dying and death were removed or glossed over in children's reading material. Concurrently, religious material was also removed from children's schoolbooks. Only since the late 1970s and early 1980s has this tendency begun to reverse. Children's books of the twenty-first century frequently deal with feelings, divorce, sex, and death. Religion is still taboo in schoolbooks—in contrast to colonial America when ministers wrote many of the schoolbooks and the local minister often oversaw the school. The town school was considered an appropriate place for children to be taught not only their letters but also religion.

Basal Readers

Books designed to teach children to read are known as basal readers. They use material from a variety of sources. From the early 1800s until the 1920s, American children were commonly taught to read with basal readers edited by Lyman Cobb, Samuel T. Worcester, Salem Town, William Russell, William D. Swan, and William McGuffey, among others. In *McGuffey's Eclectic Readers,* published continuously from 1879 to 1920, the subject of many of the selections was the death of a mother or child, typically presented as a tragic but inevitable part of life. For example, *McGuffey's Third Eclectic Reader* (1920) contains William Wordsworth's poem "We Are Seven," in which a little girl describes her family as having seven children, even though two are dead. The experience of the death of the older sister is also described. Some of the other short stories and poems in McGuffey's Readers that deal with death as a theme are: "Old Age and Death" by Edmund Waller, "The Death of Little Nell" by Charles Dickens, "Elegy Written in a Country Churchyard" by Thomas Gray, and "He Giveth His Beloved Sleep" by Elizabeth Barrett Browning. Unlike early basal readers, today there are no poems or stories that deal with death nor are there prayers in books used in public schools.

An anonymous selection in *McGuffey's Fourth Eclectic Reader,* entitled "My Mother's Grave," provides an emotional account of a young girl's experience with her dying mother. The story aims to make children polite and obedient to their parents. Through recounting the author's thoughts on revisiting her mother's grave, she remembers being unkind to her dying mother after a trying day at school. She realizes her lapse in manners later that evening and returns to her mother's room for forgiveness and finds her asleep. She vows to waken early to "tell how sorry I was for my conduct," but when she rushes into the room in the morning she finds her mother dead, with a hand so cold "it made me start" (p. 253). Even thirteen years later the author finds her remorse and pain almost overwhelming. This is not the type of subject matter and emotional content considered appropriate for twenty-first century basal readers. Commonly used basal readers rarely contain references to dying or death. If they do include a chapter from a book that deals with death, such as E. B. White's *Charlotte's Web* (1952), it is not the chapter in which Charlotte dies.

Storybooks

Insight into how dying and death were portrayed in the nineteenth century can be found in the still widely read storybook *Little Women,* written in 1869 by Louisa May Alcott. Alcott described the death of young Beth in a straightforward manner uncommon for her day. Recognizing that her depiction was at odds with the melodramatic scenes current in more romantic literature, Alcott added in the paragraph following Beth's death: "Seldom, except in books, do the dying utter memorable words, see visions, or depart with beatified countenance . . ." (Alcott 1947, p. 464).

Between 1940 and 1970 few children's books contained references to death. Two that have become classics are Margaret Wise Brown's *The Dead Bird* (1965) and *Charlotte's Web.* White's publisher initially refused to publish *Charlotte's Web* unless the ending was modified allowing Charlotte to live, which White refused. Critical reviewers of the era found death not "an appropriate subject for children" (Guth 1976, p. 531).

Separating children from an awareness of dying and death has diminished since the 1970s. Although Robert Fulton and Herman Feifel taught and wrote about dying and death before the 1960s, it was the early work of Elisabeth Kübler-Ross in 1969 that helped make death a subject for discussion and study. During the 1970s and 1980s over 200 fiction books for children contained death as a major theme. Few measured up to the standard set by *Charlotte's Web, Little Women, The Yearling* (1938), or *The Dead Bird.* During this same period some very well-written nonfiction books about death were published for children of various ages, making it a more acceptable subject. These included *About Dying* by Sara Bonnett Stein (1974), *When People Die* (1977) by Joanne Bernstein and Stephen J. Gullo, *Learning to Say Good-by: When a Parent Dies* by Eda J. LeShan (1976), *The Kids' Book about Death and Dying* and *The Unit at Fayerweather Street School* (1985) both by Eric E. Rofes, and *Living with Death* (1976) by Osborn Segerberg Jr.

Fairy Tales

Fairy tales provide an excellent example of the way society deals with themes considered distressing to children. The insulation of children from death can be traced through progressive versions of typical stories. A generalization can be made about fairy tales that can also apply to all early stories for children: As sexual content diminished, violent content increased. An analysis of successive editions of *Grimms' Fairy Tales* provides insight into the manner in which stories were modified to shield children from exposure to dying and death.

To understand this evolution, it is necessary to understand the milieu in which it took place. In the 1700s children were not perceived as needing protection from portrayals of violence primarily because life was harsh and most children died during infancy or childhood. Violence and death in children's stories of the 1700s take on a different light when viewed in the context of high infant and child mortality and the increasing, universal practice of abandoning unwanted children at the local foundling hospital or on church steps. In the seventeenth and eighteenth centuries, children were routinely required to attend public executions to witness the cost of criminal behavior. The romanticized depiction of an afterlife, superior to the life of this world, served to help children cope with the brutal facts of their lives.

Given these realities, children's literature was motivated by a belief that children needed written material to educate them and prepare them for life. The majority of books published for children through the 1800s can be compared to James Janeway's *A Token for Children: Being an Account of the Conversion, Holy and Exemplary Lives, and Joyful Deaths of Several Young Children* (Parts 1 and 2, 1671–1672). Writers of this era commonly agreed with Janeway's position that they held a sacred duty to salvage the souls of those who were not too young to go to hell. The exemplary stories in *A Token for Children* were also designed to pro-

Hänsel und Gretel._ Nº4. Knupper Knupper Kneischen,
Wer knuppert an meinem Häuschen?

Like many of Grimms' fairy tales, Hansel and Grethel *(1823) provides a vivid description of violence not only toward the characters' antagonist, but children as well.* BETTMANN/CORBIS

vide comfort to children facing the tragedy of a sibling's death or confronting their own mortality when visited by some dreaded disease.

Wilhelm and Jacob Grimm's *Cinderella* stressed punishment more than earlier oral versions. In the first version (1697), taken by Perrault from the oral tradition, Cinderella forgave her stepsisters for mistreating her and introduced them at court. The Grimms' first version (1815) has Cinderella's sisters turning pale and being horrified when she becomes a princess, while in the second edition sisters' punishment is to be blinded by pigeons pecking out their eyes.

In the Grimms' *Hansel and Grethel* (1823), there is a description of how horribly the witch howled when Grethel pushed her into the oven and how ". . . Grethel ran away leaving the witch to burn, just as she had left many poor little children to burn" (Owens 1981, p. 57). The use of violence as punishment is typical in fairy tales, even for minor misdeeds. This tendency is evident in the stories found in *Struwwelpeter.* In these tales, Little Pauline plays with matches and goes up in flames, and Conrad the Thumbsucker has his thumbs sliced off. Maria Tatar observes that "the weight is given to the punishment (often fully half the text is devoted to its description) and the disproportionate relationship between the childish offense and the penalty for it make the episode disturbing" (Tatar 1992, p. 34).

The removal of sexuality from children's fairy tales paralleled the evolution of housing in Europe. By the seventeenth century, living arrangements had evolved to provide segregation between quarters for working, food preparation, and sleeping. Usually there was a main room used for dining, entertaining, and receiving visitors, but servants and children began to have their own smaller, adjacent rooms. During this same century fairy tales began to transform into works intended primarily for children. The transformation of living spaces parallels the changes that greatly impacted children, including attitudes regarding teaching proper behavior and attitudes toward dying and death.

The obvious changes over time in one fairy tale—*Little Red Riding Hood*—parallel the changes in attitudes toward death, children, and their education. The earliest known oral version from Brittany would not be considered suitable children's entertainment in the twenty-first century. In this early version, Little Red Riding Hood is unwittingly led by the wolf to eat her grandmother's flesh, to drink her blood, and to perform a provocative striptease for the disguised wolf before climbing into bed with him. She escapes from the wolf when she goes outside to relieve herself. Because its primary purpose was to entertain adults, the story was not encumbered with the admonitions and advice that later came to distinguish versions intended for children.

The earliest written version of *Little Red Riding Hood* was in French, in 1697, by Charles Perrault. In this version, the grandmother and Little Red Riding Hood are eaten by the wolf and perish. Although Perrault did not have Little Red's mother warning her before leaving for her grandmother's house, he did conclude the story with a moral suitable for the intended children's audience: Do not speak to strangers or you, too, may provide a wolf with his dinner. The death in this story is later moderated in the Grimms' retelling. They introduce an additional character, a hunter or woodcutter, who slices the wolf open and releases the victims alive.

In a popular nineteenth-century retelling of Little Red's tale, the grandmother is eaten by the wolf, but Little Red survives, learning to pay closer attention to her mother's words: "For she saw the dreadful end to which / A disobedient act may lead" (Tatar 1992, p. 39). Another version emphasizes avoiding needless suffering. Here is the depiction of the wolf killing the grandmother: "[The Wolf] jumped up on the bed, and ate her all up. But he did not hurt her so much as you would think, and as she was a very good old woman it was better for her to die than to live in pain; but still it was very dreadful of the wolf to eat her" (1933, p. 20).

In later versions of *Little Red Riding Hood* the hunter arrives in time to shoot the wolf before he eats either Little Red or her grandmother, or the wolf escapes through an open window or becomes Little Red's pet. The moral, or message, of the story also evolves with the transformation of events. In the traditional, oral version Little Red was not warned by her mother of the dangers of talking to strangers, and cannot be seen as naughty or disobedient. In Perrault's original written version, the mother does not give Little Red any cautions, while in later versions she often gives Little Red many instructions and admonitions. Upon rescuing Little Red from the dire misfortune she brings upon herself, the hunter/woodcutter inevitably lectures her on obedience and on what can happen if she disregards her mother's warnings. The role of death in the changing tale diminishes as the tale evolves. Rather than being the graphic and unmourned event Perrault depicted, it becomes muted and is eventually relegated to the periphery of the readers' attention or disappears entirely.

Fairy tales do not always hold the promise of a happy ending. For example, Hans Christian Andersen's *The Little Mermaid* (1846) has been distorted over time. In the original version the Little Mermaid chooses death for herself rather than murdering the Prince, and thus leave her form as a mermaid. The Little Mermaid would only regain her form as a mermaid if she murdered the prince. She does not do this and so she dies and becomes a daughter of the air. After 300 years of good deeds she then can gain a human soul and enter heaven and join the prince there. The very morning that the Little Mermaid sacrifices herself and spares the Prince, he marries a princess from another land whom he mistakenly believes rescued him. Only in Disney's bowdlerized version does the Little Mermaid manage to displace the "other woman" and marry the Prince, an alteration partly justified by casting the other princess as the evil sea-witch in disguise.

The classic fairy tale *Bluebeard* (1729) also presents a problematic ending. In this tale, one of three sisters marries a wealthy but mysterious man, distinguished primarily by his blue beard. After the wedding she is given access to all of Bluebeard's possessions, but is forbidden to use one small golden key. She inevitably uses the key, and discovers the bloody bodies of Bluebeard's previous wives. Upon discovering his wife's transgression, Bluebeard prepares to add her to his collection. At the last moment, her brothers suddenly appear and save her by hacking Bluebeard to pieces before her eyes. Although the latest wife did not meet the fate of her predecessors, is it really a happy ending to have her brothers murder her husband? Her disobedience is a necessary part of the story, yet there is no clear resolution of her dilemma. The fast and easy way to conclude a fairy tale is to recite, "and they lived happily ever after," yet a close look shows that many fairy tales do not have a "perfect" ending.

When fairy tales existed solely as oral tradition, storytellers could personalize their version to suit the time, place, and audience. As stories were printed, they began to reflect more enduringly the nature of the time and place in which they were recorded. Thus it seems odd that parents continue to read to their children—often without the slightest degree of critical reflection—unrevised versions of stories imbued with values of a different time and place. L. Frank Baum, the originator of *The Wonderful Wizard of Oz* (1900), recognized this predicament and recommended that it was time for a new set of "wonder tales"; he suggested that previous fairy tales be classed as "historical" (Tatar 1992, p. 19). Indeed, denoting traditional fairy tales as "historical" would help distinguish the changes that have occurred in the years since they were recorded. It would also encourage parents and teachers to critically examine the material available to children.

Modern Themes

There is a growing perception that children are capable of understanding dying and death as natural processes, and that over time they assimilate a number of such experiences. Since the 1970s adults have begun to recognize the difficulties they experienced as a result of being sheltered from awareness of death and have begun to seek ways to allow children to become aware of the reality of dying and death. Since the mid-1970s hospice programs have enabled several million dying persons to receive care in their homes. As a result, some children have been exposed to meaningful death experiences. Increased awareness of the lethality of AIDS (acquired immunodeficiency syndrome) also makes it important that even the tales told to children reflect current perceptions of dying and death.

Scholars maintain it is important to consider the implications of fairy tales in modern times. Perhaps it is time to begin transforming them to reflect the tremendous changes that have occurred in a world increasingly forced to accept the limits of medical technology, with death again being acknowledged as a necessary and inevitable counterpart to life.

The terrorist attacks of September 11, 2001, taught children that the world is not a safe place. The *New York Times* best-seller list for September 30 revealed that the new Lemony Snicket book, *The Hostile Hospital,* outsold any of the *Harry Potter* titles that week. Also that week there were four Snicket books and four *Harry Potter* titles in the Top 10. The Lemony Snicket books are an eight-book series dubbed "A Series of Unfortunate Events." The series tells the story of the Baudelaire orphans, good children to whom bad things happen. In the first book Mr. Poe, a family friend, comes to the beach to tell the children that their parents have died in a fire, and their mansion is destroyed. The narrator cautions that everything to come is rife with misfortune, misery, and despair. Children who are protected by parents from awful truth instinctively know the world is not an absolutely safe place and one way of releasing the tension is to read about someone who is much worse off than they are. Each time the Baudelaire children find a satisfactory situation, something goes wrong. Count Olaf, a distant cousin who takes them in first, is interested only in their money. Kindly Uncle Monty, with whom they next reside, is murdered. Aunt Josephine throws herself out of a window, or at least that is the way it appears. In spite of all the terrible things that happen to the three children, they manage to survive.

See also: CHILDREN; CHILDREN AND ADOLESCENTS' UNDERSTANDING OF DEATH; CHILDREN AND MEDIA VIOLENCE; HOSPICE OPTION; LITERATURE FOR ADULTS

Bibliography

Alcott, Louisa M. *Little Women.* New York: Grosset and Dunlop, 1947.

Dowd, Maureen. "When Bad Things Happen to Good Children." *New York Times,* 30 December 2001, 9.

Guth, D. L. *Letters of E. B. White.* New York: Harper & Row, 1976.

Hunt, Peter. *Children's Literature: An Illustrated History.* New York: Oxford University Press, 1995.

Johnson, Clifton. *Old-Time Schools and School Books.* 1904. Reprint, New York: Dover, 1963.

Kübler-Ross, Elisabeth. *On Death and Dying.* New York: Macmillan, 1969.

McGuffey, William. *McGuffey's Eclectic Readers,* 7 book series, Primer–Sixth Reader. New York: Van Nostrand, 1920.

Mulherin, Jennifer, ed. *Favorite Fairy Tales.* London: Granada Publishing, 1982.

Owens, Lily. *The Complete Brothers Grimm Fairy Tales.* New York: Avenel, 1981.

Tatar, Maria. *Off with Their Heads! Fairy Tales and the Culture of Childhood.* Princeton, NJ: Princeton University Press, 1992.

ELIZABETH P. LAMERS

LIVING WILL

A living will is a written document that declares what life-sustaining medical interventions a person wants if she becomes terminally ill with little or no hope of recovery and is unable to communicate her wishes. It was created in response to the increasing ability of medical technology to prolong dying, frequently in a painful and undignified way. Often at the time life supports are needed patients are unable to communicate their wishes. A patient's autonomy and right to privacy may be violated in such circumstances when it is medical personnel or others, and not the patient, who make crucial decisions regarding life supports. Living wills are designed to permit patients to "speak" when they are unable to by providing directions in advance. It is also a way of giving meaning to the doctrine of informed consent, which requires physicians to obtain the consent of their patients before beginning any medical treatment.

The first living will was conceived in 1967 by Luis Kutner, a human-rights lawyer in Chicago and cofounder of Amnesty International, in conjunction with the Euthanasia Society of America (now called Partnership for Caring). The living wills were distributed by the Euthanasia Society, and in addition to their practical use, they served as a way of promoting education and dialogue about end-of-life issues.

The use of living wills was further popularized by the Karen Ann Quinlan case in 1976. Quinlan was twenty-one years old when she was placed on a respirator after she stopped breathing for unexplained reasons and entered a chronic persistent vegetative state. Her parents were forced to turn to a court to have her respirator removed so she could die naturally, thus bringing attention to the fact that few if any mechanisms existed for making these crucial decisions. The case acted as a catalyst for state legislatures throughout the 1970s and mid-1980s to pass living will laws.

Living wills are narrowly tailored documents that generally apply only when a person has a terminal illness, although some states allow living wills to be used when a person is in an "irreversible coma" or "persistent vegetative state." Living wills do not apply to all types of medical treatment but are limited to life-sustaining treatment or to maintenance medical care. State living will laws differ in their definitions of what constitutes life-sustaining treatment. Generally it includes artificial technology that postpones death, but not care that eases pain. In over half of the states in the United States nutrition and hydration are not considered life-sustaining treatment (although these types of provisions may conflict with court decisions that have held otherwise). In some states, persons must specifically state in their living will whether or not they want nutrition and hydration withdrawn.

Under most state laws, living wills never expire, although some states require them to be renewed periodically. Living wills can be revoked or changed at any time. Living wills must be signed by witnesses, usually two, who cannot be family members or health care workers. Some states provide mandatory living will forms; other states are more flexible. It is not clear that a living will executed in one state will be effective in another state. Only a handful of states have laws that expressly provide that another state's living will be accepted, although this does not mean that a state without such a law will not honor a living will executed in another state.

Even a properly executed living will poses obstacles to compliance. Many living wills consist of a one- to two-page form that contains standardized and broad language that is too vague to provide enough guidance to physicians. For example, one state's statutory living will form provides, in part, that if the person has "an incurable and irreversible injury, disease, or illness judged to be a terminal condition by my attending physician . . . such procedures that will only prolong the dying process [are to] be withheld or withdrawn." Such language leaves open to interpretation what is meant by a terminal condition. For some it means imminent death and for others it means an irreversible condition that will ultimately result in death. It also provides only vague guidance as to what procedures shall not be used. A feeding tube may be considered a comfort measure to some and a life support to others.

Even those forms that permit people to insert their own language often suffer from similar deficiencies, with people often using the same broad language to record their wishes. On the other hand, using more specific language can also have its pitfalls. It may make the living will difficult to apply if it does not fit the situation exactly. And even if the directions are clearly understood, when treatment should be stopped may also not be clearly spelled out in the living will. Finally, for many people, it is difficult to predict in advance what one would want in the event of a life-threatening or terminal illness. Not all possible scenarios can be anticipated.

For these and other reasons, many health care providers and advocacy groups suggest that living wills may provide a false sense of security. Physicians may not comply with them for a variety of reasons, including that they are often not available when needed (many people keep their only copy locked away in a security box) or because they do not provide specific enough instructions. To overcome these deficiencies, advocacy groups and legal organizations suggest that in addition to a living will, a person should execute a health care proxy, which appoints a person to make medical decisions when the patient can no longer do so. Several states are now combining health care proxies and living wills into one document. This permits a person who knows the patient, including his values, lifestyle, and religious beliefs, to provide guidance in making a decision that will best reflect the patient's wishes. It is also suggested that people complete a values history to aid the health care proxy in making decisions. A values history includes a description of the person's overall attitude toward life and health, dependency, his personal relationships, religious background and beliefs, finances, and other issues that may affect what type of medical intervention he wants at the end of life.

Living wills have served as an important educational tool in educating the public about end-of-life issues. They have been criticized as ineffective, however, because they are often too vague to provide guidance. Increasingly, other forms of advance directives that more clearly set out a patient's preferences and designate a person to make decisions when the patient cannot are being recommended.

See also: ADVANCE DIRECTIVES; CRUZAN, NANCY; END-OF-LIFE ISSUES; EUTHANASIA; INFORMED CONSENT; LIFE SUPPORT SYSTEM; NATURAL DEATH ACTS; PERSISTENT VEGETATIVE STATE; QUINLAN, KAREN ANN

Bibliography

Cantor, Norman L. "Advance Directive Instruments for End-of-Life and Health Care Decision Making." *Psychology, Public Policy and Law* 4 (1998):629–652.

Emanuel, Linda L., Michael J. Barry, John D. Stoeckle, Lucy M. Ettelson, and Ezekiel J. Emanuel. "Advance Directives for Medical Care: A Case for Greater Use." *New England Journal of Medicine* 324 (1991):889–895.

Furrow, Barry R., Thomas L. Greaney, Sandra H. Johnson, Timothy Stoltzfus Jost, and Robert L. Schwartz. *Health Law*. St. Paul, MN: West Publishing, 1995.

Koch, Tom. "Life Quality vs. the Quality of Life: Assumptions Underlying Prospective Quality of Life Instruments in Health Care Planning." *Social Sciences and Medicine* 51 (2000):419–427.

LoBuono, Charlotte. "A Detailed Examination of Advance Directives." *Patient Care* 34, no. 21 (2000):92–108.

Rich, Ben A. "Advance Directives: The Next Generation." *Journal of Legal Medicine* 19 (1998):1–31.

Teno, Joan, et al. "Advance Directives for Seriously Ill Hospitalized Patients: Effectiveness with the Patient Self- Determination Act and the Support Intervention." *Journal of the American Geriatrics Society* 45 (1995):500–507.

VICKI LENS

LOPATA, HELENA Z.

Helena Znaniecka Lopata has published over ten books on the social roles of women, role modification, aging, and social support. Born in 1925 in

Poznan, Poland, she is the daughter of Florian Znaniecki, a well-known sociologist in both Poland and the United States. Lopata's family emigrated to the United States to escape Nazi occupation when she was a teenager. She is Professor Emerita of Sociology at Loyola University of Chicago and a leading expert on widowhood.

Her first book on widows, *Widowhood in an American City* (1973), focused on the metropolitan Chicago area. In *Women as Widows: Support Systems* (1979), she introduced cross-cultural studies. In a collective effort, she coauthored *Widows and Dependent Wives: From Social Problem to Federal Program* (1985) with Henry P. Brehm, and edited *Widows: The Middle East, Asia and the Pacific* and *Widows: North America,* two volumes in 1987. *Current Widowhood: Myths and Realities* (1996) culminates over thirty years of research on this topic. Her work has been supported by funding and research assistance from diverse sources, including the Midwest Council for Social Research on Aging, Social Security Administration, and a Fulbright Fellowship to India.

Her father's theory of social roles as sets of social relations has influenced much of Lopata's work. The methodology of symbolic interactionism was acquired from professors and fellow students such as Herbert Blumer, Howard Becker, Erving Goffman, Rhoda Blumberg, Gladys Lang, Joseph Gusfield, Everett Hughes, Louis Wirth, and Ernest Burgess at the University of Chicago where she received her doctorate degree in sociology in 1954.

Her work has contributed to an understanding of aging and the recognition that marriage is, in many ways, a temporary status or stage that women experience. She focuses on women and widowhood because there are many more of them than widowers, and they remarry less often than men. Her research on widowhood investigates transition and status reconceptualization. She has noted the role of modernization in shaping the various ways in which women experience this role transition (or social development) around the world; in addition, she has also studied different social, ethnic, and class positions in the United States. An important finding of her comparative and historical approach is the diversity of experience women have in the role of widows.

Lopata looks at widowhood in diverse social systems such as India, where *sati* (the widow's self-immolation on the funeral pyre of her dead husband) was once common, and Israel, where the status of wives who lose their husbands varies by whether he died from "hostile acts" of Palestinians or another cause. Her comparative analysis also covers Korea, Turkey, China, the Philippines, Canada, and Australia. She has concluded that women's loss or gain of status in old age and widowhood depends on their control over societal resources such as money (e.g., Social Security checks) and family support.

Lopata defines herself as a symbolic interactionist concerned with the construction of reality, or the meanings of life. She speaks from personal experience as well. After more than forty years of marriage, Lopata lost her husband, a successful businessman whom she describes as a "Renaissance Man," while writing her latest book on widowhood. In her transition to widowhood, Lopata found the support system she has written about through her work, colleagues, friends, children, and grandchildren.

See also: CONTINUING BONDS; WIDOW-BURNING; WIDOWERS; WIDOWS; WIDOWS IN THIRD WORLD NATIONS

Bibliography

Lopata, Helena Znaniecka. *Current Widowhood: Myths & Realities*. Thousand Oaks, CA: Sage, 1996.

Lopata, Helena Znaniecka. *Women As Widows: Support Systems*. New York: Elsevier, 1979.

Lopata, Helena Znaniecka. *Widowhood in an American City*. Cambridge, MA: Schenkman, 1973.

Lopata, Helena Znaniecka, ed. *Widows*. 2 vols. Durham, NC: Duke University Press, 1987.

Lopata, Helena Znaniecka, and Henry P. Brehm. *Widows and Dependent Wives: From Social Problem to Federal Program*. New York: Praeger, 1985.

BARBARA RYAN

M

MAHLER, GUSTAV

Gustav Mahler (1860–1911) was a Bohemian-born Austrian symphonic composer whose sprawling sonic canvases were often concerned with death, either as a spur to life or as a tragic and inconsolable end. Mahler grappled with mortality in his personal life as well as in his art.

The desperately comic and the searingly tragic coexist in the composer's ten numbered symphonies and many song cycles. His childhood shows the genesis of this strange pairing. In the building where Gustav lived as a child, the tavern owned by his father was adjacent to a funeral parlor put to frequent use by the Mahler family—eight of his fourteen siblings died before reaching adulthood. Mahler's father was a self-educated, somewhat brutal man, and fights between him and his cultured, delicate wife were common. Piano lessons were a way out of the daily misery for little Gustav, and before long, he was making up distinctive pieces of his own. Mahler's mature output seems an elaboration of that early conflation.

At age fifteen Gustav entered the Vienna Conservatory, where he received a diploma three years later. The early failure of his own music to win recognition sparked a remarkable conducting career that took Mahler to all the great opera houses and concert halls of Europe. Conducting earned him a fortune, but it also meant that composing, his first love, was relegated to the off-season. Throughout much of his life, Mahler composed in isolation in summer cottages.

From the beginning, Mahler declared that his music was not for his own time but for the future. An agnostic, he apparently saw long-term success as a real-world equivalent of immortality. "Mahler was a thoroughgoing child of the nineteenth century, an adherent of Nietzsche, and typically irreligious," the conductor Otto Klemperer recalled in his memoirs, adding that, in his music, Mahler evinced a "piety . . . not to be found in any church prayer-book." This appraisal is confirmed by the story of Mahler's conversion to Catholicism in 1897. Although his family was Jewish, Mahler was not observant, and when conversion was required in order to qualify as music director of the Vienna Court Opera—the most prestigious post in Europe—he swiftly acquiesced to baptism and confirmation, though he never again attended mass. Once on the podium, however, Mahler brought a renewed spirituality to many works, including Beethoven's *Fidelio,* which he almost single-handedly rescued from a reputation for tawdriness.

In 1902 Mahler married Alma Schindler, a woman nearly twenty years his junior. They had two daughters, and when Mahler set to work on his *Kindertotenlieder*—a song cycle on the death of children—Alma was outraged. As in a self-fulfilling prophecy, their oldest daughter died in 1907, capping a series of unrelenting tragedies for the composer. In that same year, Mahler was diagnosed with heart disease and dismissed from the Vienna Court Opera following a series of verbal attacks, some of them anti-Semitic. Mahler left for America, where he led the Metropolitan Opera from 1907 to 1910 and directed the New York Philharmonic from 1909 to 1911.

While in Vienna during the summer of 1910, Mahler discovered that Alma was having an affair with the architect Walter Gropius. He sought out Sigmund Freud, who met the composer at a train station in Holland and provided instant analysis, labeling him mother-fixated. Freud later declared his analysis successful, and indeed Mahler claimed in correspondence to have enjoyed an improved relationship with his wife. But it did nothing to stop the deterioration of Mahler's health.

The Mahler biographer Henry-Louis de La Grange has effectively contradicted the popular image of Mahler as congenitally ill. A small man, Mahler was nonetheless physically active, an avid hiker and swimmer throughout most of his life. Nonetheless, he was a man drunk on work, and he grew more inebriated with age. His response to the fatigue and illness was often simply to work more. In 1901, for example, he collapsed after conducting, in the same day, a full-length opera and a symphony concert. He immediately set to work on his Symphony no. 5, which begins with a funeral march.

Mahler's symphonies divide into early, middle, and late periods, respectively comprising the first four symphonies; the fifth, sixth, and seventh symphonies; and the eighth and ninth, plus "Das Lied von der Erde" and the unfinished Tenth Symphony.

Symphony no. 1 in D is subtitled the "Titan," not after the Greek demigods but after a novel of the same name by Jean Paul Richter. The third movement turns "Frère Jacques" into a minor-mode funeral march. Symphony no. 2 moved the symphonic form into entirely new territory. It was longer and required more forces, including a chorus and vocal soloist, and its emotional range was vast. Though subtitled "Resurrection," its texts make no religious claims. Mahler's Symphony no. 3 remains the longest piece in the mainstream symphonic repertory. Its ninety-five minutes open with a massive movement that swiftly swings from moody loneliness to martial pomp, from brawling play to near-mute meditation. An ethereal final adagio is followed by four inner movements of contrasting content, including a quiet, nine-minute solo for mezzo-soprano to a text by Nietzsche extolling the depth of human tragedy. Symphony no. 4, slender by Mahler's standards, concluded Mahler's first period, in which song played an important role.

Gustav Mahler's first composition, written at age six, combined a jolly polka with a solemn funeral dirge. CORBIS

Mahler's next three symphonies were wholly instrumental. Symphony no. 5 is easily read as a backward glance at a man's life. It begins with the most magnificent of orchestral funeral marches, announced by a brilliant trumpet solo, and then slowly moves through movements of anguish and struggle toward the penultimate "Adagietto" (Mahler's most famous excerpt), a wordless love song, and finally to the last movement, filled with the promise of youth. Symphony no. 6, subtitled "Tragic," was formally the composer's most tightly structured, and no. 7, subtitled "Nightsong," is, in its odd last movement, the composer at his most parodistic. In no. 8, "Symphony of a Thousand," Mahler returned to the human voice as symphonic instrument, setting texts from the Catholic liturgy and Goethe.

For symphonists, nine is the number to fear. It took on special status for composers when

Beethoven died after composing only nine symphonies. From Beethoven on, nine had mystical significance. Schubert died after writing nine symphonies, so did Dvorak and Bruckner. Mendelssohn, Schumann, and Brahms did not get near that number before they shuffled off the mortal coil.

Mahler completed his Symphony no. 8 in 1906. In 1907 came his triple calamities: the death of his daughter, his unamicable separation from Vienna Opera, and the diagnosis of heart disease. It was not a good time to compose a symphony whose number cried death. Mahler thought he could skirt the issue by writing an unnumbered symphony that would function as his ninth without carrying the dreaded digit. Thus, Mahler composed "Das Lied von der Erde" ("Song of the Earth"), a massive song cycle for voices and orchestra, that was in every way—except the number—his Ninth Symphony.

Fate read his Symphony no. 9 as the last and would not allow him to finish a tenth. (The one movement he completed is generally performed as a fragment.) In February 1911 Mahler led the New York Philharmonic one last time at Carnegie Hall and then returned to Vienna, where he died three months later of bacterial endocarditis. The twenty-three minutes of the Ninth's last movement, which have been described as "ephemeral" and "diaphanous," weep without apology. Somewhere near the middle of this very slow (Molto adagio) movement comes a jittery harp figure that mimics the composer's coronary arrhythmia.

In length, the size of the forces required, and emotional scope, Mahler's symphonies have rarely been equaled and never surpassed. It is difficult not to see this inflation as the composer's struggle against mortality. If the world was temporary and afterlife improbable, why not postulate immortality through art? "A symphony should be like the world," Mahler said to fellow composer Jan Sibelius, "It should embrace everything!"

See also: FOLK MUSIC; MUSIC, CLASSICAL; OPERATIC DEATH

Bibliography

Cook, Deryck. *Gustav Mahler: An Introduction to His Music*. Cambridge: Cambridge University Press, 1995.

Floros, Constantin. *Gustav Mahler: The Symphonies,* edited by Reinhold G. Pauly and translated by Vernon Wicker. Portland, OR: Timber Press, 1997.

La Grange, Henry-Louis de. *Mahler.* Garden City, NY: Doubleday, 1973.

Lebrecht, Norman. *Mahler Remembered.* New York: W.W. Norton, 1987.

Mahler-Werfel, Alma. *The Diaries,* translated by Antony Beaumont. Ithaca, NY: Cornell University Press, 2000.

Mitchell, Donald, and Andrew Nicholson, eds. *The Mahler Companion.* Oxford: Oxford University Press, 2000.

KENNETH LAFAVE

MALTHUS, THOMAS

Thomas Malthus (1766–1834) was an English clergyman whose theory on population, contained in *An Essay on the Principle of Population* (1798, and later revisions), has had a considerable impact on thinking about the limits of population growth. Malthus believed that unchecked population grows geometrically, a rate that surpasses the ability of the means of subsistence (e.g., food) to support it. To avoid overpopulation, two types of checks on population exist: preventive checks and positive checks. Preventive checks result from human actions that lower the birthrate; for Malthus, this largely meant the postponement of marriage to late ages. Positive checks include anything that operates to increase the death rate (e.g., war, famine, epidemics). While the operation of any of these checks reduces the rate of population growth, Malthus did not think that the preventive checks were powerful enough to prevent the population from growing faster than the means of subsistence. Sooner or later, the more drastic positive checks would come into play. Thus, humans were bound to over-reproduce and, in the end, human numbers would be reduced by increased deaths.

In the two centuries since the *Essay* was first published, the world's population has increased from less than 1 billion to more than 6 billion. While Malthusian theory is not a dominant theory of population growth in contemporary times, there is a group of neo-Malthusians who are concerned about this rate of population growth. They contend either that family planning and birth control are necessary to decrease fertility in third world countries or that war and other social ills are the result of scarcity and overpopulation. Contemporary neo-Malthusians include Lester Brown, Paul Ehrlich, and T. Fraser Homer-Dixon. Some leading opponents are Alexander Cockburn and Paul Athanasiou.

See also: DEMOGRAPHICS AND STATISTICS; POPULATION GROWTH; WAR

Bibliography

Brown, Lester, Gary Gardner, and Brian Halweil, eds. *Beyond Malthus: Nineteen Dimensions of the Population Challenge.* New York: Norton, 1999.

Malthus, Thomas R. *Essay on the Principle of Population.* Homewood, IL: R.D. Irwin, 1963.

ELLEN M. GEE

MARTYRS

The martyr is common to every modern culture, and all societies are proud to acclaim the sacrifices of their spiritual heroes. However martyrdom as a concept is difficult to define, let alone distinguish from simple heroism or idiotic folly, because the awarding of the martyr's crown lies as much in the eyes of the beholder as in the logic of a precise definition. Yet everyone agrees that the martyr exists and that certain acts of sacrifice can legitimately be called martyrdom because martyrdom assigns meaning to death, transforming it into an act of choice and purpose that can be remembered, treasured, and, if necessary, emulated by later generations. The complexities of martyrdom are best studied from three perspectives—historical, sociological, and psychological—because martyrdom is a performance that has evolved and changed over time, requires the interaction of the state and the individual as the martyr attempts to change the power and moral structure of society, and poses questions of motivation that lie outside both history and sociology.

Martyrdom in History

The one common denominator in all martyrdoms (the word stems from the Greek *martur,* meaning "to witness" or "to attest") is that the martyr, in attesting to his or her faith, dies for a noble cause. But even here the denominator is often discredited by controversy over what constitutes nobility and blurred by the inclusion of prolonged suffering—torture, imprisonment, and extreme asceticism—that may not end in death.

Originally the cause was invariably religious, or at least articulated in religious terms. An Athenian jury ordered that Socrates (469–399 B.C.E.), the Western world's first recorded martyr, die by poison (the hemlock cup) when he refused to give up his dangerously public insistence that all men and women possessed souls, which knew the difference between good and evil, and were obliged to question historic and religious authority so as to discover the truth for themselves. Jesus of Nazareth suffered (probably in 30 or 33 C.E.) on a Roman cross to display to the classical Judaic world the truth of his message that "the time is fulfilled and the kingdom of God is at hand" (Mark 1:15). Akiva ben Joseph (50?–135 C.E.), one of the "ten martyrs" who founded schools for the study of the Torah in defiance of a Roman decree, was flayed alive with a carding claw, rejoicing that he was "permitted to love God with my life." Al-Hallaj (858–922 C.E.), the Muslim teacher, mystic, and saint—"the one who is enraptured in God"—was flogged, mutilated, and finally beheaded, accused of usurping "the supreme power of God," placing himself above the prophet Muhammad, and challenging Islamic Law.

Essential to most definitions of martyrdom are two other characteristics: Martyrs must possess choice; they must elect to die. They cannot be helpless victims of happenstance. And they must feel that death is necessary to their cause, furthering the truth and righteousness of their beliefs. Their sacrifices cannot be simply a private matter between themselves and their deity, let alone a suicide. As the psychoanalyst Erik Erikson said of Mahatma Gandhi, it is easy "to kill and be killed"; what is hard is to "make one's death count for life" (Erikson 1969, p. 197).

Imposing upon the "true" martyr a voluntary death that contributes to the success of the cause severely limits the number of candidates and opens up a minefield of debate. Should the soldier who falls upon a hand grenade in order to save the lives of his comrades be called a martyr? His act is voluntary and his goal is surely noble. Should Martin Luther King Jr., who appears in a multitude of martyrologies, be excluded because he did not consciously elect to die in 1968 at the hands of a bigoted gunman in order to advance the cause of civil rights in twentieth-century United States? Can the term *martyr* be legitimately applied, as is so often done, to the millions who died in the Nazi holocaust? They suffered unspeakably, but they did not choose their fate. Finally, should Sir Thomas More be acclaimed a proper martyr? In 1535 he chose to be beheaded rather than to publicly sanction Henry VIII's annulment of his marriage to Catherine of Aragon and the ensuing break of the Church of England from Rome, but he did so, not for the sake of papal authority or the unity of the Catholic Church, but for his private relations with God—he "set the world at nought." He died, as he said at his execution, "the king's good servant but God's first" (Marius 1985, p. 514).

The insistence that true martyrs must deliberately close the door on escape and welcome the chance to display their faith and fortitude, using the occasion to publicize their cause, has created yet another problem. The willingness to die can so easily slide into a death wish that is indistinguishable from suicide. In Judaism, martyrs dying as witnesses to God's existence and as evidence of Israel's worthiness to be Yahweh's chosen people played a crucial function in deflecting divine wrath from the sins of the Jewish nation, but historically Jewish scholars have felt obliged to curb the urge to martyrdom and the fanaticism that so often accompanies it. They limited acceptable martyrdom to the refusal to worship strange gods or commit adultery, incest, and murder, and they warned that voluntary martyrdom is in effect a kind of infanticide since unborn progeny are condemned to oblivion.

In Christianity martyrs play an even more important role. Their courage and blood were the seeds from which the new church sprang. In "On the Glory of Martyrdom," Saint Cyprian wrote that "so great is the virtue of martyrdom, that by its means even he who has wished to slay you is constrained to believe" (Cyptian 1869, vol. 2, p. 241). Nevertheless, the early church fathers were deeply worried lest the hysteria of mass suicidal martyrdom undermine the psychological impact of the true martyr, and Clement of Alexandria warned that those "in haste to give themselves up . . . banish themselves without being martyred, even though they are punished publicly" (Clement pp. 147, 173).

Likewise, in Islam the primary place of honor is given to the battlefield martyr who dies in a holy war, or Jihad. He is assured forgiveness of sin, a crown of glory, marriage to seventy-two ravishing maidens, and the right to intercede on behalf of seventy family relations. With the delights of paradise so overwhelming, Muslim jurists, however, cautioned that no one is allowed to desire martyrdom; one can only wish for the strength to endure the pain of wounds should they be inflicted upon one's body. Allah could be depended to close the gates of paradise upon those who went into battle simply to glorify themselves or for the spoils of war. As the poet T. S. Eliot has written, the greatest temptation a martyr can face is to "do the right deed for the wrong reason" (Eliot 1935, p. 44).

If over the centuries it has been difficult not to dismiss specific acts of martyrdom as a senseless waste of lives, doing neither the martyr nor the cause any good, it has been even more difficult to decide how to handle the political martyr who is so easily branded a traitor. Early martyrs invariably had hidden political agendas or their opponents attributed to them political motives. Roman officials and the elders of the temple looked upon Jesus's actions—especially his violation of the temple—with the deepest suspicion, and although Jesus died accused of blasphemy against the one and only God, his real crime was that his vision of God's kingdom on earth had no place in the existing Roman-Judaic power structure in Judea. Later Roman emperors and provincial governors regarded early Christian martyrs as political criminals because they refused to sacrifice to the emperor as a semi-divine being, a sign of loyalty to the empire similar to saluting the flag of the United States.

Of all the Christian martyrs before the nineteenth century the martyrdom of Thomas Becket, saint of Canterbury, was the most blatantly political, involving a power struggle between two willful men—Thomas, archbishop of Canterbury and Henry II, king of England—and two institutions: church and state. The archbishop (1118–1170) was assassinated as he stood at the high altar of Canterbury Cathedral by armed men who had taken their sovereign Henry II literally when in a fury he cried out, "What miserable drones and traitors have I nourished and promoted . . . who let their lord be treated with such shameful contempt by a lowborn priest" (Grim 1876, p. 429). Henry had cause to be outraged: The archbishop had excommunicated the king's supporters in the struggle between church and state and had claimed that anyone who violated his rights as archbishop was "damned by Jesus Christ."

The papacy elevated Thomas to sainthood and bestowed the crown of martyrdom upon him with unprecedented speed on the grounds that the cause—the defense of the temporal liberties of the church—was noble, the style of his death was magnificent, and the miracles that had taken place at his grave were proof of divine approval. Although thousands worshiped at his shrine, Becket's prideful and immoderate personality and the political and secular nature of his cause bothered even contemporaries. The bishop of Hereford asked whether the archbishop should in fact be accounted a martyr if "to be a martyr is to die for the faith" (fitzStephen 1876, pt. 3, p. 60). Unfortunately, it was difficult then, as it is today, to disassociate faith from institutional self-interest.

By and large early martyrdom tended to be defensive, although Jesus may be an important exception. Socrates sought to defend an ideal, not to overthrow the laws of Athens. Early Jewish martyrs endeavored to defend themselves and Judea, first from cultural annihilation by Antiochus IV and then from Roman conquest, not to reconstitute society. Second- and third-century Christians maintained only that they should be allowed to worship their God in peace. And Thomas Becket died not to destroy the state but to defend the church. However, as the history of martyrdom reached the nineteenth and twentieth centuries, the martyr became not only increasingly political in behavior but also aggressive in spirit. More and more martyrs turned into belligerent activists against, not passive victims of, society, and therefore increasingly difficult to judge.

John Brown (1800–1859) is the prime nineteenth-century example, melding the demands of a righteous and wrathful Calvinistic God with the cry for social justice on Earth. He cast himself in the role of the Lord's revolutionary instrument to bring about the necessary apocalyptic fury to purge the nation of the sin of slavery. When he was executed for terrorism and treason by the Commonwealth of Virginia for having led an insurrection against slavery, he insisted that he died not solely for "the cause of God" but also for "the cause of humanity" (Villard 1910, p. 540). But in joining the two, he so mixed martyrdom with political activism that history has been unable to clearly say whether John Brown died a martyr or a terrorist and traitor.

In the twentieth century the death of Dietrich Bonhoeffer generated equal uncertainties. There are those who would call the German pastor a martyr to humanity. Others would argue that, as a would-be assassin of the legal head of state, he violated his Christian beliefs and rightfully paid the price of treason. Bonhoeffer was part of a semi-aristocratic conspiracy to murder Adolf Hitler, having reached the decision that the sixth commandment—"thou shall not kill"—had to be set aside when warring against unspeakable evil. But after Bonhoeffer's execution in April 1945, only days before Hitler took his own life, ministers of Bonhoeffer's own Confessing Church were reluctant to have the names of their "colleagues, who were killed for their faith, lumped together with political martyrs" (Bethge 1970, p. 834).

From the start the presence of political martyrs has bedeviled martyrdom, and in the eighteenth century Pope Benedict XIV established guidelines for determining martyrdom. In regulations that operate to this day, he insisted that the acclaimed martyr had to have died for the faith as laid down by the church, the executioners had to be motivated by "hatred of the faith," and the martyr's motivation had to be purely spiritual and religious. For these reasons the Catholic Church refused to grant archbishop Oscar Romero, "the people's saint of El Salvador," the title of martyr even though he was shot down in 1980 while saying mass in the hospital chapel of the Carmelite sisters. Though the outcry was worldwide, battling against evil and social injustice in the name of the kingdom of God was not sufficient to overcome the concern that the archbishop had been assassinated for his politics, not his faith.

The Sociological Explanation

Martyrs have rarely appeared singly making it tempting to explain their presence in terms of the societies that spawned them. Martyrdom tends to be a group phenomena, drawing strength from a collective identity and representing serious cultural divisions within the state. In contrast to the hero, who is the product of a consensus society where the quality and worth of the heroic act is undisputed, the martyr is the offspring of a community at war with itself. Such societies are unable to agree whether the martyr's death should be praised as the highest service that can be rendered God or humanity, be dismissed as pointless folly, or be branded as the proper punishment reserved for traitors. Unstable societies experiencing cultural, economic, and political change are particularly likely to generate martyrs as in the case of the classical world during the second and third centuries. Beleaguered communities also spawn men and women who prefer death, often collectively, to surrender or assimilate. Jewish history abounds with this kind of response. Finally, expanding or crusading societies produce those who are eager to give their lives for their religious faith or for their political-social ideology.

Societies such as medieval Europe regarded the martyr as the paramount role model, the stories of their sacrifices being part of the culture and their tombs and relics crucial contact points between heaven and the earth. But so far the martyr has eluded demographic classification by age, class, or sex. In those situations where reliable statistics exist martyrs come from all walks of life. Of the 288 or so English Protestants who were burned at the stake under Catholic queen Mary between 1555 and 1558, only a handful were politically or socially prominent, the vast majority were artisans and agricultural laborers (fifty-one were women), and surprisingly few (7.3%) were clergymen. A generation later, however, of the Catholics executed by Elizabeth I most came from the upper stratum of sixteenth-century society and they were predominantly clerics and males. It would appear that the martyr is far too individualistic to fit into tidy social-scientific categories.

Because of the controversy surrounding Sir Thomas More's execution, the Roman Catholic Church took 400 years to confer full sainthood. ARCHIVE PHOTOS, INC.

The Psychological Explanation

The principle of reverse optics operates when viewing martyrs: The more distant they are, the more attractive they appear. Close-up martyrs are often found to be harsh, unyielding, and self-absorbed individuals. As the self-proclaimed possessors of the truth, be it social, political, or religious, martyrs find it difficult to live in the world as it is, and more often than not their determination to sacrifice their own lives to a higher purpose is accompanied by an equal willingness to sacrifice other people's lives as well. Martyrs have been the subjects of psychoanalytic study to explain such obsessive behavior, and scholars have suggested that self-interest as well as altruism lies behind their actions. Undeniably religious martyrs, no matter their creed, expect to achieve in martyrdom that uncontroversial act of heroism that makes them memorable in the eyes of both God and man, assuring them a place in heaven and in history books. As Zackary Cawdrey proclaimed in *A Preparation for Martyrdom,* a martyr's death is greater than that of other saints "who did not pass through that Red Sea of Blood" (Cawdry 1672, p. 48). "The Christian tradition of martyrdom was absolutely clear: The greater the suffering, the more glorious the reward in heaven. So much so that the early Christian fathers regarded too great an eagerness for martyrdom to be tantamount to the sin of suicide" (Smith 1997, pp. 90–96).

Other authors have argued that martyrs are deeply disturbed men and women devoured by their obsession. The early Christian and sixteenth-century Marian martyrs in particular have been researched, and hints of paranoia, masochism, and manic depression observed in their response to torture and painful death. Some martyrs are said to be socially ill–adjusted people who seek to draw attention to themselves, their behavior psychologically no different from the exhibitionism of the psychopath who, in a rage against society, shoots down dozens of innocent people in order to be noticed if only in the next day's headlines. Equally disturbing is the role of pride in the martyrs' motivation. It is difficult to find a humble martyr. The possessors of absolute truth are rarely retiring and submissive people; their sense of self is swollen by pride of mission, and they are deeply solicitous of their reputations on earth and in heaven. As Raghavan Iyer has written, "It is at the fire of exceptional and spiritually subtle egotism that many of the saints and mystics . . . have warmed their hands" (Iyer 1978, p. 126). It is that same heat that drives the martyr to acts of sublime heroism and folly.

Impact of Martyrdom

Martyrdom can be a politically and spiritually explosive performance, profoundly dangerous to society. Nothing gives greater credence to the truth of the martyr's message than the spectacle of dying for it. Jesus's death upon the cross seared itself upon the minds and imaginations of later generations who harkened to his words: "Whosoever will come after me, let him deny himself and take up the cross and follow me" (Mark 8:34). The endless storytelling of the suffering and sacrifices of past martyrs can be a potent incentive to action, be it Buddhist, Christian, Jewish, or Muslim.

As a consequence, martyrs are generally viewed by the state as peculiarly dangerous criminals because they commit offenses of the heart, mind, and soul, striking at society's definition of duty, honor, and loyalty. Common criminals—murderers, thieves, and vandals—can be summarily executed and forgotten. Martyrs, however, live on after death. Not only their bodies but also their reputations and the validity of their ideas must be destroyed. Initially the state branded martyrs as perverts and lunatics, and in the eyes of Rome all Christians were sodomites, cannibals, and "enemies of the human race."

In the twentieth century, totalitarian governments have attacked martyrs' individuality and exceptionality, dismissing them as social deviants in need of rehabilitation. They have been denied the chance to stand out from the herd and deprived of the publicity so necessary to their cause. The public Roman arena and the Spanish *auto-da-fé* have been replaced by the high walls of the prison and the mental hygiene clinic, where technicians, armed with electric probes and "truth"-inducing drugs, reshape the strongest personality. As Russian novelist Alexander Solzhenitsyn wrote in 1970, "The incarceration of free-thinking healthy people in madhouses is SPIRITUAL MURDER; it is a variation on the GAS CHAMBER, but is even more cruel: the torture of the people being killed is more malicious and more prolonged" (Rubenstein 1985, p. 137). In their battle to rearrange society more in accord to the truths they hold dear, martyrs must display great strength of body and mind, but in the face of modern technology they may well be an endangered species.

There are all sorts of martyrs. Some seek to test themselves and their faith upon the cross of martyrdom. Some regard themselves as the athletes of truth and God's instruments on earth. Still others pursue paradise and reputation through heroic deaths or nurture stubborn and overly tender consciences that cannot yield or compromise. There are the forgotten or defrocked martyrs such as Thomas Becket, whose bones 358 years after his death were tossed out upon the dunghill, his shrine destroyed, and his reputation in the eyes of the sixteenth-century English state changed from martyr to traitor. Finally, there are the unknown martyrs whose numbers are beyond reckoning. But one and all have possessed the conviction that they could "serve as well by dying as by living" (Gandhi 1958–1984, vol. 54, p. 269).

See also: BROWN, JOHN; HOLOCAUST; IMMORTALITY, SYMBOLIC; ISLAM; JESUS; SACRIFICE; SOCRATES

Bibliography

Barlow, Frank. *Thomas Becket.* Berkeley: University of California Press, 1986.

Bethge, Eberhard. *Dietrich Bonhoeffer: Man of Vision, Man of Courage.* New York: Harper and Row, 1970.

Brown, Judith. *Gandhi, Prisoner of Hope.* New Haven, CT: Yale University Press, 1989.

Cawdrey, Zackary. *A Preparation for Martyrdom*. London: Tho. Parkhurst, 1672.

Clement of Alexandria. "Miscellanies" In *The Writings,* Vol. 2. Edinburgh: T & T Clark, 1872.

Cyprian, Saint. "On the Glory of Martyrdom" In *The Writings of Cyprian,* Vol. 2 Edinburgh: T & T Clark, 1869.

Erikson, Erik. *Gandhi's Truth on the Origins of Militant Nonviolence*. New York: Norton, 1969.

Fackenheim, Emil. *The Jewish Return to History: Reflections in the Age of Auschwitz and a New Jerusalem.* New York: Schocken Books, 1978.

fitzStephen, William. "Vita Sancti Thomae" *Rerum Britannicarum,* Vol. 67, pt. 3. London: Longman & Co., 1876.

Foxe, John. *Acts and Monuments,* edited by George Townsend. 7 vols. London: R. B. Seeley and W. Burnside, 1837–1841.

Frend, W. H. C. *Martyrdom and Persecution in the Early Church: A Study of a Conflict from the Maccabees to Donatus*. Oxford: Blackwell, 1965.

Gandhi, Mahatma. *Collected Works,* Vol. 54. Delhi: Ministry of Information, Government of India, 1984.

Grim, Edward. "Vita Sancti Thomae" *Rerum Britannicarum,* Vol. 67, pt. 2. London: Longman, 1876.

Hastings, James ed., *Encyclopaedia of Religion and Ethics,* Vol. 11: *Saints and Martyrs*. New York: Charles Scribner's Sons, 1951.

Iyer, Raghavan. *The Moral and Political Thought of Mahatma Gandhi*. Oxford: Oxford University Press, 1978.

James, William. *The Varieties of Religious Experience*. New York: The Modern Library, 1936.

Klausner, Samuel. "Martyrdom." In *The Encyclopedia of Religion,* Vol. 9. New York: Macmillan, 1987.

Marius, Richard. *Thomas More*. New York: Vintage Books, Random House, 1985.

Massignon, Louis. *The Passion of al-Hallaj; Mystic and Martyr of Islam*. 4 Vols. Princeton, NJ: Princeton University Press, 1982.

Musurillo, Herbert. *The Acts of the Christian Martyrs*. London: Clarendon Press, 1972.

Oates, Stephen. *To Purge This Land with Blood: A Biography of John Brown*. New York: Harper Torchbooks, 1970.

Purcell, William. *Martyrs of Our Time*. St. Louis, MO: CBP Press, 1983.

Riddle, Donald. *The Martyrs: A Study in Social Control*. Chicago: University of Chicago Press, 1931.

Rubenstein, Joshua. *Soviet Dissidents: Their Struggle for Human Rights*. Boston: Beacon Press, 1985.

Smith, Lacey. *Fool, Martyrs, Traitors: The Story of Martyrdom in the Western World*. New York: Alfred A. Knopf, 1997.

Villard, Oswald. *John Brown, 1800-1859: A Biography Fifty Years After*. Boston: Houghton Mifflin, 1910.

Weiner, Eugene, and Anita Weiner. *The Martyr Conviction*. Atlanta, GA: Scholars Press, 1990.

Weinstein, Donald, and Rudolph Bell. *Saints & Society: The Two Worlds of Western Christendom, 1000–1700*. Chicago: University of Chicago Press, 1982.

Woodward, Kenneth. *Making Saints*. New York: Simon & Schuster, 1990.

LACEY BALDWIN SMITH

MASS KILLERS

When terrorists attacked the World Trade Center in New York City and the Pentagon in Washington, D.C., on September 11, 2001, it was not the most extensive example of mass murder ever committed, but it did have a great impact on the world, launching an extensive "war on terrorism." This incident is just one of thousands of examples of mass murder perpetrated throughout human history.

Mass Murder Defined

Murder is the killing of one person by another person with "malice aforethought"; there may or may not be premeditation. Generally, a person who murders restricts his or her act to one victim. A mass murderer, however, slays three or more victims over a short period of time. The duration is typically hours but can be days. If the act takes place in one location, it is usually continuous. *Murder spree* is a term that criminologists use if the victims are killed at more than one location. Michael Kelleher, in his 1997 book *Flashpoint,* also adds the phrase "mass murder by intention," providing the 1996 example of Larry Shoemake in Jackson, Mississippi, who killed only one victim even though he fired more than a hundred rounds of ammunition and torched a restaurant. Mass killers differ from serial killers in that serial killers murder their victims separately and over a period of time, with a cooling-off period between murders. Serial killers may slay victims for years until they are caught or turn themselves in to the authorities.

Historical Overview

The site and time of the first mass murder is unknown. The Bible delineates numerous examples of mass murder including Samson's slaying of the Philistines (Judges 16:27–30) and King Herod's order for the murder of all male children who were two years old or less in the region of Bethlehem while trying to kill Jesus (Matt. 2:16). The thanatologist Panos Bardis notes that in ancient Greece it was common to cremate a fallen Greek hero with several enemy soldiers who were still alive. Archaeological excavations have revealed the murder and burial of a royal court with a deceased king. The purpose was to serve their leader in the afterlife. One of the earliest examples of mass murder in the United States took place on August 10, 1810, at Ywahoo Falls, Kentucky, when racist whites murdered over 100 Cherokee women and children. Since the Ywahoo Falls incident the number and examples of mass murders in the United States and other parts of the world have been numerous and varied. Perhaps the most extreme example of late-twentieth-century mass genocide occurred in 1993 when nearly 1 million Rwandans were slaughtered over a period of 100 days by the Presidential Guard, elements of the Rwandan armed forces, and extremist military.

Psychological Profiles of Mass Murderers

One of the difficulties in gathering data on the mass murderer is that he or she often commits suicide. The terrorists involved in the World Trade Center and Pentagon tragedies died when the planes they hijacked hit their objectives. Dylan Klebold and Eric Harris committed suicide after their mass murder at Columbine High School in Littleton, Colorado, on April 20, 1999. Therefore some information about types listed in this entry is limited.

Kelleher outlines seven categories of mass murderers who have somewhat different motivations and profiles. These categories include perverted love, politics and hate, revenge, sexual homicide, execution, psychotic, and unexplained. Ronald and Stephen Holmes, in their book *Mass Murder in the United States* (2000), provide a different typology. Holmes and Holmes use some types from Park Dietz, including the family annihilator, the disgruntled type, and the set-and-run type. The authors then added the disciple killer, the ideological mass murderer, the disgruntled employee, and the school shooter. Both Holmes and Holmes' and Kelleher's typologies were created before the attack on the World Trade Center and the rash of suicide bombings; however, the string of early-twenty-first-century events falls under Kelleher's category of politics and hate.

Perverted love. Kelleher's first category is defined by the concept of perverted love, with an example being the family man who kills his entire family out of his own depression or pathology. Perverted love killings may be either of two types: family murder/suicide or a family killing. In the first category, more commonly done by males, the individual commits *suicide by proxy,* a term from the psychiatrist Shervert Fraser used by James Fox and Jack Levin in their book *Overkill* (1994). The families of the offender are seen as part of the self. If there is no happiness in life for the self, then, he reasons, there is no happiness in life for the extended self. He views himself as saving his family from future suffering. The egocentrism of this individual does not allow for his family to have a different opinion on life.

The individual who engages in a family killing without suicide is demonstrated by the example of Ronald Gene Simmons, the father of his daughter's son, who killed fourteen members of his family on Christmas in 1987 when his wife threatened to divorce him. Mass murderer Julio Gonzalez became jealous of his girlfriend in 1990 and torched the Bronx's Happy Land Social Club, killing nearly all ninety-seven persons inside. There have been other instances where a mass murder has been committed to protect a family member or members. During the Allen-Edwards feud in Hillsville, Virginia, on March 13, 1912, feudists entered the courtroom where a family member was being tried, and killed the judge, sheriff, commonwealth attorney, a juror, and an innocent bystander.

Politics and hate. The second type of mass murder involves politics and hate. Adolf Hitler blamed the Jews for Germany's problems, and the result was genocide. The terrorists who attacked the World Trade Center and other suicide bombers perceive the victims as violating one of the terrorists' political or religious goals. From his or her perspective, the death is viewed as for the greater good because the individual has eliminated a number of people whose views differ from his or hers. Even this minimal expectation may not always be true due to the randomness of the victims. Galvanizing the alienated opposing side into political action and a cycle of revenge is also an obvious and frequently counterproductive consequence of such a terrorist choice for mass murder. According to the September 24, 2001, issue of *Time,* the profile of the suicide bomber before September 11 had been of a young man, aged eighteen to twenty-four, who had been born in poverty and was full of both despair and zealotry, having nothing to lose. But the suicide bombers of September 11 showed a shift in profile. These men were older and had the option of middle-class lives because of their education and technical skills. One of them left behind a wife and children.

According to the April 15, 2002, issue of *Newsweek,* there have been 149 suicide bombing attacks against Israel since 1993, with the perpetrators being most often single (87.2%), from Hamas (47%), residing on the West Bank (59%), between seventeen and twenty-three years of age (67.1%), and possessing some or a full high school education (37.6%).

A differing example of mass murder involving politics and hate includes Timothy McVeigh and Terry Nichols, who bombed the federal building in Oklahoma City on April 19, 1995, because they were angry at the federal government over the 1993 Waco, Texas, raid against the Branch Davidians. They are classified as set-and-run murderers in the Holmes and Holmes typology, for this type of killer sets the killing device in motion, then leaves the location, as McVeigh did before killing 168 people, including twenty children.

Revenge. Revenge killings involve a murderer who gives "payback" to someone who is perceived to have humiliated him or her. The killer's own personal responsibility is rationalized away and blame is conveniently placed on others. One subtype of this motivation is the Holmes and Holmes type of disgruntled employee, the workplace murderer. David Burke, a fired airline employee, followed his boss onto a plane on December 7, 1987, shot him, and caused the plane to crash, killing forty-three people. Pat Sherrill, fearing that he might be fired from his postal job, killed fourteen coworkers and wounded six others in the Edmond, Oklahoma, post office on August 20, 1986. Mark Barton, a day trader, became angry after losing a great deal of money and on July 29, 1999, killed his family and entered two brokerage firms, slaying nine and wounding twelve.

Though innocent victims are frequently killed in this type of assault, workplace mass murderers typically plan the assault and are selective in their hunt for particular prime victims. The depersonalization of others is viewed by Kelleher as symbolically eliminating the whole organization or school and is called *murder by proxy* by Fox and Levin. They also point out that murderers in general have an average age of twenty-nine, but workplace mass murderers have an average age of thirty-eight. While a younger man can still see opportunities in the future, the older man sees his salary and/or status disappearing, with no satisfactory substitute in sight. Although many people experience job loss without becoming mass murderers, workplace murderers have frequently experienced chronic or recent social isolation. The only factor in their lives that is meaningful to them is their job or career, and they are incapable of coping with their problems in adaptive ways by changing their behavior. Interestingly, the workplace mass murderer will often have no significant criminal record, and others will perceive him or her to be reasonable or at least harmless. Typically, many years of frustration have occurred before the fatal event.

Fox and Levin's analysis of workplace killers also showed that 93 percent were male and more than 70 percent were white. Female mass murderers in general are less likely to choose guns or bombs, leaning more toward poison or accidents. Even in suicide, females are less likely to use firearms and more likely to use drugs, indicating that males are more acculturated to lethal mass weapons.

Some individuals, whatever the source of their frustration, lash out at random victims, such as the case of Thomas Hamilton. Upset at losing his volunteer position as a scoutmaster in Dunblane, Scotland, he entered the Dunblane Primary School twenty years later and killed seventeen children on March 13, 1996. James Oliver Huberty, after losing both his job with Babcox and Wilcox and his job as a private security guard, entered a McDonalds restaurant on July 18, 1984, and over a period of one hour and fifteen minutes killed twenty-one victims and wounded twenty. Holmes and Holmes categorize him as a disgruntled citizen because his victims were complete strangers.

A second subtype of revenge killer identifies his or her problems as coming from a particular "target group" in society. The target group killer may have a vendetta against the persons killed and/or blame the group for personal or societal problems. Marc Lepine, an avid woman hater, slaughtered fifteen "feminists" studying engineering in a Montreal, Canada, school in 1989, then committed suicide.

A third subtype of revenge killing is the school killing. Eric Harris and Dylan Klebold murdered their thirteen victims at Columbine High School on April 20, 1999, in response to societal hatred, a search for fame, and revenge resulting from ridicule by fellow schoolmates. The researchers J. Reid Meloy, Anthony Hempel, and their colleagues analyzed a sample of thirty-four adolescent mass murderers whose median age was seventeen and who had killed alone or in pairs between 1958 and 1999. They divided the sample into five types, as follows: the classroom avenger, the family annihilator, the bifurcated killer (family and classroom), miscellaneous, and the criminal opportunist. The criminal opportunist simply commits a mass murder during the course of another crime and falls into Kelleher's execution classification.

Meloy and Hempel found that 70 percent of their sample were termed "loners," 62 percent abused alcohol or drugs; many were preoccupied by violent fantasies; 42 percent had a credible history of violence against a person, animal, or property; and 43 percent were bullied by others. Forty-one percent had a history of at least one sexual-affectional bond with a female. Only 23 percent had a history of psychiatric hospitalization or at least one visit to a mental health professional, and only 6 percent showed evidence of psychosis.

The authors cite the researchers McGee and DeBernardo's 1999 study of fourteen cases of mass murder, with the murderer profiled again as a "loner or outcast" with no violent history and a middle-class suburban or rural family. According to their study, this type of mass murderer had many violent fantasies, and there was a precipitating event of peer rejection or authority discipline. They showed atypical depression or mixed personality disorders.

The authors point out several differences distinguishing adolescent from adult mass murderers. First, adolescents experience a high rate of bullying, even compared to a baseline of most students, who report being bullied at least once, and a baseline of 14 percent of both boys and girls who say they suffer severe trauma from bullying abuse. When the killer reciprocates that violence with lethal violence, he or she shows identification with the aggressor, now reversing roles and assuming the aggressive posture.

A second difference pointed out by the authors is that one out of four mass killings by adolescents involve killings in pairs. The authors view this as seeking approval from a peer, which is part of adolescent development. In each of the seven pairs in their sample, one perpetrator was dominant.

A third difference among adolescents is discussed by the scholars George Palermo and Lee Ross, who note that there are few suicides of adolescents after their murders. The authors hypothesize that adults have a higher level of moral conscience and recognize in some way the horror of their behavior on a conventional level and the subsequent social and moral consequences. Juveniles feel that because they were wronged it is acceptable to behave at a level of reciprocity, which is a premoral level in the psychologist Lawrence Kohlberg's theory of moral development.

Sexual homicide. A significant number of killings have been perpetrated by a desire to achieve sexual gratification through inflicting pain on the victims (sadism) and/or receiving pain by being kicked, scratched, pinched, or bitten by the victim. Richard Speck was influenced by drugs and alcohol when he killed eight student nurses, raping some of them in the process, on July 13, 1966, in Chicago. Numerous mass murderers such as Peter Manual and "sex beast" Melvin Rees were sadists and derived sexual pleasure from killing their victims and mutilating the corpses. The ultimate pleasure for some masochistic killers is being executed.

Execution. The execution mass murderer kills for greed and personal gain and may engage in either cold-blooded killing for profit or the unplanned execution of witnesses. The St. Valentine's Day Massacre of 1929 was a result of turf rivalry between Al Capone and "Bugs" Moran concerning the whisky business. William Burke and William Hare, Irish laborers and body snatchers living in

Edinburgh, Scotland, killed approximately eighteen persons in 1829 and delivered their bodies (for dissection purposes) to medical schools, impelled by a desire for money. Jack Gilbert Graham, irritated at his mother when she came to visit him in Denver Colorado, in 1955, decided to murder her for insurance money. He presented her with a bomb wrapped as a Christmas present to take home with her on the plane. It exploded, killing forty-three people on board. Belle Guinness, America's most notorious murderess, killed several people on her Indiana farm in 1908, including her husbands (and potential husbands), adopted daughter, and biological children for monetary reasons.

Psychotic. The psychotic type is a category used to describe a murderer who has a significant mental disorder. Charles Whitman was suffering from a brain tumor when he randomly killed eighteen people at the University of Texas on July 31, 1966. Martin Bryant was suffering from a mental disorder when he went on a rampage on April 28, 1996, in Port Arthur, Tasmania, killing thirty-five people. Howard Unruh, a World War II veteran suffering from posttraumatic stress disorder, became upset with his neighbors in East Camden, New Jersey, and went on a murder spree in September 1949, slaying thirteen individuals. Mental disorder has been an issue in numerous cases in the first two years of the twenty-first century, when a mother has slain her dependent children. Examples include Marilyn Lemak in Naperville, Illinois, who killed three children and Andrea Yates in Houston, Texas, who killed five. Although only a minority of mass murderers are actually severely mentally ill or psychotic, many have other psychological disorders, according to Kelleher. These include clinical depression, as well as antisocial personality disorder, paranoia, alcohol and/or drug abuse, and obsessions of control. Kelleher points out that these types of murderers frequently have a childhood that includes separation, physical or sexual abuse, and family violence.

Unexplained. Those murders that cannot be explained fall into the unexplained group. For example, authorities could never figure out why Thomas Eugene Braun went on his killing spree in 1967. While several hypotheses exist, there is no definitive explanation of why Charlie Lawson, a North Carolina farmer, killed his wife, six children, and himself on Christmas Day, 1929.

Weapons and Media Influences

Influences on mass murder that come not from the individual's personal life but from society include media news or motion pictures about mass killers. Adolescent murderers mentioned *Natural Born Killers* (1994) and *The Basketball Diaries* (1995) as movies that had influenced them, according to Meloy and Hempel. The *copycat effect* is a term that criminologists use to describe society's increased rate of a low-probability event—such as a suicide, skyjacking, or suicide bombing—after such an event is publicized in the media. This phenomenon was clearly operating when James Wilson shot children at a Greenwood, South Carolina, school in September 1988. He had been saving a photo of Laurie Dann, who had appeared on the cover of *People* magazine after committing a similar crime. On May 20, 1988, Dann entered a classroom in Winnetka, Illinois, carrying three pistols, and began shooting children—killing one and wounding five others before killing herself.

Mass murderers have used a variety of weapons. Anton Probst and Lizzie Borden used an axe to slay their victims. Timothy McVeigh, Terry Nichols, Jack Gilbert Graham, and numerous suicide bombers used explosives to perform their acts of murder. Most contemporary mass murderers in the United States employ automatic weapons, particularly hand guns. Males in many parts of the United States feel comfortable with guns as a part of the gun culture; men have been hunting together for both food and recreation since the days of the early republic.

The future for prevention of mass murder is somewhat pessimistic. As long as there is a gun culture or a means for mass destruction, there will be mass murder. As long as the mass media exists, there will be examples for copycat killings. However, the less publicity, glamorization, and reward these actions receive, the less likely it is that individuals will choose such actions in the future.

See also: GENOCIDE; HOMICIDE, DEFINITIONS AND CLASSIFICATIONS OF; ORGANIZED CRIME; SERIAL KILLERS; TERRORIST ATTACKS ON AMERICA

Bibliography

Allen, J. Sidna. *Memoirs of J. Sidna Allen.* Mount Airy, NC: Daniel Gardner, 1991.

Bardis, Panos D. *History of Thanatology.* Washington, DC: University Press of America, 1981.

Dickey, Christopher. "Inside Suicide, Inc." *Newsweek,* 15 April 2002, 26–32.

Dietz, Park. "Mass, Serial, and Sensational Homicide." *Bulletin of the New England Medical Society* 62 (1986):477–491.

Fox, James Alan, and Jack Levin. *Overkill: Mass Murder and Serial Killing Exposed.* New York: Plenum, 1994.

Holmes, Ronald M., and Stephen T. Holmes. *Mass Murder in the United States.* Upper Saddle River, NJ: Prentice Hall, 2000.

Jones, M. Bruce, and Trudy J. Smith. *White Christmas, Blood Christmas.* Trinity, NC: UpWords Publications, 1990.

Kelleher, Michael D. *Flash Point: The American Mass Murderer.* Westport, CT: Praeger, 1997.

Kohlberg, Lawrence. *The Psychology of Moral Development: The Nature and Validity of Moral Stages.* New York: Harper and Row, 1984.

McGeary, Johanna, et al. "The New Breed of Terrorists." *Time,* 24 September 2001, 28–36.

Meloy, J. Reid, Anthony G. Hempel, Kris Mohandie, Andrew A. Shiva, and B. Thomas Gray. "Offender and Offense Characteristics of a Nonrandom Sample of Adolescent Mass Murderers." *Journal of the American Academy of Child and Adolescent Psychiatry* 40, no. 6 (2001):719–728.

Nash, Jay Robert. *Bloodletters and Badmen.* New York: M. Evans and Co., 1973.

Palermo, George B., and Lee E. Ross. "Mass Murder, Suicide, and Moral Development: Can We Separate the Adults from the Juveniles?" *International Journal of Offender Therapy and Comparative Criminology* 43, no. 1 (1999):8–20.

Wilson, Colin, and Damon Wilson. *The Killers among Us: Sex, Madness and Mass Murder.* New York: Warner Books, 1995.

JAMES K. CRISSMAN
SANDRA BURKHALTER CHMELIR

MAYA RELIGION

At the time of Spanish contact in the sixteenth century the Maya were not a single, unified political or cultural entity, but rather were composed of competing as well as allied city states and kingdoms, many of which spoke mutually unintelligible Mayan languages, including Quiche, Tzotzil, and Yucatec. Thus, to avoid overgeneralizations it is important to specify particular Maya cultures when mentioning sixteenth-century accounts. Aside from the sixteenth-century contact period, documents written in Spanish and Mayan languages, there is the rich corpus of texts and imagery pertaining to the Classic Maya (c. 250–900 C.E.), much of which can be read and interpreted for a detailed look at Maya religious practices.

One of the most important sources concerning the contact period is the *Relación de las Cosas de Yucatan,* (Account of the Things of Yucatan) written by the Franciscan Priest Diego de Landa in the 1560s. Landa described in some detail the burial customs of the Yucatec Maya, including a period of fasting and mourning, especially for the husband and wife of the deceased. The corpse was wrapped in a shroud, with maize gruel and a precious bead placed in the mouth. The body was then interred in the house floor, which then was usually abandoned. Landa also noted that people of high rank were often cremated. In this case, the Mayan elite may have been evoking Central Mexican burial practices. Although cremation is generally rare in the Mayan region, it is well documented for the Aztec. According to Landa, the bead placed in the mouth would serve as money in the afterlife. However, it is more likely that the stone signified the life spirit, as in the case of the Aztec, who considered the mortuary bead as the symbolic heart of the deceased. In a description of royal funerary rites in highland Guatemala, the Dominican cleric and chronicler Fray Bartolome de las Casas noted that a precious bead was passed before the mouth of the dying king to capture his expiring breath soul. In ancient Maya art, this breath soul is commonly portrayed as a jade bead or flower floating before the face. Moreover, one of the more common death expressions appearing in Classic Maya texts concerns the expiration of a floral breath soul.

According to Landa, the Yucatec Maya conceived of two afterlife realms, the dark underworld known as *Metnal* and a paradisal place of plenty, where the souls would be shaded by a tree in the center of the world. The underworld was the foul realm of the skeletal death god *Ah Cimih,* also know as *Cizin,* meaning "flatulent one." The

Mayan Temple I is characterized by multiple steps and located at the religious site of Tikal in Guatemala. Aside from the planting and growth of corn, the dawn rising of the sun was another basic metaphor for resurrection and rebirth in the Maya religion. CORBIS

sixteenth-century *Popol Vuh* (a text concerning the mythology and history) of the Quiche Maya of highland Guatemala gives a very detailed description of the underworld, here known as *Xibalba,* or "place of fright." The lords of Xibalba were malevolent gods of death and disease who, although deceitful and cunning, were eventually defeated by a mythic pair of hero twins.

Many mythic episodes of the sixteenth-century *Popol Vuh,* including Xibalba and the hero twins, are present among earlier Classic Maya. Perhaps because of the abundant death imagery on Classic Maya vases, scholars have often assumed that hellish Xibalba constituted the only afterlife destination. However, one of the more common classic period themes concerns the hero twins reviving their father, the maize god. In Classic Maya thought the burial and resurrection of the deceased was compared to the planting of the moribund maize kernel, temporarily buried but destined to reemerge. One extraordinary carved vessel, commonly referred to at the "Death Vase," portrays both metaphors of death and resurrection. On one side of the vase three anthropomorphic cacao trees rise out of the skeletal corpse. The central tree is clearly the Maya maize god. The opposite side of the vase portrays the maize god as a supine, bundled corpse. Floating directly above the corpse is a solar disk, quite probably denoting the ascension of the soul into the sky. In Classic Maya art, deceased kings are commonly shown in solar disks or apotheosized as the sun god. Given the identification of the Maya sun god with war and warriors, the Classic Maya may have conceived of a celestial paradise similar to that of the later Aztec, a brilliant, flower-filled realm of heroic kings and warriors.

See also: AZTEC RELIGION; INCAN RELIGION

Bibliography

Coe, Michael D. "The Hero Twins: Myth and Image." In Justin Kerr ed., *The Maya Vase Book.* New York: Kerr Associates, 1989.

Tedlock, Dennis. *Popol Vuh: The Mayan Book of the Dawn of Life,* revised edition. New York: Simon & Schuster, 1996.

Tozzer, Alfred M. *Papers of the Peabody Museum of American Archeology and Ethnology, Harvard University.* Vol. 18: *Landa's Relación de las Cosas de Yucatan.* Cambridge, MA: Harvard University, 1941.

KARL A. TAUBE

MEMENTO MORI

The Latin term *memento mori* has long served as a reminder of mortality. Literally meaning, "Remember you will die," the term has traditionally been linked with striking images and stories of dying. Exceptionally clear examples of this tradition can be seen in New England graveyards, where tombstones from the late seventeenth and eighteenth centuries often contain two phrases: "*Memento mori*" and "*Hora fugit,*" which means, "The hour flees." These lines explain the accompanying images of hourglasses, skulls, bones, and winged death's heads. The gravestones thus ask passersby to remember not only the deceased but their own mortality as well.

The memento mori reached extravagant heights in Europe between 1300 and 1600 with four new motifs. First, the Dance of Death featured skeletal figures leading people of every rank—from pope to plowman—into a final dance. The historian Jean Delumeau discovers the dance's moral in a fourteenth-century manuscript of the Catalan poem, *Dansa de la Mort*: "Toward death we hasten, / Let us sin no more, sin no more" (Delumeau 1990, p. 74). Second, in the Triumph of Death, an armed death figure drives a chariot drawn by oxen. As the French social historian Philippe Ariès comments, this image of "collective" death recalls both the processions honoring a prince's arrival and royal funeral processions. Third, the era's most individualized and grittily realistic memento mori motif occurs in double-decker tombs. The top carvings portray the deceased lying dressed in full regalia; but the carvings beneath present the deceased as exposed *transi,* or decaying corpses. Finally, in the legend of the Three Living and the Three Dead, three well-dressed men are out hunting, and as they approach a cemetery three dead men attack them. This image accompanies the prayers for dead in a *Book of Hours,* a prayer book from the late fifteenth century. The margins reinforce the image's point with skulls and scrolls reading "Memento mori."

The prevalence of these motifs has been explained in several ways. Beginning in 1347 the Black Death decimated Europe. Coupled with wars and failing crops, disaster of this scale reshaped society. As Delumeau and Ariès have shown, these empirical forces reacted with a culture of guilt and emerging individualism. Both perspectives found a compelling message in the memento mori motifs. As sermons constantly proclaimed, life is short, status and wealth will not last, so prepare to die. Only the prepared will avoid hell and enjoy heavenly life. In all its forms, the memento mori thus incited people to learn the *Ars moriendi,* or "art of dying well," which required one to live righteously in preparation for death. New England tombstones undoubtedly continued this message.

When memento mori images appear apart from explanatory sermons and verses, they remain deeply ambiguous. Their focus on the body and its

In Guyot Marchant's 1485 version of the story, The Three Living and the Three Dead, the living survive the encounter, pray before a cross, and resolve to change their lives. FREE LIBRARY OF PHILADELPHIA, RARE BOOK DEPARTMENT

decay led historians like Emile Mâle and Alberto Tenenti to contrast these motifs with Christian belief. And as both Delumeau and the art historian Paul Binski note, being reminded of one's mortality can lead in directions that preachers would not approve: Because life is short, one should enjoy its pleasures while they last. These ambiguities also permit the tradition's images of skulls, bones, and decaying flesh to be used and manipulated in popular culture. They can fuel horror films and give an ironic edge to rock bands. Yet the tradition also retains possibilities for more probing, reflective efforts like the "Memento Mori" episode of television's *X-Files,* where Agent Scully confronts her diagnosis of a brain tumor. Remembering one's death can still exert a transforming power.

See also: ARIÈS, PHILIPE; ARS MORIENDI; BLACK DEATH; DANSE MACABRE; ONTOLOGICAL CONFRONTATION

Bibliography

Ariès, Philippe. *The Hour of Our Death,* translated by Helen Weaver. New York: Knopf, 1981.

Binski, Paul. *Medieval Death: Ritual and Representation.* Ithaca, NY: Cornell University Press, 1996.

Delumeau, Jean. *Sin and Fear: The Emergence of a Western Guilt Culture, 13th–18th Centuries,* translated by Eric Nicholson. New York: St. Martin's Press, 1990.

Ludwig, Allan I. *Graven Images: New England Stonecarving and Its Symbols, 1650–1815.* Middletown, CT: Wesleyan University Press, 1996.

DONALD F. DUCLOW

MEMORIALIZATION, SPONTANEOUS

Spontaneous memorialization is a rapid public response to publicized, unexpected, and violent deaths, typically involving the accumulation of individual mementos to create a shrine at the death site. Most spontaneous memorials start within hours of death notification; someone leaves a candle or bouquet of flowers, which is followed quickly by contributions from others. Well-documented spontaneous memorials have appeared near mass death sites like the park overlooking Columbine High School in Littleton, Colorado (the site of fifteen fatal shootings in 1999), the fence surrounding the Alfred P. Murrah Federal Building in Oklahoma City (where a bomb blast killed 168 people in 1995), and the homes of celebrities (e.g., mountains of bouquets were left at the palace of Great Britain's Lady Diana, Princess of Wales, when she died in an auto accident in 1997). Spontaneous memorials also occur in response to less celebrated deaths: the local store owner who died in a robbery, the pedestrian hit by a drunk driver, the child too near the window when a gang member started shooting.

The sociologist C. Allen Haney and colleagues have noted several ways in which spontaneous memorialization is less restrictive than traditional memorial formats, including the following:

- There are no rules of inclusion/exclusion. Anyone (including those who had never met the deceased) can participate, but no one is expected to do so.

- Timing is flexible. Typically one can join the memorial process at any time of day and for however long the memorial is in place. In Oklahoma City, for example, objects were left on the fence for years after the bombing.
- There is no expected ritual behavior. Mourners have been known to weep, pray, curse, gawk, and even videotape at the scene; some express emotions that are taboo at more traditional memorials, especially anger and guilt. Correspondingly, objects left behind do not follow a single theme; traditional death offerings, religious symbols, and idiosyncratic secular objects are common.
- The focus of memorialization varies. While those who knew the deceased mourn the loss of the individual, others grieve over the social pathologies that might have contributed to the death.

Spontaneous memorials also differ from traditional forms of memorialization by appearing where the death occurred (or at a location associated with the deceased) rather than in a site reserved for the dead. Spontaneous memorials thus tend to be impermanent but are an everyday reminder that death can happen to anyone, anywhere, at any time.

Haney and his colleagues postulate that the prevailing death practices in the United States (e.g., the removal of death, dying, and mourning from everyday life), coupled with the spread of the belief that the timing of death can be controlled, contribute to spontaneous memorialization. They suggest that unexpected, violent deaths, especially where the deceased is engaged in mundane, everyday (and presumably safe) behavior, openly violate the assumptions that death can be controlled and that death happens elsewhere. As a consequence, such deaths not only compel the immediate community to mourn but also broaden the community to include those whose lives were shaken by the death because of a perceived connection with the deceased. Members of this broader community, connected by collective mourning, go one by one to the death site to acknowledge their grief and to create a single memorial composed of their diverse, individual offerings. In this practice of honoring their dead, mourners define and reinforce their community connections.

See also: BEREAVEMENT, VICARIOUS; CELEBRITY DEATHS; FUNERAL INDUSTRY; LINCOLN IN THE NATIONAL MEMORY; ROYALTY, BRITISH; SYMPATHY CARDS

Bibliography:

Carlson, Paul. "Images of Lives Cut Short: As a Chill Wind Blows across Columbine's Campus, Thousands Remember Young People Killed in Murderous Rampage." *The News Tribune,* 1 May 1999.

Fox, Catherine. "Expressing Our Sorrow in Aftermath of Tragedy, Mourning Takes Shape in Spontaneous Memorials after the Assault." *The Atlanta Constitution,* 19 September 2001.

Haney, C. Allen, Christina Leimer, and Juliann Lowery. "Spontaneous Memorialization: Violent Death and Emerging Mourning Ritual." *Omega: The Journal of Death and Dying* 35 (1997):159–171.

Jorgensen-Earp, Cheryl R. and Lanzilotti, Lori, A. "Public Memory and Private Grief: The Construction of Shrines at the Sites of Public Tragedy." *The Quarterly Journal of Speech* 84, no. 2 (1998):150–170.

Mack, Sharon. "Roadside Remembrances: Shrines at Crash Sites Help Bereaved Connect to Where Loved Ones Were Lost." *Bangor Daily News,* 25 April 1998.

Pekkanen, Sarah. "Enshrining Shared Grief: Spontaneous Memorials Are a Testament to the Victims of Tragedy—and Therapy for Bereaved Communities." *The Sun,* 30 May 1999.

PAMELA ROBERTS

MEMORIAL, VIRTUAL

Virtual memorials, also called web memorials, are web pages or sites specifically dedicated to honoring the dead. Cyberspace tributes to the dead appeared shortly after the creation of computer-based communication. Initially most tributes were responses to death notifications on billboards and in listserv formats. While such tributes continue to appear in most cyberspace community venues, many individuals are utilizing a more permanent and accessible form of acknowledging their dead.

Memorial Types

Web memorials vary by individual involvement, cost, and connection to established ritual. The most individualized of web memorials are freestanding web pages, which are rapidly increasing in number as the Internet and web page technology become more accessible. Because they are freestanding and there is no single term to describe them, these web pages may be overlooked by search engines, making an estimate of their number difficult. However, even incomplete searches indicate that there are a myriad of memorials for individuals as well as for group tragedies, including airplane crashes, school shootings, and other sudden violent deaths.

More accessible are the growing number of web rings devoted to memorializing the dead. Web rings are individual web pages with a common theme that are linked together so that one can travel from page to page until one comes full circle, returning back to the first web page. Most memorial web rings are run by volunteers who created the web ring in reaction to their own loss. Usually there are no charges and few requirements for linking individual memorial pages to the web ring.

Most memorial web rings are grouped by the relationship of the deceased to the memorial author or by cause of death. Web rings devoted to deceased children are the most common. Generally, there is an opening page that describes the web ring, its mission, and a list of the children memorialized. Clicking on the child's name will take the visitor directly to his or her memorial, or one can view memorials in sequential fashion, using the links at the bottom of each web page to view the next memorial in the ring. Like freestanding memorial web pages, memorials linked to web rings are often elaborate, with pictures (sometimes video) and music. Many memorials have multiple pages devoted to the story of the child's life and death and links to bereavement resources. Most memorial web pages have a guestbook or an e-mail link so visitors can contact the author directly.

Both freestanding web memorials and those linked to web rings are created and maintained by the bereaved. However, Internet services change periodically and volunteer managers vary in their ability to maintain web rings. Consequently, creating and maintaining memorial web pages requires some computer expertise and the willingness to make modifications as they become necessary.

An alternative to creating individual web pages is placing a memorial in a web cemetery, of which there are several. The oldest web cemeteries are Virtual Memorial Gardens (VMG) http://catless.ncl.ac.uk/vmg/) and Dearly Departed (www.dearlydeparted.net), both free services that began in 1995. VMG is the largest web cemetery, housing thousands of human memorials. Both VMG and Dearly Departed accept e-mail tributes to the dead, which the cemeteries convert into web memorials and arrange alphabetically. Other than requesting the name of the deceased and their birth and death dates, neither service specifies format, content, or length requirements. Consequently, the size of memorials varies, from the simple recording of names and dates to memorials that exceed two single-spaced pages of text. Content also varies, with the majority of memorials emphasizing personal stories about the deceased, while fewer than 10 percent include the accomplishments and affiliations stressed in newspaper obituaries. Another variable is audience; approximately 30 percent of memorials are written as letters to the dead. Once a memorial is posted in either of these web cemeteries, it is maintained by them and considered permanent, much like the graves in traditional cemeteries.

Freestanding web memorials, memorials linked to web rings, and memorials sent by e-mail to the above online cemeteries are free, once one has gained access to the web. Other free web cemeteries include several sites devoted to the memorialization of pets, the largest of which is the Virtual Pet Cemetery (www.mycemetery.com) and sites that include pet memorials along with human memorials, like Virtual Memorial Gardens. All of the free web cemeteries were created and are maintained by either a single individual or a small group of unpaid volunteers, which can affect their services. For example, in 1998 all of the cemeteries previously mentioned requested help from those who utilized their services because of the increasing volume of memorial submissions.

Although there are free services, the majority of web cemeteries charge some fee for the posting and upkeep of memorials. Fees range from ten to fifty dollars for most web cemeteries and generally do not reflect the breadth of services provided by each site. For example, World Wide Cemetery (www.cemetery.org), one of the oldest and best organized sites, has all the amenities of other web cemeteries but charges a one-time fee of ten dollars. Their memorials have an individual guestbook, can include pictures and links, and are arranged alphabetically on individual web pages.

Most web cemeteries evoke images of traditional cemeteries, with pictures of cemetery gates or gardens on their opening pages. Opening pages often invite visitors to "enter" their cemetery, and once inside, web cemeteries tend to be visually consistent; memorials have similar features and there are simple methods of traveling from one memorial to another (usually through a list of links to memorials or letters of the alphabet). This visual continuity provides a sense of place and to many, a feeling of community; as with traditional cemeteries, other losses and the people who mourn them are nearby.

Most web cemeteries were started in the mid-1990s; since that time, closely related services called "online memorial sites" have appeared on the web. Rather than employing one general format for memorials, most online memorial sites provide a variety of prototype memorials from which the bereaved can choose, making online memorial sites more diverse than web cemeteries. Online memorial sites generally utilize a search engine for locating memorials, so that typing a name on the opening page takes the visitor directly to a particular memorial. This feature provides quick access for the visitor, but limits the experience of the memorial site as a whole that is provided by the listing of names in most web cemeteries. Therefore most online memorial sites are more difficult to browse than web cemeteries where the visitor can stroll from memorial to memorial as easily as in any graveyard.

Online memorial sites and web cemeteries also differ in the cost and length of time memorials are posted. In general, online memorial sites are more costly, with prices reflecting the number of pictures and links included in the memorial, as well as the addition of audio and video clips and e-mail guestbooks. Many online memorial sites also charge according to the length of time the memorial is posted, charging by the month or year. Therefore, unlike the majority of web cemeteries (where permanent memorials are free or provided at a one-time cost), many online memorial sites use the model of the newspaper obituary for their pricing; the more elaborate and longer running tributes are more expensive. In general, costs at online memorial sites are at least $100 for posting a memorial for one to three years. Although the initial involvement by the bereaved is similar, online memorial sites may provide less sense of community than web cemeteries because of their potential lack of permanence, increased diversity, and more limited access to other memorials. Examples of online memorial sites are Perpetual Memorials (www.memorials.com) and Virtual Memorials (www.imminentdomain.com).

The popularity of web memorialization has not escaped the funeral industry; many mortuaries are adding the creation and maintenance of web memorials to their list of services. For example, Flintofts Funeral Home and Crematory in Issaquah, Washington, offers a web memorial at no extra charge with all memorial packages, and attached over 400 memorials to their web site from 1999 to June 2001. While their memorials have individualized backgrounds, the general format is the same, with at least one picture of the deceased, information on services and viewings, and a general biography. Unlike other web memorials where the text is written by the bereaved, mortuary-based memorials are written by funeral directors and read more like extended obituaries. Therefore, there is an emphasis on accomplishments, memberships, and survivors, rather than the stories and letters favored by the bereaved. While mortuary-based memorials remove the bereaved from direct involvement in their creation, web technology is utilized to better inform the community and to extend their communication with the bereaved. At the bottom of each memorial are buttons for printing, signing the memorial guestbook, and viewing their list of memorials.

Functions

All web memorials provide a tribute to the dead that can be accessed anytime from almost anywhere. Those lacking an internment site or who live too far away can visit a web memorial when it is most meaningful to them—whether at midnight or midday. Many memorials are visited frequently, and the authors of freestanding or web ring memorials return to maintain them, much like one tends a grave.

Most web memorials provide a way to contact the bereaved, typically through an e-mail guestbook. Guestbooks give anyone the opportunity to offer condolences, potentially expanding the support network available to the bereaved. Also, guestbooks remain available to visitors and the bereaved long after the normal condolence cycle.

Most web memorials are not limited to a certain size, allowing the bereaved to create more lengthy and personal tributes than in other forms of memorialization. The psychologists Marcia Lattanzi and Mary E. Hale found that after traditional postdeath rituals have ended writing to and about the dead can aid in the expression of emotion, creating a sense of perspective and sharing about the death. Web memorials can be a catalyst for talking with others about the dead as well as a method for sharing with those who never knew the deceased. In addition, creating the web memorial can be a group activity, where sharing strengthens existing relationships.

However, the function of web memorials depends on the type of memorial established. Death educators have argued that the more removed the bereaved are from the ritual process, the less beneficial the rituals will be. From this perspective, mortuary-based memorials may be the least useful, while freestanding memorials or memorials linked to web rings may provide the greatest benefits to the bereaved.

All web memorials except mortuary-based tributes (with their ties to the timing and purchase of traditional services) provide opportunities for publicly memorializing the dead that are not available in other venues. There are no restrictions on who writes a memorial (and for whom); those who have felt disenfranchised in the death system are given the opportunity to engage in this public ritual when they may have been denied access to others. Traditionally disenfranchised groups like parents of miscarried babies, pet owners, and friends of the deceased are frequent authors of web memorials. Web memorials can be created at any time (even years after the death), providing the opportunity to honor continuing bonds with the dead. In addition, the cost of web memorials is not prohibitive—even the most expensive web memorial services are cheaper than most traditional obituaries or grave markers.

Questions and Concerns

The web has created new opportunities for memorializing the dead that appear to enhance the lives of the bereaved. However, because web memorialization is a late-twentieth-century phenomenon, many issues concerning the future of web memorials remain unresolved. Three of the most troubling issues are:

1. Web memorials could substitute ritual: Web memorialization appears beneficial when used as a supplement to traditional rituals, with time and greater acceptance, web memorials may be considered a substitute instead, perhaps taking the place of rituals that foster direct human contact.
2. Web memorials could remove the bereaved from the process of death: Positive elements of web memorialization include writing, constructing, and maintaining one's own memorial to the dead. As more services remove the bereaved from this process, the abilities to express emotions, share thoughts with others, and continue caretaking activities for the deceased are compromised.
3. Web sites may not be permanent: Web memorials depend on a stable web site and someone to periodically check their functioning. Therefore, the continued existence of web memorials depends on the bereaved themselves, volunteer site managers, and/or for-profit companies. But who will tend the memorials when the companies go out of business and the volunteers become unavailable? Physical graves remain in place after years of neglect, but will web memorials?

As the web has grown and diversified so have web memorials to the dead. Used as a supplement to traditional ritual, such memorials provide extended opportunities to honor the dead and have more meaningful communication about the dead with the living. However, the future course of web memorialization remains to be determined.

See also: BURIAL GROUNDS; CEMETERIES AND CEMETERY REFORM; GRIEF: CHILD'S DEATH, FAMILY; INTERNET; LAWN GARDEN CEMETERIES; VIETNAM VETERANS MEMORIAL

Bibliography

Argyle, Katie. "Life after Death." In Rob Shields ed., *Cultures of the Internet.* Thousand Oaks, CA: Sage, 1996.

Lattanzi, Marcia, and Mary E. Hale. "Giving Grief Words: Writing during Bereavement." *Omega: The Journal of Death and Dying.* 15, no. 1 (1984–85):45–52.

Roberts, Pamela. "Tangible Sorrow, Virtual Tributes: Cemeteries in Cyberspace." In Brian deVries ed., *End of Life Issues: Interdisciplinary and Multidisciplinary Perspectives*. New York: Springer, 1999.

Roberts, Pamela, and Lourdes Vidal. "Perpetual Care in Cyberspace: A Portrait of Web Memorials." *Omega: The Journal of Death and Dying*. 40, no. 4 (2000):521–545.

PAMELA ROBERTS

METAPHORS AND EUPHEMISMS

Twenty-first-century human beings live in a culture in which "dead" is a four-letter word. Because four-letter words have a reputation for being obscene, death is obscene to modern sensibilities; that is, to those in modern death-denying cultures who rarely have firsthand experiences with the dying and the dead. Modernity has afforded people the ability to hide the dying process from public view; and often people see the dead body of a loved one to be so polluting that they pay strangers to dispose of "it" properly. The modern mind can abstract death, further buffering itself from death's horror, through the use of metaphor and euphemism when describing the dead. In daily conversations the deceased tend to pass or fade away, embark on a desired trip to meet their eternal reward or loved ones ("Grandpa is back with Grandma"), or merely fall asleep ("She earned her rest").

Some scholars argue that our circumlocutions should be understood as evidence of death denial, as should such colorful expressions as "buying the farm," "pushing up daisies," or "kicking the bucket." On the other hand, euphemism has a long tradition of use when dealing with the topic of death, and the use of metaphor is often inevitable when trying to explain certain facets of the human condition, particularly death.

Humans are symbolic creatures, perceiving and experiencing their social worlds largely through their symbols, many of which are figurative and metaphoric. Instead of understanding metaphors as embellishments of facts, they are better conceived as ways in which these facts are experienced, filtering and shaping apprehensions of social reality and understandings of things about which they are unfamiliar—like death.

Distinctive metaphors and euphemisms have emerged from the various social institutions directly involved with death. The more powerful the institution, the more likely its metaphors leak into everyday parlance and produce common worldviews. Over the twentieth century, these have included the military, medical, and political orders—the social institutions primarily responsible for death control.

Twentieth-century militarism had a powerful effect on death's metaphoric framings. In George Orwell's futuristic novel *Nineteen Eighty-four* (1949), the Ministry of Truth proclaimed "War is peace." In the twenty-first century war is "pacification." The military sanitizes its lethal activities through benign labels (e.g., the Nazis assigning carloads of concentration camp–bound to *Sonderbehandlung,* meaning "special treatment") or by dehumanizing its enemies (who are "fumigated," "exterminated," or "wasted" like cockroaches and rats). In *Doublespeak* (1989), William Lutz distinguishes euphemism, which covers the unpleasant, from doublespeak, whose purpose is to deceive and mislead. To illustrate the latter, he noted how the U.S. State Department replaced "killing" with "unlawful deprivation of life." Dead enemy soldiers are "decommissioned aggressor quantum." Deaths of innocent civilians are referred to as "collateral damage." When commandos parachuted in the early 1980s American invasion of Grenada, the Pentagon referred to the action as a "predawn vertical insertion."

In *Illness As Metaphor* (1978), Susan Sontag describes the military metaphors applied to disease, the alien invaders that breach bodily defense systems necessitating surgical, chemical, or radiation counterattacks. The frontline in the cultural war against death is the medical establishment. Here death has long been viewed as failure, giving rise to a host of clinically detached euphemisms. Patients "go sour," their respirations cease, or they are simply "no longer with us." Emergency room nurses make references to someone being "DDD" ("definitely done dancing") or "getting bagged."

The euphemisms extend to those most likely to die—those who have lived the longest lives. The most death prone are not "old people" but rather "senior citizens," "Golden Agers," or simply "the mature." They die in "homes"—rest homes, nursing homes, retirement homes—where they are too often deindividualized and victimized by underpaid staff.

In the political arena, heated battles on the moralities of abortion and euthanasia have produced a new language for death-related matters. In the contest between social movements supporting or opposing legalized abortion and euthanasia has emerged the self-referencing "pro-choice" and "pro-life" labels. For those opposing assisted or accelerated death, "active euthanasia" is a euphemism for murder. For proponents, the practice of keeping the terminally ill alive on hi-tech life supports is "technological torturing" of the dying.

Crisp mortality references often enter into American parlance when referring to nonthanatological matters. People often "die" symbolically, as when failing in their social performances. One certainly does not want to be "dead wrong," an office "deadwood," a "deadbeat" father, or within a "dead-end" job. Companies may adopt a "poison pill" defense against a hostile takeover attempt, leaving workers worried about being "axed" or appearing on "Schindler's List." The symbolic potency of such death metaphors rise with increases in the centrality of work roles to the identities of men and women. Studies have shown that when a business facility shuts down workers often go through the deathlike stages described by the death expert Elisabeth Kübler-Ross. A late 1980s survey of Richmond, Virginia, entrepreneurs published in the *Wall Street Journal* cited nearly six in ten saying failure was the incident they feared most, with fear of death being but a distant third for both sexes. And when the worker actually does die, he or she dies metaphorically in occupationally unique ways: Deceased soldiers "answer their last roll call," chefs "lay down their knife and fork," actors "make a final exit," and boxers "take the last count."

Among those whose job it is to deal with the dead, death professionals as scholar Michael Lesy calls them, metaphors arising from their humor produce the death desensitizations required for them to cope with society's "dirty work." Among themselves, funeral directors, for instance, refer to embalming as "pickling" or "curing the ham," cremation as "shake and bake," and coffins as "tin cans." When dealing with the public, the "patient" (not the corpse) is "interred" (not buried) within a "casket" (not coffin) beneath a "monument" (not tombstone).

So what do all of these colorful, humorous, consoling, deceptive, demeaning, and frightful framings of death mean? Are they useful? The metaphors and euphemisms that people apply to the dying and the dead shape the way the living now see their connection with the dead. They can sanitize the profound pollution posed by a decaying corpse and assuage the profound moral guilt of collective murder during times of war. They can reaffirm the meaningfulness of the deceased's life ("He lives with us all") or degrade their very existence ("The vermin were whacked").

Perhaps another way to think about the matter is to ask how many words there are that solely capture the single fact that this person or creature is no more. "He died" is the simplest way English speakers can make the point. From there on, everything is an elaboration of a phenomenon of which none of the living has any direct knowledge. The military borrows from the medical when it conducts its surgical operations to remove "the cancer"; the medical from the military in its "wars against enemy diseases." In sum, metaphors and euphemisms for death are employed as both shields and weapons, to cover the unpleasant or distasteful aspects of mortality, or to apply the power of death to reinforce the significance of certain events among the living.

See also: CHILDREN; COMMUNICATION WITH THE DYING; SHAKESPEARE, WILLIAM; TABOOS AND SOCIAL STIGMA

Bibliography

Bailey, William. *Euphemisms and Other Double-Talk.* New York: Doubleday, 1983.

Brown, Richard. *A Poetic for Sociology: Toward a Logic of Discovery for the Human Sciences.* Cambridge, MA: Cambridge University Press, 1977.

"Fear of Death Takes a Back Seat." *Wall Street Journal,* 23 July 1987, 1.

Friedrich, Otto. "Of Words That Ravage, Pillage, Spoil." *Time,* 9 January 1984, 76.

Lesy, Michael. *The Forbidden Zone.* New York: Farrar, Straus and Giroux, 1987.

Lutz, William. *Doublespeak: From "Revenue Enhancement" to "Terminal Living": How Government, Business, Advertisers, and Others Use Language to Deceive You.* New York: Harper and Row, 1989.

Orwell, George. *Nineteen Eighty-four, A Novel.* New York: Harcourt, Brace, 1949.

Sontag, Susan. *Illness As Metaphor.* New York: Farrar, Straus and Giroux, 1978.

Turner, Ronny, and Charles Edgley. "Death As Theatre: A Dramaturgical Analysis of the American Funeral." *Sociology and Social Research* 60, no. 4 (1975):377–392.

Internet Resources

Stein, Howard F. "Death Imagery and the Experience of Organizational Downsizing: Or, Is Your Name on Schindler's List?" In the Psychoanalytic Study of Organizations [web site]. Available from www.sba.oakland.edu/ispso/html/stein.html

MICHAEL C. KEARL

MIND-BODY PROBLEM

What color is a thought? How much does a thought weigh? How tall or short or how fat or skinny is a thought? Precisely where in space and time are thoughts located? What is the temperature of a thought? What is the speed of a thought?

Indeed these are very odd sorts of questions. The oddity itself is revealing: Thoughts do not seem to belong to the class of things that can submit to such questions or provide their answers. Thoughts do not seem to have size, shape, weight, color, velocity, mass, temperature, or location. Sometimes, of course, a thought can be described as "heavy" or "weighty," as in a philosophical discussion that considers such profound thoughts as "Is there a God?" and "Does my life have an objective meaning?" Thoughts can also be described as "dark," as in the statement, "The psychotic mind engages in dark thoughts such as murder and suicide." And people can speak of a "hot" idea, as in the slogan, "Wireless computers are now a hot idea." But these are all metaphorical uses of language. These statements do not literally mean that thoughts can have weight, color, or temperature. In short, the very nature of thought itself raises some serious questions.

Thought, or consciousness itself, does not seem to easily fit into the world of physical nature. In nature, people constantly encounter things with physical characteristics—trees, animals, automobiles, rocks, and other objects, all of which have physical properties such as weight, shape, and color. The human body, too, seems to belong to this world of nature, for it has size, weight, mass, and color. However, physical characteristics do not seem to be appropriate when discussing mental realities such as thoughts or consciousness in general. Does this mean that the mental world is somehow different from the physical? Does this mean that there are at least two separate realities or substances in the world: minds and bodies? Consequently, what will be the relevance of these questions to issues concerning death?

Dualism

Dualism is the view that there are, indeed, at least two kinds of realities: the physical—characterized by measurable properties such as weight, location, size, and color; and the mental—characterized by nonphysical and immeasurable qualities such as immateriality. Dualism is a very old tradition, having many proponents. Some scholars claim that Plato (428–348 B.C.E.) was the first to make a sharp distinction between the mind and body. For Plato, the relationship between the mind and body is not an ideal one—in fact, the body can be seen as the "prisoner" of the mind or soul, which is the true person. In death, the mind and soul are separated. The body decomposes into its original elements, but the mind or soul cannot decompose because it is not a composed material substance. Therefore, the mind or soul cannot die. In Plato's works one sees the direct result of dualism with regard to the question of death: It provides hope for survival of the person after the death of the body.

However, other scholars argue the tradition of dualism did not begin with Plato. Perhaps the first philosopher to offer this position was Pythagoras (6th century B.C.E.). Pythagoras believed in the transmigration of the soul—the view that the soul is immortal and is bound up with the divine soul, to which it may return when "purified" after its separation from its temporary physical house (the body). Presumably there are any number of transmigrations of the same soul, as taught in the doctrine of reincarnation in religions like Hinduism.

Although Plato is not the "father" of dualism, certainly he provided a far more extended treatment and defense of the doctrine than anyone who came before him. The Platonic dualism had great influence on Christian thinking, though it could not be made perfectly consistent with scriptural views since Plato shared the Pythagorean belief in transmigration of the soul. The greatest of the early Medieval thinkers was Augustine (354–430) who held,

> Man is not a body alone, nor a soul alone, but a being composed of both . . . the soul is not the whole man but the better part of man; the body is not the whole but the inferior part of man . . . and when both are joined they received the name of man. *(Dods 1872, p. 24)*

We can say that Christianity, for the most part, adopted a form of Platonic dualism as its official view, which went more or less unchallenged until Aquinas (1225–1274) who followed Aristotle's line of thinking on the mind-body relationship. Aristotle (384–322 B.C.E.) disagreed with Plato, his mentor and teacher, and provided a closer relationship between the mind and the body, claiming that the soul is the "form" of the body.

In modern philosophy it is René Descartes (1596–1650) who is most associated with dualism. Descartes's philosophy radically separates the mental and the physical, by claiming that they are, indeed, two very different kinds of substances. In his *Meditations,* he writes:

> There is a great difference between the mind and the body, inasmuch as the body is by its very nature always divisible, while the mind is utterly indivisible. For when I consider the mind, or myself in so far as I am a thinking thing, I am unable to distinguish any parts within myself. . . . By contrast, there is no corporeal or extended thing that I cannot think of which in my thought I cannot easily divide into parts; and this very fact makes me understand that it is divisible. This one argument would be enough to show me that the mind is completely different from the body, even if I did not already know as much from other considerations *(Cottingham 1966, p. 9)*

But Cartesian dualism suffered from the beginning under the criticism of the "interaction problem." Namely, if mind and body are radically distinct substances, how is it that the mind and body can interact at all, as they obviously do?

Dualism has been under severe attack in the twentieth century, especially since Gilbert Ryle's book *The Concept of Mind* (1949). Some support for dualism, however, can be found in works such as Arthur Koestler's *The Ghost in the Machine* (1967); Karl Popper and Sir John Eccles's *The Self and Its Brain* (1977); and Zeno Vendler's *Res Cogitans* (1972) and *The Matter of Minds* (1984).

Monism

Those who deny that mind and body are two different and distinct realities, are called monists. Monism holds that there is only one ultimate reality, and that mind and body are essentially reducible to it. The oldest tradition within this view is known as materialism, which states that the ultimate reality is physical matter, and all that is or ever was arises out of and is ultimately reducible to matter. Perhaps the first real materialism is the view of atomism as proposed by Leucippus (c. fifth century B.C.E.) and Democritus (c. 460–360 B.C.E.). According to this view, all things are composed of indivisible particles of matter (atomoi). The human soul, too, is composed of "soul-atoms" which may be different from others in being smooth and spherical, but they are atoms nonetheless. Epicurus (342–270 B.C.E.) later adopted the Democritean materialism to argue that death is nothing to be feared since it is simply the dissolution of the soul into its original atoms. The Roman philosopher-poet Lucretius (c. 95–55 B.C.E.) also developed materialism as an attempt to rid human beings from religious fears by arguing against any nonphysical soul, and therefore proposing the mortality of all human beings.

The most important materialist in the modern period is the English philosopher Thomas Hobbes (1588–1679), who was greatly impressed by the progress during his day within science and mathematics. Galileo and Johannes Kepler, in particular, had shown the importance of using mathematics with careful observation of moving bodies in space. True knowledge, Hobbes felt, seeks to observe and understand true reality, which for him, is made up simply of "bodies in motion." For Hobbes, all reality and substance is corporeal or material. He firmly believed that someday science would be able to offer a full account of all reality based on a materialistic model, without recourse to a transcendent, incorporeal God. Nearly two centuries after Hobbes's death, Charles Darwin's *Origin of Species* (1859) and Thomas Henry Huxley's

Man's Place in Nature (1863) provided scientific support for just such a materialistic explanation for the origins and development of life, without resort to any outside immaterial agency or deity.

In contemporary times, science has made some progress in showing that life itself may be understandable in terms of biological and biochemical terms. Much of the focus in the twenty-first century has centered on the question whether the mind can be completely reduced to materialistic and mechanistic functions. Many philosophers, beginning with the analytic thinkers, began to hold to a materialist or "physicalist" position. A variety of more or less materialistic views have emerged. One of the most popular theories to emerge since the 1950s is the "mind-brain identity theory," developed by Herbert Feigl, U. T. Place and J. J. C. Smart, which holds that "mental states are quite literally identical with brain states" (Borst 1970, p. 13). Other forms of materialism contend that mental states are reducible to "statements about behavior" and are therefore referred to as "behaviorism" (p. 15).

Perhaps the most famous philosophical behaviorist is Gilbert Ryle. His book, *The Concept of Mind* (1949), has had a major impact for many in discrediting dualism. Ryle refers to the concept of dualism as "Descartes' Myth" and as "the dogma of the Ghost in the Machine." The myth of dualism, he contends, is the result of a type of mistaken thinking which he calls a "category mistake." The example Ryle uses illustrates it best. Imagine someone on a campus visit of a university. He receives a full tour of the university, visiting the classroom buildings, the library, and the dormitories. At the end of the tour, the visitor then asks, "But where is the university?" He has mistakenly assumed that the university is some separate entity existing apart from all of its constituents. He has mentally placed "university" in the same category as "classroom buildings," "library," and "dormitories." But the university is not some separately existing entity alongside of the buildings that make it up; rather it stands for the entire collection. So, too, Ryle contends, the "mind" should not be thought of as some separate entity in the same category as "body" (or brain).

Partly because of Ryle's arguments, many philosophers have ceased to talk about "the mind" as a separate category. The focus since the 1970s has been on mental activity or consciousness in general. Perhaps the most audacious work comes in Daniel Dennett's *Conciousness Explained* (1991), which provides more attacks on dualism, but attempts to explain consciousness in terms of brain events has not avoided its critics either. Dennett himself agrees the task is difficult: "Scientists and philosophers may have achieved a consensus of sorts in favor of materialism, [but] getting rid of the old dualistic visions is harder than contemporary materialists have thought" (Dennett 1991, p. 37). Thinkers who have provided serious obstacles to any simple materialism include Jerry Fodor's *A Theory of Content and Other Essays* (1990), Roger Penrose's *The Emperor's New Mind* (1989), and John Searle's *Intentionality: An Essay in the Philosophy of Mind* (1983).

Relation to Death

The mind-body issue has crucial impact on questions concerning death. In the end, the materialist's position is that a person is identical with his or her body; or that the "mind" is identical with the brain and its functioning. When the body/brain dies, therefore, there is no continuation of the person; there is no hope for an afterlife. The dualist position does not identify the person with his or her body/brain. Therefore dualism leaves open the door for belief in an afterlife. For most, this is primarily a religious question that cannot be resolved by philosophy or science.

The mind-body issue has bearing on how one defines death. Does death occur only when the body expires? When exactly does this happen? The Harvard Brain Death criterion defines death as including a flat electroencephalogram (EEG). The materialist position would seem supportive of such a view. If death is the end of the person, and if the person is to be identified with something like brain functioning, then it would follow that one should define death as an event tied to something like a flat EEG.

But is there something like a mental death as well, which is totally separate from physical death? Consider such medical cases as Karen Ann Quinlan and Nancy Cruzan, where the brain is still functioning, but where the forebrain—the most human part of the brain—is destroyed. Both cases were famous U.S. euthanasia cases and each had their forebrains destroyed through illness. Cruzan's case (request for euthanasia by family) went to the U.S.

Supreme Court (1989). Some scientists, along with the Quinlan and Cruzan families, argued that the patients in those cases (referring to the person as identified with some qualitative, human, mental life) were already dead; that is, Quinlan and Cruzan, as the persons the families knew before their accidents, were already gone. Keeping their bodies alive was, they argued, a grotesque injustice.

According to death researchers like R. S. Morison, the human being does not die as a unit. According to this view, life in any organism has no real sharp beginning and end points. Defining death is all the more difficult with a complex organism such as a human being. The dualist would seem supportive of this recognition that mental death (or the death of the person) may occur before and apart from physical death, because it does not identify the person with brain functioning. The mind-body debate, therefore, has relevance for a number of issues concerning death, such as religious concerns about an afterlife and moral issues such as euthanasia.

See also: AFRICAN RELIGIONS; BUDDHISM; CHINESE BELIEFS; CHRISTIAN DEATH RITES, HISTORY OF; IMMORTALITY; ISLAM; JUDAISM; NEAR-DEATH EXPERIENCES; PHILOSOPHY, WESTERN

Bibliography

Aristotle. *Metaphysics,* translated by W. D. Ross. In Richard McKeon ed., *The Basic Works of Aristotle.* New York: Random House, 1941.

Augustine. *The City of God,* translated by M. Dods. Edinburgh: T & T Clark, 1872

Borst, C. V. *The Mind/Brain Identity Theory.* New York: St. Martin's Press, 1970.

Dennett, Daniel C. *Consciousness Explained.* Boston: Little, Brown, 1991.

Descartes, René. *Meditations on First Philosophy,* revised, edited, and translated by John Cottingham. Cambridge: Cambridge University Press, 1966.

Fodor, Jerry. *A Theory of Content and Other Essays.* Cambridge, MA: MIT Press, 1990.

Guthrie, W. K. C. "Pythagoras and the Pythagoreans." In *A History of Greek Philosophy.* Cambridge: Cambridge University Press, 1971.

Hobbes, Thomas. *Leviathan.* New York: Dutton Press, 1950.

Morison, R. S. "Death: Process or Event?" In P. Steinfels and R. M. Veatch eds., *Death Inside Out: The Hastings Center Report.* New York: Harper and Row, 1974.

Penrose, Roger. *The Emperor's New Mind.* Oxford: Oxford University Press, 1989.

Plato. *Phaedo.* In Edith Hamilton and Huntington Cairns eds., *The Collected Dialogues of Plato.* Princeton, NJ: Princeton University Press, 1961.

Pojman, Louis P. "What is Death? The Crisis of Criteria." In *Life and Death: Grappling with the Moral Dilemmas of Our Time.* Boston: Jones and Bartlett Publishers, 1992.

Ryle, Gilbert. *The Concept of Mind.* New York: Barnes and Noble, 1949.

Searle, John. *Intentionality: An Essay in the Philosophy of Mind.* Cambridge: Cambridge University Press, 1983.

Vendlar, Zeno. *The Matter of Minds.* Oxford: Clarendon Press, 1984.

WILLIAM COONEY

MISCARRIAGE

Miscarriage, or in medical terminology spontaneous abortion, is the termination of a pregnancy from natural causes before the time the fetus can survive for even a few minutes outside the uterus. (Induced abortion is the term used for those expulsions of an embryo or fetus that are artificially induced by mechanical means or drugs.) Miscarriage generally occurs before the twentieth week of pregnancy. A fetus born dead from natural causes after twenty weeks is called stillborn. Perhaps 50 to 78 percent of all fertilized eggs spontaneously abort. Only about 10 to 15 percent of the time are women aware that they have miscarried. Spontaneous abortions often seem to be functional in that they naturally eliminate many fetuses that may have birth defects.

Before miscarrying, a woman usually has spotting or more obvious bleeding and discharge from the vagina. The uterus contracts, causing pelvic cramps. Bleeding, discharge, and cramps become more severe if the miscarriage continues, and part or all of the contents of the uterus may be expelled. One miscarriage does not mean that later pregnancies will spontaneously abort, however, and about 70 to 90 percent who have miscarried eventually become pregnant again. Only about 1 percent of women suffer three or more miscarriages, perhaps because of anatomical, hormonal, genetic, or immunological factors.

About 85 percent of miscarriages happen in the first twelve weeks of pregnancy; the remaining 15 percent occur between thirteen and twenty weeks. The most likely reason is an abnormality in fetal development, usually as a result of extra chromosomes (about 60% of miscarriages). Occupational exposure to some chemicals may increase the chances of having a miscarriage. Other possible causes include chronic infections, unrecognized diabetes in the mother, and defects in the uterus. About one-third of the time there is no known cause for the miscarriage. Many studies have indicated that emotional disturbances in the mother's life are not usually linked with miscarriage. Miscarriage does, however, cause emotional disturbance in the lives of many women. Women tend to blame themselves: "I exercised too hard"; "Stress at work caused this"; "I fell down and hurt the baby." However, stress or physical trauma rarely results in a miscarriage, and health care professionals advise women not to blame themselves.

American society tends to define the loss of the fetus as "just a miscarriage," but most women who experience a miscarriage see the loss as a death—the death of a life or the death of a dream. Research indicates that losing a baby due to miscarriage can be a devastating experience for family members. Some women consider suicide after a miscarriage. Some couples' relationships are thrown into turmoil as a result of the loss. Some surviving siblings will feel guilt that they somehow caused the death, and will grieve in silence. However, researchers have found that families who support each other through these difficult times are likely to end up feeling stronger and more deeply committed to each other.

See also: ABORTION

Bibliography

Beers, Mark H., and Robert Berkow, eds. *The Merck Manual of Diagnosis and Therapy*. Whitehouse Station, NJ: Merck Research Laboratories, 1999.

Berkow, Robert, and Mark H. Beers, eds. *The Merck Manual of Medical Information, Home Edition*. Whitehouse Station, NJ: Merck Research Laboratories, 1997.

DeFrain, John, Elaine Millspaugh, and Xiaolin Xie. "The Psychosocial Effects of Miscarriage: Implications for Health Professionals." *Families, Systems, and Health: Journal of Collaborative Family Health Care* 14, no. 3 (1996):331–347.

Hyde, Janet Shibley, and John D. DeLamater. *Understanding Human Sexuality,* 7th edition. Boston: McGraw Hill, 2000.

Insel, Paul M., and Walton T. Roth. *Core Concepts in Health,* 8th edition. Mountain View, CA: Mayfield, 2000.

Larson, David E., ed. *Mayo Clinic Family Health Book,* 2nd edition. New York: William Morrow, 1996.

Olds, Sally B., Marcia L. London, and Patricia A. Wieland Ladewig. *Maternal-Newborn Nursing: A Family and Community-Based Approach,* 6th edition. Upper Saddle River, NJ: Prentice Hall Health, 2000.

JOHN DEFRAIN

MISSING IN ACTION

It is a value of possibly all known cultures that the remains of their fallen warriors be retrieved so that they can be buried with all the honor due those who sacrificed their lives for the group. It is also one of the greatest indignities for an enemy to deny such ritualization. Today there are teams of American civilian and military personnel scouring the jungles, mountains, and waters of Southeast Asia for the remains of military servicemen who were listed as missing in action (MIA) from the Vietnam War. In addition, forensic teams are pursuing leads in recovering and returning remains of MIA servicemen from both the Korean War and World War II. These search teams are a direct result of the efforts of the Vietnam-era wives who, unlike the wives of previous wars, banded together to improve the living conditions in which the American POWs were living in. After the return in 1973 of the American POWs in Operation Homecoming, the group's focus shifted to the return of all U.S. prisoners, the fullest possible accounting for those still missing, and repatriation of all recoverable remains.

Military Missing Personnel

The United States' Department of Defense (DOD) lists a military serviceman as MIA if "he or she was not at their duty location due to apparent involuntary reasons as a result of hostile action and his/her location is not known" (Department of Defense 1996, p. 5). In addition, three criteria guide the accounting process for missing personnel by the Defense Prisoner of War/Missing Personnel Office:

(1) the return of a live American; (2) the return of identifiable remains; and (3) provision of convincing evidence why the first two criteria are not possible. Since the 1950s the DOD has listed thousands of military personnel as missing in action. There are more than 2,600 American servicemen listed as MIA from the Vietnam War; approximately 8,900 from the Korean War; and an additional 80,000 from World War II. If one considers only the immediate family members missing servicemen, the number of people affected by the MIA tragedy is in the hundreds of thousands.

In past wars, when military personnel were listed as MIA, their status was reviewed after one year according to the Military's Missing Persons Act. A tribunal of fellow military personnel familiar with the war situation was convened. Evidence was presented as to whether the serviceman should continue to be carried as MIA or changed to the status of killed in action/body not returned (KIA/BNR). Most MIA statuses in the Vietnam War were not changed, as had been done in prior wars, because of reliable U.S. intelligence reports indicating hundreds of MIA servicemen possibly being alive and held in captivity. By the 1980s the U.S. government changed all but one MIA to a presumptive finding of death (PFOD), despite the official position that "we cannot rule out the possibility that American POWs or MIAs were left behind at the end of the [Vietnam] war" (The National League of Families, October 1997). The goal of the United States continues to be the return of any live Americans, the repatriation of all recoverable remains, and the fullest possible accounting for those still missing.

Known Death versus Unknown Death

Normally, when one thinks of grief it is in the context of the loss of a loved one through a "known" death. A known death is when a person dies and there is a body that gives physical testimony to that individual's death. For the bereaved, the grieving cycle can begin as the body confirms, against deepest wishes, that the deceased no longer lives in the physical world (Attig 1991). Therefore, when one thinks of a loss it is usually equated with a documented death and a physical body to mourn over.

The missing in action status is unique in that the loss is not final. There is no certainty of death, no "physical body" to identify or mourn over, and no official documentation of the person's death. The MIA situation is similar to individuals who are lost through natural or human disasters (i.e., floods, tornadoes, shipwrecks, or airplane crashes) and whose bodies are never recovered. The difference between the two losses lies in the cognitive realization that death is certain even though there is no body to identify.

Grief and the MIA Loss

When the bereaved learn of the death of a loved one they begin a process of grief and, after a culturally accepted period of time, achieve grief resolution. When the military authorities first notify the MIA families that their loved one is "missing in action" the initial shock is typically followed by the hope for rescue or the known status of prisoner of war (POW). When this hope is not immediately realized, the family members begin exhibiting the first symptoms of the grief cycle, such as shock, numbness, and disbelief (Freud 1917, 1957; Bowlby 1961; Parkes 1970). Thus, the MIA wartime casualty is a paradox. On the one hand grieving is triggered by the MIA loss, which causes the family members to try and make sense of the loss, break their emotional and internal attachments to the deceased, and reintegrate the deceased within one's self, thereby reaching closure. On the other hand, MIA family members have largely been unable to bring grief to closure due to the lack of evidence to support the death and the persistent belief (hope) that the missing serviceman may still be alive. Further complicating the picture is the fear that by letting go and reaching grief closure, the MIA family members are abandoning the missing serviceman. This fear can give rise to feelings of guilt and betrayal. The result is that, for many MIA family members, the grieving process is interrupted and drawn out indefinitely. In the absence of any credible evidence the MIA family members remain in bereavement limbo, "figuratively 'stuck in time' and unable to go forward" (Hunter 1988, p. 312).

The clinical psychologist Pauline Boss argues that MIA families face another type of challenge. She describes the concept of boundary ambiguity in which the family does not know with certainty "who is in" and "who is out" of the family system. Boss posits that as long as there is ambivalence about the role of the husband/father and when the

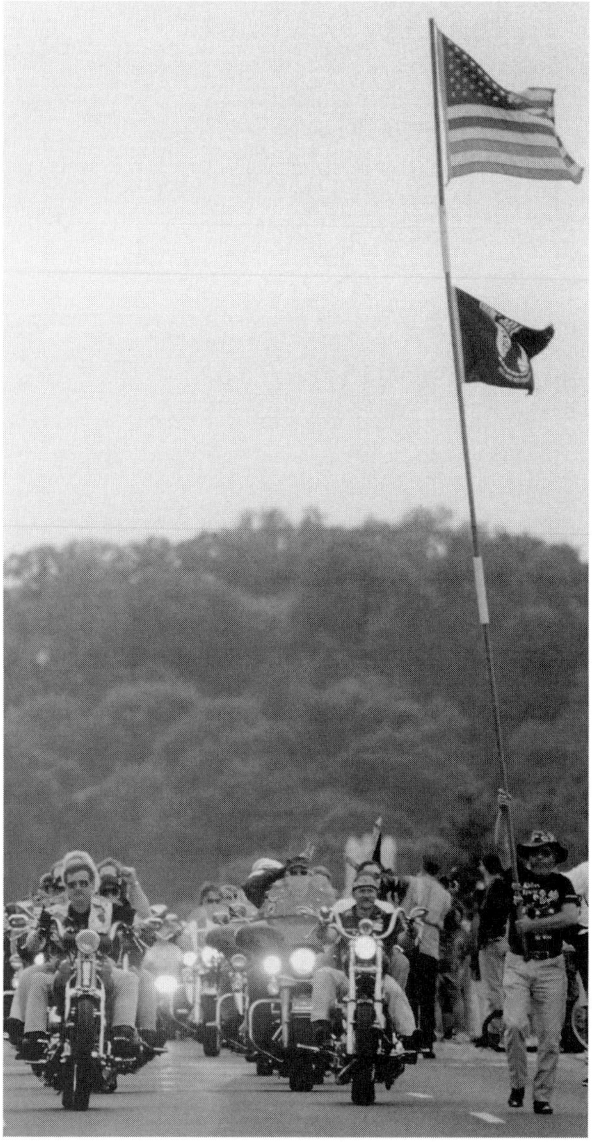

Motorcyclists, during the eleventh Annual Memorial Weekend Rolling Thunder Rally, ride in protest of the U.S. military's unwillingness to acknowledge prisoners of war and failed attempts to find those missing in action. AP/WIDE WORLD PHOTOS

psychological husband/father presence is maintained, "the family system, systemic communication, feedback, and subsequent adjustment [to the ambiguous loss] over time are curtailed" (Boss 1977, p. 141). This ambivalence can lead to family members feeling helpless and more prone to depression and anxiety, leaving them poorly equipped to achieve closure to their grief work.

When the Vietnam War officially ended in 1975, some of the wives of the missing were able to accept the fact that their loved ones were probably never coming home—they were dead. Some of the wives eventually remarried and moved on with their lives. But have these wives or their children forgotten the husbands/fathers that they waited so many years for? More important, have these family members been able to fully accept their loss and attain a state of grief closure? Edna Hunter-King suggests that this is not so. The following is an excerpt from a 1983 interview of a wife who had "closed the book and got on with living" by remarrying:

> I've come to realize that his remains have not been returned so there is no finality to it. Also, all the news in the papers recently [about the possibility of American POWs still being held in Southeast Asia after the war ended] has upset me. I didn't know I was still vulnerable. . . . What if he were still there? I can't even think about it! . . . Looking at this thing 10 years later, I feel less removed now than I did, say, seven years after Homecoming. *(Hunter 1988, p. 323)*

For many MIA families the uncertainty and ambiguity of the wartime loss have transformed the journey of grief from one with a clear endpoint and closure into one of extended, indefinite grief (Hunter 1998). Many MIA family members exhibit patterns of grief, including avoidance, denial, guilt, intrusive thoughts, and preoccupation with the loss. However, because these symptoms are prolonged, they are often misinterpreted as dysfunctional and in many cases can lead to an assessment of frozen, impacted or unresolved grief—all "maladaptive" forms of grief. The MIA trauma highlights the misunderstanding that an ambiguous loss can engender. The ambiguous nature of the MIA loss challenges grief therapists and researchers alike to devise new models of therapies, which may help the MIA families find meaning in the loss, learn to live with the uncertainty, and move forward with their grief.

Several family members have offered the following suggestions to help others move forward in their grief. Family members, relatives, and friends can perform a small burial service wherein personal items associated with the missing serviceman are placed in a box and buried. Others have suggested that, when possible, visiting the physical location of the loss can bring a sense of "realness" and even "finality" to the ambiguous wartime loss. Finally, dedicating a small area in a room and placing pictures, letters, medals, and memorabilia belonging to the serviceman can give meaning to the loss by creating a physical memorial to the missing serviceman, thereby making the loss more tangible.

For most MIA family members, however, the ambiguous MIA loss will be forever troubling and in many cases grief resolution will remain elusive due to the lack of finality regarding the fate of their missing loved one. As the grief experts S. Zisook and S. R. Shuchter wrote in 1986, "There is no prescription for how to grieve properly . . . and no research-validated guideposts for what is normal versus deviant mourning. . . . We are just beginning to realize the full range of what may be considered 'normal' grieving" (Zisook and Shuchter 1986, p. 288).

See also: CEMETERIES, MILITARY; CONTINUING BONDS; GRIEF: OVERVIEW, FAMILY; GRIEF AND MOURNING IN CROSS-CULTURAL PERSPECTIVE; WAR

Bibliography

Archer, John. *The Nature of Grief: The Evolutions and Psychology of Reactions to Loss.* New York: Routledge, 1999.

Attig, Thomas. *How We Grieve: Relearning the World.* New York: Oxford University Press, 1996.

Boss, Pauline. "A Clarification of the Concept of Psychological Father Presence in Families Experiencing Ambiguity of Boundary." *Journal of Marriage and the Family* 39 (1977):141–151.

Boss, Pauline. "The Relationship of Psychological Father Presence, Wives' Personal Qualities and Wife/Family Dysfunction in Families of Missing Fathers." *Journal of Marriage and the Family* 42 (1980):541–549.

Boss, Pauline. *Ambiguous Loss: Learning to Live with Unresolved Grief.* Cambridge: Harvard University Press, 1991.

Bowlby, John. "Process of Mourning." *International Journal of Psycho-Analysis* 42 (1961):317–340.

Campbell, Cathy. L., and A. S. Demi. "Adult Children of Father's Missing in Action (MIA): An Examination of Emotional Distress, Grief and Family Hardiness." *Journal of Family Relations* 49, no. 3 (2000):267–276.

Clark, Michael. S. *Patterns of Grief Reactions in the Families of the Unaccounted for POW/MIA Servicemen from the Vietnam War.* Ann Arbor, MI: UMI Dissertation Publishing, 2000.

Department of Defense. *Department of Defense POW/MIA Newsletter* (Spring 1996).

Freud, Sigmund. *Mourning and Melancholia. Standard Edition of Complete Psychological Works of Sigmund Freud,* Vol. 14. Reprint, London: Hogarth Press and Institute of Psychanalysis, 1957.

Hunter-King, Edna. J. "Children of Military Personnel Missing in Action in Southeast Asia." In Y. Danieli ed., *International Handbook of Multigenerational Legacies of Trauma.* New York: Plenum, 1998.

Hunter, Edna. J. "Long-Term Effects of Parental Wartime Captivity on Children of POW and MIA Servicemen." *Journal of Contemporary Psychotherapy* 18, no. 4 (1988):312–328.

National League of Families of Prisoners of War and Missing in Action in Southeast Asia. *National League of Families of Prisoners of War and Missing in Action in Southeast Asia Newsletter* (September 1997).

Parkes, Colin. M. "Seeking and Finding a Lost Object: Evidence from Recent Studies of the Reaction to Bereavement." *Normal and Pathological Responses to Bereavement.* New York: MSS Information Corporation, 1974.

Rando, Therese. A. *Treatment of Complicated Mourning.* Champaign, IL: Research Press, 1993.

Wortman, C. B., and R. C. Silver. "The Myths of Coping with Loss." *Journal of Consulting and Clinical Psychology* 57 (1989):349–357.

Zisook, S., and S. R. Shuchter. "The First Four Years of Widowhood." *Psychiatric Annals* 15 (1986):288–516.

MICHAEL S. CLARK

MOMENT OF DEATH

Is there a moment of death? Millions of death certificates provide abundant evidence—or do they? Many world religions also envision an awesome moment in which the soul departs from the body to continue its existence in another form. Furthermore, the moment of death is the signal for an abrupt change in society's way of dealing with the individual: Medical attention gives way to mortuary services and rites of passage; the death is announced through formal and informal channels;

personal records are reclassified; the deceased person's assets are redistributed (or become the subject of conflict and litigation); and there is additional tension in situations such as organ donation and cryonic suspension. In each of these scenarios there is often a sense of urgency to move on to the next step whether this be the removal of organs to save another person's life or the preparation for cryostasis. The moment of death, then, has both symbolic resonations and practical consequences. Nevertheless, despite the definitions, assumptions, and beliefs that surround it, the moment of death can be quite an elusive concept.

Is There a Final Moment of Life?

The most common assumption in Western society is that life gives way to death in a "razor-thin" moment. This image has been reinforced by numerous movie and television scenes in which a sick or injured person suddenly falls silent and lies still, the struggle is then over. These depictions are also consistent with the inclination to see much of reality in dichotomous terms. One either wins or loses; one's conclusions are either right or wrong; a person is either good or bad, a friend or an enemy, and dead or alive. This way of thinking has the advantage of reducing complexity and ambiguity, but the disadvantages of oversimplification and premature judgment. By contrast, Eastern religions and scientific thought are more likely to emphasize process and flow. Buddhists and Hindus, for example, regard perpetual change as a basic feature of the universe. Within this worldview, living and dying can be regarded as a tidal play of forces that occur throughout life.

Death certificates seem to support the assumption that there is a clear and definitive moment of death when time of death is recorded. Often, though, this information is based on estimates rather than direct observation. A resident of a long-term care facility or a hospital patient may have been seen alive at Time A and then discovered dead at Time B. Precisely when the death occurred between A and B is unknown, but a time is recorded to complete the certificate. It is not unusual for the death certificate to be signed by a physician who was not there at the specified time. There can also be a strategic basis for selecting the moment of death. For example, a patient who dies in the operating room may not be pronounced dead until moved to a postsurgery unit.

No reliable information is available on the number of deaths that are actually witnessed, whether at home, in the community, or in medical care settings. Patients enrolled in hospice programs seem to have a better chance for companionship at the time of death, but even then this does not always happen. The collective experience of caregivers and researchers suggests that many people pass from life to death without another person at their side. Nobody knows if they experienced a definitive moment of death.

It can be difficult to identify a moment of death when the person has not been able to respond and communicate effectively for some time. This situation may arise after a stroke, drug reaction, or catastrophic failure of the cardiovascular or some other system. A nurse could detect the cessation of vital functions if the patient is on life support, and this might be considered the moment of death. Not all unresponsive patients are under this kind of intensive observation, however, and nurses may have conflicting duties to perform even when they are trying to monitor vital signs.

The moment of death has become a more problematic concept with the changing definitions of death and the technological advances that can keep basic physiological systems going even if there is no discernible mental functioning. The person may seem to have perished some time ago, and the moment of death may become a matter of professional, family, and legal decision making. Even a slight possibility of recovery, though, can create the lingering question of whether or not the moment of death has actually occurred.

How one decides to define the moment of death also depends on one's willingness to consider rigor mortis and other physiological processes that continue for some time afterward. The person is dead, but organic processes still have their sequences to complete.

The Mystery of the Moment

The moment of death is not as clear and firm a fact as many people have often supposed. It has been defined and assessed in many ways throughout history, and there may be other changes yet to come. For personal, religious, and bureaucratic purposes it is often useful to assume that a specific, identifiable moment separates life from death. Biomedical research and experience offers only mixed support for this belief. The body becomes cooler after death, for example, but people have survived at even lower temperatures. A sudden "flat-line" shift in electrical brain activity is considered evidence for death, yet the readings may be continued for another twenty-four hours just to be sure.

Nevertheless, there have also been many observations to verify an obvious moment of death for some people. Companions have seen a person change in an instant, as though a subtle wave had passed through them (or a subtle something had passed from them). Everything seems to be as it was a moment before—except that a vital quality is missing and a shell of the person left behind. The sense of moment has occasionally been intensified by the feeling that an energy has been shared from the dying person to the companion. Known as the "death flash," this phenomenon has not been successfully studied but has experiential validity for those who feel that they have been part of a mysterious transfer.

The moment of death is unlikely to be the same for the dying person and the other people who may be in attendance. The dying person might have a final experience before the signs become visible to others. Similarly, a person might be considered by others to have passed into death but actually retain some form of mental life, possibly even continuous awareness of the situation. Still again, death might occur so suddenly that the afflicted person has no time to register any experience. Battlefield deaths have provided many examples. Some soldiers killed in the battle of Gettysburg, for example, remained frozen in their active positions, such as scaling a wall. For these victims there may not have been a moment of death, but their last moments remained as though fixed forever in time for those who later entered the killing ground.

Depending on the perspective one takes, then, the moment of death can be seen to be a religious image, a bureaucratic convenience, or a sociomedical complexity.

See also: COMMUNICATION WITH THE DYING; CRYONIC SUSPENSION; GOOD DEATH, THE; LAST WORDS; LIFE SUPPORT SYSTEMS; ORGAN DONATION AND TRANSPLANTATION; SYMPTOMS AND SYMPTOM MANAGEMENT

Bibliography

Binski, Paul. *Medieval Death*. Ithaca, NY: Cornell University Press, 1996.

Coco, Gregory A. *A Strange and Blighted Land. Gettysburg: The Aftermath of a Battle*. Gettysburg, PA: Thomas Publications, 1995.

Nuland, Sherwin B. *How We Die*. New York: Knopf, 1994.

Stein, Arnold. *The House of Death: Messages from the English Renaissance*. Baltimore, MD: Johns Hopkins University Press, 1986.

Wilkins, Robert. *Death: A History of Man's Obsessions and Fears*. New York: Barnes & Noble, 1990.

ROBERT KASTENBAUM

MORTALITY, CHILDBIRTH

Until the late twentieth century, and then only in developed countries, the mortality risks associated with childbearing were substantial. Although there are risks to infants, the following entry focuses on the mortality risks faced by mothers. Maternal mortality is measured by the maternal mortality ratio, which is the number of deaths related to pregnancy per 100,000 live births.

Getting an accurate measure of the maternal mortality ratio in many parts of the world is difficult primarily because one needs reliability in both the number of pregnant women and in the number of live births. A pregnant woman may die, perhaps due to an illegal abortion, but her death is not counted as pregnancy related either because her pregnant status is not ascertained or that information is withheld due to religious/moral convictions. In addition, maternal deaths extend to forty-two days past delivery or past pregnancy termination; if a woman is not receiving any medical care in the immediate postpartum period, her death may not be attributed to childbearing. The number of live births is not available in the countries that do not have a birth registration system. Even among countries that do, there may be systematic differences between countries in the designation of a birth as "live." Thus statistics on maternal mortality for all but the most developed countries are best-guess estimates only.

Global Variation in Maternal Mortality

At the turn of the twenty-first century, there were substantial differences in maternal mortality. According to Women's International Network News figures, the number of maternal deaths worldwide per 100,000 live births is 430, with a sharp division between developing countries, where the maternal mortality ratio is estimated to be 480, and developed countries, where the ratio is 27. These ratios can be translated into women's lifetime risk of dying from pregnancy/pregnancy-related reasons: 1 chance in 48 in the third world contrasted with 1 in 1,800 in developed countries. The highest maternal mortality levels are found in eastern and western Africa; Mozambique's maternal mortality ratio is among the highest in the world at 1,500. The lowest levels occur in northern Europe.

Causes of Maternal Mortality around the World

Maternal mortality is the result of any number of complications that beset pregnant women worldwide. The most common direct causes of maternal death are severe bleeding (25%), infection (15%), unsafe abortion (13%), eclampsia (pregnancy-induced hypertension, often accompanied by seizures, 12%), and obstructed labor (8%). Fundamental to the reduction of maternal mortality is the identification of the wider social, economic, health, and political factors that are associated with it, an area that is the subject of considerable debate among policymakers. Some argue that maternal mortality is an unusual public health problem in that it is primarily affected by institutionally based medical interventions. This viewpoint is unusual in that most causes of death have responded more to public health initiatives (e.g., clean drinking water, sanitation) than to medical interventions. According to this view, the way to reduce maternal mortality is through the provision of emergency obstetrical care. In contrast, others argue that the key factor in maternal mortality is the disadvantaged status of women, a position that reframes maternal death as a social justice issue. Maternal mortality is viewed as the accumulation of a number of risks that girls and women face (e.g., malnutrition, female genital mutilation, premature marriage and pregnancy, lack of family planning mechanisms for child spacing) that reflect the relative lack of status and worth accorded to them in certain countries.

Both medical and social factors play important roles in maternal mortality. There is clear evidence that medical interventions are important in reducing maternal mortality, as long as those interventions are performed by trained personnel. Especially important is competent emergency obstetrical care. Research done in rural Gambia shows that prenatal care is far less effective than emergency care in reducing the rate of death related to childbirth. This fact may be because many of the life-threatening complications that accompany pregnancy and delivery cannot be predicted for individual women. Also important is the provision of family planning services, which operate to lower the number of births and thus reduce the risk of maternal death. Evidence on the importance of social factors in maternal mortality is less well documented. Overall maternal mortality is much lower in societies in which women have higher educational levels and higher social status. However, there is no direct one-to-one relationship between improvements in women's social conditions and reductions in maternal mortality. Nevertheless, access to legal abortion is important in reducing deaths because legal abortions are more likely to be performed in a clean environment by trained medical personnel. It is estimated that about one-half of abortions lead to maternal death in Indonesia where abortion is illegal; this translates to the deaths of nearly 1 million women per year. In certain third world countries, the provision of safe and legal abortion is bound up with cultural views about gender roles, and is intimately related to women's position in society.

Maternal Mortality in the United States

Figure 1 shows the trend in the maternal mortality ratio in the United States over the course of the twentieth century. Maternal mortality ratios were over 600 (somewhat higher than in the contemporary developed world) until the early 1930s, when decline commenced. (The high rates around 1920 are likely due to the global influenza epidemic.) Compared to general American mortality decline, this is a late starting date; reductions did not occur despite an increasing proportion of deliveries in hospitals, the introduction of prenatal care, and the increased used of antiseptics in labor and delivery. Two reasons have been given for the lack of reduction in maternal mortality during the first third of the twentieth century: Women either received no care or care in which the attendant did not recognize the severity of complications; and women received improperly performed medical interventions. It is likely that the second reason was more of a factor because unnecessary or improperly performed interventions and a lack of careful antiseptic procedures were common during that time period.

The huge decline from the mid-1930s to the mid-1950s (from 582 to 40) has been attributed to a number of factors: the shift in responsibility for maternity care to obstetricians; the introduction of new antibiotics, the establishment of blood banks (along with blood typing and transfusion procedures); the introduction of safer types of anesthesia; and safer use of forceps. A good portion of the decline from the mid-1950s is due to declining infections related to septic abortion, resulting from the liberalization of abortion laws starting in the early 1960s and the legalization of abortion in 1970.

Although the timing of the decline in maternal mortality was late in the United States relative to general declines in mortality, the same can be observed for England and Wales. With improved living conditions (e.g., nutrition, sanitation), the nineteenth century saw reductions in infant mortality and in deaths due to infection, with little benefit from medical advances. However, reduction in maternal mortality had to wait upon the development of medical interventions and procedures, and their proper use. While later declines were dependent upon social and political change (i.e., acceptance of abortion), the early and very large decline in maternal mortality was the product of medical advance. The dependence of safe childbirth on medicine is at odds with a trend commencing in the late twentieth century in Western societies to return to an idealized demedicalized childbirthing past. The evidence is compelling that medicine is key to safe childbirth.

The contemporary maternal mortality ratio in the United States is 7.7, a level that has remained unchanged since the early 1980s despite reductions in general and infant mortality and despite a national goal to reduce maternal mortality to no more than 3.3 by 2000. Part of the reason for the failure to meet this goal is the existence of a persistent and large racial difference in maternal mortality. African-American women—who bear 16 percent of U.S. babies—have a maternity mortality ratio (19.6) that is nearly four times higher than white women (5.3). The reasons for the racial disparity are not clear. Some of the factors that are likely involved include racial differences in susceptibility to high blood pressure, a leading cause of maternal death; general health; and receipt of high-quality prenatal care. However, generalizations are difficult, especially given state differences. For example, the maternity mortality ratio for African Americans varies from a low of 8.7 in Massachusetts to a high of 25.7 in Washington, D.C.

FIGURE 1

Material mortality ratios: United States, 1915–1998.

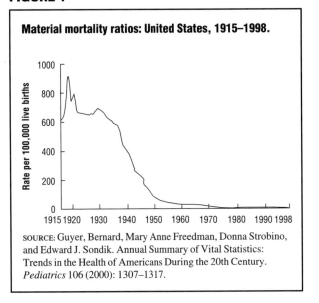

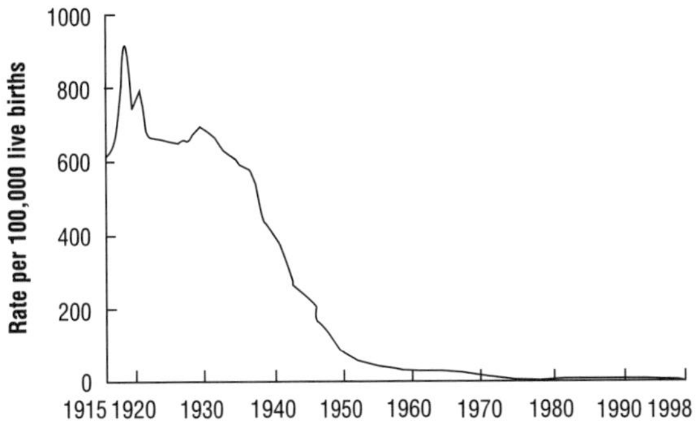

SOURCE: Guyer, Bernard, Mary Anne Freedman, Donna Strobino, and Edward J. Sondik. Annual Summary of Vital Statistics: Trends in the Health of Americans During the 20th Century. *Pediatrics* 106 (2000): 1307–1317.

The rate of decline in maternal deaths had stalled, and persistent racial differences—showing a substantial African-American disadvantage—remain. Yet, almost no research, either by biomedical or by social scientists, is addressing these issues. As a result, the safe motherhood goal of maternal mortality less than 3.3 has not been achieved in America.

See also: CAUSES OF DEATH; GENDER AND DEATH; MORTALITY, INFANT

Bibliography

Cook, Rebecca J. "Human Rights Law and Safe Motherhood." *Women's International News Network* 25, no. 3 (1999):20.

Greenwood, A. M., B. M. Greenwood, A. K. Bradley, et al. "A Prospective Study of the Outcome of Pregnancy in a Rural Area of Gambia." *Bulletin of the World Health Organization* 65 (1987):635–643.

Guyer, Bernard, Mary Anne Freedman, Donna Strobino, and Edward J. Sondik. "Annual Summary of Vital Statistics: Trends in the Health of Americans during the 20th Century." *Pediatrics* 106 (2000):1307–1317.

"Indonesia: Up to 50% of Abortions Lead to Maternal Death." *Women's International Network News* 26, no. 2 (2000):52.

Luker, Kristin. *Abortion and the Politics of Motherhood.* Berkeley: University of California Press, 1984.

Maine, Deborah, and Allan Rosenfield. "The Safe Motherhood Initiative: Why Has It Stalled?" *American Journal of Public Health* 89 (1999):480–483.

"Maternal Mortality: A Global Review." *Women's International Network News* 24, no. 3 (1998):15–18.

Population Reference Bureau. "Mozambique's High Rate of Maternal Mortality." *Population Today,* (April). Washington, DC: Author, 2000.

"Racial Divide in Maternal Mortality." *Society* 27, no. 3 (2000):4–6.

"State-Specific Maternal Mortality among Black and White Women: United States, 1987–1996." *Morbidity and Mortality Weekly Report* 48, no. 23 (2000):492–497.

Wertz, Richard W., and Dorothy C. Wertz. *Lying In: A History of Childbirth in America.* New Haven, CT: Yale University Press, 1989.

ELLEN M. GEE

MORTALITY, INFANT

Infant mortality refers to deaths of children under the age of one year. It is measured by the infant mortality rate, which is the total number of deaths to children under the age of one year for every 1,000 live births. The infant mortality rate is often broken down into two components relating to timing of death: neonatal and postneonatal. The neonatal mortality rate refers to the number of deaths to babies within 28 days after birth (per 1,000 live births). Sometimes a special type of neonatal mortality is assessed. The perinatal mortality rate measures the number of late fetal deaths (at or after 28 weeks gestation) and deaths within the first 7 days after birth per 1,000 live births. The postneonatal mortality rate involves the number of deaths to babies from 28 days to the end of the first year per 1,000 live births. The distinction between neonatal (and perinatal) and postneonatal mortality is important because the risk of death is higher close to the delivery date, and the causes of death near the time of birth/delivery are quite different from those later in infancy. Therefore, effective interventions to reduce infant mortality need to take into account the distribution of ages at death of infants.

Many developing countries lack the resources to keep track of infant deaths; therefore data for these areas are estimates only. Another methodological problem in measuring infant mortality is ascertaining the number of live births. Sometimes this problem is one of undercounts of births (i.e., births are not registered and thus not counted); sometimes the difficulty lies in inconsistently differentiating stillbirths and live births, especially across countries because this distinction is not as clear-cut as one might imagine.

Infant Mortality in International Perspective

Table 1 provides infant mortality rates for the world, for developed and developing countries, and by continent, with some selected countries that highlight the range of levels. At 57, the world's infant mortality rate has never been lower; however, differences across the world are substantial. Africa's rate (88) is ten times higher than the average rate (8) for the developed countries. Within Africa the highest levels of infant mortality in the world are experienced, with rates as high as 157 in Sierra Leone. On average the rate for Asia (56) is somewhat lower than for Africa, but some Asian countries such as Afghanistan have rates (150) as high as anywhere in the world. On the other hand, Hong Kong's rate (3.2) is very low, illustrating that the most variation in infant mortality level occurs in Asia. Both Europe and North America (the United States and Canada) have low levels of infant mortality, with average rates well under 10. However, European variation is not inconsequential; rates in at least some parts of Eastern Europe are nearly 10 times higher than in northern European countries such as Iceland and Sweden.

Overall, income and education, both at the societal and individual levels, are closely associated with infant mortality. While the relationship between infant mortality and level of socioeconomic development is not perfect, the infant mortality rate is commonly used more than any other measure as a general indicator of socioeconomic well-being and of general medical and public health

TABLE 1

Infant mortality rates by region (and selected countries), 2001

Area	Rate
World	57
Developed Countries	8
Less Developed Countries	63
Africa	88
Sierra Leone	157
Western Sahara	150
Liberia	139
Asia	56
Afghanistan	150
East Timor	143
Hong Kong	3.2
Europe	9
Iceland	2.6
Sweden	3.5
Albania	22
Romania	20.5
Latin America (and the Caribbean)	35
North America (U.S. and Canada)	7

SOURCE: Population Reference Bureau. *2001 World Population Data Sheet.* Washington, DC: Population Reference Bureau, 2001.

conditions in a country. Richer countries can provide the basic ingredients for infant survival: clean water, sanitary surroundings, adequate food and shelter, and access to health care services. A large portion of infant mortality is due to infectious and communicable diseases, which sanitary practices and an adequate diet do much to prevent.

At the individual level mothers (and fathers) with higher income and education are more likely to possess knowledge of sanitary behaviors and the money for adequate food, as well as to take their babies to a health service if needed. Especially important in the latter regard is oral rehydration therapy, which is effective in saving babies from dying from the dehydration that accompanies diarrhea.

Causes of Infant Deaths

Postneonatal mortality is most often caused by infectious diseases, such as pneumonia, tetanus, and malaria. An important factor in reducing postneonatal mortality is adequate nutrition, particularly breast milk, which provides babies with both the nourishment and the antibodies to fight infectious diseases. Of course adequate breast milk depends upon adequately nourished mothers. Also important is the proper use of breast milk substitutes—mixing formula with unclean water and/or diluting formula for cost-savings reasons, both known to occur in developing countries, have negative affects on the health of infants. The promotion by multinational corporations of breast milk substitutes to women in poorer countries has been one of the travesties of our times; it is estimated that 1.5 million deaths a year could be prevented by breast-feeding.

The issue of HIV-infected mothers' breast-feeding has become controversial. A number of countries have instituted policies that recommend that mothers with HIV (human immunodeficiency virus) not breast-feed, based on some evidence of mother-to-child transmission of HIV through breast-feeding. In contrast are policies that promote breast-feeding in areas with high HIV prevalence. Because breast-feeding protects against the infectious diseases that take the lives of millions of infants every year, there is policy debate about the best course of action. Researchers do not know if the protection against infectious diseases afforded by breast-feeding outweighs the risks of HIV transmission to children, so it is not possible to make a definitive conclusion about the risks and benefits of breast-feeding by mothers with HIV. However, a 2000 study by the World Health Organization (WHO) Collaborative Study Team on the Role of Breastfeeding on the Prevention of Infant Mortality determined that the breast-fed babies of mothers with HIV had six times the protection against diarrheal deaths in the first few months of life than babies not breast-fed. In the second half-year of life, protection against both diarrheal and acute respiratory infections was about double that for non-breast-fed babies. Protection declined with age of child, and was greatest for the children of the least educated women. It appears the benefits may outweigh the risks for limited (in time) breast-feeding and for poorer women, who are unable to afford safe substitute milk substitutes. However, another issue to consider is that breast-feeding may negatively affect the health of mothers with HIV/AIDS (human immunodeficiency virus/acquired immunodeficiency syndrome).

Another cause of infant mortality is violence. Research conducted in two areas in India show that wife beating, closely linked with patriarchal social structures, leads to both pregnancy loss and infant mortality. Other violence, such as infanticide, the deliberate killing of infants, is extremely difficult to document, but it seems likely that some portion of the "missing girls" in India and China were the victims of infanticide. When infanticide is practiced, it is most likely a response to difficult economic circumstances (and coercive population policy, in the case of China) in conjunction with male-child preference.

Violence against babies is not limited to developing countries. Violence to infants in the form of head trauma, including shaken baby syndrome (SBS), has been studied in America. In 2000 the researchers Suzanne Starling and James Holden found that in both a western and southern U.S. sample men are more likely (70 percent) to be perpetrators of violence, with biological fathers (not necessarily married to the mother or living with the child) the most likely to cause fatal (and nonfatal) head trauma to infants, followed by boyfriends. The victims were more likely to be boys, with an average age of six months.

Excluding violence, neonatal mortality (in contrast to postneonatal mortality) is less likely to be the direct result of social, economic, and environmental conditions. Major causes of neonatal mortality include low birthweight, preterm (premature) birth, congenital malformations, and sudden infant death syndrome (SIDS). In developed countries most infant mortality is concentrated in the early neonatal period, with the aforementioned causes of death predominant.

Infant Mortality in the United States

Over the course of the twentieth century, each developed country has a somewhat unique trend in the timing and tempo of infant mortality decline, an examination of the American case provides a general sense of the Western pattern. In the early part of the twentieth century, the infant mortality rate was in excess of 100—much higher than in the developing countries (on average) of the twenty-first century. In other words, more than 10 percent of children born died in the first year of life. In the earlier stage of decline, postneonatal mortality was reduced. Over the period from 1915 to around the end of World War II, postneonatal mortality experienced a steady and dramatic decline to a level of approximately 10 (Wegman 2001). At the same time, deaths of babies from 28 days to one year of age decreased as a proportion of total infant deaths (i.e., all death under the age of one). This decline was due to improvements in nutrition and in public health, such as clean drinking water, sewage disposal, and personal hygiene. Deaths due to diarrhea and infectious diseases such as pneumonia, diphtheria, and typhoid fever were reduced dramatically. In the post–World War II era, vaccines and other medical interventions such as antibiotics played a role in further declines.

Neonatal mortality declined more slowly and later than postneonatal mortality. It was not until around 1975 that the neonatal rate reached 10—lagging behind neonatal mortality by a generation. Neonatal mortality decline is much less dependent on nutrition and public health measures; rather, it requires more sophisticated medical interventions, especially to keep low birthweight babies alive. In the twenty-first century, approximately two-thirds of all infant deaths occur in the neonatal period, with the leading causes of death associated with low birthweight, congenital malformations, and SIDS.

The latest data available reveal that the United States' rate for infant mortality is not as low as one might expect. According to the Population Reference Bureau, its rate of 7 is surpassed by several European countries (Denmark, Iceland, Finland, Germany, Netherlands, Switzerland, and the Czech Republic all have rates under 5), several Asian countries (Singapore, Hong Kong and Japan all have rates under 4), Canada (5.5), Australia (5.3), and New Zealand (5.5) (Wegman 2001). Countries in the 7 to 8 range in infant mortality, along with the United States, include Cyprus, Malaysia, and Cuba—all considerably less developed than the United States. The United States' comparatively poor ranking in infant mortality has led to concern at the national level, especially relating to racial inequalities. The figures for African Americans show a consistent disadvantage in infant mortality, a disadvantage that is increasing, especially with regard to neonatal mortality.

An important factor influencing the relationship between race and infant mortality is birthweight. At the end of the twentieth century, 13 percent of (non-Hispanic) African-American babies were born in the low birthweight category (under 2,500 grams or approximately 5 pounds), compared with approximately 6.5 percent of (non-Hispanic) Caucasian babies and Hispanic infants.

The reasons why African-American women are so much more likely to give birth to high-risk, low birthweight infants remain unclear, although differences in prenatal care may be implicated, as may the absence of a national health care system and inadequate social welfare. Another factor to note is that the infant mortality of whites is lowered by the contribution of immigrants who have lower infant mortality than the native born.

In the decade of the 1990s, Caucasian women (and American Indian and Asian/Pacific Islander women) experienced some increase in low birthweight babies. This statistic has been attributed in part to an increase in multiple births (e.g., twins, triplets), which are more likely to be low birthweight newborns. Increases in multiple births are associated with fertility drugs and reproductive technologies such as in vitro fertilization and, to some degree, later age at childbearing. This increase in low birthweight infants does not bode well for future declines in neonatal mortality.

The Future

In developing countries considerable progress against infant mortality, especially postneonatal mortality, can be accomplished through the implementation of basic public health measures that will reduce infant deaths due to diarrhea and infectious disease. However, the HIV/AIDS epidemic places some countries, especially sub-Saharan Africa and parts of Southeast Asia, in a difficult position since HIV/AIDS kills infants directly and, through lowering immune functioning, indirectly. In developed countries, the major immediate challenge is to reduce the proportion of low birthweight infants. While improved prenatal care will advance that goal, restructuring (i.e., dismantling) of welfare states presents a possible barrier, as does the continuing popularity of technologies to increase fertility. Another unknown factor in all countries is the future role of re-emerging old and emerging new viruses and pathogenic bacteria; these microbes could significantly increase postneonatal mortality.

See also: CAUSES OF DEATH; GENDER AND DEATH; INFANTICIDE

Bibliography

Coale, Ansley J. "Excess Female Mortality and the Balance of the Sexes." *Population and Development Review* 17 (1991):517–523.

Guyer, Bernard, Mary Anne Freedman, Donna Strobino, and Edward J. Sondik. "Annual Summary of Vital Statistics: Trends in the Health of Americans During the 20th Century." *Pediatrics* 106 (2000):1307–1317.

Hummer, Robert A., Monique Biegler, Peter B. DeTurk, Douglas Forbes, W. Parker Frisbie, Ying Hong, and Starling G. Pullum."Race/Ethnicity, Nativity, and Infant Mortality in the United States." *Social Forces* 77 (1999):1083–1118.

Jejeebhoy, Shireen J. "Associations Between Wife-Beating and Fetal and Infant Death: Impressions from a Survey in Rural India." *Studies in Family Planning* 29 (1998):300–308.

Kposowa, Augustine J., and Pamela J. Preston. "Linking Racism to Birth Weight Disparities in the United States." *Research in Social Stratification and Mobility* 16 (1998):181–224.

Kramer, Michael S., Kitaw Demissie, Hong Yang, Robert W. Platt, and Reg Sauvé. "The Contribution of Mild and Moderate Preterm Birth to Infant Mortality." *Journal of the American Medical Association* 284 (2000):843–849.

Lewis, Michael. "A Path Analysis of the Effect of Welfare on Infant Mortality." *Journal of Sociology and Social Welfare* 26 (1999):125–136.

Liston, Robert. "The Contribution of Mild and Moderate Preterm Birth to Infant Mortality." *Journal of the American Medical Association* 284 (2000):843–849.

Newell, Marie-Louise. "Does Breastfeeding Really Affect Mortality among HIV-1 Infected Women?" *Lancet* 357 (2001):1634–1636.

Population Reference Bureau. *2001 World Population Data Sheet*. Washington, DC: Author, 2001.

Sen, Amartya "Missing Women." *British Medical Journal* 304 (1992):587–588.

Starling, Suzanne P., and James R. Holden. "Perpetrators of Abusive Head Trauma: A Comparison of Two Regional Populations." *Southern Medical Journal* 93 (2000):463–465.

Wegman, Myron E. "Infant Mortality in the 20th Century, Dramatic but Uneven Progress." *Journal of Nutrition* 131 (2001):401S–408S.

Wise, Jacqui. "Baby Milk Companies Accused of Breaching Marketing Code." *British Medical Journal* 314 (January 1997):167–169.

World Health Organization Collaborative Study Team on the Role of Breastfeeding on the Prevention of Infant Mortality. "Effect of Breastfeeding on Infant and Child

Mortality Due to Infectious Diseases in Less Developed Countries: A Pooled Analysis." *Lancet* 355 (2000):451–455.

ELLEN M. GEE

MOURNING

The term *mourning* is probably the single most inconsistently used term in thanatology. Traditionally it has been used to refer to the cultural and/or public display of grief through one's behaviors. This usage focuses on mourning as a vehicle for social communication. In this regard, mourning can pertain at various times to specific rituals, particular outward signs (e.g., black clothes or an armband), the identification of who is to be recognized as bereaved, and a specified time period during which signs of grief can be shown. However, the term has been assigned other meanings that contribute to its being used interchangeably with the terms "grief" and "bereavement" to denote personal and subjective responses to loss. As yet there is no total consensus on the use of the term; however, in this essay mourning is discussed as a distinct phenomenon that is stimulated by the experience of loss (i.e., bereavement). While it encompasses "acute grief," it includes and implies substantially more than that experience.

Conceptual Development

Theories of mourning have changed significantly over time. Initially psychoanalytic conceptualizations held sway. There was particularly strong, early input from Sigmund Freud, whose oft-quoted 1917 paper "Mourning and Melancholia" tends to be cited by scholars erroneously as the first work on the topic. (Among others, there was Karl Abraham's 1911 paper on the treatment of manic depression and allied conditions, which partially prompted Freud's classic paper.) Later substantial psychoanalytic refinement was provided by Erich Lindemann, whose 1944 paper "Symptomatology and Management of Acute Grief" shared with Freud's particular prominence as a basis for later observers's comparisons, agreements, and disagreements. Coming originally out of the psychoanalytic school, John Bowlby, the chief architect of attachment theory, then incorporated the philosophical tenets of that theory into the theory of mourning a number of publications during the 1960s through 1980s. Bowlby dispensed with abstract and unverifiable psychoanalytic concepts and incorporated principles from ethology, control theory, and cognitive psychology. Early-twenty-first-century thanatologists hold views that are strongly influenced, at least in large part, by attachment theory. This makes it the predominant, although not exclusive, perspective from which mourning is currently explained. While Bowlby's protégé, Colin Murray Parkes, has continued to expand understanding of mourning in numerous ways along attachment dimensions, he also has promoted the concept of psychosocial transitions that has been well incorporated into contemporary mourning theory.

Concepts from three theoretically and clinically related domains are being incorporated into the thinking about mourning. Each has generated a number of important implications about mourning, selected examples of which are noted herein.

From the generic psychological arena of *stress, coping, and adaptation theory* comes the notions that mourning involves more than merely reacting to loss, but active attempts to contend with it; that the individual's cognitive appraisal of the loss, its implications, and one's coping attempts is a critical factor determining response and accounting for its idiosyncrasy; and that successful outcome of mourning appears to require both problem- and emotion-focused coping.

Out of the realm of *traumatic stress and victimization theories* are being adopted into scientific understanding of mourning the ideas that assumptive world revision is necessary after major loss; that acute grief is a form of traumatic stress reaction; and that posttraumatic growth is possible as a positive consequence of loss.

From the province of *cognitive theory,* particularly *constructivism,* stems the belief that much of the painfulness of bereavement comes from disruption of the mourner's personal construct system caused by the death; the expectation that personal meaning reconstruction is at the heart of mourning; and the realization that there is traditionally an insufficient appreciation of cognitive processes in bereavement due to relative overfocus upon affective processing and failure to comprehend the two main sets of cognitive processes (i.e., the mourner's learning about the reality and implications of the loved one's death, and the mourner's transforming to incorporate the changes necessitated by the death).

Eight specific bereavement-related notions are also becoming assimilated into contemporary understanding of mourning:

1. Mourning does not necessarily proceed in invariant sequences; staged-based models of mourning are inaccurate in implying that all mourners undergo the same processes in the same order.
2. Continued connections to the deceased are not necessarily pathological and, if appropriate, can be therapeutic.
3. People do not necessarily "get over" major loss, but learn to live with it, with struggles to do so persisting far longer than previously thought.
4. Routinely suggesting professional intervention for all mourners can be harmful; it tends only to be regularly needed by bereaved persons who are at high risk.
5. There is no one way to respond to loss; Western mental health has been biased in favor of emotional expressiveness and this has been harmful to people with other styles.
6. Mourning and meaning making occur not only on an intrapersonal individual level, but also on an interpersonal familial/social level.
7. Mourning can become complicated; this need not automatically suggest pathology on the mourner's part, but may be due to other factors (e.g., circumstances of the death, the role of the deceased, and availability of support, among others).
8. Mourning is culturally relative.

Taken together, these associated concepts and specific bereavement-related notions have significantly broadened and deepened the comprehension of mourning, and enhanced appreciation of the complex challenges and experiences that it brings to mourners.

Mourning and Grief: Definitions and Distinctions

To comprehend mourning, it is necessary first to understand its distinctions from and relationship to grief. There is much to be gained by distinguishing between acute grief reactions to loss and the psychosocial labors of mourning undertaken over time to live with that loss. To assert that they are the same disregards two very different sets of experiences and demands, and seriously compromises bereavement intervention and research efforts. This discussion is predicated upon Therese A. Rando's 1993 model of mourning, which was developed specifically in relation to Western society. Consistent with the action-oriented nature of mourning, a process rather than content focus is maintained in this discussion.

Grief refers to the process of experiencing the psychological, behavioral, social, and physical reactions to the perception of loss. A grief response expresses one or a combination of four things: (1) the mourner's feelings about the loss and the deprivation it causes (e.g., sorrow, depression, guilt); (2) the mourner's protest at the loss and wish to undo it and have it not be true (e.g., anger, searching, preoccupation with the deceased); (3) the effects caused by the assault on the mourner as a result of the loss (e.g., traumatic stress, disorganization, physical symptoms); and (4) the mourner's personal actions stimulated by any of the previous three (e.g., crying, social withdrawal, increased use of medication or psychoactive substances).

However, the ultimate goal in contending with any major loss is for the individual experiencing it to be able to recognize that the loved one truly is gone and to make the necessary internal (psychological) and external (behavioral and social) changes to incorporate that loss into his or her ongoing life. Grief in itself cannot accomplish what is required to reach this goal. As solely a complex set of passive reactions to the loss, it fails to take the individual far enough.

Accommodation suggests an adaptation to make room for a particular circumstance. Clinical experience suggests that it is to be preferred over the term *resolution,* which insinuates a once-and-for-all closure that typically is not achieved—or even desirable—after the death of a dearly loved one. The bereaved must make a series of readjustments to cope with, compensate for, and adapt to the absence of what has been lost physically and/or psychosocially. Failure to make the proper adaptations and re-orientations necessitated by the loss leaves the survivor related inappropriately to the lost person and the now-defunct old world.

For these reasons, grief is a necessary, but not sufficient, condition to come to successful accommodation of a loss. Grief is to mourning like infancy is to childhood: It is the beginning, but not the entire course, of events. However, it is pivotal because without the experiences and learning provided by acute grief—where the mourner confronts and is taught the reality of the loss and the need for the mourner to change is made clear—the rest of mourning cannot take place.

Mourning, then, encompasses much more than grief, which starts it off. It refers as well to the consequent conscious and unconscious processes and courses of action that promote three operations, each with its own particular focus, that enable the individual ultimately to accommodate the loss. The first operation promoted by mourning is the undoing of the psychosocial ties that had bound the mourner to the loved one when that person was alive, with the eventual facilitation of new ties appropriate to that person's now being physically dead. The focus is internal, upon the mourner's readjustment vis-à-vis the deceased. In the second operation, mourning processes help the mourner to adapt to the loss. The focus again is internal, upon the self and the making of revisions in one's assumptive world and one's identity insofar as the loss invalidates certain of one's assumptive world elements and aspects of one's previous identity. The third operation promoted by mourning helps the mourner learn how to live healthily in the new world without the deceased. Here, the focus is external, upon the physical and social world as the mourner attempts to move adaptively into it without the loved one through the adoption of new ways of being in that world and reinvestment in it.

Uncomplicated reactions of acute grief may last many months and in some cases even longer. In contrast, because of its myriad aspects and demands, uncomplicated mourning can last a number of years, long after acute grief is spent. In fact, it lasts forever for many people, as there often is revisiting and reworking of major loss over time. This does not necessarily mean that the individual is in acute grief all that time (that would be considered pathological), nor that the reality of the loss and its implications were not fully comprehended earlier on. It merely speaks to the ongoing nature of living with major loss.

The distinction between grief and mourning is crucial not only to the maintenance of appropriate expectations for mourners, but also for helping them cope. Many individuals assist the bereaved with the beginning processes of acute grief by enabling their reactions to the loss, but do not assist sufficiently, if at all, with the important latter processes of readjustment. Consequently, mourners are frequently left alone to reshape themselves and their world after the loss of a loved one, and suffer additionally as a result.

Requirements for Healthy Mourning

For healthy mourning to take place, a number of actions must be undertaken. These vary depending upon the model utilized, yet there is remarkable overlap. According to Rando, there are six specific "R" processes that must be completed successfully by the individual in order for the three reorientations—in relation to the deceased, self, and external world—of healthy mourning to occur.

1. Recognize the loss. Recognizing the loss involves acknowledging the reality of the death and understanding what caused it.
2. React to the separation. This process involves experiencing the pain; and feeling, identifying, accepting, and giving some form of expression to all the psychological reactions to the loss. It also involves identifying and mourning the secondary losses that are brought about by the death.
3. Recollect and reexperience the deceased and the relationship. Healthy mourning involves reviewing and remembering realistically, with reviving and reexperiencing being the associated feelings.
4. Relinquish the old attachments to the deceased and the old assumptive world.
5. Readjust to move adaptively into the new world without forgetting the old. This process, involves revising the assumptive world, developing a new relationship with the de-

ceased, adopting new ways of being in the world, and forming a new identity.

6. Reinvest. The emotional energy once invested in the relationship with the deceased eventually must be reinvested into other people, objects, pursuits, and so forth in order that emotional gratification can be received by the mourner.

Each person undertakes these processes (or not) in his or her own fashion and to his or her own depth. This is because each individual's mourning is determined by a constellation of thirty-seven sets of factors that renders the mourner's response as unique as his or her fingerprint. To be able to understand any mourner adequately, one must know the factors circumscribing the particular loss of that individual at that precise point in time. A response that is perfectly appropriate for one person in one set of circumstances may be pathological for another person in those circumstances or for the same person under different circumstances. These factors cluster under three main areas: (1) psychological factors, which are subdivided into characteristics pertaining to the nature and meaning of the specific loss, the mourner, and the death; (2) social factors; and (3) physiological factors.

Duration and Course of Mourning

There is no general time frame for the length of mourning, it is dependent upon the unique constellation of factors associated with the mourner's particular bereavement. It is important to differentiate between the duration of acute grief and of mourning. The former may be very time limited; whereas the latter, technically, can go on forever in some ways. Contrary to the myth that mourning declines linearly over time, its course often fluctuates significantly. Fluctuations occur over both the short (e.g., hourly basis) and long (e.g., a period of months or more) terms. Different types of losses are associated with diverse patterns of fluctuations (e.g., sudden death, parental loss of a child).

Even long after a death has occurred and acute grief has subsided, a wide variety of circumstances can produce within the mourner subsequent temporary upsurges of grief (STUG) reactions. These are brief periods of acute grief for the loss of a loved one that are catalyzed by a precipitant that underscores the absence of the deceased or resurrects memories of the death, the loved one, or feelings about the loss. Although such reactions previously have been inappropriately construed as being pathological, they typically are a normal part of uncomplicated mourning. This is not to say that they cannot be a manifestation of some problem, only that they are not necessarily so. There are fourteen types of STUG precipitants. These are classified under the three categories of cyclic precipitants (i.e., experiences that occur repeatedly over time), linear precipitants (i.e., experiences that are one-time occurrences), and stimulus-cued precipitants (i.e., those that involve stimuli unrelated to time).

Mourning in a Changing Sociocultural Milieu

Any person's mourning is powerfully influenced by the sociocultural context within which it occurs. This affects all manner of factors circumscribing an individual's mourning—from the type of loss that transpires to the reactions exhibited; from the meaning of that loss to the characteristics of the mourner and the types of support received or not.

Twentieth-century sociocultural and technological trends in Western society have significantly increased the prevalence of complicated mourning by causing a rise in virtually all of the seven high-risk factors predisposing to complicated mourning. The trends that have contributed most substantially to this include, among others, urbanization, technicalization, secularization, deritualization, increased social mobility, social reorganization, multiculturalism, escalating violence, wide economic disparity, medical advances, and contemporary political realities.

On the other hand, improved, and improving, bereavement research is providing more accurate information, pointing the way to primary prevention on personal and social levels and to a spectrum of interventions for bereaved persons at all degrees of risk. Socially, bereavement is more accurately understood and more visible as a legitimate topic for discussion than ever before; nevertheless, there remains significant room—and need—for improvement in these areas.

See also: GRIEF; GRIEF AND MOURNING IN CROSS-CULTURAL PERSPECTIVE; THANATOLOGY

Bibliography

Abraham, Karl. "Notes on the Psycho-Analytical Investigation and Treatment of Manic Depressive Insanity and Allied Conditions." In *Selected Papers on Psycho-Analysis.* 1911. Reprint, London: Hogarth, 1949.

Bonanno, George, and S. Kaltman. "Toward an Integrative Perspective on Bereavement." *Psychological Bulletin* 125 (1999):760–776.

Bowlby, John. *Attachment and Loss,* Vol. 3: *Loss: Sadness and Depression.* New York: Basic Books, 1980.

Corr, Charles, and Donna Corr. "Anticipatory Mourning and Coping with Dying: Similarities, Differences, and Suggested Guidelines For Helpers." In Therese A. Rando ed., *Clinical Dimensions of Anticipatory Mourning: Theory and Practice in Working with the Dying, Their Loved Ones, and Their Caregivers.* Champaign, IL: Research Press, 2000.

Doka, Kenneth. "Grief." In Robert Kastenbaum and Beatrice Kastenbaum eds., *Encyclopedia of Death.* Phoenix, AZ: The Oryx Press, 1989.

Folkman, Susan. "Revised Coping Theory and the Process of Bereavement." In Margaret Stroebe, Robert Hansson, Wolfgang Stroebe, and Henk Schut eds., *Handbook of Bereavement Research: Consequences, Coping, and Care.* Washington, DC: American Psychological Association, 2001.

Freud, Sigmund. "Mourning and Melancholia." In *The Standard Edition of the Complete Psychological Works of Sigmund Freud,* edited and translated by James Strachey, Vol. 14. 1917. Reprint, London: Hogarth, 1957.

Janoff-Bulman, Ronnie. *Shattered Assumptions: Towards a New Psychology of Trauma.* New York: The Free Press, 1992.

Lindemann, Erich. "Symptomatology and Management of Acute Grief." *American Journal of Psychiatry* 101(1944):141–148.

Neimeyer, Robert. *Lessons of Loss: A Guide to Coping.* New York: McGraw-Hill Companies, Inc./Primis Custom Publishing, 1998.

Parkes, Colin. "Attachment, Bonding and Psychiatric Problems after Bereavement in Adult Life." In Colin Parkes, J. Stevenson-Hinde, and P. Marris eds., *Attachment Across the Life Cycle.* London: Routledge, 1991.

Parkes, Colin. "Bereavement As a Psychosocial Transition: Processes of Adaptation to Change." *Journal of Social Issues* 44, no. 3 (1988):53–65.

Parkes, Colin, and Robert Weiss. *Recovery from Bereavement.* New York: Basic Books, 1983.

Rando, Therese A. "Grief and Mourning: Accommodating to Loss." In Hannelore Wass and Robert Neimeyer eds., *Dying: Facing the Facts,* 3rd edition. Washington, DC: Taylor and Francis, 1995.

Rando, Therese A. *Treatment of Complicated Mourning.* Champaign, IL: Research Press, 1993.

Rando, Therese A. *Grief, Dying, and Death: Clinical Interventions for Caregivers.* Champaign, IL: Research Press, 1984.

Rando, Therese A., ed. "On the Experience of Traumatic Stress in Anticipatory and Postdeath Mourning." In *Clinical Dimensions of Anticipatory Mourning: Theory and Practice in Working with the Dying, Their Loved Ones, and Their Caregivers.* Champaign, IL: Research Press, 2000.

Raphael, Beverley. *The Anatomy of Bereavement.* New York: Basic Books, 1983.

Raphael, Beverley, Christine Minkov, and Matthew Dobson. "Psychotherapeutic and Pharmacological Intervention for Bereaved Persons." In Margaret Stroebe, Robert Hansson, Wolfgang Stroebe, and Henk Schut eds., *Handbook of Bereavement Research: Consequences, Coping, and Care.* Washington, DC: American Psychological Association, 2001.

Rosenblatt, Paul. "A Social Constructionist Perspective On Cultural Differences in Grief." In Margaret Stroebe, Robert Hansson, Wolfgang Stroebe, and Henk Schut eds., *Handbook of Bereavement Research: Consequences, Coping, and Care.* Washington, DC: American Psychological Association, 2001.

Rubin, Simon. "A Two-Track Model of Bereavement: Theory and Application In Research." *American Journal of Orthopsychiatry* 51 (1981):101–109.

Schut, Henk, Margaret Stroebe, Jan van den Bout, and Maaike Terheggen. "The Efficacy of Bereavement Interventions: Determining Who Benefits." In Margaret Stroebe, Robert Hansson, Wolfgang Stroebe, and Henk Schut eds., *Handbook of Bereavement Research: Consequences, Coping, and Care.* Washington, DC: American Psychological Association, 2001.

Stroebe, Margaret, Robert Hansson, Wolfgang Stroebe, and Henk Schut. "Future Directions for Bereavement Research." In Margaret Stroebe, Robert Hansson, Wolfgang Stroebe, and Henk Schut eds., *Handbook of Bereavement Research: Consequences, Coping, and Care.* Washington, DC: American Psychological Association, 2001.

Stroebe, Margaret, Robert Hansson, Wolfgang Stroebe, and Henk Schut, eds. *Handbook of Bereavement Research: Consequences, Coping, and Care.* Washington, DC: American Psychological Association, 2001.

Stroebe, Margaret, and Henk Schut. "Models of Coping with Bereavement: A Review." In Margaret Stroebe, Robert Hansson, Wolfgang Stroebe, and Henk Schut eds., *Handbook of Bereavement Research: Consequences, Coping, and Care.* Washington, DC: American Psychological Association, 2001.

Stroebe, Margaret, and Henk Schut. "The Dual Process Model of Coping with Bereavement: Rationale and Description." *Death Studies* 23 (1999):197–224.

Tedeschi, Richard, and Lawrence Calhoun. *Trauma and Transformation: Growing in the Aftermath of Suffering.* Thousand Oaks, CA: Sage, 1995.

Woodfield, Robert, and Linda Viney. "A Personal Construct Approach to the Conjugally Bereaved Woman." *Omega: The Journal of Death and Dying* 15 (1984–85):1–13.

Worden, J. William. *Grief Counseling and Grief Therapy: A Handbook for the Mental Health Practitioner,* 2nd edition. New York: Springer, 1991.

THERESE A. RANDO

MUMMIFICATION

The word *mummy* comes from a procedure often used by families in the Middle East to prepare a corpse for burial. During this procedure, the body is washed and then wrapped in strips of linen. To secure and protect this wrapping, a coating of Bitumen tar—also known as mum—may be applied. The effectiveness of this substance has been demonstrated in its preservation of extinct animals for long periods of time, as exemplified by the La Brea Tar Pits of Los Angeles. "Ice mummy" has also become a familiar term as both human and animal corpses have been discovered in a state of remarkable preservation.

It is this apparent resistance to decay that has made the mummy such a compelling object, whether achieved by technical knowledge and skill or by circumstance and whether intended or unintended (as were the ice mummies). There has long been a widespread aversion to the sight and smell of a decaying body, as well as the fear that one can be contaminated by contact with the dead. A corpse that appears intact, and even lifelike, deflects these anxieties. The mummified corpse also stimulates curiosity: What secret knowledge might be discovered, what elusive mysteries brought to light? And—for those not afraid to ask—can the mummy walk again?

Mummies have been most closely associated with Egypt ever since ancient tombs were opened in a continuing series of archeological discoveries (preceded by centuries of grave looting and destruction). There is good reason for this emphasis. The numbers alone are striking: Researchers estimate that about 70 million people were mummified in Egypt in addition to a large number of animals. The spectacular nature of the royal chambers and the remarkable condition of some of the mummies have well deserved their attention. Moreover, scholars have provided invaluable information about the ancient world through their studies of mummies, their surroundings, and their artifacts. The story of mummies, though, neither begins nor ends with the Egyptians. Attention is given to mummies in other times and places after visiting the ancient dynasties that flourished by the banks of the Nile.

The Egyptian Way of Life and Death

Egypt's large and largely arid land has been populated for at least a half million years. Drought, disease, and other hardships required a determined communal effort for survival as well as ingenuity in problem solving and a viable belief system. Death was an insistent part of everyday experience (the average life expectancy has been estimated as not much more than twenty years). Nothing was more predictable than the rising of the sun, the flooding of the Nile, and the transformation from life to death. About 7,000 years ago the Egyptians started to create a civilization that was a marvel in its own time and a source of inspiration to the present day. Astronomy, mathematics, engineering, and the healing, cosmetic, and textile arts were all brought to a new level. With every advance in their civilization the Egyptians brought additional skill, finesse, and grandeur to their dealings with death, their ancient nemesis.

The art of mummification underwent its own lengthy period of development. A small and hard-pressed population functioning on the edge of survival could only dig resting places for their dead in the dry desert sands. The historian Bob Brier noted, "Because these graves were shallow, on occasion the sand would blow away to reveal the shocking sight of a dead body that had retained its flesh and hair—a still-recognizable individual" (Brier 1996, p. 19). The lack of moisture in the parched sands was responsible for the preservation of the general shape and features of the deceased. Extremely dry and extremely cold conditions both inhibit the bacterial activity that usually consumes flesh and organs.

Belief in some form of afterlife was widespread in the ancient world. The Egyptians' encounters with sand-dried corpses might have influenced their particular beliefs and practices regarding the afterlife. Although mummification is the most striking feature of the Egyptian way of death, it draws its meaning from a more encompassing view of the world. Both beliefs and practices continued to evolve over the long span of Egyptian history. The Predynastic period dates from approximately 5,000 years before the Common Era. The Egyptian nation came into existence about 2,000 years later during what is known as the Archaic period. Egyptian history has been divided into many other phases, but it is the Old Kingdom (starting about 2660 B.C.E.) and the New Kingdom (about 1500 B.C.E.) that are of most interest to the discussion of mummification. Pyramids were built and bodies mummified in the Old Kingdom, but the sands of time (along with many acts of vandalism and looting) have left only scattered and often enigmatic traces of the civilization. Also, mummification techniques were not as effective in the earliest years. Nevertheless, some elements of the most ancient beliefs and customs have survived within writings, illustrations, and wall paintings from the New Kingdom.

Remarkable survivors from the past are five sets of documents that reveal much about the ways in which Egyptians conceived of death and the afterlife. Most renown of these documents is a work whose title was originally translated as *Book of the Dead,* but which has had its more accurate title restored, *Book of Going Forth by Day*. The other documents are *The Pyramid Texts, The Coffin Texts, The Books of Breathing,* and *The New Kingdom Books of the Netherworld.* Earliest of these is *The Pyramid Texts* that were found in the tombs of Old Kingdom kings and queens (though not the whole remains of the royal personages themselves). *The Pyramid Texts* consists of 227 magical spells to help the deceased Pharaoh ruler to pass through the various checkpoints in the postmortem journey. It was not for the common person, nor was it an explicit statement of religious principles.

One idea embodied in *The Pyramid Texts* has especially impressed later historians and theologians: The dead will be judged. In fact, all the dead will be judged, even the mighty Pharaoh who judged others. The history of religion scholar S. G. F. Brandon credits the ancient Egyptians with introducing and elaborating the belief that how a person has lived will have a profound effect on the afterlife. Christian concepts of faith, good works, salvation, and damnation were yet to come, but the Egyptians had made the basic link between the quality of life and afterlife. These early texts, though, are guides not to a higher level of morality but to strategies for negotiating the perilous passage to the netherworld. The flourishing New Kingdom society provided elaborate funerals for its most illustrious people. These rituals offered channels for expressions of grief and mourning and affirmed the power of the family line—but also launched the departing soul on its journey with all the right moves. Specialists in funerals, tomb construction and decoration, and mummification were valued members of society, as were the priests with their incantations and gestures.

Inspiring and justifying all these practices were two myths that each contributed to a view of the afterlife. Osiris was revered as the person who showed the Egyptians how to create their great civilization, but his murdered corpse was hewn into many pieces. Through heroic efforts, his wife (or sister-wife) Isis put him back together again. This myth has been interpreted as a fertility and renewal symbol: Life passes into death, but from death life emerges anew. Egyptologists have noted that the Osiris myth emphasizes the importance of an intact corpse, and that their funerary art often depicted this mythological figure. The other myth centers around Atum-Re, a local god who was closely associated with the life-giving force of the sun. The pharaohs were the incarnated sons of Atum-Re and would rejoin him in the skies at the end of their days on the earth.

The corpse was regarded as more than a lifeless body. It included several spiritual forces or entities. The *ka* was a spirit-twin that accompanied the person throughout life and, surviving death, preserved individual identity. It remained within a ka statue created in the likeness of the living person. In turn, the ka needed to be fed and looked after by mortuary attendants. The *ba,* often represented as a soul-bird, lingered in the vicinity of the corpse as a faithful companion. If all went well with the funeral ritual and mummification, the deceased would achieve the status of an *akh* (translated by Brandon as "glorified being"). The rules for achieving a glorified afterlife were not quite the same for royalty and commoners: Other affluent members of society benefited from quality mummification and other funerary amenities, while the general population had to make do with much simpler arrangements and with less expert mummification procedures.

The Making and Unmaking of Mummies

Transforming a royal corpse into a mummy in the New Kingdom period involved the following actions, many or all of which would be accompanied by prayers and magic spells:

1. Remove the internal organs by incision and pull the brain through the nostrils on an iron hook.
2. Replace the heart with the carved replica of a scarab (the dung-beetle, symbolizing the recycling transactions between life and death).
3. Rinse the body cavity with palm wine.
4. Reshape face and body as necessary to repair damages caused by the final illness.
5. Place aromatic substances within the body, sew it up, cover with "divine salts" and allow seventy days for drying and other preparations.
6. Wash the body, wrap in undercoated linen sheets, draw facial features in ink to recreate the appearance of the living person.
7. Place in a tapered coffin and the coffin into a sarcophagus (stone vessel).
8. Add objects that could be useful to the deceased in the next life.
9. Seal the tomb.

The results were sometimes magnificent. Even so, the preserved body itself was but a shell in artistic disguise. Lacking internal parts, there was no way the mummy could walk again, and the Egyptians did not have this expectation. The mummy was part of a spirit communication system, not a dead person waiting to be resuscitated.

Mummies could also be unmade. Some attempts at mummification failed. Looters destroyed many presumably successful mummies in ancient times. Royal remains were often removed from their original lodgings for safekeeping, but some nevertheless became casualties. The slaughter of the mummies began in earnest as tombs were discovered and their contents plundered by outsiders. Mummies were powdered into medicines that were sure to cure what ailed the medieval person, or so the alchemists promised. Bits of mummy remains also had commercial value as relics. Wholesale destruction of mummies occurred during the heyday of European colonialism and the Industrial Revolution. Showing no regard for religious belief or history, exploiters consigned thousands of mummies into the flames as fuel for the railroads, or held mummy unwrapping parties that destroyed the remains. Even a museum official casually tossed away a preserved arm from the Old Kingdom, in all likelihood the most ancient mummy part ever discovered. Fortunately, some of the most illustrious tombs were not unearthed until a more responsible attitude had developed in the late nineteenth and twentieth centuries.

Mummies As Frozen Time

Mummies are far from an Egyptian exclusive. As with the pharaohs, however, every mummy, wherever found, has the potential for revealing something about the ways in which people have lived and died. The ancient people of Chile, for example, developed complex mummification techniques at least 2,000 years before the Egyptians. These mummies were notable for having no tooth decay, a finding that is thought to be related to their diet as foragers. Researchers were also able to determine that there were clear divisions of labor in the society, gender-related and otherwise. Laborers, for example, had more skeletal distortion than did priests.

Discoveries in the towering and icy peaks of the Andes have added substantially to scientists' knowledge of past societies. Ceremonial sites have been excavated on mountain peaks from central Chile to southern Peru. Here chilling discoveries were made: the mummies of Inca children—by the hundreds—who were sacrificed to the mountain gods and their supreme deity, the sun. There is one obvious similarity to the Egyptians: the belief in a sun god. The differences, though, are profound. These were children put to death in order

Wealthy and valued members of Egyptian society, such as this priestess, benefited from a quality mummification.
BRIDGEMAN ART LIBRARY

to placate the gods and therefore receive rain, bountiful crops, and protection from disasters.

These human sacrifices occurred in relatively modern times, only 500 years ago. In September 1995, anthropologist Johan Reinhard discovered 18,000 feet high atop Mount Ampato a fourteen-year-old girl whose body was accompanied by gold and silver dolls. The remarkable state of preservation was attributed to the freezing temperatures and high altitude. The life of the "Ice Maiden," as she has been called, was almost surely offered to the gods. The relationship, if any, between the Inca practices and those of Chileans almost 8,000 years ago remains to be determined.

Archeologists and anthropologists could add that ice is also sufficient for preservation. Notable discoveries of ice mummies have been made in other places. For example, at about the same time that Incan priests were sacrificing children on mountaintops, the Inuit were burying six women and two children in a small settlement on the west coast of Greenland. As the anthropologist Hart Peder Hensen and his colleagues reported in *The Greenland Mummies* (1991), the deceased were provided with warm clothing and useful items for their journey to the land of the dead. The cold terrain and the dry air had preserved their bodies until they were discovered in the twentieth century. The relatively intact bodies and their undisturbed burial hut have enriched sociologists' understanding of Inuit history and culture (for example, people living in the rigors of the extreme north were up-to-date in European fashions and also dressed their children as miniatures of adults). It is clear that the same form of mummification—in this case, freezing—can occur within situations as different as ritual murder and loving farewell.

Researchers are still studying and learning from the highly publicized Ice Man (also known as Otzi), whose mummified body was discovered in a glacier in the Otztaler Alps on the Austrian-Italian border in 1991. Remarkably well preserved, Otzi was a Neolithic hunter more than 5,000 years ago. The exceptional condition of the permafrost-protected corpse, his clothing, and his tools has provided scientists with invaluable information about the Neolithic way of life, although not necessarily about their way of death, since the Ice Man died while apparently on a hunting expedition. Konrad Spindler's *The Man in the Ice* (1994) is a major contribution for readers who want to explore mummies and mummification beyond the Egyptian Valley of the Kings.

The Mummies of Urumchi tells still another story. The earliest of these mummies are contemporaneous with the most renowned Egyptian examples from the New Kingdom period, but even better preserved. The people are Caucasian, tall, blond, and apparently blue-eyed. They are dressed in brightly colored woolen clothing and high-peaked hats. The surprise is their place of death: the desert wilderness of China's Uyghur Autonomous Region. Controversy immediately engulfed this discovery: Was it possible that 4,000 years ago the people of China included Caucasians who were sporting the most advanced textiles? Does world history have to be rewritten to accommodate this find? Anthropologist Elizabeth Wayland Barber makes a strong case for the proposition that many great people migrated across Europe and Asia during the Bronze Age, bringing a variety of skills with them. Furthermore, what has long been a desert may once have been fertile land.

Every now and then mummies return from various times and places. Peat bogs in Denmark, England, Germany, Ireland, and the Netherlands have reluctantly yielded their cache of bodies—some deposited there as long as 6,000 years ago. The cool, damp soil, perhaps with the help of a tanning action, seems responsible for the preservation. The deaths themselves often seem to have been caused by murder, perhaps ritualistic.

Attempts to protect a corpse from deterioration have also been motivated by the reluctance to let go of a beloved or powerful person. For example, the body of Suzanne Curchod was preserved in alcohol by her loving husband, a minister under France's Louis XVI, to honor her wishes to remain near him. As early as the eighteenth century suggestions were made to vitrify the more notable dead, transforming them into a kind of stone-glass. As the French sociologist Philippe Ariès observes, both the actual and the proposed acts of preservation were in accord with the spirit of the times. Even the halls of academia have surrendered to the impulse. When death claimed Jeremy Bentham, a trenchant social philosopher whose writings have remained influential over the years, his colleagues at University of London had him mummified and placed in a closet. Legend has it that he has been invited as honored guest to attend occasional faculty meetings.

An ironic attempt at mummification occurred following the death of Vladimir Lenin, the founder of the Soviet Union, in 1924. The Bolshevik party, seeking complete domination, tried to replace religion with its own version of science. Before long, though, the secret police virtually kidnapped physicians and required them to mummify the fallen leader. This endeavor proved to be a tragicomedy as described by the biochemist Ilya Zbarsky in *Lenin's Embalmers* (1997). The political imperative that Lenin's body appear intact and robust was at odds with its condition when physicians were summoned to the task, and they had no effective procedures at hand. Trial-and-error ingenuity was required to create the desired but misleading impression that a high quality of mummification had been achieved. Despite all of the medical advances made since the New Kingdom, there had also been a loss of knowledge specific to mummification. Lenin's embalmers did what they could to make a sacred icon of his body while party officials twisted in anxiety. The desire to preserve the remains of a powerful person had persisted from the sun god worshippers of ancient times to a modern society whose leaders were determined to get along without any gods at all.

In the twenty-first century mummies continue to hold interest to researchers for what they can reveal of history, illness, and past ways of life. They are also subjects of ethical and legal disputes as part of the general concern about the proper treatment of human remains. Perhaps more attention could be given to the simple fact that so much loving and often creative attention has been given by the living to those who have passed on.

See also: CRYONIC SUSPENSION; EGYPTIAN BOOK OF THE DEAD; HUMAN REMAINS; IMMORTALITY; KENNEWICK MAN; OSIRIS; PYRAMIDS; SACRIFICE; TOMBS

Bibliography

Ariès, Philippe. *The Hour of Our Death.* New York: Alfred A. Knopf, 1981.

Barber, Elizabeth Wayland. *The Mummies of Urumchi.* New York: W. W. Norton, 2000.

Brandon, S. G. F. *The Judgment of the Dead.* New York: Charles Scribner's Sons, 1967.

Brier, Bob. *Egyptian Mummies.* London: Michael O'Mara, 1996.

Budge, E. A. Wallis. *The Mummy: Chapters on Egyptian Funereal Archeology,* 2nd edition. New York: Biblo and Tannen, 1964.

Cockburn, Aidan, Eve Cockburn, and Theodore A. Revman, eds. *Mummies, Disease and Ancient Cultures.* Cambridge: Cambridge University Press, 1998.

Deem, James J. *Bodies from the Bog.* Boston: Houghton Mifflin, 1998.

Harris, James E., and Kent R. Weeks. *X-Raying the Pharaohs.* New York: Charles Scribner's Sons, 1973.

Hensen, Hart Peder, Meldgaard Jorgen Jens, and Jorgen Nordqvist, eds.*The Greenland Mummies*. Washington, DC: Smithsonian, 1991.

Hornung, Erik. *The Ancient Egyptian Books of the Afterlife*. Ithaca, NY: Cornell University, 1999.

Ikram, Salina, and Aidan Dodson. *The Mummy in Ancient Egypt*. London: Thames and Hudson, 1998.

Kastenbaum, Robert. *Death, Society, and Human Experience,* 7th edition. Boston: Allyn and Bacon, 2001.

Mallory, J. P., and Victor H. Mair. *The Tarim Mummies: Ancient China and the Mysteries of the Earliest People from the West*. London: Thames and Hudson, 2000.

Reinhard, Johan. *Discovering the Inca Ice Maiden: My Adventures on Ampato*. Washington, DC: National Geographic Society, 1998.

Spindler, Konrad. *The Man in the Ice*. New York: Random House, 1994.

Von Dassow, Eva, ed. *The Egyptian Book of the Dead: The Book of Going Forth by Day,* 2nd edition. San Francisco: Chronicle Books, 1998.

Weeks, Kent R. *The Lost Tomb*. New York: William Morrow, 1998.

Zbarsky, Ilya. *Lenin's Embalmers*. London: Harvill Press, 1997.

ROBERT KASTENBAUM

MUSEUMS OF DEATH

In Western Europe there are a variety of museums, and in several countries the scenery is enriched by special museums that are dedicated exclusively to the topics of death, dying, funerals, and remembrance. Because these entities are largely considered social taboos, the existence of such institutions appears to be anachronistic. Therefore, one is forced to question their origin and goals, as well as their social and political acceptance.

The fact that the museums are relatively new or still in their founding or building phases seems to indicate a changing attitude toward death and dying. Questions about dying with dignity, modern forms of funeral services, or an adequate way of mourning and remembrance are more insistent in the twenty-first century than they were in the 1980s. Regardless of a societal change in attitude, these museums are neither called museums of death or dying nor do they otherwise bear the terms *dying* or *death* in their names. Instead, they bear more culturally accepting translations, calling themselves, for example, Museum of Piety (Budapest, Hungary), Funeral Museum (Vienna, Austria) or Museum for Sepulchral Culture (Kassel, Germany). Despite their often misleading names, none of these museums makes any effort to hide its subject; notably, death and dying.

These museums primarily foster a culture-historical approach related to the public interest in history, culture, and the arts. Therefore, collections and exhibitions focus strongly on the impressive examples of funeral and cemetery culture, pictorial documents of these events, and curiosities. In comparison to other specialized museums, like museums of bread, glass, or chinaware, the funeral museums have above all a responsibility for their visitors, who always react very sensitive to the subject of death and dying.

The Vienna Funeral Museum best exemplifies a museum of funeral culture. Founded in 1967 as a branch of the Vienna Municipal Funeral Department, the museum is a business museum whose goal is to present the history of the company in objects, pictures, and written documents. Accordingly, the collection comprises many of the company's products and equipment such as coffins, urns, funeral vehicles, shrouds, and more. However, the Vienna Funeral Museum also documents the entire funeral culture in Austria, with an emphasis on Vienna. Of particular emphasis is the history of the funeral in Vienna. At the beginning of the twentieth century numerous competing private funeral homes were replaced by a municipal funeral company. The main reason behind this move was a social concern: The desire for evermore luxurious funerals—as exemplified by the proverbial *Schoene Leich* ("beautiful corpse") in Vienna—had driven the citizens to excessive expenditures that were even pushed further by the commercial interests of the funeral directors.

The Vienna Funeral Museum became the model for a similarly organized museum in Budapest whose Hungarian name, *Kegyleti Muzeum,* may be best translated as Museum of Piety. Opened in 1991–1992, this museum is associated with Vienna and Austria due to the long-lasting common history within the Habsburg monarchy. In addition, the Museum of Piety strives to consider the regional and confessional differences of Hungary. Both the Vienna and the Budapest museums are branches of their respective Municipal Funeral Departments and receive no public funding.

Unlike the Vienna Funeral Museum, the *Museum fuer Sepulkralkultur,* (Museum of Sepulchral Culture) in Kassel must meet public and political acceptance. Although it is supported by the *Arbeitsgemeinschaft Friedhof und Denkmal* (Association for Cemetery and Memorial), it was built entirely with public funding. The costs of running the museum are mostly paid by the federal and state government, the municipality, and churches.

In accordance with the statute of its governing body, the mission of the Museum of Sepulchral Culture is to promote public understanding of the culture of funerals, cemeteries, and mourning. In addition to its permanent exhibition, which presents objects of funeral culture within Germany, Austria, and Switzerland on a total area of 1,400 square meters, the museum features special exhibitions that focus on various aspects of the cultural history of funerals, current developments and trends, and artistic confrontations with death, dying, and mourning. An affiliated library consists of a large stock of monographs, catalogues, and offprints, as well as an extensive collection of original source material. The museum is home to various archives, such as a collection of graphic art consisting of 15,000 pieces, which serve as a resource for research and scientific studies throughout Europe.

The two cemetery museums in Riehen near Basel, Switzerland, and in Hamburg, Germany, owe their existence to the personal commitment of single individuals. The collection *Friedhof Hoernli* (Hoernli Cemetery) was compiled in a tireless effort by an employee of the cemetery and has been on display since 1994. It was the goal of the collector to preserve old and vanishing items used in everyday funeral and cemetery activities; its purpose is to document the history of less-recognized professions dealing with death. The museum is supported by a private association, receives some funds from the cemetery administration, and otherwise relies on donations from sponsors.

The situation was similar in Hamburg. Individuals with a strong interest in preserving the world's largest cemetery formed the *Förderkreis Ohlsdorfer Friedhof* (Society for the Promotion of the Ohlsdorf Cemetery), and opened the *Museum Friedhof Ohlsdorf* (Museum of the Ohlsdorf Cemetery). The museum is dedicated to raising public interest for the Friedhof Ohlsdorf cemetery, and for promoting historical and contemporary funeral culture. The collection in the museum, on display since 1996, focuses mainly on the history of Hamburg's cemetery culture. Since the Ohlsdorfer Friedhof was opened in 1877 as the first American-style park cemetery in Germany, it is of significant importance to the European cemetery culture.

The National Funeral Museum in London, which was initiated by an undertaker from London's West End, has a status all its own. It was the growing public desire to reintroduce the old horse-drawn hearses that provided the impetus to start the museum. The result is an impressive collection comprised of both historical hearses and one of the oldest motorized funeral vehicles. The collections have been complemented by historical funeral equipment, old drawings and prints, shrouds, mourning dresses, and mourning jewelry. In addition, an extensive library was founded. Since the museum is entirely a private institution, the funeral company covers all expenses. Training and seminars are other sources of income.

The Netherlands' *Uitvaartmuseum,* known as the Museum of Exit, is still in its initial phase. Supported by a private association, it has a complete collection that has attracted considerable attention. The museum is an important impetus for a renewal of the funeral culture in the Netherlands, where in a liberal and open-minded atmosphere new funeral rites have developed. The Netherlands have become famous for a remarkable variety of funeral-related artistic forms.

Finally, the *Museu de Carrosses Funebres* (Museum for Hearses) in Barcelona, Spain, which specializes in the collection of historical funeral vehicles.

Increasing public awareness and presenting the goals of the museums is part of the mission of the European Federation of Funeral Museums (EFFM). Founded in Vienna in 1998, the association unites museums that specialize in the culture of funerals, cemeteries, and mourning, and whose common intention is to disseminate historical and contemporary values in this field.

See also: CEMETERIES, MILITARY; CEMETERIES, WAR

REINER SÖRRIES

MUSIC, CLASSICAL

Western classical music has commemorated death in ritual and pondered it in concert works. A deeper relationship to death exists in the very syntax of Western harmony.

Origins of Classical Music

Western art music has its origins in the system of tonality developed in the Medieval Church. That system, which grew out of the church modes, consists of two or more tones sounding at once in a pattern of tension and release ("dissonance" and "consonance"). This was unique among the musical forms of the globe until the twentieth century when Western tonality, through popular music, essentially preempted other local musical forms.

This dominating pattern of tension and release means that Western tonality, unlike all other known musical systems, mimics a natural cycle of birth/growth/decay/death/new birth. The simplest chord progression initiates a home key (birth), develops relationships to other keys by venturing from the home key (growth), reaches a knot of dissonance requiring relief (decay), and finally resolves to the home key again (death, with an implied rebirth). In other cultures, ritual and art music sought to transcend the natural process through hypnotic repetition or intricate, non-tonal patterning. Western classical music embraced it, and accompanied the rise of material science.

Death Motifs

Death is built into the syntax of Western music. When portrayed as the subject of a composition, mortality has certain specific musical characteristics; the mood is somber, the tonality almost always minor, and the tempo slow. Yet the most famous recurring death motif in classical music, the Dies Irae, which dates to the Dark Ages, is more sinister than somber. Its text, "Day of wrath, day of doom," conjures the Christian last judgment in its most horrible aspect. The first eight notes are distinctive, with or without the sung text, and they fit into the format of many common chords and progressions. Composers, therefore, have employed the Dies Irae often, both in sung works (the text forms part of the Requiem Mass which has been set to music by countless composers) and in purely instrumental contexts. The Russian post-Romantic Sergei Rachmaninov employed it almost obsessively, not only in appropriate works such as his tone poem, *Isle of the Dead,* but in such unlikely places as the playful pages of the *Rhapsody on a Theme of Paganini.*

The Requiem Mass is probably the largest and most dramatic classical musical form borrowed from ritual. Composers who set its Latin text for use in concert rather than liturgy have included Palestrina, Vittoria, Mozart, Cherubini, Berlioz, Faure, Bruckner, Verdi, and Stravinsky. Brahms, vigilantly Protestant, composed a German Requiem to biblical rather than Catholic liturgical texts. The Passion, a liturgical text relating the death of Jesus Christ, has also been used by composers as concert works. Two extraordinary Passions by Johann Sebastian Bach (one *According to St. John,* another *According to St. Matthew*) belong at the pinnacle of the repertoire.

Another smaller and more universal ritual that became an instrumental form was the funeral march. Mozart's Masonic Funeral Music, the second movement of Beethoven's Symphony no. 3 ("Eroica"), and the penultimate movement of Chopin's B-flat minor Piano Sonata, are excellent examples. The latter has become boilerplate, often simply referred to as "The Funeral March." Mahler used funeral marches throughout his oeuvre, perhaps most spectacularly (and unexpectedly) in the opening movement of his Symphony no. 5.

Death Myths of the Great Composers

Death holds a prominent place in the mythos of great composers. Existential defiance was a favored theme for composers dying in the nineteenth century. Beethoven died at age fifty-six, reputedly shaking his fist at a clap of thunder as at God. Schumann went insane and walked into the Rhine to drown himself; the attempt failed. Recent, controversial scholarship seems to support the idea that Tchaikovsky, long thought to have died from accidentally contracted cholera, committed suicide on the discovery of his homosexuality. The truth of his death has yet to be established beyond doubt.

The number of composers who died young is greater even than that of great poets. In addition, their modes of death were diverse and often disturbingly colorful or mysterious. The most famous case is that of Mozart. The theories of Mozart's death, numerous and ever-growing, have become a part of the composer's identity. The most notorious is that Mozart was murdered by his rival Antonio Salieri, which was the subject of a play by Alexander Pushkin and an operatic setting by Nikolai Rimsky-Korsakov nearly a century before it became the subject of Peter Shaffer's play (later made into a popular film) *Amadeus*.

Mozart was thirty-five when he died in 1791. Franz Schubert was thirty-one years old when he died in 1828; syphilis was the probable cause. Chopin and Mendelssohn both died before their fortieth birthdays. The dubious prize for the youngest death of a composer with any still-active repertoire goes to the eighteenth-century Belgian Guillaume Lekeu, who succumbed at age twenty-five to an intestinal infection brought about by tainted ice. Charles-Valentin Alkan, a nineteenth-century French composer of exorbitantly difficult piano music, was also a Talmudic scholar who died when his bookshelves collapsed and the heavy volumes of his library crushed him. The Second Viennese school of Arnold Schoenberg and his students were obsessed with number. When Schoenberg's great student Alban Berg suffered an insect bite that infected him, Berg calculated his chances based on a personal numerology, and died on the day he predicted.

In 1937 the musicologist Alfred Einstein put forth the theory that great composers die with a "swan song," a final masterpiece before death. He supported this idea with numerous examples, including Bach, whose masterful *Art of the Fugue* was left unfinished at death, and Mozart, who left behind the trunk of a Requiem, begun shortly before he died. The theory hardly applies universally, however, and it is ironic to note that the single terminal work actually titled "Swan Song," was a compilation of Schubert songs slapped together posthumously by a publisher looking to trade on the sensation of it.

Though George Frideric Handel, Franz Josef Haydn, Franz Liszt, and Giuseppe Verdi all lived and worked past seventy, composers who enjoyed their full share of three-score-and-ten are rare before 1900. Twentieth-century composers who lived and thrived into their eighties include Igor Stravinsky, Aaron Copland, Leos Janacek, Ralph Vaughan Williams, and Elliott Carter.

See also: DANCE; FOLK MUSIC; MAHLER, GUSTAV; OPERATIC DEATH

Bibliography

Einstein, Alfred. "Opus Ultimum." *Musical Quarterly* 23 (July 1937):269–286.

Landon, H. C. Robbins. *1791, Mozart's Last Year.* New York: Schirmer Books, 1988.

Levinson, Jerrold. *Music in the Moment.* Ithaca, NY: Cornell University Press, 1997.

Monson, Karen. *Alban Berg.* New York: Houghton Mifflin, 1986.

Neumayr, Anton. *Music and Medicine.* 2 vols. Bloomington, IN: Medi-Ed Press, 1994–96.

KENNETH LAFAVE

N

NATIVE AMERICAN RELIGION

Because they lived so close to nature, all Native American peoples from the Stone Age to the modern era knew that death from hunger, disease, or enemies was never far away. The various death customs and beliefs, which first evolved during the invasions of Asians from Siberia to Alaska across a land bridge during the last Ice Age at least 12,000 years ago, gave them the means to cope with that experience. Individual tribes maintained their own death customs and adapted them to their regional environments into which they migrated, although such rituals and beliefs could pass from one group to the other through trade and intermarriage. Most Native American tribes believed that the souls of the dead passed into a spirit world and became part of the spiritual forces that influenced every aspect of their lives. Many tribes believed in two souls: one that died when the body died and one that might wander on and eventually die.

Burial customs varied widely from tribe to tribe. Indians disposed of their dead in a variety of ways. Arctic tribes, for example, simply left their dead on the frozen ground for wild animals to devour. The ancient mound-building Hopewell societies of the Upper Midwest, by contrast, placed the dead in lavishly furnished tombs. Southeastern tribes practiced secondary bone burial. They dug up their corpses, cleansed the bones, and then reburied them. The Northeast Iroquois, before they formed the Five Nations Confederation in the seventeenth century, saved skeletons of the deceased for a final mass burial that included furs and ornaments for the dead spirits' use in the afterlife. Northwest coastal tribes put their dead in mortuary cabins or canoes fastened to poles. Further south, California tribes practiced cremation. In western mountain areas tribes often deposited their dead in caves or fissures in the rocks. Nomadic tribes in the Great Plains region either buried their dead, if the ground was soft, or left them on tree platforms or on scaffolds. Central and South Atlantic tribes embalmed and mummified their dead. But during outbreaks of smallpox or other diseases leading to the sudden deaths of many tribe members, survivors hurriedly cast the corpses into a mass grave or threw them into a river.

Rites among Native Americans tended to focus on aiding the deceased in their afterlife. Some tribes left food and possessions of the dead person in or near the gravesite. Other groups, such as the Nez Perce of the Northwest, sacrificed wives, slaves, and a favorite horse of a dead warrior. Among many tribes, mourners, especially widows, cut their hair. Some Native Americans discarded personal ornaments or blacked their faces to honor the dead. Others gashed their arms and legs to express their grief. California tribes engaged in wailing, staged long funeral ceremonies, and held an anniversary mourning ritual after one or two years. Southwest Hopi wailed on the day of the death, and cried a year later.

Some Southwestern tribes, especially the Apache and Navajo, feared the ghosts of the deceased who were believed to resent the living. The nomadic Apache buried corpses swiftly and burned the deceased's house and possessions. The mourning family purified itself ritually and moved to a new place to escape their dead family member's ghost. The Navajo also buried their dead quickly with little ceremony. Navajos exposed to a corpse had to undergo a long and costly ritual purification treatment.

See also: AFTERLIFE IN CROSS-CULTURAL PERSPECTIVE; GHOST DANCE

Bibliography

Garbarino, Merwyn, S. *Native American Heritage.* Boston: Little, Brown, 1976.

Josephy, Alvin M., Jr. *The Indian Heritage of America.* New York: Houghton Mifflin Company, 1991.

Underhill, Ruth. *Red Man's America: A History of Indians in the United States.* Chicago: University of Chicago Press, 1953.

KENNETH D. NORDIN

NATURAL DEATH ACTS

Natural Death Acts (also known as Death with Dignity Acts and Living Will Acts) are laws that determine in what situations, and how, people can refuse life-sustaining medical interventions. The purpose of these laws is to permit patients to choose a "natural" death, unencumbered by medical technology. The laws are a response to the great strides made by medical science over the last half of the twentieth century in prolonging the life of the chronically and severely ill. Concerns arose that medical technology that could forestall death, such as respirators and feeding tubes, increased the agony of dying. It also spawned concerns that an individual's right to autonomy and self-determination could be infringed by such invasive technology.

Origins in the United States

The first law in the United States that clarified the right of persons to refuse life-sustaining medical technology was passed in California in 1976. It permitted patients whose condition was terminal and death imminent to stop or refuse medical treatment. Throughout the late 1970s and 1980s other states began passing similar laws. At the start of the twenty-first century, every state had laws protecting the rights of dying patients.

There are several legal principles underlying these laws. The common law recognizes the right of each individual to control his own person without interference from others. This right extends to the medical arena, requiring doctors to obtain the consent of their patients before treating them. As stated by U.S. Supreme Court Justice Benjamin Cardozo, "every human being of adult years and sound mind has a right to determine what shall be done with his own body; and a surgeon who performs an operation without his patient's consent commits an assault, for which he is liable" (*Schloendorff* v. *Society of New York Hospital,* 1914). This consent must be informed, requiring doctors to disclose the nature of what they are doing and the risks and benefits. The principle of informed consent to medical procedures governs all medical care, including life-sustaining treatment, and includes the right to refuse such treatment.

The U.S. Constitution also protects the right of dying patients to refuse medical care. This right was first established in the case of *In re Quinlan,* decided by the New Jersey Supreme Court in 1976. It involved a twenty-one-year-old woman who had been placed on a respirator after she stopped breathing for unexplained reasons and then entered a chronic persistent vegetative state. The court granted her parents' request for removal of the respirator, finding that it infringed upon her right to privacy as protected under the Constitution. Fourteen years later, the U.S. Supreme Court, in the case of *Cruzan* v. *Director, Missouri Department of Health,* also involving a young woman in a coma, found that the Fourteenth Amendment to the Constitution, which provides that a person may not be deprived of her liberty without due process of law, includes a liberty interest in refusing heroic medical measures.

Advance Directives

These legal principles are embodied in Natural Death Acts, which outline the procedures for exercising the right of dying patients to refuse life supports. Because many dying patients are incompetent at the time the crucial decision to withdraw or refuse life supports must be made, these laws provide mechanisms for patients to exercise their rights in advance. The primary mechanism is the advance directive, which is a statement, usually in writing, that declares what kind of lifesaving medical treatment a patient wants after he has become incompetent or unable to communicate to medical personnel. One form of an advance directive, the living will, provides specific instructions on whether or not a person wants to accept life-sustaining medical interventions. Another form of advance directive is a health care proxy (or power of attorney), which appoints another person to make the decision and which may also include instructions on life supports. The laws also set forth what is required to prove the wishes of the patient when he has failed to complete an advance directive. Many Natural Death Acts also provide for the appointment of a surrogate decision maker.

While each state has its own Natural Death Act, there is also a federal law, the Patient Self-Determination Act (PSDA), which is designed to encourage patients to exercise their rights by completing advance directives. The PSDA requires hospitals, health maintenance organizations, and others that receive federal funds to tell patients of their rights under the applicable state law to make end-of-life medical decisions. The PSDA also requires that advance directives be maintained in patients' charts.

Despite these laws, the vast majority of people—between 80 and 90 percent—never execute advance directives. Nevertheless, largely through the passage of such laws, and the publicity generated by various right-to-die cases, a consensus has emerged over the years that patients have a right to refuse life-sustaining medical intervention. In one poll, 84 percent of Americans said they would not want life supports if they had no chance of recovery. How far that right should extend, however, is still a matter of controversy.

Right-to-Die Opposition

Initial opposition to the "right to die" was based on a state's interest in protecting the sanctity of life, preventing suicide, and protecting innocent third parties (i.e., a patient's children). These interests, however, become less significant in cases where a patient is terminally ill or severely incapacitated with no hope of improving. The ethical integrity of the medical profession, whose primary mission is to enhance life, is also cited as a reason for opposing the right to die. Nevertheless, virtually every professional organization, including the American Medical Association, recognizes that patient autonomy and good medicine may require the withdrawal of life supports. Natural Death Acts also typically include a "conscientious objection" exception that permits physicians with religious or moral objections to refuse to honor a request to withhold or withdraw life supports so long as alternative accommodations, such as transfer to another hospital, are madc.

Natural Death Acts also do not distinguish between withholding and discontinuing life supports. Thus, for example, removing a ventilator from a patient is considered the same as never starting it. One reason for this is that it encourages heroic measures be taken in times of uncertainty, with the understanding that they can be discontinued at a later point if found to be of little benefit or a burden to the patient.

There is some disagreement over whether nutrition and hydration should be treated the same as other forms of mechanical life support, such as respirators. This is primarily because of the emotional and symbolic significance of food and water. To some, withholding water and food, even if it must be supplied though such mechanical means as inserting a gastrostomy tube in a patient's stomach, is causing death by starvation or thirst. Courts, however, do not distinguish between the two, viewing artificial nutrition and hydration as medical interventions as invasive as other forms of life-sustaining technology. Many Natural Death Acts, however, do treat the provision of nutrition and hydration differently. Some prohibit their withdrawal (although a court will likely ignore this prohibition). Others require people completing a living will to explicitly state whether artificial hydration and nutrition is to be included as a form of life support.

Assisted Suicide

Whether the right to die includes the right to ask others, such as a physician, for assistance in dying, is an intensely debated issue. Such assistance usually means the prescription of drugs, self-administered by the patient, which will hasten death. Physicians do engage in the practice, but until the late twentieth century remained silent about it. In 1991 the physician Timothy Quill brought the issue to the public's attention by publishing an article in the *New England Journal of Medicine* describing how he provided a prescription of barbiturates to a patient with instructions on how to use them to hasten the patient's death. A subsequent study, published in the *New England Journal of Medicine* in 1996, found that 20 percent of the physicians surveyed had knowingly and intentionally prescribed medication to hasten a patient's death. Other times, physicians will prescribe medication to ease pain, knowing that it will hasten death.

There appears to be some support for physician-assisted suicide among the general public. The same 1996 *New England Journal of Medicine* study found that 66 percent of the public supported its legalization. Supporters of the right contended that there was no difference, in hastening death, between the removal of life supports and the self-administering of a prescribed drug. They contended that writing a prescription required a less active role for the physician than physically removing equipment and caused less agony and pain.

Opponents believed that permitting assisted suicide violated the sanctity of life, and would open the door to more active forms of euthanasia, such as a physician administering a lethal injection or even ending a patient's life without his or her consent. They were also concerned that elderly and dependent people, who might perceive themselves as a burden to family and society, would feel an obligation to die sooner rather than later if physician-assisted suicide were made legal. They also argued that it would change the role of the medical profession from protectors of life to agents of death. As of 2001, the American Medical Association (AMA) opposed physician-assisted suicide, because "the physician's role is to affirm life, not to hasten its demise." Instead, the AMA recommended that physicians focus on making the dying more comfortable through the provision of palliative care which seeks to provide comfort, not a cure, including the full use of pain medication (even if it hastened death).

The law has been hesitant to recognize a right to assisted suicide. In 2001 every state, except Oregon, had laws prohibiting assisted suicide, making it illegal for anyone, including physicians, to assist in another's death. In 1997 the U.S. Supreme Court, in the case of *Vacco* v. *Quill,* refused to overturn such laws on the grounds that they violated a person's constitutional right to privacy. The Court distinguished between the right to refuse life-sustaining medical interventions and requesting that affirmative acts be taken, such as prescribing a lethal dose of drugs, to hasten death. The Court explained the distinction by noting that "when a patient refuses life sustaining medical treatment, he dies from an underlying fatal disease or pathology; but if a patient ingests lethal medication prescribed by a physician, he is killed by that medication."

The Court left it to individual states to decide whether to legalize physician-assisted suicide. The only state to do so was Oregon, which passed the Death with Dignity Act in 1994, permitting physicians to prescribe medication that enhanced death, generally barbiturates, to patients under certain circumstances. It applied only to terminally ill persons with less than six months to live. Two physicians had to agree on the prognosis. A referendum to appeal the act was rejected by 60 percent of Oregon voters, thus demonstrating that there was considerable public support for physician-assisted suicide. As of 2001, only a handful of people had requested assisted suicide since the law went into effect. The law has also been upheld by the federal courts.

The Exceptional Case of the Netherlands

Most other countries recognize the right to refuse life-sustaining treatment but do not recognize the right to physician-assisted suicide. The one exception is the Netherlands, which permits not only assisted suicide but also other more active forms of euthanasia, including permitting a physician to actually administer the cause of death, such as a lethal injection. This right was first recognized by the Dutch Supreme Court, who excused from criminal culpability physicians who assist in the suicide of a dying patient when ethics and the good practice of medicine required it. It has since been codified into law, which requires that the patients are competent, have voluntarily and repeatedly over time requested assistance in dying, and are enduring unacceptable suffering, and where a second physician agrees assisted suicide is appropriate. A commission to study the effects of this initially judicial-made law, the Remmelink Committee, found that 2,300 deaths resulted from euthanasia in 1990. It is not known whether any of these deaths were involuntary, a concern of people who oppose assisted suicide. Some contend that the rates of euthanasia in the Netherlands are no different than those in other countries, just more visible.

The Societal Consensus

By the early twenty-first century, the existence of Natural Death Acts in every U.S. state reflected a societal consensus that people should be able to control the manner and timing of their own death in the face of medical technology able to prolong life. There were limits, however, to this right. Physician-assisted suicide and more active types of euthanasia had not, with some exceptions, been recognized under the law.

See also: ADVANCE DIRECTIVES; CRUZAN, NANCY; EUTHANASIA; INFORMED CONSENT; LIVING WILL; QUINLAN, KAREN ANN; RIGHT-TO-DIE MOVEMENT; SUICIDE TYPES: PHYSICIAN-ASSISTED SUICIDE

Bibliography

Bachman, Jerald G., Kirsten H. Alcser, David J. Doukas, and Richard L. Lichenstein. "Attitudes of Michigan Physicians and the Public toward Legalizing Physician-Assisted Suicide and Voluntary Euthanasia." *New England Journal of Medicine* 334 (1996):303–309.

Emanuel, Ezekiel J., Diane L. Fairclough, and Linda L. Emanuel. "Attitudes and Desires Related to Euthanasia and Physician-Assisted Suicide among Terminally Ill Patients and Their Caregivers." *Journal of the American Medical Association* 284 (2000):2460–2468.

Emanuel, Linda L. *Regulating How We Die: The Ethical, Medical, and Legal Issues Surrounding Physician Assisted Suicide.* Cambridge, MA: Harvard University Press, 1998.

Florencio, Patrik S., and Robert H. Keller. "End-of-Life Decision Making: Rethinking the Principles of Fundamental Justice in the Context of Emerging Empirical Data." *Health Law Journal* 7 (1999):233–258.

Fried, Terri R., Michael D. Stein, Patricia S. O'Sullivan, et al. "Physician Attitudes and Practices Regarding Life-Sustaining Treatments and Euthanasia." *Archives of Internal Medicine* 153 (1993):722–728.

Glasson, John. "Report of the Council of Ethical and Judicial Affairs of the American Medical Association: Physician-Assisted Suicide." *Issues in Law and Medicine* 10 (1994):91–97.

Gorsuch, Neil M. "The Right to Assisted Suicide and Euthanasia." *Harvard Journal of Law and Public Policy* 23 (2000):599–710.

Keigher, Sharon. "Patient Rights and Dying: Policy Restraint and the States." *Health and Social Work* 19 (1994):298–306.

Orentlicher, David. "Trends in Health Care Decision Making: The Limits of Legislation." *Maryland Law Review* 53 (1994):1255–1305.

Powell, John A., and Adam S. Cohen. "The Right to Die." *Issues in Law and Medicine* 10 (1994):169–182.

Quill, Timothy. "A Case of Individualized Decision Making." *New England Journal of Medicine* 324 (1991):691–694.

Scherer, Jennifer M., and Rita James Simon. *Euthanasia and the Right to Die: A Comparative View.* Lanham, MD: Rowman & Littlefield, 1999.

Silveira, Maria J., Albert DiPiero, Martha S. Gerrity, and Chris Feudtner. "Patients' Knowledge of Options at the End of Life: Ignorance in the Face of Death." *Journal of the American Medical Association* 284 (2000):2483–2488.

VICKI LENS

NEAR-DEATH EXPERIENCES

Near-death experiences (NDEs) have been reported for much of human history. There is evidence in early Greek and Roman literature, in medieval Western religious literature, ancient literature of Buddhism, and the oral history and folklore of aboriginal societies in Australia, North and South America, and Oceania. The parapsychological literature has discussed NDEs since the nineteenth century, however the popular discussion of these experiences only dates from the early 1970s with the publication of Raymond Moody's best-selling *Life After Life* (1975). Moody coined the term *near-death experience* but later regretted its overidentification with physical death and changed the term for these experiences to *paranormal deaths.*

In *Life After Life* Moody discussed fifty individual cases of people who, when unconscious and apparently near death and then resuscitated, reported conscious social and psychological experiences. Some people reported sensations of traveling in a dark tunnel. Others reported meetings with bright beings of light or deceased relatives and friends.

Since this early book of casual observations from an author who had been an academic philosopher retrained as a medical practitioner first appeared, other more research-based books have been published. Among these are the behavioral and clinical studies of the psychologist Kenneth Ring (*Life At Death* 1980), the cardiologist Michael Sabom (*Recollections of Death* 1982), and the psychotherapist Margot Grey (*Return from Death* 1985). These were soon followed by other studies from parapsychology, religious studies, sociology, philosophy medicine, and particularly psychiatry.

Among the many studies that have been published since Moody's work include several that have been conducted with children. Childhood NDEs are similar to those reported by adults with some minor differences in phenomenology. Life review, for example, is present for those with a long enough life to recall. Children seem to more often see animals in their NDEs than do adults, suggesting that perhaps animals are one of the few "dead beings" a child might expect to see in such a state. The incidence of NDEs is extremely difficult to assess and depends much on the definition one uses as much as the methodology one employs. In clinical settings, frequently employing cardiac patients, the incidence has been reported in the vicinity of between 9 percent and 18 percent.

Estimates of incidences within the general population have been attempted with surveys. Researchers estimate that approximately 5 percent of the United States population has experienced an NDE, which has led researchers in the U.S. to suggest that some 10 million Americans have had an NDE and in Germany over 3 million people have experienced NDEs.

Some twenty years after the initial observations and theories studies have uncovered and discussed negative NDEs—experiences near death that are less than pleasant for the person in this near-death state. In these accounts, people visit dark places, encounter cruel or taunting beings, and experience feelings of sadness or anxiety. As of 2001 there have been few psychological or social correlates to predict NDEs, either of the positive or negative variety. Gender, age, class, and religious affiliation do not appear to play any role in predicting these experiences. There are some circumstantial correlates, such as surgical or suicide patients who appear not to experience life review compared to those whose injuries or illnesses are of sudden onset. But most of these predictive correlates appear to predict one or more NDE features (e.g. lights, life-reviewed, tunnel sensations, etc.) rather than actual incidence.

The professional and popular profile of NDEs has exploded since the 1970s. It is not immoderate to claim the NDE has become an important and central subject of study and entertainment since the late twentieth century. Moody's book has sold some 12 million copies to date. Film and video consistently employ NDE imagery in their scenes of death—from *Flatliners* (1990) to *What Dreams May Come* (1998). Several autobiographical NDE accounts have made the *New York Times* best-seller list.

The International Association for Near-Death Studies was established in the early 1980s in the United States, with chapters in the United Kingdom, Europe, Canada, and Australia. The association has an academic peer-review journal—*Journal of Near-Death Studies*—edited from the Department of Psychiatry at the University of Virginia Medical School. Articles about the NDE have appeared in prestigious medical journals including *Lancet, British Medical Journal, Journal of Nervous and Mental Disease,* and the *American Journal of Psychiatry,* among many others.

Theories

Understandably, near-death studies have drawn major theoretical debate from several quarters, in particular New Age and skeptical writers. Church leaders and writers are divided. Some side with materialist medical theories, while others argue that such experiences are the work of darker forces. Others allow that such experiences may be revelations into some larger human and perhaps divine dimension.

New Age writers, influenced by modern spiritualism and Eastern religions, have found the afterlife imagery rich in suggestion and confirmation about the eschatological theories of these influences. Skeptics, wary of religious resurgence and supernatural explanations, have tended to scrutinize the case details and research methodologies more carefully. They have tended to favor neuroscientific theories of explanation, particularly those with behavioral and psychobiological models of consciousness.

Among the chief psycho-neuro-biological theories of NDE have been theories of sensory deprivation and cerebral anoxia. Both events have been traced to abnormal temporal lobe seizure activity or the release of ketamines or other hormonal and chemical reactions in the brain. There have been theories about the role of drugs—both medical and illicit—but these took less prominence as more NDEs were reported in situations where these drugs were not implicated. The central problem with biological theories of NDEs is that most of these assume the experience to be closely associated with unconscious states. Increasingly this appears to be less the case.

There has been less effort in surveying the cross-cultural evidence around these experiences, yet it is here where the diversity of NDEs becomes increasingly apparent. What examination there has been in this area seems to indicate that the stereotypical profile of NDEs as an unconscious experience enjoys significant variation. Experients (people who experience NDEs) from hunter-gatherer societies, for example, tend not to report tunnel sensation or life review—an important observation that could undermine the credibility of attempts to create particular neurophysiological theories based up on these two details.

However, taking the stereotypical NDE profile of sensations of euphoria, out-of-body experience, tunnel sensation, life review, and meetings with beings of light or deceased people has also opened up another model of near-death experiences as experiences *not* near death and *not* unconscious. Here, similar phenomenology has been reported in connection with shamanic initiation rites, castaway experiences, experiences of trapped miners, mountaineering accidents, and bereavement experiences.

Further complicating the question of causation is the finding that near-deathlike experiences may be induced in therapeutic settings through use of eye-movement desensitization and reprocessing (EMDR) techniques in psychotherapy. During grief therapy using EMDR techniques, patients may experience reunion with deceased relatives and friends, tunnel sensation, experiences of light and peace, and the observation of supernatural vistas. Near-death experiences are no longer phenomena simply associated with unconscious experiences of cardiac arrest and resultant resuscitation.

The examination of these kinds of conscious experiences has lead to the recognition of two important points. First, NDE phenomenology is not always associated with real, physical experiences of death but merely the expectation of dying and loss. Second, NDE phenomenology is associated with conscious as well as unconscious experience. These observations immediately call into question theories of NDE that rely on unconscious cases and that employ cerebral anoxia (oxygen deprivation of the brain) as their primary mechanism of causation. Any physiological theories of NDE must take into account that the phenomenology spans conscious and unconscious experiences and enjoys significant cultural variation.

Notwithstanding these qualifications, it is important to note that physiological theories have no more power in undermining supernatural explanations than New Age theories have of establishing them. The issue of whether consciousness is merely a function of physical processes or is mediated by them is not settled by biological debate, least of all one with obvious materialist assumptions.

The issue of the nature of consciousness and death, specifically the fate of consciousness beyond death, is a philosophical question. It is not settled by empirical claims if only because all scientific conclusions are subject to revision. And because they are ipso facto empiricist models of explanation, such models are biased against theories of experience not subject to these types of tests and proofs.

The nature of death or of consciousness is also not settled by logical argument if only because there are always better arguments to be made, and will need to be made, by the changeable requirements of a diverse and evolving professional and academic culture. The arguments about human survival are made in the service of persuasion and are rarely definitive except to those with faith—in religious or scientific, materialist ideas. Evidence and argument must have a context to be persuasive within. They are most effective among a community of believers. This remains true of twenty-first-century skeptics and religious adherents.

Even away from the ideological posturing of the more extreme opinions from religion and science, NDEs are not readily explained by current neurophysiology. Some researchers have argued that drugs may be implicated, but often they are

Some people who have had near-death experiences (NDEs) reported an experience of life review or the sight of supernatural vistas such as cities or blissful rural scenes of beauty. In these early accounts nearly every NDE was reported to have feelings of great peace and happiness, even euphoria. GEORGE D. LEPP/CORBIS

not. Other researchers have argued that tunnel sensation is due to the side effects of oxygen deprivation to the brain, but NDEs occur to people who are fully conscious as well.

Personality changes linked to disturbances to temporal lobe, such as religiosity, philosophical pursuits, widening affect and so on, have been associated with obsessiveness, humorlessness, anger, and sadness—qualities not normally associated with NDEs. There have been claims that NDEs have occurred when patients were connected with electroencephalograph (EEG) machines, but these claims were subsequently proven false. There are now documented cases, but the reliability and validity issues behind measurement of brain activity are far from certain and so such cases are intriguing at best and irrelevant at worse.

What scientists are able to say is that the research to date has provided fruitful indicators of the type of brain/consciousness models that are needed to further explore and understand the physiological basis of these experiences. Advances in this scientific area will undoubtedly supply researchers with a basic benchmark for understanding the broad biological context of NDEs but they do not solve, and probably will never solve, the diverse incidents and experiences that are regularly reported near death. In this context, the best answer researchers will ever have when it comes to the question of whether or not NDEs represent evidence of human survival of death is that perhaps they might, but rarely conclusively.

Implications of Near-Death Experiences

Aside from the professional debates about the causes of NDEs there lies a major discussion about their consequences. Those whose NDEs are clinically derived from close physical encounters with death often report changed values and lifestyles. Those whose NDEs are derived from initiation rites, castaway experiences, or mining accidents also report life changes. These changes to values or lifestyles are associated with both positive and negative NDEs, although such changes may be dissimilar from each other. For people whose NDE is a positive experience, many report a lessening or disappearance of any personal fear of death. These people also report a greater "love of humanity," often expressed as a desire to change career or work aspirations so as to work for the good of others.

There is a greater expressed desire to be more tolerant or patient of human foibles and a greater appreciation for the interconnectedness of all living things. Those who encounter near-death experiences report an increase in their interest in spirituality but often expressly distinguish this from a church-going religiosity. Many other people have reported an increased interest in education or higher learning. This is often associated with a simple post-NDE desire for learning, but also for retraining into some kind of helping profession to meet their newly found ambition to "help others." People who have experienced a negative NDE will often, understandably, report a greater fear of death, and are more likely than those with positive experiences to return to church attendance.

There has been some suggestion that those who experience near-death experiences encounter a new type of consciousness. NDEs create human beings that have higher spiritual values and such people are important to an evolution of improved social and political values within humanity. But it is not at all clear that the research on post–NDE changes in individuals reflects genuine changes or simply new attitudes and hopes in these people. People often report stigma and rejection of their new attitudes and values, while many others are even skeptical of the actual NDE itself. Many near-death participants have reported being withdrawn or depressed about such responses and more than one book has recorded that the diverse reactions of people and their networks have lead to job loss and marital breakdown.

It appears that experiences of light and love near death no more makes a better person than any other experience of crisis. Experiences that are testing and challenging to one's personal values and character can transform one for the better or may destroy that person. But it is not the experience that holds the key, but one's capacity to learn and be changed by that experience. In this way, NDEs occupy similar psychiatric and social space as bereavement, job loss, poverty, personal failure, and social rejection. They may be sufficient but not guaranteed grounds for personal growth and change.

As mentioned previously, the NDE is not confined to people near death or loss. It may also take "passengers." In his book *The Last Laugh* (1999), Moody calls these experiences "empathic," "conjoint," or "mutual" NDEs. People caring for dying people may report some actual NDE phenomenology—experiences of light, out-of-body experiences, meeting supernatural or deceased beings, and enjoying sensations of peace and joy. These are part of a discreet subset of near-death phenomenology such as shared near-death visions, shared near-death experiences, and shared illness experiences. They have been reported in early-nineteenth-century parapsychology literature and in late-twentieth-century near-death studies and literature.

The social and psychological pattern for their appearance seems to be a personal journey that takes the dying or ill person through similar stages of social isolation and reintegration. The number of reported cases of shared NDE are small and their documentation inconsistent in thoroughness. Yet, such cases continue to strengthen the importance of the social and psychological nature and complexity of NDEs. There can be no doubt that biological factors play a role but it may yet turn out to be a diverse mediating one, subject to equally complex social factors. Just as the physiology of smiling is no key to the secret of happiness, the physiology of NDEs may not unlock the secret of the fate of the soul nor even of its whereabouts.

The problem of NDEs appears to tread similar territory to other problems of social and psychological marginalization. In that space, NDEs are areas of contested social meanings between modern-day "experts" of one persuasion or another, and individuals trying to make sense of experiences for which science and religion have poorly prepared them. Without a settled, agreed-upon set of meanings, the status of NDEs, their passengers, and their public relationships with the outside world will always be ambiguous and problematic.

See also: COMMUNICATION WITH THE DEAD; COMMUNICATION WITH THE DYING; IMMORTALITY; MOMENT OF DEATH; REINCARNATION

Bibliography

Anderson, John. *Life, Death and Beyond.* Grand Rapids, MI: Zondervan, 1980.

Becker, Carl. "The Centrality of Near-Death Experiences in Chinese Pure Land Buddhism." *Anabiosis* 1 (1981): 154–171.

Blackmore, Susan. *Dying to Live: Science and the Near-Death Experience.* London: Grafton, 1993.

Botkin, Allan. "The Induction of After-Death Communications Utilizing Eye-Movement Desensitization and Reprocessing: A New Discovery." *Journal of Near-Death Studies* 18, no. 3 (2000):181–209.

Flynn, Charles. *After the Beyond: Human Transformation and the Near-Death Experience.* Englewood Cliffs, NJ: Prentice-Hall, 1986.

Gallup, George. *Adventures in Immortality.* London: Souvenir, 1982.

Grey, Margot. *Return from Death: An Exploration of the Near-Death Experience.* London: Arkana, 1985.

Greyson, Bruce. "The Incidence of Near-Death Experiences." *Medicine and Psychiatry* (December 1998):92–99.

Greyson, Bruce. "A Typology of Near-Death Experiences." *American Journal of Psychiatry* 142 (1985):967–969.

Greyson, Bruce, and Nancy Evans-Bush. "Distressing Near-Death Experiences." *Psychiatry* 55 (1992):95–110.

Hick, John. *Death and Eternal Life.* London: Collins, 1976.

Kellehear, Allan. *Experiences near Death: Beyond Medicine and Religion.* New York: Oxford University Press, 1996.

Kung, Hans. *Eternal Life?* London: Collins, 1984.

Lorimer, David. *Whole in One: The Near-Death Experience and the Ethic of Interconnectedness.* London: Penguin, 1990.

Moody, Raymond. *The Last Laugh: A New Philosophy of Near-Death Experiences, Apparitions, and the Paranormal.* Charlottesville, VA: Hampton Roads Publishing, 1999.

Moody, Raymond. *Life After Life.* New York: Bantam, 1975.

Morse, Melvin. *Closer to the Light: Learning from Children's Near-Death Experiences.* New York: Villard Books, 1990.

Rawlings, Maurice. *Before Death Comes.* London: Sheldon Press, 1980.

Ring, Kenneth. *Life At Death: A Scientific Investigation of the Near-Death Experience.* New York: Coward, McCann and Geoghegan, 1980.

Ritchie, George. *Return from Tomorrow.* Grand Rapids, MI: Fleming H. Revell, 1978.

Sabom, Michael. *Recollections of Death: A Medical Investigation.* New York: Harper and Row, 1982.

Shapiro, Francis. *Eye-Movement Desensitization and Reprocessing: Principles, Processes and Procedures.* New York: Guilford, 1995.

Sutherland, Cherie. *Transformed by the Light: Life After Near-Death Experiences.* New York: Bantam, 1992.

Zaleski, Carol. *Otherworld Journeys.* New York: Oxford University Press, 1989.

ALLAN KELLEHEAR

NECROMANCY

Necromancy (derived from the Greek *nekros,* meaning "dead," and *manteia,* meaning "divination") is the evocation of the dead to obtain omens about future events or secret facts. It is based upon the belief that the deceased, free of physical limits, holds the power to obtain information that is not accessible to the living.

Necromancy is a practice that originated in ancient Persia, Greece, and Rome, but was most popular during the Middle Ages, and is rare today. The most common form of necromancy is to summon the spirit of the corpse by sacrifices and incantations but there is also the less common practice of attempting to raise the corpse to life. The rituals demand meticulous execution and exacting preparations involving the choice of a proper place, for example a cemetery or the ruins of an ancient monastery; the choice of the right time, usually between the hours of midnight and one in the morning; use of specific incantations; and accessories, such as bells. One of the most important elements is the use of a magic circle which protects the necromancer and his or her assistant from being harmed by provoking the dead.

There are many examples of necromancy throughout history, but the best-known necromancer was the witch of Endor, who, according to the Bible, summoned the spirit of Samuel to answer Saul's questions. Often considered a sinister practice, necromancy was condemned by the Catholic Church and was outlawed by the Witchcraft Act of 1604 in Elizabethan England.

See also: COMMUNICATION WITH THE DEAD; DEAD GHETTO

Bibliography

Drury, Nevill. *Dictionary of Mysticism and the Occult.* San Francisco: Harper and Row, 1985.

Guiley, Rosemary E. *The Encyclopedia of Witches and Witchcraft.* New York: Facts on File, 1989.

Shepard, Leslie A. *Encyclopedia of Occultism & Parapsychology,* 3rd edition. Detroit: Gale Research Inc., 1991.

ISABELLE MARCOUX

NECROPHILIA

The term *necrophilia* is mostly used as a psychiatric expression for a pathological sexual attraction to corpses. It is a very rare and poorly understood phenomenon. In his seminal 1894 work, *Psychopathia Sexualis,* Richard von Krafft-Ebing, one of the first psychiatric writers, called it a horrible manifestation of sadism. Abraham A. Brill, who published the first comprehensive examination of the subject in 1941, characterized necrophiles as many other authors had—mentally deficient, psychotic, and incapable of obtaining a consenting partner. Necrophilia has been associated with cannibalism and vampirism as all are considered perversions.

In 1978 Neville Lancaster reported in the *British Journal of Psychiatry* the case of a twenty-three-year-old student of music at a teacher's training college in England. He was convicted of the murder of a young woman, and sentenced to imprisonment for life. The defendant admitted that he had broken into a mortuary on two occasions prior to the murder and had sexual intercourse with female corpses. The prosecution saw him as a necrophile who desired a dead body and therefore decided to kill the victim. The student was tested with an IQ of 153, and no evidence of psychiatric illness was found. The defendant had a normal romantic relationship with a music teacher. The three necrophilic incidents occurred after the student was drinking extensively and taking other chemical agents, so the previous incidents of sexual intercourse with corpses completely disquieted him the following morning. Necrophilia seemed to upset him as much as the murder itself.

This report demonstrates how difficult it is to draw any generalizations from a single case history. In 1989 Jonathan Rosman and Phillip Resnick reviewed 122 cases manifesting necrophilic acts or fantasies. They distinguish genuine necrophilia from pseudonecrophilia and classify true necrophilia into three types: necrophilic homicide (murder to obtain a corpse for sexual purposes); "regular" necrophilia (the use of already dead bodies for sexual pleasure); and necrophilic fantasy (fantasizing about sexual activity with a corpse, without carrying out any necrophilic acts). The pseudonecrophile has a transient attraction to a corpse, but a corpse is not the object of his sexual fantasies. According to Rosman and Resnick, neither psychosis, mental retardation, nor sadism appears to be inherent in necrophilia. The most common motive for necrophilia is possession of an unresisting and unrejecting partner. Necrophiles often choose occupations that put them in contact with corpses.

Based on single case histories, many researchers offer psychoanalytic explanations for necrophilia. Rosman and Resnick developed an empirical model to get a deeper understanding of how psychodynamic events could lead to necrophilia: "(1) The necrophile develops poor self-esteem, perhaps due in part to a significant loss; (a) He (usually male) is very fearful of rejection by women and he desires a sexual object who is incapable of rejecting him; and/or (b) He is fearful of the dead, and transforms his fear of the dead—by means of reaction formation—into a desire for the dead; (2) He develops an exciting fantasy of sex with a corpse, sometimes after exposure to a corpse" (Rosman and Resnick 1989, p. 161). Because no therapist has treated a sufficient number of necrophiles, research literature on effective treatments does not exist.

See also: GRIEF; NECROMANCY; VAMPIRES

Bibliography

Brill, Abraham A. "Necrophilia." *Journal of Criminal Psychopathology* 2 (1941):433–443.

Krafft-Ebing, Richard von. *Psychopathia Sexualis: With Especial Reference to the Antipathic Sexual Instinct: A Medico-Forensic Study,* Burbank, CA: Bloat, 1999.

Lancaster, Neville P. "Necrophilia, Murder and High Intelligence: A Case Report." *British Journal of Psychiatry* 132 (1978):605–608.

Rosman, Jonathan P., and Phillip J. Resnick. "Sexual Attraction to Corpses: A Psychiatric Review of Necrophilia." *Bulletin of the American Academy of Psychiatry and the Law* 17 (1989):153–163.

RANDOLPH OCHSMANN

NEONATAL INTENSIVE CARE UNIT

Neonatology is a specialty within pediatric medicine that provides care for sick and/or premature infants. It is an area of medicine that is very young in comparison to other areas of medicine. This is also true for the newborn babies that begin their lives in the neonatal intensive care unit (NICU). Infants less than one month old are often referred to as "neonates." These neonates can be born as early as twenty-four weeks gestation (five months of pregnancy) and spend several months in the NICU. The NICU is a highly technical specialized unit in a hospital that provides medical/nursing care and technological support to sick and/or high-risk premature infants. Premature infants (infants born before thirty-seven weeks gestation) are the largest group of infants who require this high-tech environment to survive. Most preterm infants stay in the NICU until their due date. Thus, if a child was born six weeks early, parents can expect that their child will be in the NICU for six weeks. The NICU often becomes a second home for many families, where parents spend many hours each day with their infants. For the most part, these tiny infants must learn to breathe and grow before they can go home.

Other infants who require this specialized medical/nursing care are either born sick with some kind of disease or have a congenital defect or syndrome. These infants require specialized care until they can be easily cared for by their families at home. This medical/nursing care may be supportive, palliative, or surgical in nature and is determined by the individualized needs of the child.

The NICU did not exist until the early 1960s and the specialty of neonatology did not begin until the 1970s. These special units were established soon after the death of President John F. Kennedy's newborn son, who died of respiratory distress and immature lungs. He was born at thirty-four weeks gestation. His death brought increased awareness in the United States to the numbers of preterm infants who were dying because of immature lung development shortly after their births. Knowledge and expert care of these infants increased, and by the early 1990s more than 90 percent of these premature infants were surviving, including those infants born as early as twenty-four weeks gestation. There are more than 1,500 NICUs in the United States. Most are regional centers that provide training and consultation to a network of newborn nurseries in several communities. Regionalized care brings perinatologists (specialists who treat high-risk pregnant mothers) and neonatologists together to provide the best possible support and care to this special dyad. This is necessary because even though the NICU team can support the infant, most often the best place for the child is in the womb of his or her mother until forty weeks gestation, the normal length of a pregnancy.

The ability to better support these vulnerable infants and families has changed primarily because of a substantial increase in knowledge and understanding of the physiologic, psychosocial, and neurobehavioral capabilities of high-risk infants. In addition to this enormous growth in knowledge, there have been many advancements in technology, such as the development of surfactants and the refinement of mechanical ventilation, that have greatly influenced the ability of medical personnel to physiologically support infants in the NICU. Research findings have contributed many facets and dimensions to providing care that further enhance the long-term outcomes for high-risk infants and their families. For example, although there is still some mystery to the underlying pathophysiology of retinopathy of prematurity (retinal damage related to immature developing retina of preterm infants, once believed to be related to too much oxygen therapy), refined management of the progression of the disease often minimizes long-term problems for these infants. The delivery of expert medical/nursing care requires the artful use of technology and the integration of developmentally supportive and family-centered concepts into routine medical practices.

There are many different kinds of technology in the NICU, including different types of infant ventilators, monitors, and supportive devices, such as infusion pumps, oxygen hoods, and incubators. Although this equipment has become more responsive to the needs of the infants, there is still much the scientific and medical communities can learn about the use of technology to support neonates. The benefits of these machines are often coupled with iatrogenic hazards that may lead to long-term complications and increased numbers of chronic patients in the NICU. Although this equipment is intended to support infants in the NICU, many times all it does is increase the time infants spend in the NICU with little improvement in long-term outcomes. Technology must be used prudently with outcomes and cost-benefit as part of the decision-making process. Even with the technological advances and neurobehaviorally based interventions that are available to the premature infant, nothing can substitute for the normal environment of the womb.

More than any other phenomenon, technological developments seem to have become the most transforming force in the advancement of neonatal care. It was the development of the first infant ventilator that many medical professionals believe actually "birthed" the NICU. Prior to that time, incubators kept infants warm but only the strongest survived in the small isolated special care nurseries. The equipment in the twenty-first-century NICU has evolved significantly since the 1980s and 1990s. Previously, equipment used in the NICU was developed as scaled-down versions of technology used to support adults. These adult designed machines, however, did not meet the very different and unique physiologic needs of the infant. Providing care in the highly technical environment of the NICU is challenging. Technologic interventions allow for greater medical support and management of sicker and smaller preterm infants. And, although these infants are indisputably more vulnerable and dependent on the care of others, they are continually developing and maturing into amazingly independent and resilient human beings.

The professionals who work in the NICU are highly trained in the care of preterm babies. There are neonatologists, neonatal nurse practitioners, staff nurses, respiratory therapists, developmental specialists, occupational therapists, and physical therapists. This team of professionals works together with the family to provide a holistic approach to the management of the child's needs.

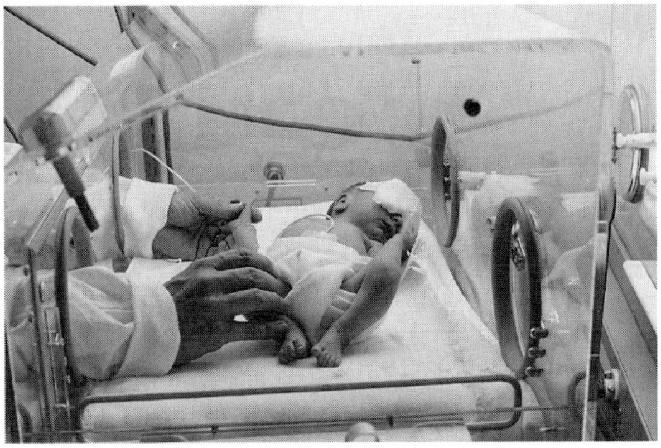

Newborns can be treated for jaundice with phototherapy in NICUs, one of the many technologies available in intensive care units. AMERICAN ACADEMY OF PEDIATRICS

Sometimes pediatric specialists are used as a resource when, for example, an infant requires cardiac surgery for a congenital defect. The neonatal team requests a specialized consultant, who is then invited to examine the child and his or her medical records and provide focused input with regard to the continued management of the child. Sometimes management requires surgery. Because the infants are so small and so susceptible to infection, this surgery is often performed within the confines of the NICU rather than the institution's operating room. The decision regarding the operation's location is based on how well the NICU is equipped to handle the type of surgery required and the comfort of the surgeon with the NICU environment.

Neonatal intensive care has become a leader in the provision of family-centered care, which recognizes the unique and individual needs of each infant and family. Family-centered care is a philosophy of care in which the pivotal role of the family is acknowledged and respected in the lives of children. Within this philosophy, families are supported in their natural caregiving and decision-making roles, and medical professionals respect their unique strengths as people and families. Family-centered care recognizes and promotes normative patterns of living at home and in the community. Parents and professionals are seen as equals in a partnership committed to the child and the development of optimal quality in the delivery of all levels of health care. Family-centered care also helps the family achieve the best possible environment for promoting the growth and development of individual members of the family. Family-centered care strengthens the family unit through advocacy, empowerment, and enabling the family to nurture and support their child's development.

Family centered caregiving interventions include individualizing care to include providing clustering of caregiving tasks. "Clustering" caregiving increases rest periods for the infant, providing medical and supportive interventions based on the individualized behavioral cues of the infant, supporting the infant's long-term development by acknowledging the infant's post-conceptional age when choosing interventions, paces procedures, and integrates the family into the interdisciplinary caregiving team. Particular interventions might include providing developmentally supportive positioning, skin-to-skin (kangaroo) holding, music therapy, infant massage, and/or cuddler programs. However, individualized interventions unique to the needs of each child are the key to success with a particular infant and family. Although some infants die in the NICU, the number is relatively low compared to the number who are cared for and discharged home as relatively "normal" with their families.

See also: INFANT MORTALITY; LIFE EXPECTANCY

Bibliography

Albritto, Sabra, Donna Acosta, Deanna Bellinger, and Denise Farmer. *You Are Not Alone: The NICU Experience.* Boston: Children's Medical Ventures, 1998.

Als, Heidelise. "Developmental Care in the Newborn Intensive Care Unit." *Current Opinion in Pediatrics* 10 (1998):138–142.

Als, Heidelise, and Frank Duffy. "Neurobehavioral Assessment in the Newborn Period: Opportunity for Early Detection of Later Learning Disabilities and for Early Intervention." *Birth Defects: Original Article Series* 25 (1989):127–152.

D'Apolito, Karen, Jacqueline McGrath, and Andrea O'Brien. "Infant and Family Centered Developmental Care Guidelines." In *National Association of Neonatal Nurses Clinical Practice Guidelines,* 3rd edition. Des Plaines, IL: National Association of Neonatal Nurses, 2000.

Gibbons C., S. Geller, and E. Glatz. "Biomedical Equipment in the Neonatal Intensive Care Unit: Is It a Stressor?" *Journal of Perinatal and Neonatal Nursing* 12 (1997):67–73.

Graham, Susan. "Futile Care in the Neonatal Intensive Care Unit: Is Aggressive Care Always Justifiable?" *Journal of Neonatal Nursing* 5 (1999):23–26.

Jamsa, K., and T. Jamsa. "Technology in Neonatal Intensive Care—A Study of Parents' Experiences." *Technology and Healthcare* 6 (1998):225–230.

Johnson, Beverly, E. S. Jeppson, and L. Redburn. *Caring for Children and Families: Guidelines for Hospitals.* Washington, DC: Association for the Care of Children's Health, 1992.

Merenstein, Gerald B., and Sandra L Gardener. *Handbook of Neonatal Intensive Care,* 4th edition. St. Louis, MO: Mosby, 1998.

Miles, Margaret, S. G. Funk, and M. A. Kasper. "The Neonatal Intensive Care Unit Environment: Sources of Stress for Parents." *American Association of Critical Care Nurses: Clinical Issues* 2, no. 2 (1991):346–354.

Zaichkin, Janette. *Newborn Intensive Care: What Every Parent Needs to Know.* Santa Rosa, CA: NICU Ink, 1996.

JACQUELINE M. MCGRATH

NOTIFICATIONS OF DEATH

One of the most important messages communicated in human societies has always been the notification that one of their members has died. The news spreads outward—like ripples in a pond—from family members to friends, to employers, and to fraternal orders and other organizations to which the deceased belonged. Various bureaucracies, too, must be informed, such as Social Security, insurance agencies, and voters' registration, as the deceased is no longer entitled to the benefits of the living. A death notice announces a void in the social fabric and the survivors' entry into the bereavement role. Who delivers the death notification, and to whom it is delivered, reveals much about the nature of individuals' ties to the broader society.

The order and nature by which notifications are made reveal a prioritizing of the importance of the social bonds between the deceased and his or her kinship groups, friends, work and civic associates, and the wider public. If the wrong approach is employed when informing someone of a death,

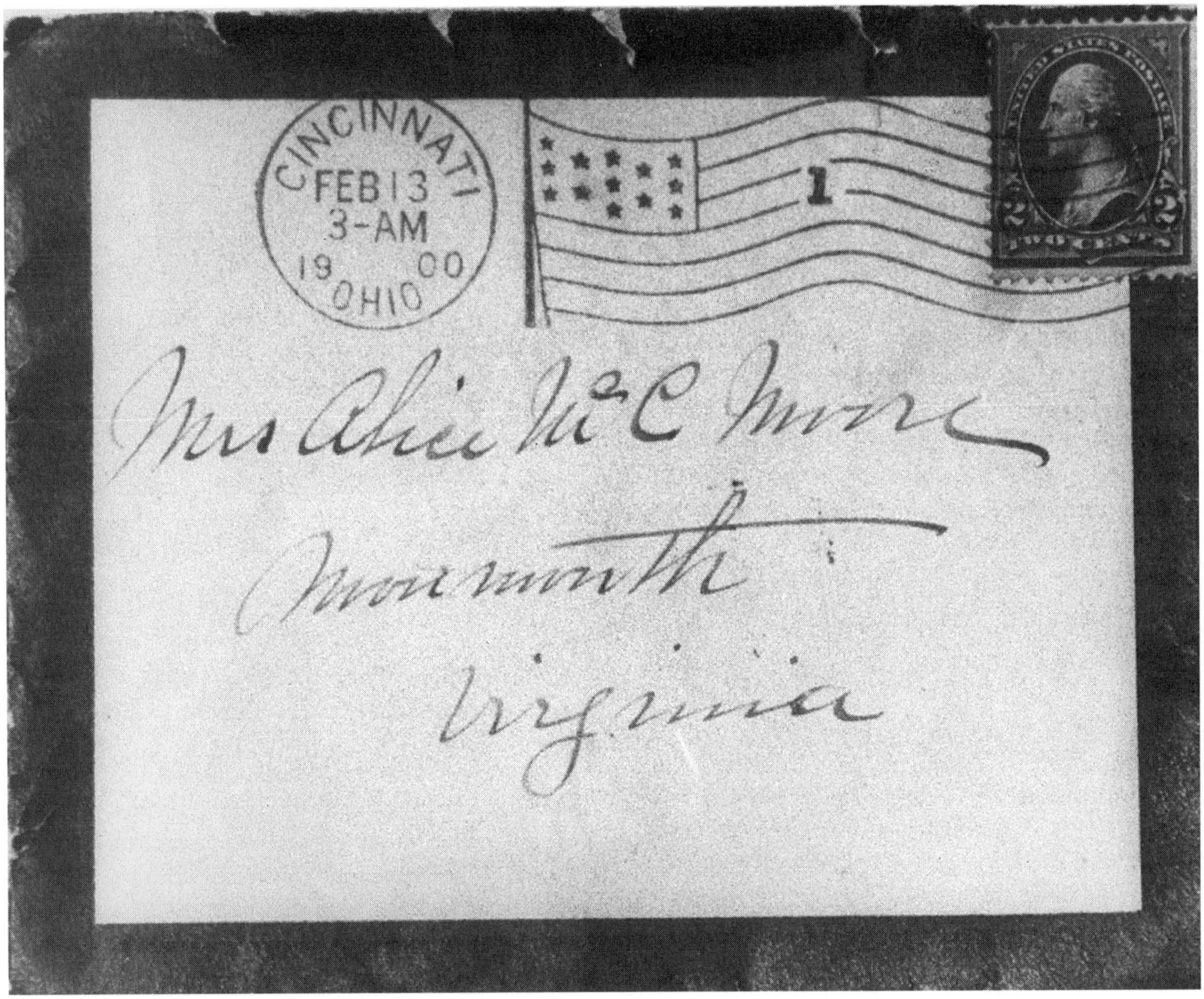

Until the early twentieth century an individual did not attend a funeral without an invitation. One way of providing an invitation was a letter edged in black, generally enclosed in a black-edged envelope. The invitation served the dual purpose of notifying the receiver of the death and inviting him or her to the deceased's funeral. JAMES CRISSMAN

as when a distant cousin is informed before a sibling of the deceased, people may feel slighted and ill feelings can result. Therefore, a "ranking" process usually exists with regard to whom the contact person(s) should be and the order in which survivors should be notified of a death. Each family unit usually has its own plan of contact order for those who should be a part of the notification process.

Traditional Methods of Delivering Death Notifications

When societies were rural, small, and members lived near one another, it was feasible to walk from residence to residence and personally spread the news that someone had died. When horses were available, riding, rather than walking, was an option.

The custom of ringing a bell to announce a death originated in Europe and became a cultural trait. In Tudor England, it was called a "Passing Bell" or "Soul Bell" (Montell 1975, p. 68). Tolling the bell was used in different ways depending on the community. The bell might simply be sounded several times and people would understand its meaning. It could be rung several times, there would be a pause, and it would be tolled again each hour for several hours. In some societies, the number of times the bell was rung reflected the age of the person. The famous English poet, John Donne, obsessed with his own death and lying in bed suffering from a serious illness, wrote "For Whom the Bell Tolls" while listening to the tolling of a distant funeral bell. The custom of ringing the bell was brought to early America and utilized in areas such as Central Appalachia for many years.

In the small American towns of the nineteenth and twentieth centuries, where no newspapers, telephones, or other means of fast conveyance were extant, it was common to place a funeral notice in the window of a business establishment. People who lived in the community, or were visiting, would go to the window of the business to see who had died and then respond accordingly. In some areas of Europe and America it was also a custom to place a black badge or flower wreath on the door of a residence or business to denote a death.

When telephones were introduced, for people who could afford them, tolling bells and other forms of notification were no longer necessary. Messages could be sent to people who lived a long distance from where the death occurred. With the phone, the message which had been public, now became privatized. The advent of the telephone brought a new form of death anxiety. When the knowledge of an impending death exists, there is a degree of anxiousness every time the telephone rings. There is the certainty that "this call is the one" and there is an element of hesitancy to answer the phone. If it is not answered, the bad news will not be received, and the death can be denied for a while longer.

Twentieth-Century Death Notifications

From the early 1900s to the present, many radio stations have a daily broadcast, usually in the morning, to inform the listening public of those who have died, with a biographical summary similar to an obituary and notice of the time and place of the funeral. These programs are usually supported by local funeral establishments.

While one might consider the obituary that appears in newspapers to be a modern contrivance, it actually dates to at least the Middle Ages. The obituary is a published announcement of a death. It includes a brief biography of the deceased and information concerning the funeral, but the quantity and type of data included vary from one obituary to another. Symbolically reaffirmed is the community's social hierarchy. Occasionally the person's standing in the social hierarchy is denoted, and in rare instances there may be a photograph of the deceased.

Sudden Death Notification

In the hospital setting, it is generally the duty of the physician to notify the next of kin that a death has taken place, but there are instances in which the task has been assigned to a nurse, clergyperson, or social worker. In the case of accidental death, vehicular or nonvehicular, it often is a police officer, accompanied when possible by a chaplain, who delivers the news. When death occurs, the victim's name is withheld from the public pending notification of the family as family members who have proprietary rights to being first informed.

To soften the impact of a death notice, the police and military have developed their own system of informing survivors of the demise of a loved one. While procedures vary from department to department, generally when a police officer is killed the chief of police and the officer's immediate supervisor go to the residence of the deceased to deliver the news. If a chaplain is available, he or she will take part in the notification process. When a death occurs in the military, a chaplain or high-ranking officer will go to the home of the survivors. During a war, when there are not enough personnel to deliver the news directly, a registered letter is sent to the home. The Louvin Brothers' 1991 song "Robe of White" best describes the process:

> "I'm sorry," said the postman, "I must ask you to sign
> This little book that I have brought along.
> You see this letter's registered." He slowly bowed his head.
> And then she knew that there was something wrong.
> The address on the corner of this envelope of blue
> Told her that her darling son was dead.
> Where Jimmy's name and number had always been before,
> His captain's name was written there instead.

When there is a lingering illness prior to a death, survivors have a chance to adjust to the demise of their loved one. Some thanatologists even refer to a process of "anticipatory grief" where the person actually ends the grieving process (and sometimes abandons the dying person) prior to the death. However, when there is a sudden death, whether it is the result of an accident, suicide, murder, fatal heart attack or stroke, disaster, or war wound, sudden death notification can have a traumatic impact on the recipient of the news. Grief may be more intense than in instances where there is time to prepare for a death.

There is always a right way and a wrong way to notify someone of a sudden death. Neither the military nor the police should send a lone novice to notify the family or next of kin; however, it may be a good idea to have an inexperienced person accompany someone who is experienced to learn the correct process of notification). The notifier should be someone who is experienced in interpersonal relations (e.g., a clergyperson) or someone who has either received a notification of death at some point or has been a notifying agent at least once. A death notice should not be sent directly through the mail, it should be hand delivered. The deliverer should not walk up to the door, hand the letter to the survivor, and leave. It is best to deliver it to a friend of the family and have them carry it by hand to the survivors.

When a sudden death notice is delivered, the message should be short and to the point. The bearer should simply say that they have bad news and then tell the survivor(s) that their loved one is dead. According to the sociologists Michael Leming and George Dickinson, "Because the recipient of the news will probably be in shock and will disbelieve immediately after receiving the news, then is the time to add the simplest of details"—the person is dead, place of death, brief description of how they died, and where the deceased is located (Leming 2002, p. 477). No matter how well the deliverer of bad news may do his or her job, the survivor will in most cases accept the news with great difficulty.

See also: DEATH SYSTEM; GENDER DISCRIMINATION AFTER DEATH; GRIEF: FAMILY; SYMPATHY CARDS

Bibliography

Ariès, Philippe. *The Hour of Our Death*. New York: Vintage Books, 1982.

Crissman, James K. *Death and Dying in Central Appalachia*. Urbana: University of Illinois Press, 1994.

Gerbner, George. "Death in Prime Time: Notes on the Symbolic Functions of Dying in the Mass Media." *The Annals* 447 (1980):64–70.

Leming, Michael R., and George E. Dickinson. *Understanding Dying, Death & Bereavement,* 5th edition. Fort Worth, TX: Harcourt, 2002.

Montell, William Lynwood. *Ghosts along the Cumberland: Deathlore in the Kentucky Foothills*. Knoxville: University of Tennessee Press, 1975.

The Louvin Brothers. "Robe of White." *Songs That Tell a Story*. Rounder Records C-1030.

JAMES K. CRISSMAN
MARY A. CRISSMAN

NUCLEAR DESTRUCTION

The Nazi death camps and the mushroom cloud of nuclear explosion are the two most potent images of the mass killings of the twentieth century. As World War II ended and the cold war began, the fear of nuclear annihilation hung like a cloud over the otherwise complacent consumerism of the Eisenhower era. The new technologies of mass death exacted incalculable costs, draining the treasuries of the United States and the Soviet Union and engendering widespread apocalyptic fatalism, distrust of government, and environmental degradation.

The advent of nuclear weapons fundamentally altered both the nature of war and the relationship of the military with the rest of society. A 1995 study by John Pike, the director of the space policy project at the Federation of American Scientists, revealed that the cost of nuclear weapons has constituted about one-fourth to one-third of the entire American military budget since 1945. President Eisenhower, in his farewell speech on the threats posed by the "military-industrial complex," warned of the potential of new technology to dominate the social order in unforeseen ways. The "social system which researches, chooses it, produces it, polices it, justifies it, and maintains it in being," observed British social historian E. P. Thompson, orients its "entire economic, scientific, political, and ideological support-system to that weapons system" (Wieseltier 1983, p. 10).

Throughout the cold war, U.S. intelligence reports exaggerated the numbers and pace of development of the Soviet Union's production of bombs and long-range nuclear forces, thus spurring further escalations of the arms race and the expansion of the military-industrial complex. In the 1950s there was the bomber gap, in the 1960s it was the missile gap, in the 1970s the civilian defense gap, and in the 1980s the military spending gap. The Soviet Union and the members of the NATO alliance developed tens of thousands of increasingly sophisticated nuclear weapons and delivery systems (e.g., cannons, bombers, land- and submarine-based intercontinental ballistic missiles) and various means of protecting them (e.g., hardened underground silos, mobile launchers, antiballistic missiles). With the possible exception of the hydrogen bomb, every advance in nuclear weaponry—from the neutron bomb and X-ray warheads to the soldier-carried Davy Crockett fission bomb—was the product of American ingenuity and determination.

A Brief History of Cold War Nuclear Developments

During World War II, while German research resources were largely invested in developing the V-1 and V-2 guided missiles, similar investments were being made by the United States and selected allies in producing the ultimate bomb through the highly secret Manhattan Project. The first nuclear device was detonated before dawn on July 16, 1945, at the Alamogordo Test Range in south central New Mexico. Within two months, atomic bombs were dropped on the Japanese cities of Hiroshima and Nagasaki. The U.S. government claimed that these bombings were necessary to shorten the war and avoid the anticipated heavy casualties of a land invasion of Japan, but later revisionist historians have disputed that motivation, claiming rather that the blasts were intended as an advertisement of American power over the Soviet Union.

The United States continued to develop the new weaponry despite the fact the war had concluded. Whether this was the reason why the Soviet Union embarked on its own weapon program, or if it would have done so if the U.S. had ceased production, remains a matter of debate. The Soviets deeply feared that the United States, having demonstrated its willingness to use the weapon on civilian populations, might not hesitate to do so again during the cold war. Two weeks after Hiroshima's destruction, Stalin ordered a crash program to develop an atomic bomb using Gulag prisoners to mine uranium and construct weapons facilities, putting the needs of his people behind those of the bomb. The race for nuclear supremacy had begun.

The 1940s saw the dawn of the cold war: the Soviet blockade of Berlin, Mao's victory over the Nationalists in China, discoveries and accusations of espionage, and, in September 1949, evidence that the Russians had tested their own bomb. Major General Curtis LeMay, head of the newly formed Strategic Air Command, was ordered to prepare his Air Force unit for possible atomic attack. His first war plan, based on a concept called "killing a nation," involved attacking seventy Soviet cities with 133 atomic bombs.

Fears of imminent nuclear war swept the globe. President Truman believed that if the Russians had the bomb, they would use it. The physicist Edward Teller pushed for a thermonuclear weapon whose virtually unlimited power would dwarf the atomic bombs produced under the Manhattan Project. The "Super," as it would be called, was the hydrogen bomb. In January 1950 Truman approved its development. Five months later, North Korea, with Stalin's support, attacked South Korea. Later that year, when in retreat, the North Koreans were reinforced by another Russian ally, Communist China. The cold war was in full swing, and the climate of fear and suspicion fueled McCarthyism. In 1952 the first hydrogen bomb was detonated, releasing a force some 800 times greater than the weapon that had destroyed Hiroshima. The bomb, initially sixty-two tons, was later made smaller and lighter, allowing its placement on missiles.

It was then that President Eisenhower's Secretary of Defense, John Foster Dulles, presented the impression that the United States would instigate nuclear war if there were any communist encroachments upon the "free world." Peace was maintained through the deterrent of fear: "Mutually Assured Destruction" (MAD) became the principle nuclear strategy for the rest of the twentieth century, making it inconceivable that politicians would risk the destruction of the planet by actually deploying the weapons they were so busily and alarmingly developing and stockpiling. To ensure retribution following a first strike, stockpiles continued growing to the point where human populations could be killed many times over.

Nuclear anxieties intensified with the development of strategic intercontinental rockets capable of delivering a nuclear warhead anywhere in the world within minutes. Because atomic war would basically be a one-punch affair, the alacrity and thoroughness of the first strike became the preoccupation of strategic planners. The race between the United States and Russia to refine German rocket technology intensified during the 1950s. When Russia launched the first satellite, *Sputnik,* in 1957, Americans panicked at the thought of Soviet hardware overhead and its ability to drop weapons from orbit. To recoup lost face and bolster national confidence, the United States entered the space race with its own orbital missions and even considered a plan to detonate a Hiroshima-size nuclear bomb on the moon that would be visible to the naked eye. In 1961 the Soviets placed the first man, Yuri Gargarin, into orbit as the nuclear-arms race combined with the space race as the key instruments of cold war rivalry between the Soviet Union and the United States.

But the critical event of the 1960s was the 1962 discovery that Russians had deployed forty-eight offensive ballistic missiles in Cuba. In a showdown of nuclear brinkmanship, both the Soviet Union and the United States went on highest alert in their preparations for war. For thirteen days the cold war almost went hot. As the Russian nuclear missiles were nearing operational status the Kennedy administration weighed such options as mounting an air strike, staging an invasion, or conducting a naval blockade. After the latter was selected, a Russian fleet steamed west to break it; a U.S. spy plane was shot down over Cuban territory killing the pilot. Eventually, though, diplomacy and level heads prevailed. The missiles were removed in exchange for a U.S. pledge not to invade the communist country and to remove its obsolete Jupiter missiles from Turkey. The nations' closeness to the unthinkable contributed to their agreeing on the 1963 Nuclear Test Ban Treaty.

There was one final peaking of fears and expenditures before the collapse of the Soviet Union: the entry of another communist superpower on the nuclear game board. China, which had detonated its first atomic bomb in 1964, claimed thirteen years later to have successfully tested guided missiles with nuclear warheads. Reports surfaced of nuclear shelters being constructed in Manchuria. The 1970s concluded with six members in the nuclear club and with memories associated with the seventy-fifth anniversary of the beginning of World War I and how an unpredictable chain of events could set into motion unwanted global conflict.

In 1982 President Reagan unilaterally discontinued negotiations for a comprehensive test ban of nuclear weapons, echoing the military's claims of a "testing gap" with the Soviet Union. In fact, as of the beginning of 1985, the United States had over the previous four decades (since 1945) conducted some 200 more nuclear tests than had the Soviets. The President proposed the Strategic Defense Initiative, popularly known as "Star Wars," to protect the nation from missile attack by using exotic technologies that were still on the drawing board. Pure scientific research in physics, lasers, metallurgy, artificial intelligence, and dozens of other areas became largely focused on direct military uses. By the mid-1980s, 70 percent of American programs in research and development and testing and evaluation were defense-related, and nearly 40 percent of all U.S. engineers and scientists were involved in military projects.

Compounding public anxieties was a 1982 forecast by U.S. intelligence agencies that thirty-one countries would be capable of producing nuclear weapons by 2000. From the scientific community came highly publicized scenarios of a postwar "nuclear winter," possibly similar to conditions that led to the extinction of dinosaurs following the impact of an asteroid. Groups such as Physicians for Social Responsibility warned that such a conflict would lead to the return to the Dark Ages. Books like Jonathan Schell's *The Fate of the Earth* (1982) and media images such as ABC television's special *The Day After* (1983) produced a degree of public unease not seen since the 1962 Cuban Missile Crisis.

The collapse of the Soviet Union and the end of the cold war in the late 1980s did not conclude American research and development—nor fears of a nuclear holocaust. In Russia, equipment malfunctions have accidentally switched Russian nuclear missiles to a "combat ready" status, and deteriorating security systems have increased the likelihood of weapons-grade materials falling into the hands of rogue states and terrorists. In the United States, major military contractors sought long-term sources of revenue to compensate for their post–cold war losses, and Republicans continued pushing for a defensive missile shield. In the mid-1990s the Department of Energy approved expenditures of hundreds of millions of dollars for superlasers and supercomputers to simulate weapons tests. A sub-critical nuclear weapons test, called Rebound, was conducted in 1997 at the Nevada Test Site. At the beginning of President George W. Bush's term, the 2001 Defense Authorization Bill was passed requiring that the Energy and Defense Departments study a new generation of precision, low-yield earth penetrating nuclear weapons to "threaten hard and deeply buried targets."

The Proliferation

Through espionage, huge national investments, and a black market of willing Western suppliers of needed technologies and raw materials, the American nuclear monopoly was broken with the successful detonations by the Soviet Union (1949), the United Kingdom (1952), France (1960), China (1964), India (1974), and Pakistan (1998).

Although the Western allies made the Soviet Union the scapegoat for the proliferation of nuclear weapons, it has been the export of Western technology and fuel that has given other countries the capability of building their own bombs. Although publicly dedicated to controlling the proliferation of "the bomb," in the fifty years following the Trinity detonation the United States shipped nearly a ton of plutonium to thirty-nine countries, including Argentina, India, Iran, Iraq, Israel, Japan, New Zealand, Pakistan, South Africa, Sweden, Turkey, Uruguay, and Venezuela.

The countries suspected of having (or having had) nuclear weapons programs include Iraq, Romania, North Korea, Taiwan, Brazil, Argentina, and South Africa. There is little doubt that the sixth member of the nuclear club is Israel, which was supplied a reactor complex and bomb-making assistance by the French as payment for its participation in the 1956 Suez Crisis. Despite its concerns over nuclear proliferation, the United States looked the other way as the Israeli nuclear program progressed, owing to the country's strategic position amid the oil-producing countries of the Middle East. When a Libyan airliner strayed over the highly secretive Negev Nuclear Research Center in 1973, Israeli jets shot it down, killing all 104 passengers.

Living with the Bomb

In *By the Bomb's Early Light* (1985) Paul Boyer asks how a society lives with the knowledge of its capacity for self-destruction. However such thinking was in vogue with the approach of the West's second millennium, with the media saturated with doomsday forecasts of overpopulation, mass extinctions, global warming, and deadly pollutants. By the end of the 1990s, half of Americans believed that some manmade disaster would destroy civilization.

The real possibility of nuclear war threatens the very meaning of all personal and social endeavors, and all opportunities for transcendence. In 1984, to dramatize the equivalency of nuclear war with collective suicide, undergraduates at Brown University voted on urging the school's health service to stockpile "suicide pills" in case of a nuclear exchange.

Such existential doubts were not mollified by the government's nuclear propaganda, which tended to depict nuclear war as a survivable natural event. Americans were told that "A Clean Building Seldom Burns" in the 1951 Civil Defense pamphlet "Atomic Blast Creates Fire," and that those who fled the cities by car would survive in the 1955 pamphlet "Your Car and CD [civil defense]: 4 Wheels to Survival."

Not even the young were distracted from thinking about the unthinkable. Civil defense drills became standard exercises at the nation's schools during the 1950s, including the "duck and cover" exercises in which students were instructed to "duck" under their desks or tables and "cover" their heads for protection from a thermonuclear blast. In the early 1980s, a new curriculum unit on nuclear war was developed for junior high school students around the country. Psychologists wrote about the implications of youngsters expecting never to reach adulthood because of nuclear war.

The Impacts of the Nuclear Arms Race on Culture and Society

In the words of Toronto sociologist Sheldon Ungar, "Splitting the atom dramatically heightened the sense of human dominion; it practically elevated us

The 1945 atomic bomb in the Japanese city of Hiroshima, one of the only times that nuclear weapons were used in warfare, instantly killed 100,000 people and injured thousands more, with the majority of its victims being civilians. GETTY IMAGES

into the empyrean. The control over nature's ultimate power was also taken as a sign of grace, an indication of America's moral superiority and redemptive capacity" (1992, p. 5). But this seeming benefaction turned into a nightmare, destroying Western faith in moral progress and providential history.

Scholars and essayists have speculated liberally on the psychological and cultural effects of growing up with the possibility of being vaporized in a nuclear war. For instance, did it contribute to permissive parenting strategies by older generations seeking to give some consolation to their children? Or the cultural hedonism and dissolution of mores evidenced when these children came of age? It certainly did contribute to the generational conflicts of the 1960s, as some baby boomers laid blame for the precarious times on older generations.

It is in the arts that collective emotions and outlooks are captured and explored, and fears of the atomic unknown surfaced quickly. As nuclear weapons tests resumed in Nevada in 1951, anxieties over radioactive fallout were expressed cinematically in a sci-fi genre of movies featuring massive mutant creatures. These were to be followed by end-of-the-world books (e.g., *Alas, Babylon* in 1959), films (e.g., *On the Beach* in 1959, *Fail-Safe* in 1964, *Dr. Strangelove* in 1964), television series *Planet of the Apes,* and music (e.g., Bob Dylan's "Hard Rain" and Barry McGuire's "Eve of Destruction").

The bomb also opened the door to UFOs. In the same state where the first nuclear bomb exploded two years earlier, near Roswell, New Mexico, an alien space ship supposedly crashed to Earth, although later reports have debunked that story despite the stubborn beliefs in an alien visitation by various UFO aficionados. Were they contemporary manifestations of angels, messengers carrying warnings of humanity's impending doom? Or did our acquisition of the ultimate death tool make our neighbors in the cosmos nervous? The latter idea was the theme of the 1951 movie *The Day the Earth Stood*

Still, where the alien Klaatu issued an authoritarian ultimatum to earthlings to cease their violence or their planet will be destroyed.

Harnessing the Atom for Peaceful Purposes

The logic of the death-for-life tradeoff runs deep throughout all cultural systems. It is a price we see exacted in the natural order, in the relationship between predator and prey, and in the economic order in the life-giving energies conferred by fuels derived from the fossils of long-dead animals. Over 80 percent of American energy comes from coal, oil, and gas, whose burning, in turn, produces such environment-killing by-products as acid rain.

This logic extends to attempts to harness nuclear energy for peacetime uses. In theory, such energy can be virtually limitless in supply. In the words of the science writer David Dietz, "Instead of filling the gasoline tank of your automobile two or three times a week, you will travel for a year on a pellet of atomic energy the size of a vitamin pill. . . . The day is gone when nations will fight for oil . . ." (Ford 1982, pp. 30–31). But it is a Faustian bargain because the by-products, most notably plutonium, are the most lethal substances known to man. Thousands of accidents occur annually in America's commercial nuclear plants. Collective memory remains vivid of the meltdown at the Chernobyl nuclear plant in the former Soviet Union in 1986 and the 1979 accident at Three Mile Island in Pennsylvania.

The Ecological Legacy

A comprehensive 1989 study by Greenpeace and the Institute for Policy Studies estimated that at least fifty nuclear warheads and 9 nuclear reactors lie on ocean floors because of accidents involving American and Soviet rockets, bombers, and ships. Radiation leaks south of Japan from an American hydrogen bomb accidentally dropped from an aircraft carrier in 1965. In the 1990s equipment malfunctions led to Russian missiles accidentally being switched to "combat mode," according to a 1998 CIA report.

The cold war rush to build nuclear weapons in the 1940s and 1950s led to severe contamination of the land and air. In one 1945 incident at the 560-square-mile Hanford nuclear reservation in Washington State, over a ton of radioactive material of roughly 350,000 to 400,000 curies (one curie being the amount of radiation emitted in a second by 1,400 pounds of enriched uranium) was released into the air. There, the deadly by-products of four decades of plutonium production leaked into the area's aquifer and into the West's greatest river, the Columbia. Fish near the 310-square-mile Savannah River site, where 35 percent of the weapons-grade plutonium was produced, are too radioactive to eat. Federal Energy Department officials revealed in 1990 that 28 kilograms of plutonium, enough to make seven nuclear bombs, had escaped into the air ducts at the Rocky Flats weapons plant near Denver.

Such environmental costs of the cold war in the Untied States are dwarfed by those of the former Soviet Union. In the early years of their bomb program at Chelyabinsk, radioactive wastes were dumped into the Techa River. When traces showed up 1,000 miles away in the Arctic Ocean, wastes were then pumped into Karachay Lake until the accumulation was 120 million curies—radiation so great that one standing on the lake's shore would receive a lethal dose in an hour.

The Corruption of Public Ethics

Perhaps even more devastating than the environmental damage wrought by the nuclear arms race was its undermining of public faith in government. Public ethics were warped in numerous ways. Secrecy for matters of national security was deemed paramount during the cold war, leaving Americans unaware of the doings of their government. The secrecy momentum expanded beyond matters of nuclear technologies and strategies when President Truman issued the first executive order authorizing the classification of nonmilitary information as well.

Some instances of severe radioactivity risk were kept secret from the public by federal officials. Thousands of workers—from uranium miners to employees of over 200 private companies doing weapons work—were knowingly exposed to dangerous levels of radiation. Though many of these firms were found by various federal agencies to be in violation of worker safety standards set by the Atomic Energy Commission, there were no contract cancellations or penalties assessed that might impede the pace of weapons production. After three decades of denials and fifty-seven years after the Manhattan Project began processing radioactive materials, the Federal government finally conceded in 2000 that nuclear weapons workers had been exposed to radiation and chemicals that produced cancer in 600,000 of them and early death for thousands of others.

The dangers extended well beyond atomic energy workers; ordinary citizens were exposed to water and soil contaminated toxic and radioactive waste. From 1951 to 1962, fallout from the Atomic Energy Commission's open-air nuclear blasts in the Nevada desert subjected thousands to cancer-causing radiation in farm communities in Utah and Arizona. According to a 1991 study by the International Physicians for the Prevention of Nuclear War, government officials expected this to occur but nevertheless chose this site over a safer alternative on the Outer Banks of North Carolina, where prevailing winds would have carried the fallout eastward over the ocean. The study predicted that 430,000 people will die of cancer over the remainder of the twentieth-century because of their exposures, and millions more will be at risk in the centuries to come.

According to a 1995 report of the Advisory Committee on Human Radiation Experiments, between 1944 and 1974 more than 16,000 Americans were unwitting guinea pigs in 435 documented radiation experiments. Trusting patients were injected with plutonium just to see what would happen. Oregon prisoners were subjected to testicular irradiation experiments at doses 100 times greater than the annual allowable level for nuclear workers. Boys at a Massachusetts school for the retarded were fed doses of radioactive materials in their breakfast cereal. And dying patients, many of whom were African Americans and whose consent forms were forged by scientists, were given whole-body radiation exposures.

Conclusion

Nuclear anxieties have migrated from all-out war among superpowers to fears of nuclear accidents and atomic attacks by rogue nations. According to Valentin Tikhonov, working conditions and living standards for nuclear and missile experts have declined sharply in post–Communist Russia. With two-thirds of these employees earning less than fifty dollars per month, there is an alarming temptation to sell expertise to aspiring nuclear nations. During its war with Iran, Iraq in 1987 tested several one ton radiological weapons designed to shower radioactive materials on target populations to induce radiation sickness and slow painful deaths. And during May of 1998, two bitter adversaries, India and Pakistan, detonated eleven nuclear devices over a three-week period.

Some believe that with the advent of nuclear weapons, peace will be forever safeguarded, since their massive use would likely wipe out the human race and perhaps all life on Earth. Critics of this outlook have pointed out that there has never been a weapon developed that has not been utilized, and that the planet Earth is burdened with a store of some 25,000 to 44,000 nuclear weapons.

See also: APOCALYPSE; DISASTERS; EXTINCTION; GENOCIDE; HOLOCAUST; WAR

Bibliography

Associated Press. "16,000 Now Believed Used in Radiation Experiments." *San Antonio Express-News,* 18 August 1995, 6A.

Boyer, Paul. *By the Bomb's Early Light: American Thought and Culture at the Dawn of the Atomic Age.* New York: Pantheon, 1985.

Broad, William J. "U.S. Planned Nuclear Blast on the Moon, Physicist Says," *New York Times,* 16 May 2000, A17.

Broad, William J. "U.S., in First Atomic Accounting, Says It Shipped a Ton of Plutonium to 39 Countries." *New York Times,* 6 February 1996, 10.

"Brown Students Vote on Atom War 'Suicide Pills.'" *New York Times,* 11 October 1984.

Ford, Daniel. *The Cult of the Atom: The Secret Papers of the Atomic Energy Commission.* New York: Simon and Schuster, 1982.

Institute for Energy and Environmental Research and the International Physicians for the Prevention of Nuclear War. *Radioactive Heaven and Earth: The Health and Environmental Effects of Nuclear Weapons Testing In, On and Above the Earth.* New York: Apex Press, 1991.

Leahy, William D. *I Was There: The Personal Story of the Chief of Staff to Presidents Roosevelt and Truman Based on His Notes and Diaries.* New York: Whittlesey House, 1950.

Maeroff, Gene I. "Curriculum Addresses Fear of Atom War." *New York Times,* 29 March 1983, 15, 17.

Maloney, Lawrence D. "Nuclear Threat through Eyes of College Students." *U.S. News & World Report,* 16 April 1984, 33–37.

Rosenthal, Andrew. "50 Atomic Warheads Lost in Oceans, Study Says." *New York Times,* 7 June 1989, 14.

Subak, Susan. "The Soviet Union's Nuclear Realism." *The New Republic,* 17 December 1984, 19.

Tikhonov, Valentin. *Russia's Nuclear and Missile Complex: The Human Factor in Proliferation.* Washington, DC: Carnegie Endowment for International Peace, 2001.

Toynbee, Arnold. *War and Civilization.* New York: Oxford University Press, 1950.

Ungar, Sheldon. *The Rise and Fall of Nuclearism: Fear and Faith As Determinants of the Arms Race.* University Park: Pennsylvania State University Press, 1992.

Welsome, Eileen. *The Plutonium Files: America's Secret Medical Experiments in the Cold War.* New York: Dial Press, 1999.

Werth, Alexander. *Russia at War.* New York: E. P. Dutton, 1964.

Internet Resources

Department of Energy. "Advisory Committee on Human Radiation Experiments: Final Report." In the Office of Human Radiation Experiments [web site]. Available from http://tis.eh.doe.gov/ohre/roadmap/achre/report.html.

Jacobs, Robert A. "Presenting the Past Atomic Café as Activist Art and Politics." In the Public Shelter [web site]. Available from www.publicshelter.com/main/bofile.html.

Public Broadcasting System. "The American Experience: Race for the Super Bomb." In the PBS [web site]. Available from www.pbs.org/wgbh/amex/bomb/index.html.

Wouters, Jørgen. "The Legacy of Doomsday." In the ABCnews.com [web site]. Available from http://abcnews.go.com/sections/world/nuclear/nuclear1.html.

MICHAEL C. KEARL

NURSING EDUCATION

Nurses spend more time with patients who are facing the end of life (EOL) than any other member of the health care team. In hospice, nurses have been recognized as the cornerstone of palliative care, and it is increasingly apparent that nurses play an equally important role in palliative care across all settings. Studies have documented that nurses and other members of the health care team are inadequately prepared to care for patients with pain at the EOL. Inadequate care of the dying continues to be a problem in the twenty-first century. Many reasons have been cited for this failure, including inadequacies in the basic and continuing education of health care providers.

Challenges to EOL Care

Numerous studies during the 1980s and 1990s have documented that nurses lack knowledge about pain control, one key aspect of EOL care. Pain management has been described as a situation in which physicians continue to underprescribe, nurses inadequately assess and undermedicate patients, and patients take only a portion of the analgesics prescribed or underreport their pain. Generally, physicians and nurses have an inaccurate knowledge base about common pharmacologic agents used in pain control and have exaggerated fears about the likelihood of addiction. The fear of addiction continues to be a major obstacle to adequate treatment of pain at the EOL.

However, pain management is only one aspect of EOL care. Other EOL needs include management of other physical and psychological symptoms, communication with patients and families, preparation of the staff and family care at the time of death, and many other aspects of care of the dying. Attention to EOL issues, such as a report by the Institute of Medicine on EOL care and action by the U.S. Supreme Court on the right to die, have prompted a focus beyond pain management to include other dimensions of EOL care.

Improving EOL Care

Two milestones, a key EOL care project supported by the Robert Wood Johnson Foundation conducted between 1997 and 2000 and its resultant recommendations and the 1997 Institute of Medicine report on EOL care, have addressed these deficiencies, resulting in increased awareness of EOL issues and spurring changes to EOL care and nursing education.

The Robert Wood Johnson Foundation Project. The Robert Wood Johnson Foundation funded study was conducted by the City of Hope investigators. The overall purpose of this project was to strengthen nursing education to improve EOL care by accomplishing three goals: (1) to improve the content regarding EOL care included in major textbooks used in nursing education; (2) to insure the adequacy of content in EOL care as tested by the national nursing examination, the NCLEX; and (3) to support the key nursing organizations in their efforts to promote improved nursing education and practice in EOL care.

The primary activity for the first goal, improving the content regarding EOL care in nursing textbooks, was a review of fifty major textbooks used in nursing education. These fifty texts were selected from a list of over 700 textbooks used in schools of nursing, and then were stratified by topic areas. The areas selected and number of books included were AIDS/HIV (1), assessment/diagnosis (3), communication (2), community/home health (4), critical care (4), emergency (2), ethics/legal issues (5), fundamentals (3), gerontology (3), medical-surgical (5), oncology (2), patient education (2), pediatrics (3), pharmacology (4), psychiatric (3), and nursing review (4).

A detailed framework for analyzing the content of the textbooks was developed by the City of Hope investigators. This framework was based on a review of current literature and expert opinion about optimum EOL care. Nine critical content areas were selected: palliative care defined; quality of life (physical, psychological, social, and spiritual well being); pain; other symptom assessment/management; communication with dying patients and their family members; role/needs of caregivers in EOL care; death; issues of policy, ethics, and law; and bereavement.

The fifty texts encompassed a total of 45,683 pages. Each text was reviewed using the framework. The reviewer scanned the complete index, table of contents, and all text pages for possible content. The reviewers were very inclusive and liberal in their approach, and when any EOL content was identified, those pages were copied. The copied pages then were analyzed for content using a "cut-and-paste" approach in which the content was placed on the analysis grid within the appropriate framework section. Key findings of the study were:

- Of the 45,683 pages of text reviewed, 902 pages were related to EOL content, representing only 2 percent of the total content.
- Of 1,750 chapters included in the texts, 24 were related to EOL, representing 1.4 percent of all chapters.
- The nine EOL topic areas reviewed were included infrequently in the texts' tables of contents or indexes. At least one chapter was devoted to an EOL-related topic in 30 percent of the texts.
- The EOL topics with the poorest focus in the texts were quality-of-life issues at EOL and role/needs of family caregivers. The areas of strongest content were pain and policy/ethics issues.
- Overall, 74 percent of the content in the framework was found to be absent from the texts, 15 percent was present, and 11 percent was present and commendable.

Recommendations from this analysis were presented to a conference of publishers and the City of Hope investigators continue follow up with the editors of these texts and other books in order to improve EOL content in future editions. Major progress has been made to date and the textbook editors and authors have been very responsive.

The second goal of the project, ensuring the adequacy of content in EOL Care, as tested by the NCLEX exam, was also successfully implemented. City of Hope investigators worked with the staff of the National Council of State Boards of Nursing to increase the emphasis of EOL care within the exam to increase its priority for nursing education, and thus the knowledge of practicing nurses. Goal three, supporting key organizations in their efforts to promote nursing education and practice in EOL care, was also achieved. Many nursing organizations have been mobilized to address the deficiencies in EOL care.

In addition to studying nursing education, City of Hope nurse researchers also surveyed over 2,300 practicing nurses to determine their perspectives on EOL care. Respondents were asked to rate these dilemmas based on their occurrence as "not common," "somewhat common," or "very common." The most frequently occurring dilemmas were use of advance directives and preserving patient choice/self-determination, which 37 percent and 23 percent, respectively, cited as very common. Interestingly, 93 percent of respondents cited requests for assisted suicide and requests for euthanasia as not common dilemmas, and 6 percent cited these requests as somewhat common. More than one-third of all nurses reported seven of the nine dilemmas, excluding those of assisted suicide and euthanasia, as somewhat common or very common. Acknowledging the diversity in responses to these dilemmas is important. For example, although 37 percent of respondents reported use of advance directives as very common dilemmas, 31 percent of the respondents reported this area as not common.

Respondents were also asked to rate how much of a barrier each factor was to providing good EOL care in their settings. The items were rated as "not a barrier," "somewhat of a barrier," or "a severe barrier." Respondents most frequently cited "influence of managed care on end-of-life care" (25%) as a severe barrier followed closely by "lack of continuity of care across settings" (23%). The barriers that were reported as common and the diversity of these barriers illustrate the complexity of effective EOL care. The respondents identified not only system barriers (e.g., continuity of care, influence of managed care) but also cited patients' (70%) and family members' (73%) avoidance of death as somewhat of a barrier. Other prominent barriers were health care providers' lack of knowledge and personal discomfort with death.

Institute of Medicine report. The Institute of Medicine report on improving EOL care concluded with seven recommendations, two of which spoke directly to the need for improved professional knowledge:

- Physicians, nurses, social workers, and other health care professionals must commit themselves to improving care for dying patients and using existing knowledge effectively to prevent and relieve pain and other symptoms.
- Educators and other health care professionals should initiate changes in undergraduate, graduate, and continuing education to ensure that practitioners have relevant attitudes, knowledge, and skills to provide good care for dying patients.

End-of-Life Nursing Consortium

The studies of the 1990s lead to the End-of-Life Nursing Education Consortium (ELNEC) project—a comprehensive, national education program to improve EOL care by nurses. Primary project goals include developing a core of expert nursing educators and coordinating national nursing education efforts in EOL care. This project points to the future of nursing education in the twenty-first century.

This three-and-a-half-year ELNEC project began in February 2000, and is a partnership of the American Association of Colleges of Nursing (AACN) and the City of Hope Cancer Center (COH). A primary goal of the project is to bring together leading nursing groups and perspectives to form a collaborative approach to improve EOL education and care. The ELNEC curriculum has been developed through the work of highly qualified subject matter experts serving as consultants, with extensive input from the advisory board and reviewers. Courses are designed to prepare educators to be instructional resources for their schools and organizations, and serve as a vital force in the dissemination of this important content.

ELNEC includes a total of eight courses, five of which are offered for baccalaureate and associate degree faculty who can then facilitate integration of EOL nursing care in basic nursing curricula. Two courses are planned for school-based, specialty organization, and independent nursing continuing education providers in order to influence practice of nurses in their target groups. The final course will be for state board of nursing representatives to strengthen their commitment to encourage end-of-life education and practice initiatives in their states. In addition, five regional ELNEC courses will be offered.

See also: COMMUNICATION WITH DYING; DEATH EDUCATION; PAIN AND PAIN MANAGEMENT; SYMPTOMS AND SYMPTOM MANAGEMENT

Bibliography

American Association of Colleges of Nursing. *A Peaceful Death.* Report from the Robert Wood Johnson End-of-Life Care Roundtable. Washington, DC: Author, 1997.

American Nurses Association. *Position Statement on Active Euthanasia and Assisted Suicide.* Washington, DC: Author, 1994.

Ferrell, Betty R. "End-of-Life Care: How Well do We Serve Our Patients?" *Nursing* 28, no. 9 (1998):58–60.

Ferrell, Betty R., Marcia Grant, and Rose Virani. "Strengthening Nursing Education to Improve End-of-Life Care." *Nursing Outlook* 47, no. 6 (1999):252–256.

Ferrell, Betty, Rose Virani, and Marcia Grant. "Analysis of End-of-Life Content in Nursing Textbooks." *Oncology Nursing Forum* 26, no. 5 (1999):869–876.

Ferrell, Betty, Rose Virani, Marcia Grant, Patrick Coyne, and Gwen Uman. "Beyond the Supreme Court Decision: Nursing Perspectives on End-of-Life Care." *Oncology Nursing Forum* 27, no. 3 (2000): 445–455.

Field, Marilyn J., and Chris K. Cassel, eds. *Approaching Death: Improving Care at the End of Life.* Report of the Institute of Medicine Task Force. Washington, DC: National Academy Press, 1997.

Internet Resources

American Association of Colleges of Nursing. "ELNEC Project." In the American Association of Colleges of Nursing [web site]. Available from www.aacn.nche.edu/ELNEC.

BETTY R. FERRELL

NUTRITION AND EXERCISE

Since the mid-1990s health practitioners, researchers, and scientists have learned that regular exercise and nutritional balance can significantly reduce degenerative diseases associated with aging and extend the human life span. The mechanism by which this occurs involves numerous physiological and biochemical mechanisms. For instance, researchers know that exercise improves neurological function by improving the transmission of nerve impulses in nerves and brain pathways. When this occurs, the human body experiences improved mood, faster reflexes, and better endocrine control.

Diabetes and Heart Attack Prevention

When engaged in a regular routine of exercise and a balanced diet, the human body experiences a reduction in many diseases that are associated with shortening of life, such as diabetes, hypertension, atherosclerosis, heart attack, and stroke. Cardiovascular disease is the number one killer in the industrialized world. In the United States alone, every year there are approximately 1 million deaths due to heart attacks. Hundreds of thousands more are left cardiac cripples, unable to work or enjoy life to the fullest. In addition, there are 16 million people diagnosed with diabetes every year and the numbers keep rising. Even more frightening is the fact that the disease is occurring at a younger age. Previously, non-insulin-dependent, or Type II, diabetes mellitus was considered a disease of middle age. Now it is being diagnosed in children as young as ten years of age. The incidence of this disease increased 40 percent from 1990 to 2000, with a 70 percent increase in thirty-year-olds during this same decade. Given these statistics, the benefits of regular exercise and good nutrition should be seriously considered by those who live in the Western world.

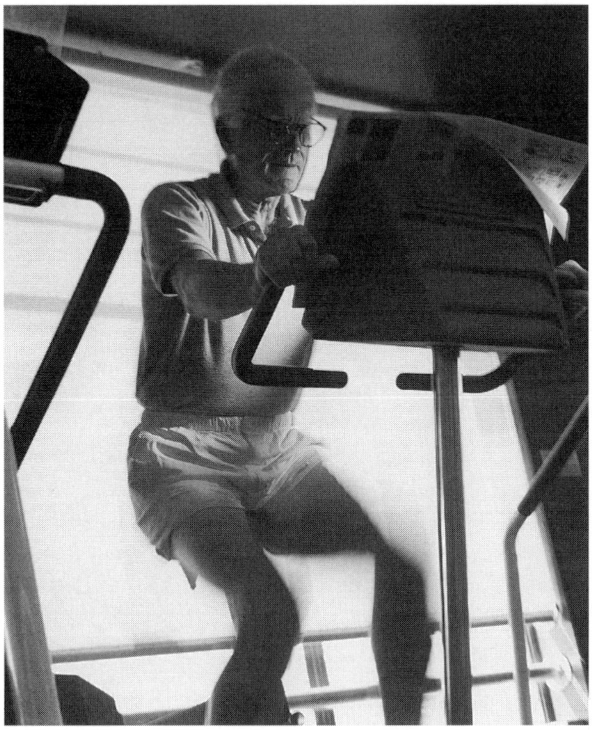

Regular exercise and the consumption of nutrient-dense vegetables help reduce the incidence of cardiovascular disease, diabetes, certain cancers, and brain aging. RAOUL MINSART/CORBIS

In addition, heart failure and diabetes are linked because diabetes accelerates atherosclerosis and can increase the risk of heart attacks and strokes by as much as sixfold. Diabetes is also associated with damage to numerous organs and tissues, including the kidneys, eyes, and nervous system. Diabetes is recognized as the leading cause of blindness and kidney failure in the United States.

These two conditions can be drastically reduced by a combination of regular exercise and balanced nutrition. For example, it has been recognized that there is a strong link between childhood Type II diabetes and obesity, with 90 percent of such children being obese. Conversely, while other factors play a role, lack of exercise and poor nutritional choices play a major role in both diseases. By flooding the body with a high intake of fats and simple sugars, cells become resistant to insulin function. That is, the pancreas is able to manufacture enough insulin but it is unable to transfer the glucose into the cell. If the process continues, the pancreas will eventually exhaust itself and be unable to produce more insulin. When this occurs, the diabetic person becomes insulin dependent, and is characterized as having Type I diabetes mellitus.

Medical professionals recognize that exercise improves glucose entry into the muscles and that many Type II diabetics can be managed or, in some cases, cured through a regular program of exercise and nutritional changes. Nutritional changes are particularly important and many failures are caused by the diabetic's failure to adhere to these dietary changes.

Numerous diseases are related to the production of free radicals by cells. Free radicals are destructive chemicals, mostly produced during metabolism that oxidize fats, DNA, and proteins within cells and tissues. For example, oxidation of fats within the walls of blood vessels is thought to result in the formation of atherosclerotic plaques that clog the arteries. Likewise, when diabetes develops the number of free radicals formed increases significantly, and when complications develop the rate increases dramatically. These free radicals begin to damage cells and tissues, resulting in the numerous complications associated with the disease.

Exercise not only reduces the incidence of the diseases responsible for many of these free radicals, but it induces the tissues and cells to produce more antioxidant enzymes. A diet high in fruits and vegetables, especially the more nutrient-dense vegetables, significantly reduces the incidence of cardiovascular disease and diabetes and reduces the severity of these disorders by providing the body with very powerful and versatile antioxidants.

Brain Aging and Cancer Prevention

Most people are aware of the vitamin-based antioxidants, such as vitamins A, C, and E, and the carotenoids (i.e., beta-carotene and lycopene), but of equal or greater importance are the plant-based flavonoids. Researchers have identified over 5,000 flavonoids, which have been shown to be powerful and versatile antioxidants against numerous types of free radicals—including many that are not neutralized by vitamins A, C, and E.

A multitude of studies have shown that a diet high in nutrient-dense vegetables and fruits can significantly lower the incidence of many cancers, hypertension, diabetes, and atherosclerosis, and delay nervous system aging. In one study, in which various fruits and vegetables were tested, it was found that blueberries, strawberries, and spinach were the most powerful in slowing brain aging, as measured by careful studies of brain chemistry and function. Regular exercise has also been shown to slow brain aging changes. When combined with good nutrition, an even greater effect can be expected.

Regular exercise and good nutrition have been shown to reduce the incidence of certain cancers as well. This is especially true for colon cancer and breast cancer. The explanation may lie in the improved immune function, increasing the number of antioxidant enzymes, and metabolic efficiency induced by exercise. Numerous nutritional components, such as vitamins, minerals, and flavonoids, have also been shown to significantly inhibit cancer formation, growth, and spread. Studies have shown that nutrients do this by a multitude of methods involving cell biochemistry and enhanced immunity.

Avoiding Overexercising

While exercise is critical to good health, too much exercise can be harmful, and even bring on many of the diseases human beings are attempting to prevent. This is because extreme exercise, by significantly increasing metabolism, also dramatically increases free radical production. As the human body ages, it produces more free radicals and accumulates more free radical damage in cells. Studies have shown that after age seventy DNA accumulates free radical damage ten times faster than at a younger age. Extreme exercise would be especially hazardous for the elderly. Moderate exercise has been shown to provide the same amount of health benefits as more vigorous exercise programs.

For ultimate benefits, doctors generally recommend that individuals exercise at a moderate level at least three times a week, avoid simple sugars, eat complex carbohydrates low on the glycemic index, maintain a fat intake slightly below 30 percent of caloric intake, and include a small amount of lean meats in their diets.

Bibliography

Berenson, Gerald S., et al. "Association between Multiple Cardiovascular Risk Factors and Atherosclerosis on Children and Young Adults." *The New England Journal of Medicine* 338 (1998): 1650–1656.

Blair, Stephen N., Harold W. Kohl, and Carolyn E. Barlow. "Physical Activity, Physical Fitness, and All-Cause Mortality in Women: Do Women Need to be Active?" *Journal of the American College of Nutrition* 12 (1993):368–371.

Blaylock, Russell L. "Neurodegeneration and Aging of the Central Nervous System: Prevention and Treatment by Phytochemicals and Metabolic Nutrients." *Integrative Medicine* 1 (1999):117–133.

Drake, D. A. "A Longitudinal Study of Physical Activity and Breast Cancer Prediction." *Cancer Nursing* 24 (2001):371–377.

Fliatarone, Maria A., et al. "Exercise Training and Nutritional Supplementation for Physical Frailty in Very Elderly People." *The New England Journal of Medicine* 330 (1994):1769–1775.

Kramsch, D. M., et al. "Reduction of Coronary Atherosclerosis by Moderate Conditioning Exercise in Monkeys on an Atherogenic Diet." *New England Journal of Medicine* 305 (1981):1483–1489.

Kujala, Urho M., Jaakko Kaprio, Seppo Sarna, and Markku Koskenvuo. "Relationship of Leisure-Time, Physical Activity and Mortality: The Finnish Twin Cohort." *Journal of the American Medical Association* 279 (1998):440–444.

Leon, A. S., J. Connett, D. R. Jacobs, and R. Rauramaa. "Leisure-Time Physical Activity Levels and Risk of Coronary Heart Diesease and Death: The Multiple Risk Factor Intervention Trial." *Journal of the American Medical Association* 285 (1987):2388–2395.

Littman, A. J., L. F. Voigt, S. A. Beresford, and N. S. Weiss. "Recreational Physical Activity and Endometrial Cancer Risk." *American Journal Epidemiology* 154 (2001):924–933.

Packer, Lester. "Oxidants, Antioxidant Nutrients and the Athlete." *Journal of Sports Science* 15 (1997):353–363.

Powell, Kenneth, Carl J. Caspersen, Jeffrey P. Koplan, and Earl S. Ford. "Physical Activity and Chronic Disease." *American Journal Clinical Nutrition* 49 (1989): 999–1006.

RUSSELL L. BLAYLOCK

O

Office of the Dead

See Christian Death Rites, History of.

Omens

Humans have always desired to break free from the "custody of time," to shed the anxiety engendered by uncertainty over the time of one's own death. The creation of death omens in nearly all cultures has, perhaps, arisen from a deep-seated yearning to quell this gnawing doubt. Such omens might take several various forms: the prediction of approaching death may be connected with specific dreams (whitewashing, tooth extraction, the fence falling, drowning in muddy water, and so on) or to the strange behavior or sudden appearance of certain animals (e.g., hens crowing or a visit from an owl, which are called "death-birds" in many cultures). Some death omens not only predict the fact of approaching death but also disclose its location and precise circumstances.

The following function analysis intends to examine the syncretic death omens of European peasants (the above mentioned examples are also taken from the experience of this cultural segment), in which both Christian and non-Christian elements may be found.

The Structure of Omen Beliefs

In traditional European peasant societies—the main focus of the ensuing remarks—death omens have functioned as a kind of code recognizing mechanism and as a guide to action. The most important task of code recognition is for the individual to connect and store the knowledge concerning the interdependence of the signifier, the signified, and the traditional meaning of the symbol as cultural code. This interdependence is necessary for the observer, for instance, to be able to associate the hooting of the owl landing upon the granary (as signifier) with death (as signified) and to draw a conclusion from the association that is considered conventional by the given culture.

Action strategies fall into three categories: The first category is group of communication rules that define the way in which the news of the omen may spread. It is a generally accepted rule that nobody should talk about bad dreams before sunrise and that news of bad omens should not be given to a dying person, especially someone in great pain, so that the victim should not fear that the relatives are looking forward to his or her death. Such omens are discussed among the neighbors or distant relatives. Nevertheless, if the critically ill person's condition is worsening—and the relatives seem to reject the possibility of the approaching exit—the neighbors may send for the priest to prevent the dying person from leaving this life without receiving the last rites.

Additionally, action strategies contain a preventive-evasive behavior model. Following such a model, the observer of the omen may try to prevent the impending death by means of various sacred magical rites. Prayers to saints, in particular to Saint Job, are said to cast off the realization of death-prophesying dreams. These should be offered immediately after awakening, before sunrise, or facing the rising sun. Praying in a group, crossing, practicing charity, asking the priest to say a mass—or a combination of the foregoing—are also frequently applied preventive measures.

If nobody is seriously ill or elderly in the neighborhood and the observer cannot therefore infer who the target of the omen is, he will decide to wait and will warn his family members to be exceedingly cautious. If the bad dream or other omen is not followed by a death until the end of the consensually established "incubation" period (generally three days, three weeks, or three months), the omen will cease to have any significance in the future.

Should the preventive-evasive acts prove ineffective, or if they seem worthless because of the advanced state of illness, an awaiting-preparing behavior model will be activated. If it can be inferred who is about to die in this case, the omen urges the observer to start realizing the possibility of an impending death and to measure its consequences.

On the other hand, the omen might warn the observer to prepare for the ritual group activity following the onset of death (e.g., vigil, funeral feast, burial) and to provide for the spiritual needs of the dying person (such as receiving the last rites). Consequently, the main purpose of the systems of behavior and beliefs connected with the portents is to ensure that neither the observer nor his immediate environment (nor indeed the dying person) is left entirely unprepared for the challenges of the approaching crisis.

The omens of death contain code recognizing techniques and sophisticated action strategies that are developed and inherited through direct communication. The latter constituent involves communicative rules as well as preventive-evasive and awaiting-preparatory behavioral instructions intended to prevent the realization of the ill omen and prepare all the affected members of the community for the approaching loss.

The Role of Death Omens in the Death Rituals

There are three partially overlapping, organically social and psychological functions of death omens. First, the conditioned sphere of activity in life periods when the observation of omens is not followed by death (within the culturally regulated "incubation period"); second, the realization-rationalization-preparation occurring in the crisis period preceding death; and, finally, the reorganizational function during the period of mourning.

Unfulfilled Omens

If approaching death cannot be anticipated by any other means than the observed omen, the observers will pay special attention to the surroundings, lamenting whomever the ill omen could refer to. When they cannot attribute the omen to a definite person, they forget it. In this way "there are always a few individuals in the community who are in a 'state of being warned.'" (Kunt 1980, p. 326) Although a number of omens remain unfulfilled, the individuals are never discouraged and do not consider this fact a failure of the omens' functioning mechanism. These omens are forgotten, and the next omen is received in the usual way.

In the state of "being warned," the observer individual recalls all the basic beliefs and behavior instructions of peasant attitudes toward death (the above mentioned action strategies; the belief in resurrection or heaven as "healing theories") that help to prevent the occurrence of death or conduce to survive the event with the smallest possible shock. In this way a background of worries triggering the observation of the omen or activated by the observation is brought to the "surface" in a culturally regulated frame and may be kept partially under cultural control.

In order to avoid a possible disturbance caused by the unfulfilled omen and to prevent the emergence of doubts about the reality and validity of omen beliefs, the peasant community has a number of plausible and unquestionable explanations at hand that help to interpret the situation in a "reassuring way." It is generally agreed that the absence of death is attributed to the devout intervention of transcendent powers (St. Job or Jesus). Occasionally it is explained by the success of danger-averting magic activities (i.e., killing the crowing hen.) The generally accepted interpretation is that the clearing of the danger is not due to "malfunctioning" of the omen but to the favorable influence and mercy of transcendent powers.

It is precisely for this reason that if the omen is not followed by a death within the conventionally accepted "incubation" period, the "preshock" state results in a new equilibrium, relegitimizing the faith in the basic Christian regulating principles of the peasant world-and-death concept, and the particular omen is forgotten. (Naturally, the omen may well be related to deaths occurring years after its appearance.)

In that case the omen's conditioning function becomes significant, which serves to strengthen fundamental principles, beliefs of peasant death concept (belief in life after death and resurrection, adhering to the prescriptions of Christian ethics, and so on). This is precisely why all unfulfilled omens are "really a symbolically expressed 'Memento mori' " (Kunt 1980, p. 327).

Omens Appearing Immediately Prior to Death

In traditional accounts, members of peasant communities are far more likely to observe omens portending death (especially in the form of negative dreams) if they have been tending a seriously ill or dying relative. In this period, anticipation of death may be more manifest in the dream-work, which makes possible the activation of the realization function. In the European peasant communities predictions based upon dreams have always been considered an accepted, legitimate method of gaining knowledge of reality. The world of dreams is outside the observer; it is interpreted as an authentic and objective system of prophecy. Thus, dreams as widely accepted form of knowledge, are particularly suitable for transforming negative foreboding into a realization of the inevitability of the impending death; they foretell and realize the fact of death of the ill relative in the form of a confirming feedback.

Traditional explanations about omens that appear immediately before death may contain estimates of the expected length of the expected interval before the onset of death. It is a common belief, for example, that the strange behavior of animals only briefly precedes the onset of death—twenty-four hours at the most. The last phase of dying is marked by the death-bed visions (Kastenbaum 2000; Parkes 1998; Rososenblatt, Walsh, and Jackson 1976; Zaleski 1987) in which the deceased relatives of the ill person appear and he or she talks to them aloud, tussles with them. (The arrival of deceased relatives is signaled by such events as the door of the dying person's room opening by itself or by the mirror falling from the wall.) The family standing around the deathbed interprets this phenomenon of visitation by the dead as if the deceased are waiting for the dying person, calling him or her to them, and that after the person's departure from this life it is they who will lead the way to the other world.

The significance of the rationalizing function exemplified above is that through the approximate time coordinates built upon traditional experience, death omens play a significant part in distinguishing the stages of the dying process. In this sphere of activity at least two advantageous effects are worth mentioning.

The first is that these time coordinates mark the events leading up to death as a gradual process and are thus able to alleviate the elemental feeling of anxiety connected with the unpredictability of the exact time of the death. Second, these temporal reference points may help the relatives to carry out their duties properly because their observation has an activating function; they urge and warn the observers to fulfill their tasks accompanying the final stages of death (i.e., calling for the priest to perform the last rites). In this way the omens immediately preceding death have a preparatory role as well: They inform the immediate environment of the dying person of the approaching death, and they prompt the family to start accustoming themselves to the situation and to concentrate their spiritual energy.

The survival of portents appearing immediately prior to death is primarily due to the fact that they were able to provide approximate points of reference and time coordinates in cases where official Christian guidance regarding the crisis period left people without counsel (or the guidance provided tended to be generalizing and impersonal). In other words, these omens essentially filled the "blank areas" of Christian interpretations of the death process.

Retrospective Interpretation: The Reorganizational Function

Often, in peasant death culture, after the last respects are paid to the next of kin, close neighbors convene to discuss and evaluate the events in the crisis period leading to the death. These discussions cover the portents of death, the process of dying, the number of people attending the funeral, their behavior, and so on.

Several studies have made it clear that in such discussions a number of events and episodes were identified as omens that had not been deemed as such earlier—occasionally because they trusted in the sick person making an unexpected recovery, so they tried to ignore any signs to the contrary.

This process, defined as retrospective meaning attribution, may contribute significantly to the success of the grief-work process, the fast and successful modification of the survivor's "assumptive world to incorporate loss, thereby achieving a new sense of normalcy and purpose" (Gilbert 1995, p. 310).

Its foremost support in the grief work is in the way in which the closest relatives build into their memory of the dying process motifs retrospectively identified as omens, thereby partly modifying their original impressions. The retrospectively incorporated omens are interpreted in the final, modified narrative about death as indicator elements (which help the survivors to cut the process of dying into discrete segments), thus helping to alleviate the relative's own painful vulnerability to death.

Through retrospective meaning attribution the close relatives partly rewrite their memories of the dying process, unconsciously adapting it to the prerequisites of successful grief work by comprehending the process of departure in a manner more rational and foreseeable than reality—thus facilitating the coping with loss.

However, if the dying person was not cared for properly (e.g., could not receive the last rite because the family misinterpreted the situation), the evaluation of omens may also bring about remorse—and that could lead to a breakdown in grief work and the appearance of pathological reactions.

Conclusion

While all omens preceding death are considered to be elements of rites of separation (Gennep 1960; Littlewood 1993), retrospective meaning attribution incorporates rites that help to humanize and rationalize the preserved impressions of dying and death; it also fosters the development of a new relationship between the surviving kin and the departed individual by transforming their relationship into "an inner representation based on memory, meaning and emotional connection" (Romanoff and Terenzio 1998, p. 701). It may also facilitate the mourners' early reintegration into the wider community, into the traditional order of peasant life, and help to strengthen their faith in its essential principles and values.

See also: GRIEF AND MOURNING IN CROSS-CULTURAL PERSPECTIVE; GRIEF: ANTICIPATORY, THEORIES; NEAR-DEATH EXPERIENCES; MEMENTO MORI

Bibliography

Fulton, Robert, and Julie Fulton. "A Psychosocial Aspect of Terminal Care: Anticipatory Grief." In Richard A. Kalish ed., *Caring Relationships: The Dying and the Bereaved.* New York: Baywood, 1977.

Gennep, Arnold van. *The Rites of Passage.* 1909. Reprint, Chicago: University of Chicago Press, 1960.

Gilbert, Kathleen R. "Family Loss and Grief." In Randal D. Day, Kathleen R. Gilbert, Barbara H. Settles, and Wesley R. Burr eds., *Research and Theory in Family Science.* Pacific Grove: Brooks/Cole, 1995.

Gilliland, Glenda, and Stephen Fleming. "A Comparison of Spousal Anticipatory Grief and Conventional Grief." *Death Studies* 22 (1998):541–570.

Kastenbaum, Robert. *The Psychology of Death,* 3rd edition. London: Free Association Books, 2000.

Kunt, Erno. "Hiedelemrendszer És társadalmi parancs" (Systems of Popular Belief and Social Directives.) In Frank Tamás and Hoppál Mihály eds., *Hiedelemrendszer És társadalmi tudat I-II.* Budapest: Tömegkommunikációs Kutatóközpont, 1980.

Lindemann, Erich. "The Symptomatology and Management of Acute Grief." *American Journal of Psychiatry* 101 (1944):141–148.

Littlewood, Jane. "The Denial of Death and Rites of Passage in Contemporary Societies." In David Clark ed., *The Sociology of Death.* Oxford: Blackwell, 1993.

Parkes, Colin Murray. *Bereavement Studies of Grief in Adult Life.* Harmondsworth: Penguin Books, 1998.

Romanoff, Bronna D., and Marion Terenzio. "Rituals and the Grieving Process." *Death Studies* 22 (1998): 697–711.

Rosenblatt, Paul C., R. Patricia Walsh, and Douglas A. Jackson. *Grief and Mourning in Cross-Cultural Perspective.* New Haven, CT: Human Relations Area Files Press, 1976.

Stroebe, Margaret. "Coping with Bereavement: A Review of the Grief Work Hypothesis." *Omega: The Journal of Death and Dying* 26 (1992–1993):19–42.

Zaleski, Carol. *Otherworld Journeys. Accounts of Near-Death Experience in Medieval and Modern Times.* Oxford: Oxford University Press, 1987.

PETER BERTA

ONTOLOGICAL CONFRONTATION

Human beings have a degree of awareness of personal existence not found among other species. This awareness, the province of ordinary people as much as philosophers and theologians, encompasses the finitude of life, the personal existence of others, the possibility of other worlds, and the questions of when people came into the world, why they are on Earth, and what happens when they die. Asking these questions is motivated not merely by curiosity but also by the anguish inspired by the prospect of one's own death or that of a loved one.

The most powerful ontological confrontation occurs when facing the inevitability of one's own death, whether as an immediate reality or as an imagined, distant eventuality. How does one confront his or her own real death? In the highly developed countries, more people die a long and slow death (e.g., from cancer or from AIDS). People experience ever longer waits for life-saving surgery. Although little is known about how individuals cope with impending death, there does seem to be a common avoidance of ontological questions, even on the deathbed.

What about the anticipation of death? How does one confront the finite nature of life? These questions arise persistently in philosophy and literature. For example, psychotherapist Jeffrey Kauffman presented the philosophical perspective by editing the book *Awareness of Mortality* (1995). He stated that awareness of mortality is the alpha and omega of thanatology (where it starts from and where it is heading). But what are the consequences of this confrontation for the individual? There is various anectodal evidence but little in the way of systematic research. This question has, however, come under experimental scrutiny, and there are only a few areas of thanatology where results of experimental studies provide new insights. In everyday life, the idea of death may enter the mind many times a day even for individuals unconcerned with death. This kind of ontological confrontation can also take place in a laboratory, where researchers have discovered that the confrontation with death leads to cognitive reactions and to various emotional responses that can have positive or negative effects.

Consequences of Confrontation with Death

Existential philosophers and psychotherapists focus on the positive consequences of ontological confrontation. For example, Irvin Yalom emphasizes that the idea of death is a powerful agent of change. Facing one's own death is the highest challenge to the individual, potentially imparting greater intensity to life and even leading to a radical personal transformation. A literary example of this process is Leo Tolstoy's classical story "The Death of Ivan Ilych." Faced with imminent death, Ilych taps previously dormant resources of empathy for his family and friends, and his former fear of death is replaced by a fulfilling sense of well being. Working with cancer patients in a therapeutic group setting, Yalom has shown that cancer can heal psychoneurosis. It is astonishing that tragedies such as life-threatening illnesses or losses of significant others can be followed by an increase of personal maturity.

In his book *Is There an Answer to Death,* Peter Koestenbaum also wants to show the positive consequences of ontological confrontation by demonstrating that there are times when dealing with existential questions can bring a greater meaning to life. He argues that the anticipation of death reveals who one really is. Intellectually, death helps to define human nature and brings people into contact with their deepest feelings, needs, and opportunities.

According to Koestenbaum, anticipation of death can have the following ten consequences:

1. By accepting the fact of being condemned to death, the individual can start living and thereby then neutralize fear.
2. By recognizing death, the individual is on the way to becoming decisive.
3. By remembering death, the individual concentrates on essentials.

4. By being aware of death, the individual achieves integrity.
5. Through knowing about death, the individual finds meaning in life.
6. By recognizing death, the individual will become honest.
7. Through the realization of death, the individual will gain strength.
8. By accepting death, the individual is motivated to take charge of his or her own life.
9. Through the thought of death, the individual is willing to assume a total plan for life.
10. By being aware of death, the individual escapes the stranglehold of failure.

From an existential and phenomenological perspective, meditation on personal death is a precondition for achieving meaning and freedom of fear in everyday life. Adrian Tomer has shown, however, that other philosophical approaches contend that reflection on death does not necessarily confer meaning on life and that it is even questionable whether facing death is the best way to deal with the problem of death. The psychologist Patrick C. Thauberger and his colleagues used the construct labeled "avoidance of ontological confrontation" as the basis of an empirical study whose results challenge the notion that awareness is the answer to the problem of death. Individuals classified as "existential confronters" did report significantly more use of stimulants and soft drugs. Being that ontological confrontation is also negatively related to self-reported health and quality of life, it seems that one must pay a price when trying to face death. Confronters were no better off than "avoiders of the confrontation with death," who required a few agents (e.g., tranquilizers) of their own to deal with reality. Overall, the results suggest a rather complex network of relationships among avoidance/-confrontation strategies, various kinds of social behavior, and health-related variables.

There is also empirical evidence that ontological confrontation leads to changes of beliefs. Investigating the notion that belief in afterlife serves the function of helping the individual to deal with fear of death, Michael Osarchuk and Sherman Tatz selected subjects scoring high and low on a belief-in-afterlife scale and exposed them to stimuli designed to arouse fear of death, to the threat of being shocked, or to a nonthreatening task. Comparing the scores on an alternate belief-in-afterlife scale, only the high believers exposed to death threat intensified their belief that there is a life after death. Data obtained by Randolph Ochsmann, however, does not support this notion because strengthening belief-in-afterlife was not accompanied by lower scores of anxiety. With highly religious subjects, confrontation with death did not intensify this belief. The low religionists, however, showed even less of an inclination to believe in an afterlife and intensified their hedonistic preferences.

The consequences of ontological confrontation can be discerned empirically. In one experimental study, Christian subjects either considered or not considered the question of their own death, and were then asked to rate target persons on an interpersonal attraction scale. Ontological confrontation caused them on the one hand to rate a target peron significantly more favorable who was presented as a fellow Christian, that is an ingroup member. On the other hand, thinking of their own death led to much less favorable ratings of target persons who were presented as Jews, that is outgroup members. The same pattern was found in a second study when subjects rated target persons who either held very similar or very dissimilar attitudes. Thus it seems that mortality salience leads to more negative evaluations of outgroup members and those who criticize one's culture. It provokes harsher punishment for moral transgressors and increased aggression against those who challenge one's beliefs. Another study has shown that for individuals for whom driving ability is a barometer of self-esteem, mortality salience leads to increased risk-taking while driving and while driving in a simulator task.

Implications

Results of experimental studies cannot be applied directly to everyday life, of course. Most likely, there are psychological factors that will weaken the effects of mortality salience. But it cannot be ruled out that other interactive forces will lead to an increase of negative consequences, for example, and even stronger favoritism of ingroup members and discrimination of outgroup members. Nonetheless, reported results do raise some serious questions.

For example, it seems necessary to discuss the situation of individuals who care for the terminally ill. Basic fears of death caused by the salience of mortality are prominent among caregivers. While attending to the dying, professional and nonprofessional helpers sometimes fend off their fears, but this defensive repression is less successful when confrontation with death is very frequent. Does mortality salience contribute to emotional exhaustion and depersonalization "burnout"? Knowing that ontological confrontation will lead to greater anxiety among individuals with low self-esteem, one should reconsider demands of institutional caregivers who are expected to subordinate their own psychological well-being to that of the patient. Professional helpers themselves should be more sensitive to their own "terror management" to improve interaction with the terminally ill and persons who suffer severe loss. Discrepancies between the altruistic motivations of caregivers and their actual behavior might well be linked to low self-esteem and the necessity of defensive reactions. Considering the potentially negative consequences of ontological confrontation, death-education programs should receive much more attention.

Research also indicates that mortality salience may lead to hostile reactions toward "outsiders," members of other cultures who might present a threat to the individuals' self-esteem, especially in homogeneous cultures that do not prize diversity. Under such conditions, hostility toward foreigners might increase proportionately with the anxiety arising from confronting death. It might not be accidental that far-right groups often stage meetings at cemeteries to honor so-called heroes, and publicly wear death symbols (e.g., skulls and crossbones). The individual's fundamentally defensive need to protect himself from anxiety must therefore be incorporated into programs developed to fight intolerance, racism, and xenophobia.

There is evidence that mortality salience has an effect on intentionally risky behavior such as unsafe sex, extreme sports, which is a growing problem in advanced industrial societies. Among adolescents and young adults, car accidents are one of the most common causes of death. Appeals to fear evidently do not work when the self-esteem of a person is linked to driving or other kinds of risky behaviors. On the contrary, people may be motivated to take even greater risks after confronting death.

Robert Kastenbaum has discussed the negative consequences of ontolological confrontation in the context of possible links between terror management and some major social problems, such as murder, suicide, alcohol, and drugs. What happens when there is no management of terror? What happens when there is neither individual self-esteem nor a cultural belief system to defend against death anxiety? There is ample reason to doubt that contemporary industrialized cultures are fostering a meaningful conception of reality that instills self-esteem and hence respect for the humanity of others inside and outside the culture.

See also: AIDS; ANXIETY AND FEAR; BECKER, ERNEST; BONSEN, F. Z.; CANCER; KIERKEGAARD, SØREN; MEMENTO MORI; NEAR-DEATH EXPERIENCES; PSYCHOLOGY; TERROR MANAGEMENT THEORY

Bibliography

Greenberg, Jeff, Tom Pyszczynski, and Sheldon Solomon. "The Causes and Consequences of a Need for Self-Esteem: A Terror Management Theory." In Roy Baumeister ed., *The Private and the Public Self.* New York: Springer, 1986.

Greenberg, Jeff, Tom Pyszczynski, Sheldon Solomon, et al. "Evidence for Terror Management Theory II: The Effects of Mortality Salience on Reactions to Those Who Threaten or Bolster the Cultural Worldview." *Journal of Personality and Social Psychology* 58 (1990):308–318.

Harmon-Jones, Eddie, Jeff Greenberg, Sheldon Solomon, and Linda Simon. "The Effects of Mortality Salience on Intergroup Bias Between Minimal Groups." *European Journal of Social Psychology* 25 (1996):677–681.

Kastenbaum, Robert. *The Psychology of Death,* 3rd edition. New York: Springer, 2000.

Kauffman, Jeffrey, ed. *Awareness of Mortality.* Amityville, NY: Baywood, 1995.

Koestenbaum, Peter. *Is There an Answer to Death?* Englewood Cliffs, NJ: Prentice-Hall, 1976.

McGregor, Holly, Joel Lieberman, Jeff Greenberg, Sheldon Solomon, Jamie Arndt, and Linda Simon. "Terror Management and Aggression: Evidence That Mortality Salience Motivates Aggression against Worldview-Threatening Others." *Journal of Personality and Social Psychology* 74 (1998):590–605.

Ochsmann, Randolph. *Angst vor Tod und Sterben: Beiträge zur Thanato-Psychologie.* Göttingen: Hogrefe, 1993.

Osarchuk, Michael, and Sherman J. Tatz. "Effect of Induced Fear of Death on Belief in Afterlife." *Journal of Personality and Social Psychology* 27 (1973):256–260.

Rosenblatt, Abram, Jeff Greenberg, Sheldon Solomon, Tom Pyszczynski, and Deborah Lyon. "Evidence for Terror Management Theory I: The Effects of Mortality Salience on Reactions to Those Who Violate or Uphold Cultural Values." *Journal of Personality and Social Psychology* 57 (1989):681–690.

Smith, Marion Brewster. "Perspectives on Selfhood." *American Psychologist* 33 (1978):1053–1063.

Solomon, Sheldon, Jeff Greenberg, and Tom Pyszczynski. "A Terror Management Theory of Social Behavior: The Psychological Functions of Self-Esteem and Cultural Worldviews." In Mark P. Zanna ed., *Advances in Experimental Social Psychology,* Vol. 24. New York: Academic Press, 1991.

Taubman Ben-Ari, Orit, Victor Florian, and Mario Mikulincer. "The Impact of Mortality Salience on Reckless Driving: A Test of Terror Management Mechanisms." *Journal of Personality and Social Psychology* 76 (1999):35–45.

Thauberger, Patrick C., John F. Cleland, and Eileen M. Thauberger. "Some Indices of Health and Social Behavior Associated with the Avoidance of the Ontological Confrontation." *Omega: The Journal of Death and Dying* 14, no. 3 (1983–1984):279–289.

Tomer, Adrian. "Death Anxiety in Adult Life—Theoretical Perspectives." In Robert A. Neimeyer ed., *Death Anxiety Handbook.* Washington, DC: Taylor & Francis, 1994.

Yalom, Irvin D. *Existential Psychotherapy.* New York: Basic Books, 1980.

RANDOLPH OCHSMANN

OPERATIC DEATH

Opera began in the last decades of the sixteenth century in Florence, Italy, when a group of music and drama enthusiasts called the Camerata decided that ancient Greek drama must have been sung throughout. While there is evidence that music played a role in the theater of ancient Greece, this surmise of the Camerata involved a leap of the imagination: What if the words were declaimed as song? From this idea sprang opera. The form has gone through so many changes according to era, national, and individual temperament that it challenges common sense to draw it all under one umbrella. Yet the constant of sung drama has remained.

As the earliest operas were modeled after a certain conception of Greek drama, the tragic ones among them naturally reflected an idea of death in line with their model. The first operas took plots from mythology, including Claudio Monteverdi's *Orfeo* (1607), the oldest opera still produced with any regularity. The story is the familiar one that begins when the happy marriage of Orpheus to Euridice is terminated by Euridice's death. The gods then give Orpheus permission to travel into the underworld to retrieve his wife, such is his love for her. Their single prohibition: "Do not look at her until you reach the sunlight." Of course, he cannot resist a glance backward and the entire enterprise is ruined. The story links love and death; in a very broad sense, the ensuing history of tragic opera has been an elaboration on that theme.

Love and Death

Peter Conrad's *A Song of Love and Death: The Meaning of Opera* (1987) addresses this confluence of Eros and Thanatos. Conrad espouses the theory that desire and annihilation in opera directly parallel their respective personifications in Greek mythology: Apollo (god of the sun and reason, and therefore of individual desire) and Dionysus (god of wine and therefore of the obliteration of individual consciousness). He uses the theory of the nineteenth-century German philosopher Friedrich Nietzsche in support of his idea that the history of opera forms a kind of dialectic in which desire fulfilled is desire destroyed (Conrad 1987).

In the beginning, however, opera was less a quest to bind love and death than to portray them as mutually exclusive opposites. Death in the earliest operas is accompanied neither by the quest for Apollonian individuation nor a need for self-forgetting, though both emotional states play roles in later operas. Instead, many characters in early operas die simply for lack of love, frequently accompanied by the most wretched self-pity. In Henry Purcell's *Dido and Aeneas* (1689), the first English opera to find a permanent place in the repertoire, the climax of the score occurs when Dido, deserted by the Trojan Aeneas so that he may go found the city of Rome and father Western civilization, cries in music her famous Lament. "Death must come when he is gone," she sings, weeping herself to death, though in "reality" she dies atop a funeral pyre. This mood of pulling one's own tragic death around the shoulders like a blanket would be revived briefly in the nineteenth century and given to the same character, when Berlioz's Dido in *Les Troyens* sings in French: "Je vais mourir / Dans ma douleur immense submergee," which is interpreted as, "I wish to die, In my immense anguish submerged."

In the early eighteenth century opera became highly formalized. *Opera seria* (tragic opera) and *opera buffa* (comic opera) both took on rigid formulas in which certain sorts of characters recurred and a handful of librettos (texts) were recycled among composers such as Gluck and Handel, less as inspiration to tell stories in music than as excuses to display technique. This was the age of the castrato, the castrated male singer whose unnaturally high, pure sound was relished by knowledgeable opera goers. Opera seria was chorus-less, representing a disappearance of society from the stage. Without the presence of society, and without the threat of sex (the castrato was, after all, harmless) opera took on a strange coolness. Sexual love was replaced by fanciful sentiment, tragedy was muted by its isolation.

Wolfgang Amadeus Mozart is a singular case with regard to the subject of opera, just as he was exceptional in most other regards. In a short span of time, he virtually founded modern opera, fulfilling and then abandoning the old opera seria, reinvigorating the German form known as Singspiel and, with librettist Lorenzo da Ponte, inventing a new form in which full-blooded characters experienced life in ways that conformed neither to tragic nor comic preconceptions.

Although as a Freemason he espoused belief in death as "man's best friend," and while one of his last completed pieces was a work for use in Masonic funeral ceremonies, Mozart seemed to shy away from death in certain key operatic and even religious scores. In his setting of the Latin Mass in C Minor (1781), Mozart waxed operatic, with solos and choruses worthy of the stage. Left unfinished, its omissions are telling. The twenty-five-year-old composer did not merely take the Latin text as far as he could, one movement after another, but instead stopped cold at the point in the credo in which Jesus is made man—the extraordinarily beautiful Et Incarnatus Est. The remainder of the credo deals with Jesus's crucifixion, death, and resurrection, yet Mozart skipped over this to the following movement, the *Sanctus-Benedictus,* and never returned to finish it. This deliberate avoidance of portions of text dealing with death is all the more peculiar, as the score was composed as a memorial for his mother.

Mozart loved opera from early in life and composed for the theater until his death at age thirty-five. He composed his first opera seria, *Mitridate,* at age fourteen and his last, *Idomeneo,* at age twenty-three. In both, fathers wrong their sons, to whom it is left to redeem the fathers' actions. King Mitridate distrusts both sons and envies the love one of them enjoys with the beautiful Aspasia. Only in death does he see the truth and ask his sons' forgiveness. The unlucky title character in *Idomeneo* pledges his son, Idamante, in sacrifice, but this is avoided and the son, at close, is morally triumphant.

As soon as he was done with opera seria, Mozart was, for all intents and purposes, done with death onstage. In his triptych of operas made in collaboration with Lorenzo Da Ponte—*The Marriage of Figaro, Don Giovanni,* and *Cosi fan tutte*—life takes center stage and is flooded with light. Forgiveness among quarreling and conspiring lovers is the theme of both *The Marriage of Figaro* and *Cosi fan tutte.* Death figures only in *Don Giovanni,* when the famous lover (Don Juan of legend) kills the father of one of his conquests in a duel, and is later himself dragged to hell by the dead father's shadow. Even so, Giovanni's killing of the Commendatore is an act of self-defense, not premeditated murder, and when Giovanni is pulled to hell, the punishment seems inappropriate. In some versions of the opera an ensemble of Giovanni's friends and enemies sing about life after his death and the distinct feeling is one of loss. An aspect of life has been condemned by moral agent (the Commendatore) and snuffed out.

In *The Magic Flute,* Mozart's penultimate opera and one steeped in Masonic ritual and symbolism, the characters do not die, though at the end several of them are vanquished from the holy realm of the supremely wise Sarastro. Flute is a psychological study, and just as the early degrees of Freemasonry are initiations into one's own inner states, the various characters in the opera may be seen as parts of one ideal character. The hero Tamino is that character's questing self, while the sidekick Papageno calls himself the "doppelganger," or Tamino's superficial double. Tamino contains within himself the archetype of the Mother, personified as the Queen of the Night, and an anima figure with a name much like his, Pamina. The evil Monostatos is his shadow, and the great Sarastro the Wise Man he would become. The dark archetypes are vanquished, but death as such does not appear in *The Magic Flute*.

The title says all in Mozart's final opera, *La Clemenza da Tito*. The clemency of the Emperor Titus is the subject and the end of an opera that commemorates forgiveness, reason, and free will, completely contradicting the operatic tradition of revenge, emotional chaos, and fate. But all of that made a quick comeback.

Bel canto ("beautiful singing") opera was the most popular in early-nineteenth-century Italy. Vincenzo Bellini and Gaetano Donizetti were among its greatest practitioners. Donizetti was unusual in his ability to compose very effectively in both comic and tragic modes. His *Daughter of the Regiment* (1840) is so light that it could fly away, while *Lucia di Lammermoor* (1835) probably deserves the prize for the bloodiest opera written before the twentieth century.

In *Lucia,* love and death make a huge return. The Scottish lass Lucy, of the castle Lammermoor, is in love with Edgar of Ravenswood and he with her. But her brother Henry has other plans and forces Lucy to marry a man named Bucklaw for money and advantage. On her wedding night, Lucy goes insane and stabs Bucklaw to death, then sings a very long and very effective insanity scene, accompanied by flute and usually draped in a bloody nightdress, then collapses, dead of sheer sorrow. Not to leave anyone innocent alive, Donizetti has Edgar stab himself to death at Lucy's grave.

Thus did the bel canto tradition revive the marriage of Eros and Thanatos. Society was back, too, in the form of large choruses that sang commentary on the action while distancing themselves from the horror. Death does not happen to crowds; it comes only to individuals.

Giuseppe Verdi summed up the traditions that had gone before and created, over a period of several decades, a body of work that forms the very center of most opera houses, at least in the United States. He was much stronger a tragedian than he was a comedian, and the sense of doom forecast in a typical Verdi opera is palpable from the start. Love and death now started to merge. Verdi's *Aida* (1872) offers perhaps the clearest single example of the purity of their union. The Egyptian Radames loves the enslaved Aida and proclaims it in the aria "Celeste Aida," translated as "Heavenly Aida." The beauty of the music and the extra-earthly location of Radames' praise immediately signal death at the end of the tunnel. And indeed, at the end, Radames and Aida, the victims of political wrangling and the circumstances of birth, are together in a tomb, awaiting their suffocation together song singing, "O terra, addio!" or "O earth, farewell!"

Dying for love is permitted, even praiseworthy, but murder for revenge will get its karmic due. In Verdi's *Rigoletto* (1851), the hapless title character, a hunchbacked jester, believes the dying human in a sack he is about to throw into the river is the Duke of Mantua, whose murder he has plotted. Instead it is his own daughter, Gilda, who dies in the duke's place.

The Verdi opera that most crucially mixes love and death with greatest intensity is also the composer's most unusual opera, *La Traviata* (1853). Alone among his works, *La Traviata* takes place in the composer's own time; every other Verdi opera happens among ancient nobility or in biblical times. Based on the play *The Lady of the Camelias* by the French novelist and playwright Alexandre Dumas, *La Traviata* finds the courtesan Violetta in love with dashing, callow, young Alfredo Germont. When the elder Germont, Alfredo's doleful father, wishes to forbid the relationship, he addresses not his son, but Violetta. His admonition to her takes the form of a warning that his son's future will be irredeemably tarnished by association with such a woman as she. Violetta gives up Alfredo, and dies of tuberculosis.

In *La Traviata* the themes of love and death come together. Old Germont, the voice of the crowd, society, and its morals, severs the sexual from the personal and thus condemns Violetta to death, for without love she cannot live. The tuberculosis is either a punishment for her sexual liaison, a symbol of her airless life without Alfredo, or both.

The advent of Richard Wagner's music dramas ushered in an entirely reformed view of death. While the death of the individual was the cornerstone of tragedy for the Italians, it took on a transcendent meaning for Wagner. In a Wagner music drama (a term he preferred to the Italian "opera"), individual death is nearly always a meaningful sacrifice to a greater whole. Death is no longer punishment, it is a kind of reward in the form of escape from desire. In Wagner's *Tristan und Isolde,* the title characters find true love only in death; in fact, the musical climax is a passage called the "Liebestod," or "Love-Death." Their ends as individuals return them to a transcendent unity. Desire and death are one.

The opera-obsessed German philosopher Friedrich Nietzsche, whose views Peter Conrad draws upon, saw clearly that Wagner's innovation advanced the transcendental over the real. Yet Nietzsche's view of the role of opera as musical tragedy changed markedly over the course of his short professional life. In his first major, published essay, *The Birth of Tragedy out of the Spirit of Music* (1872), he announced himself as a Wagnerian. German music has "Dionysian root" he wrote, starting in Bach and culminating in Wagner. The Dionysian death-ecstasy in German music contradicted the Apollonian habit of placing importance on individual ego, replacing it with the superiority of Dionysian sacrifice of the individual.

Late in life Nietzsche contradicted himself. In an essay titled *The Case of Wagner* (1888), he condemned Wagner's embrace of death and praised Georges Bizet's *Carmen* (1875) for its sunniness and embrace of life. *Carmen,* of course, ends with the death of its heroine, and she even sees it coming. She has rejected her former lover for a new one and the former will stab her to death outside the bullring. She has seen this in the cards—literally. But her death is not a sacrifice, it is an affirmation of the values by which she has chosen to live. Nietzsche at the last saw in this a greater, larger thing than Wagner's "love-death."

For most of the nineteenth century the Italian and German models existed side by side. Giuseppe Verdi continued, and brought to a climax, operatic death as the portrayal of individual tragedy. In Verdi, death is punishment, from god or at least from some faceless universal fate. In Wagner's four-part *Ring of the Nibelung* (completed 1876), death is the supreme reward, coming only to great heroes such as Siegfried, and to his female counterpart Brunnhilde, who rides her horse Grane onto Siegfried's funeral pyre.

In both Wagner and Verdi, the action was nearly always removed from contemporary realities. All Wagner is myth-ridden and Verdi preferred to distance his characters from immediate relevance by placing them in the past or upon a throne. Toward the end of the nineteenth century a school of Italian composers brought about a revolution that turned this upside down.

It was called *verismo,* literally "realism," and it transposed the traditional subjects of betrayal, revenge, and murder among nobility to those of betrayal, revenge, and murder among everyday people. The first verismo opera to enter the repertoire was a one-act, unusual in the operatic realm. *Cavalleria Rusticana* marked the debut of twenty-eight-year-old composer Pietro Mascagni. Terse, intense, and violent, *Cavalleria* was shocking in its time, as much for its directness of expression as for what it expressed. Here were revenge and murder stripped bare of any noble pretence or mythological garment. The story is a simple one involving a Sicilian soldier, his burning lust for a married woman, and the inevitable outcome.

The composer Ruggero Leoncavallo tried to duplicate the success of *Cavalleria* in *I Pagliacci* (1892), cast in two short acts and a prologue, but short enough to be produced in tandem with another brief opera. (Today, in fact, it is usually teamed with *Cavalleria.*) In *I Pagliacci* there is the added element of layered reality: A player (*un pagliacco*) acts out in character the very feelings of jealousy and revenge he is feeling as a private individual. Again, jealousy leads to murder, but what "on stage" has been merely a distraction becomes, in real life, shocking tragedy. The famous final line sums up this irony: "La commedia e finita!" ("The comedy has ended!)"

With Giaccomo Puccini, the greatest name of the verismo school, all sacrifices are love offerings, and they are made exclusively by women. Between 1896 and 1904, Puccini composed three of the most enduring tragic operas in Italian: *La Boheme, Tosca,* and *Madama Butterfly.* In *La Boheme* Mimi dies of

In Puccini's Madama Butterfly, *a Japanese woman commits hara-kiri when her American husband returns home to Nagasaki with an American bride. This is one of Puccini's three tragic operas where each ends with the dramatic passing of its central heroine.* BETTMANN/CORBIS

tuberculosis—Violetta's disease—while the title characters of the others snuff themselves in contrasting emotional modes. In *Tosca* the eponymous heroine attempts to foil fate and fails when her lover, Cavalradossi, is shot to death by a Napoleonic firing squad. Tosca had thought the muskets to be loaded with blanks; in horror, she flings herself from the parapet of the castle of Saint Angelo-Rome. And in *Madama Butterfly,* a Japanese wife commits hara-kiri when her American husband returns to Nagasaki with an American wife after not taking the Japanese ceremony seriously.

In Puccini's *Girl of the Golden West* and *La Rondine,* nobody dies. They are his least produced works. In *Suor Angelica* of his *Trittico*—a set of three one-act operas—Puccini presents what is perhaps the most poignant death of any in his works. The title character, who has taken vows as expiation for having had a child out of wedlock, finds out that her child has died, and so ends her own life.

Death figures oddly in the sole comedy of *Trittico,* the enduringly charming *Gianni Schicchi.* In this opera after Dante, the title character feigns to be the voice of a dying man (who is, in fact, already dead) in order to will himself the man's fortune. This is not selfishness, but a distorted nobility, the opera implies, as Schicchi does this in order to produce a proper dowry for his love-stricken daughter. In *Turandot,* left incomplete at Puccini's death in 1924, the gentle Liu sacrifices herself for her master Calaf so that he can claim as his own the moon goddess Turandot. This role of woman as sacrificial object was uniquely nineteenth century and predominantly Mediterranean.

There is nothing in opera before bel canto, nor after Puccini, to match the regularity with which women die in Romantic Italian operas. (German operas offer up gender-neutral sacrifices.) They do not languish, like Dido, but either give themselves willingly or are punished for sin—theirs or another's. This almost certainly reflected the role of women in Catholic countries of the time, at once relegating them to secondary status and elevating them to a kind of deity. When Gilda dies willingly for the worthless Duke in *Rigoletto,* it confers on her a sainthood no male character in Italian opera comes remotely near achieving.

Russian opera of the nineteenth century had a distinct political bent. The death of the czar in Mussorgsky's *Boris Godonuv* is also the temporary death of the state. The title character, who has seized power through an innocent's murder, is toppled by a pretender; his personal tragedy is merely symbolic of the national tragedy his fraud has initiated. In Tchaikovsky's *Eugene Onegin,* the death of one of the characters in a duel is rendered nearly meaningless by his killer's lack of regard for Tatiana, the woman they have fought over. Russian society at large—has the final say, rejecting the killer's eventual advances and propping up the stability of her conventional marriage.

The twentieth century saw an explosion of opera, which took on myriad forms and generated many subgenres. Richard Strauss announced in *Salome* (1905) and *Elektra* (1908) a new and heightened dissonance, all the better to accompany the beheading of John the Baptist in the former and the bloodbath of the latter. But he soon dropped this innovative language for operas that cradled gentle melodies set to more optimistic stories, such as *Der Rosenkavalier.* The ceaseless anxiety produced by the unrelieved dissonances of *Elektra* is a cue for future work that Strauss himself never took up. The musical language hangs on to dissonance as to some painful reminder of life; to achieve cadence, to dissolve into consonance, would mean death.

The Czech composer Leos Janacek bloomed late, composing a first opera of any significance (*Jenufa*) at age fifty, and his greatest operas after age sixty-five. This imbued his works with the glow of wise emotional distance. Forgiveness and understanding, not revenge and murder, are the dominant themes. In *Jenufa,* the title character is repeatedly wronged by those around her. Her fiancé's jealous brother disfigures her, her fiancé leaves her, and her stepmother drowns her illegitimate baby. Through it all, Jenufa finds opportunity to grow emotionally. In *The Cunning Little Vixen,* the story is set among animals. The title creature escapes a gamekeeper to found a family, only to see her path lead to death. Yet, it is a death absorbed into a cycle of life. Nature has taught humankind a lesson. *The Makrapulos Affair* concerns an opera singer as old as her art. In the course of the opera, 337-year-old Emilia Marty (one of many names she has had over the centuries) must learn how to die.

Death seems to be the least of worries for the characters in Alban Berg's two operas, *Wozzeck* (1921) and *Lulu* (left unfinished at the composer's death in 1935). The titular character in *Wozzeck* is a simple-minded soldier and fool of nature. He makes extra money by shaving his captain and by offering his body as a guinea pig for a doctor bent on proving arcane theories, the funds from which he gives to his common-law wife, Marie, and their child. But when he finds that Marie has bedded the handsome Drum Major of his battalion, he slits her throat under a blood-red moon and then, in remorse and confusion, drowns himself. In *Lulu,* the title character is cut to pieces by Jack the Ripper. Sex and death meet here in the most hideous fashion. Notably, the only "pure" character in the opera is the Countess Geschwitz, a lesbian. All male advances made to Lulu, with their potential for procreation and the regeneration of life—and therefore death—are treated essentially as acts of violence. Only the Countess, whose sexual relation with Lulu cannot continue the wheel of life/death, is pure. Here Wagnerian "transcendence" is given modern meaning.

In English, composer Benjamin Britten's operas, death usually involves the sacrifice of an innocent for the supposed good of the greater whole. In *Peter Grimes* (1945), a misfit suffers under the watchful eyes of a judgmental society. In *Billy Budd,* after Herman Melville's novella, the title character is made a scapegoat and in *Death in Venice,* after Thomas Mann's work, life itself is viewed as sacrifice.

In the French composer Francis Poulenc's *Dialogues of the Carmelites* (1958), death is the very subject. A young woman fears death and, seeing the tumult of life around her and the threat of the 1789 French Revolution, escapes to a convent. At length, it becomes clear that the other nuns have taken vows in order to embrace death, not avoid it. The final scene, one of the most chilling in the repertoire, calls for the sisters to chant a *Salve Regina* (Hail Queen of Heaven) as they exit the stage, one by one, to be guillotined. Periodically, the guillotine falls. The chilling effect is a constant diminuendo, until at last only one voice is heard singing, and that, too, is terminated.

No other theatrical form treats death in the heated and often terrifying way opera treats it. Opera's stepchild, the musical play, may involve death but it is infrequently given emotional coloring. The deaths in four of Rodgers and Hammerstein's musicals—*Oklahoma!, Carousel, South Pacific,* and *The King and I*—are nearly incidental to the stories. Only in the 1990s, with Stephen Sondheim's *Passion* and Adam Guettel's *Floyd Collins,* did American musical theater come to treat death with a sobriety approaching that of opera.

Tragic drama without music can convey horror, pity, fear, and sorrow, but music adds a dimension of unsettling personal involvement. Aristotle's famous dictum to the effect that drama is a purgation of the emotions does not really fit opera. One might leave *Aeschylus* feeling grateful that one is not among the characters, yet likely to leave Strauss's *Elektra* feeling very much like one or more of the characters. In the end, opera has become a form vastly distanced from the ancient Greek drama it was originally designed to emulate.

See also: FOLK MUSIC; GREEK TRAGEDY; MAHLER, GUSTAV; ORPHEUS; SHAKESPEARE, WILLIAM

Bibliography

Berger, William. *The NPR Curious Listener's Guide to Opera.* Washington, DC: Perigee, 2002.

Chailley, Jacques. *The Magic Flute, Masonic Opera.* New York: Alfred A. Knopf, 1971.

Conrad, Peter. *A Song of Love and Death: The Meaning of Opera.* New York: Simon & Schuster, 1987.

Kerman, Joseph. *Opera As Drama.* Berkeley: University of California Press, 1988.

Monson, Karen. *Alban Berg.* New York: Houghton Mifflin, 1986.

Nietzsche, Friedrich. *The Birth of Tragedy and the Case of Wagner,* edited by Walter Kaufman. New York: Alfred A. Knopf, 1972.

Osborne, Charles. *Complete Operas of Puccini.* New York: Da Capo Press, 1990.

Osborne, Charles. *Verdi: A Life in the Theatre.* New York: Alfred A. Knopf, 1987.

Sadie, Stanley, ed. *The New Grove Book of Operas.* New York: St. Martin's Press, 1996.

Weiss, Piero, comp. *Opera: A History in Documents.* New York: Oxford University Press, 2002.

KENNETH LAFAVE

ORGAN DONATION AND TRANSPLANTATION

Since the eighteenth century researchers have been experimenting with organ transplantation on animals and humans. However, the modern era of organ transplantation really began in the 1950s. In its early years, these were truly perilous procedures, fraught with danger, very likely not to be successful in particular instances, and rightly characterized as involving "the courage to fail"—a seminal work of the same name was written by Renée Fox and Judith Swazey in 1974.

Over time a combination of advances in knowledge, technology, pharmacology, and practice made it possible to transplant specific organs successfully from one human to another. In North America some milestones in this work include the first successful transplants of a kidney (Boston in 1954); pancreas/kidney (Minneapolis in 1966); liver (Denver in 1967); pancreas (Minneapolis in 1968); heart (Stanford in 1968); heart/lung (Stanford in 1981); single lung (Toronto in 1983); double lung (Toronto in 1986); living-related liver (Chicago in 1989); and living-related lung (Stanford in 1990). Transplants of kidneys, livers, hearts, pancreases, lungs, and heart-lungs are an accepted part of twenty-first-century medical treatment.

Twentieth-century specific achievements rested on two important developments. The first was tissue typing, or the ability to classify and compare human tissues. This led to the realization that a graft or transplant will have the greatest likelihood of success when it is most closely matched to the biological characteristics of the recipient. For example, a transplant is most likely to succeed when it takes place between identical twins who share a high degree of genetic material.

The second important breakthrough, which has been termed "the most notable development in this area" by the United Network for Organ Sharing, was the scientist Jean Borel's discovery of an immunosuppressant drug called cyclosporine in the mid-1970s. This drug was approved for commercial use in November 1983. Effective immunosuppression prevents the recipient's immune system from attacking and rejecting the transplanted organ as a foreign body. There are side effects to using this drug and clinicians must balance the threat of rejection against the dangers of rendering the transplant recipient susceptible to infection and other life-threatening assaults. When properly managed, however, immunosuppression has saved hundreds of thousands of lives and greatly enhanced quality in living.

The Need for Donations and Available Transplants

The growing need for transplantable human organs arises mainly from nonfunctioning or poorly functioning organs in potential recipients. With improved screening practices and diagnostic techniques, individuals who might benefit from transplantation have been identified earlier and more effectively. At the same time, transplant centers have advanced their technical abilities to transplant major organs.

Recognizing these developments, in 1984 the U.S. Congress enacted the National Organ Transplant Act (NOTA), which established the national Organ Procurement and Transplantation Network to facilitate the procurement and distribution of scarce organs in a fair and equitable way. The United Network for Organ Sharing (UNOS) administers this network under contract to the government's Division of Transplantation in the Department of Health and Human Services. NOTA also created the Scientific Registry of Transplant Recipients, a system to measure the success of transplantation by tracing recipients from time of transplant to failure of organ (graft) or patient death, which is administered under contract by the University Renal Research and Education Association at the University of Michigan.

The need for organ transplantation can be seen in data from the National Transplant Waiting List (see Table 1). The top line of this table identifies the major bodily organs that can currently be transplanted: individual kidneys, livers, and hearts; entire lungs, pancreas, and intestines, or portions thereof; and joint transplants of a kidney/pancreas or heart/lung. Clearly, the greatest numbers of transplant candidates are waiting for kidneys and livers. Table 1 also offers a snapshot, as of May 31, 2001, of the estimated number of patients (76,555) registered on the waiting list by gender, age, and race or ethnicity. Among registrants on the waiting list, the ratio of males to females is nearly 60/40, the largest numbers by age are 18 to 49 years old (followed closely by those 50 to 64 years of age), and the largest numbers by race or ethnicity are Caucasian Americans and African Americans.

Table 1 discloses two distinguishing features about African-American candidates on the waiting list. First, they are disproportionately in need of kidney transplants. More than 90 percent of African-American registrants are waiting for a kidney transplant by contrast with 70 to 77 percent of individuals from other minority groups who need such a transplant. This appears to result from elevated rates of high blood pressure, diabetes, and sickle cell anemia in the African-American community, all of which can have a deleterious effect on kidney functioning. Second, African Americans who make up about 12 percent of the overall U.S. population, are present in unusually high numbers on this list—more than 24 percent of all those registered with a U.S. transplant center.

Developments in Organ Donation and Transplantation

Table 2 reports end-of-year data for numbers of patient registrations on the transplant waiting list from 1988 through 2000, as well as the number of transplants accomplished and the numbers of donors from whom organs were recovered in each of those years. These data and Figure 1 show that during the last twelve years of the twentieth century in the United States the number of patient registrations on the transplant waiting list increased by over 360 percent, while numbers of transplants and donors increased only about 81 percent and 96 percent, respectively. In other words, during this time period the United States witnessed a gradual or incremental increase in the availability of transplantable organs, while there was a huge growth in the need for such organs.

Consequently, the single largest obstacle to organ transplantation in the twenty-first century is the scarcity of transplantable organs. In fact, there would be no transplantation of organs if the concept of donation did not exist. For that reason, it is helpful to consider some facts about organ donation and to take note of some efforts that have been made to increase the pool of organs available for transplantation.

Organ Donation and Consent to Donation

Organ donation is only possible when: (1) the organ in question is not uniquely vital to the donor's health; or (2) the donor is already dead when the organ is retrieved from his or her body. Living donors can offer replaceable materials (such as blood or blood products), one of a pair of twinned organs (such as kidneys), or a portion of certain organs (such as a liver, lung, or pancreas). Nonliving donors—individuals who have died prior to donation and the subsequent recovery of their organs (sometimes called "cadaveric donors")—can donate all of these and other transplantable organs provided that conditions preceding, at the time of, and immediately following their

TABLE 1

Number of individuals (patients or registrations) on the National Transplant Waiting List as of May 31, 2001, by organ, gender, race, and age [a]

Number / Percentage	Kidney	Liver	Pancreas	Kidney - Pancreas	Intestine	Heart	Heart-Lung	Lung	Total
Total:[b]	49,203	17,733	1,133	2,502	165	4,250	217	3,673	76,555
By Gender:									
Females	22,056	7,661	518	1,147	72	952	125	2,161	34,692
	42.5	42.4	45.1	44.4	42.6	22.3	57.3	58.1	42.3
Males	29,860	10,399	630	1,439	97	3,309	93	1,556	47,383
	57.5	57.6	54.9	55.6	57.4	77.7	42.7	41.9	57.7
By Age:									
0–5	90	547	7	2	99	127	16	22	910
	0.2	3.0	0.6	0.1	58.6	3.0	7.3	0.6	1.1
6–10	121	207	1	0	16	39	3	44	431
	0.2	1.1	0.1	0.0	9.5	0.9	1.4	1.2	0.5
11–17	426	361	7	0	15	86	19	138	1,052
	0.8	2.0	0.6	0.0	8.9	2.0	8.7	3.7	1.3
18–49	25,644	6,807	970	2,158	29	1,227	146	1,731	38,712
	49.4	37.7	84.5	83.4	17.2	28.8	67.0	46.6	47.2
50–64	19,824	8,435	161	420	10	2,268	33	1,686	32,837
	38.2	46.7	14.0	16.2	5.9	53.2	15.1	45.4	40.0
65+	5,811	1,703	2	6	0	514	1	96	8,133
	11.2	9.4	0.2	0.2	0.0	12.1	0.5	2.6	9.9
By Race or Ethnicity:									
Caucasian Americans	22,555	13,412	980	1,977	104	3,325	171	3,111	45,635
	43.4	74.3	85.4	76.5	61.5	78.0	78.4	83.7	55.6
African Americans	18,169	1,311	108	380	42	563	23	382	20,078
	35.0	7.3	9.4	14.7	24.9	13.2	10.6	10.3	24.5
Hispanic Americans	7,144	2,244	46	171	17	288	18	160	10,088
	13.8	12.4	4.0	6.6	10.1	6.8	8.3	4.3	12.3
Asian Americans	2,895	702	7	36	4	49	3	33	3,729
	5.6	3.9	0.6	1.4	2.4	1.1	1.4	0.9	4.5
Others	1,152	391	7	22	2	36	3	31	1,645
	2.2	2.2	0.6	0.9	1.2	0.8	1.4	0.8	2.0

[a]Some patients are multiply listed at different transplant centers for the same organ or at the same transplant center for multiple organs (e.g., kidney and heart). The data in this report are not adjusted for multiple listings at different centers. However, the data are adjusted for multiple listings at the *same* center; thus, a patient is counted only once per center. The degree of multiple listing of the same patient at different centers has been difficult to determine accurately, but is estimated to involve less than five percent of all patients and appears to have declined over time.

[b]The numbers in this line represent current estimates of *patients* listed on the waiting list. Note that the overall total in this line (= 76,555) is less than the sum of the organs (= 78,876) because some patients are listed for multiple organs. Such patients are counted separately under each organ for which they are waiting, but only once in the overall total. All other figures in the remainder of this table reflect numbers of *registrations* (whose total = 82,075) rather than numbers of patients.

SOURCE: Adapted from United Network for Organ Sharing, 2001. Available from www.unos.org.

death do not damage the organs or otherwise render them unsuitable for transplantation.

For nonliving donors, this usually means that organs must be recovered shortly after the death of an otherwise healthy donor and before they have begun to deteriorate (the time frame depends on the particular organ in question). In most instances, the donor will have died of external trauma to the head (e.g., as associated with an accident, homicide, or suicide) or a cerebrovascular incident (e.g., resulting from cranial hemorrhage or stroke), and will have been pronounced dead ("brain dead"). Often, some bodily functions in a potential organ donor will be artificially sustained by external intervention for a limited period of time in order to preserve the quality of transplantable organs while decisions are made about donation and a search for appropriate recipients is undertaken. This does not mean that an already-dead donor is "being kept alive"; only some biological functions are being supported externally, not the life of the person.

As reported in Table 2, the ratio of nonliving to living donors has declined over time from 69/31 percent to approximately 52/48 percent. That appears to reflect the increasing willingness of living donors, whether or not they are related by blood or

TABLE 2

Number of patient registrations on the National Transplant Waiting List, number of U.S. transplants, and number of U.S. organ donors, end of year 1988–1994

	Year						
	1988	1989	1990	1991	1992	1993	1994
Number of Patient Registrations on the National Transplant Waiting List	16,026	19,095	20,481	23,198	27,563	31,355	35,271
Number of Transplants							
Non-living donors	10,803	11,225	12,879	13,327	13,559	14,735	15,206
Living	1,823	1,918	2,123	2,423	2,572	2,899	3,086
Total:	12,626	13,143	15,002	15,750	16,131	17,634	18,292
Number of Donors							
Non-living	4,080	4,012	4,509	4,526	4,520	4,861	5,100
Living	1,827	1,918	2,124	2,425	2,572	2,906	3,102
Total:	5,907	5,930	6,633	6,951	7,092	7,767	8,202

Number of patient registrations on the National Transplant Waiting List, number of U.S. transplants, and number of U.S. organ donors, end of year 1995–2000

	Year						
	1995	1996	1997	1998	1999	2000	Total
Number of Patient Registrations on the National Transplant Waiting List	41,179	46,925	53,123	60,299	67,079	73,951	515,545
Number of Transplants							
Non-living donors	15,902	15,965	16,253	16,943	16,946	17,255	190,998
Living donors	3,438	3,735	4,009	4,473	4,768	5,653	42,920
Total:	19,340	19,700	20,262	21,416	21,714	22,908	233,918
Number of Donors							
Non-living	5,359	5,416	5,477	5,799	5,822	5,984	65,465
Living	3,458	3,756	4,021	4,496	4,748	5,600	42,053
Total	8,817	9,172	9,498	10,295	10,570	11,584	108,418

SOURCE: Adapted from United Network for Organ Sharing, 2001. Available from www.unos.org.

marriage to a potential recipient, to offer a part of their bodies for transplantation. At the same time, although the ratio of organs that are actually transplanted from nonliving donors to those from living donors has declined from 86/14 percent to 75/25 percent, transplantation remains much less frequent from living donors than from nonliving donors.

One reason for the infrequency of donation is that living persons can only donate one of a pair of organs or a portion of an organ to a single recipient, while a nonliving donor can donate six to eight major organs, along with ocular components and numerous other tissues that can affect the lives of fifty or more recipients. Still, living donation offers advantages in that the donor's medical history is known, an extensive evaluation can be done beforehand, the organ is removed under elective circumstances, and the donated organ is out of the body only a very short period of time.

Consent for donation is obtained from potential living donors after a suitable screening and evaluation process to determine that they understand the procedure that will be undertaken, are consenting freely, are a good tissue match to the potential recipient, are likely to be able to withstand the surgical donation process, and can be expected to cope effectively with the aftermath of the experience however that may work out. In the case of a potential donor who has died, health care professionals who are not part of the transplant

FIGURE 1

Transplant Candidates, Organ Transplants, and Organ Donors, United States, 1988–2000

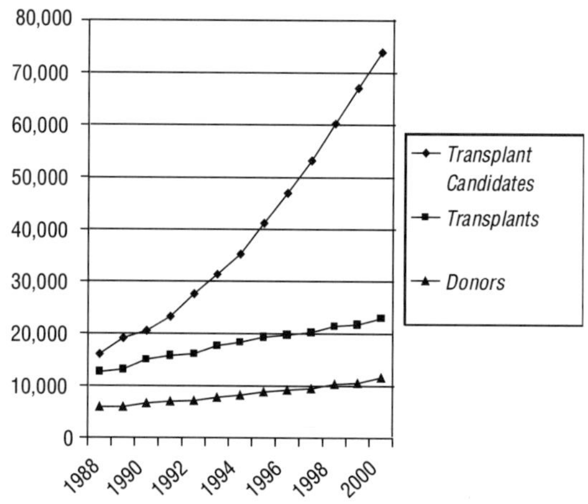

SOURCE: Adapted from United Network for Organ Sharing, 2001. Available from www.unos.org.

team will determine death and communicate that diagnosis to next of kin. Wherever possible, an effort will be made to disassociate this declaration of death from issues associated with organ donation.

Donation of major organs in the United States does not follow a policy of "presumed consent," although such policies are practiced elsewhere around the world. In the United States, the Uniform Anatomical Gift Act (1968, with amendments in 1987) regulates who may make or receive an anatomical gift, under what conditions, and for what purposes. Permission to donate from nonliving donors must be obtained from an appropriate source. Furthermore, under a government regulation called the Medicare and Medicaid "Conditions of Participation" that went into effect in 1998, hospitals must: (1) report all patients whose deaths are imminent or who have died in their institution to their local or regional Organ Procurement Organization (OPO); (2) ensure the right of next of kin to choose donation; and (3) arrange for trained personnel (members of the OPO staff or hospital personnel whom they have trained for this purpose) to offer the opportunity to donate.

It is difficult to approach grieving family members shortly after the (often sudden and traumatic) death of a loved one to discuss organ donation. However, many believe it would be even worse to fail to make this option available to family members at a time when they have been victimized by death and when so little else is within their control, or to have them realize later that they could have found some measure of solace in a dark time if someone had only mentioned the possibility of making a "gift of life." Done properly, offering the opportunity of donation can provide a way of continuing the legacy of an individual's life, assisting family members in their bereavement, and helping others through transplantation.

Efforts to Increase Organ Donation

Efforts to increase organ donation have taken many forms. Among them, public education projects have sought to emphasize a number of relevant facts, including "brain-dead" individuals cannot return to life; donor families incur no costs to donate; human tissues and organs cannot legally be bought and sold in the United States; and organ donation usually has no substantive effect on desired funeral practices, other than the possibility of a brief delay. In addition, transplantation is encouraged and supported by nearly all religious communities in the United States; members of minority groups are most likely to find a close tissue match with other members of similar groups and gene pools; a large and growing number of individuals on the transplant waiting list are in desperate need of a transplanted organ; an average of fifteen persons on the waiting list (5,597 in 2000) die each day in the United States because a transplantable organ does not become available for them. These public education efforts are summarized by the slogan, "Don't take your organs to heaven . . . heaven knows we need them here!"

Similar efforts involve urging potential donors to sign, date, and have witnessed an organ donor card. Such cards can be obtained from the federal government's Division of Transplantation and local, regional, or national organizations, such as the Coalition on Donation, the United Network for Organ Sharing, or the National Kidney Foundation. Many states have a donor card on the reverse side of their driver's licenses and/or encourage applicants for new or renewed driver's licenses to indicate willingness to donate by registering in a computer database.

However, individuals who wish to donate should discuss this matter with their next of kin.

Regardless of any written or oral expression of wishes that an individual might make, next of kin are likely to be key decision makers in this matter. Lack of discussion among family members about their wishes is the single most significant barrier to organ donation. Thus, public education campaigns have urged potential donors to "Share your life. Share your decision."

Xenotransplantation and Non–Heart Beating Donors

Two other efforts to enlarge the pool of potential organ donors involve xenotransplantation and what are called "non–heart beating donors." Xenotransplantation is transplantation across species, that is, from animals to humans. At present, xenotransplantation has been successful in cases like heart valves from pigs, but that success has been limited to certain tissues. Non–heart beating donors are individuals in permanent vegetative states who are not yet dead but for whom competent decision makers (their next of kin or those authorized to act for them as substitute decision makers) might decide: (1) to withdraw life-sustaining interventions; and (2) to authorize donation. In such circumstances, the interventions are withdrawn and a brief interval is allowed during which the individual is observed to determine whether or not he or she resumes spontaneous functioning. If the individual is pronounced dead, interventions are resumed as needed to permit recovery of donated organs. From 1993 to 2000 in the United States, organs were recovered from a total of 581 non–heart beating donors.

Issues and Controversies

At present, attempts to meet the need for transplantable organs and tissues depend primarily on human donors, generating numerous social, personal, professional, ethical, and legal issues.

One set of issues concerns the types of physical, psychosocial, and spiritual care that are appropriate or mandatory for living and nonliving donors, donor family members, and transplant candidates and recipients both before and after donation and transplantation. When a loved one has died and he or she is approached about donating his or her organs, donor family members have been especially concerned that: (1) the need for information and care should be addressed at a time when they are first learning about the death and about the implications of donation; (2) determination of death should be made without regard to donation and their loved one should be cared for with respect and dignity; and (3) their subsequent needs for follow-up bereavement care after the donation decision should be met in appropriate ways. To that end, the National Donor Family Council published in 1994 a "Bill of Rights for Donor Families." Similarly, concerns about specific needs of transplant recipients for ongoing, seamless, and high quality medical, psychosocial, and spiritual care led the transAction Council of the National Kidney Foundation to develop and publish in 2001 a "Transplant Recipients' Bill of Rights and Responsibilities." Further, all of these parties are concerned about implications of donation as a "gift of life" and what may follow from that decision (e.g., are there implied obligations and/or bonds?).

Another set of issues involves efforts to increase the availability of transplantable organs. Campaigns to increase public awareness about organ donation and the need for transplantation have not substantially increased the number of available organs. Here, the key issue has to do with consent for donation. In cases involving nonliving donors, some have proposed that formal indications of an individual's desire to donate made prior to death (e.g., through a signed donor card or consent for inclusion in a state donor registry) should become legally definitive, sufficient in themselves, and not subject to being overruled by next of kin.

For non–heart beating donors, issues of consent relate to the fact that decisions to withdraw life support and then (after death has been determined) to recover organs are made by next of kin or substitute decision makers acting on the authority of an advance medical directive. There are potential issues about whether the individual is really dead before being returned to interventions designed to preserve the quality of the organs to be transplanted. If so, on what basis is that determined? How long does one have to wait after withdrawing life support before pronouncing death? Why are pain medications sometimes administered to such patients, if they are in fact dead? In addition, there are issues regarding whether decisions to authorize withdrawal of life support and donation are properly made by a substitute decision maker who may be the individual's beneficiary or have some other personal interest in the outcome.

In the case of living donors, consent to donate may become problematic if psychosocial pressures or familial influences impose coercion on the potential donor. This would be especially true in cases of child donors. And in all cases of living donors there can be questions as to whether it is appropriate, even with their consent, to impose the risks of major surgery and all that entails on healthy individuals who derive no direct physical benefit from that procedure. An issue for professionals who work with living donors concerns the injunction to "do no harm" because organs do not regenerate and the donor will be permanently impaired.

Further, while the buying and selling of human organs is not legal in the United States, some have suggested that funding of some type should be made available, either directly or indirectly, to donor families to facilitate decisions to donate. For example, funds might be paid directly to funeral homes to alleviate some financial burdens on families who agree to donate organs from a loved one. Surveys of family members who have agreed to donate do not report them as favoring such proposals. However, views of family members who declined to donate are not well-known.

The first issue that faces potential transplant candidates involves gaining access to the national transplant waiting list. This issue has particular relevance for those who are economically disadvantaged or who are members of minority groups. When such individuals receive their health care services from impersonal institutions or systems in which they do not have full confidence, they may not be adequately informed about how they might benefit from transplantation or not sufficiently empowered to bring up their interest in that possibility. By contrast, individuals with sufficient time, energy, and other resources may be able to gain access to the waiting list more easily and may be able to do so at more than one transplant center. Further, in order to be accepted by a transplant center, one must demonstrate ability to pay for this expensive procedure. There are not any hospitals that can afford to offer many free organ transplants. People who cannot show that they have adequate resources available to them—in the form of funding from Medicare, state assistance, private insurance, or money that they themselves raise—may not be accepted as transplant candidates.

Once on the transplant waiting list, discrimination is less likely because organs are allocated to those at the top of the list as determined by criteria that strive to ensure equity in terms of antigen matching, how sick the person is, and how long he or she has been on the list. However, when insufficient numbers of transplantable organs are available (as in the United States), issues still exist concerning whether these scarce resources should be allocated: (a) locally or regionally before being made available nationally or (b) to the sickest individuals first on the waiting list (regardless of geography). It has been argued that local or regional allocation would encourage individuals to donate in support of their local communities. The counterargument is that allocation without regard to geography would direct organs in the first place to individuals on the waiting list who are the sickest and most in need of a transplant. Proponents speaking on behalf of the primacy of local and regional allocation reply that those who are sickest have a lower likelihood of long-term success as transplant recipients. From another perspective, in light of the typical pool of patients that each serves, it has been suggested that giving primacy to local or regional organ allocation tends to favor smaller transplant centers over larger, national transplant centers that tend to enroll sicker patients on their waiting lists.

Further, funding is an ever-present issue in this field for the recovery of transplantable organs and tissues, for transplantation itself, and for the long-term support of transplant recipients. To the issue of funding, one can add issues involved in the "commodification" of transplantable organs and especially human tissues that, once processed, have a long shelf life and seem to many to lose their connection to their original source in a human body. Has this led to excess profit making by some tissue banks and processors? Does it all imply an unwillingness to realize that in the end death is part of the human condition?

Tissue Donation and Transplantation

In addition to organs, it is also possible to transplant human tissues such as skin grafts for burn and accident victims; heart valves and aortic patch grafts to sustain heart functioning; saphenous and femoral veins, which are used in cardiac bypass surgery; eye and ocular components to restore or improve sight; and bone and connective tissue grafts, which make possible periodontal and trauma reconstructions, as well as spinal fusions. Because blood and fat cells are removed during the processing of donated tissues, there is usually no issue of rejection after transplantation and many tissues can be sterilized, frozen, and kept in storage often for many years. Upwards of 400,000 tissue transplants are accomplished each year in the United States.

Conversations about retrieval of transplantable tissues may be part of the overall discussion of organ donation or they may occur independently—often in the form of a telephone conversation rather than a face-to-face interaction. In the former instance a procurement coordinator from an OPO might be the principal professional in the discussion; in the latter instance a staff member from a specialized eye or tissue bank might assume that role.

See also: BIOETHICS; DEFINITIONS OF DEATH; INFORMED CONSENT

Bibliography

Authors for the Live Organ Donor Consensus Group. "Consensus Statement on the Live Organ Donor." *Journal of the American Medical Association* 284, no. 22 (2000):2919–2926.

Caplan, Arthur L., and Danile H. Coelho, eds. *The Ethics of Organ Transplants: The Current Debate*. Amherst, NY: Prometheus Books, 1998.

Corr, Charles A., Lucy G. Nile, and the Members of the National Donor Family Council. *Bill of Rights for Donor Families*. New York: National Kidney Foundation, 1994.

Fox, Renée C., and Judith P. Swazey. *Spare Parts: Organ Replacement in American Society*. New York: Oxford University Press, 1992.

Fox, Renée C., and Judith P. Swazey. *The Courage to Fail: A Social View of Organ Transplants and Dialysis*. Chicago: University of Chicago Press, 1974.

Prottas, Jeffrey. *The Most Useful Gift: Altruism and the Public Policy of Organ Transplants*. San Francisco, CA: Jossey-Bass, 1994.

The transAction Council. *Transplant Recipients' Bill of Rights and Responsibilities*. New York: National Kidney Foundation, 2001.

U.S. Department of Health and Human Services, Health Care Financing Administration. "Medicare and Medicaid Programs; Hospital Conditions of Participation; Identification of Potential Organ, Tissue, and Eye Donors and Transplant Hospitals' Provision of Transplant-Related Data." *Federal Register* 63 (1998):33856–33874.

U.S. Department of Health and Human Services, Health Resources and Services Administration, and Health Care Financing Administration. *Roles and Training in the Donation Process: A Resource Guide*. Rockville, MD: Author, 2000.

Wendler, Dave, and Neal Dickert. "The Consent Process for Cadaveric Organ Procurement: How Does It Work? How Can It Be Improved?" *Journal of the American Medical Association* 285, no. 3 (2001):329–333.

CHARLES A. CORR
DONNA M. CORR

ORGANIZED CRIME

In the pantheon of the American violent antihero, the gangster has occupied an enduring price of place second only to the cowboy; both have enjoyed the distinction of inspiring an entire genre of popular music. Whether the cinematic iconography is that of the loyal family operative—*The Godfather* (1972)—or the brutal sadist—*The Untouchables* (1987)—the adventure, violence, and bloodshed of the American gangster continues to grip the imagination of the world.

In reality, organized crime is mainly another business—the bursts of machine-gun fire and "rubouts" that dominate the movie version of gangland are really only the occasional means to a higher (or lower) end—money. Like rogue nation-states securing their national interests, organized criminal syndicates aggressively defend their profits and business "turf" by any means necessary.

In distinction to other forms of criminality, organized crime is a conspiratorial activity involving the collaboration of numerous people over a prolonged period. Unlike other criminal groupings, syndicates have maintained enough organizational strength to allow continued operation in the face of the loss of one or more members. Criminal syndicates rely on rules and regulations to maintain discipline and control within their ranks. Breaking the rules typically results in verbal or physical punishment, including death.

Organized crime groups are motivated by money rather than ideology—a characteristic that distinguishes them from organized terrorism. Although there are occasional links between terrorist groups and organized criminals (e.g., the Russian Mafia is often accused of supplying Russian nationalists with weapons), organized criminals generally avoid connections with terrorists and are much more restrained and functional in their use of violence.

Like other plunderers, from the state level to the back alleys, organized criminals are willing to use violence and murder to accomplish their goals. Although reliable statistics on mob murder and violence are unavailable, the level of bloodshed seems proportional to the vigor of the market for mob-supplied goods. Expanding markets and profits associated often intensify competition between existing groups and spawn new ones; violence tends to flare when several groups are jockeying for the same market niche. Violence also plays an important internal role among criminal groups who use it as a deterrent to insubordination. Violence can also be the price of failure. Mexican organizations, for example, kidnap, torture, and execute members whose drug shipments are confiscated by U.S. border agents.

Gangsters themselves are the most likely victims of organized-crime-related violence; however, bystanders sometimes get caught in the middle. The DeMeo crew of the Gambino family murdered well over a hundred people; while most of them were criminals, several were simply in the wrong place at the wrong time.

Criminal syndicates tend to specialize in the provision of illicit goods and services. Organized crime is not limited to any one kind of activity, illegal or otherwise, but syndicates tend to focus on gambling, drug trafficking, loan sharking, prostitution, and extortion. To accomplish their goals, participants function in hierarchical networks, with each member assigned a particular task. The structure of organized crime insulates the leadership from direct criminal involvement. The subordinates are willing employees with specialized skills, such as computer hacking or contract murders.

Organized criminals often make use of government corruption to accomplish their organizational goals. Bribery and extortion are necessary tools for the survival of their enterprise. For example, a recent federal investigation in Arizona resulted in the arrest of ten federal officers, two deputy sheriffs, three local police officers, and one local judge. In another investigation, federal agents discovered that four Immigration and Naturalization Service inspectors were paid over $800,000 to pass more than twenty tons of cocaine into the United States.

Traditional Organized Crime

The origins of organized crime in the United States date back to at least the early 1800s, when criminal gangs victimized the residents of New York, Boston, and other cities. By the middle of the nineteenth century, at least some of these gangs had emerged in a sufficiently structured and prominent form to warrant public recognition of "organized crime."

One of the first criminal groups with a tightly organized and acknowledged leadership was New York's Forty Thieves Gang, which thrived from 1820 to about 1860 (another gang by the same name operated between 1930 and 1940). Throughout the early and mid-nineteenth century, many sons of poor Irish immigrants formed gangs and participated in criminal activities, including theft, burglary, and extortion. The Forty Thieves and groups like them were also heavily involved in local politics. In fact, New York's infamous Tammany Hall politicians used the brawling Irish gangs as tools of political power, selectively procuring their services for such unlovely reasons of state as breaking up picket lines, intimidating voters, and stuffing ballot boxes. In return for their help, the gangs received protection from the police, access to political power, and jobs for their relatives.

Other immigrant groups were associated with organized crime in the nineteenth and early twentieth centuries—among them Jewish, Polish, Chinese, and Italian—leading many criminologists to suspect that immigration may have facilitated the growth of organized criminal activity in the United States. One scholar has argued that because early immigrants were wedged into poverty-stricken ghettos with few legitimate opportunities for conventional success, they were more likely to turn to crime to escape poverty. "The aspiring ethnic, blocked from legitimate access to wealth and power, is permitted to produce and provide those illicit goods and services that society publicly condemns but privately demands" (Ianni 1975, p. 89). In short, organized crime provided the immigrant and his family a means to escape the penury and indignity of the ghetto. The same processes may still be at work in the twenty-first century with more recent immigrants to U.S. cities.

Like many other immigrants groups, the Irish-American population found increasingly legitimate avenues for success outside the ghetto. With fewer members of their own ethnic group willing to support or even tolerate their criminal ventures, Irish syndicates found it difficult to maintain control over the criminal rackets. For the most part, the Irish were slowly, sometimes violently, replaced by other criminal groups.

However, while Irish and other ethnic groups have come and gone on the American organized crime scene, none have rivaled the impact or resilience of the Italian-American syndicates. Between 1820 and 1930 almost 5 million Italians immigrated to the United States—more than 2 million between 1900 and 1920. Like the Irish before them, Italian immigrants found themselves isolated in ghetto areas with few legitimate opportunities to realize the American dream, so that some of their number sought to escape poverty by supplying the illicit goods and services demanded by the local populace.

Some argue that the Italian experience was even more conducive to the formation of criminal syndicates. Because many Italian immigrants did not speak English, they were even more isolated and had even fewer opportunities for positive influence outside their ethnic enclaves. Moreover, the organizational antecedents of organized crime, including secret societies such as the Italian Mafia and the Camorra already permeated southern Italian culture. Thus, Italian immigrants brought with them knowledge of the ways of secret societies and the spirit of the Mafia that they used to construct a uniquely American organization that emerged later, with the advent of Prohibition.

In 1919 the passage of the Volstead Act made it illegal to produce, distribute, or sell alcoholic beverages. Prohibition (1920–1933) provided the context for the rapid development of a new illegal enterprise and the necessity for a more complex division of labor between and within the criminal groups responsible for bringing in and distributing illegal alcohol. In essence, the large profits that could be made by satisfying the public demand for alcohol motivated small-time, local Italian gangs to expand beyond the ghetto.

While it is easy to focus on the violence associated with gang wars during Prohibition, the breadth of the market induced many Italian gangs to work more extensively with other criminal groups than they ever had before. At times, however, cooperation failed and resulted in bloody conflicts. For example, in Chicago a four-year feud between rival Irish and Italian forces culminated on February 14, 1929, when members of the Capone mob, disguised as police officers, systematically executed seven members of the Moran gang in the aptly named "St. Valentine's Day Massacre." Interestingly, collaboration with non-Italians increased profits, and most syndicate leaders recognized that gang wars were bad for business. Working with non-Italian groups also demonstrated the utility of other models of organization that departed radically from the family patronage model of the traditional Italian Mafia that many of the young American-born Italians rejected.

The violence reached its peak in the Castellammarese War of 1930–1931, when the Old World faction headed by Salvatore Maranzano was nearly exterminated by younger, Americanized factions under the direction of Giuseppe Masseria. By the end of the war, Maranzano was dead along with many of his compatriots, clearing the way for the Americanized gangsters to assume new levels of leadership in Italian-American crime syndicates. In the shadow of Prohibition, newer, younger leaders replaced their fractious elders with an organization that was on the whole more cooperative, stable, and profitable. Some criminologists contend that by the end of Prohibition, U.S. organized crime had developed a national, rigidly hierarchical framework under almost exclusive control of the Italian Mafia. Others cite evidence that indicates the criminal syndicates maintained a fluid, decentralized, ethnically diverse structure that has promoted their interests in an environment hostile to their very existence. As of the twenty-first century, the Mafia (also known as La Cosa Nostra) remains the most powerful organized-crime group in the United States, but most criminologists deem it a declining force.

Nontraditional Organized Crime

The contemporary war on drugs, like Prohibition in an earlier generation, has drawn the attention of organized crime, generating expanded opportunities for cooperation and competition among the various criminal groups seeking entry into this illegal market. While the Mafia may be the best-established criminal group involved in the American drug trade, many of the nontraditional groups vying for a share of the action are better organized, both nationally and internationally, and more violent. Specialization in drug trafficking is one of the hallmarks of the emerging criminal syndicates that experts refer to as nontraditional organized crime; they can also be found operating in other criminal rackets like gambling and prostitution. Although various Asian gangs, primarily of Chinese origin, have been active in the United States since the 1850s, they are also labeled nontraditional organized crime.

The Chinese Triads are among the most feared and interesting criminal syndicates that operate in the United States. Overseas the Triads are heavily engaged in illegal gambling, prostitution, and extortion; inside the United States they generate millions of dollars trafficking in opium products such as heroin. Like many criminal syndicates, Triads are principally involved in the importation and wholesale distribution of narcotics; however, because of their close ties with American Tongs and Chinese-American youth gangs, Triads have ready access to street-level markets. Youth gangs are also instrumental in protecting the Triad/Tong narcotics turf from infiltration by competitors (i.e., rival African-American groups) through intimidation and violence.

Mexico is also home to a number of powerful organized crime groups. Mexican cartels, also considered nontraditional organized crime, vividly illustrate the brutality of drug trafficking. For many years the Juarez Cartel has controlled the El Paso, Texas, gateway for drug traffic. Authorities believe that the Juarez Cartel is responsible for more than 300 drug-related disappearances in Mexico, more than 120 drug-related homicides, and 73 disappearances in El Paso. In a separate incident in 1998, a U.S. border patrol agent confronted and was murdered by narcotics smugglers along the Arizona-Mexico border. Events such as these along the U.S. border with Mexico are part of a larger pattern in which organized criminals attempt to maximize its profits by protecting shipments and territory through the use of deadly force.

Another nontraditional organized-crime group making headway in the United States is the Russian Mafia. With the collapse of the Soviet Union, the Russian Mafia, or *vorovskoi mir,* emerged as an important criminal organization in both Russia and America, supplying coveted but illegal goods and services in both markets. In addition, the Russian Mafia is intimately tied to the political and economic structure of Russia, much more so than most organized crime groups. Russian businesses, for example, often have little choice but to turn to criminal syndicates for investment capital. While many Russian gangs are local or national, more and more are establishing international links, including links to the United States, where they are involved in multiple rackets, including drug trafficking and securities fraud.

Organized Crime and the Media

The mass media both reflect and shape public perceptions of organized crime. Films such as *Goodfellas* (1990), televisions shows like *The Sopranos* (1999), and books like Mario Puzo's *The Godfather* (1969) all portray Italian-Americans as the primary perpetrators of organized crime. Furthermore, stories of organized crime in the news often focus on only the most superficial and sensational crimes. This coverage leaves the public with the view that this type of criminal behavior, while somewhat romantic, is excessively violent. In all likelihood, members of crime syndicates go out of their way to avoid exposure to such violence. Thus the media has fueled society's appetites for stories about mobsters while at the same time obscuring the reality of organized crime groups by providing stereotypical images of their members, their modes of organization, and their activities. Suffused with the romance of death and daring in the popular imagination, the bulk of organized-crime activities carry all the panache of a corporate board meeting or an accountant's balance sheet.

See also: FIREARMS; HOMICIDE, DEFINITIONS AND CLASSIFICATIONS OF; HOMICIDE, EPIDEMIOLOGY OF

Bibliography

Abadinsky, Howard. *Organized Crime,* 6th edition. Belmont, CA: Wadsworth, 2000.

Barlow, Hugh D. *Introduction to Criminology,* 7th edition. New York: Harper Collins, 1996.

Ianni, Francis A. J. *Black Mafia: Ethnic Succession in Organized Crime.* New York: Pocket, 1975.

Lyman, Michael D., and Gary W. Potter. *Organized Crime,* 2nd edition. New Jersey: Prentice Hall, 2000.

Mustain, Gene, and Jerry Capeci. *Murder Machine: A True Story of Murder, Madness, and the Mafia.* New York: Onyx, 1993.

Internet Resources

McCraw, Steven C. "Organized Crime, Drug Trafficking, and Terrorist Acts." In the Federal Bureau of Investigation [web site]. Available from www.fbi.gov/congress/congress00/mccraw.htm.

JOHNETTA M. WARD
JASON D. MILLER

Orpheus

Orpheus, according to Greek myth, is one of the few who descended into Hell and lived to tell about it. The son of Oeagrus (King of Thrace) and the muse Calliope, he is famous for his musical and poetic gifts inherited from Apollo and the Muses. His lyre and his odes were so charming that upon hearing them, wild animals became quiet, and trees and rocks started to move.

Orpheus fell in love with the nymph Eurydice and married her, but she died suddenly from a snake bite. In despair, Orpheus followed Euridyce into Hades (Hell) to bring her back. His music and lyrics enchanted Hades' protectors, even the triple-headed dog, Cerberus, and the gods of Hades were persuaded to bring back to life his dead wife. One condition of Eurydices' return was that he could not look back at her until he reached the threshold of Hades. Orpheus looked back to see whether Eurydice was following him and lost her forever.

Orpheus's death is subject to many interpretations, but the most common is that the Thracian women, jealous of his love and fidelity toward his deceased wife and hurt by his indifference, tore his body to pieces and threw his head and lyre into the river Hebre. His remains finally reached Lesbos Island, the cradle of lyric poetry. Orpheus is also considered an initiate, a prophet who retained secrets from the afterlife, having brought back revelations from his descent into Hell.

The Orpheus myth has inspired many forms of artistic representation, among them the vanished Polygnote fresco (fifth century B.C.E.), which presented Orpheus during his descent into Hell, that has now disappeared; *Orfeo,* a musical drama by Monteverdi (1607); *Orph'ee aux Enfers,* a spectacular opera by Offenbach (1858) and *Le testament d'Orph'ee,* a film by Jean Cocteau (1959).

See also: Charon and the River Styx; Operatic Death

Bibliography

Coulter, Charles R., and Patricia Turner. *Encyclopedia of Ancient Deities.* Jefferson, NC: McFarland and Company, 2000.

Sacks, David. *A Dictionary of the Ancient Greek World.* New York: Oxford University Press, 1995.

Warden, John. *Orpheus: The Metamorphoses of a Myth.* Toronto: University of Toronto Press, 1982.

ISABELLE MARCOUX

Osiris

In Ancient Egyptian mythology, Osiris was the god of the beyond whose death and resurrection brought a guarantee of an afterlife to mortals. He was a kindly Pharaoh, teaching agriculture, music, arts, and religion to his people. Jealous of his successful reign, his brother Seth killed him with the help of many accomplices and took control of Egypt. However, Seth's reign was foreshortened by Isis's great love for her husband and brother Osiris, whom she brought back from the dead. A skillful magician, she gave Osiris breath by flapping her wings above him while she transformed into a bird. Osiris and Isis then conceived Horus, their beloved son. Seth, seething in anger, killed Osiris once again, this time by cutting his body to pieces and throwing them into the Nile River. Isis, with the help of Anubis, the god with the jackal head, reconstituted Osiris's body with bandages and embalming rites, thus creating the first mummy. During this act, the god Thoth recited an incantation. Finally, Horus avenged his father Osiris in a bloody duel with Seth in which Horus lost his eye, which was then given as a food offering to Osiris.

Each of the ceremonies which were followed after Osiris' death, became the actual rituals that the Egyptians performed to ensure access to the eternal life after death. Egyptians performed mummification of the body to preserve it eternally, recited incantations to facilitate access to the hereafter and provide gifts to help them on their voyage. The deceased's soul proceeds to Hell and must appear before Osiris's Court, which weighs the soul's good and bad actions; the heart must be light as a feather to obtain salvation. Otherwise, the consequence is torment and destruction.

In pictorial representations, Osiris is portrayed wearing the white clothes used in mummification; he typically holds the king's scepter and the judge's whip, symbols of supreme authority.

See also: CANNIBALISM; GODS AND GODDESSES OF LIFE AND DEATH; JESUS; SACRIFICE

Bibliography

Coulter, Charles R., and Patricia Turner. *Encyclopedia of Ancient Deities.* Jefferson, NC: McFarland and Company, 2000.

Griffiths, John Gwyn. *The Origins of Osiris and his Cult.* Leiden, Netherlands: E. J. Brill, 1980.

Mercatante, Anthony S. *Encyclopedia of World Mythology and Legend.* New York: Facts on File, 1988.

ISABELLE MARCOUX

P

Pain and Pain Management

In June 2001 a California jury awarded $1.5 million to the family of a terminally ill eighty-five-year-old man, finding the doctor liable for elder abuse and reckless negligence because he had failed to order appropriate pain medication. This court judgment brought the issue of pain control for the terminally ill into sharper focus. The thought of dying in pain can contribute to the desire for suicide or assisted suicide. Since the 1990s a movement has emerged to improve pain management and thereby reduce the anxiety of both patients and caregivers.

What Is Pain?

Pain has been characterized in a variety of ways. There are physical definitions such as an unpleasant sensation; a warning that something is wrong; or the body's response to a thermal, chemical, or mechanical injury. There are also definitions that attempt to provide a meaning or explanation. For example, pain is a punishment; it lets the body know it is alive; it is a teacher helping to modify future behavior; or it is "all in one's head."

Two definitions have become particularly influential among health care providers, educators, and researchers. The International Association for the Study of Pain (IASP) proposes that pain is an unpleasant sensory and emotional experience associated with actual or potential tissue damage. Margo McCaffery suggested as early as 1968 the widely accepted definition, "Pain is whatever the experiencing person says it is, existing whenever the experiencing person say it does" (McCaffery and Beebe 1989, p. 7). Both definitions point to the fact that pain is much more than tissue damage that triggers a response from the nervous system. The management of pain therefore involves more than treating the tissue injury. The individual's cultural background, present circumstances, and state of mind all require assessment and attention. It has become clear that cultural learning leads to differences in the way that people express pain. Furthermore, it is also becoming increasingly accepted among the medical community that, in contrast to previous medical beliefs, children feel pain even when they are too young to express it effectively. Elderly people may also have different, less obvious, ways of expressing pain, especially if affected by Alzheimer's disease. Health care providers are therefore improving their expertise in recognizing signs of pain across a broad span of patients.

How Does Pain Work?

Research about pain is still limited, but is going forward on many fronts. A major focus is the search for a molecular description of how a pain stimulus is signaled to the brain and how the brain signals its response. Until that process has been firmly identified, caregivers and researchers can utilize the following overview of pain pathways.

Cell damage occurs. Proteins trigger specific channels that set off the pain signal. As chemicals are released the area becomes inflamed and swollen. Identification of the specific pain channels may lead to the development of highly selective local anesthetics with reduced side effects for the rest of the body.

When the tissue damage threshold is reached, nerve fibers in the area carry a message to the spinal column. There are three types of nerve fibers, each of which has a distinctive role in producing pain sensations. Small, myelinated fibers known as *A delta* carry localized and sharp thermal and mechanical impulses to the neospinothalamic tract. The small, unmyelinated *C fibers* carry aching, throbbing, burning, dull, unlocalized messages to the paleospinothalamic tract and on to the brain stem and thalamus. *A beta fibers,* which are large and myelinated, serve to inhibit impulses from the A delta and C fibers, thereby modulating the number and intensity of impulses sent up the spinal tracts.

The physiologist Patrick Wall, one of the world's foremost authorities on pain, describes what happens in the dorsal horn of the spinal cord, "If the input message comes only from the large A beta fibers as a result of touch, the cell fires briefly and then is turned off. If, however, the input volley comes from tissue damage detection fibers, A delta and C, the cell fires more vigorously and exaggerates the output. During all this time, the brain is sending down control messages to amplify, diminish, or ignore the signal" (Wall 2000, p. 40). An example of this occurs when hitting one's shin on a sharp object. The immediate response is to reach down and rub the area. The rubbing message is carried by the A beta fibers closing the gate to messages from the A delta and C fibers.

Once in the spinal cord the messages cross to the opposite side of the spinal column. Next they travel upward through the spinothalamic tract, conveying information about the nature and location of the stimulus to the thalamus, cerebral cortex, and spinoreticular tract. This process activates autonomic and limbic (motivational-affective) responses in the brain stem and thalamus. Messages descend the spinal cord as a result of these responses.

It is in the brain stem and the cerebral cortex that the pain messages are analyzed. Here the body meets the mind. While little research is available, there are theories and some pieces of the puzzle to suggest what is happening.

Endorphins. Endorphins are important pieces of the puzzle. Scientists know something of the body's defenses against pain. Some neuropeptides, such as Substance P, appear to be pain specific transmitters. Other peptides, such as the endorphins and enkephalins, provide profound analgesic (pain-relieving) effects. Morphine and other opioid medications were in use long before the opioid receptor sites in neural tissue were discovered in the 1970s. The word *endorphin* was coined as a contraction to the terms *endogenous* (meaning "a natural property of the body") and *morphine.* Methods to turn on secretion of the endorphins have been studied. Massaging or moving a painful part may owe some of its effectiveness to stimulating endorphin production. The "runner's high," a good feeling as a result of exercise, has also been attributed to endorphin release.

Placebo response. Less well explained is the "placebo effect." This occurs when a treatment produces an effect primarily because of its intent rather than its specific therapeutic physical or chemical properties (e.g., taking a pill that actually contains no medicine). People sometimes report that they feel better even though they have had only the expectation and appearance of a treatment. The double-blind research technique that pits a new drug against an inactive substance has been developed to offset the placebo effect. The placebo would be expected to produce no effects. In actuality, however, placebo users frequently report positive effects. An important aspect of the placebo effect seems to be that the person trusts the person administering the treatment and believes that the treatment will be effective. The placebo effect can be a useful supplement to therapeutic treatment but its effectiveness differs markedly from person to person and is not entirely reliable.

Both the presence of endorphins and the well-documented placebo response point to the power of the mind-body connection in pain management.

Treatment of Pain in the Terminally Ill Person

Pain is the most common symptom experienced by hospice patients. The World Health Organization has estimated that more than two-thirds of patients in the advanced stages of cancer experience pain. Other studies confirm this estimate. Unrelieved pain leads to fatigue, nausea, and loss of appetite.

Daily activities and sleep patterns are disrupted. The patient may experience depression and anxiety that damage relationships because loved ones do not know what to say or do.

Careful assessment of the patient's pain is the starting point for achieving adequate control. Patient and family understanding of the purpose and goals of assessment enhance communication with the health care provider. Patient communication starts with awareness of the location, quality, and intensity of the pain. "Stabbing," "throbbing," "burning," or "cramping" help identify the quality of the pain. Choosing words carefully can help the health care provider understand the pain and monitor changes in the quality over time.

The intensity of pain is often monitored through the use of a pain scale, typically asking the patient to choose a number from one (no pain) to ten (worst pain). The Waley/Baker Faces Rating scale, depicting five faces (from smiling to frowning with tears) assists children and some adults to indicate pain intensity. Health care providers also ask about the factors that precipitate or aggravate the pain. Patients are asked to identify any ways they may have discovered to control the pain and how they carry on with their activities of daily living.

Understanding the meaning of pain can be elusive for both the patient and his or her family and the health care provider. The patient's background, beliefs, and values can affect how the pain is interpreted and consequently the expectations for pain control. For example, some children have been raised to bear scrapes and injuries without tears and sobs, and some have learned to keep their vulnerabilities to themselves when in the company of strangers. Still others have been taught that suffering is a test of spiritual strength, therefore it is a moral weakness to admit to pain. People with such backgrounds may inhibit their expressions of pain even during a terminal illness. It is then up to the caregivers to detect signs of suffering and provide relief without challenging the patient's intention to appear in control of herself.

Thorough assessment of the many factors of pain is essential when selecting appropriate treatment. The patient and health care provider form an active collaboration. Confidence that the health care provider understands the patient and that the pain will be managed is a crucial first step to achieving control. The partnership with the health care provider is even more important when the patient is facing the end of life. Pain, with no prospect of relief, leads to profound hopelessness in many patients.

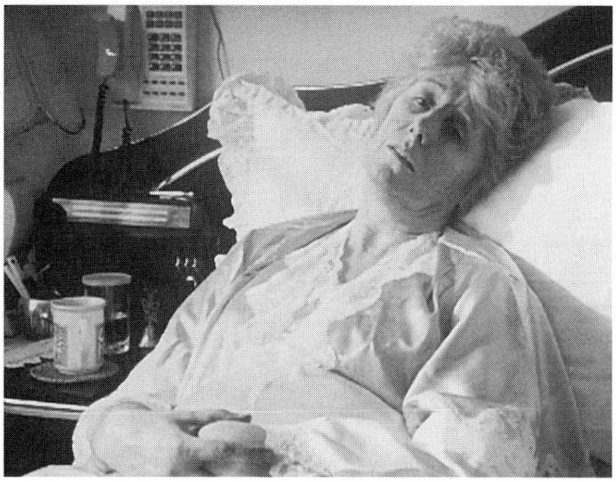

A terminally ill cancer patient who advocated for euthanasia in a 1999 Australian television commercial, said that she takes twenty pills a day in addition to three doses of morphine but is still in pain. Control of pain is a major concern at end-of-life treatment because terminally ill patients tend to have suicidal thoughts or make suicide attempts. AFP/CORBIS

Techniques to Control Pain

Often patients and family assume that new and increasing pain must be expected. In actuality, a search for cause should be conducted at the earliest possible time. Identifying potential causes of pain can lead to effective prevention and control. The same approach should also be used with regard to other symptoms, such as constipation, pressure ulcers, and respiratory difficulties. These symptoms can often be prevented with attentive care.

Regular comfort measures deserve constant attention. As energy for activities of daily living and self-care wanes near the end of life, it is not uncommon for the patient to omit regular movement, mouth care, and basic physical cleanliness. Assistance with passive exercises, bathing, tooth brushing, and hair care may not seem like pain control, but in actuality these details can play a big part in maintaining comfort. A warm shower, if possible, provides dermal stimulation, relaxation of muscles, and a decrease in anxiety because it is such a routine part of life.

Use of Noninvasive Pain Control Measures

The first methods of pain control probably included stimulation of the skin with heat, cold, massage, and vibration, all of which have the ability to relieve pain without causing injury, at a low cost, and with little experience. Other types of stimulation of the skin include massage with menthol-based lotions, transcutaneous electrical nerve stimulation (an electrical current administered through skin patches), and acupressure (gentle pressure applied to acupuncture points).

Rubbing a bumped shin or applying a cool cloth to a forehead works to relieve discomfort. A parent's kiss to make everything "all better" helps a child through a painful experience. It reminds the individual that the presence of a loved one has a role in relieving pain.

Assisting the patient to focus attention on stimuli other than pain is another effective noninvasive pain control measure. Because the pain stimulus does not go away, but instead becomes "more bearable," this strategy has the advantage of being under the patient's control. It is also inexpensive. Many patients use the distraction strategy without realizing it by watching television, reading, doing crossword puzzles, listening to music, or attending to the company of friends and relatives. Meditation and guided visual imagery are also in this group of therapies. A disadvantage is that the existence of the pain may be doubted by others if the patient can be distracted. Distraction requires concentration and may drain the energy resources of the patient, perhaps leading to increased fatigue and irritability. The method is particularly effective for brief painful episodes.

Freedom from skeletal muscle tension and anxiety produces the relaxation response, characterized by specific physiological responses (decreased oxygen consumption, decreased respiratory rate, decreased heart rate, decreased muscle tension, normal blood pressure, and increased alpha brain waves) and a lowering of the subjective sense of distress. Conscious attempts can be made to interrupt the cycle of pain that leads to anxiety and muscle tension with increased pain as a result. The relaxation response requires active patient involvement. Many patients need specific instruction to invoke the relaxation response effectively. Some techniques include deep breathing exercises, jaw relaxation, review of peaceful past experiences, and a meditative or progressive relaxation script or tape.

Use of medication. While the noninvasive therapies are useful for mild pain, they should be considered supplements to the effective management of moderate to severe pain. Moderate to severe pain are often treated with medication and invasive pain control measures.

The World Health Organization developed the "analgesic ladder" to illustrate a systematic plan for the use of pain medication. Mild pain is treated with medications such as aspirin, acetominophen, and non-steroidal anti-inflammatory drugs (NSAIDs). Maximum recommended doses of these drugs restrict amounts in order to prevent toxicity and damage to the liver and kidneys. As pain increases, opioids such as oxycodone may be used. Severe pain requires morphine or other long-acting opioids. The dose is matched to the pain level. Although there are side effects to these drugs, the amount of drug is not limited. If pain level increases, the route by which the medication is given may change from the slower acting oral route to a faster route, whether transdermal, transmucosal, or intravenous. It is important to avoid routes that actually cause pain, such as intramuscular injection.

For continuous pain, medical practitioners often maintain that continuous pain medication should be available. This requires drugs that are long acting and given on a continuous schedule. The goal is to keep pain in check, rather than waiting until it is out of control before administering more medication.

Side effects of the drugs should be anticipated and prevented. The most common and preventable side effect of the opioids is constipation. Prevention includes adequate fluid and fiber intake and the possible use of stool softeners and laxatives.

It is important to remember that withstanding pain uses energy. When pain is first adequately relieved with medication, the patient may sleep for an extended period of time. This sleeping does not indicate that too much medication is being taken, it means that the person's body is recuperating and regaining energy. This sleepiness can lead family and caregivers to fear that the disease is progressing or that too much medication is being given. If the person arouses easily, then it is an indication that he or she is not taking too much medication.

Invasive Pain Relief Strategies

Some approaches to pain relief are called invasive because tissue damage may be caused by the procedure itself. The procedure may involve stimulation of nerves, the spinal cord, or areas of the brain. Blocking the nerves with medication or by actually cutting the nerve may reduce pain. These approaches may be useful if the patient is not able to withstand extensive surgical procedures. Acupuncture is considered an invasive approach to pain because the needles enter the skin. It is unknown whether acupuncture analgesia is superior to placebo analgesia or other types of hyperstimulation procedures.

Self-Management Concept

The fear of unrelieved pain raises anxiety for terminally ill patients and their families. Many caregivers remember instances when they felt helpless in the face of pain. Giving the patient information about pain leads to better pain control and lowered anxiety. The confidence that pain will remain in control and the continued presence of the health care provider can go a long way to assure that pain will not be an issue at the end of life.

The patient plays a significant role in providing information about the pain and in selecting and using diverse pain control methods. The patient is the best judge of the adequacy of control. Caregivers may hear statements such as the following that express personal preference:

- "It is okay if I only have pain when I move."
- "I want to continue to be up and walking, so I will need more medication."
- "A warm shower, meditation, and pain medication at bedtime helps me get a good night's sleep."
- "I just want to have no pain. I don't care if all I do is sleep."

The adequacy of pain control can be judged by the patient's feeling of comfort and ability to participate in activities of daily living. The goal of complete freedom from pain may not be achievable.

Fear of addiction is often an issue with pain control, especially when opioids are used. Psychological dependence is a pattern of compulsive drug use characterized by a continued craving for an opioid and the need to use the opioid for effects other than pain relief. Addiction resulting from medical treatment regimen is extremely rare. On the other hand, the need to increase doses over time is not uncommon because of tolerance for the drug or changes in the disease process. Other drugs may be added to the regime. Medical practitioners cite the importance of not abruptly stopping the medications.

Health care providers themselves may be a barrier. It is important to seek out providers who believe the pain is real, who are willing to provide diverse approaches to the pain, and who plan for continued contact. Concerns about providing sufficient medication to relieve pain without precipitating the death of a terminally ill person should be discussed openly. If large doses of opioids are required, the physician may be hesitant to order them and nurses may be reluctant to administer the needed dose because the actions might be considered performing euthanasia or assisting suicide. The line between relieving pain and hastening death may not be clear. Patients can help with the ethical issues by making their wishes clear and by seeking the assistance of a like-minded counselor or medical professional in explaining their preferences.

Pain Management: The Future

Research concerning the physiologic mechanisms of pain continues in the early twenty-first century. These research efforts will most likely reveal new, more specific pain control measures. In the meantime, the controversy between governmental control of opioids to prevent abuse and the need for opioid use for pain relief continues. Professional care providers need education and organizational support that establishes standards and accountability for pain management. A recent initiative to require that pain be assessed as often as the patient's temperature, heart rate, respiratory rate, and blood pressure are taken provides a starting place for standards and accountability. Dissemination of information about pain-relieving drugs and other interventions remains crucial to quick, effective responses to pain. Access to analgesic medication and pain is crucial. Paying for the cost of health care should not become a barrier to pain management. Professionals must continue to advocate for patients in pain as American society struggles to afford health care for the entire population.

The public should be appropriately educated about pain and pain relief if it is to advocate for the use of pain medications. Fears that medication will cause addiction and the inability to experience and control life decisions prevents use of some effective pain measures. Patients' fear of stigma if they offer complaints of pain can keep providers from understanding patients' extent of pain and thus appropriately treating it.

Researchers and leading edge practitioners agree that people in pain can be empowered by knowing what to expect from health professionals in relation to pain management. Assessment of the pain and its causes is the first step. Professionals should seek a clear understanding of the meaning of the pain to the patient and family. Multiple approaches to the pain can be recommended. Concerns about addiction and other effects of the controls measure can be addressed through patient education and referral to pain specialists. The knowledge, skills, and tools exist to meet the goal that no one should die in pain.

See also: CHILDREN, CARING FOR WHEN LIFE-THREATENED OR DYING; SYMPTOMS AND SYMPTOM MANAGEMENT

Bibliography

Agency for Health Care Policy Research. "Management of Cancer Pain. Clinical Practice Guidelines No. 9." AHCPR Publication No. 94-0592. Rockville, MD: U.S. Department of Health and Human Services, 1994.

International Association for the Study of Pain, Subcommittee of Taxonomy. "Pain Terms: A Current List with Definitions and Notes on Usage. Part II." *Pain* 6 (1979):249–252.

McCaffery, Margo, and Alexandra Beebe. *Pain: Clinical Manual for Nursing Practice*. St. Louis, MO: C. V. Mosby, 1989.

McMillan, S. C. "Pain and Pain Relief Experienced by Hospice Patients with Cancer." *Cancer Nursing* 19, no. 4 (1996):298–307.

Morris, Jon, et al. "The Effect of Treatment Setting and Patient Characteristics on Pain in Terminal Cancer Patients: A Report from the National Hospice Study." *Journal of Chronic Disease* 39, no. 1 (1986):27–35.

World Health Organization. *Cancer Pain Relief and Palliative Care*. Technical Report Series 804. Geneva: Author, 1990.

BEATRICE KASTENBAUM

PALLIATIVE CARE

See HOSPICE OPTION.

PARAMEDICS

See EMERGENCY MEDICAL TECHNICIANS.

PERSISTENT VEGETATIVE STATE

Individuals in persistent and permanent vegetative states (both called PVS) are not dead, although philosophers still debate whether they are "people." Their brains still function at a very rudimentary level; they have sleep-wake cycles; and they normally can breathe without assistance. According to the American Academy of Neurology, about 10,000 to 25,000 PVS individuals exist in the United States at any one time. Approximately 50 percent of them have been in this state less than six months and 70 percent for less than a year.

People go into PVS after their brains suffer a lack of oxygen, a lack of sugar, or a similar event. Normally, the onset of a coma is the first stage. If they neither die nor awaken, they lapse into a "vegetative state." Usually, only young trauma victims awaken from this state; older or oxygen-deprived individuals, which is the more common situation, usually do not. After one month health practitioners call the condition a "persistent vegetative state." If their brain damage is the result of a non-traumatic event, adults and children rarely emerge from a persistent vegetative state after being in it for three months. If the damage results from trauma, children rarely recover after being in the state for one year; adults rarely emerge after six months in that state. At some indeterminate time later, the patient's condition transforms into an irreversible "permanent vegetative state."

Physicians with training and experience in PVS make the diagnosis on clinical grounds established by the American Academy of Neurology, which include:

- no awareness of themselves or their environment—an inability to interact with others;
- no reproducible, purposeful, or voluntary responses to visual, auditory, tactile, or noxious stimuli; and
- no ability to speak or to understand language; sleep-wake cycles with intermittent wakefulness without awareness; sufficiently preserved lower brain and brain stem functions to permit survival with medical and nursing care; bowel and bladder incontinence; variably preserved cranial nerve (pupillary, oculocephalic, corneal, vestibulo-ocular, gag) and spinal reflexes.

No diagnostic study can make the diagnosis with certainty. Except in the case of infants with anencephaly, reliable criteria do not exist for making a diagnosis of PVS in infants less than three months of age.

The American Academy of Neurology states that of the adults in a persistent vegetative state for three months after brain trauma, 35 percent will die within a year after the injury. Another 30 percent will go into a permanent vegetative state, 19 percent will recover with severe disabilities, and 16 percent will recover with a moderate or minimal disability. If they remain in a persistent vegetative state for six months, 32 percent will die, 52 percent will go on to a permanent vegetative state, 12 percent will recover with severe disabilities, and 4 percent will recover with moderate or minimal disability. Nontraumatic brain damage markedly decreases the chance of any recovery. After such patients have been in PVS three months, only 6 percent will recover with severe disabilities and 1 percent will recover with a moderate or minimal disability. After six months, no adults who remain in that state recover.

Children have a better chance of recovering from brain trauma than adults. Virtually all children in a persistent vegetative state from causes other than trauma go on to a permanent vegetative state rather than to death. Unlike adults, about 3 percent of these children recover, but always with severe disabilities.

Medical experts differ in opinion as to exactly how those in PVS should be classified. These individuals cannot interact with or experience their environment, feel pain, or communicate in any way—their thinking, feeling brain is gone. Their condition will not improve, but they can live with medical and nursing support for many decades.

See also: CRUZAN, NANCY; DO NOT RESUSCITATE; END-OF-LIFE ISSUES; LIFE SUPPORT SYSTEM; QUINLAN, KAREN ANN; RESUSCITATION

Bibliography

American Academy of Neurology Quality Standards Subcommittee. "Practice Parameters: Assessment and Management of Patients in the Persistent Vegetative State." *Neurology* 45 (1995):1015–1018.

Iserson, Kenneth V. *Death to Dust: What Happens to Dead Bodies?,* 2nd edition. Tucson, AZ: Galen Press, 2001.

Iserson, Kenneth V. *Grave Words: Notifying Survivors about Sudden, Unexpected Deaths.* Tucson, AZ: Galen Press, 1999.

KENNETH V. ISERSON

PERSONIFICATIONS OF DEATH

Visitors to the Church of St. Nicholas in Tallinn, Estonia, will recall the representation of death as a bony, dark figure with a skull, as depicted in Bernt Notke's famous canvas, *Danse Macabre* (c. 1460). Many others are acquainted with the image of death as the reaper in Ingmar Bergman's dramatic film *The Seventh Seal* (1957).

Through the ages people have tried to personify death by giving it a humanlike form. Personification is used in this context as the mental transformation of inner thoughts and feelings into autonomous figures. The term *personify* is defined as giving inanimate objects or abstract ideas human characteristics. Formed in this way, death personifications can be considered culture-bound channels to transfer invisible phenomena into external patterns.

Death Personifications in History

In the ancient world, life and death were perceived as two forces of the Great Mother, the oneness of everything. Life was associated with the Good

Mother, and death with the Evil Mother. According to the psychologist Erich Neumann, death is the hungry earth, devouring its own children.

In classical Greek tradition, the unity of life and death is split into opposites. Life is personified as feminine, and death as masculine. Death is named Thanatos, the twin brother of Hypnos, the god of sleep. His mission is to accompany the departed to Hades, the underworld, where the aged boatman Charon ferries them across the Sinister River, which separates the underworld from the world above. In Greek mythology, death is considered inevitable, but not purely evil. Illustrations on Greek vases depict Thanatos and Hypnos as two young men. In European art, literature, and iconography, Thanatos is often portrayed as an earnest, winged youngster holding an extinguished flare.

In Judeo-Christian religion, death is considered exceedingly evil. It is not personified as a humanlike figure; rather it is described by its actions. The Old Testament says that humans are cast down in the kingdom of death, which resembles Hades, where the wicked are punished. The Christian concept of death associates death with sin. Sin is regarded as opposition to the will of God, requiring repentance and God's forgiveness. Only in apocalyptic writings is death personified as a human figure, a pale horseman who kills people using violence.

Death Dance

During the plagues (the Black Death) and wars of the fourteenth and fifteenth centuries, personifications of violent death were popular. Throughout this time there was a belief that the skeletonized dead rose from their graves and tempted the living of all ages and ranks to join them in a dance to the death. The "dance of death," or dance macabre, was an allegorical theme in art, literature, and music. It was first embodied in murals, then in woodcuts. The Parisian painter Guyot Marchaut published a portrayal of the death dance in woodcuts and verse (1486), which was circulated throughout Europe. Best known are the fifty-one drawings of the German painter Hans Holbein the Younger (1497–1543), where death is personified as a skeleton, and each individual dances through life embracing his own death.

Death Personifications in Art

This theme of personifying death as a skeleton or a reaper has continued into the twenty-first century. In Sweden the dramatist August Strindberg's play *The Dance of Death* (1901) is filled with macabre medieval symbolism. Bergman's film *The Seventh Seal* personifies death as a man with a hood obscuring his face. In "La Mort et le Bûcheron" (Death and the woodcutter) the French landscape painter Jean François Millet depicts death as the grim reaper. Alfred Kubin paints death as a skeleton in "Blätter mit dem Tod." The Austrian painter Gustav Klimt personifies death in the flamboyantly dressed skeleton in his "Tod und Leben" (Death and life, 1916). Musical renderings of the personification of death include *Totentanz* (1864) by the Hungarian composer Franz Liszt, *Danse Macabre* (1874) by the French composer Camille Saint-Saëns, and *La danse des morts* (1940) by the French composer Arthur Honneger.

Personification of Death in Children and Adults

In 1948 the researcher Maria Nagy observed that Hungarian children had a tendency to personify death as "the reaper" or "the skeleton," a figure that appeared in order to carry people off. Later research in the United States could not confirm Nagy's findings. American children showed no signs of personifying death. In Canada more than thirty years later, Richard Lonetto showed that children tended to personify death as exemplified through their drawings. In Sweden, Maare E. Tamm and Anna Granqvist observed that less than 10 percent of children and adolescents personified death. The personifications of younger children were ideographic, a "death man," while those of older children were formed from cultural symbols. All children personified death as masculine.

Personification of death in adults is studied in the United States by Robert Kastenbaum and Carol Herman. In 1997 they found that females most often select "kind and gentle" imagery, as "the gentle comforter" or "the gay deceiver," while males are more likely to see death as a "cold, remote" person. Grim and terrifying personifications of death were infrequent. In Sweden, Maare E. Tamm found that a majority of the adults studied personified death as an old man, the reaper figure being the most apparent personification.

Similar to Gustave Doré's nineteenth-century engraving Death on a Pale Horse, *death is most commonly personified as a skeleton or reaper by children and adults.* BETTMANN/CORBIS

Conclusion

Death has been personified through the ages; in the ancient world as a feminine figure, and from classical Greek civilization to the present as a masculine figure. When the plague raged throughout Europe, death acquired a violent, frightening, and macabre image. The image of the "grim reaper" is preserved in art and literature, and in people's minds, to the present day. It is hard to say how death will be portrayed in future decades, when new technology like the Internet and virtual reality introduces new ways of thinking in philosophy, theology, and the human mind. Certainly people will continue to personify death in some way because there is a universal tendency among humankind to understand the world as a humanlike entity, and personification of an image—in this case death—makes its qualities more palpable and less terrifying.

See also: ARS MORIENDI; BLACK DEATH; BLACK STORK; DANSE MACABRE; VAMPIRES

Bibliography

Holbein, Hans. *The Dance of Death.* New York: Dover, 1971.

Kane, Barbara. "Children's Concepts of Death." *Journal of Genetic Psychology* 134 (1979):141–153.

Kastenbaum, Robert, and Carol Herman. "Death Personification in the Kevorkian Era." *Death Studies* 21, no. 2 (1997):115–130.

Le Goff, Jacques. *Medieval Civilization, 400–1500.* Oxford: Basil Blackwell, 1998.

Lonetto, Richard. *Children's Conceptions of Death.* New York: Springer, 1980.

Neumann, Erich. *The Great Mother. An Analysis of the Archetype,* 2nd edition. New York: Bollingen Series/Princeton, 1974.

Sorvinou-Inwood, Chistiane. *Reading Greek Death: To the End of the Classical Period.* Oxford: Oxford University Press, 1994.

Tamm, Maare E. "Personification of Life and Death among Swedish Health Care Professionals." *Death Studies* 20, no. 1 (1996):1–22.

Tamm, Maare E., and Anna Granqvist. "The Meaning of Death for Children and Adolescents: A Phenomenographic Study of Drawings." *Death Studies* 19 no. 3 (1995):203–222.

MAARE E. TAMM

PHILOSOPHY, WESTERN

"The hour of departure has arrived, and we go our own ways—I to die, and you to live. Which is better God only knows" (Edman 1930, p. 88). These dramatic lines, spoken by Socrates at the end of Plato's *Apology,* are among the most memorable in the history of Western philosophy. Their implication that death is a blessed relief from the suffering that is life has proved a watershed in Western philosophical attitudes toward life and death, with some subsequent thinkers echoing their otherworldly metaphysics and others, like Nietzsche, countering with a passionate affirmation of life against death. Because a philosophical verdict on death entails a judgment on life as well, no issue is more central to the metaphysical controversies that have marked the history of Western philosophy nearly from the beginning.

Ancient Period

The first philosophers in ancient Greece (c. 600 B.C.E.) were cosmologists chiefly concerned with the origin and nature of the universe, so the meaning of death to humans was not a prominent issue in their work. The first of these thinkers was Thales, who described the universe as "full of gods," a view that seems to imply that the universe is alive and that there is no such thing as dead, inert matter. Anaximander, who was Thales's student, seems to have been the first to suggest an evolutionary mechanism for life and for the human species. About death he says, "Things perish into those things out of which they have their being, as is due . . ." (Guthrie 1971, p. 76), seeming to imply that death and change are natural parts of the cycle of life. For Anaximenes, life occurs through the breathing in of air, seen as a divine element and the nature of soul itself. He offers the first purely naturalistic explanation of death. It occurs, he explains, when the creature is no longer able to respire and the outside air can no longer enter in to counteract compression.

Heraclitus spoke of death more often than his contemporaries. For him death is a basic feature of the universe, for he believed in the periodic consumption of the universe by fire. In his cosmology, the whole world and each creature in it are in a constant state of flux, and each element lives by the death of the other. The processes of life and death are a necessary feature of the world; he argues that without them the cosmos would disintegrate. Heraclitus was among the first to suggest that not all souls perish at death; virtuous souls, he believed, may rejoin the divine spark itself. Pythagoras, the philosopher and mathematician, elaborated a doctrine of reincarnation or transmigration of the soul; in his view, life and death involve a process and a progress through many series of physical forms (human and animal) with the goal of achieving a spiritual purity leading to an ultimate reunion with the state of divine origin.

The survival of the spirit or mind after the death of the body is supported in other pre-Socratic thinkers such as Empedocles and perhaps Anaxagoras. But this view met a stiff challenge in the materialist metaphysics of the atomists Leucippus and Democritus. The atomistic theory suggests that all things in the universe are composed of indivisible particles of matter (*atomoi*); at death the atoms simply disperse, and there is no survival of the individual. Atomism is the last great theory offered by the philosophers before Socrates, and the theme is picked up again by Epicurus, with important consequences for human dealings with death.

With Socrates, the gadfly-philosopher of the ancient Greek agora, the topic of death achieves more focus. The *Apology,* recounts Socrates' (469–399 B.C.E.) unjust condemnation to death by a court in Athens. Before leaving the court, Socrates requests to speak to his friends on the subject of his impending execution. He reasons that death is not an evil; in fact, he argues, "There is much reason to hope for a good result. . . . Death is one of two things. Either it is annihilation, and the dead have no consciousness of anything, or, as we are told, it is really a change—a migration of the soul from this place to another" (Hamilton and Cairns 1961, p. 25). If death is a state of nothingness, he argues, it will be like an eternal sleep and therefore will be a gain and nothing to fear. If death is migration of the soul into another world, a spiritual world of true judges, then there is also nothing to fear because no evil can await a good and just person. So, Socrates concludes, the good person can be of good cheer about death, and know for "certain—that nothing can harm a good man either in life or after death" (p. 41).

Plato (428–348 B.C.E.) took a more definite stand than his mentor Socrates (though because Plato made Socrates the major character in *Dialogues,* it is sometimes hard to distinguish between the two). Plato believed that death is most definitely not an eternal sleep but rather the moment at which the soul (that is, the true person) is finally released from the body (its earthly prison). In the *Phaedo,* there is no either/or argument. Rather, Plato attempts to prove the immortality of the soul, offering reasons why the real philosopher, who is "always pursuing death and dying," should never fear the end. In the *Phaedo* no less than four arguments or proofs are offered; all of them, however, depend on two main Platonic premises: a dualistic view of the relation between the body and soul, and the conviction that the core of true being is the soul, which survives the death of the body. Perhaps the most widely discussed argument is the last offered by Plato: The soul is incapable of death because death is, after all, decomposition (wherein the dying subject is dissolved), but the soul, being simple and uncompounded, cannot decompose.

Aristotle (384–322 B.C.E.), Plato's greatest student, did not share a similar conviction about the immortality of the soul. In *De Anima* (On the Soul) he denies the Platonic dualism of soul and body, arguing instead for a far closer relationship: the soul, he says, is the "form" of the body. The comparison he makes is that between the pupil and the power of sight: "As the pupil *plus* the power of sight constitutes the eye, so the soul *plus* the body constitutes the animal. From this it indubitably follows that the soul is inseparable from its body, or at any rate that certain parts of it are (if it has parts) . . ." (McKeon 1941, p. 556). As the son of a physician, Aristotle was much more closely attuned to the material world than Plato; he viewed the human being as a preeminently biological creature, a member of the animal kingdom. Aristotle was the first of the philosophers to carry out detailed study and writings on animals in *De Partibus Animalium* (On the Parts of Animals), a topic he pursued in such biological writings as *De Generatione et Corruptione* (On Generation and Corruption), where he studies "coming-to-be and passing-away" as changes uniformly found in all of nature, and *Historia Animalium* (The History of Animals).

While it is clear that Aristotle denies the Platonic dualism and the consequent views on immortality—indeed, he seems to suggest that a desire for immortality is a wish for the impossible—it is not certain that he believes that death is the final end of the soul entirely. The highest part of the soul, the purely intellectual part, is akin to the divine, he argues, and may survive death. Aristotle does not elaborate on this possibility, but it is clear that this cannot be a belief in the survival of the whole person (such as in Plato's view), since for him the person is a union of body and soul together, and at death that union no longer exists.

Classical philosophy after Aristotle concerned itself with practical issues of living, especially the quest for happiness and peace of mind. Epicurus (341–271 B.C.E.), who was introduced to the writings of Democritus in his early teens, propounded an atomistic metaphysics and the attendant skepticism toward an afterlife. For epicureanism, the goal of each human being is tranquility (*ataraxia*) of soul. This tranquility can be achieved only after certain fears are conquered—chiefly, the fear of the gods and of death. Atomism solves both fears at once, he argues, while at death the subject ceases to exist and therefore is touched neither by the gods or the experience of death itself.

As Athens gave way to Rome as the cultural epicenter of the ancient world, the philosophy of stoicism grew in prominence and influence. Among its most eloquent expositors was the Roman emperor Marcus Aurelius (121–180), whose *Meditations* is an especially rich source of reflection on the meaning of life in the face of death. Stoicism emphasizes acceptance of that which is outside of human control, in particular, the workings of nature, seen as a divine and governing force. Aurelius viewed death as either a cessation of sensation or as an ascent to the divine—and hence nothing to fear in either case.

Medieval Period

The Middle Ages saw a gradual convergence of philosophical and theological concerns. The great thinkers of this age were theologians first and philosophers second. Augustine (354–430) held firm to the Christian notions of the human predicament. The human being is in a state of misery because of a diseased condition brought on by original sin, for which the chief punishment is death. In Augustine's view, God created human beings to live according to his commandments. In the *City of God,* Augustine argues that should the human being live righteously,

> He should pass into the company of angels, and obtain, without the intervention of death, a blessed and endless immortality; but if he offended the Lord his God by a proud and disobedient use of his free will, he should become subject to death, and live as the beasts do, the slave of appetite, and doomed to eternal punishment after death. *(Dods 1872, XII, p. 21)*

But there is a way out of this misery. Augustine, accepting the Platonic dualism, believed that the soul was the true person and can exist apart from the body. The soul, therefore, can escape the misery endemic to earthly life, but only with God's help and grace.

For many medieval thinkers, Plato's thinking provided the necessary philosophical groundwork for belief in an afterlife. For the most part, the medieval theologian/philosophers welded Platonism to Christianity so firmly that criticism of the synthesis was nearly tantamount to heresy. This dogmatism was reflected clearly in Bonaventure (1221–1274), a Franciscan and Augustinian thinker who rejected the influx of Aristotelian ideas in his time because they seemed to deny the immortality of the soul.

There was the occasional crack in the Platonic/Christian foundation of medieval philosophy. The Islamic theologian/philosophers Avicenna (980–1037) and Averroes (1126–1198) appear to have interpreted Aristotle in such a way to raise doubts about individual immortality. According to this perspective, if anything of the soul survives, it is not the individual person but some divine spark that rejoins its supra-individual source.

It took the towering intellect of Thomas Aquinas (1225–1274) to come to terms with the powerful Aristotelian system and the consequences for Christianity of its clear-cut denial of the mind-body dualism. For Aristotle, the soul is not trapped in a body but is naturally allied with it. Although this conception makes it harder to disentangle a distinctly immortal soul from the mortal body at death, Aquinas elicits from it support for the Christian notion of an afterlife—that is, a bodily resurrection. Since the soul is united with a particular body, at death this natural unity will be restored through a physical resurrection that reunites body with soul. Christ's own resurrection was, after all, a bodily resurrection.

Modern Period

The Frenchman René Descartes (1596–1650), the father of modern philosophy, provides support for belief in an afterlife. In *Discourse on Method* he writes,

> Next to the error of those who deny God . . . there is none which is more effectual in leading feeble minds from the straight path of virtue than to imagine that . . . after this life we have nothing to fear or to hope for, any more than the flies or the ants. *(Haldane and Ross 1931, p. 276)*

Further, the original subtitle to Descartes's major work, the *Meditations,* was "In which the existence of God and the Immortality of the Soul are demonstrated." Descartes provides an argument for the immortality of the soul by suggesting a radical difference between the two substances, mind and body, such that mind is in no way dependent on the body for its existence.

Arguments like Descartes's were rejected by those who did not share his radical dualism. The Englishman Thomas Hobbes (1588–1679), for instance, held that belief in an afterlife is a result of religious superstition driven chiefly by the fear of death. David Hume (1711–1776), in "Of the Immortality of the Soul," argues that the case for mortality was strong and asked, "What reason is there to imagine that an immense alteration, such as made on the soul by the dissolution of the body, and all its organs of thought and sensation, can be effected without the dissolution of the soul?" (Hume 1993, p. 406).

An entirely different approach was taken by Immanuel Kant (1724–1804), who provided what has come to be known as the "moral argument" for the immortality of the soul. Kant acknowledged that humankind cannot demonstrate, as a matter of certainty, things like the existence of God and the immortality of the soul. However, in *Critique of Practical Reason,* he writes, "It is morally necessary to assume the existence of God" and that morality requires humankind to pursue a state of complete virtue (*summum bonum*), which is "only possible on the supposition of the immortality of the soul" (Abbot 1927, pp. 218–219).

Among the other major moderns who grappled with human mortality, the French thinker Blaise Pascal (1623–1662) argued in *Pensées* that the human being is unique in having the knowledge of death. In *Ethics*, the Dutchman Baruch Spinoza (1632–1677) wrote that "a free man thinks of nothing less than death, and his wisdom is a meditation not of death but of life" (Elwes 1919, p.113). Some interpret these lines as simply a recommendation to avoid consideration of death because it arouses wasteful fears. On this interpretation, Spinoza's advice is similar to that of the French essayist Michel de Montaigne (1533–1592), who, in *Essays* wrote that humans should adopt the attitude of the simple, nonphilosophical person and not "have death constantly before our eyes" because "nature teaches [him] not to think of death except when he actually dies" (Zeitlin 1936, p. 208). Others see in Spinoza one who became a free and wise man only after much thought about death and much grappling with his fears about it, so that what he really meant was that a wise and free man will become so only after confronting and conquering death.

Contemporary Period

Reflections on death and dying in the nineteenth and twentieth centuries extended and reshaped the themes discussed in the modern period. The existentialists, in particular, follow the lead of the German Arthur Schopenhauer (1788–1860), who called death the "muse of philosophy." Schopenhauer, in *The World As Will and Idea,* states "all religious and philosophical systems are principally directed toward comforting us concerning death, and are thus primarily antidotes to the terrifying certainty of death" (Haldane and Kemp 1948, p. 378).

Existentialist thinkers, beginning with Søren Kierkegaard (1813–1855) and Friedrich Nietzsche (1844–1900), were directly concerned with contemplating the deeper meanings of death. Kierkegaard, the father of religious existentialism, begins by contemplating the meaning of existence itself, rather than engaging in philosophical abstractions; he wrote that it was easier to indulge in abstract thought than it was to exist. For him, existence requires passion and truth—and not just any truth, but a truth for which he can live and die. The most important existential truths for Kierkegaard were not those available to objective reason, but those which require subjectivity (or passionate inwardness), courage, commitment, and faith. For Nietzsche, the father of atheistic existentialism, truth required courage. The courageous individual, however, will have the courage to face the inevitable fact for Nietzsche that "God is dead." For Nietzsche, this means that there is no cosmic order, purpose, or meaning in the universe or in human life. What is required is to create one's own order, purpose, and meaning by facing and then slaying death. In *Thus Spake Zarathustra,* he says that what is required is courage which "is the best slayer—courage which attacks: which slays even death itself" (Kaufmann 1954, p. 269).

The twentieth-century existentialists continued the exploration into death as a necessary theme for anyone seeking "authenticity," as Martin Heidegger (1889–1976) put it. In his view, it was all too easy to fall back into an artificial, inauthentic life by ignoring the reality of death and by failing to recognize that the human being is, after all, a "being towards death" (Heidegger 1962, p. 296). Heidegger argues that authenticity comes only in the recognition of human temporality and finitude. For the French thinker Albert Camus (1913–1960), the reality of death must not only be accepted, but it also provides evidence of the "absurd," the lack of any real correspondence between the desires of humankind and the cold, dark universe. The French existentialist Jean-Paul Sartre (1905–1980) followed Nietzsche in rejecting God or any attempt to ground meaning objectively in the universe itself. For Sartre, meaning was found in human freedom, but death was not an obstacle to an individual's freedom. As he states in *Being and Nothingness,* "Death is not an obstacle to my projects; it is only a destiny of these projects elsewhere. And this is not because death does not limit my freedom but because freedom never encounters this limit" (Barnes 1956, p. 547). In a sort of atheistic existentialist version of Epicurus, death is seen as that which a meaningful life never encounters. As Sartre explains, meaning requires subjectivity (as in Kierkegaard), and "I myself escape death in my very project. Since death is always beyond my subjectivity, there is no place for it in my subjectivity" (p. 548).

The analytic philosophers, being drawn to issues of language and logic, perceived the whole topic of death as being outside the proper study of philosophy since, in their view, it is hopelessly bound up with religion and metaphysics. The English philosopher A. J. Ayer (1910–1989), in *Language, Truth, and Logic,* is typical in demanding empirical evidence for belief in an afterlife because "all the available evidence goes to show that it is false" (Ayer 1946, p. 117). Bertrand Russell (1872–1970) went further in *Why I Am Not a Christian,* declaring:

> Man is the product of causes which had no prevision of the end they were achieving; that his origin, his growth, his hopes and fears, his loves and beliefs, are but the outcome of accidental collocations of atoms; that no fire, no heroism, no intensity of thought and feeling, can preserve an individual life beyond the grave; that all the labors of the ages, all the devotion, all the

> inspiration, all the noonday brightness of human genius, are destined to extinction in the vast death of the solar system, and that the whole temple of man's achievement must inevitably be buried beneath the debris of a universe in ruins. *(Russell 1957, p. 107)*

The French religious existentialist Gabriel Marcel (1889–1973) countered this point of view. In *Homo Viator* he states, "If death is the ultimate reality, value is annihilated in mere scandal, reality is pierced to the heart" (Crauford 1951, p. 152). Marcel discusses death from several unique perspectives. He speaks of the "death of man" as following upon the heels of Nietzsche's "death of God." Marcel does not refer to the death of the human species itself because of some catastrophe such as a nuclear war. Rather, he refers to a radical change stemming from what he calls "techniques of degradation," wherein the human person is degraded, dehumanized, and treated as a thing or an object rather than as a person. Under this system of depersonalization, the person is already "dead." However, Marcel finds the possibility for hope. In *Being and Having,* he says that death can be "considered as the springboard of an absolute hope" (Farrer 1949, p. 93). How can death provide hope? An essential part of one's personhood, he argues, lies in one's relationship with others, for humans are intersubjective beings. And while other thinkers have focused on what death and dying means to the individual, Marcel explores what death may mean as an avenue for fuller relationships with others—in particular, those that we love. For Marcel, loving transcends the world of things—and nothing that can happen to the world of things (including death) can affect the person.

In the last few decades of the twentieth century, certain postmodern thinkers have revisited the "death of man" theme. The French thinker Michel Foucault (1926–1984), for instance, speaks of the "death of man," and his countryman Jacques Derrida (1930–) refers to the "ends of man." Foucault, following Heidegger, also examines death in terms of an "analytic of finitude" (Shuster 1997).

See also: BUDDHISM; CHINESE BELIEFS; HEIDEGGER, MARTIN; HINDUISM; ISLAM; KIERKEGAARD, SØREN; MIND-BODY PROBLEM; PLATO; PLOTINUS; SARTRE, JEAN-PAUL; SCHOPENHAUER, ARTHUR; SOCRATES; ZOROASTRIANISM

Bibliography

Aristotle. *The Basic Works of Aristotle,* translated by Richard McKeon. New York: Random House, 1941.

Augustine. *The City of God,* translated by M. Dods. Edinburgh: T & T Clark, 1872.

Aurelius, Marcus Antoninus. *Marcus Antoninus Aurelius,* translated by C. R. Haines. Cambridge, MA: Harvard University Press, 1916.

Ayer, A. J. *Language, Truth and Logic.* New York: Dover Publications, 1946.

Derrida, Jacques. "The Ends of Man." In Alan Bass tr., *Margins of Philosophy.* Chicago: University of Chicago Press, 1982.

Descartes, René. *Discourse on Method,* translated by R. B. Haldane and G. R. T. Ross. In *The Philosophical Works of Descartes.* Cambridge: Cambridge University Press, 1931.

Edman, Irwin, ed. *The Works of Plato.* New York: Modern Library, 1930.

Epicurus. "Letter to Menoeceus," translated by C. Bailey. In *Epicurus: The Extant Remains.* Oxford: Clarendon Press, 1926.

Foucault, Michael. *The Order of Things.* New York: Random House, 1970.

Guthrie, W. K. C. *A History of Greek Philosophy.* Cambridge: Cambridge University Press, 1971.

Heidegger, Martin. *Being and Time,* translated by John Macquarrie and Edward Robinson. New York: Harper and Row, 1962.

Hume, David. "On the Immortality of the Soul." In Stephen Copley and Andrew Edgar eds., *Selected Essays.* Oxford: Oxford University Press, 1993.

Kant, Immanuel. *Critique of Practical Reason,* translated by T. K. Abbot. London: Longmans Green, 1927.

Kierkegaard, Søren.*Concluding Unscientific Postscript,* translated by D. F. Swenson. Princeton, NJ: Princeton University Press, 1941.

Kirk, G. S., and J. E. Raven. *The Presocratic Philosophers.* Cambridge: Cambridge University Press, 1957.

Marcel, Gabriel. *Searchings.* New York: Newman Press, 1976.

Marcel, Gabriel. *The Mystery of Being,* translated by R. Hague. 2 vols. Chicago: Henry Regnery Company, 1960.

Marcel, Gabriel. *Homo Viator,* translated by Emma Crauford. Chicago: Henry Regnery Company, 1951.

Marcel, Gabriel. *Being and Having,* translated by Katherine Farrer. London: Dacre Press, 1949.

Montaigne. *Essays,* translated by Jacob Zeitlin. New York: Dover Publications, 1936.

Nietzsche, Friedrich. *Thus Spake Zarathustra.* In *The Portable Nietzsche,* edited and translated by Walter Kaufmann. Princeton, NJ: Princeton University Press, 1954.

Pascal, Blaise. *Pensees and The Provincial Letters,* translated by W. F. Trotter and Thomas M'Crie. New York: The Modern Library, 1941.

Plato. *The Collected Dialogues of Plato,* translated and edited by Edith Hamilton and Huntington Cairns. Princeton, NJ: Princeton University Press, 1961.

Russell, Bertrand. *Why I Am Not a Christian.* New York: Simon & Schuster, 1957.

Sartre, Jean-Paul. *Being and Nothingness,* translated by Hazel E. Barnes. New York: Philosophical Library, 1956.

Schopenhauer, Arthur. *The World As Will and Idea,* translated by R. B. Haldane and J. Kemp. London: Routledge & Kegan Paul, 1948.

Schuster, Joshua. "Death Reckoning in the Thinking of Heidegger, Foucault, and Derrida." *Other Voices* 1, no. 1 (1997).

Spinoza. *Ethics,* translated by R. H. M. Elwes. London: Bell Publishing, 1919.

Thody, Philip. *Albert Camus: A Study of His Work.* New York: Grove Press, 1957.

WILLIAM COONEY

PHOENIX, THE

In ancient Greek and Egyptian mythology, the phoenix is a mythical bird associated with the Egyptian sun god Ra and the Greek god Phoibos Apollo. The bird symbolizes resurrection and immortality and has retained its symbolic connotation of life arising anew from the ashes of death. The Romans compared the phoenix with the Eternal City, and even put it on a coin as a symbol of the undying Roman empire. The phoenix as a symbol of resurrection might have appealed to early Christians as well.

According to the Egyptians, the phoenix was as large as an eagle or as a peacock, with brilliant plumage and a melodious cry. According to the Greeks, the bird lived in Arabia. Each morning at dawn the phoenix would bathe in the water and sing so beautifully that the sun god would stop to listen. Both the Egyptian and the Greek traditions mention that only one phoenix could exist at any time and that it had a long life (from 500 to 1,461 years). Upon sensing its approaching death, the phoenix would build a nest of aromatic wood, set it on fire, and allow itself to be consumed by the flames. From the ashes in the pyre a new phoenix would spring to life that would then embalm the ashes of its father in an egg of myrrh and fly with them to Heliopolis ("the city of the Sun") in Egypt. There it would deposit the egg on the altar of the sun god.

See also: OSIRIS; REINCARNATION

Bibliography

Bonnefoy, Yves. *Greek and Egyptian Mythologies.* Chicago: University of Chicago Press, 1992.

Burkert, Walter. *Structure and History in Greek Mythology and Ritual.* Berkeley: University of California Press, 2001.

Lançon, Bertrand. *Rome in Late Antiquity: Everyday Life and Urban Change: A.D. 312–609.* Edinburgh: Edinburgh University Press, 2000.

Sissa, Giulia, and Marcel Detienne. *The Daily Life of the Greek Gods,* translated by Janet Lloyd. Stanford, CA: Stanford University Press, 2000.

JEAN-YVES BOUCHER

PLATO

The poet Ralph Waldo Emerson once remarked, "Plato is philosophy and philosophy is Plato" (Emerson 1996, p. 21). No less adulation came from the philosopher Alfred North Whitehead, who claimed that Western philosophy was a "series of footnotes to Plato," (Whitehead 1929, p. 63). These kinds of acclamations give one a sense of the major importance of the thinker originally named Aristocles, who came to be called Plato because of his robust figure. Born into one of the most distinguished families in Athens, Plato (428–348 B.C.E.) seemed destined for a career in politics. This changed mainly because of the influence of his great mentor Socrates (470–399 B.C.E.), who was falsely accused of impiety and corrupting the youth and executed by the state. Becoming distrustful of politics, Plato decided to carry on the philosophical traditions of his mentor. He founded the Academy, considered the first university in Western civilization, and wrote the *Dialogues,* which continue the eternal questions raised by Socrates.

Plato was especially interested in his mentor's pursuit of real, eternal truths (Justice, Beauty, Goodness), which Plato believed had an existence beyond the mere physical world of flux and change. Accordingly, Plato developed a dualism: There is the physical and changing world (to which the body belongs), and the permanent and immaterial world (to which the mind or soul belongs). The body is then seen as the prisoner and temporary residence of the soul, which has existed before its imprisonment and which will exist again after its release from the body at death. In this way, says Plato, the true philosopher is "always pursuing death and dying" (Emerson 1996, p. 21).

The *Dialogues* offer a variety of arguments for the immortality of the soul. In the *Republic,* Plato argues that the soul cannot be destroyed by any inherent evil or by anything external to it. In his *Phaedrus* he reasons that the soul is its own "self-moving principle" and is therefore uncreated, eternal, and indestructible. And in the *Phaedo* a series of arguments are offered based on the cyclical nature of life and death; knowledge the soul could only have gained in a pre-existence; the incorporeal or spiritual nature of the soul; and the view that the soul is the essence and principle of life itself.

The argument regarding the nature of the soul is perhaps the one that gets discussed by scholars most often. If the soul is incorporeal, it is simple or uncomposed (not made up of parts). But death is the decay and corruption of a thing into its elementary parts (decomposition). The soul, therefore, cannot die since an uncomposed entity cannot be decomposed. The logic of this argument is compelling; however, it depends entirely on its key premise: that the soul is spiritual, not corporeal. This is a major point of contention for many, including Plato's greatest student—Aristotle (384–322 B.C.E.). Though he firmly believed in the immortality of the soul, Plato never considered his arguments to be conclusive proofs and recognized the need for further discussion and consideration, saying that one can only "arrive at the truth of the matter, in so far as it is possible for the human mind to attain it" (Hamilton and Cairns 1961, p. 107).

See also: PHILOSOPHY, WESTERN; PLOTINUS; SOCRATES

Bibliography

Emerson, Ralph Waldo. "Plato; or, The Philosopher." *Representative Men.* Cambridge, MA: Harvard University Press, 1996.

Friedlander, Paul. *Plato: An Introduction.* New York: Harper and Row, 1964.

Plato. *The Collected Dialogues of Plato,* edited and translated by Edith Hamilton and Huntington Cairns. Princeton, NJ: Princeton University Press, 1961.

Whitehead, Alfred North. *Process and Reality.* New York: Macmillan, 1929.

WILLIAM COONEY

PLOTINUS

Plotinus (c. 204–270) was the leading exponent of Neoplatonic thinking, which blended Plato's philosophy with religious mysticism. Born in Egypt, he grew up in Alexandria (located on the central coast of Egypt, just west of the Nile Delta) and was educated in the classics. His own teachings quickly gained notoriety, especially in Rome. He did not begin to write until late in life, and his lectures were edited by his student, Porphyry, for the *Enneads.*

Plotinus was attracted to the Platonic metaphysics of transcendence; that is, the location of reality outside of this physical, sensory world, in a suprarational, spiritual world of the "Good." Plotinus used religious/mystical phrases to refer to this reality, such as "the One," "All-Transcending," "Author at once of Being," "The First," and the "Indefinable." His religious views have typically been described as pantheistic, which holds that the divine principle is present in and throughout the entire universe, although a dualistic representation (where the divine and the created universe are seen as separate) could also be supported, given the subtleties of Neoplatonic thought.

Plotinus saw life in the universe as a double movement—first as an emanation from the source (as light emanates from the sun), and then a return back to the divine. The human soul lives in exile on this earth, and desires the return home. One can achieve "home" in this life through a mystical union with God. Porhyry relates that his master had achieved a mystic state quite often in his life, and that this experience could not be given a completely rational account. One can also reach home through reincarnation (another Platonic influence) —where one can achieve higher forms of life until eventually passing out of the cycle of birth and death. This "emancipation of souls" is accomplished only by a "purification" whereby the soul avoids attachments to the body, in particular, lusts and sensual desires and impulses.

Neoplatonism was one of the chief ways in which the Platonic philosophy was introduced to Medieval thinkers like Augustine, and therefore had major impact on the Christian world.

See also: PHILOSOPHY, WESTERN; PLATO

Bibliography

O'Daly, J. P., *Plotinus' Philosophy of The Self.* Shannon, Ireland: Irish University Press, 1973.

Plato. *The Republic.* In Benjamin Jowett trans., *The Dialogues of Plato.* New York: Random House, 1937.

Plotinus. *Enneads.* In G. H. Turnbull trans., *The Essence of Plotinus.* New York: Oxford University Press, 1934.

WILLIAM COONEY

POLYNESIAN RELIGIONS

In treating all subjects, including death, Polynesian religions are based on experience rather than faith. Prominent among those experiences are encounters with many different types of gods and spirits. These include human beings who have died and assumed one of several possible forms. For instance, miscarried or aborted fetuses can be transmuted into vicious demons. Neglected souls can become wandering, homeless, pathetic ghosts. Revered relatives can be transformed into family gods. The diversity of such experience stimulates a wide variety of beliefs and practices.

Polynesians believe in life after death. Indeed, the wall between the living and the dead is more permeable than in modern Western culture. When a person is about to die, one of his or her souls can—unbeknownst to him or her—warn the immediate family. Shortly after dying, a person can visit relatives and friends. The family of the deceased prays for the soul's successful journey to the land of the dead. The dead can linger, however, around the living to whom they were especially attached. Elderly couples continue to converse long after one of them has died. The surviving lover can be pulled toward the new home of the beloved. According to the Polynesian belief system, the world of the living is in continual communion with that of the dead.

Family and friends must, therefore, establish methods for both detachment and attachment. The clothes and belongings of the deceased can be destroyed. At the wake of the deceased, the New Zealand *mâori* "trample" through the house to reclaim it for the living. In formal oratory, they call upon the ancestors for their blessing but dismiss them before the body of their speech. Throughout Polynesia, the troublesome presence of a dead person reveals the existence of unfinished business that must be resolved before the soul can depart in peace.

The positive relation to the ancestors and the recently dead is, however, one of the strengths of Polynesian culture. Genealogy provides identity as well as individuals upon whom one can call for help. An elder who has been revered as a leader in life does not lose his or her love of family after death. If the family feels the need for his or her continuing care, they can strengthen the soul's presence with offerings and prayer. Hawaiian families conduct ceremonies to transform the deceased into the body of the animal to whom the family is related. A fisherman of the shark family is guarded by his embodied relative. Children of the owl family can be led out of danger by the bird who appears to help them. Similarly, family and even friends can use body parts of the dead to create servant spirits, which lack the full personality of a family god but are obedient servants for limited tasks.

Polynesian spiritual practices are possible because souls are physical. At death, a soul exits the body from a tear duct and begins a tentative, instinctive journey into the uplands for a time and then proceeds along the path of the spirits to the place on each island where the souls jump off into the land of the dead. If a soul expert feels the person should not have died, he or she can find the soul, "snatch" it between cupped hands, reinsert it

Ancient Polynesian temple platforms, marae, *are still considered to be holy places by many Polynesians although indigenous religious practice has largely ceased. Ritual dances and sacrifices are sometimes re-enacted for tourists and guests of the islands.* JACK FIELDS/CORBIS

under the big toe, and massage it up the body until the person revives. On the other hand, an enemy can capture the soul and destroy it, annihilating the deceased. Polynesians believe in life after death, but not necessarily immortality.

As in all aspects of Polynesian religion, human beings are seen as powerful and capable. They are not terrified and overpowered by phenomena of the dead. Inborn talent, trained sensitivity, and education enable them to handle gods and spirits as naturally as they do the winds and the waves. Indeed, Polynesian Christians, living in the same world as their ancestors, often supplement their new religion with such traditional beliefs and practices. The combinations they create are compelling and broadening. The Polynesian's understanding of family as a spiritual power, of deceased family members as continuing sources of love and care, of the closeness and communion of the living and the dead, and of the human being's capacity to manage death as well as life are a genuine contribution to the world.

See also: African Religions; Afterlife in Cross-Cultural Perspective; How Death Came into the World

Bibliography

Kamakau, Samuel M. *Ka Po'e Kahiko: The People of Old.* Honolulu: Bernice Pauahi Bishop Museum.

Moyle, Richard. *Fâgogo: Fables from Samoa in Samoan and English.* Auckland: Auckland University Press, 1981.

Orbell, Margaret. *The Illustrated Encyclopedia of Mâori Myth and Legend.* Canterbury: Canterbury University Press, 1995.

Pukui, Mary Kawena, E. W. Haertig, and Catherine A. Lee. *Look to the Source.* Honolulu: Hui Hânai, 1979.

JOHN P. CHARLOT

Population Growth

Population growth refers to change in the size of a population—which can be either positive or negative—over time, depending on the balance of births and deaths. If there are many deaths, the world's population will grow very slowly or can even decline. Population growth is measured in both absolute and relative terms. Absolute growth is the difference in numbers between a population over time; for example, in 1950 the world's population was 4 billion, and in 2000 it was 6 billion, a growth of 2 billion. Relative growth is usually expressed as a rate or a percentage; for example, in 2000 the rate of global population growth was 1.4 percent (or 14 per 1,000). For every 1,000 people in the world, 14 more are being added per year.

For the world as a whole, population grows to the extent that the number or rate of births exceeds the number or rate of deaths. The difference between these numbers (or rates) is termed "natural increase" (or "natural decrease" if deaths exceed births). For example, in 2000 there were 22 births per 1,000 population (the number of births per 1,000 population is termed the "crude birth rate") and 9 deaths per 1,000 population (the "crude death rate"). This difference accounts for the 2000 population growth rate of 14 per 1,000, which is also the rate of natural increase. In absolute numbers, this means that approximately 78 million people—or about the population of the Philippines—are added to the world each year. For countries, regions, states, and so on, population growth results from a combination of natural increase and migration flows. The rate of natural increase is equivalent to the rate of population growth only for the world as a whole and for any smaller geographical units that experience no migration.

Populations can grow at an exponential rate, just as compound interest accumulates in a bank account. One way to assess the growth potential of a population is to calculate its doubling time—the number of years it will take for a population to double in size, assuming the current rate of population growth remains unchanged. This is done by applying the "rule of seventy"; that is, seventy divided by the current population growth rate (in percent per year). The 1.4 percent global population growth rate in 2000 translates into a doubling time (if the growth rate remains constant) of fifty-one years.

History of Global Population Growth

As can be seen in Figure 1, the world's population grew very slowly until about 1750. There was a long period of stationary growth (no growth) until 1000 B.C.E., when the world's population was approximately 300 million; this was followed by a period of slow growth from 1000 B.C.E. to approximately 1750, at which time global population was an estimated 800 million. Until this time, the world's population was kept in check by high death rates, which were due to the combined effects of plagues, famines, unsanitary living conditions, and general poverty. After 1750, the world's population grew substantially; by 1950 it had tripled to around 2.5 billion. In this 200-year period, the doubling time was 122 years. Growth from 1950 to 1985 was even more dramatic; by 1985, the human population was 5 billion. World population had doubled in thirty-five years. By 2000 global population was 6 billion and is projected to be 9 billion in 2050.

Population growth did not become exponential until around 1750. Before that, high mortality counterbalanced the high fertility needed by agrarian parents. Death rates were high and life expectancy was low; life expectancy at birth was in the range of twenty to forty years (most likely around thirty years) until the middle of the eighteenth century. This high mortality was a function of several factors, including poor nutrition, which led directly to deaths through starvation and indirectly through increasing susceptibility to disease; epidemics; and, quite possibly, infanticide and geronticide, especially during times of food shortage.

Starting in the middle of the eighteenth century, the mortality rate began to decline in the West, the first place in the world where the natural balance between births and deaths was altered by humans. This decline in deaths occurred not because of major medical breakthroughs (e.g., penicillin was first used only in the 1940s) but rather because of improvements in food availability, housing, water cleanliness, personal hygiene, and public sanitation. Later, in the twentieth century, medical advances, particularly vaccinations against infectious diseases, accelerated mortality decline.

FIGURE 1

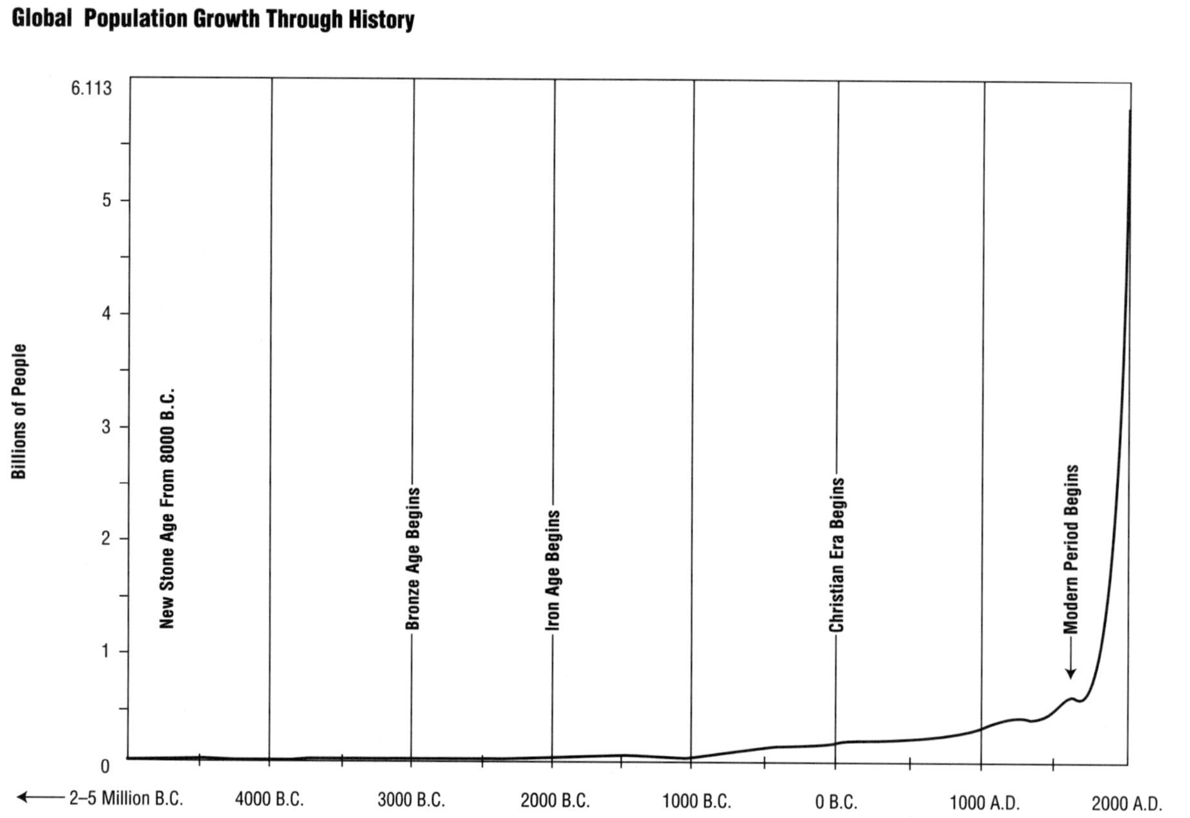

SOURCE: Yaukey, David, and Douglas L. Anderton. *Demography: The Study of Human Population.* Prospect Heights, IL: Waveland Press, 2001.

Western mortality decline was relatively slow, paralleling socioeconomic development, and it occurred in a global context in which European population "surplus" (arising from gaps between lowering mortality and more slowly lowering fertility) was able to migrate to new areas (e.g., the United States, Canada, and Australia) that were very sparsely populated by Aboriginal peoples (whose numbers were reduced even more by contagious diseases brought by Europeans).

Mortality decline in less developed countries followed a different path. First, mortality decreases did not begin until around 1950, much later than in the West. Second, in many less developed countries, substantial mortality reductions occurred in a short period of time. A classic example is Ceylon (now Sri Lanka), where the death rate was halved in less than a decade, starting in the early 1950s. (In the West, a comparable reduction typically took around one century.) In these less developed countries, mortality decreases were not matched by fertility decreases, where they produce population growth rates much greater than those experienced in the West. So the demographic transition that took two centuries to unfold in the West occurred (or is occurring) within the span of a single life. Third, mortality decline did not parallel economic development. Rather, the impetus behind third world mortality reductions originated, for the most part, in factors external to the society. For example, the speedy mortality decline in Ceylon was due to the importation of American technology (pesticides and the airplanes for spraying them) that killed the mosquitoes that were responsible for malaria, the leading cause of death. During the cold war, it was not uncommon for the United States to provide nonaligned countries with such assistance in the hopes of wooing them away from the Soviet Union and a communist development model.

As a result, the world witnessed unprecedented rapid population growth between 1950 and 1985, owing, in large part, to third world increases.

FIGURE 2

World Population and Population Growth Rate, 1950–2050

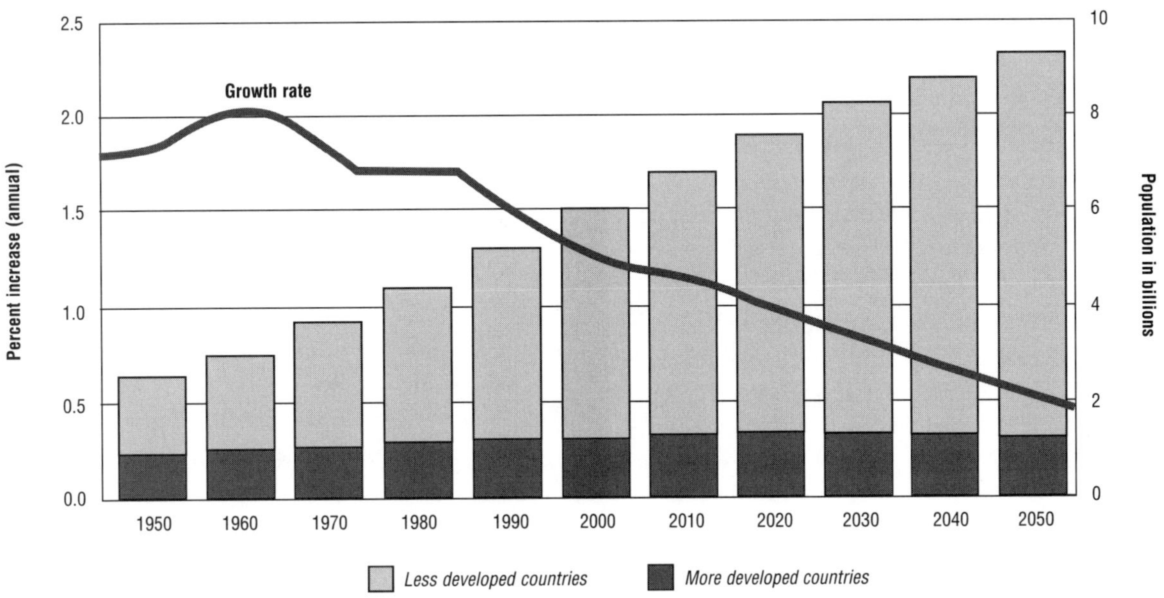

SOURCE: United Nations. *World Population Prospects: The 2000 Revision*. New York: United Nations, 2001.

Further, the phenomenal increase in human numbers over the past 250 years is largely the consequence of mortality declines—not fertility increases. The first deaths to be reduced were those due to infectious diseases, the victims of which were most often children. The old killers of the past were to be replaced by chronic and degenerative diseases; the primary victims shifted from the young to the old.

Population Growth 1950–2050

The rate of global population growth has declined significantly from its 1970s highs (see Figure 2). Current estimates anticipate a continued decline to about 0.5 percent in 2050. This corresponds to a doubling time of 140 years, a rate that has fostered concern about how the world will cope with 18 billion people in 2190.

It is in the less developed countries that the continued growth in population will occur in the twenty-first century. Even though mortality is much higher in less developed countries (e.g., life expectancy at birth in 2000 was 75 years in the more developed countries and 62 to 64 years in the less developed countries), fertility remains even higher, thus accounting for relatively high growth in the third world. However, projections are not guarantees. Population may grow more slowly if, optimistically, fertility declines more quickly than experts expect (e.g., between just 1965 and 1987 the average number of children born to Thai women dropped from 6.3 to 2.2) or, pessimistically, if mortality increases, especially in light of the persistence of HIV/AIDS pandemic and other communicable diseases.

Theories of Population Growth

While theories about population growth first appeared in ancient Greece, the English clergyman and economist Thomas Malthus (1766–1834) is considered to be the pioneering theorist of the modern age. Malthus formulated a "principle of population" that held that unchecked population grows more quickly than the means of subsistence (food and resources) to sustain it. Population will be controlled either by preventive checks (lowering the number of births, particularly by postponement of marriage age) or by positive checks (increasing deaths as a result of famines, plagues, natural disasters, war). Given a morally based preference for preventive checks, later followers of Malthus (neo-Malthusians) have supported family planning and contraception even though Malthus himself felt that contraception was unacceptable. Other neo-Malthusians have focused upon the claimed negative effects of rapid population growth: war, violence, and environmental degradation.

Karl Marx's views on population were directly opposed to those of Malthus. Marx disagreed with the Malthusian idea of a universal principle of population that applied to all societies. For Marx, population growth depended upon the economic base of society. Thus, capitalist society is characterized by its own population principle, which Marx termed the "law of relative population surplus." He argued that capitalism creates overpopulation (i.e., a surplus of people relative to jobs), leading to increased unemployment, cheap labor, and poverty. Also, capitalism requires unemployment in order to ensure a docile, low-paid class of laborers. Marx envisioned that overpopulation would not occur in postcapitalist, communist society.

In the middle of the twentieth century, demographic transition theory became the dominant theory of population growth. Based on observed trends in Western European societies, it argues that populations go through three stages in their transition to a modern pattern. Stage One (pretransition) is characterized by low or no growth, and high fertility is counterbalanced by high mortality. In Stage Two (the stage of transition), mortality rates begin to decline, and the population grows at a rapid pace. By the end of this stage, fertility has begun to decline as well. However, because mortality decline had a head start, the death rate remains lower than the birth rate, and the population continues to experience a high rate of growth. In Stage Three (posttransition), the movement to low fertility and mortality rates is complete, producing once again a no-growth situation. The theory of demographic transition explains these three stages in terms of economic development, namely industrialization and urbanization. Since about 1980, demographic transition theory has been criticized on a number of grounds, including its assumption that the demographic experience of non-Western societies will inevitably follow that of the West; its failure to consider cultural variables; and its hypothesized relationship between population growth and economic development. Indeed, all three theories above contain assumptions about population growth and economic development; however, there is mounting evidence that this relationship is complex and varies from context to context. As the twenty-first century begins, the attempt to erect a general theory of population growth has been abandoned, signaling for some an alarming trend in population studies.

See also: CAUSES OF DEATH; DEMOGRAPHICS AND STATISTICS; LIFE EXPECTANCY; MALTHUS, THOMAS; SOCIAL FUNCTIONS OF DEATH; TECHNOLOGY AND DEATH

Bibliography

Brown, Lester R., Gary T. Gardner, and Brian Halweil. *Beyond Malthus: Nineteen Dimensions of the Population Challenge*. New York: W. W. Norton, 1999.

Coale, Ansley J. "The History of the Human Population." *Scientific American* 231 (1974):40–51.

Ehrlich, Paul R., and Anne H. Erhlich. *The Population Explosion*. New York: Simon and Schuster, 1990.

Furedi, Frank. *Population and Development: A Critical Introduction*. Cambridge, England: Polity Press, 1997.

Homer-Dixon, Thomas. *Environment, Scarcity, and Violence*. Princeton, NJ: Princeton University Press, 1999.

Keyfitz, Nathan. "Population Theory and Doctrine: A Historical Survey." In Alex Inkeles and Masamichi Sasaki eds., *Comparing Nations and Cultures: Readings in a Cross-Disciplinary Perspective*. Englewood Cliffs, NJ: Prentice-Hall, 1996.

Livi-Bacci, Massimo. *Population and Nutrition: An Essay on European Demographic History*. Cambridge: Cambridge University Press, 1991.

McKeown, Thomas. *The Origins of Human Disease*. Oxford: Basil Blackwell, 1988.

McKeown, Thomas. *The Modern Rise of Population*. London: Edward Arnold, 1976.

Overbeek, Johannes. *History of Population Theories*. Rotterdam, Netherlands: Rotterdam University Press, 1974.

Petersen, William. *From Birth to Death: A Consumer's Guide to Population Studies*. New Brunswick, NJ: Transaction Publishers, 2000.

Population Reference Bureau. *World Population Data Sheet, 2000*. Washington, DC: Author, 2000.

United Nations. *Population Growth, Structure and Distribution: The Concise Report*. New York: United Nations, Department of Economic and Social Affairs, 1999.

ELLEN M. GEE

PROTESTANTISM

Protestantism is the collective term applied to Christian denominations originating in groups that separated from the Roman Catholic Church in Europe's sixteenth-century Reformation. Reformers challenged the Church's manipulation of concerns about death and destiny to achieve temporal power and raise revenue. Church responses to the reformers' challenge, and the social and political alliances shaped by the debate, led to the major reform movements becoming churches independent of Rome.

At this time society was preoccupied with death. The Roman Catholic Church occupied a central role mediating between the living and the dead, who were in purgatory—a place of purification for souls readying themselves to enter heaven. The period of suffering in purgatory could be reduced by masses and prayers endowed by family and friends. It was also possible to obtain a special gift of pardon, or indulgence, and by the late Middle Ages indulgences had become commodities sold by the Church.

The reformers asserted that God saved souls by a free, unmerited gift of grace, not through church practices or decrees. They rejected purgatory, prayers for the dead, and the invocation of the saints, adopting an agnostic stance concerning such matters that were not directly attested to by Scripture. Their insistence that the living could no longer work on behalf of the dead brought significant changes to beliefs and practices concerning death, dying, and disposal.

On their death beds Protestants no longer made provision for the repose of their souls through endowing masses, purchasing indulgences, or providing alms for the poor so as to be remembered by them in their prayers. Rather, they sought to testify to the faith they held and in which they now died. A good death was calm, peaceful, and assured; although later in Puritan New England, especially belief in predestination required necessary doubt of salvation, assurance being replaced by anxious repentance.

While Catholic funerals eulogized the deceased and interceded for them in their entry into eternal life, Protestants preached to the living, avoiding any suggestion of intercessions on behalf of the dead. The performative ritual of Catholicism was abandoned: Protestants simply remembered the deceased and sought to learn from their example. Both Catholicism and Protestantism continued to evangelize by heightening the fear of death, fostering contempt for the world and emphasizing suffering as a route to salvation.

The social reorganization that accompanied industrialization changed European burial practices. Garden cemeteries replaced churchyards, separating places of worship from the place of burial. Undertakers appeared to prepare and transfer bodies and, in due course, to coordinate the religious services involved. Further, as medicine became dominant later in the nineteenth century, death was regarded increasingly as a medical challenge, not a spiritual transition. This secularization of dying and disposal initially affected Protestants more than Catholics, as the latter retained their ritual requirements.

The first half of the twentieth century saw the end of any distinctive idea of a Protestant death, and an increasing silence (except in some fundamentalist circles) about the afterlife issues that had dominated earlier religious discourse. By the 1970s these remaining distinctions eroded. Purgatory effectively disappeared from Catholic discourse. Cremation, since World War II a more usual mode of disposal among Protestants, became common among Catholics as well. In the twenty-first century both Catholicism and Protestantism focus upon the living rather than the dead, and both struggle to address the renewed interest in connection with the dead which is emerging in Western societies.

See also: CATHOLICISM; CHRISTIAN DEATH RITES, HISTORY OF

Bibliography

Ariès, Philippe. *The Hour of Our Death.* New York: Alfred A. Knopf, 1981.

Delumeau, Jean. *Sin and Fear: The Emergence of a Western Guilt Culture 13th–18th Centuries.* New York: St. Martin's Press, 1990.

Huizinga, Johan. *The Waning of the Middle Ages.* New York: St. Martin's Press, 1949.

Jupp, Peter, and Glennys Howarth, eds. *The Changing Face of Death: Historical Accounts of Death and Disposal.* Basingstoke, United Kingdom: Macmillan, 1996.

McDannell, Colleen, and Bernhard Lang. *Heaven: A History.* New Haven, CT: Yale University Press, 1988.

Stannard, David E. *The Puritan Way of Death*. New York: Oxford University Press, 1977.

Walter, Tony. *The Eclipse of Eternity: A Sociology of the Afterlife*. New York: St. Martin's Press, 1996.

Walter, Tony. *The Revival of Death*. New York: Routledge, 1994.

BRUCE RUMBOLD

PSYCHOLOGY

For much of its 125-year history, psychology, the study of human behavior, could not find a place for death and dying among the topics that it considered worthy of scientific attention. Although psychology was derived from philosophy, a system that gives death a central role in shaping human thought and conduct, early on there was a schism between those who wanted to study behavior from an experimental, physiological perspective and those who wanted to keep a broader, person-based focus. In Europe during the late 1800s, experimental psychology was advanced by such pioneers as Wilhelm Wundt, Francis Galton, and Alfred Binet, and in the United States by E. L. Thorndike, G. Stanley Hall, James McKeen Cattell, and John Dewey. A more encompassing, holistic approach was advanced in Europe by Sigmund Freud and in America by William James.

With late-nineteenth-century science dominated by Charles Darwin's theory of evolution, it was perhaps inevitable that the fledgling science of psychology steered itself toward the experimental, psychophysiological side of investigation and away from philosophy. Although there were voices in the field hinting at the importance of death for understanding human behavior, psychology as a whole paid little attention.

Logical positivism, a method of inquiry that rejects transcendental metaphysics and requires as proof verifiable consequences in experience, held center stage in psychology until the events of World War II fundamentally changed the way psychologists considered their task. Many of the early experimental theories of behavior emphasized evolutionary (genetic) determinism. However, nothing in the psychologist's laboratory manual could predict or explain the wholesale human destruction of two world wars in fewer than thirty years. Science the savior turned out to be the specter of death in the guise of Nazi Germany and the atomic bomb.

In the wake of World War II, psychology turned its attention to social and organizational behavior, as well as to explanations of racism and violence in the development of malignant personality patterns. It was again willing to consider philosophical approaches to behavior that emphasized the whole person. Logical positivism was eclipsed by existential and humanistic philosophies that grappled with the nature of humanity and the meaning of behavior.

In this context, psychology's first organized approach to death was a symposium titled "The Concept of Death and Its Relation to Behavior," chaired by clinical psychologist Herman Feifel and presented at the 1956 annual meeting of the American Psychological Association in Chicago. The symposium served as the basis for the 1959 book *The Meaning of Death,* edited by Feifel, which is widely recognized as the single most important influence in galvanizing what has since become the multidisciplinary field of thanatology (the study of death, dying, and bereavement).

During the two decades that followed publication of Feifel's book, psychologists began to fully participate in the thanatological community by making important contributions to theory, research, education, and service delivery. Empirical and clinical advances were made in understanding how people construct their ideas and attitudes about death, how ideas about death change from childhood through old age, the nature and meaning of death anxiety, the biological basis of attachment and grieving, and why people commit suicide. Psychologists such as Daniel Leviton and Robert Kastenbaum helped spearhead the death education movement, and the latter built one of the first university centers devoted to the study of death at Wayne State University in Detroit, Michigan. Two of the premier research journals devoted to this topic area were created by psychologists: *Omega: The Journal of Death and Dying* edited by Robert Kastenbaum, and *Death Education,* now called *Death Studies,* edited by Hannelore Wass.

The last two decades of the twentieth century saw a maturing of the field of thanatology, the role played by psychologists in shaping the future of death studies, and the treatment of dying and bereaved persons. During this time psychologists were at the forefront in research on death attitudes and death anxiety; coping with life-threatening illnesses such as cancer, heart disease, and AIDS; grief and bereavement; and the study of suicide. Psychologists helped build and staff hospices for terminally ill patients. Many colleges and universities hired psychologists who made death studies a major focus of their work as part of an expansion of research and coursework in thanatology for students in developmental, clinical, counseling, and school psychology programs.

Empirical and Clinical Findings

From its inception, thanatology has been a multidisciplinary field encompassing anthropology, education, medicine, nursing, philosophy, psychiatry, religion, social work, sociology, the arts, and the humanities. In contrast to this ecumenical trend, research on death attitudes and death anxiety has been conducted mostly by psychologists. Perhaps this is why the literature has shown a strong focus on methodological issues rather than broader sociocultural and applied concerns. By 1995 there were more than 1,000 published studies in this field that addressed diverse subjects, including children, adolescents, adults, the elderly, and the mentally ill. Almost all of these studies involved descriptive, atheoretical, single-assessment designs and used self-report questionnaires. In spite of the limitations inherent in these studies, four themes have emerged from their findings:

1. Most people think about death to some extent and report some fear of death, but only a small subset exhibit a strong preoccupation with death or fear of death.
2. Women consistently report more fear of death than men, but the difference is typically minor to moderate.
3. Fear of death does not increase with age among most people.
4. When considering their own death, people are more concerned with potential pain, helplessness, dependency, and the well-being of loved ones than with their own demise.

Studies have also demonstrated that fear of death is not a unidimensional variable. Various subcomponents are evident in fear of a painful or unpleasant afterlife, fear of the unknown, and fear of a loss of dignity or individuality. In addition, some research has shown that fear of death may take different forms on the conscious and unconscious levels. For example, low levels of self-reported death anxiety may be an outright aversion and avoidance at an unconscious level.

Death possesses many meanings for people and is an important psychological element for all persons, not just the elderly, dying persons, and those facing potential death in their daily activities (e.g., military and police). People think about death and experience the deaths of others throughout life. Adult conceptions of death can be quite complex and involve multiple abstractions, among them the concepts of futurity, inevitability, temporal uncertainty, universality, personal inclusion, and permanence. As humans develop from early childhood into adulthood, their ability to think abstractly also increases. Research has confirmed that among children and adolescents, comprehension of death is related to general levels of cognitive development and personal experiences with death-related phenomena.

The pioneering work of the Hungarian psychologist Maria Nagy identified three stages of development in children's ideas about death. In children from three to five years old she found great curiosity about death and a widespread view of death as a separation where the dead are not as alive as the rest of us but can come back to normal living status. From ages five to nine children begin to understand that death is final but they persist in believing that one might avoid it. Death also becomes personified at this age. From age nine into adulthood there is recognition of death as personal, universal, final, and inevitable.

Research on the death attitudes of children and adolescents demonstrate that they must not be shielded from knowledge of death and should be included in discussions about death at appropriate times. Even the youngest children are aware of separation and its threat to their well being. Young people are inquisitive about death. Adults who exclude children from death-related conversations and experiences do them a disservice by removing them from important sources of information and thus reinforcing anxiety and fear. Adults who wish to participate in educating their children about death must be aware of their own attitudes and values, be prepared to share their feelings and experiences, and serve as models for a healthy appreciation of the importance of death.

Treatment of the Dying and Bereaved

Medical advances have extended the human life span, yet created a growing population of persons (particularly the elderly) who die with chronic diseases. Too often the focus of professionals has been on the physical disease rather than the experiences of the victims. Both clinical and research findings underscore that dying is not just a biological process but also a psychological one. There is an essential need for open and honest communication between the dying person, health-care providers, family, and friends.

The attitudes and fears of caregivers strongly influence the way in which they view and treat the dying and bereaved. Most dying persons and their families want to be apprised of the processes of death, communicate about death and its consequences, and be included in decision-making as it applies to treatment and end-of-life issues. Unless health-care providers can become aware of their own feelings and attitudes, receive education about dying and grief, and become comfortable with the knowledge of death as a multifaceted process that has many derivatives and outcomes, their patients will often be ill-served or even harmed.

The psychiatrist Elisabeth Kübler-Ross conceived a five-stage model of dying and grief that has helped to increase death awareness in the general public and has spawned numerous research investigations. She proposed that as individuals respond to awareness of impending death (their own or that of a loved one), they move through stages of denial, anger, bargaining, depression, and acceptance.

Empirical and clinical investigations inform us that grief unfolds in many different ways and demonstrates not weakness but rather a necessary and deep human need most of us have in reacting to the loss of our own life and that of a loved one. Hard data do not support the existence of stages or schedules through which all persons move as they experience and respond to death. For example, studies of Kübler-Ross's model have shown a simultaneity, omission, or reversal of stages in some individuals.

Because of a lack of precise clinical criteria, healthy and unhealthy grief can be difficult to distinguish. Hence practitioners must be cautious in encouraging survivors to abandon grief prematurely or to wallow in it. They must be alert to signs of personal denial, avoidance, or antipathy among the dying and bereaved so that meaningful interventions can be considered early enough to have the greatest positive impact.

Current and Future Directions

Among the areas of current interest and importance to psychologists are the development of comprehensive theories of dying and bereavement; studies of death and dying among children; theory-based, experimental, longitudinal, and cross-cultural investigations of how death attitudes are related to diverse human behaviors; and development of empirically-validated models and methods for treating the dying and bereaved.

Although thanatology is still waiting for a compelling, realistic framework for understanding death, progress is being made by psychologists in conceptualizing dying and bereavement. People in the field have moved away from viewing grief as a series of predictable stages to seeing it from a task-based perspective. Charles Corr identified four dimensions of tasks: physical, psychological, social, and spiritual. Kenneth Doka suggested a five-phase model of life-threatening illness: prediagnostic, acute, chronic, terminal, and recovery. Clinical psychologist Therese Rando advanced the concept of anticipatory grief to include not only one's reactions to an impending death but also all of the losses experienced throughout one's life. Robert Neimeyer, clinical psychologist, and colleagues have developed their view of bereavement as a task of meaning reconstruction. Robert Kastenbaum has argued for a life-span-developmental approach to death and dying that incorporates a biopsychosocial perspective, stressing an awareness of what anthropologists call etic and emic frames of reference; that is, viewing death from the outside (as observer) and inside (from the point of view of the dying person). He has drawn attention to deathbed scenes as a way of developing a more complete understanding of dying at what is arguably the single most critical point in the process. The social psychologists Tom Pyszczynski, Jeff Greenberg, and Sheldon Solomon applied terror management theory to the fear of death. They argued that a wide variety of behaviors, many of them seemingly unrelated to death, guard against conscious and unconscious fear of personal death.

Since 1956 psychology has moved from its original ostrich approach to death to a recognition of death studies as among the most important in the field. The bounty of books and hundreds of research articles published each year portend a continued flourishing of thanatology in the twenty-first century.

See also: ANTHROPOLOGICAL PERSPECTIVE; ANXIETY AND FEAR; DEATH EDUCATION; DYING, PROCESS OF; FEIFEL, HERMAN; KÜBLER-ROSS, ELISABETH; SOCIOLOGY; STAGE THEORY; TERROR MANAGEMENT THEORY

Bibliography

Corr, Charles A., Kenneth J. Doka, and Robert Kastenbaum. "Dying and Its Interpreters: A Review of Selected Literature and Some Comments on the State of the Field." *Omega: The Journal of Death and Dying.* 39 (1999):239–259.

Feifel, Herman. "Psychology and Death: Meaningful Rediscovery." *American Psychologist* 45 (1990):537–543.

Feifel, Herman. *The Meaning of Death.* New York: McGraw-Hill, 1959.

Freud, Sigmund. *Beyond the Pleasure Principle,* edited and translated by James Strachey. New York: Norton, 1975.

Hall, G. Stanley. "Thanatophobia and Immortality." *American Journal of Psychology* 26 (1915):550–613.

James, William. *The Varieties of Religious Experience.* New York: Modern Library, 1994.

Kastenbaum, Robert. *The Psychology of Death,* 3rd edition. New York: Springer, 2000.

Kübler-Ross, Elisabeth. *On Death and Dying.* London: Macmillan, 1969.

Nagy, Maria. "The Child's Theories Concerning Death." *Journal of Genetic Psychology* 73 (1948):3–27.

Neimeyer, Robert A., ed. *Meaning Reconstruction and the Experience of Loss.* Washington, DC: American Psychological Association, 2001.

Neimeyer, Robert A., and David Van Brunt. "Death Anxiety." In Hannelore Wass and Robert A. Neimeyer eds., *Dying: Facing the Facts,* 3rd edition. Philadelphia: Taylor & Francis, 1995.

Pyszczynski, Tom, Jeff Greenberg, and Sheldon Solomon. "A Dual-Process Model of Defense against Conscious and Unconscious Death-Related Thoughts: An Extension of Terror Management Theory." *Psychological Review* 106 (1999):835–845.

Rando, Therese A., ed. *Loss and Anticipatory Grief.* Lexington, MA: Lexington Books, 1986.

Shneidman, Edwin S. *The Suicidal Mind.* New York: Oxford University Press, 1996.

Strack, Stephen, ed. *Death and the Quest for Meaning.* Northvale, NJ: Jason Aronson, 1997.

Wass, Hannelore, and Robert A. Neimeyer, eds. *Dying: Facing the Facts,* 3rd edition. Philadelphia: Taylor & Francis, 1995.

STEPHEN STRACK
HERMAN FEIFEL

PSYCHOPOMPS

See DEATHBED VISIONS AND ESCORTS.

PUBLIC HEALTH

Public health services can prevent premature death from epidemics such as the plague, cholera, and many other infectious and environmentally determined diseases; and enhance the quality of life. Public health is among the most important institutions of organized societies, almost entirely responsible for the immense improvements in life expectancy everywhere in the world in the past 150 years. Its aims are to promote, protect, and preserve good health, and to sustain people when disabilities render them incapable of fending for themselves. Public health is practiced by a team of specialists trained in medicine, nursing, sanitary engineering, environmental, social, and behavioral sciences, health education, administration, and a variety of other fields. In many nations, including the United States, public health is organized hierarchically at national, regional, and local levels.

Public health services are distinguished from other aspects of the health care system because they are financed by taxation, with no fees paid by the users of these services. This phenomenon can lead to funding crises and staff layoffs when there is political pressure to cut taxes. People and their political representatives often take their health for granted when no epidemics threaten them, so they are not motivated to maintain public health services, staff, and infrastructure at a high level of efficiency and effectiveness, even though ensuring public health is an essential component of the health care system. No nation remains healthy if public health services break down, as they did in Russia after the collapse of the Soviet Union. In this case, infant mortality rates rose, life expectancy fell, and epidemics of diphtheria, typhoid, and other lethal infections occurred. Public health services are as vital to national security as efficient armed forces and the police and fire services. The people of the United States recognized this fact when cases of anthrax occurred in 2001, caused by the introduction of anthrax spores into letters sent through the U.S. Postal Service.

Deadly Epidemics

Since the origins of agriculture and permanent settlements 10,000 years ago, human progress has been punctuated by deadly epidemics. Often arising seemingly out of nowhere, they cut a swath through the population, arousing fear among victims and survivors alike. They were perceived as due to the wrath of a vengeful god, retribution for sinful conduct, or manifestations of evil spirits. Before their causes were understood, survivors full of grief and rage sometimes blamed witches, or those perennial scapegoats, the Jews, extracting vengeance by burning them at the stake or conducting pogroms. Epidemics of plague, smallpox, typhus, cholera, malaria, influenza, and measles have contributed to the fall of civilizations and the defeats of campaigning armies, and they have long fascinated historians as well as epidemiologists. Biblical stories of epidemics indicate the people of those times encountered smallpox and bubonic plague. The historian Thucydides described the plague that decimated the Athenian forces at the end of the first year of the Peloponnesian War (426 B.C.E.), but despite his meticulous description (based partly on having had it himself) the cause remains uncertain. It may have been influenza complicated by bacterial infection. The vitality of the late Roman Empire (200–400 C.E.) was sapped by two diseases better described as endemic than epidemic—malaria, spread by mosquitoes in the Pontine marshes nearby, and lead poisoning, caused by drinking from cups made of tin-lead alloys.

The greatest of all epidemics was the Black Death, which entered Europe at Genoa on ships trading from Asia Minor in 1347, and spread over the next two to three years until it had laid waste to the entire continent. The Black Death killed at least one-third of the population. Sometimes whole villages were wiped out and, in cities such as Paris, organized life and everyday commerce came to a halt. Plague had struck before, for instance at the time of Justinian (543 C.E.), and continued to cause occasional epidemics such as the one in London in 1665 described in Samuel Pepys's diary. However, society had not seen anything on the scale of the pandemic of 1347–1349. The plague bacillus primarily infects rodents and is transmitted by the rats' fleas. Human epidemics occur when ecological conditions bring rats, their fleas, and people together at close quarters in dirty, verminous conditions.

Typhus, caused by a microorganism called Rickettsia, a small bacterium, is spread by the body louse. Epidemics of typhus occur when large numbers of people are confined in close quarters in dirty, verminous clothing (e.g., war refugees and campaigning armies). An impending epidemic that would have had a serious strategic impact was stopped in Naples in 1944 by liberal use of the insecticide DDT. In his classic work *Rats, Lice and History* (1935), the microbiologist Hans Zinsser vividly describes how the outcome of wars has often been decided by which side was more successful in withstanding the deaths from typhus among its fighting forces. The European conquest of the Americas and colonization of the rest of the world was materially assisted by the impact of measles, smallpox, and tuberculosis on the people who had been there before them. Europeans had some inherent resistance to those diseases after many centuries of exposure had weeded out those most susceptible. The Allied campaigns in the Pacific during World War II were facilitated by the fact that American, Australian, Indian, and British forces had effective anti-malarial agents and their Japanese adversaries did not. This fact may have played a larger part in the victory than the atom bombs dropped on Hiroshima and Nagasaki.

In the eighteenth and nineteenth centuries an arrogant assumption by medical men that they could lay their healing hands upon women in childbirth—even when those hands were laden with dangerous bacteria—led to a tragic epidemic of fatal childbed fever. The epidemic ended only when the studies of Ignaz Semmelweiss in Vienna and Budapest and Oliver Wendell Holmes in Boston in the 1840s were translated into hand washing in antiseptic lotion. The use of antisepsis in labor wards and operating rooms, as practiced and advocated by the surgeon Joseph Lister, followed hand washing more than twenty years later.

In the late twentieth and early twenty-first centuries, the HIV/AIDS (human immunodeficiency virus/acquired immunodeficiency syndrome) pandemic had a catastrophic impact on sub-Saharan Africa, comparable to the Black Death in medieval Europe except for the different course of the disease. The plague killed in a few days and HIV/AIDS takes a few years, but the ultimate death rate is higher, approaching 100 percent, whereas at its worst the Black Death killed between 70 percent and 80 percent of its victims. By the end of the twentieth century, HIV/AIDS afflicted more than 40 million people and killed 30 million people.

With the insights of modern evolutionary biology and medical sciences, researchers know that epidemics and many other widely prevalent diseases originated from and are perpetuated by a combination of ecological conditions. Malaria, yellow fever, other vector-borne diseases, and many parasitic infections probably first occurred in humans as a result of evolutionary developments in the causative agents and their vectors. Smallpox, influenza, measles, plague, and several other epidemic diseases probably first afflicted humans by "jumping species" from their origins as diseases of animals that were domesticated by Palaeolithic humans.

In the second half of the twentieth century, most people in the rich industrial nations were able to live long and healthy lives, but as many as 30 to 40 percent of middle-aged men were dying before their potential life span of lung cancer or coronary heart disease, two modern epidemic diseases often attributable to tobacco addiction. Undeterred by the massive evidence that their product is the most powerful addictive substance known, and lethal if used as the manufacturers intended, the tobacco manufacturers embarked upon aggressive and successful campaigns to market cigarettes to girls and women who had previously not often smoked. The result is that lung cancer death rates among women began to rise sharply in the final two decades of the twentieth century, and can be confidently predicted to keep rising so long as women continue to fall victim to tobacco addiction. Similar aggressive and unprincipled tobacco marketing campaigns are being conducted throughout the developing nations in the early twenty-first century. The World Health Organization estimates that the annual number of deaths from tobacco-related diseases could reach 8 to 10 million worldwide by 2025 as a result. This would make tobacco addiction a lethal epidemic disease comparable to if not greater in magnitude than HIV/AIDS.

Historical Origins of Public Health

Contemporary public health services began in the middle of the nineteenth century in response to the squalid conditions that existed in the rapidly growing cities and towns of the industrial revolution. These cities and towns were dangerous places. In the early nineteenth century, a newborn had about one chance in four or five of dying before his or her first birthday, and only about half survived long enough to grow up and have children of their own. They died of diarrheal diseases, including cholera, or of respiratory infections, such as bronchitis, measles, croup, pneumonia, and tuberculosis. Life expectancy in the new industrial towns was only about thirty-five years. This appalling situation challenged the emerging medical sciences and the social reformers to act. Aided by an expanding knowledge and understanding of the times, their efforts led to reduction of infant mortality rates and rising life expectancy. By 1900 infant mortality rates in the industrial nations had fallen to about 100 per 1,000 live births, and life expectancy had risen to about 45 to 50 years. By 1950 infant mortality rates were down to about 40 per 1,000 live births and life expectancy was at or above seventy to eighty years in most of the industrial nations. By 1999 infant mortality rates were below 10 per 1,000, and life expectancy approached 80 years, even in the United States, which has traditionally lagged behind many other wealthy industrial nations.

Social, medical, and public health reform originated largely in England, but took place almost simultaneously throughout much of Western Europe and the United States. A combination of several essential factors made possible these reforms, collectively known as the sanitary revolution. The same essential factors must exist before almost any public health problem can be resolved. These include an awareness that the problem exists; an understanding of what is causing it; the capability to control the cause or causes; belief that the problem is important enough to tackle; and political will.

An awareness that the problem exists. In the middle to late nineteenth century, awareness was facilitated by rising literacy, the availability of newspapers, and the development of vital statistics that provided documentary evidence of the magnitude of the problem of deaths from diarrheal diseases and respiratory infections in infancy, childhood, and early adult life. Since the mid–twentieth century, television has played an increasingly important role in drawing attention to new public health problems, such as those associated with toxic pollution of the environment.

An understanding of what is causing it. John Snow, the English physician who investigated the cholera epidemics in London in the 1840s and 1850s, provided evidence that the disease was spread by polluted drinking water. The cholera vibrio, the causative organism, was not discovered until about thirty years later, but recognition that polluted water was spreading cholera enabled some preventive action—provision of clean water supplies—to begin.

Capability to control the cause or causes. Oliver Wendell Holmes and Ignaz Semmelweis demonstrated that washing hands in a disinfectant could prevent most cases of childbed fever. Both men were vilified by their colleagues who regarded it as an insulting slur on their character to imply that their dirty hands caused the disease. Joseph Lister was successful because his carbolic spray implied that the cause was not necessarily the unhygienic habits of the doctors but rather bacteria in the air in operating rooms and lying-in wards in hospitals. By then, many varieties of dangerous bacteria had been discovered and linked to the diseases that they caused.

Belief that the problem is important enough to tackle. Historically, a mounting emotion of public outrage about what is perceived to be an intolerable burden upon the people is the catalyst for change. The phrase "filth diseases" evokes the distaste for unhygienic conditions that contributed to the burden of premature deaths in nineteenth-century industrial Britain. Geoffrey Vickers, a British social policy specialist, referred to this rising public outrage as "redefining the unacceptable"—a phrase that captures the essential factor in setting a new goal for public health.

Political will. A public health problem will persist unless there is determination to correct the conditions that cause it. This usually means disturbing the status quo and encroaching upon the livelihood of individuals and often powerful interest groups—slum landlords, nineteenth-century water supply companies, twentieth-century tobacco manufacturers, and twenty-first-century industry, energy, and transport sectors resisting action to control global climate change. Moreover, it costs money to make the necessary changes, which usually results in additional taxes and extended political debate.

Methods of Public Health

Health can be preserved, protected, and promoted in several ways, including ensuring the environment is safe, enhancing immunity, and living a healthy lifestyle.

Ensuring the environment is safe. A safe environment includes drinking water that is free from dangerous pathogenic organisms and toxic substances. This requires purification of public water supplies, a sanitation service with efficient sewage disposal, and safeguards against contamination of water and food supplies by pathogens and toxic chemicals. In modern urban industrial societies clean air is another part of the natural environment that must be protected: clean indoor air, free from tobacco smoke, as well as urban air free from smog. Efforts to clean both outdoor and indoor air are often initially resisted by various interest groups.

Enhancing immunity. Immunity is enhanced by vaccination or immunization against infectious diseases in infancy and childhood. Vaccination against smallpox began after Edward Jenner, a physician in Gloucestershire, England, experimented on his patients with cowpox lymph in the late eighteenth century. His results, published in *An Inquiry into the Variolae Vaccinae* (1798) were perhaps the single most important public health advance of the second millennium. Smallpox had long been one of the great epidemic scourges. It killed 40 percent or more of all who were infected by the virus, and disfigured, sometimes blinded, many more. Within one hundred years it had been brought under control in most parts of the world and in 1980, after a determined global eradication campaign, the World Health Organization proclaimed the worldwide eradication of smallpox. Vaccines and sera containing immunizing agents have been developed against many other dangerous and often lethal infectious agents. See Table 1 for a list of the most important, all of which (except polio) caused innumerable premature deaths. Vaccines to prevent smallpox and rabies, two deadly virus diseases, were developed long before the agent was discovered, which had to await the invention of the electron microscope. Discovery of the bacterial agents responsible for many other dangerous infections occurred rapidly in the late nineteenth century, following the development of high-quality microscopes and the techniques of bacterial culture.

Living a healthy lifestyle. Living a healthy lifestyle means abiding by the maxim of the ancient Greeks, "Nothing to excess." It includes avoiding harmful addictive substances, especially tobacco, and adhering to a balanced diet and regular exercise program. Living a healthy lifestyle can be encouraged by health education campaigns. Adhering to a balanced diet—comprised of the right mix of protein, fats, and carbohydrates, with vitamins and essential trace elements—is necessary to achieve good health and prevent premature death. Famine conditions have killed populations of people in the past, partly from starvation itself but also because malnutrition makes people, especially children, vulnerable to deadly infections such as measles, and reduces resistance to tuberculosis.

Other methods of public health include carefully nurturing the next generation; ensuring that children are well-borne and do not have inherent genetic defects or malformations that result from exposure to toxic substances; and prudent use of diagnostic and therapeutic medical services (i.e., avoiding multiple and often needless exposures to diagnostic X rays, coronary artery surgery for elderly people at the upper extremity of the life span, and cosmetic breast implants), which can be harmful if improperly applied.

See also: AIDS; BLACK DEATH; CAUSES OF DEATH; DEATH SYSTEM; LIFE EXPECTANCY; TECHNOLOGY AND DEATH

Bibliography

Last, John M. *Public Health and Human Ecology,* 2nd edition. New York: McGraw-Hill, 1997.

McMichael, A. J. *Human Frontiers, Environment, and Disease: Past Patterns, Uncertain Futures.* Cambridge: Cambridge University Press, 2001.

McNeill, William Hardy. *Plagues and Peoples.* Garden City, NY: Anchor Press, 1976.

Snow, J. *Snow on Cholera,* edited and annotated by W. H. Frost. 1936. Reprint, New York: Hafner Publishing, 1965.

Zinsser, Hans. *Rats, Lice and History.* Boston: Little, Brown, 1935.

JOHN M. LAST

PURGATORY

From the third century onward, Christian theologians developed a theory of psychic postdeath purification on the basis of the words of St. Paul: "Fire shall try every person's work." He continues by saying that those who have built their lives upon shoddy foundations "shall be saved, yet saved through fire" (1 Cor. 3:11–15). Paul's was a doctrine of postdeath purification that was shared with late Judaism and early rabbinic thought. From the beginning of their organized existence, therefore, both the synagogue and the early Christian church prayed extensively for their dead, and many of the most ancient prayers to this effect are still found in the liturgies of the Greek and Latin churches.

Several early theologians reflected on the obscurities of the primitive Christian teaching on the state of the soul after death and deduced that between the death of the individual and the final judgment at the end of time there would be an intermediate state. During this state the souls of the dead inhabited a place where, according to their deeds, they were either happy or wretched. Those souls who required purification of their past lives would experience the purifying fire (in Latin *purgatorium*) more drastically than those who were more advanced in holiness before their death. The Greek theologians generally regarded the posthumous purification by fire in the "spiritual" or symbolic sense of psychic transfiguration into a higher condition. Clement and Origen of Alexandria had envisaged that the soul of the departed would be made to learn all the things it had refused to learn on the earth through the strenuous ministrations of correcting angels until it had been purified enough to ascend closer to God. The fourth-century teacher Gregory of Nyssa expressed the idea more generically: "We must either be purified in the present life by prayer and the love of wisdom (*philosophias*) or, after our departure from this world, in the furnace of the purifying fire." And Gregory of Nazianzus, his contemporary, writes in his poetry of the "fearful river of fire" that will purify the sinner after death.

The idea of purgatorium as a place of after-death purification distinct from the finality of the place of the elect and the damned (heaven or hell) that would be determined by God only on Judgment Day was put forward as a learned opinion by leading Western theologians, particularly Jerome, Augustine, and Gregory the Great. These thinkers seemed to wish more than the Easterners to bring some systematic order into the diffuse doctrine of the afterlife and judgment. It was Pope Gregory in the seventh century who elevated the opinion of the earlier thinkers into a more or less formulated doctrine: "Purgatorial fire will cleanse every elect soul before they come into the Last Judgement." So began the divergent thought that developed over the course of centuries between the Byzantines and Latins.

The Eastern Christian world retained a simpler doctrine of the afterlife that maintained that the souls of the elect, even those who were not particularly holy, would be retained in "a place of light, a place of refreshment, a place from which all sorrow and sighing have been banished." This view reflected the statement in Revelation 14:13 that "those who die in the Lord rest from their labors." In short, the state of afterlife as it was envisaged in the Eastern church was generally a happy and restful condition in which the departed souls of the faithful were not divorced from God, but waited on Judgment Day with hopeful anticipation, as the time when they would be admitted to a transfigured and paradisial condition in proximity to God.

The Latin church, on the other hand, developed its doctrine of purgatory with a more marked stress on that state of painful purification that would attend the souls of all those who had not reached a state of purity before their death.

Aptly titled The Burden of Pride *(1868), French printmaker Gustave Doré recreated a scene from Dante's* Purgatory. *Quite possibly the greatest medieval work on the topic,* Purgatory *was the second book in his* Divine Comedy. CHRIS HELLIER/CORBIS

In the tradition of both churches, the state of the souls after death called out to the living to assist them in prayers, both public and private, so that God would show them mercy. In the tenth century, under the influence of Odilo of Cluny, the Feast of All Souls (November 2) was established in the Western calendar as a time when the living prayed for the release from sufferings of all departed Christians. The popularity of this feast helped to fix the idea of purgatory in the religious imagination of Latin Christians. After the twelfth century, Western theology further rationalized the state and purpose of purgatory in arguing that it was a cleansing by fire of the lesser sins and faults committed by Christians (venial sins), and the payment of the debt of "temporal punishment," which medieval theologians taught was still owed by those who had committed grave offenses (mortal sins) even though the penalty of such sins (condemnation to an eternity in hell) had been remitted by God before death. The later rationalization for purgatory, therefore, stood in close relation to the highly developed Western church's penitential theory, as the latter had devolved from feudal ideas of penal debt and remission. The theological tendency is best seen in the work of the scholastic theologian Anselm, who reflects on the nature of eternal penalties incurred by mortals who offend against the prescripts of the deity, in his influential study of the atonement *Cur Deus Homo* (On Why God was Made Man), published in 1098.

Purgatory, as it developed in the West through the later Middle Ages, became more and more of a dismal idea, linked to the understanding of redemption as a penal substitutionary sacrifice, and increasingly distanced from the early Christian notion that the redemption represented God's glorious victory given as a gift to liberate the world. The medieval obsession with the state of the souls after death led to a flourishing of legends and popular narratives of the sufferings of the souls in purgatory. They were, in a sense, the prelude to the greatest medieval work of graphic imagination relating to the subject, Dante's *Purgatory,* the second book of the *Divine Comedy.* Mystics such as Catherine of Genoa also made it a central theme of their visionary teachings, further fixing the idea in the Western mind. In the medieval Latin church the desire to assist the departed souls in their time of sorrow led to a thriving demand for masses and intercessions for the dead, and for "indulgences," which were held to lessen the time of suffering that the souls in purgatory would be required to undergo. This led soon enough to the concept of purgatory being one of the early points of contention in the great religious crisis known subsequently as the Reformation.

Protestant theologians rejected the doctrine of purgatory as one of their first public departures from medieval theological speculation, and the English church censured the "Romish doctrine of Purgatory" outright in its Article 22. The Orthodox churches had much earlier censured the whole idea when ecumenical union was being contemplated in the thirteenth and fifteenth centuries. On each occasion, the Latin Church defended its position in conciliar statements (the Council of Lyons in 1274 and the Council of Florence in 1439). The rejection of the idea by the Reformation teachers led to its defense once again in the sixteenth-century Council of Trent, which led to renewed focus on the idea of purgatory as a distinguishing mark of the authority of the Roman Catholic Church in the domain of defining dogmas not clearly distinguished in the scriptural accounts.

As an idea it lives on in Dante's writings, and in dramatic poems such as John Henry Newman's nineteenth-century "Dream of Gerontius." As a religious factor it is still very much alive in Western Catholicism in the celebration of various Feasts of the Dead, and in the liturgical commemorations of the departed on November 2. Modern Roman Catholic theology, after Trent, has clearly moved away from emphasizing the purifying pains of purgatorial fire and instead highlights the need for the living to commemorate the dead who have preceded them.

See also: AFTERLIFE IN CROSS-CULTURAL PERSPECTIVE; HEAVEN; HELL

Bibliography

Atwell, Robert. "From Augustine to Gregory the Great: An Evaluation of the Emergence of the Doctrine of Purgatory." *Journal of Ecclesiastical History* 38 (1987):173–186.

d'E Jesse, Eustace T. *Prayers for the Departed, Purgatory, Pardons, Invocations of Saints, Images, Relics: Some Remarks and Notes on the 22nd Article of Religion.* London: Skeffington & Sons, 1900.

Hubert, Father. *The Mystery of Purgatory.* Chicago: Franciscan Herald Press, 1975.

Le Goff, Jacques *The Birth of Purgatory.* Chicago: University of Chicago Press, 1984.

Ombres, Robert. *The Theology of Purgatory.* Cork: Merces Press, 1979.

J. A. MCGUCKIN

PYRAMIDS

Historians have said that most of what humans know about ancient cultures is based on funerary artifacts. Certainly no other example of mortuary culture stands out in modern consciousness than the Egyptian pyramids. The first large-scale stone construction in Egypt was the funerary complex of the Third Dynasty king, Netjerikhet Djoser at Saqqara, demonstrating already at this point in history the strong connection between the pyramid and the royal afterlife. This monument was designed by the king's famous vizier and overseer of

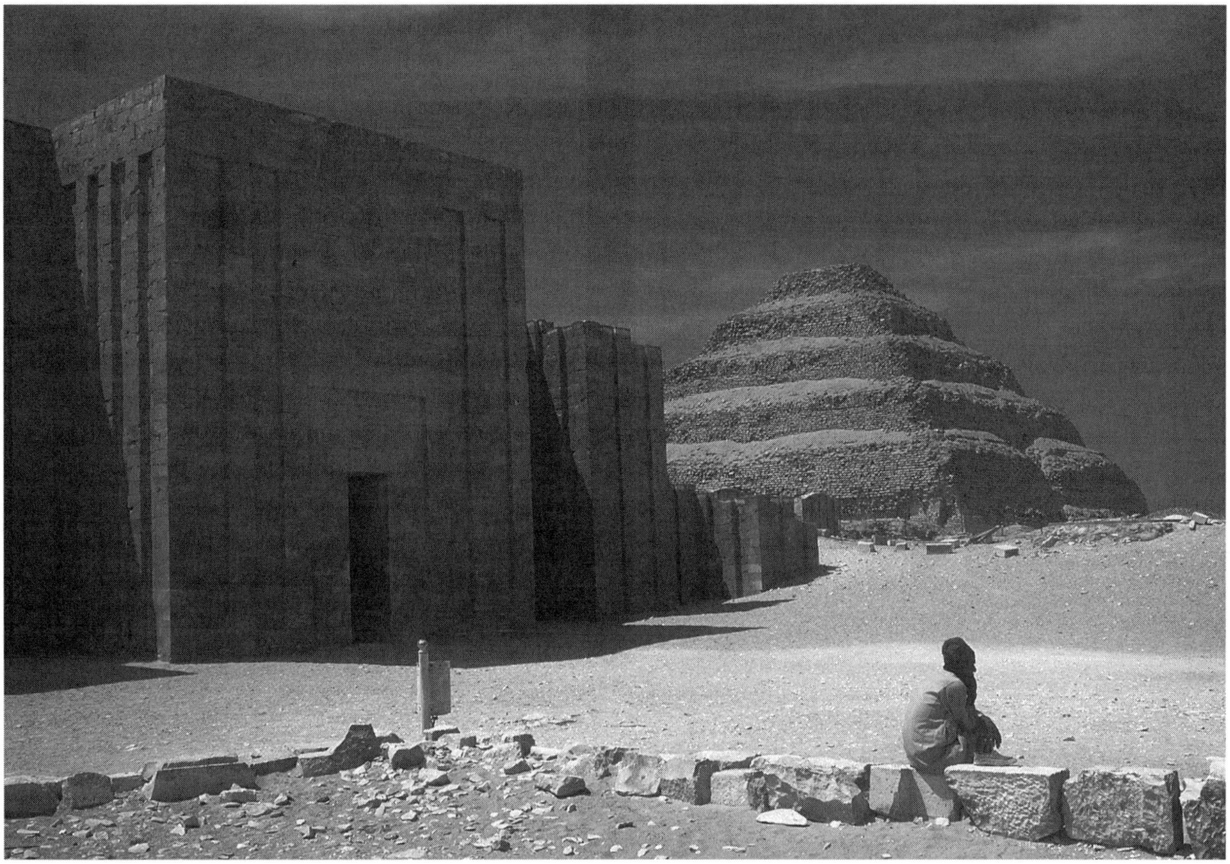

The first pyramid of Egypt, designed by Imhotep in the Third Dynasty, was made for the pharaoh Zoser. The stepped pyramid at the center of the funeral complex, reaches a height of 200 feet, with Zoser's original burial chamber 90 feet below ground. RICHARD T. NOWITZ/CORBIS

works: Imhotep. At its center stood a step-pyramid rising in seven stages to approximately 240 feet in height. Pyramid building reached its climax during the Fourth Dynasty. The first king of the dynasty, Snofru, constructed the first true pyramid, but it was his son Khufu (Kheops) who built the first and largest of all the pyramids at Giza. Over 2.3 million blocks of stone averaging around 2.5 tons apiece were used to erect this enormous structure, which attained a height of about 481 feet and whose square base was 756 feet at each side.

These enormous constructions must have placed a considerable strain on the nation's resources, so it is not surprising that after the Fourth Dynasty both pyramids and royal mortuary complexes and their pyramids dramatically decreased in scale and their construction was shoddier. After some rather small monuments at the beginning of the Eighteenth Dynasty, pyramids ceased to be used for royal burials. Nevertheless, the Egyptians continued to consider pyramids as the most preferable tomb form so that small versions were occasionally incorporated into the superstructure of private tombs during the New Kingdom and Ramesside periods.

The fact that such an inconceivable amount of energy would be expended on these massive funerary structures has given rise to many fantastical alternative explanations as to their origin and purpose. Even though texts explain little specifically about the meaning of the pyramids and say virtually nothing about how they were built, the preponderance of evidence clearly shows that they were intended as the kings' funerary monuments. A combination of archaeological evidence from the sites along with some sparse textual material clearly demonstrates a connection between these monuments and the royal mortuary cult. However, there was a strong association with worship of the sun god Re, the chief religious belief during the

Old Kingdom. The pyramids' shape reminds some of a staircase, but a similarity with a sunburst seems a more probable intent.

Normally the pyramid was the largest part of a vast, tripartite temple enclosure whose purpose was to maintain the king's cult, theoretically in perpetuity. The design details changed constantly, but retained essentially the same pattern. The main access to the pyramid complex was at the valley temple at the edge of the cultivation in the Nile valley, usually affording access to a canal. The valley temple was connected to the high desert plateau by a covered causeway. Finally, the pyramid precinct itself was surrounded by an enclosure wall behind which were subsidiary temples and satellite pyramids intended for the king's soul or family members.

The very fact that the pyramids were intended for the king meant that they had a much broader connection with religion. In Egyptian religious and political ideology, the king—who was both the earthly incarnation of the god Horus and the son of the sun god Ra—was always the nexus between humanity and the realm of the gods. Therefore the pyramids were not merely royal tombs but national endeavors that could help all Egyptians in terms of the gods and the afterlife, reminiscent of the spirit that one can sense behind the great European cathedrals. Interestingly, they did provide at least symbolic immortality to their occupants.

See also: EGYPTIAN BOOK OF THE DEAD; IMMORTALITY; MUMMIFICATION; TOMBS

Bibliography

Edwards, I. E. S. *The Pyramids of Egypt*. Harmondsworth: 1985.

Lehner, Mark. *The Complete Pyramids*. New York: Thames and Hudson, 1997.

OGDEN GOELET JR.

Q

QIN SHIH HUANG'S TOMB

Until 1974, thousands of statues remained to be unearthed on the archaeological site at Shaanxi province, where Qin Shih Huang (c. 221–210 B.C.E.), the first unifier of China, was buried. For more than 2,200 years, these statues had been buried together with the Emperor in a massive city surrounded by two walls some twenty meters high (about 65 feet), and punctuated with gates on the northern, southern, western, and eastern sides and square towers at each corner. The excavation near Qin Shih Huang's tomb also uncovered four pits containing a total of nearly 8,000 figures. The soldiers are organized according to the military conventions of the time. In December 1987 the mausoleum was included in the World Heritage List by United Nations Educational, Scientific, and Cultural Organization.

Emperor Qin Shih Huang, who was only thirteen years old when he became king of Qin, ordered an underground palace to be built as his burial place. PUBLIC DOMAIN

Qin Shih Huang (259–210 B.C.E.) was king of Qin, the largest warrior state in ancient China. One of the most powerful and innovative monarchs in Chinese history, he decreed the building of the Great Wall. He also created many extravagant palaces. Wishing to retain his riches in the afterlife, upon taking the throne he began to build a magnificent underground palace in which he was to be buried. The tomb took some 700,000 workers thirty-eight years to complete. The details of the tomb's scale and contents were recorded in the Shiji, an ancient historical record. Relics excavated from the mausoleum are rich in contents and great in quantity. The king was buried with a symbolic force of life-sized terracotta soldiers, chariots, and horses assembled to protect him in the next world. Other sculptured animals include oxen, dogs, sheep, and pigs. Also, a clay soldier lies beside two iron cooking pots, two large ceramic soup bowls, and some smaller bowls. The figures are all impressively lifelike in their degree of detail.

The arrangement of a tomb was not only an important life event but also a religious rite. Qin

Shih Huang believed that some people could escape from death, either by living for a very long time or by being reborn in a new form. Therefore, he sent people to find drugs that would grant him longevity. He also prepared replicas of worldly goods to help him in his new life. People believed that if the spirit of the deceased were happy, it would intercede in the spirit world on behalf of its descendants and they would do well.

See also: CHINESE BELIEFS; DEATH SYSTEM; IMMORTALITY; TOMBS

Bibliography

First Emperor of China, The. Produced by Ching-chih Chen. Santa Monica, CA: Voyager Company, 1991. Videorecording.

Kern, Martin. *The Stele Inscriptions of Ch'in Shih-huang: Text and Ritual in Early Chinese Imperial Representation.* New Haven, CT: American Oriental Society, 2000.

Lazo, Caroline. *The Terra Cotta Army of Emperor Qin.* New York: New Discovery Books, 1993.

Li Yu-ning, ed. *The First Emperor of China.* White Plains, NY: International Arts and Sciences Press, 1975.

MUI HING JUNE MAK

QUINLAN, KAREN ANN

On April 15, 1975, Karen Ann Quinlan, seventeen years old, presumably ingested barbiturates and alcohol at a party. She became comatose and experienced two periods of apnea (absence of breathing) of about fifteen minutes each, which resulted in irreversible brain damage. She was placed on a respirator and was fed nutrition and fluids by a gastrostomy tube. Her parents were told that she was in a persistent vegetative state from which there was no hope of recovery. Her physician, Robert Morse, considered the ventilator medically appropriate. He claimed that allowing a person in a persistent vegetative state to die was in violation of the professional standard of the time. Quinlan was still in a vegetative state five months later. The electroencephalogram (EEG) showed no signs of brain function, and she did not respond to verbal, visual, or even painful stimuli.

The Quinlan family priest told the parents that they had no moral obligation to continue extraordinary means (the respirator) to support their daughter's life, but that artificial feeding and fluids were "ordinary means" and should be maintained. Quinlan's father said he did not want to kill his daughter but merely wanted the respirator removed so that she had the option of dying a natural death. The Quinlans petitioned the New Jersey Superior Court for permission to remove the respirator. On November 10, 1975, that court denied the parents' request based on its contention that people have a constitutional right to life but do not have a parallel constitutional right to death. The lower court decision was appealed to the New Jersey Supreme Court, which in 1976 decided that "refusal of life-saving treatment" fell under the constitutional "right to privacy." They ruled that Quinlan could be removed from the respirator. However, hospital staff had already weaned her from the respirator, so the court decision was moot. She lived for ten years with the aid of artificial nutrition and hydration. She finally died in December 1985 of pneumonia. Since the Quinlan decision, a number of other states have permitted families to withdraw life support from comatose or terminally ill patients.

The Quinlan case is significant for several reasons. The definition of death, once linked to brain damage and the cessation of heart and lung functioning, had to be modified to accommodate technological advances in life support systems. Patients who formerly would have died can now be maintained indefinitely on life support. Further, considerations to maintain or withdraw life support raised moral and legal issues involved in the nationwide debate on abortion rights, patient's rights, and as well as organ and tissue retrieval for the burgeoning field of organ transplantation. The Quinlan case provided a focus for energetic and productive discussion of the complex and interrelated moral, ethical, and legal issues related to the definitions of life and death, the right to die, and the freedom of choice. The Quinlan case therefore stimulated intensive and productive national debate, discussion, and research on the related subjects of physician-assisted suicide, the quality of life, and the quality of dying.

See also: ADVANCE DIRECTIVES; CRUZAN, NANCY; DO NOT RESUSCITATE; LIVING WILL; NATURAL DEATH ACTS

Bibliography

Angell, M. "After Quinlan: The Dilemma of the Persistent Vegetative State." *New England Journal of Medicine* 330 (1994):1524–1525.

Gordon, M., and P. Singer. "Decisions and Care at the End of Life." *Lancet* 346 (1995):163–166.

The Multi-Society Task Force on PVS. *Medical Aspects of the Persistent Vegetative State* 330 (1994):1499–1508, 1572–1578.

WILLIAM M. LAMERS JR.

R

Rahner, Karl

The Jesuit priest Karl Rahner is widely regarded to have been one of the leading Catholic theologians of the twentieth century. Rahner's early writings on death were published at a time when academic theology gave little serious consideration to the topic. Less sophisticated believers generally assumed that they knew what death was, and quickly moved on to mythological conjectures about the afterlife. Rahner sought to illuminate death's religious and theological significance. These initial publications and later writings are typical of his pioneering investigations, which creatively appropriate diverse theological and philosophical sources (e.g., Ignatian spirituality, Thomas Aquinas, Catholic neoscholasticism, Kant, Hegel, and Heidegger). Notwithstanding their uncompromising rigor, most of his articles had a broadly pastoral concern to explore ways of recovering the meaning of Catholic doctrine in an intellectually plausible and contemporary idiom.

The density of Rahner's work is rooted in the subject matter itself. God, Rahner insisted, is not—and cannot—be an object for thought the way the things of our world are. But a person can know God by attending to the movement of knowing itself toward its objects, which reveals that human thinking always reaches beyond its immediate objects toward a further horizon. The movement of knowing, and the ultimate "goal" toward which it reaches, can be grasped only indirectly (or "transcendentally") as one's thinking turns back on itself reflexively. Rahner identified the elusive and final "term" of this dynamism of knowing with God, and argued that the same kind of movement toward God as "unobjectifiable" horizon is entailed in freedom and love.

By conceiving God, who always exceeds human reach, as the horizon of the movement of knowing, freedom, and love, Rahner emphasized that God is a mystery—a reality who is known and loved, but only reflexively and indirectly, as the ever-receding horizon of the human spirit. God remains a mystery in this sense even in self-communication to humanity through Jesus and the Holy Spirit. With this participation of God in an earthly history of human interconnectedness, something of God is anticipated—known reflexively and indirectly—at least implicitly whenever we know, choose, or love a specific being, particularly a neighbor in need. Conversely, God is implicitly rejected in every refusal of truth, freedom, and love.

Because it is often the good of a neighbor or the world, rather than God or Jesus which is directly affirmed or refused, it is quite possible that the one deciding will be unconscious or even deny that the act is a response to God. In either case, however, one turns toward or away from God and Jesus in turning one's mind and heart freely toward or away from the realities of the world.

Death is a universal and definitive manifestation of this free acceptance or rejection of God's self-communication ("grace"). In that sense, death is the culmination and fulfillment of a person's freedom, the final and definitive establishment of personal identity. It is not simply a transition to a new or continued temporal life. If there were no

Karl Rahner's wide-ranging concerns encompassed questions about the nature of God, Christ, and the relation of the Christian belief to modern understandings of the world. BETTMANN/CORBIS

such culmination, no ability to make a permanent and final commitment of self, then freedom would be an illusion. Genuine self-determination would be denied because every choice could be reversed. If everything is reversible, no act or succession of acts could definitively express an individual's identity. The Christian conviction that this life is the arena in which human fate is worked out, requires the freedom for such definitive acceptance or rejection of God's self-communication. But any anthropology that takes seriously the human capacity for free self-determination would also be required to see death as a kind of culmination and definitive expression of personal identity. Hence death is not something that happens only to the physical body. Death involves and affects the person as a whole. It involves consciousness, freedom, and love. It is not endured passively.

Hence, death as a personal and spiritual phenomenon is not identical with the cessation of biological processes. For example, illness or medication can limit personal freedom well before the onset of clinically defined death. Moreover, insofar as all the engagements of one's life anticipate death, Rahner maintained that every moment of life participates in death. Hence he disputed the notion of death as a final decision if this is understood to be an occurrence only at the last moment.

The Christian tradition has emphasized the definitive and perduring character of personal existence by affirming the soul's survival after death. Rahner warned that this way of conceiving of death can be misleading if one imagines that the separation of soul and body, entails a denial of their intrinsic unity. The contemporary appreciation of the bodily constitution of human reality was anticipated by the scholastic doctrine of the soul as the "form" of the body and thus intrinsically, not merely accidentally, related to it. Personal identity is shaped by one's embodied and historical engagement with the material world. So the culmination of freedom in death must entail some sort of connection with that embodiment. Rahner's notion of God as mystery, beyond objectification in space and time, provides a framework for affirming a definitive unity with God that does not imagine the unity as a place or as a continuation of temporal existence. In the early essays, Rahner addressed the problem of conceiving the connection to embodiment, particularly in the "intermediate state" before the resurrection of the dead on judgment day, with the hypothesis that death initiates a deeper and more comprehensive "pancosmic" relationship to the material universe. In later essays, he recognized that it was not necessary to postulate an intermediate state with notions such as purgatory if one adopts Gisbert Greshake's conception of "resurrection in death," through which bodily reality is interiorized and transformed into an abiding perfection of the person's unity with God and with a transformed creation.

The Christian doctrine of death as the consequence and punishment of sin underscores its ambiguous duality and obscurity. If the integrity of human life were not wounded by sinfulness, perhaps death would be experienced as a peaceful culmination of each person's acceptance of God's self-communication in historical existence. But death can be a manifestation of a definitive "no" to truth and love, and so to God, the fullness of truth and love. Ironically, this results in a loss of self as well because it is unity with God's self-communication that makes definitive human fulfillment possible. In the "no," death becomes a manifestation of futile self-absorption and emptiness, and as such punishment of sin. Moreover, everyone experiences death as the manifestation of that possibility. As a consequence of sin, people experience death as a threat, loss, and limit, which impacts every moment of life. Because of this duality and ambiguity, even a "yes" to God involves surrender. Just as God's self-communication to humanity entailed fleshing out the divine in the humanity of Jesus, including surrender in death on the cross, so death-to-self is paradoxically intrinsic to each person's confrontation with biological death.

See also: HEIDEGGER, MARTIN; KIERKEGAARD, SØREN; PHILOSOPHY, WESTERN

Bibliography

Phan, Peter C. *Eternity in Time: A Study of Karl Rahner's Eschatology.* Selinsgrove, PA: Susquehanna University Press, 1988.

Rahner, Karl. "The 'Intermediate State.'" *Theological Investigations,* translated by Margaret Kohl, Vol. 17. New York: Crossroad, 1981.

Rahner, Karl. "Ideas for a Theology of Death." *Theological Investigations,* translated by David Bourke, Vol. 13. New York: Crossroad, 1975.

Rahner, Karl, ed. "Death." *Encyclopedia of Theology: The Concise Sacramentum Mundi.* London: Burns and Cates, 1975 .

Rahner, Karl. *On the Theology of Death,* translated by Charles H. Henkey. New York: Herder and Herder, 1961.

ROBERT MASSON

REINCARNATION

The concept of reincarnation, that of an individual dying and then being reborn into another body, has existed in various religions for at least 3,000 years. The belief most likely arose independently in different areas, and this was followed by periods in which the concept spread to other regions. It has now spread to the point that there are probably more people alive who believe in reincarnation than do not. Even in cultures such as the United States and Western Europe that do not have a predominant belief in reincarnation, 20 to 30 percent of the population holds the belief. While the general concept is present in a number of religions and people groups, there are also significant differences between the various belief systems.

Hinduism

In Hinduism, it is believed that an enduring soul survives after death, spends a variable amount of time in another realm, and then becomes associated with a new body. Rebirth into the opposite sex or, under certain circumstances, into a nonhuman animal form is considered possible. Hinduism includes the concept of *karma,* the idea that the conditions into which one is born are determined by one's conduct in various previous lives. Life on Earth is considered undesirable, and an individual may engage in religious practices in each life until eventually earning release from the cycle of rebirth, losing individuality, and achieving union with the infinite spirit (*nirvana*).

Buddhism

Buddhism shares some concepts with Hinduism but also has some significant differences. In particular, Theravada Buddhism, found in the southern parts of Asia, emphasizes in the doctrine of *anatta,* or no soul, which states there is no enduring entity that persists from one life to the next. At the death of one personality, a new one comes into being, much as the flame of a dying candle can serve to light the flame of another. When an individual dies, a new personality is born, generally first into a nonterrestrial plane of existence followed later by a new terrestrial personality. As in Hinduism, karma determines the circumstances of subsequent lives, so there is continuity between personalities but not persistence of identity. For this reason, Theravada Buddhists prefer the term *rebirth* to *reincarnation.*

In Buddhism, the law of karma is viewed as naturalistic, akin to the laws of physics. Thus, circumstances of rebirths are not seen as rewards or punishments handed out by a controlling God but are simply the natural results of various good deeds and misdeeds. The cycle of rebirths has involved innumerable lives over many eons, including ones in both sexes, in nonhuman animals, and in other realms. It inevitably involves suffering and continues until all cravings are lost and nirvana is achieved.

Shiite Muslims

A number of groups of Shiite Muslims in western Asia, such as the Druses of Lebanon and Syria and the Alevis in Turkey, have a belief in reincarnation that does not include the concept of karma. Instead, they believe that God assigns souls to a series of lives in different circumstances that are generally disconnected from one another until the ultimate Judgment Day, when God sends them to heaven or hell based on the moral quality of their actions during all the various lives. The Druses also believe that rebirth occurs immediately after death with no discarnate existence possible. While the Alevis believe that rebirth in nonhuman animals can occur, the Druses do not, and, in fact, they believe that they can only be reborn as other Druses. Neither group believes that they can be reborn as members of the opposite sex.

Judaism and Christianity

While reincarnation is not a belief in mainstream Judaism and Christianity, it has been part of the belief system of some of their groups. In Judaism, the Kabbalah, the body of teaching based on an esoteric interpretation of Hebrew scriptures, includes reincarnation, and Hasidic Jews include it in their belief system. In Christianity, some groups of early Christians, particularly the Gnostic Christians, believed in reincarnation, and some Christians in southern Europe believed in it until the Council of Constantinople in 553 C.E. Some Christians find support for reincarnation in the passage in the New Testament Book of Matthew in which Jesus seems to say that John the Baptist is the prophet Elijah returned.

Ancient Greece

The Greek philosophers wrote extensively about the concept of reincarnation, beginning with the legendary Orpheus and with Pythagoras. After Socrates, Plato, whose ideas about reincarnation became particularly influential, taught that one's soul is immortal, preexists before birth, and is reborn many times. Each soul chooses its next life, guided by its experiences in the previous lives. Aristotle initially accepted the ideas of his teacher Plato, but later largely rejected the concepts of reincarnation and immortality, becoming the father of materialism in Western thought.

West Africa

The concept of reincarnation is common among the various peoples of West Africa. In general, unlike Hindus and Buddhists, they believe that rebirth is desirable and that life on Earth is preferable to that of the discarnate, limbo state. They believe that individuals are generally reborn into the same family and that their souls may split into several rebirths simultaneously. Some groups believe in the possibility of rebirth into nonhuman animals while others do not. Many have the concept of "repeater children," in which one soul will harass a family by repeatedly dying as an infant or young child only to be reborn into the family again.

Native Americans and Inuit

The Inuit and many other Native American tribes, particularly those in the most northern and northwestern parts of North America, also believe in reincarnation. The details of the beliefs have varied greatly across different groups. Many do not necessarily expect all individuals to be reborn, but they instead focus on those who have had premature deaths, such as deceased children being reborn into the same family or dead warriors being reborn with birthmarks corresponding to their wounds. Some have believed in human to nonhuman rebirth and in cross-sex reincarnation. Many of them also believe that an individual may be reborn simultaneously as several different people.

Evidence for Reincarnation

In the twentieth century, researchers began exploring possible evidence for reincarnation. In 1961 Ian Stevenson, then the chairman of the Department of Psychiatry at the University of Virginia, began investigating cases of young children who claimed to remember previous lives. In a typical case, a child at the age of two or three would begin to speak spontaneously about another life. Some children described the life of a stranger while others talked about a deceased individual known to the child's family. In the cases involving a stranger, the child would often persist with the claims until the family eventually made efforts to locate the family of the previous personality; that is, the person whose life the child was describing. In many cases, their efforts were successful, and the child would then meet the family. At these meetings, the child would often be said to identify members of the previous family as well as items belonging to the deceased individual.

Stevenson discovered that such cases were fairly easy to find in many parts of the world, particularly in Asia, and he eventually relinquished his position as departmental chairman to pursue the research full time. Since that time, he and other researchers have collected over 2,500 cases of children claiming to remember previous lives. As of 2002, such cases were still being collected regularly. While they each have individual variations, they generally share certain characteristics.

Location of cases. Cases are most easily found in cultures with a belief in reincarnation, and the most common areas for cases include India, Sri Lanka, Turkey, Lebanon, Thailand, Myanmar, West Africa, and among the tribal groups of northwest North America. Cases have been found, however, wherever they have been sought, and they include well over 100 nontribal American ones.

Types of lives described. The children who spontaneously report past lives generally describe a life as someone in their own culture. Even the exceptions usually show some geographical connection, such as Burmese children who describe the lives of Japanese soldiers killed in Burma during World War II, and cases of children describing lives in faraway countries are very rare.

In addition, the lives described are almost always ordinary ones, as the children describe typical family life and routine occupations. Claims to have been a famous person or royalty are essentially nonexistent in the spontaneous child cases. The children also tend to describe recent lives; the average interval between the death of the previous personality and the birth of the child is around fifteen months.

One exceptional part of the lives described is the percentage of violent deaths reported. Stevenson found that approximately 60 percent of the children who talk about the mode of death of the previous personality describe a violent one. Compared to cases with a nonviolent mode of death, the cases that involve violence have a shorter interval on average between the death of the previous personality and the birth of the subject.

Age and manner of speaking. The children studied almost always start talking about the previous lives between the ages of two and five years. Some with unusual verbal skills may make statements earlier, and some make gestures earlier that are not understood until they develop the verbal skills to make statements that connect the gestures to a previous life. They almost always stop talking about the previous life between the ages of five and eight, which is generally the age when children branch out from the family and begin school, and also the age when children tend to lose early childhood memories.

Many of the children show extreme seriousness or great emotion when they talk about the previous life. They may cry as they talk about missing their previous family or show great anger in describing their killer. The children in the stronger cases, such as ones with more verified statements about the previous life, tend to show more emotion in describing the previous life than those in the weaker cases. Some children may talk about the previous life with great emotion one minute and then go off to play the next, and some parents say that their child has to be in the "right" state of mind to discuss the previous life. In U.S. cases, this is often during relaxed times such as during a car ride or after a bath. Other children, however, appear to have access to the memories at all times.

Themes of the past life statements. The children in the studies who talk about previous lives do not tend to make statements indicating great wisdom. Instead, they generally talk about events from the end of the previous life; almost three-quarters of the subjects describe the mode of death of the previous personality. They are also much more likely to talk about people from the end of that life than about people from earlier in it. Thus, a child who describes the life of an adult tends to talk about a spouse or children rather than parents.

Few subjects talk about any time between lives. Of those that do, some describe staying near their homes or the site of their deaths, and they may describe seeing their funerals or other events that occurred after their deaths. Others report going to a discarnate realm, at times describing meetings with other beings such as sages or guides.

Birthmarks and birth defects. In about 35 percent of the cases, the child bears a birthmark or birth defect that matches a wound of the previous personality, usually the fatal wound. The birthmarks tend to be unusual ones, often being puckered scarlike areas, and some of them are said to have oozed or bled for some time after the child was born. The birth defects are often ones that are extremely rare. In the late 1990s Stevenson published a series of over 200 such cases in which he documented the correspondence of the marks to wounds on the previous personality, using postmortem reports whenever possible. Examples include cases in which children had birthmarks that matched the bullet entrance and exit wounds on the previous personality and others with multiple marks matching the wounds from the shotgun blasts that killed the previous individuals.

Behaviors related to the previous life. Many of the children in these studies show behaviors that suggest a connection to the previous individual. They often show emotions toward the various members of the previous family that are appropriate: demurring to a husband, being bossy to a younger sibling (who is now, in fact, much older than the subject), and so forth.

Many of the children show phobias related to the mode of death; 50 percent of those describing a violent death show a phobia of the instrument of that death. At times, the phobia will be present long before the child talks about the previous life; for example, a baby may show an intense fear of water, and that child later reports a memory of having drowned in the previous life.

Some children show likes and dislikes that match those of the previous personality. For example, Burmese children who describe lives as Japanese soldiers may complain about the spicy Burmese food while requesting raw fish to eat.

Many of the children show connections to the previous life in their play. For example, some act out the occupation of the previous personality. At times, this can reach compulsive proportions so that, for instance, the child misses school because of the insistence on continuing with this play. Others repetitively act out the death that they describe in what appears to be posttraumatic play. Many of the children who report previous lives as members of the opposite sex show behaviors appropriate to that sex. They may dress, play, and think of themselves as members of the opposite sex, and this behavior can be of such severity to warrant a diagnosis of gender identity disorder. Most of the children, however, show a normal course of development that is indistinguishable from their peers.

Methods and Interpretations

In the vast majority of cases, the investigators do not get to a case until after the subject's family and the previous personality's family have met, often not until years after. This leads to the need to interview as many firsthand witnesses as possible. These include, of course, the subject, but he or she may not still be reporting memories of the previous life by the time of the interview. The child's parents are always important witnesses, since the young child has often told more to them than to others. In addition, other family members and family friends can be important witnesses. After they have been interviewed and the information recorded, the previous personality's family is interviewed. Those family members can confirm both the details of the previous personality's life that are relevant as well as any recognitions or information that the child demonstrated when the two families met. In all instances, firsthand knowledge rather than hearsay is sought. Interviews are conducted with the use of an interpreter in countries where one is needed.

Repeat interviews are often conducted, both to obtain additional details that were missed during the first ones and to determine whether the reports remain consistent. In addition, other evidence is gathered when relevant. For example, postmortem reports may be obtained, both to confirm the details that the child gave about the death as well as to confirm, when applicable, that the child's birthmarks do match wounds on the deceased. In the cases in which the previous personality was unknown to the subject's family, investigators also attempt to learn whether the child or the family may have had a connection to the previous personality or possible access to information about that life that is not immediately apparent.

There are also times when the researchers find a case in which the previous personality has not yet been identified. The information from the subject and his or her family is recorded, and it is then used in an effort to identify the deceased individual whose life the child is describing.

There are several possible ways in which these cases could arise through normal means. One is fraud, but this is quite unlikely for the vast majority of cases, given the number of witnesses often involved, the amount of effort that would be necessary to perpetrate such a fraud, and the lack of motive to do so.

Another possibility is that the children have learned about the deceased person through normal means but then forgotten where they acquired the information. This would not explain the birthmarks that match the wounds of the deceased. Also arguing against this interpretation are the lack of opportunity in many cases for the child to have heard anything at all about the previous personality, the mention by some children of information known to only a select few intimates of the previous personality, the child's strong sense of identification with the previous personality, and other behavioral features that the children often show. In addition, the stronger cases, such as ones with more verified statements about the previous life, tend to involve greater distance between the homes of the child and the previous personality than the weaker ones.

A third possibility is that after the families of the subject and the previous personality have met, the family members credit the subject with having had more knowledge of the prior life than he or she actually had. According to this interpretation, the evidence for a connection with a previous life is not valid due to faulty memory on the part of the participants. While this possibility would not explain the birthmark cases or the ones in which a written record was made of the child's statements before the previous personality was identified, it could explain many others. Two studies, however, argue against this hypothesis. In 2000 Stevenson and Jürgen Keil conducted a study in which Keil reinvestigated cases twenty years after Stevenson's initial investigation. They found that the cases had not become stronger in the participants' minds over the years, and, in fact, some had become somewhat weaker as witnesses recalled less specific details of what the child had said. In the other study, Schouten and Stevenson in 1998 compared cases from India and Sri Lanka in which written records had been made before the two families met with other thoroughly investigated cases without such written records. The two groups had the same percentage of correct statements, and the overall number of statements was actually lower in the cases without a written record made beforehand.

In addition to normal means, a possible way to explain the cases would be that the children gain knowledge of the previous personality through extrasensory perception. This seems unlikely because most of these children show no other extrasensory ability and because the cases involve multiple features—birthmarks, identification with the previous personality, longing for the previous family, phobias, repetitive play—other than the knowledge of the previous life.

Another possible explanation is reincarnation. These cases, taken at face value, suggest that memories, emotions, a sense of identification, and even physical features can carry over from one life to the next. This does not necessarily mean that these characteristics carry over for other individuals who do not remember previous lives, or that other individuals have even had previous lives. The cases do, however, provide evidence that should be considered in any evaluation of the concept of reincarnation.

See also: African Religions; Afterlife in Cross-Cultural Perspective; Buddhism; Hinduism; Islam; Phoenix, The; Plato

Bibliography

Harvey, Peter. *An Introduction to Buddhism: Teachings, History and Practices.* Cambridge: Cambridge University Press, 1990.

Head, Joseph, and Sylvia L. Cranston, eds. *Reincarnation: The Phoenix Fire Mystery.* New York: Warner Books, 1979.

Mills, Antonia, and Richard Slobodin, eds. *Amerindian Rebirth: Reincarnation Belief among North American Indians and Inuit.* Toronto: University of Toronto Press, 1994.

Schouten, Sybo A., and Ian Stevenson. "Does the Socio-Psychological Hypothesis Explain Cases of the Reincarnation Type?" *Journal of Nervous and Mental Disease* 186 (1998):504–506.

Stevenson, Ian. *Children Who Remember Previous Lives: A Question of Reincarnation,* revised edition. Jefferson, NC: McFarland and Company, 2001.

Stevenson, Ian. *Reincarnation and Biology: A Contribution to the Etiology of Birthmarks and Birth Defects.* Westport, CT: Praeger, 1997.

Stevenson, Ian. "The Belief in Reincarnation among the Igbo of Nigeria." *Journal of Asian and African Studies* 20 (1985):13–30.

Stevenson, Ian. *Cases of the Reincarnation Type,* Vol. 4: *Twelve Cases in Thailand and Burma.* Charlottesville: University Press of Virginia, 1983.

Stevenson, Ian. *Cases of the Reincarnation Type,* Vol 3: *Twelve Cases in Lebanon and Turkey.* Charlottesville: University Press of Virginia, 1980.

Stevenson, Ian. *Cases of the Reincarnation Type,* Vol 2: *Ten Cases in Sri Lanka.* Charlottesville: University Press of Virginia, 1977.

Stevenson, Ian. *Cases of the Reincarnation Type,* Vol 1: *Ten Cases in India.* Charlottesville: University Press of Virginia, 1975.

Stevenson, Ian, and Jürgen Keil. "The Stability of Assessments of Paranormal Connections in Reincarnation-Type Cases." *Journal of Scientific Exploration* 14 (2000):365–382.

Tucker, Jim B. "A Scale to Measure the Strength of Children's Claims of Previous Lives: Methodology and Initial Findings." *Journal of Scientific Exploration* 14 (2000):571–581.

JIM B. TUCKER

REPLACEMENT CHILDREN

When a family suffers the death of a child, the reverberations can extend beyond the immediate period of bereavement. When a child is born into a family that has suffered such a loss, there is concern that the new child might be compromised in his or her development. Such a baby is often described as a "replacement child," a substitute or replacement for the child who died. This baby is thought to be at risk for later psychological difficulties because of an inability to form an identity separate from the dead child. It is thought that parents who are unable to fully and completely mourn the death of their child may compromise a subsequent child's mental health by imbuing that child with the qualities and characteristics of the dead sibling and by continuing to mourn the earlier death.

Parental Bereavement

The death of a child is among the most profound losses that an individual can suffer, and the resulting grief can be especially intense and prolonged. This is in part due to the uniqueness of the parent-child relationship. From the moment of conception, the parents fantasize about the child-to-be, investing in him or her their hopes and dreams for the future. Parents see themselves in their children, and when the child dies, it is as if a part of the parent dies, too. Parents also feel acutely the loss of the parenting role when their children die. The social role of parent, which can begin at conception, is an important organizer of time, activity, and identity. The loss of the parental role often challenges the parent's sense of meaning or purpose in life. The death of a child also changes the nature and composition of the family constellation and alters the family story.

Parents cope with the death of a child in multiple ways. Often, particularly when the death occurs during or shortly after birth, parents express the desire to have another child. They feel a strong need to fulfill the expectations created by the previous pregnancy and assume the parenting role. When the child that dies is older, parents may feel the need to fulfill the expectations, hopes, and dreams engendered by the dead child.

The Replacement Child As a Clinical Phenomenon

There has been much concern in mental health literature about families inadvertently creating replacement children. This phenomenon was first described in a 1964 paper by Albert and Barbara Cain, who reported on six families receiving psychiatric treatment following the death of a child or adolescent and the birth of a subsequent child who later developed psychiatric problems. This clinically important paper led to the prominence of the term *replacement child* in the mental health field. The parents in the Cain and Cain study were characterized by intense idealization and investment in the dead child, maternal personality dysfunction that predated the child's birth, and a history of losses in the mother's own childhood. The parents were restrictive and overprotective, and the children were fearful, anxious, morbidly preoccupied with death, and lacking in self-esteem. The authors of this study warned that parents should not have another child until they have had the opportunity to completely mourn the death of their child.

Although Cain and Cain note that the replacement of a child who dies at birth or in infancy is less likely to be complicated by confused identifications and comparisons with siblings, other clinicians suggest there may be some risk when a child dies at or near birth as well. In this case, the parents' experience with their baby is very limited. They have few memories to mourn and instead must mourn the wishes and expectations that they held for the child. The baby remains an abstraction even after the death.

The replacement-child concept has influenced contemporary obstetric and neonatal caregiving practice. When a child dies during the perinatal period (at or near birth), parents are encouraged to have contact with the dead baby, including holding and naming him or her, taking pictures, and making memories. It is suggested that parents who have these experiences are better able to grieve the loss, can separate the real baby from the fantasy image they hold, and thus may be better able to parent a subsequent child. Medical personnel have often counseled parents who have experienced perinatal loss to wait before attempting subsequent pregnancies in order to grieve fully for the dead child.

Research into Parents' Opinions

There is a considerable body of psychiatric case studies on the pathology of the replacement child. Studies that solicit parents' opinions suggest that giving birth after the death of a child may be helpful to the parents and help families grow through loss. One researcher found that recently bereaved parents experienced their loss as a void or hole in the family. For some parents, the decision to have another child provides a reason to begin living again. Although parents indicate that they could not replace the dead child, many want another child of the same sex as soon as possible and often give the subsequent child a name that resembles that of the dead child.

It is important to directly assess the psychological functioning of children born subsequent to parental bereavement. Parental attitudes toward the decision to have other children, parental beliefs about practices, and parents' interpretation of the family structure directly and indirectly affect child mental health. Parental interpretations of the family constellation and stories about family life determine family practices and, through these practices, child development. Family stories give meaning to the past and direction to the future, shaping subsequent development.

What Family Practices Say about Subsequent Children

By listening to and analyzing the stories of parents who have lost children at or near birth and who have gone on to have subsequent children, it is apparent that many parents do not replace the dead child with a child born later. Some parents continue to represent their family as including their deceased child and maintain an imagined relationship with the dead child that is separate and apart from their relationship with their living children. Other parents continue for years to feel the death of their child as a hole or void in the family constellation. Other parents may, in fact, fill in the gap in the family with a newborn "replacement child." Many parents continue to remember and pay homage to their dead child long past the initial mourning period. None of these arrangements or representations of family are necessarily pathological.

Theoretical Constructions of Grief and the Replacement Child: Stage Models

Concerns about the risk of having a replacement child are derived from a stage model of grieving. This way of understanding grief suggests that there is a typical pathway through grief and a "good" and "bad" way to grieve. The "good" way consists of moving from a period of shock or denial, through an intensely painful period during which the deceased is acutely missed and the bereaved may feel guilty and angry as well as sad, followed by a period of grief resolution characterized by changed or diminished attachment to the deceased, loosened emotional bonds, reinvestment in the social world, and return to preloss levels of functioning. A "bad" way would include denial of the loss or premature focus on moving forward. Cain and Cain note that the replacement children in their study represent a "pseudoresolution" of mourning because there is a denial of loss and a retention of intense emotional ties to the dead child.

Meaning Reconstruction

Some psychologists suggest that the grieving is a means of reconstructing meaning in the face of a world that has irrevocably changed. Making meaning is, of course, highly personal, and the meanings a grieving individual creates are unique. Hence there is no universal path through grief, and no practice (i.e., replacing a child) can be prescribed or be considered detrimental on its face. Rather, the place the child holds in the family story and the meanings the parents ascribe to the dead child and the surviving and subsequent children require individual assessment. Further, contemporary models of grief note the commonality and normalcy of maintaining continuing bonds to the deceased. Thus, a continued relationship with the dead child, considered pathological in the Cain and Cain study, is increasingly noted as common practice and one that does not necessarily interfere with the growth and development of surviving children.

Conclusion

While the replacement-child construct may have clinical utility, especially in cases where parents may have preexisting dysfunction and/or a significant history of losses, it seems clear that clinical axioms like "replacement child" do not do justice to the complexity of parental interpretations of the child and the family constellation. When parents are asked to describe how they coped with the loss of a child, and when families who have experienced the birth of a child subsequent to a loss describe their experiences, it becomes clear that there are many paths through this grief that do not result in the anticipated pathology. As caregivers for families who have experienced the death of a child, one must seek to understand the meaning of the dead child and subsequent children, and what those children represent to their families. Without listening closely to the stories that parents tell, mental health practitioners are in danger of assuming psychological risk when there may be none.

See also: CHILDREN; GRIEF: CHILD'S DEATH, FAMILY; GRIEF COUNSELING AND THERAPY; MORTALITY, INFANT

Bibliography

Bowlby, John. *Attachment and Loss,* Vol. 3: *Loss: Sadness and Depression.* New York: Basic Books, 1980.

Cain, Albert C., and Barbara S. Cain. "On Replacing a Child." *Journal of the American Academy of Child Psychiatry* 3 (1964):443–456.

Grout, Leslie A., and Bronna D. Romanoff. "The Myth of the Replacement Child: Parents' Stories and Practices after Perinatal Death." *Death Studies* 24 (2000):93–113.

Johnson, Sherry. "Sexual Intimacy and Replacement Children after the Death of a Child." *Omega: The Journal of Death and Dying* 15 (1984):109–118.

Klass, Dennis, Phyllis R. Silverman, and Steven L. Nickman. *Continuing Bonds: New Understandings of Grief.* Washington, DC: Taylor & Francis, 1996.

McClowery, S. G., E. B. Davies, K. A. May, E. J. Kulenkamp, and I. M. Martinson. "The Empty Space Phenomenon: The Process of Grief in the Bereaved Family." *Death Studies* 11 (1987):361–374.

Neimeyer, Robert A. *Meaning Reconstruction and the Experience of Loss.* Washington, DC: American Psychological Association, 2001.

Rando, Therese A., ed. "Parental Bereavement: An Exception to the General Conceptualizations of Mourning." *Parental Loss of a Child.* Champaign, IL: Research Press, 1986.

Raphael, Beverly. *The Anatomy of Bereavement.* New York: Basic Books, 1983.

LESLIE A. GROUT
BRONNA D. ROMANOFF

RESUSCITATION

The term *resuscitation,* as used by medical personnel, means both trying to revive those who have gone into cardiac arrest (cardiopulmonary resuscitation or CPR) and any intense intervention that will prevent imminent death. Such interventions usually include helping people get oxygen and breathe, restoring the amount of fluid and blood in their system, keeping their hearts beating effectively, and halting any process that is interfering with their ability to survive. Some of these processes merge almost seamlessly with the process of "life support."

The simplest resuscitation procedure to assist oxygenation and breathing is to position the head and body so that the airway (e.g., nose, mouth, pharynx, and trachea) remains open. In some cases, clinicians may insert an oral or nasal airway device to help keep it open while patients continue breathing on their own. If the clinician believes that they may stop breathing, do not have control of their airway, may aspirate stomach contents, or have stopped breathing (apnea), he or she will usually put a tube into the trachea. These endotracheal tubes, made of clear polyvinyl, protect the airway or are used to attach patients to a mechanical ventilator (sometimes referred to as a respirator). In some cases, clinicians cannot pass the tube orally or nasally into the trachea because of damage to the area, swelling, or a person's unusual anatomy. In those cases, the clinician uses an emergency surgical technique, a cricothyrotomy, to pass the tube into the trachea through a hole made in the neck just below the thyroid cartilage (Adam's apple). An alternative surgical technique, more difficult to perform in emergencies, is the tracheotomy, in which physicians insert a smaller "trach" tube low in the neck.

Once the clinician places a tube in the trachea, patients may simply have humidified oxygen administered through the tube if they are still breathing adequately on their own. More commonly, they will first be "bagged" by hand, using a bag-valve mask, and then attached to a mechanical ventilator. These ventilators force oxygenated air into the lungs in the amount and at a pressure appropriate for each patient.

Sometimes, most frequently after trauma, one or both lungs collapse and may accumulate blood around them in the "pleural space." This often causes patients to have difficulty breathing. In some cases, it may decrease the oxygen getting into their systems and diminish the ability of their hearts to pump blood. In such cases, the clinician must immediately place a tube (chest tube or thoracostomy tube) into the pleural space through the chest wall. He or she then connects it to suction and removes the air and blood.

IVs, Fluids, Blood

Another common resuscitation measure is to administer fluids into a patient's veins. This helps improve the blood flow and thus the amount of oxygen and nutrients available to the body's tissues, thereby facilitating the cells' ability to discard waste products. Used for patients who are dehydrated, bleeding, or who simply cannot take adequate amounts of fluid orally, this procedure often includes inserting intravenous catheters with large internal diameters (large-bore IVs), into the arm, foot, neck, shoulder area, or groin. Through these IVs, medical personnel may administer large amounts of fluids, such as Normal Saline, Ringers Lactate Solution, plasma, or blood.

During resuscitations, medical personnel may place a large monitor/infusion catheter, such as Swan-Ganz or triple-lumen catheter, to assess a patient's state of hydration, heart functioning, and the amount of fluid in the lungs. Personnel may also place a catheter into the bladder to assess how the patient is producing urine, which is a simpler measure of how well the kidneys are functioning and an indirect measure of a patient's fluid status.

Heart

Clinicians often must concentrate on correcting cardiac (heart) abnormalities while resuscitating a patient. The most obvious and dramatic measure is cardiopulmonary resuscitation (CPR), in which clinicians pump on the sternum to generate circulation of blood. Resuscitation, however, may include many other activities before the clinician resorts to this procedure.

One of the most common resuscitative measures is to administer antiarrhythmic drugs to stop abnormal heart rhythms, such as overly rapid or slow heartbeats. In either case, the heart is not pumping effectively and so is not supplying enough blood to the brain and the rest of the body. The drugs may also be used when the heart is producing beats from an abnormal site, such as from the ventricle. This can either be an ineffective rhythm (not producing good blood flow) or a forewarning of cardiac arrest and so must be corrected. If the antiarrhythmic drugs prove ineffective, the patient may require an electrical shock to restore the heart to a normal rhythm. This can either be synchronized with the heartbeat (often at a relatively low voltage), called "cardioversion," or at higher energies and unsynchronized, called "defibrillation." Defibrillation is generally used to resuscitate patients in cardiac arrest.

Other measures to improve heart activity during resuscitations include inserting a temporary pacemaker, administering thrombolytics (clot busters), performing angiography, and doing pericardiocentesis. Temporary pacemakers, often placed through the same large IV sites as are used for fluid resuscitation, are inserted when the heart is beating too slowly to be effective, or to override an abnormally fast and life-threatening heart rate that they cannot stop any other way. Clinicians use thrombolytics, one of a class of medications, to help open coronary arteries during or immediately after a heart attack. If these drugs prove unhelpful (or sometimes even if they are working), physicians may take patients to the cardiac catheterization laboratory for coronary angiography. This procedure visualizes and opens coronary (heart) vessels and is particularly useful in patients in cardiogenic shock. In some patients, a sudden accumulation of blood or fluid around the heart (pericardial tamponade, often due to trauma) causes their heart to pump ineffectively. In those cases, physicians may need to put a needle into the sac around the heart to withdraw enough fluid, usually less than 50 cc, so that the heart can again pump normally. After this procedure, called pericardiocentesis, cardiac surgeons generally must take patients to the operating room for a definitive procedure.

Treating Underlying Problems

An essential step in resuscitations is for clinicians to definitively remedy underlying problems. Among other things, this may include stopping bleeding, halting or preventing infection, controlling blood pressure, and treating poisoning.

While external bleeding can be easily controlled with direct pressure, surgeons often need to operate on patients to halt bleeding in the chest, abdomen, or head. They may perform laparotomies (abdominal operations), thoracotomies (chest operations), and craniotomies (entering the skull) if bleeding does not stop spontaneously. Patients with continuing bleeding, such as from a torn artery, will die without such surgery. When necessary, neurosurgeons also perform craniotomies to relieve pressure on the brain from blood that has accumulated within the skull. In some cases, rather than operating, radiologists control bleeding with small pledgets of material that they put into the vessels through arterial catheters. In an even simpler procedure, orthopedic surgeons may slow or stop bleeding by stabilizing fractured bones (particularly the pelvis and femur). Physicians administer a variety of medications and clotting factors to reverse the process in patients bleeding due to hemophilia, liver failure, disseminated intravascular coagulation (DIC), platelet dysfunction, or other abnormalities related to the blood-clotting system. Unlike mechanical interventions, treatment for bleeding disorders may last for days until patients improve.

Infections still cause many deaths, and not all infections can be treated effectively. Yet, when possible, clinicians treat or try to prevent infections in patients undergoing resuscitations. For example, patients with perforated intestines may need broad-spectrum antibiotics administered both before and after surgery. Those with open fractures need similar antibiotic coverage, both to prevent and to treat infections. These patients, if they are not already immunized, also must receive immunizations against tetanus.

Patients undergoing resuscitation often have an altered blood pressure. Blood pressure is a measure of the effectiveness of cardiac activity (the pump), the distention and porosity of the blood vessels (the pipes), and the amount of blood in the circulatory system (fluid). The brain (control station) regulates these elements, directly or indirectly. When illness or injury alters any of these factors, blood pressure moves out of the safe and healthy range. Low blood pressure (hypotension) usually accompanies serious illness. Clinicians must frequently administer intravenous vasopressors to such patients to help elevate their blood pressure and to assure that adequate blood is flowing to their vital organs. In some cases, blood pressure is too high, a development that can be accompanied by or lead to strokes, heart attacks, dissecting aortas, and other life-threatening events. Physicians must use antihypertensive drugs to help resuscitate such patients.

Resuscitations often occur in patients who have taken overdoses of dangerous medications or illicit drugs, or who have come into contact with a dangerous poison. Treatment for such events includes using medications to reverse a drug's effect, when possible. There are few specific antagonists for common drugs, with the exceptions being narcotics, benzodiazepines (i.e., Valium) and Tylenol. Other antidotes also exist for some exotic poisons, such as cyanide, snake and insect toxins, heavy metals, and industrial chemicals similar to those used as warfare agents. Treatment for most drug overdoses, however, employs measures to support the affected systems, especially breathing, the heart and blood pressure, and the kidneys. Treatment often includes using charcoal to bind any of the medication still in the gut or washing off any toxin that is on the skin. Occasionally, clinicians must use renal dialysis or other supportive measures. Patients may also have severe reactions to a normal medication dose, an event termed "anaphylaxis," including a closed airway, impaired breathing, and falling blood pressure. Resuscitation involves supporting each of these systems.

Other resuscitations involve patients with severely abnormal temperatures (usually from environmental exposure or medications), acid-base and electrolyte abnormalities (sodium, potassium), and protracted seizures. These may occur alone, or in combination with other problems that also require resuscitative efforts and aggressive, organ-specific support while the clinician attempts to treat the problem's underlying cause.

Calling for Help, Viewing Resuscitations, and Stopping Resuscitative Efforts

In many U.S. jurisdictions, ambulance personnel must attempt resuscitation when patients are not clearly dead. Many people have received unwanted resuscitation attempts after their loved ones simply tried to notify authorities that the person had died. Most states have statutes or protocols whereby individuals can prevent unwanted resuscitation through an out-of-hospital Do Not Resuscitate (DNR) order or an advance directive that is recognized by ambulance personnel. Often referred to as "orange forms" because of their common color, prehospital advance directives allow medics to not begin resuscitative measures in cases of cardiac arrest. They are usually used for homebound, hospice, and nursing home patients.

The paramedic profession was formed primarily to implement new cardiac resuscitation methods and to "raise" the clinically dead from cardiac arrest. Yet, for patients on whom medics perform out-of-hospital CPR, only about 1 to 7 per every 100, on average, are discharged from hospitals alive. In those who have a cardiac arrest after trauma and are brought to a hospital, only about 5 per 200 survive, with only about 3 per 200 being able to function, meaning that many patients are pronounced dead on the scene, either after failed resuscitative efforts or where CPR was not begun because it would have been futile. As paramedic Mike Meoli wrote, "No matter how quickly we are summoned or how well we perform, the usual outcome of a CPR call is the same: death" (1993). While the phrase "dead on arrival" once meant that no resuscitation was attempted, the media now often use it for many patients who actually died in the emergency department, sometimes after a resuscitation attempt.

Family members who arrive during resuscitations should be allowed in the resuscitation area, if they wish. Senior staff (nurse, social worker, chaplain) should quickly brief them on what they will see and then accompany them throughout the procedure. When survivors witness resuscitative efforts, the resuscitations often run more smoothly (and more quietly), and the survivors have fewer problems accepting both the death and the notion that significant efforts were made to save their loved one. Studies show that they do not disrupt the resuscitative efforts. Subsequently, they also have lower levels of anxiety, depression, posttraumatic avoidance behavior, and grief. If the family is present when it is clear that resuscitative efforts have been unsuccessful, this should be explained to the family before supportive measures are discontinued, to provide them with a chance to "say goodbye" before death is pronounced.

Patients are dead when a physician declares them dead. Because errors are occasionally made, care must be taken to assure that patients declared dead are, in fact, dead. Such precautions also prevent implementing unnecessary resuscitative efforts. These errors can be avoided by checking vital signs and observing isoelectric cardiac activity in at least three ECG readouts (leads). This can be omitted when anatomical injuries (i.e., decapitation) are incompatible with life.

Prehospital personnel (EMTs, paramedics) should not begin or should halt resuscitative efforts if it would jeopardize their safety, if they cannot physically continue, or if there is a valid prehospital advance directive specifying not to resuscitate. This also applies when any of the following are present: rigor mortis, livor mortis, evidence of decomposition, bodies burned beyond recognition, or injuries clearly incompatible with life. Hospital personnel should not begin or should stop resuscitative efforts when the patient has declined them, in situations in which inadequate resources exist to treat all patients (e.g., disasters), or when appropriate resuscitative efforts have not been effective. Following resuscitation, physicians have two responsibilities: pronouncing the person dead and notifying the survivors.

See also: ADVANCE DIRECTIVES; DO NOT RESUSCITATE; END-OF-LIFE ISSUES; LIFE SUPPORT SYSTEM; NECROMANCY; PERSISTENT VEGETATIVE STATE

Bibliography

Iserson, Kenneth V. *Death to Dust: What Happens to Dead Bodies?,* 2nd edition. Tucson, AZ: Galen Press, 2001.

Iserson, Kenneth V. *Grave Words: Notifying Survivors of Sudden, Unexpected Deaths.* Tucson, AZ: Galen Press, 1999.

Iserson, Kenneth V. "Terminating Resuscitation." In Peter Rosen, Roger M. Barkin, Stephen R. Hayden, Jeffrey Schaider, and Richard Wolfe eds., *The 5-Minute Emergency Medicine Consult.* Philadelphia: Lippincott Williams and Wilkins, 1999.

Iserson, Kenneth V. "A Simplified Prehospital Advance Directive Law: Arizona's Approach." *Annals of Emergency Medicine* 22, no. 11 (1993):1703–1710.

Lombardi, Gary, John E. Gallagher, and Paul Gennis. "Outcome of Out-of-Hospital Cardiac Arrest in New York City: The Pre-Hospital Arrest Survival Evaluation (PHASE) Study." *Journal of the American Medical Association* 271, no. 9 (1994):678–683.

Meoli, Mike. "Supporting the Bereaved: Field Notification of Death." *Journal of Emergency Medical Services* 18, no. 12 (1993):39–46.

Robinson, Susan Mirian, Sarah Mackenzie-Ross, Gregor L. Campbell-Hewson, Conor Vincent Egleston, and Andrew T. Prevost. "Psychological Effect of Witnessed Resuscitation on Bereaved Relatives." *Lancet* 352 (1998):614–617.

KENNETH V. ISERSON

REVOLUTIONARIES AND "DEATH FOR THE CAUSE!"

Willingness to die for a religious or political cause has long been recognized as a key measure of an activist's commitment. To supporters of the activist's cause, such sacrifice amounts to martyrdom, whereas critics are more likely to view it as a triumph of irrational extremism.

Literature on the subject of dying for a cause divides between analyses of two frequently overlapping categories: religious and political causes. While there are striking parallels between self-sacrifice for religious and political purposes, particularly in their intended impact on observers, there are also significant differences pertaining to belief in an afterlife.

Religious Self-Sacrifice

Dying for a religious cause is predictably linked with religious persecution, with self-sacrifice justified as a means to the salvation of others. Persecution may take several forms, including an established religious system attempting to suppress a new, emerging faith that poses a threat; the consequence of political activities that threaten those practicing a particular faith; or an intragroup battle to prevent an established faith from changing its beliefs too radically. The functions of self-sacrifice under such situations include generating negative publicity which may prevent further threats to the faith, establishing the viability of the faith as one for which people are prepared to lose their lives, or exonerating prophecies that foretold the demise of a true believer.

Heresy trials. In medieval Europe, particularly the period of 1200–1500 C.E., the Roman Catholic Church often undertook investigations of heresy accusations. Individuals charged with subscribing to and disseminating heretical beliefs could escape severe punishment by confessing ignorance of proper views, assisting the inquisition that had condemned them by identifying other heretics, and accepting nonlethal sanctions. Refusing to confess or to assist the inquisition led to the heretic's death, either during interrogation or at a public execution. Self-sacrifice in this setting was the act of an individual who refused to implicate others or to accept the established faith's legitimacy.

It is difficult to measure the effect such deaths had on rallying supporters. Inquisitorial hearings were protracted and thorough, and appear to have been effective at ending specific heresies, such as the Cathars (persecuted and wiped out during the twelfth and thirteenth centuries), but their frequency suggests that heresy (or belief that heresy was a problem) was widespread. Awareness of the severe sanctions meted out to heretics may have made many people reluctant to listen to them, but such sanctions may also have made those risking heresy charges appear more appealing for their willingness to undertake the risk of persecution and certain death.

Religious expectation of self-sacrifice. Several religious traditions include an expectation that devoted followers will willingly risk their lives in defense of the faith. Proclamations of this sort often accompany a call to battle in which true believers are expected to take the lives of nonbelievers at great risk to themselves. Given widespread reluctance to undertake such risks, other assurances are often added, such as absolution of sins, certainty of salvation, and eternal life in paradise.

The religious beliefs of the early Normans, which did not emphasize an afterlife, carried similar expectations. A glorious life was to be ended with an equally glorious death, preferably in a battle where chances of survival were nonexistent.

Death of charismatic leaders. As sociologists have long believed, one test of a new belief system constructed around the life and works of a charismatic leader involves his or her death. Can the belief system make the transition to a new period in its existence when it is denied its most attractive spokesperson? Chances of success are enhanced if the charismatic leader foretold his or her death or consciously pursued it, presenting followers with the explicit challenge of responding appropriately. The death of such a figure also creates a role model for others to follow. Lacking the leader's bearing and vision, followers nonetheless can revere their leader's life and extol the virtues of self-sacrifice to new generations of believers. That new generation, then, is socialized to appreciate, accept, and adopt the value of self-sacrifice in defense of the faith.

This does not mean that all followers of a faith with a long tradition of self-sacrifice are themselves destined to commit such acts, but rather that any religious tradition that recognizes and celebrates self-destruction spawns future generations of martyrs.

Political Self-Sacrifice and Marxism

Revolutionary Marxists view revolution as a necessary and natural component of history. Violent upheaval is thought to be essential to moving society from one stage of development to the next, ending with the arrival of communism. It is the clash between antagonistic classes that propels history onward, with ascending classes violently displacing obsolete ruling classes whose political and economic structures obstruct the rise of more progressive systems. The key to this analysis is the creation of class consciousness, whereby members of exploited classes realize not only their existence as a class with a common condition but also their historic mission of bringing about inevitable change. Because ruling classes cannot imagine themselves as being obsolete and justify their continued control with the belief that those that they dominate are incapable of self-rule, they do not relinquish power voluntarily. This means that violent revolution is the only way to remove them and advance the course of history.

Marxists also recognize the variability of conditions under which a revolution can be expected to succeed. Many unsuccessful, premature uprisings misread the strength of ruling classes or the loyalty of armies and police. Quite often, the cost of a failed revolution is execution for its principal supporters, such as occurred after the many European revolutions of 1848. In Paris, for example, 3,000 insurgents were killed and another 4,000 deported while the 1871 Paris Commune was suppressed at the cost of 20,000. Given these contingencies and the likelihood of violent opposition, revolutionaries must be prepared to die for their political activities and may very well be killed during a failed uprising.

One key motivation for this willingness to die for the cause is a deep-rooted belief in the cause's inevitability. Sooner or later, substantial change will be needed. An activist who chooses to hasten that day may succeed and become a hero of the revolution or else fail and eventually become recognized as a martyr. While ruling classes portray those whom they dominate as unintelligent, leftist revolutionaries believe they have extensively studied and fully understand human history. While ruling classes often employ religious ideology to justify their domination, revolutionaries believe that their scientific analysis of economic development reveals a more substantial truth: that their success is ultimately both progressive and inevitable. Because they usually reject organized religions for their role in supporting oppressive political systems, revolutionaries typically dismiss the idea of an afterlife. Any form of immortality they can hope for, then, can be achieved only by a posthumous reverence among the living.

Some revolutionaries undertake great risks and court self-destruction because the political system that they attack is seen as responsible for having killed members of their family or community. For such individuals, there is no reason to continue living, beyond exacting revenge. Vladimir Ilyich Ulyanov (Lenin), for example, became a dedicated political activist and revolutionary after his brother

Police attempt to control a crowd of University of Wisconsin students protesting Dow Chemical's Napalm in 1967. The first requirement for a social movement is the potential for strain, characterized by genuine conflict or contradiction within a society. AP/WIDE WORLD PHOTOS

was executed for having participated in a failed attempt to assassinate the czar.

Stages in Social Movements

According to the sociologist Neil Smelser, successful political movements proceed in several stages. Smelser's ideas, while most commonly applied to social movements such as the American civil rights movement, can also aid in an understanding of revolutionary uprisings, especially in identifying potential junctures of self-destruction.

The first requirement is the potential for strain, some genuine conflict or contradiction within a society, for the possibility of angry demands for change to develop. Sociologists believe that most simple societies and all complex societies possess significant potential for strain. This strain must be sufficiently strong or durable to generate a reaction. For example, a society engaged in war initially may find its people united behind it. If the conflict is short and victory complete, that unity will remain strong. However, if combat persists and there are significant losses, demands for radical change are certain to appear.

A third stage is characterized by the formation of a generalized belief. Individuals seeking to thwart change may characterize the strain as inevitable, normal, not severe, or soon to end. Others may claim a variety of causes for the strain, none requiring dramatic change. Still others may recognize a need for significant change but claim that reform rather than radical overhaul of the current society or political or economic system would be sufficient. Finally, some may diagnose the problem as fundamental to the system and requiring radical, even violent, change to eliminate it. It is at this point that some supporters of extreme solutions may use the occasion of their own destruction to draw attention to their analysis of the situation.

Intellectuals are important for providing generalized beliefs that transcend the often splintered and localized beliefs of oppressed groups. If those beliefs include a justification for violence to bring significant change, then death may appear very early in a movement's development. Quite common, for example, is a distinction between violence used to bring needed change and violence used to prevent such change from occurring. The writings of political theorist Herbert Marcuse, for example, were popular with elements of America's New Left in the 1960s. Marcuse's distinction between what he called "red terror" and "white terror" was intended to evoke comparisons with the Bolshevik-Menshevik clash during the revolution and the ensuing counter-revolution in Russia during World War I. For Marcuse, violence was justifiable if its objective was to bring an end to all violence, to end a system that routinely relied upon violence to keep itself in place. This liberating (red) violence was regrettable but largely reactive, brought on by oppressive (white) violence that was used to keep privileged groups in place. If this perspective had dominated the American antiwar movement, protests against the country's involvement in Vietnam would have been far more violent.

Social movements enter a new phase with the appearance of precipitating incidents. A string of events can persuade large numbers of individuals that the strain is not going away and that many of the attempts to explain the strain are incorrect. People can quickly cluster around a given belief system. In the context of an evolving revolution, precipitating incidents are often violent and reveal how much force an oppressive system is prepared to employ to keep itself in power. For that reason, self-destruction is sometimes seen as a necessary step to show potential followers of the revolution both the bravery of revolutionaries and the callous attitude toward life of those they are challenging. One motive behind terrorist attacks is to provoke a brutal reprisal that might be viewed as disproportionate to the initial assault. Intended as a deterrent that will show the high price to be paid for the use of violence by revolutionaries, under some circumstances such reprisals can have the opposite effect of generating widespread sympathy for rebels. The persistent conflicts between Palestinians and the Israeli government, for example, have created this sort of assault-and-retaliation sequence.

Mobilization of opposition is essential for movements to progress to their next level of development. Unless opponents are able to mobilize, there may not be any significant social change. Just as important, control of key resources is necessary, such as mass media, systems of transportation, and power grids. Mobilization of opposition also means the generation of crowds and new opportunities for violence, as explained by two popular theories of crowd behavior: convergence and emergent norm.

Because people with similar backgrounds and beliefs are likely to gather together, any decision to employ violence may spread to others in the group. This would occur not because of Gustave LeBon's once-popular belief that a crowd's excitement can produce a kind of "group mind," but rather because of the similarity of the crowd's constituents, many of whom may be persuaded that violence is necessary or even essential.

While everyday life has predictable continuity, individuals joining large, unregulated, expressive crowds are unsure of what sort of behavior is expected of them. They search for information about their situation and thus are responsive to rumor. If a rumor becomes widespread, it may be seen by several crowd members to justify aggressive action, such as a violent confrontation with police. Others witnessing the aggression come to believe that anger and hostility are expected, conform to the newly emergent norms of behavior, and so place themselves at more risk than they might otherwise have. Emergent norm theory does not claim that any specific norms are certain to develop in crowds but rather that most people are unsure of just what constitutes appropriate behavior because of their lack of familiarity with the setting.

If agents of social control, such as the police, army, and judicial system, are unable to restrain mobilized groups, then dramatic social change is inevitable. In the example of revolutionary movements, this stage can entail full-scale physical assault on the agents of social control and thus the clear risk of self-destruction. Less dramatically, it can involve political prisoners either working to create uprisings, escapes, or widely publicized starvation campaigns, such as that effectively employed by Irish Republican Army member Bobbie Sands.

Conclusion

Despite the aforementioned differences, religious and political martyrs share certitude in their causes' ultimate truths. For this reason, they must be distinguished from self-destructive, isolated bands of individuals lacking a larger agenda, such as those involved in the Columbine High School attack in April 1999.

See also: ASSASSINATION; CULT DEATHS; DEATH SYSTEM; MARTYRS; SOCIAL FUNCTIONS OF DEATH

Bibliography

Brown, Harold O. J. *Heresies: Heresy and Orthodoxy in the History of the Church*. Peabody, MA: Hendrickson Publishers, 1998.

Gerth, Hans, and C. Wright Mills, eds. *From Max Weber: Essays in Sociology*. New York: Oxford University Press, 1958.

Lambert, Malcolm. *The Cathars*. London: Blackwell, 1998.

LeBon, Gustave. *The Crowd: A Study of the Popular Mind* London: T. F. Unwin, 1925.

Leff, Gordon. *Heresy in the Middle Ages*. New York: Manchester University Press, 1967.

Marcuse, Herbert. *Five Lectures: Psychoanalysis, Politics, and Utopia*. Boston: Beacon Press, 1970.

Smelser, Neil. *Theory of Collective Behavior.* New York: Free Press, 1963.

JONATHAN F. LEWIS

RIGHT-TO-DIE MOVEMENT

In 1976 the New Jersey Supreme Court handed down its decision in the case of Karen Ann Quinlan, and in 1989 the U.S. Supreme Court ruled in the case of Nancy Beth Cruzan. The issue in both cases concerned whether the parents of these two women, who were both in a persistent vegetative state (PVS), could withdraw life-sustaining treatment when their daughters' preferences were unknown. Quinlan's treatment was a ventilator; and Cruzan's a feeding tube. The courts ultimately ruled the life-sustaining treatment could be withdrawn, although each court required a different process for doing so. It is these two court decisions that are considered America's landmark right-to-die cases.

In 1976 Quinlan, who was twenty-one, suffered a respiratory arrest that resulted in a PVS. After it became evident that she would never recover, her parents decided to take her off the ventilator; however, the hospital and medical staff refused their request. Her parents asked the courts to grant them the power to authorize the ventilator's withdrawal. Almost a year later the New Jersey Supreme Court held that the state's interest in protecting Quinlan's life was outweighed by her right of privacy, given her poor prognosis and the invasion of her body that would be necessary to keep her alive.

In 1983 twenty-five-year-old Cruzan was found lying in a ditch after a car accident. This too resulted in a PVS, but without the need of a ventilator. As with the Quinlans, Cruzan's parents came to accept the fact that she would never recover. With this realization they asked her health care providers to withdraw her feeding tube; their request was also refused. The legal odyssey that ensued ended at the U.S. Supreme Court. The Supreme Court upheld the Missouri Supreme Court, which required "clear and convincing" evidence that Cruzan would forgo artificial nutrition and hydration given her current state before her parents could remove the feeding tube.

After the Supreme Court's decision was handed down several of Cruzan's friends came forward with recollections of statements she had made regarding patients who were in similar circumstances to hers. They said Cruzan had stated she would never want to live like that. These friends gave her parents the "clear and convincing" evidence they needed to have the feeding tube withdrawn.

Out of the Quinlan and Cruzan cases, particularly the latter, came the Federal Patient Self-Determination Act (PSDA). The PSDA went into effect on December 1, 1991, and requires all hospitals, nursing homes, hospices, and health maintenance organizations (HMOs) to provide patients with information on advance directives. The PSDA also requires these organizations to provide educational programs to their staff and community on advance directives.

An advance directive is a legal document that allows adults to state their preferences for end-of-life treatment. There are typically two kinds of advance directives: The first is a living will, which allows adults to state what treatments they would or would not want at the end-of-life such as cardiopulmonary resuscitation, a ventilator, or antibiotics. The second kind is a Durable Power of Attorney for Healthcare, which allows an adult to appoint someone, such as a friend or family member, to make health care decisions for him or her should he or she lose decision-making ability. It is through an advance directive that patients can meet the "clear and convincing" evidence standard as required by some states, such as Missouri. However, advance directives are of little help to end-of-life patients who are not dependent on life-sustaining treatment. As a result, it was just a matter of time until the public demanded the next logical step after the right to refuse treatment—the right to end their lives with their physician's help.

In fact it took less than five years from the passage of the PSDA for the federal courts to hear arguments that patients ought to have the right to end their lives with the assistance of their physicians by way of an intentional overdose; in short, they wanted to legalize physician-assisted suicide. Pushing the courts was a newly passed voter-approved referendum that allowed just that.

The Oregon Death with Dignity Act was passed in 1994 by popular referendum with a 2 percent margin. The act allows adult residents of Oregon who are capable of making health care decisions and are terminally ill to request from their physician a prescription for a lethal dose of a medication. Immediately after its passage an injunction preventing its implementation was imposed. After three years of legal battles all hurdles were finally cleared, or so the general public believed. Oregon's legislators placed on the November 1997 ballot a measure calling for the repeal of the act. The measure was voted down by a 20 percent margin.

Following the second passage of the act another injunction was issued, pending court appeals. On March 6, 1996, the 9th Circuit Court of Appeals in *Compassion in Dying* v. *Washington* held that preventing a competent adult from seeking physician assistance in committing suicide interfered with an individual's liberty interest and, therefore, violates an individual's substantive due process rights. Less than a month later in a similar case, the 2nd Circuit Court of Appeals in *Quill* v. *Vacco* held that the New York statute criminalizing assisted suicide violated the equal protection clause of the Fourteenth Amendment. The court reasoned that the state has no rational or legitimate interest in preventing a mentally competent terminally ill patient in the final stage of his or her illness from taking a lethal dose of a physician-prescribed medication. Ultimately, the U.S. Supreme Court overturned both decisions; the Washington case became known as *Washington* v. *Glucksberg*.

On June 27, 1997, the Supreme Court ruled that a state's ban on suicide is rationally related to a legitimate government interest and therefore there is no constitutional right to physician-assisted suicide; however, states are free to decide for themselves whether to allow physician-assisted suicide. Currently, Oregon is the only state that allows physician-assisted suicide, as voter referendums that sought to legalize it have failed in Washington (1991), California (1992), Michigan (1998), and Maine (2000).

The Oregon Death with Dignity Act took effect on October 27, 1997. To date, ninety Oregon patients have died after the intentional overdose of medication that was prescribed by their physician for that exact purpose: 15 patients in 1998, 27 in 1999, 27 in 2000, and 21 in 2001.

See also: CRUZAN, NANCY; DEFINITIONS OF DEATH; DO NOT RESUSCITATE; EUTHANASIA; QUINLAN, KAREN ANN; SUICIDE TYPES: PHYSICIAN-ASSISTED SUICIDE

Bibliography

Battin, Margaret, Rosamond Rhodes, and Anita Silvers. *Physician Assisted Suicide: Expanding the Debate.* New York: Routledge, 1998.

Cassel, Eric. *The Nature of Suffering and the Goals of Medicine.* New York: Oxford University Press, 1991.

Dubler, Nancy. "The Doctor-Proxy Relationship: The Neglected Connection." *Kennedy Institute of Ethics Journal* 5, no. 4 (1995):289–306.

Humphry, Derek. *Final Exit: The Practicalities of Self-Deliverance and Assisted Suicide for the Dying.* New York: Dell, 1996.

Kliever, Lonnie, ed. *Dax's Case: Essays in Medical Ethics and Human Meaning.* Dallas, TX: Southern Methodist University Press, 1989.

Schmitz, P. "The Process of Dying with and without Feeding and Fluids by Tube." *Journal of Law, Medicine and Health Care* 19, no. 1–2 (1991):23–26.

MATT WEINBERG

RIGOR MORTIS AND OTHER POSTMORTEM CHANGES

Once the heart stops beating, blood collects in the most dependent parts of the body (livor mortis), the body stiffens (rigor mortis), and the body begins to cool (algor mortis).

The blood begins to settle in the parts of the body that are the closest to the ground, usually the buttocks and back when a corpse is supine. The skin, normally pink-colored because of the oxygen-laden blood in the capillaries, becomes pale as the blood drains into the larger veins. Within minutes to hours after death, the skin is discolored by livor mortis, or what embalmers call "postmortem stain," the purple-red discoloration from blood accumulating in the lowermost (dependent) blood vessels. Immediately after death, the blood is "unfixed" and will move to other body parts if the body's position is changed. After a few hours, the pooled blood becomes "fixed" and will not move. Pressing on an area of discoloration can determine this; if it blanches (turns white) easily, then the blood remains unfixed. Livor mortis is usually most pronounced eight to twelve hours after death. The skin, no longer under muscular control, succumbs to gravity, forming new shapes and accentuating prominent bones still further. The body then begins to cool.

At the moment of death, the muscles relax completely—a condition called "primary flaccidity." The muscles then stiffen, perhaps due to coagulation of muscle proteins or a shift in the muscle's energy containers (ATP-ADP), into a condition known as rigor mortis. All of the body's muscles are affected. Rigor mortis begins within two to six hours of death, starting with the eyelids, neck, and jaw. This sequence may be due to the difference in lactic acid levels among different muscles, which corresponds to the difference in glycogen levels and to the different types of muscle fibers. Over the next four to six hours, rigor mortis spreads to the other muscles, including those in the internal organs such as the heart. The onset of rigor mortis is more rapid if the environment is cold and if the decedent had performed hard physical work just before death. Its onset also varies with the individual's age, sex, physical condition, and muscular build.

After being in this rigid condition for twenty-four to eighty-four hours, the muscles relax and secondary laxity (flaccidity) develops, usually in the same order as it began (see Table 1). The length of time rigor mortis lasts depends on multiple factors, particularly the ambient temperature. The degree of rigor mortis can be determined by checking both the finger joints and the larger joints and ranking their degree of stiffness on a one- to three- or four-point scale. Many infant and child corpses will not exhibit perceptible rigor mortis. This decreased perceptible stiffness may be due to their smaller muscle mass.

During this period, the body gradually cools in a process called algor mortis. The best way to accurately assess a corpse's temperature is with a core (tympanic membrane, liver, or rectal) thermometer. Rectal insertion may be difficult and cause postmortem injury.

A few adult corpses may not undergo perceptible rigor mortis. Folklore in Britain, the Philippines, and elsewhere ascribed fearsome supernatural powers to these "limber corpses."

In the early nineteenth century, the American and British poor often prepared their own dead for burial in a process called "laying-out," "streeking," or rendering the "last offices." Women normally washed the corpse, plugged its orifices, closed its eyes and mouth, straightened its limbs, and dressed or shrouded it. It was ritually important to close the eyes quickly, being that they are the first to rigidify in rigor mortis, and it was thought that a corpse with open eyes posed a threat to its kin. As has long been the case in many cultures, they used coins to keep the corpse's eyes closed. The practice of using coins endures, representing a feeling that money, so important in life, may also be important in death.

TABLE 1

Approximate times for algor and rigor mortis in temperate regions

Body temperature	Body stiffness	Time since death
warm	not stiff	dead not more than three hours
warm	stiff	dead 3 to 8 hours
cold	stiff	dead 8 to 36 hours
cold	not stiff	dead more than 36 hours

SOURCE: Stærkeby, M. "What Happens after Death?" In the University of Oslo Forensic Entomology [web site]. Available from http://folk.uio.no/mostarke/forens_ent/afterdeath.shtml.

In the embalming process, embalmers first position the body. They then relieve rigor mortis by flexing, bending, and massaging the arms and legs. They then move the limbs to a suitable position, usually with legs extended and arms at the sides or hanging over the sides of the table, so that blood can drain into and expand the vessels for better embalming. They need to position the body before injecting embalming fluid, for no matter what stage of rigor mortis a body is in, once embalming fluid is injected, the muscles begin to firm up, or "set." (Without embalming, they would become flaccid over a period of hours.) After embalming, the muscles harden gradually over the next eight to twelve hours. Once they are set, embalmers cannot alter the body's position.

Putrefaction

In the absence of embalming or relatively rapid cremation, the body putrefies. The first sign of putrefaction is a greenish skin discoloration appearing on the right lower abdomen about the second or third day after death. This coloration then spreads over the abdomen, chest, and upper thighs and is usually accompanied by a putrid odor. Sulphur-containing intestinal gas and a breakdown product of red blood cells produce both the color and smell. The ancient Greeks and the Etruscans paid homage to this well-recognized stage of decomposition by coloring a prominent god aquamarine, considered the color of rotting flesh.

Bacteria normally residing in the body, especially the colon, play an important part in digestion of food during life. They also contribute mightily to decomposition after death—the process of putrefaction. The smell, rather than the sight, is the most distinctive thing about a putrefying body.

Under normal conditions, the intestinal bacteria in a corpse produce large amounts of foul-smelling gas that flows into the blood vessels and tissues. It is this gas that bloats the body, turns the skin from green to purple to black, makes the tongue and eyes protrude, and often pushes the intestines out through the vagina and rectum. The gas also causes large amounts of foul-smelling bloodstained fluid to exude from the nose, mouth, and other body orifices. Two of the chemicals produced during putrefaction are aptly named putrescine (1,4-diaminobutane) and cadaverine (1,5-pentanediamine). If a person dies from an overwhelming bacterial infection, marked changes from putrefaction can occur within as few as nine to twelve hours after death.

By seven days after death, most of the body is discolored and giant blood-tinged blisters begin to appear. The skin loosens and any pressure causes the top layer to come off in large sheets (skin slip). As the internal organs and the fatty tissues decay, they produce large quantities of foul-smelling gas. By the second week after death, the abdomen, scrotum, breasts, and tongue swell; the eyes bulge out. A bloody fluid seeps out of the mouth and nose. After three to four weeks, the hair, nails, and teeth loosen and the grossly swollen internal organs begin to rupture and eventually liquefy. The internal organs decompose at different rates, with the resistant uterus and prostate often intact after twelve months, giving pathologists one way to determine an unidentified corpse's sex.

Aside from the action of microbes, the breakdown of cells (autolysis) helps destroy the body unless the corpse is kept at or below 32 degrees Fahrenheit. Cells die (necrosis) through the progressive destruction of their various parts. First, the cellular fluid (cytoplasm) and the energy-releasing mechanism (mitochondria) swell. Various products, including calcium, begin to coalesce in the mitochondria as other mechanisms within the cell dissolve. Next, loss of energy causes the cell to lose its connections with neighboring cells (tissue destruction) and to further lose control over the fluid within its outer barrier, much like an overfilled water balloon. The cell controller (nucleus) fails, and the packs of destructive acids (enzymes) within the cell break loose. These enzymes complete the work of destroying the cell.

The sociologist Ruth Richardson summed up decomposition aptly: "The physicality of a human corpse is undeniable. It is a carcass, with a predisposition to decay, to become noisome, obnoxious to the senses, and harrowing to the emotions. Disposal of such perishable remains is imperative" (1987, p. 15).

See also: AUTOPSY; BURIED ALIVE; CRYONIC SUSPENSION; DEFINITIONS OF DEATH

Bibliography

Eckert, William G. "Timing of Death and Injuries." *Medico-Legal Insights.* In *Inform Letter,* 1991.

Iserson, Kenneth V. *Death to Dust: What Happens to Dead Bodies?* 2nd edition. Tucson, AZ: Galen Press, 2001.

Oever, R. van den. "A Review of the Literature as to the Present Possiblitilies and Limitations in Estimating the Time of Death." *Medicine, Science and the Law* 16 (1976):269–276.

Randall, Brad. *Death Investigation: The Basics.* Tucson, AZ: Galen Press, 1997.

Richardson, Ruth. *Death, Dissection and the Destitute.* London: Routledge and Kegan Paul, 1987.

KENNETH V. ISERSON

RITES OF PASSAGE

Rites of passage are special rituals societies employ to assist their members at key times of biographical change. These life transitions follow a recognizable pattern of behavior in many cultures; for example, babies are given a name and social identity, youths enter adulthood or marry, others retire, gain particular qualifications such as degrees or enter particular professions, or pass from the world of the living to the world of the dead. Changes of status can be related to changes in identity because the term *identity* embraces social and psychological aspects of life. The term *status* tends to refer to sociological values without reference to the personal feelings and self-evaluation of individuals. In this entry, the term *status* emphasizes the social dimension and identity of the psychological aspects of an individual's life.

The idea of status passage rituals was first introduced by the anthropologist Arnold van Gennep, who saw regeneration as the law of life and described rites of passage as a threefold process with phases of separation, segregation, and integration. For there to be a new self the old self must ritually die. Candidates for some rite would be separated from the status to be left behind, leaving familiar companions, surroundings and home, perhaps encountering actual or symbolic aggression in being wrenched away or carried off. Second, they enter a "between" period devoid of distinguishing marks of status and expressions of their old identity, such as names or clothing. In the case of passage to adulthood, adolescents may together undergo a degree of discipline and share a mutual sense of hardship, bonding them together. Their curtailed freedom begins a reorientation toward their future status and life obligations. This may involve learning the traditions of their society or the skills of some particular profession or trade. Only after this period of learning and endurance is complete do they undergo the third phase of reincorporation into society. However, they do so with their new status and identity, perhaps involving a new name or title, forms of dress or style of language and, almost certainly, new patterns of behavior with appropriate duties and responsibilities.

Van Gennep likened society to a house with people moving over thresholds from room to room. The Latin word for threshold is *limen,* hence his three phases of rites of passage as preliminal, liminal, and postliminal. He also argued that, depending upon the final goal of a ritual, the preliminal, liminal, or postliminal phase would be stressed over and above the others. Rites of passage sometimes involve more than one type of status change. In a marriage, for example, it is not only the bride and groom that pass from being single or divorced to being married but their parents also become parents-in-law. Parents, siblings, and friends may all enter new relationships.

Van Gennep's scheme was constructed to describe patterns of life in those traditional societies often described as primitive or tribal societies. In such communities of relatively few people and high levels of face-to-face contact, many would acknowledge the change of status and identity of an individual during rites of initiation into manhood, womanhood, or motherhood. However, caution is required when the idea of rites of passage is applied to events in contemporary and large-scale societies where little such recognition exists.

Such understandings of ritual permit insight into the significance of funerary ritual, a rite of passage observed in a great majority of human societies. Numerous changes of identity are associated with funeral rites, affecting the statuses of the dead, surviving relatives, and members of the broader community.

Death separates the deceased from their statuses of living parent, spouse, or coworker. The period of preparing the dead for burial or cremation moves them into a transitional phase when they are neither what they have been nor yet what they will become. Such moments of transition often involve uncertainty and potential danger. The ritual impurity of the corpse derives from its inability to respond to others, yet is still "present" in their everyday routines. Accordingly, people pay their respects to the dead, marking their former identity with them, express sorrow for the bereaved and, by so doing, reaffirm their continuing relationship with them. Stories recounting the achievement or character of the dead and supernatural powers may be invoked to forgive any evil the deceased may have perpetrated and to guide them into the afterlife. Gifts and goods may be provided to assist the individual to depart from this world to the next.

Just as initiates in their liminal period may be taught mysteries of their culture so the dead may be given their own form of education in the form of guidance provided in sacred texts, chants and prayers assist their journey, as in texts like the Egyptian *Book of the Dead* and the Tibetan *Book of the Dead.* Very often there are special priests or ritual experts to attend to this task. Sometimes additional rites are performed to assist the departed, often referred to as soul or life forces, to settle in their new world. A major goal of death rites is to ensure that the individual who has died leaves the realm of the living for the realm of the afterlife. Liminal periods of change include uncertainty and are often regarded as potentially dangerous, with the case of death providing powerful examples as

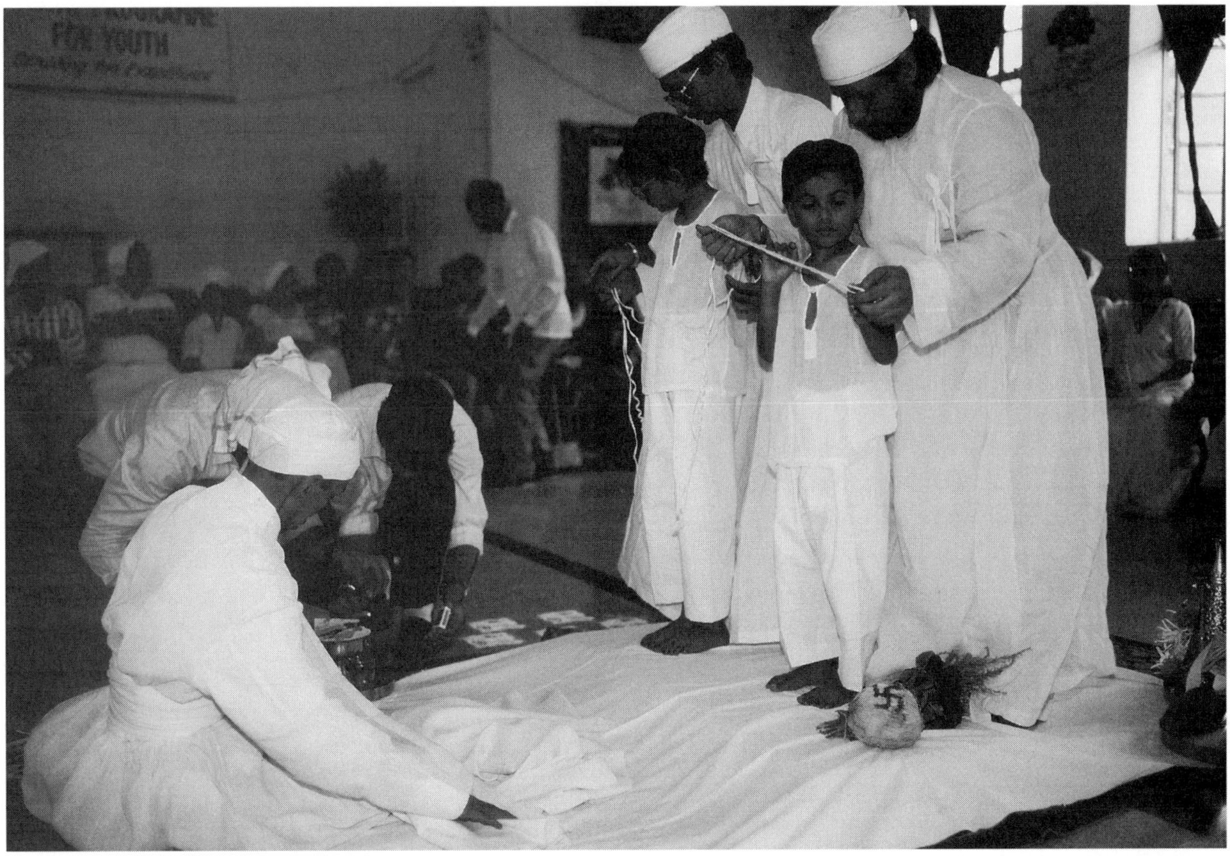

During the Indian Navjote ceremony, the ritual rite of passage where the person is accepted into the Parsi community, a priest ties a sacred thread around the child's waist as he or she chants the Ahuna-Vairya (ancient prayers). LINDSAY HEBBERD/CORBIS

key social members depart and others have to take their place.

Just as living persons become ancestors or souls in heaven so the living undergo changes in relation to them. Robert Hertz argues that funeral rites involve a kind of parallel process in which the decay of the dead reflects the path of grief in the bereaved. Bereavement involves both the social change of status of people—from, say, being a wife to being a widow, from being a child to being an orphan, or from being a subordinate adult to becoming the head of the family. It also involves psychological changes of identity associated with such shifts. Human beings become dependent upon each other and, in a sense, each identity is made up of elements of other people's influence. People become "part of" each other, and thus when one dies a portion of one's self perishes as well. Some theories of grief discuss this in terms of attachment and interpret bereavement as the loss that follows when attachments are removed.

The fear of ghosts or spirits, for example, can be related to both the dimensions of status and identity. In terms of status, ghosts and spirits can be seen as the dead who have not been successfully moved from their place in this world to that of the next. They are those who are caught in the between realm of an unintended liminal state, potentially dangerous liminal entities, or phenomena as they symbolize radical change that challenges the social life set up against such change. Sometimes further rites exist to try to get such spiritual forces finally to leave the world of the living and get on with their future destiny. At its most extreme, rites of exorcism serve to banish the dead or other supernatural entities and prevent them from influencing the living. In terms of identity, this time the identity of the living, ghosts and spirits and perhaps we should also include vivid dreams of the dead, all reflect the individual experience of a bereaved person who is still, psychologically speaking, caught up with the identity of the deceased person. Physical death has also been widely employed as an idiom to describe the leaving of an old status and the entry into a new one.

Two other anthropologists, Victor Turner and Maurice Bloch, have developed van Gennep's scheme. Turner explored liminality as a period in which human beings found great strength in the mutual support of others in the same situation. He coined the word *communitas* to describe this feeling of shared unity among those who, for example, were initiated together. The same might also apply to groups of people in the army or at college together, groups of people at carnivals or in pilgrimages, and those who are bereaved. Together they share the succor of their common humanity as they come together in adversity. For a moment they forget their different statuses and the symbols that divide them to enter into the shared emotional experiences associated with grief. To be with others at such a time is to acknowledge what it means to be human and to be mortal. In these types of situations, people sometimes speak of finding a strength they did not know they possessed, or they speak of the support they felt from others over a period of bereavement.

Maurice Bloch extensively modified van Gennep's scheme, criticizing its stress on the social status aspects of life and its ignoring of more psychological aspects. Bloch added the emphasis upon the psychological realm of experience as basic to human beings. This existentialist-like stress provides a welcomed realization that the anthropology of ritual is, ultimately, about people with feelings. Bloch stressed that while a threefold ritual scheme of preliminal, liminal, and postliminal phases may suffice to describe changes in social status, it does not do justice to the changes individuals experience. It is not that an individual is simply removed from social life, taught new things, and given a new status on re-entry to ordinary social life. Far from it, that individual changes not least because of the experiences of bereavement and grief.

Bloch makes a significant contribution to rites of passage in his theory of rebounding conquest, or rebounding violence. He describes the ordinary facts of life in terms of people being born, maturing, and then dying. Most human cultures, however, are unhappy with this simple progression. Through ritual forms they take living people and in a symbolic sense cause them to "die" and be "reborn" as new kinds of individuals, shedding old, used-up selves so new ones can take their place. Not only are they given a new status but they will also have experienced inner changes to their sense of identity. Many rituals of initiation in religions as well as in some secret societies use the natural idioms of birth and death but reverse them to speak of death and rebirth. It is as though the ordinariness of human nature is "killed" and a new and higher nature is bestowed. In some religious traditions this scheme of rebounding conquest can be applied to death rites when physical death is said to be the basis for a new and spiritual life either in future transmigration of the soul or in some form of resurrection.

See also: GENNEP, ARNOLD VAN; GRIEF AND MOURNING IN CROSS-CULTURAL PERSPECTIVE; HERTZ, ROBERT

Bibliography

Bloch, Maurice. *Prey into Hunter.* Cambridge: Cambridge University Press, 1992.

Gennep, Arnold van. *The Rites of Passage.* 1909. Reprint, London: Routledge and Kegan Paul, 1960.

Rappaport, Roy A. *Ritual and Religion in the Making of Humanity.* Cambridge: Cambridge University Press, 1999.

Turner, Victor. *The Ritual Process.* London: Routledge and Kegan Paul, 1969.

DOUGLAS J. DAVIES

ROYALTY, BRITISH

The large-scale public reactions that followed the death of Diana, Princess of Wales, on August 31, 1997, and that of Queen Elizabeth the Queen Mother on March 30, 2002, illustrate the long-standing tendency of prominent British royal deaths to stir an emotional response from millions who had never personally been acquainted with the deceased. Royal deaths have also evoked important forms of ritual and symbolic commemoration that are significant both in the context of the evolution of British civil religion and national identity, and in shaping and representing wider social and cultural responses to death. Despite occasional subversive undertones, the expression of such collective grief usually provided a potent legitimation of the institution of the monarchy and the existing social and political order.

Historical Survey

The deaths of Tudor monarchs such as Henry VIII in 1547 and Elizabeth I in 1603 were followed by elaborate ceremonics, combining religious and secular elements, and apparently reflecting genuine depth of public feeling. During the reign of James I from 1603 these rituals were developed further into a "theatre of death" through which the new Stuart dynasty sought to assert its prestige, but in so doing it began to outrun popular sentiment. At this period royal funeral ceremonies—like those of all members of the elite—were controlled by precise regulations from heralds designed to ensure that they reflected, sustained, and stabilized a social and political order that had been disrupted by the death.

A seeming low point in the fortunes of the monarchy came in January 1649 when, following its victory over King Charles I in the English Civil War, Parliament sentenced him to death "by the severing of his head from his body." When, however, the king was publicly executed on the balcony of Whitehall Palace, one observer recorded that the fall of the axe was greeted with "such a groan by the thousands then present as I never heard before" (Bland 1986, p. 54). Charles, who conducted himself at the last moments with great dignity, claimed that he died a martyr, and subsequent religious veneration for his memory and the restoration of the monarchy in 1660 indicated that his enemies had indeed overreached themselves by committing regicide.

From the seventeenth century until the early nineteenth century royal funerals—in common with those of the nobility—took place at night. This custom was intended to lessen the burden of precise heraldic regulation, which was already beginning to seem anachronistic. It had the effect of giving enhanced drama to the occasions, lit by torchlight, but reduced the scope for public participation. In the meantime, few royal deaths inspired strong public emotions. Notable exceptions were the untimely demise of Mary II in 1694, a victim of smallpox at the age of thirty-two, and the death in childbirth in 1817 of Princess Charlotte, then the only legitimate grandchild of George III and second in line to the throne. In 1821 the funeral procession of George IV's estranged wife Queen Caroline was accompanied by demonstrations against the king and the government, who were held responsible for shabby treatment of the deceased. In general, however, the late Stuart and Hanoverian royal family inspired dutiful observance rather than intense feeling in an era that in its overall response to death tended to emphasize ritual rather than emotion.

There was a gradual change in attitudes during the long reign of Queen Victoria (1837–1901). The funeral of the queen's husband, Prince Albert, in 1861 was a private one, but it was accompanied by strong expressions of collective public grief, and in the decades that followed his widow appeared to make continued mourning a way of life. In this period the royal family came to be seen increasingly as paradigmatic of the joys and sorrows of ordinary families, and hence there was a growing tendency for the public to view its bereavements in a quasi-personal way. This phenomenon was strikingly illustrated by sentiment following the early death of the queen's grandson, Prince Albert Victor, in 1892, and on Victoria's own demise in 1901. Meanwhile precedents for a more grandiose form of public mourning were set by two major non-royal funerals, those of Lord Nelson in 1806 and the Duke of Wellington in 1852. These trends combined to produce extensive popular engagement with large-scale funerals for Queen Victoria and, in 1910, Edward VII.

During the period since World War I there have only been two deaths of reigning monarchs, George V in 1936 and George VI in 1952. Both gave rise to strong and extensive public emotion, which was focused by repetition of essentially the same forms of ritual used in 1910. Until the end of the twentieth century, responses to the deaths of other members of the royal family were relatively low-key. In 1997, however, the tragic and untimely nature of Princess Diana's death following the very high profile nature of her life ensured that feelings would run high. The Queen Mother's death at the age of 101 in 2002 was, by contrast, hardly unexpected, but it evoked a widespread mood of sadness at her passing and of celebration of her life. Her funeral followed a broadly similar pattern to that of her husband George VI. Even here, though, there were innovations that reflected the social changes of the intervening half century, including the presence of the Princess Royal among the male mourners following the coffin, and the conveyance of the body to its final resting place at Windsor by road rather than railway.

Organizing and Performing Rituals

Overall responsibility for the funerals of sovereigns rests with the Earl Marshal, an office of state held on a hereditary basis by the dukes of Norfolk, who are assisted by the heralds of the College of Arms. The funerals of other members of the royal family are organized by Lord Chamberlain's office, which is part of the permanent royal secretariat. Numerous other agencies are involved in more complex and large-scale rituals. These have included the Office of Works (for temporary additions to buildings), the church, the armed services, the police, and the railways.

Until the beginning of the nineteenth century royal funerals were usually held in London with interments in Westminster Abbey. George III, however, moved the royal burial place to St. George's Chapel in Windsor Castle, thus focusing ceremonially on what was then a relatively small country town, several hours journey from the capital in pre-railway days. Scope for public participation was therefore limited. Only following the death of Queen Victoria was there a decisive move back to a more public and large-scale ceremonial. Her funeral, which included a spectacular naval review and a military procession through central London, represented a return to a "theatre of death" on a scale not seen since the early seventeenth century. The trend was confirmed upon the death of her son Edward VII when a further ritual of a public lying-in-state in Westminster Hall was added and proved enormously popular.

Major royal funerals, especially those of sovereigns, were made up of a series of ceremonies extending over several days, public and private, religious and secular, and presenting different aspects of the deceased. For example, Edward VII's body initially lay privately in his bedroom at Buckingham Palace, before being moved ceremonially to the Throne Room, and then in a street procession to Westminster Hall. After the three days of the public lying-in-state, there was a further street procession to Paddington Station, a train journey to Windsor, a procession from the station to the Castle, and a culminating religious service in St. George's Chapel.

The apparent seamlessness of such events conceals a reality of extensive improvisation and last-minute decision making. Royal funerals—unlike coronations, jubilees, and weddings—need to be arranged in a timescale measured in days rather than months. Although Queen Victoria was eighty-one at the time of her death, no developed plans for her funeral were in place and the ten days between her death and funeral were marked, according to one participant, by the most "extraordinary hurly burly of confusion" (Wolffe 2000, p. 235). Although some discreet advance planning can be made, the exact circumstances of a death are unforseeable and, in particular, the unexpected death of a relatively young person, as in the case of Princess Diana, is likely to catch the authorities almost wholly unprepared.

During the nineteenth and early twentieth centuries the days of royal funerals were increasingly marked by parallel processions and church services in provincial towns and cities. By this means many people remote from London or Windsor were able to achieve a sense of participation in a national ritual. Solidarity in grief was expressed by the wearing of mourning clothes and emblems such as black armbands. In this period instructions for the general wearing of mourning for periods of several weeks drew general compliance, giving a somber atmosphere to the streets. From the mid–twentieth century onward, the advent of radio and, eventually, television intensified this sense of involvement while shifting it from the communal public religiosity of streets and places of worship to the individualistic and domestic environment of people's homes. Film and television have increased consciousness of royal funerals as mass spectacles, as manifested in the unprecedented size of the worldwide television audience that watched Princess Diana's funeral.

Functions and Effects

As in the aftermath of death in private life, responses to royal deaths have been shaped by contingent circumstances and emotions, which were often fluid and fast moving. Explicit social, cultural, and political agendas were seldom articulated. Nevertheless, a number of strong implicit functions

Princess Diana's funeral, with novel elements such as the Elton John song "Goodbye England's Rose/Candle in the Wind," showed the way in which long-standing tradition is continually being reshaped by the British community—just as Diana reshaped the traditions of royalty while alive. CORBIS

and more or less intentional consequences can be identified.

First, there was the need to reaffirm the social and political hierarchy that had been disrupted by the death. This function was especially strong in the early modern era of close heraldic regulation, but persisted in the nineteenth and twentieth centuries, with processions and other rituals being designed to display order and stability. At the same time, from the early twentieth century onward, public lyings-in-state, and large crowds—whether present in person or participating at a distance through radio and television—constituted a democratic element. Conversely, however, on some occasions responses to royal deaths have had a subversive dimension. Public reactions to the deaths of Princess Charlotte in 1817 and Queen Caroline in 1821 were colored by hostility to the Tory government of the day and to the Prince Regent, who succeeded to the throne as George IV in 1820. Such a tendency to question rather than sustain the existing order recurred in the hostility expressed toward the surviving royal family following Princess Diana's death.

Second, the aftermath of royal deaths has provided an opportunity for affirming or reshaping the image of the deceased. In life Prince Albert was liable to be seen as a meddling foreigner exercising an inappropriate influence over the government, but in death he became a symbol of ideal English manhood. Queen Victoria was celebrated as an ideal of motherhood, but the reality of her relationships with her children and grandchildren was much more ambivalent. Princess Diana, perceived in life as sometimes wayward and manipulative, became a quasi-saint in death.

Third, collective mourning for royalty has been a focus for common identity within the multinational United Kingdom state and, in the past, the diverse and scattered territories of the British Empire.

Royalty are perceived to transcend social and political divisions to a degree that has only been matched by exceptional non-royal figures (i.e., Sir Winston Churchill, who died in 1965). The psychological constraints imposed by a sense of decency in the face of death made open dissent very rare, even in countries such as India and Ireland where British rule was otherwise strongly contested.

Fourth, royal deaths have served as a communal representation of private fears and griefs. Thus Princess Charlotte was identified with the numerous early-nineteenth-century young women who died in childbirth, just as Princess Diana's car crash painfully reminded the public of this characteristic form of death for late-twentieth-century young women. Prince Albert's early death was a focus for the personal bereavements of other widows and young children, while in responding to the deaths of Queen Victoria and subsequent monarchs, members of the public showed themselves to be recalling or anticipating losses of their own parents and grandparents.

Finally, royal deaths have marked the passage of time. Many people recall their own exact circumstances when they heard of the death of Princess Diana, or among an older generation, George VI. Monarchs who reigned for a long period, such as George III (1760–1820), seemed to symbolize a whole era, and their passing therefore stirred a sense of discontinuity and new beginnings. This phenomenon was especially pronounced in the case of Queen Victoria, whose death coincided closely with the beginning of the twentieth century, and has recurred in relation to Queen Elizabeth the Queen Mother, whose long life spanned the whole of that same century.

Conclusion

Overall, responses to British royal deaths can be set within a broadly Durkheimian theoretical perspective. In other words they serve as a ritual expression of social solidarities and a means for regenerating and sustaining the fabric of national life. They are also a significant component of a British form of civil religion, being an occasion for the affirmation both in rituals and in speeches and sermons of the perceived fundamental spiritual values focused upon the institution of the monarchy. For example, at the lying-in-state of Edward VII, the Archbishop of Canterbury spoke of a renewing of a sense of national mission. Upon the death of George VI the February 15, 1952, edition of the *Times* affirmed that "the sentiments evoked by the death and accession of monarchs have a quality that it is no impiety to call religious." By the time of Princess Diana's death the explicitly Christian content of such religiosity had become significantly more attenuated, but the sense of a spiritual dimension to national grief remained.

The British experience invites comparison with other countries that have remained monarchies in the contemporary era. The deaths of King Olaf V of Norway in 1991 and of King Baudouin of Belgium in 1993 were followed by widespread public grief, which gave occasion for significant reaffirmations of national unity and identity. Further afield the elaborate rituals that follow the deaths of Thai monarchs constitute politically significant affirmations of continuity and royal prestige, while the assassination of King Birendra of Nepal in 2001 evoked intense and emotionally charged reactions. Monarchs, in contrast to most presidents and prime ministers, normally hold office for life, and accordingly become for their generation seemingly permanent carriers and symbols of national identity. Their deaths, inevitable as they are in the course of nature, are therefore particularly psychologically disorienting for their people. Study of the ways in which nations react to this disruption of the fabric of seeming normality both adds to understanding of attitudes to death itself, and illuminates wider historical and social processes.

See also: CELEBRITY DEATHS; DURKHEIM, ÉMILE; LINCOLN IN THE NATIONAL MEMORY; QIN SHIH HUANG'S TOMB; TOMBS

Bibliography

Behrendt, Stephen C. *Royal Mourning and Regency Culture: Elegies and Memorials of Princess Charlotte.* Basingstoke, England: Macmillan, 1997.

Bland, Olivia. *The Royal Way of Death.* London: Constable, 1986.

Cannadine, David. "The Context, Performance and Meaning of Ritual: The British Monarchy and the 'Invention of Tradition,' c. 1820–1977." In Eric Hobsbawm and Terence Ranger eds., *The Invention of Tradition.* Cambridge: Cambridge University Press, 1983.

Cannadine, David. "War and Death, Grief and Mourning in Modern Britain." In Joachim Whaley ed., *Mirrors of Mortality: Studies in the Social History of Death.* London: Europa, 1981.

Darby, Elisabeth, and Nicola Smith. *The Cult of the Prince Consort.* New Haven, CT: Yale University Press, 1983.

Davies, Douglas J. *Death, Ritual and Belief: The Rhetoric of Funerary Rites.* London: Cassell, 1997.

Fritz, Paul S. "From 'Public' to 'Private': The Royal Funerals in England, 1500–1830." In Joachim Whaley ed., *Mirrors of Mortality: Studies in the Social History of Death.* London: Europa, 1981.

Huntington, Richard, and Peter Metcalf. *Celebrations of Death: The Anthropology of Mortuary Ritual.* Cambridge: Cambridge University Press, 1979.

Kuhn, William M. *Democratic Royalism: The Transformation of the British Monarchy, 1861–1914.* Basingstoke, England: Macmillan, 1996.

Schor, Esther. *Bearing the Dead: The British Culture of Mourning from the Enlightenment to Victoria.* Princeton, NJ: Princeton University Press, 1994.

"Throne and Church," *The Times,* 15 February 1952, 7.

Walter, Tony, ed. *The Mourning for Diana.* Oxford: Berg, 1999.

Wolffe, John. *Great Deaths: Grieving, Religion and Nationhood in Victorian and Edwardian Britain.* Oxford: Oxford University Press, 2000.

Woodward, Jennifer. *The Theatre of Death: The Ritual Management of Royal Funerals in Renaissance England 1570–1625.* Woodbridge, England: The Boydell Press, 1997.

JOHN WOLFFE

S

SACRIFICE

Prayer is a form of communication with a deity or other spiritual being. Words addressed to a deity usually offer praise or seek guidance, blessing, forgiveness, fertility, victory, or protection. Like prayer, sacrifice is a form of communication with a deity for similar purposes. The word itself means "to make holy." As distinct from prayer, sacrificial offerings include objects of value and symbolic significance that are given to the gods to earn their favor. The gifts can take many forms, becoming sacred themselves through ritual consecration. The gods might be offered the most desirable foods or provided with the finest vessels, carvings, tools, and weapons. Historians, however, have often regarded blood sacrifice as the most powerful way to appease the gods. It was not unusual for societies to engage in both animal and human sacrifice, although the historical trend has been toward a sharp reduction in the latter.

Participants in blood sacrifice rituals experience a sense of awe, danger, or exaltation because they are daring to approach the gods who create, sustain, and destroy life. The buildup of tension prior to the blood sacrifice gives way to a festive sense of triumph and relief. Morale is strengthened by the ritual killing because the group has itself performed the godlike act of destruction and is now capable of renewing its own existence. The underlying philosophical assumption is that life must pass through death.

According to ancient rites of sacrifice, the sacrificial animal or human should be of high value. The gods would be offended by a sickly or inferior offering. In Old Testament tradition, Abel was obeying what was already an ancient tradition when he sacrificed the firstborn of his herds to God. Bulls were sacred to Egyptians more than 5,000 years ago, being associated with Taurus, a god with both animal and human features. For the Egyptians, then, the sacrifice of a bull was the gift of a demigod to the gods. In the years immediately preceding the emergence of Christianity some mystery cults switched from bull to human sacrifices, using the same ceremonies in which the victim was first honored as a god, then put to bloody death. Osiris, the legendary Egyptian ruler who, murdered, became the god of fertility, cast a long shadow over these proceedings. Biblical scholars have often commented that the death of Jesus had been prefigured by other events in which a person was raised to the status of a god and then sacrificed for the good of the people. The significance of blood as a link between Jesus and his followers is consistent with that tradition.

Sacrifice and Society

Human sacrifice is sometimes regarded as a bizarre practice carried out by a few scattered societies who either were uncivilized or exceptionally cruel and violent. However, there is persuasive evidence that the sacrificial impulse has been common throughout history and has played an important role in society.

The origins of blood sacrifice are lost in the mist of prehistory. Nevertheless, inferences can be drawn from archaeological research and from the practices and beliefs of people whose rituals continued into the historical period. The same societies usually performed other types of sacrifices as well, but these examples demonstrate the widespread use of ritual murder as an approved component of social policy.

Foundation and passage sacrifices. There is abundant archaeological evidence that many societies practiced both animal and human sacrifice to persuade the gods to protect their buildings and ensure safe passage through dangerous areas where their own gods might lack jurisdiction. Burials suggestive of sacrifice have been found in the sites of ancient bridges and buildings throughout Asia, Europe, and North Africa. It was widely believed that territories were under the control of local gods who might be angered by intrusions. Blood sacrifice at border crossings (often marked by rivers) and within buildings were thought to be prudent offerings. Sacrificial victims were also interred beneath city gates.

Children were often selected as the sacrificial offerings. Excavation of the Bridge Gate in Bremen, Germany, and several ancient fortresses in Wales are among the many examples of this practice. According to the Book of Kings, when Joshua destroyed Jericho he prophesized that the man who rebuilds Jericho "shall lay the foundation stones thereof upon the body of his first born and in his youngest son shall he set up the gates thereof." In rebuilding the city, Hiel later sacrificed his oldest and youngest sons in precisely this manner. The historian Nigel Davies observes that biblical accounts of foundation sacrifices have been supported by archaeological investigations:

> In the sanctuary in Gezer were found two burnt skeletons of six-year-old children and the skulls of two adolescents that had been sawn in two. At Meggido a girl of fifteen had been killed and buried in the foundations of a large structure. Excavations show that the practice of interring children under new buildings was widespread and some were evidently buried alive. *(Davies 1981, p. 61)*

Foundation sacrifices dedicated to fertility (as, for example, in storage buildings) often involved infant and child victims. Captives, slaves, and criminals have also been selected as sacrificial victims on many occasions. That foundation sacrifices belong only to the remote past could be an erroneous assumption. In early twentieth-century Borneo an eyewitness testified that a criminal was buried alive in every posthole for a new building so that he might become a guardian spirit.

Attempts to Explain Blood Sacrifice

No one attempt to explain blood sacrifice seems adequate for the variety of forms and purposes associated with this practice in many societies over many years. Nevertheless, it is useful to consider the following accounts as informed attempts to explain the relationship between blood sacrifice and society.

Male bonding and collective killing. Hunters learned to cooperate with each other to improve their chances of success. This common purpose led to a sense of brotherhood, what is often called "male bonding" in the twenty-first century. Their mutual allegiances and rituals set them apart from others as they swore their oaths on blood and became the specialists in killing. Some theorists suggest that the basic forms of society were derived from the distribution of roles within the hunting group and their codes of loyalty. The structure of society in general has been modeled on male-bonded groups who relied on blood sacrifices to achieve their own survival and success—or so upholds this theory that seems to seriously underestimate the contribution of women to the shaping of society.

Sacrifice reduces violence. It may seem peculiar to suggest that sacrifice reduces violence, but some anthropologists and historians have drawn this inference. Aggressive tensions within a society can lead toward violence against fellow members. Ritual sacrifices provide a relatively safe framework to keep violence within bounds while at the same time offering emotional release through killing substitute victims. This theory suggests that, at least in some circumstances, ritual killing of a designated victim can restrain the larger group from tearing itself apart.

Sacrificial companions to the next life. Many societies have considered their leaders as representative of their people both in this life and the next. It was important, then, to make sure that the ruler of the land (be it a king or otherwise) was accompanied to the afterlife with a retinue of loyal attendants. Rulers often had their concubines and servants (as well as household animals) entombed with them. Even distinguished ministers might be among the companions who were either entombed or immolated in order to serve their ruler after death. Examples include major archaeological finds in Egypt and China where the bodies of numerous attendants were discovered in chambers adjoining the royal coffin. There is evidence that elaborate ceremonies were conducted to honor the chosen companions prior to their deaths. It appears that the sacrificial victims often were given libations that provided a drug-induced insensitivity prior to their deaths.

The practice of burying the living with the dead encountered increasing criticism through the centuries. Eventually many societies shifted to symbolic sacrifices; for example, the later Egyptian practice of placing figurines (*Shabti*) in the royal tombs. China, Japan, the Greek states, and other ancient civilizations also moved toward symbolic rather than actual sacrifice of companions upon the death of their rulers. Furthermore, with the development of Christianity and Islam, a life after death appeared more likely to be within reach of individuals other than royalty, therefore making voluntary sacrifice a less attractive proposition.

Sacrifice keeps the world going. The most sweeping theory is based on an interpretation of history that pictures the human condition as fearful and perilous, beset with threats to survival from starvation, attack, and events such as earthquakes, volcanic eruptions, and floods that were taken to be the work of angry gods. Possessing limited knowledge and technology, societies tried to find a way of negotiating with rival, demanding, and frequently unpredictable gods if the world and their own lives were to continue. Sacrifice soon became a significant form of exchange with the gods, a sort of currency in an age before the establishment of a monetary system. In modern parlance, sacrifice was a way of doing business.

Human sacrifice was considered so crucial a measure that it persisted for some time even in societies that had become more complex and sophisticated. For example, the practice of sacrificing the eldest son was a salient feature of Mediterranean cults 5,000 years ago and still a powerful theme in Judaism and early Christianity. Sacrifice would be tamed slowly as societies developed more effective ways to manage their needs and cope with their environments. The gradual and still

Among the ruins of Montsegur in southern France, a memorial stands in the Field of the Burned to commomorate the sacrifice of over 200 Cathar heretics in 1244.
FORTEAN PICTURE LIBRARY

incomplete abolition of slavery throughout the world also reduced the supply of potential victims. And, again, the slow and still incomplete movement toward according full human rights to females eventually spared many the death of a sacrificial victim.

Controversies and Unsettled Questions

Many questions and differences of opinion continue to exist around the issue of human sacrifice. This situation is not surprising, considering the limits and ambiguity of some of the evidence and the strong emotions aroused by the subject.

Death does not always signify sacrifice. Bodies dating from the first and second centuries B.C.E. have been recovered from bogs in England, Denmark, Wales, and other Northern European sites. These have often been considered sacrificial victims because the bodies showed many signs of having been subjected to ritualistic treatment. More sophisticated examination of the remains, however, indicates that at least some of the bodies had been accorded high honors, not put to death by sacrifice or punishment. It is probable that other errors have been made in identifying sacrifice victims, although enough clear and substantial data are available to demonstrate that sacrifice has been a common practice throughout much of the world.

Why child sacrifice? One of the most dramatic episodes in Judeo-Christian Scripture begins with God's command that Abraham sacrifice Isaac, his son. Abraham sorrowfully prepares to obey, but God intervenes and provides a ram as a sacrificial substitute. The meaning of this episode has been the subject of intense discussion through the centuries, although it is most often interpreted as a celebration of faith on Abraham's part and mercy on the part of God. Another human sacrifice reported in the Bible has remained more difficult to interpret in a favorable light and, therefore, has received less attention. Jepthah pledged he would sacrifice the first living creature that he saw when returning home if God would grant him victory in an upcoming battle. The victorious Jepthah was greeted by his daughter upon returning home. True to his pledge, Jepthah made a burnt offering of his daughter (who is not given a name in the biblical account). Why would God intervene for Isaac but not for Jepthah's daughter? Was Jepthah pious or callous in carrying through with the execution? These questions continue to haunt scholars and ethicists.

How many people were sacrificed by the Incas and Aztecs? This question can now be answered with confidence. Yes, the Incas of Peru and the Aztec of Mexico put a great many people to ritualistic death. This proposition was doubted for some years, in part because this kind of mass slaughter was difficult to imagine. Evidence has become increasingly clear, however, that human sacrifice was a core feature of the Inca and Aztec cultures.

Remains of Inca sacrifices have been dated from as long ago as 5000 B.C.E., sometimes on the towering peaks of the Andes, sometimes in the coastal desert. Archaeological investigations have found evidence of human sacrifice into the sixteenth century, and this practice is thought to have continued for some time afterward. Tenochtitlan (predecessor to Mexico City) is known to have been the active site of human sacrifices long before Spanish forces arrived to witness these events firsthand: There were already huge collections of skulls on display.

Twenty-first-century historians tend to agree that human sacrifice was both a unifying event and an intense demonstration of religious beliefs for these powerful empires. The Aztecs believed that the "vital energies" of one person could be transferred to another person through drinking the blood and eating the flesh. The gods also craved flesh and blood, so human sacrifice benefited both Aztecs and their ever-hungry deities. Sacrifice was an integral part of their worldview in which the threat of death was ever present, a threat that had to be countered by extreme and relentless measures that would magically transform death into life. Discoveries since the mid-twentieth century confirm that many women were sacrificed in special rituals intended to renew the fertility cycle.

Peruvian sacrifices were also concerned with encouraging the gods to bless their fertility. For reasons that are not entirely clear, the priests appear to have sacrificed an extraordinary number of children. Also somewhat obscure are the reasons for their practice of decapitating their victims. Having left no written records, the Incas and other Peruvian cultures have also taken with them their secrets and mysteries.

Do human sacrifices still exist? A few scattered reports of ritualistic murders believed to be sacrificial appear in print occasionally, usually in American and European newspapers. The reports are brief and inconclusive; for example, one October 1999 *Irish Times* article read, "Police in the eastern Indian state of Bihar yesterday dug up the remains of two teenage girls allegedly killed by their father in a ritual human sacrifice this week." It is probable that at least some such killings are the work of deranged individuals rather than religious celebrants. It is also possible, however, that credible evidence of contemporary human sacrifice may come to light.

A controversial theory suggests that patriotism, war, and adherence to the flag are incitements to a disguised form of sacrifice. Generally, the homicide rate decreases when a nation is involved in a popular war. Although there are other ways to interpret this fact, it is a challenging thought that patriotism might be regarded as "a civil religion of blood sacrifice, which periodically kills its children to keep the group together" (Marvin and Ingle 1999, p. 315).

See also: AZTEC RELIGION; CANNIBALISM; CHILDREN, MURDER OF; GODS AND GODDESSES OF LIFE AND DEATH; HUNTING; INCAN RELIGION; OSIRIS

Bibliography

Benson, Elizabeth P., and Anita G. Cook. *Ritual Sacrifice in Ancient Peru: New Discoveries and Interpretations.* Austin: University of Texas Press, 2001.

Brown Burkett, Walter. *Homo Necans: The Anthropology of Ancient Greek Sacrificial Ritual and Myth.* Berkeley: University of California Press, 1983.

Carrasco, David L. *City of Sacrifice: The Aztec Empire and the Role of Violence in Civilization.* Boston: Beacon Press, 1999.

Davies, Nigel. *Human Sacrifice in History and Today.* New York: William Morrow and Co., 1981.

Eliade, Mircea. *A History of Religious Ideas,* 3 vols., translated by Willard R. Trask. Chicago: University of Chicago Press, 1978.

Foss, Martin. *Death, Sacrifice, and Tragedy.* Lincoln: University of Nebraska Press, 1966.

Gennep, Arnold van. *The Rites of Passage.* 1900. Reprint, Chicago: University of Chicago Press, 1960.

Girard, René. *Violence and the Sacred.* Baltimore, MD: Johns Hopkins University Press, 1977.

"Girls Killed in 'Sacrifice.'" *Irish Times,* 23 October 1999, 14.

Green, Miranda Aldhouse. *Dying for the Gods: Human Sacrifice in Iron Age and Roman Europe.* Charleston, SC: Tempus, 2001.

Harris, Marvin. *Our Kind.* New York: Harper Perennial, 1990.

Hughes, Dennis D. *Human Sacrifice in Ancient Greece.* New York: Routledge, 1991.

Levenson, Jon D. *The Death and Resurrection of the Beloved Son.* New Haven, CT: Yale University Press, 1993.

Marvin, Carolyn, and David W. Ingle. *Blood Sacrifice and the Nation.* Cambridge: Cambridge University Press, 1999.

Peires, J. B. *The Dead Will Arise.* Bloomington: Indiana University Press, 1989.

Read, Kay Almere. *Time and Sacrifice in the Aztec Cosmos.* Bloomington: Indiana University Press, 1998.

Ulansey, David. *The Origin of the Mithrac Mysteries: Cosmology and Salvation.* New York: Oxford University Press, 1991.

Westermarck, Edward. *The Origin and Development of the Moral Ideas.* London: Macmillan, 1906.

Young, Dudley. *Origins of the Sacred.* New York: St. Martin's Press, 1991.

ROBERT KASTENBAUM

SAFETY REGULATIONS

Safety regulations are defined as mandatory requirements that aim to prevent or reduce injury. They include laws and regulations, such as prohibiting the sale of fireworks, and mandatory standards, such as specifying that children's nightwear be fire resistant. Table 1 presents examples of safety regulations that fall into a number of categories.

Environments for Safety Regulations

A common factor in whether regulation is used is the seriousness of the outcome being addressed in terms of human health. For this reason regulation is more common in transportation and the workplace, where the potential for fatal injury is perceived to be relatively great, and less common in the home and in sports environments, where the potential for fatal injury is perceived to be less. Regulations are often introduced in situations where the actions of one person can injure other persons who do not have the ability or opportunity to decide whether to accept the risks associated with those actions. The most common examples relate to regulations protecting the safety of children and of workers.

Even where a person's actions are likely to cause injury only to herself, regulation may be introduced if the costs of injury to that person are largely borne by the public. Perhaps the most contentious among this class of regulations in the United States are mandatory motorcycle helmet and safety belt laws. The overall effectiveness of safety regulations depends on whether the requirement being mandated is capable of preventing or reducing the target injury and on whether the process of regulation is effective. Some of the factors that influence the effectiveness of the process of regulation include: (1) whether the regulation requires active or passive compliance; (2) the effectiveness of enforcement; (3) public awareness of the regulation; and (4) public support for the regulation.

Regulations can require active compliance by the person being protected, for example putting on a safety belt, or they can provide passive protection, for example the temperature of hot water systems being preset before leaving the factory. Compliance with passive protection is generally much greater and there is less need for enforcement activity at the level of the individual when this approach to regulation is adopted.

To be effective the process of regulation requires sufficient public knowledge about the regulation and adequate enforcement. Promotion of voluntary compliance to achieve a level of community support before regulating has been an effective paradigm in countries such as Australia with respect to issues such as the mandatory use of safety belts and bicycle helmets. Once there is a high degree of public acceptance, there is less need for widespread enforcement and greater potential to focus enforcement on the nonconforming minority.

The most productive role of enforcement is to increase compliance, rather than detect noncompliance. Public education about the regulation that stresses the likelihood of detection has been found to increase compliance with drunk driving and speeding laws. There is little evidence that very large penalties produce significantly greater compliance by individuals than sizable, but not extreme, penalties. For companies, penalties are generally larger to minimize noncompliance based on commercial reasons. Selective enforcement of regulations can lead to ineffectiveness of the regulations for the group that is not being enforced and concerns about victimization from those groups being enforced. The police generally enforce traffic safety regulations. In the workplace, the enforcement role is sometimes undertaken by labor unions or by government workplace safety bodies.

TABLE 1

Aim of safety regulations

Aim of regulation	Examples
Limit access to dangerous products or activities	Graduated driver licensing Machine operator licensing Restrictions on the sale of alcohol to minors Child-resistant closures on pharmaceuticals or cleaning products Firearm regulations
Limit levels of harmful substances	Lead in paints Speed limits Power restrictions on motorcycles Temperature of hot water systems Manual handling limits
Require the use or installation of particular protective devices	Safety belts Motorcycle helmets Protective gear in workplaces Smoke detectors Electrical safety switches
Prescribe protective performance	Motor vehicle safety standards Standards for personal protective equipment Fire-resistant nightwear Isolation pool fencing Safety glass
Require information to be provided to consumers about likely hazards	Labeling of poisons and pharmaceuticals Alcohol content labeling on beverage containers

SOURCE: Courtesy of Haworth, 2001.

In other arenas, community groups or local government enforce.

Regulations can be prescriptive or performance based. In relation to a product, prescriptive regulations prescribe how the product must be constructed but performance-based regulations require that the product meet certain performance criteria (e.g., acceleration values on a crash test dummy). Manufacturers have argued that prescriptive regulation has the potential to impede the development of innovative solutions and possibly safer products.

Effects of Safety Regulations

Improving safety by regulation is a relatively slow process. It can take many years to have regulations passed by the government. In addition, most regulation is not retrospective and only applies to products manufactured or activities commenced after the implementation of the regulation (or even some years after implementation). For example, a regulation that requires electrical safety switches to be fitted to new homes constructed after a certain date will take many years to permeate a significant proportion of homes.

The levels of safety performance required by legislation may be very low. An alternative approach that is becoming more common in transport safety is to combine regulation with encouraging consumer pressure to drive the market to produce something safer than is required by regulation. For example, the Snell Memorial Foundation tests motorcycle helmets to what is generally considered a more rigorous standard than that required by the U.S. Department of Transportation standard. Many manufacturers submit their helmets for Snell testing because they perceive that certification to this standard provides a market advantage. In such instances, the role of regulation may become that of providing a minimum standard to prevent unacceptably poor performance, rather than encouraging good safety performance.

However, regulation may sometimes result in counterproductive behavior. Those who resist the regulation may attempt to circumvent it. One example of this problem is the phenomenon of "toy" motorcycle helmets that provide little or no head protection. Some objectors to compulsory helmet wearing legislation wear these helmets to avoid detection by police.

Sometimes there are objections to safety regulations on the grounds that they subjugate individual rights to the public good, particularly in the United States. Mandatory-helmet-wearing legislation has been extremely contentious on these grounds. Helmet use reduces motorcyclist fatalities, injuries, and treatment costs and universal helmet laws increase helmet use substantially. The requirement is capable of preventing or reducing the target injury and the process of regulation is effective; however, the price for these benefits is that individual actions are restricted. Through a helmet use law, society requires each motorcyclist to take an action that appears to affect only him- or herself, but a motorcyclist's injury or fatality affects many others, directly and indirectly. Family, friends, and coworkers must adapt to the personal consequences of an injury or fatality. Society as a whole bears many of the direct and indirect costs, and these issues must be weighed against individual freedom of action.

See also: CAUSES OF DEATH; INJURY MORTALITY; TRIANGLE SHIRTWAIST COMPANY FIRE

Bibliography

Barss, Peter, Gordon Smith, Susan Baker, and Dinesh Mohan. *Injury Prevention: An International Perspective.* New York: Oxford University Press, 1998.

National Committee for Injury Prevention and Control. *Injury Prevention: Meeting the Challenge.* New York: Oxford University Press, 1989.

Preusser, David F., James H. Hedlund, and R. G. Ulmer. *Evaluation of Motorcycle Helmet Law Repeal in Arkansas and Texas.* Washington, DC: U.S. Department of Transportation National Highway Safety Administration, 2000.

NARELLE L. HAWORTH

SAINTS, PRESERVED

The lives and deaths of saints have long occupied a distinctive place in Christian belief. Other religious traditions have also revered certain individuals as embodying their most admired virtues and having a special relationship with God. Christian saints, however, became such powerful figures that church authorities have had to balance carefully between supporting and moderating their influence. This influence includes the veneration of objects said to have been used by or associated with a saint and, even more precious, their physical remains.

Martyrs, Hermits, and Town Saints

Christianity was but one of many religious sects that were active within the extended reach of the Roman Empire as disciples started to disseminate the teachings of Jesus. The zeal of the early Christian converts brought them into conflict with their Roman overlords, who feared any destabilizing movements. Some Christians were executed by the authorities, others were slaughtered. The persecutions continued into the fourth century before abating. Those who died for their beliefs became the first martyrs, and the first martyrs became the first saints. Sanctification occurred by acclaim of their fellow believers; it would be another millennium before the pope and the church acquired authority over this process.

An early example of spontaneous sanctification was Polycarp of Smyrna (second century). He was admired as a person who had sacrificed himself in emulation of Jesus and therefore strengthened the faith. Polycarp's bones were buried in a secret and safe place. This action could be regarded simply as a sign of respect, but eventually veneration of physical remains of saintly persons would become a widespread and intense phenomenon. Martyrs predominated among the earliest saints. There is no comprehensive record of all the men and women who were martyred in the early Christian centuries, and many of the names have been lost. Another type soon emerged: the desert hermits, most notably Anthony (fourth century), who chose an ascetic and isolated life in the desert wilderness to overcome the temptations of the spirit and the flesh. Having accomplished this daunting task, he laid down guidelines for other Christians and became the inspiration for monasticism.

As time went on the number of saints increased greatly. Local and regional saints appeared in profusion throughout the Western domains of Christianity. Most of these saints were people who had impressed their community but were not known beyond their limited area. High church officials had little influence over the creation of town saints or the cult practices that formed around them.

Solace for the People, Challenge for the Papacy

Christianity struggled with dissension and numerous practical problems through the first millennium. The organizational effectiveness of the Roman Catholic Church gradually improved, however, and popes were in position to exercise a greater degree of control. One of the issues that needed serious attention was the status and function of saints. Many of the faithful relied heavily on both local and universally acclaimed saints. Images, statues, and shrines represented and honored the saints. People overwhelmed by anxiety and suffering turned to their favorite saints for help. The saints of choice were compassionate. They listened to the fears and sorrows. They certainly had more power than the people, whose sense of hopelessness and despair led them to beg for intercession.

Church leaders knew that the venerated saints represented an accessible point of comfort for the great mass of believers who, illiterate and poorly educated, had only limited understanding of the more subtle and abstract ideas that comprised Christian theology. The saints were mercy and salvation brought near. At the same time, though, there were also problems that could not be ignored. The numerous saint cults often seemed more pagan than Christian. Purists were dismayed by what appeared to be the worship of images that drew attention away from the true meaning of Christianity. There was also concern that the status of saint had been seriously debased by the uncritical and unrestrained enthusiasm of people who had been carried away by their emotional needs.

One other phenomenon required special attention: the ever-growing fascination with the bones and other remains of saints. Many of the people acclaimed as saints since the fourth century had been credited with miracles either while alive or dead. It was widely believed that their physical remains could also be invoked to produce miracles, usually of healing the desperate and incurable. Aside from the medical and religious questions involved there were also the economic and power issues. Churches were competing with each other for relics and remains (including even body parts claimed to have belonged to Jesus). The church that had no illustrious saint remains was in a difficult position in attracting parishioners and donations. Saint remains were offered for sale to the highest bidder, and many a church official suspected their authenticity, yet hesitated to challenge or withdraw from the bidding.

The church worked hard to sort things out, starting in the eleventh century, and continuing into modern times. Many local saints were dropped from the lists. Guidelines and procedures were established to rule out weak and spurious claims for new candidates. It was a hard blow when very popular saints such as Christopher were eliminated on the grounds that no such person had actually existed (although Christopher has continued to thrive despite this directive). The investigative techniques developed by the church helped to lay the foundation for present-day detective work and intelligence analysis. This dedication to ensuring that only the deserving are venerated was accompanied by a reaffirmation of the power of saints. Any lingering doubts were put to rest by the Council of Trent (1563), which made belief in the efficacy of saintly intervention a core article of Catholic faith.

The church did little, though, to subdue the fixation on saintly remains or to dry up the commerce of same. It is unlikely that any such campaign would have been very successful because there was a widespread horror of the decomposing body during the Middle Ages (to the extent that the illustrious dead would often be boiled until the flesh separated from the bones, with the former then tossed and the latter buried). It was therefore a most welcome miracle when a corpse did not decay, when divine intervention had spared a person the indignity of decomposition. Some of the most beloved saints were those whose bodies had "the odor of sanctity" rather than the rank smell of decomposition when unearthed after a lengthy period of burial. The Virgin Mary escaped decomposition through her ascension to heaven and therefore also avoided corruption of the flesh. Medieval destinations for pilgrimage invariably featured saint relics and remains.

Germaine Cousin is a relatively recent example of an incorruptible. Born in rural France in 1579, she was described as an unattractive and mentally unstable person who attracted little attention when she died at the age of twenty-two. Her corpse happened to be disinterred forty years later and was reported to be perfectly preserved, even unto the garland of carnations and rye that had been placed on her hair. This preservation (like many others) could not be attributed to embalming. In due time she had become St. Germaine, provided with an altar by which her remains could perform their work of healing and protecting those who sought her intercession.

Preserved remains of saints can still be seen. Lawrence Cunningham expresses a not uncommon discomfort with viewing "the incorruptible bodies encased in glass coffins or the statues of Santa Lucia with eyeballs on a plate held in her hand or the large reliquaries with shriveled arms and tibias" (Cunningham 1980, p. 1). Anneli Rufus vividly describes several preserved saints in their contemporary settings.

A Perspective on Preserved Saints

History suggests that saints of the Roman Catholic Church achieved their distinctively influential status first as exemplars of faith and courage and then as intermediaries through which troubled people could convey their fears and hopes to God. The prospect of salvation and immediate triumph over death became attenuated as the centuries went by and people continued to suffer and die. Saints became increasingly valued as available resources to help with pressing concerns; female saints provided an alternative to the male-dominated church hierarchy.

Two themes had been widespread in world societies long before Christianity: fear of the dead and belief in sympathetic magic. These themes were often combined in cults of the dead where rituals attempted to keep the peace between the living and the dead while drawing upon the special powers of the latter. The emerging saint cults exhibited some of these features, but with a significant twist: The sacred remains of the saints were not to be feared; they were, rather, tokens of hope. The remains also functioned as objects for the working of sympathetic magic. Whatever had been close to a person—or, in this case, part of the person—could be used to make good things happen.

People who otherwise felt powerless to understand and control their fate could take inspiration from those who had become saints by virtue of their virtue, and could participate in a sense of mystic communion with those whose bodies had been preserved from the corruption of the flesh. Even the staunchest faith can sometimes use another glimmer of hope.

See also: CATHOLICISM; CHRISTIAN DEATH RITES, HISTORY OF; JESUS; MARTYRS; VIRGIN MARY, THE

Bibliography

Ariès, Philippe. *The Hour of Our Death,* translated by Helen Weaver. New York: Alfred A. Knopf, 1981.

Brown, Peter. *The Cult of the Saints: Its Rise and Function in Latin Christianity.* Chicago: University of Chicago Press, 1982.

Cruz, Joan Carroll. *The Incorruptibles.* Rockford, IL: Tan Books, 1977.

Cunningham, Lawrence. *The Meaning of Saints.* New York: Harper and Row, 1980.

Delaney, John J. *Dictionary of Saints.* New York: Doubleday, 1997.

Farmer, David H. *The Oxford Dictionary of Saints.* New York: Oxford University Press, 1987.

Huizinga, Johan. *The Autumn of the Middle Ages.* Chicago: University of Chicago Press, 1996.

Rufus, Anneli. *Magnificent Corpses*. New York: Marlowe and Company, 1999.

Tuchman, Barbara W. *A Distant Mirror: The Calamitous 14th Century*. New York: Alfred A. Knopf, 1978.

Weinstein, Donald, and Rudolph M. Bell. *Saints and Society: The Two Worlds of Western Civilization*. Chicago: University of Chicago Press, 1982.

Williams, Caroline. *Saints: Their Cults and Origins*. New York: St. Martin's Press, 1980.

Woodward, Kenneth L. *Making Saints: How the Catholic Church Determines Who Becomes a Saint, Who Doesn't, and Why*. New York: Simon & Schuster, 1990.

Wyschograd, Edith. *Saints and Postmodernism*. Chicago: University of Chicago Press, 1990.

ROBERT KASTENBAUM

SAMARITANS

See BEFRIENDING.

SARTRE, JEAN-PAUL

Traditional European Christian philosophy, particularly in the eighteenth century, was filled with images of and sermons on the fear of the judgment that would come upon the time of death. Characterized by Plato as the need to free the soul from the "hateful" company of the body, death was seen as the entrance into another world. By contrast, the efforts of nineteenth- and twentieth-century existentialists were to humanize and individualize death as the last stage of life rather than the entrance into that which is beyond life. This shift historically helped to make death conceptually a part of life, and therefore could be understood as a human phenomenon rather than speculation as to the nature of a spiritual life.

If death is the last stage of life, then one philosophical question is, What is the nature of the experience? It is to this question that the phenomenological analysis of Jean-Paul Sartre contributed significant insight. It can be said that when a child dies, the child becomes frozen in time. Always a child, the potential of that child is never realized and the experience of the life of that child ends. Sartre explains in his analysis of time that the past is fixed in the experiential history of the person. Whatever the person did, or even did not do, is simply the way it is. If a person was a coward when he or she died, then the image of that person as a coward is how the individual is remembered.

In his book *Being and Nothingness* (1956) Sartre established his early phenomenological method, exploring the nature of the human experience. Since Socrates, Western philosophers have suggested that essence or those basic aspects that make up the person are divinely preordained or predesigned prior to birth. Sartre, on the other hand, understood that the person must first exist before that which makes up the person can be identified, as human beings are not objective objects but rather subjective in their dynamic ability to change. Thus for Sartre, existence precedes essence. If analysis starts with the first human experience and ends with the last, then one's past is the past that was experienced by the individual, the present is the current reality, and the future reflects his or her potential. For Sartre, at the point of death the person does not have a past, as he or she is now dead and cannot continue to write in the log of the present. Rather, a person then becomes his or her past. Like the child who has died, in death the person is frozen in the minds of those persons who remember him or her.

Sartre used the concept of a wall to explain the transition from life to death. This concept is best understood by persons in a hospice who find that their comrades in death often understand them better than their families or those who do not understand their own finite nature. As he often did, Sartre offered his existentialist philosophy in a more academic volume and then explained it in his plays and novels. In his story *The Wall* (1964) Sartre writes about Pablo, a Spanish loyalist in his cell with two other republicans waiting execution by Generalissimo Franco's soldiers. He reflects as follows: "For twenty-four hours I have lived at Tom's side, I had heard him, I had talked to him, and I knew that we had nothing in common. And now we resemble each other like twins, only because we shall die together" (Stern 1967, p. 174). Persons faced with their own finitude often see the meaning of both their experiences and their lives from a larger perspective.

Jean-Paul Sartre and lifetime companion Simone de Beauvoir, whose ashes are buried side-by-side, share the same gravestone in the Montparnasse Cemetery in Paris, France. ROBERT HOLMES/CORBIS

Sartre would say that as he has not experienced death, he does not know what it is, but he can see that it must have some reality as others seem to experience its presence. An atheist, he believed that there is no divine being and therefore no heaven or an afterlife. Rather, there are only those aspects of the conscious choices made by the individual that live on in the lives of those the person has touched. Sartre's understanding of life is that it reflects the experience of one's existence. When the person is dead, he or she is only memories held by those who are in some way a part of the life of the individual. These contributions to the humanizing of the dying experience and the philosophical understanding of the role of death offer benchmarks in the history of the philosophy of death.

See also: FRANKL, VIKTOR; FREUD, SIGMUND; IMMORTALITY; PHILOSOPHY, WESTERN; PLATO

Bibliography

Sartre, Jean-Paul. *Truth and Existence.* Chicago: University of Chicago Press, 1992.

Sartre, Jean-Paul. *Nausea/The Wall and Other Stories: Two Volumes in One.* New York: Fine Communications Books, 1964.

Sartre, Jean-Paul. *Being and Nothingness: A Phenomenological Essay on Ontology.* New York: Philosophical Library, 1956.

Stern, Alfred. *Sartre: His Philosophy and Existential Psychoanalysis.* New York: Delta, 1967.

JAMES W. ELLOR

SAUNDERS, CICELY

The name of Cicely Saunders is synonymous with one of the major social innovations of the twentieth century: the modern hospice movement. Saunders was born in England on June 22, 1918, the first of three children of Gordon and Chrissie Saunders. She enjoyed the material comforts of a successful middle-class family, and at the age of fourteen was sent to Roedean, one of the country's exclusive boarding schools for girls. In 1938 she went to Oxford University to read politics, philosophy, and economics, but interrupted her studies two years later to become a student nurse at the Nightingale Training School of London's St. Thomas's Hospital. When a back injury forced her to leave nursing, she returned to Oxford and qualified in 1944 with a diploma in public and social administration. She then commenced training as a hospital almoner, or medical social worker.

In a large London hospital Saunders became involved in the care of a patient who was ill and dying far away from his own home. His name was David Tasma, and he had come to London as a refugee from Poland's Warsaw ghetto. In the short time that they knew each other, he proved an inspiration to Saunders, and their professional relationship turned into a deep friendship. One day he said to her, "I want only what is in your mind and in your heart." This combination of emotion and intellect proved to be a guiding theme in her subsequent work. The two discussed an idea that it might be possible to create more homelike places where people could end their lives. When Tasma died, on February 25, 1948, he left Saunders with a gift of £500 and the following encouragement: "Let me be a window in your home."

Saunders determined immediately to learn more about the care of the terminally ill. First she worked as a volunteer in St. Luke's, a home for the dying in Bayswater, London. Then she made the momentous decision to study medicine, starting in 1952 and qualifying at the age of thirty-eight. She began to see her work with dying people as a form of religious calling or vocation.

In 1958 she took up a position as Research Fellow at St. Mary's School of Medicine, conducting work at St Joseph's Hospice in Hackney, in the East End of London. Here she laid down the basic principles of modern hospice care. She developed a systematic approach to pain control in terminally ill patients; she gave attention to their social, emotional, and spiritual needs; and she began teaching what she knew to other people. Her concept of "total pain" provided a revolutionary way of conceptualizing the complexity of patients' suffering. In response to medicine's despairing rejection of the dying patient—"There is nothing more we can do"—she offered a positive, imaginative alternative that sought to ensure pain relief, maintain dignity, and enhance the remaining period of available life, however short.

Soon Saunders made plans to build her own modern hospice. To signify that it would care for people on their last journey in life, it was given the name St. Christopher's, referring to the patron saint of travelers. She gathered a group of supporters who helped to work out the plan in detail, and she traveled to the United States and other countries to promote and refine her ideas. There were huge barriers to be overcome, including the low priority assigned to the care of the dying in the British National Health Service, a lack of research, no specialized education in the field, and social indifference to matters of care at the end of life. Yet, after eight years of fund-raising, planning, and promoting the idea, Saunders saw St. Christopher's Hospice open to its first patients in 1967. As she often remarked afterwards, "It took me nineteen years to build the home round the window." Along the way she had marshaled help from major charitable donors, from senior figures in the establishment, and from a growing body of clinicians and lay people committed to the development of this work.

Cicely Saunders's approaches to pain relief and tending to the emotional and spiritual needs of terminally ill patients helped shape the modern hospice movement. ST. CHRISTOPHER'S HOSPICE

For the next eighteen years Saunders was the medical director of the hospice she had created. She quickly expanded its services to include home care; she promoted research into pain control and into the efficacy of the program; and she developed a center for specialist education. During this time she authored some eighty-five publications, some of which appeared in several languages. Constant media attention made the hospice well known throughout the world. Her work was acclaimed internationally, and she received many prizes and honors from numerous countries, including the Lambeth Doctorate of Medicine (1977); the Gold Medal in Therapeutics of the Worshipful Society of Apothecaries, London (1979); the Templeton Prize for outstanding contributions in the field of religion (1981); and entry into the

Order of Merit, the highest honor within the British system (1989). St. Christopher's received thousands of visitors each year and became a beacon of inspiration for others who came to study, develop clinical skills, and conduct research.

In 1985 Saunders retired from full-time work at the hospice but remained active in her writing, teaching, and support for developments in hospice and palliative care. Both her private and professional life continued to be matters of public interest. She became the subject of a biography and of television documentaries and press interviews. In 1980 she married the Polish artist Marian Bohusz-Sysko, whom she had first met in 1963. She continued to travel and give lectures and presentations, especially after her husband died in 1995; her work remained a source of inspiration to those endeavoring to develop palliative care around the world. Her eightieth birthday was celebrated in 1998 with a conference in her honor at the Royal College of Physicians, London. In 2000 she retired from the position of chairman at St. Christopher's Hospice to take on the role of president/founder and to assist in the development of a new palliative care institute that will bear her name.

See also: HOSPICE AROUND THE WORLD; HOSPICE IN HISTORICAL PERSPECTIVE; HOSPICE OPTION; PAIN AND PAIN MANAGEMENT

Bibliography

Clark, David. "'Total pain,' Disciplinary Power and the Body in the Work of Cicely Saunders, 1958–67." *Social Science and Medicine* 49, no. 6 (1999):727–736.

Clark, David. "Originating a Movement: Cicely Saunders and the Development of St. Christopher's Hospice, 1957–67." *Mortality* 3, no. 1 (1998):43–63.

Du Boulay, Shirley. *Cicely Saunders: The Founder of the Modern Hospice Movement.* London: Hodder and Stoughton, 1984.

DAVID CLARK

SCHOPENHAUER, ARTHUR

Arthur Schopenhauer (1788–1860) was one of the few notable thinkers of his time to regard the relationship between life and death as the central problem of philosophy. He was also among the first Western intellectuals to draw insights from Buddhist and Hindu worldviews.

The German philosopher was born into a prosperous family that had many social and cultural connections. Contemporaries described Schopenhauer as a scintillating conversationalist with discerning taste in the arts. However, he was also seen as a gloomy person whose company was difficult to bear. Even as a youth, Schopenhauer was strongly affected by the imperfections of life—one must endure suffering, loss, disappointment, and frustration until the hammer blow of death ends all. Life seemed like an all but unbearable burden. Why go on living, then? The answer was clear to him: People put up with the miseries of life because they are terrified of death. Schopenhauer's need to resolve the dilemma of a miserable life and a terrifying death would contribute much to his elaboration of a philosophical system that has continued to influence world thought. His writings often challenge the reader's stamina: Schopenhauer himself cautioned his readers that they must resign themselves to reading all three volumes of *The World As Will and Representation* (1818) twice—and then perhaps once again for good measure.

The Thing-in-Itself

Following Eastern religious perspectives, Schopenhauer rejected the assumption that the world presents itself directly to the human mind. He believed it is more accurate to say that people construct representations of the world and then respond to these ideas or images as though they were objective reality. Even such powerful ideas as life and death are framed within the conventions of language and societal custom. Not denying that there is a core of reality within representations of life and death, he argued that people often respond more to the representations than the reality.

The philosopher's quest to understand the world through words, logic, and reason had been missing the point, according to Schopenhauer. Words are usually limited to the superficial appearance of reality. Seldom do people recognize the thing-in-itself, the inner nature of both the universe and human nature. The essence of life is to be sought in a driving force, an incessant impulse that is far more powerful than reason. He called this force "The Will." The will might be regarded as the thing-in-itself in action. Life is the most significant example. The essence of life is the fierce impulse to continue, to survive. The will operates for the species as well as for the individual. The blind will of nature does not hesitate to sacrifice many individuals in order to keep the species going.

Death As the Answer to Life

Humans face a unique situation—they are driven by the will to live, like all other creatures, but are also aware of the certainty of death. In Schopenhauer's view, all religions have been motivated by the desire to find some way of coping with this dilemma. His own conclusion is, "Only small and limited minds fear death" (Schopenhauer 1957, vol. 1, p. 27). Humans have death as their destiny, their completion. Individuality ceases with death, but the essence of being is indestructible and remains part of the cosmic process.

Schopenhauer invites the reader to take a larger view of the universe instead of the usual concern for individual life. From this cosmic vantage point, life and death are reciprocals, not opposites. He notes that Eastern thought has long represented the same god as having both creative and destructive powers. Siva, for example, displays the lingam, a symbol of generation, although she is adorned with a necklace of skulls. Greeks and Romans celebrated "the full ardour of life" at their funerals to make a similar point (Schopenhauer 1957, vol. 1, p. 355). It would be wise then, according to Schopenhauer, for people to look "away from the death of the mourned individual [with] knowledge that the whole of nature is the phenomenon and also the fulfillment of the will to live" (p. 355).

The answer to death proposed by Schopenhauer has not been widely accepted, in part because many people continue to focus on individual fate rather than cosmic process. Among his many influences, however, was the life versus death instinct of Sigmund Freud, and continuing discussions about the value of death education and the ethics of rational suicide.

See also: Buddhism; Hinduism; Philosophy, Western; Plato; Thanatology

Bibliography

Choron, Jacques. *Death and Western Thought.* New York: Collier Books, 1963.

Janaway, Christopher. *Self and World in Schopenhauer's Philosophy.* Oxford: Oxford University Press, 1989.

Schopenhauer, Arthur. *The World As Will and Representation.* 3 vols. 1818. Reprint, London: Routledge & Kegan Paul, 1957.

ROBERT KASTENBAUM

SÉANCE

See Communication with the Dead.

Serial Killers

Descending into minds that people view as belonging to despicable monsters is a requirement for individuals who search for or attempt to understand serial killers. The serial murderer Jeffrey Dahmer would go to bars in Milwaukee, Wisconsin, and pick up young men, sometimes telling them he was a photographer and luring them back to his apartment with an offer of money to be his model. He would then drug their drinks to subdue them so that they would be easier to strangle. However, those factors did not tell investigators the emotional core of his killing, they were simply the modus operandi (MO) of the crime. MO includes victim type, how the criminal approached or overcame his victim, tools used, and the time and place that the crime occurred.

More revealing is what has been called a killer's "signature," which has been defined by John Douglas as "a personal detail that is unique to the individual, *why* he does it: the thing that fulfills him emotionally" (Douglas 1997, p. 26). John Douglas, the first full-time profiler at the behavioral science division of the Federal Bureau of Investigation Academy in Quantico, Virginia, thinks the killer's signature is a better guide to behavior than his MO. While the MO may change as the killer comes up with a better technique, the emotional reason he commits the crime does not change. In Dahmer's case his murder signature showed the sadistic sexual satisfaction and control of living with his victims' bodies. In his case, some of these behaviors included engaging in sex with the bodies, cutting up the victims and cannibalizing body parts such as the heart, pulling muscles from the bone and wearing them on his own shoulders, painting the skulls to put over his bed, and storing one victim's head in the refrigerator.

Characteristics of Serial Murder

What is serial murder? The British author John Brody first used the term in 1966, and the National Institute of Justice defined serial murder in 1988 as "a series of 2 or more murders, committed as separate events, usually, but not always, by one offender acting alone" (Newton 2000, p. 205). Another perspective is that of Steve Egger, who uses six characteristics in his definition of serial murder: (1) There are a minimum of two murders; (2) the killer and victim are unrelated; (3) the murders have no direct connection to each other and occur at different times; (4) the murders usually occur at different locations; (5) victims may have characteristics in common with earlier or later victims; and (6) the murders are not committed for material gain but for gratification based on fantasies.

Several of these characteristics are debatable. The material gain motive is more common with the female than the male style of serial murder, thus Egger's definition could be seen more as serial signature murder. Also, individuals such as Edmund Kemper, who killed his grandparents and mother, and Henry Lee Lucas, whose mother was his first victim, are generally classified as serial killers. The criminologist Eric Hickey states that most researchers define serial killers as having three to four victims, but also includes in his database of serial killers some individuals who "killed only two victims but were suspect in other slayings or in which evidence indicated their intent to kill others" (Hickey 1997, p.27). The problem with using a definition based strictly on three victims omits the two-time signature killer who has obsessive qualities and would be expected to continue to kill.

Serial murder differs from mass murder in that mass murder involves killings of four or more victims in the same general area and occurs as one event in a short period of time. The mass murderer "appears to give little thought or concern to his or her inevitable capture or death" and may give him- or herself up or commit suicide if not killed by police (ibid., p. 7).

Characteristics of the Serial Killer

According to Hickey's 1997 database of approximately 399 serial killers, the average age of the murderer at the time of the first killing was 27.5 years, and they typically were white males. Criminologists James A. Fox and Jack Levin (2001) found that males made up more than 90 percent of the sample. Seventy-three percent of male offenders were white, 22 percent were African-American, and the remainder were of different ethnic groups. Fox and Levin report that the researcher Grover Godwin's 1999 database of 107 serial killers revealed an average age of thirty. Ninety-five percent were males, 5 percent were females, and 16 percent were African-American. Godwin also found that only 4 percent of his sample graduated with a bachelor's degree, while most were employed in blue-collar jobs. Victims were 67 percent female, with children, prostitutes, and the elderly as other preferred victim categories, although 20 percent of Godwin's sample were males who had additionally been raped by their attackers.

In 1992 the researchers Robert Ressler, a veteran of the FBI who served as founder of the FBI's Violent Criminal Apprehension Unit; Ann Burgess and John Douglas interviewed thirty-six convicted, imprisoned, sexual murderers who had a total of 118 murder and attempted murder victims among them. The interviews with the sexual murderers showed very active, violent, sexualized fantasies, which focused on killing until the first murder occurred and perfecting the killing after the first murder had occurred. The researchers were surprised by the lack of positive childhood fantasies remembered by the offenders. They noted progression in seven of the offenders from conscious awareness of a fantasy to actually acting out the fantasy within only a year. They saw clear behavioral progressions as well. Numerous authors have cited the childhood predictive behavior for serial killers of torturing animals. Many serial killers had been arrested, or had been in mental hospitals, for less serious behaviors before the serial killing began.

Organized vs. Disorganized. There are several typologies of serial killers. Ressler, Burgess, and Douglas viewed them either as "organized" or "disorganized" based on crime scene information. The organized killer plans the murder, chooses a stranger as a victim, then engages in limited conversation with the relatively personalized victim. The crime scene is not sloppy, but controlled, as is the victim, who suffers aggressive acts before death. The weapon is not present, nor is the victim's body. The crime scene for a disorganized murderer, on the other hand, is a spontaneous offense with either the victim or the area, or both, known to the perpetrator. There is very little conversation with a depersonalized victim, who suffers sudden violence. A few personal qualities of the organized criminal are good intelligence, high birth order status, some social competence, and the use of alcohol with the crime. The disorganized killer has average intelligence, is socially immature, has lower birth order status, uses alcohol minimally, and is more likely to be psychotic than an organized killer.

Some killers have qualities of both types, such as Jack the Ripper, who operated in 1888 in Whitechapel, the east end of London. This area of poverty and misery saw the savage assaults of Jack the Ripper on a series of prostitutes. Because his true identity was never officially revealed, John Douglas profiled the killer a century later, and the biographer Phillip Sudgen believes Douglas would have labeled him "disorganized." Yet Sudgen points out that this murderer also had some organized qualities such as the ability to hold a conversation with potential victims and his typical removal of weapons and clues.

Male vs. Female. Hickey reviewed differences between male and female serial killers. Results show female serial killers are more likely to kill husbands, relatives, or people in hospitals or nursing homes where they work; murder in one specific place; poison the victims; and report money to be a motive. Males are more likely to kill strangers, be geographically mobile, torture or mutilate more often when killing, and report a sexual motive. Most females thus meet the definition of the National Institute of Justice as serial murderers but do not meet Egger's definition with its additional parameters of the killer and victim being unrelated and a murder not committed for material gain but for fantasy gratification.

The Psychological Phases of Serial Killers

In 1988 the psychologist Joel Norris described the psychological phases that serial killers experience. Norris worked on the defense teams of several convicted killers from Georgia and completed 500 interviews with such individuals, during which he identified the following phases.

The killer begins with an *aura phase,* in which there is a withdrawal from reality and a heightening of the senses. This phase may last anywhere from several moments to several months and can begin as a prolonged fantasy, which may have been active for a short time or for years. The killer may attempt to medicate himself with alcohol or drugs.

The *trolling phase* consists of the behavior patterns that a particular killer uses to identify and stalk his victim. Norris described how Ted Bundy strapped his arm in a sling and asked for help with books, packages, or even the hull of a sailboat to lure the victim into his car. Some victims escaped and said he never seemed out of control until the moment he actually attacked them.

The *wooing phase* is that time period when most killers win the confidence of victims before luring them into a trap. The *capture phase* may include the locking of a door or a blow that renders the victim helpless. The killer savors this moment. Norris described the *murder phase* as the ritual reenactment of the disastrous experiences of the killer's childhood, but this time he reverses the roles.

The next phase Norris described is the *totem phase.* After the kill, murderers sink into a depression, so many develop a ritual to preserve their "success." This is why some killers keep news clippings, photographs, and parts of the victims' bodies, or eat parts of the victims, wear their skin, or show parts of victims' bodies to later victims. The trophy is meant to give the murderer the same feelings of power he experienced at the time of the kill.

The last phase is the *depression phase.* A victim, now killed, no longer represents what the killer thought he or she represented, and the memory of the individual that tortured the murderer in the past is still there. Ressler compares the murder to a television serial with no satisfactory ending because the serial killer experiences the tension of a fantasy incompletely fulfilled. In each subsequent murder, he attempts to make the scene of the crime equal to the fantasy. Norris notes that there is an absence of the killer's sense of self and, during this phase, the killer may confess to the police before the fantasies start once more. However, because victims are not seen as people, recollections of murders may be vague or viewed as the killer having watched someone else. They may have a memory for tiny details about the murder, which is dissociated from the event as a whole.

Psychological, Social, and Biological Factors in the Serial Murder

Psychological factors in the development of serial murder have sometimes included obvious abuse or emotional isolation in childhood. An example of the obviously abusive stands out in Henry Lee Lucas's prostitute mother hitting him for years with broom handles, dressing him as a girl for school, and forcing him to watch her having sex with men who would then be violent toward him. In such cases, the child appears to identify with the aggressor and replay a childhood victimization, this time as the aggressor. But not all cases show obvious massive family dysfunction. Many cases, however, according to Ressler and his fellow researchers Ann Burgess and John Douglas, do show loss of a parent or parental rejection. Robert Keppel and William Birnes describe the formation of the diphasic personality, in which a person's life develops two phases. One phase is the fantasy life where the child has complete control, while the other phase is the shell that walks through the real world and has little energy or effort committed to it. The child is emotionally isolated with his fantasies.

From a social construction point of view, Hickey describes a trauma-control model of the serial killer. While head injury or brain pathology may be predisposing factors, the eventual offender responds to traumatization in the formative years in the negative way of having low self-esteem and increasingly violent fantasies. Traumatic experiences and feelings from the past may be dissociated from conscious feelings, and the adult offender may aid an altered state of consciousness by facilitators such as alcohol, pornography, or drugs. Finally he commits murder as a way of regaining control and may initially feel reinforced before the low self-esteem sets in again.

Biological causes of crime were hypothesized by Hans Eysenck, who believed that criminality resulted from a nervous system distinct from that of most people, and that extroverts were more likely to be involved in antisocial behavior. J. A. Gray proposed a behavioral inhibition system as the neural system underlying anxiety. This system teaches most people not to make an antisocial response because of anxiety and is called passive avoidance learning. The researcher Don Fowles continued this concept with the idea that criminal personalities have deficient behavioral inhibition systems, therefore will proceed to make the antisocial response. The second half of Gray's model is the behavioral activation system, which causes reward-seeking behavior and active avoidance of punishment, such as running away. Fowles believes this system is normal in the criminal personality. Gray's theory also says there is a nonspecific arousal system receiving excitatory inputs from both systems.

Similar ideas may be viewed directly from the brain. In a 1997 article in the *Journal of Psychoactive Drugs,* the researcher Daniel Amen reported findings with Single Photon Emission Computerized Tomography (SPECT) brain imaging, which measures metabolic activity and cerebral blood flow patterns to examine differences in the aggressive brain. He examined forty aggressive adolescents and adults from a psychiatric population that physically attacked someone or destroyed property within six months of evaluation, and compared them to an age-, sex-, and diagnosis-matched control group of forty psychiatric patients who had never had reported problems with aggression. No person was included in the study who had a history of a substance abuse problem in the last year or a history of head injury involving loss of consciousness.

Amen found aggressive individuals show significant differences from nonviolent individuals. First, there is decreased activity in the prefrontal cortex; decreased functioning would result in less impulse control, less ability to focus attention, and poor judgment of highly charged situations. He found increased activity in the left side only of the basal ganglia and limbic system. Among multiple complex functions, he noticed that overactivity in the basal ganglia is associated with anxiety, and overactivity in that part of the limbic system is associated with negative mood and a higher chance of violent behavior. He found increased activity in the temporal lobes, which, among other functions, have been connected to temper outburst and rapid mood shifts, especially noted for the left temporal lobe. He found increased activity in the anteromedial portions of the frontal lobes (anterior cingulate area), which, among other functions, results in obsessive inability to stop thinking about negative events or ideas. In his 1997 publication, Amen discusses how correct medication can improve some of these abnormalities and, along with therapy, improve problem behavior. He has also found that the use of alcohol results in overall decreased brain activity, and chronic alcoholism is associated with reduced metabolism, especially in the frontal and temporal regions of the brain. These are the same regions involved in violent behavior. Interestingly, Ressler and colleagues specifically listed alcohol use during the murder as one of the characteristics of the organized serial killer.

Violence has also been connected to a variety of serotonin abnormalities as well as reduced glucose metabolism shown by positron emission tomography. In 1997 the scholar Adrian Raine and colleagues examined glucose metabolism in forty-one murderers pleading not guilty by reason of insanity, compared to an equal number of age- and sex-matched control subjects. The murderers showed reduced glucose metabolism in the prefrontal cortex, superior parietal gyrus, left angular gyrus, and corpus callosum. The left hemispheres of their brains had lower activity than the right in the amygdala, thalamus, and medial temporal lobe.

Research has identified certain brain dysfunctions, parental loss or rejection, and the development of the diphasic personality and the trauma control model as potential factors in the development of the serial killer. In the future, identifying the diphasic, emotionally isolated child and helping him or her to connect with people could potentially occur in the school. Perhaps brain scans as well as school-based behavioral evaluations could indicate those people who might benefit from psychotherapy, social skills interventions, medication, or some combination of the above to prevent or control their aggressiveness. A society with the skills and the willingness to finance such a possibility would have to make careful decisions about the freedoms of the people it labeled as well as the rights of the public. Yet deinstitutionalization of the mentally ill, as flawed as it is, took hundreds of thousands of people out of hospitals and gave them a less restrictive life. Perhaps a similar, but well-managed, outcome could be the future of a safe public and of the murderers society must lock away.

See also: AIDS; HOMICIDE, DEFINITIONS AND CLASSIFICATIONS OF; MASS KILLERS

Bibliography

Amen, Daniel, Matthew Stubblefield, Blake Carmichael, and Ronald Thisted. "Brain SPECT Findings and Aggressiveness." *Annals of Clinical Psychiatry* 8, no. 3 (1996):129–137.

Amen, Daniel G., Stanley Yantis, John Trudeau, Matthew Stubblefield, and Jonathan Halverstadt. "Visualizing the Firestorms in the Brain: An Inside Look at the Clinical and Physiological Connections between Drugs and Violence Using Brain SPECT Imaging." *Journal of Psychoactive Drugs* 29, no. 4 (1997):307–319.

Douglas, John, and Mark Olshaker. *Journey into Darkness.* New York: Pocket Books, 1997.

Fowles, Don C. "The Three Arousal Model: Implications of Gray's Two-Factor Learning Theory for Heart Rate, Electrodermal Activity, and Psychopathy." *Psychophysiology* 17, no. 2 (1980):87–104.

Fox, James A., and Jack Levin. *The Will to Kill.* Boston: Allyn and Bacon, 2001.

Gresswell, David M., and Clive R. Hollin. "Multiple Murder: A Review." *British Journal of Criminology* 34, no. 1 (1994):1–14.

Hickey, Eric. *Serial Murderers and Their Victims,* 2nd edition. Belmont, CA: Wadsworth, 1997.

Keppel, Robert D., and William J. Birnes. *Signature Killers.* New York: Pocket Books, 1997.

Levin, Jack, and James A. Fox. "Serial Murder." In *Deadlines: Essays in Murder and Mayhem.* Boston: Allyn and Bacon, 2001.

Newton, Michael. *The Encyclopedia of Serial Killers.* New York: Checkmark Books, 2000.

Norris, Joel. *Serial Killers.* New York: Anchor Books/Doubleday, 1989.

Raine, Adrian, Monte Buchsbaum, and Lori LaCasse. "Brain Abnormalities in Murderers Indicated by Positron Emission Tomography." *Biological Psychiatry* 42, no. 6 (1997):495–508.

Ressler, Robert K., Ann W. Burgess, and John E. Douglas. *Sexual Homicide: Patterns and Motives.* New York: Free Press, 1992.

Ressler, Robert K., and Tom Shachtman. *I Have Lived in the Monster.* New York: St. Martin's Press, 1997.

Ressler, Robert K., and Tom Shachtman. *Whoever Fights Monsters.* New York: St. Martin's Press, 1992.

Seltzer, Mark. *Serial Killers: Death and Life in America's Wound Culture.* New York: Routledge, 1998.

Sudgen, Phillip. *The Complete History of Jack the Ripper.* New York: Carroll & Graf Publishers, 1995.

SANDRA BURKHALTER CHMELIR

SEVEN DEADLY SINS

Pride, Envy, Avarice, Wrath, Lust, Gluttony, and Sloth are the seven deadly sins that popes, saints, preachers, artists, writers, dramatists, and musicians have urged Christian believers to avoid at all costs. Life can be placed at risk by indulging in these sins; for example, those whose arrogant pride invites disaster, the gluttons who eat their way to the grave, or the violently wrathful who are executed according to the laws of the land. Far more significant, though, are the consequences of sin for the fate of the soul. The corruption of the soul through sinful thoughts and actions literally dis-graces the perpetrator during his or her sojourn on the earth. Having fallen out of grace with God during life, the person is in peril of damnation after death. The sins are "deadly," then, primarily in their effect on the soul as divine judgment offers salvation or hurls it to damnation.

Historical Perspective

What became crystallized as the seven deadly sins does not appear as such in the Bible, although the Old and the New Testaments identify attitudes and behaviors that violate the principles of a righteous life. Theologians compiled lists of the most serious sins as they attempted to instruct monks, priests, and laities on the requirements for a virtuous Christian life. The earliest influential list identified eight sins that were obstacles to perfection. John Cassian, a fifth-century monk and spiritual leader, specified several sins that later became part of the standard list: pride, gluttony, covetousness (envy), anger (wrath), and ennui (sloth). Two other items on his list—impurity and vanity—are related to lust and pride, and "dejection" was folded into sloth, although not until the seventeenth century.

The standard list of seven deadly sins was established by Pope Gregory the Great in the sixth century. He maintained that pride breeds all the other sins, and is therefore the most serious offense. St. Thomas Aquinas, author of the landmark thirteenth-century *Summa Theologica,* reaffirmed that pride (or "vainglory") is rebellion against the authority of God. Aquinas reasoned that some sinful acts are venial rather than deadly: They arise from the temptations of everyday life and have the effect of weakening the bonds of trust and fellowship among people. Lust, for example, threatens the crucial relationship between parents and children. Such actions become elevated to deadly sins when they arise from the spiritual failing of pride and therefore threaten the soul's acceptance into the kingdom of God.

Many ideas and images became associated with each of the deadly sins over the centuries. The particular associations varied, but specific punishments often were considered to await the perpetrator. In all instances the sinner is assumed to be alive in some form after death in order to experience the agony and despair.

- Pride=Broken on the wheel
- Envy=Encased in freezing water
- Avarice (Greed)=Boiled in oil
- Wrath (Anger)=Torn apart, limb from limb
- Lust=Roasted by fire and brimstone
- Gluttony=Forced to eat rats, snakes, spiders, and toads
- Sloth (Apathy)=Thrown into snake pits

Set against the deadly sins were the heavenly virtues, also seven in number. The first three of these virtues have remained the most widely mentioned: faith, hope, and charity. The others are fortitude, justice, temperance, and prudence. Attempts have been made to match these virtues against the sins, but it is difficult to discern a one-on-one correlation.

Influence of the Seven Deadly Sins

The medieval world was conceived largely in religious terms, and lives were to be governed by rules derived from divine authority. Morality and

Indulgence in pleasures of the flesh paved the road to damnation. Gluttons, for example, were forced to gobble down toads, rats, and snakes, as revealed by this fifteenth-century French illustration. DOVER PUBLICATIONS, INC.

order in human affairs required constant and vigorous attention, then as now. The seven deadly sins and their punishments offered a striking set of cautions, while other teachings, such as the seven heavenly virtues, limned the positive path. Creative artists in all the media contributed much to the message, some of their work becoming enduring masterpieces of Western culture.

Geoffrey Chaucer's fourteenth-century *Canterbury Tales,* Dante Alghieri's fourteenth-century *Divine Comedy,* Edmund Spenser's sixteenth-century *The Fairie Queen,* and Christopher Marlowe's sixteenth-century *Tragical History of Doctor Faustus* all feature depictions of the seven deadly sins that remained influential long after their periods of creation. When Hieronymus Bosch introduced his unique and startling visual representation of the seven deadly sins in the fifteenth century, it was with a revisionist twist. The sins were converted from theological abstractions to the follies of everyday people in their everyday lives—with a bracing addition of dark humor.

As the medieval mindset gave way to the modern there was more attention given to naturalistic explanations for events (i.e., disease, famine, and earthquake) and to human actions. The concept of sin would come under increasing pressure from rival explanations, many with psychological and sociological orientations. Nevertheless, the seven deadly sins have continued to appeal to the artistic imagination and to engage the attention of people who, in times very different from Pope Gregory's, are still attempting to negotiate their way between temptation and virtue. Examples of contemporary or near-contemporary contributions include *The Seven Deadly Sins* (1933), set as a musical theater piece by the twentieth-century composer Kurt Weill (best known for *The Threepenny Opera* (1933)), and the motion picture *Seven* (1995), starring Brad Pitt, Morgan Freeman, and Kevin Spacey. The survival of this concept has also included numerous examples of accommodation to technology and consumerism.

See also: CATHOLICISM; CHRISTIAN DEATH RITES, HISTORY OF; HELL; PURGATORY

Bibliography

Alighieri, Dante. *The Divine Comedy*. Garden City, NY: Doubleday, 1947.

Aquinas, Thomas. *Summa Theologiae*. New York: McGraw-Hill, 1976.

Chaucer, Geoffrey. *The Canterbury Tales of Geoffrey Chaucer.* New York: Simon and Schuster, 1948.

De Tolnay, Charles. *Hieronymus Bosch*. New York: Artabus, 1966.

Fairlie, Henry. *The Seven Deadly Sins Today*. South Bend, IN: University of Notre Dame Press, 1983.

Marlowe, Christopher. *Doctor Faustus*. New York: Signet, 2001.

Menninger, Karl. *Whatever Became of Sin?* New York: Hawthorne, 1973.

Schimmel, Solomon. *The Seven Deadly Sins: Jewish, Christian, and Classical Reflections on Human Psychology.* New York: Oxford University Press, 1997.

Spenser, Edmund. *The Fairie Queen*. New York: Longman, 2001.

ROBERT KASTENBAUM

SEX AND DEATH, CONNECTION OF

Sex and death have a number of connections other than having been taboo topics in polite company and controversial subjects in school curriculums. As is the case with many taboos, both can lead to fetishes and eroticisms, and their mere mention holds shock value for young adults.

Few question that life's greatest drives are to reproduce and to avoid death. The Austrian psychoanalyst Sigmund Freud and the French social theorist Michel Foucault argued that the two are fused, that the death instinct pervades sexual activity—a connection easily seen by a Frenchman whose language frames orgasms as *petit mort,* or "mini-deaths." With the AIDS epidemic their view has become particularly poignant. A 1992 study from Amsterdam, for instance, found that about one in six U.S. soldiers surveyed said that sex without condoms was worth the risk of getting the AIDS virus. A year later a story released by Planned Parenthood counselor offices in San Antonio, Texas, explained how teenage girls were demonstrating their toughness by having unprotected sex with an HIV-infected gang member. It seems that, for some, sexual desire is intensified in the presence of taboos and boundaries, even deadly ones.

The Scientific Perspective: Death As the Cost of Reproduction

Early lessons about the connection between reproduction and death often come from exceptional stories from the animal kingdom. Pacific salmon, for instance, return after three or four years in the ocean to battle hundreds of miles upstream—against gill nets, predators, and dams—to the tributaries where their lives began, to spawn and to die. Their remains fertilize the streams, providing food for the tiny microorganisms on which their offspring will feed. In addition, one cannot forget the story of how the female praying mantis bites off the head of her partner while mating. Or how in several marsupial mice species, the immune systems of the mice collapse after their first mating, leading to death shortly thereafter.

It has been observed that death is the price multicellular creatures must pay in order to reproduce. The biologist William Clark observed, "Obligatory death—as a result of senescence (natural aging)—may not have come into existence for more than a billion years after life first appeared. This form of programmed cell death seems to have arisen at about the same time cells began experimenting with sex in connection with reproduction" (Clark 1996, p. xi). Perhaps one legacy of this original immortality is the telomerase, the so-called immortality enzyme, found within the cells of testes and ovaries. Absent from normal cells that age and die, telomerase is what allows cancerous cells to reproduce without limits.

In the case of the life span of mammals, the period in which they have the greatest resistance to harmful environmental factors is when they have the greatest reproductive capacity. Evolution has little interest in the survival of those who have produced viable offspring and are in the post-reproductive period of life, hence the extreme rarity of senescent (old) animals in the natural order.

Humanity is not immune from this law of death as the cost of sex. This toll for reproduction has particularly been borne by women. Unlike at the start of the twenty-first century, when women held a seven-year life-expectancy advantage over males in developed nations, historically, because of their high maternal death rates, women were the shorter-lived sex. Maternal death rates remain high in poor nations of the world, where women are up to 200 times more likely than women in the richest countries to die as a result of complications of pregnancy, abortion, or childbirth—the causes of one-quarter of all deaths of those of childbearing age. In the United States, the Centers for Disease Control and Prevention reported in 2001 that black women were four times more likely than non-Hispanic white women to die of pregnancy-related problems.

Even the sex act itself can prove lethal. Cardiovascular specialists have long warned how extramarital sex was dangerous for heart patients, as it increased their blood pressure and pulse rate more than when having sex with a familiar partner. Such activity killed a former American vice president, Nelson Rockefeller, who died of a heart attack during an extramarital tryst in 1979. In 1998, having sex shortly after having given birth proved fatal for two British women, who died of air embolisms.

Attempts to enhance one's sexual experiences can be deadly as well. In 1998 the Food and Drug Administration reported the deaths of several men taking the highly popular Viagra impotence pill. Each year, attempts at sexual self-gratification accidentally kill between 500 and 1,000 individuals, predominantly men, because of autoerotic asphyxia. To heighten their sexual orgasm during masturbation, these individuals cut off the supply of oxygen and blood to their head, often by tying a belt or rope around their neck. Consciousness may be lost, and the individual dies by strangulation.

Relationships between Sex and Longevity

The need for species to change over time underlies evolution's mechanisms for triggering death with sex. In addition, there are genetic clocks determining the time frame for species to produce and raise the next generation to the point where it can successfully pass on its genetic code. Thus the later in life a species reproduces, the longer its life expectancy. Fruit flies with special "longevity genes" have been created, allowing them to live twice as long as their normal counterparts. By breeding them at increasingly advanced ages, Carla Sgrò and Linda Partridge also found that fruit flies that produced eggs at a young age died earlier than those that reproduced when they were older. When the younger-reproducing flies were sterilized with X rays, they began living as long as their older counterparts.

How this phenomenon might apply to humans raises interesting questions. Will the trend toward postponing parenting ultimately lead to the delaying of senescence and death? And, given the trend of affluent older males beginning second families with their young "trophy wives," will an even greater longevity advantage develop in the upper classes?

Nevertheless, postponement of parenting indefinitely can also lead to premature death. In 1986 Evelyn Talbott found that women over the age of fifty who had been married but had never had children might face an increased risk of dying suddenly of heart disease. Several studies in the early 1990s found that men who had vasectomies increased their risk of testicular cancer and prostate cancer, the latter by 56 to 66 percent at all ages.

Another 1994 study of 1,800 Seattle women by Janet R. Daling and her colleagues for the National Cancer Institute found that abortion increased women's risk of breast cancer by 50 percent. In the same year, a study directed by Mats Lambe found that having a child increased a woman's risk of breast cancer in her younger years but protected her against cancer in later life. For example, a thirty-five-year-old woman who gave birth at age twenty-five had an 8 percent higher risk of breast cancer than did a childless woman the same age; at age fifty-nine, however, the former's risk was 29 percent lower than the latter's.

On the other hand, eliminating one's ability to reproduce has also been found to reduce the likelihood of death. A 1999 study by physician Edward M. Messing and his associates showed that castration increased the survival chances of men with spreading prostate cancer. And Canadian researchers in 2001 reported that women with a high probability of developing ovarian cancer could reduce their cancer risk by up to 72 percent with tubal ligations.

Special Case of AIDS

During the late twentieth century it was the AIDS epidemic that most universally symbolized the lethal aspects of sexuality, particularly acts outside of monogamous relationships. While the popular conception in the United States initially saw the sex-death connection largely confined to specific high-risk groups, particularly homosexual populations, throughout most of the world the epidemic spread through heterosexual unions.

At the start of the twenty-first century, the highest rates of HIV infection were in sub-Saharan African countries, occurring within the most sexually active segment of the population, those fifteen to forty-nine years of age. Here the cultural sex order made for an epidemiological nightmare, where individuals were more likely than their European counterparts to have numerous sex partners. Once again women were disproportionately the victims, more likely being the one infected than infecting—owing to greater male promiscuity and female subservience—and being the sex to most quickly develop full-blown AIDS infection and dying of its effects. Projections, made in 2000, were that men would outnumber women by eleven to nine. Without AIDS, life expectancy in 2010 was projected to be 70 years in Zimbabwe, 68 in South Africa, and 60 in Zambia. With AIDS, life expectancy was expected to fall below 35 years in Zimbabwe, to 48 in South Africa, and to 30 in Zambia.

The HIV deaths resulting from sexual relations extend from individuals to entire social orders. The epidemic has killed family structures—producing a huge generation of orphans—and severely diminished chances for economic development. In 1999 at Eskom, South Africa's electric utility, 11 percent of the workers were infected with HIV, as were an estimated 40 percent of the Ugandan military and one-third of that country's teachers. In South Africa, Zimbabwe, and Kenya, some of Africa's most industrialized countries, gross domestic product was predicted to be 20 percent lower by 2005 than it otherwise would have been without the epidemic.

When the Sex Drive becomes Deadly

Evolution has endowed human males with a high sex drive coupled with considerable aggressiveness—especially regarding matters of breeding rights. In Pakistan, husbands are often acquitted for the "honor killing" of their spouses, whose "crime" may range from a simple flirtation to an affair.

Violent sexual assaults on the weak and unempowered occur throughout the world. In Juárez, Mexico, during the late 1990s, at least seventy women had been raped and murdered by sexual predators, their bodies dumped in the Chihuahua Desert. In the United States, the rape, maiming, and murder of children are frequent news items, leading to most states passing sexual predator legislation and demands that the public be informed of where these individuals reside when released.

Violence between sexual intimates is unfortunately common. Domestic violence is the leading cause of injury to women in the United States, resulting in more injuries than muggings, rape by strangers, and car accidents combined. In about one-third of killings of women, the killer is either her spouse or boyfriend. And of females murdered by strangers, prostitutes comprise a disproportionate number of victims.

Rough sex has produced its share of fatalities as well. One highly publicized death occurred in the mid-1980s in New York City's Central Park, where an eighteen-year-old woman was found strangled. Robert Chambers, a nineteen-year-old from an affluent family, confessed to having accidentally killed her while engaging in "kinky sex." This turned out not to be the case, but the defense has been used several times since for deaths resulting from sadomasochistic sexual activities.

Psychiatrists have long seen the underlying sexual motivations behind serial killers, typically featuring elements of sadism and necrophilia. Tim Cahill's psychobiography of John Wayne Gacy—who between 1972 and 1978 raped, tortured, and then murdered thirty-three young men in the Chicago area—detailed Gacy's feelings of inferiority and unworthiness in his father's eyes, guilt about his homosexual tendencies, and feelings of inadequacy in male-female relationships.

Connections between Sexual and Death Moralities in the American Mind

Moral codes often contain messages of restraint regarding matters of sex and harm of others—the antithesis of social chaos with its orgies of sex and violence. It is worth noting the internal consistencies of these issues in individuals' minds, for how they coalesce affects outlooks toward a host of political and religious matters.

Consider, for instance, attitudes toward the moralities of abortion, euthanasia, and the right of the terminally ill to commit suicide, and how they correlate with the perceived moralities of premarital sex and homosexual relations. According to the National Opinion Research Center's "General Social Surveys," (Davis and Smith 1998), between 1977 and 1998 the proportion of American adults supporting all three death matters increased from 26 to 38 percent, while the percent disapproving of all three declined from 33 to 26 percent. During the mid-1990s, 70 percent of those who endorsed all three death issues believed it was "not wrong at all if a man and woman have sex relations before marriage," compared to only 15 percent of those who opposed these three death issues. Similarly, 64 percent of those who endorsed all three death issues believed that "sexual relations between two adults of the same sex" was "not wrong at all," compared to 12 percent of those opposed to all three death issues.

Death-Sex Connections in the Arts

In a 1992 book, Camille Paglia claimed that it was in the West that sex, violence, and aggression are major motivations for artistic creativity and human relationships. There is little doubt that these are qualities of audience appeal. Hollywood has long known of the attractions to the erotic and the violent, which is why 60 percent of R-rated movies and nearly half of X-rated movies contain violence. The long-term success of the James Bond movie series derives from its fusion of sex and death.

According to Geoffrey Gorer, such seductions derive from cultural pruderies to matters of sex and death. William May observed that as sex becomes pornographic when divorced from its natural human emotions of love and affection, so death becomes pornographic when divorced from its natural emotion, which is grief. Perhaps the pornographic connotation is why designer Christian Dior chose in the 1990s to label one of its perfumes "Poison."

See also: AIDS; ANXIETY AND FEAR; DEATH INSTINCT; SERIAL KILLERS; SEVEN DEADLY SINS; THRILL-SEEKING

Bibliography

Bataille, Georges. *Death and Sensuality: A Study of Eroticism and the Taboo.* New York: Arno Press, 1977.

Batman, Philip A., John Thomlinson, Victor C. Moore, and Richard Sykes. "Death Due to Air Embolism during Sexual Intercourse in the Puerperium." *Postgraduate Medical Journal* 74 (1998):612–613.

Cahill, Tim. *Buried Dreams: Inside the Mind of a Serial Killer.* New York: Bantam, 1986.

Cale, Alexander R. J., Marwan Farouk, Richard J. Prescott, and Ian W. J. Wallace. "Does Vasectomy Accelerate Testicular Tumour?: Importance of Testicular Examinations before and after Vasectomy." *British Medical Journal* 300 (1990):370.

Clark, William. *Sex and the Origins of Death.* New York: Oxford University Press, 1996.

Daling, Janet R., Kathleen E. Malone, Lynda F. Voight, Emily White, and Noel S. Weiss. "Risk of Breast Cancer among Young Women: Relationship to Induced Abortion." *Journal of The National Cancer Institute* 86 (1994):1584–1592.

Davis, James A., and Tom A. Smith. "General Social Surveys, 1972–1998" [machine-readable data file]. Principal Investigator, James A. Davis; Director and Co-Principal Investigator, Tom W. Smith; Co-Principal Investigator, Peter V. Marsden, NORC ed. Chicago: National Opinion Research Center, producer, 1998; Storrs, CT: The Roper Center for Public Opinion Research, University of Connecticut, distributor.

Giovannucci, Edward, Tor D. Tosteson, Frank E. Speizer, et al. "A Retrospective Cohort Study of Vasectomy and Prostate Cancer in U.S. Men." *Journal of the American Medical Association* 269 (1993):878–882.

Gorer, Geoffrey. *Death, Grief, and Mourning*. New York: Doubleday Anchor, 1965.

Jeter, Jon. "AIDS Sickening African Economies." *Washington Post,* 12 December 1999, A1.

Kearl, Michael, and Richard Harris. "Individualism and the Emerging 'Modern' Ideology of Death." *Omega: The Journal of Death and Dying* 12 (1981):269–280.

Lambe, Mats, Chung-Cheng Hsieh, Dimitrios Trichopoulos, et al. "Transient Increase in the Risk of Breast Cancer after Giving Birth." *New England Journal of Medicine* 331, no. 1 (1994):5–9.

May, William. "The Sacral Power of Death in Contemporary Experience." In Arien Mack ed., *Death in American Experience*. New York: Schocken, 1973.

Narod, Steven A., Ping Sun, Parviz Ghadirian, et al. "Tubal Ligation and Risk of Ovarian Cancer in Carriers of BRCA1 or BRCA2 Mutations: A Case-Control Study." *Lancet* 357 (2001):1467–1470.

Paglia, Camille. *Sexual Personae: Art and Decadence from Nefertiti to Emily Dickinson*. New Haven, CT: Yale University Press, 1992.

Sgrò, Carla, and Linda Partridge. "A Delayed Wave of Death from Reproduction in *Drosophil*." *Science* 286 (1999):2521–2524.

Talbott, Evelyn, K. Detre, L. Kuller, and K. Baffone. "Is Childlessness a Risk Factor for Sudden Cardiac Death in Women? Results of a Case-Control Study." *Circulation* 74 (1986):333.

MICHAEL C. KEARL

SEXTON, ANNE

A number of creatively eminent individuals have taken their own lives, including John Steinbeck, Ernest Hemingway, Sylvia Plath, and many other writers. The large number of such cases suggests that there may be a functional relationship between creativity and psychological health. This relationship seems to vary across domains, with the rate of suicide especially high in certain groups of artists, suggesting that there may be something unique to those domains that either draws suicide-prone persons into the domain or has an impact on the individual such that suicide is considered and often attempted.

The American Pulitzer Prize–winning poet Anne Sexton took her own life in 1974 via carbon monoxide poisoning before reaching the age of fifty. Her life and work are especially interesting because her poetry was clearly tied to her own psychiatric treatment. She began writing with only moderate formal education (a high school diploma), but after being published she was given honorary degrees from several universities, including Tufts, Radcliffe, and Harvard. While she is probably best known for *Live or Die* (1966), which was awarded the Pulitzer Prize, Sexton also received acclaim for *The Awful Rowing towards God* (1975), *The Death Notebooks* (1974), *The Book of Folly* (1972), *Mercy Street* (1969), *Love Poems* (1969), *All My Pretty Ones* (1962), *To Bedlam and Partway Back* (1960), *Transformations* (1971), and several volumes of selected and collected poems.

Sexton was born in Massachusetts on November 9, 1928, to Mary Gray Staples and Ralph Churchill Harvey, who were known to drink regularly and sometimes heavily. They were somewhat prominent and quite socially active. Scholars suggest that they may have valued their social engagements over their family responsibilities. There is some evidence that Sexton's mother was jealous about her very early writing. Sexton did not have obvious creative aspirations, but instead seemed to think more about a family of her own. At one point her mother accused her of plagiarism and had that particular writing examined. It was deemed to be original, but many scholars suggest this incident affected Sexton's relationship with her mother. When Sexton reported feelings of guilt about her childhood, she focused on the relationship she had with her grandmother. She admitted to feeling responsible for the failure of this relationship.

Sexton had two older sisters. Biographers have noted that Sexton and her sisters were not especially close to one another, and her position as the youngest child in the family has been underscored.

Research on family structure, including birth order, often suggests that an individual's expectations and worldview are associated with ordinal positioning within the family; interestingly, it is frequently the middle-born child who grows up to be the creative rebel. Sexton was socially active as a teenager, but also showed signs of a preoccupation with death. She was active in extracurricular activities, including athletic teams and cheerleading.

Sexton's aunt on her father's side attempted suicide in early childhood, lived several decades in an apparently stable marriage, and eventually committed suicide just before she turned seventy. The family believes that if her aunt's suicide had any sort of influence on Sexton, it was probably informational (e.g., the aunt modeling suicide) rather than genetic.

Sexton eloped with Alfred Mueler Sexton II when she was twenty years old, maintaining the view that she would become a traditional housewife. She apparently got along no better with her mother-in-law than she did her own mother. There were instances of various kinds of misbehavior, ranging from cigarette smoking to angry outbursts in the home of her in-laws. There were also instances of depression, especially after the birth of her two children: Linda in 1953 and Joyce in 1955. Sexton's first attempted suicide was not long after the birth of her second child. Although Sexton had planned to be a housewife and mother, she had difficulties coping with life, especially when her husband was away on business, falling into bouts of depression during the times he was gone.

Sexton was a bit of a rebel and nonconformist, or at least had difficulty with certain social norms. There is, for example, some indication that she was promiscuous, and she eloped with Alfred after knowing him for a very brief period of time—and while engaged to a different man. Scholars note that this type of behavior was not unusual given Sexton's creative temperament.

Other researchers suggest that the social and historical milieu of Boston in the 1950s was a factor in Sexton's troubled life. Sexton's expectation of being a housewife could easily have reflected social norms and pressures rather than a true inclination and intrinsic interest. Perhaps Sexton had a creative drive that she could not reconcile with the pressures placed on her to move in a more conventional direction. Depression could have easily resulted from the incompatibility between her creative temperament and social expectations.

Sexton was apparently addicted to sleeping pills and perhaps also to alcohol, further evidencing serious psychiatric disorders. At one point she had an affair with one of her therapists, further supporting the idea that she was not bound by most social norms.

Another explanation for Sexton's suicide involves the domain of poetry. Poets often invest a great deal of themselves into their work. Even if the poetry is eventually critically acclaimed, the writing of poetry can be quite stressful because on one hand the individual exposes a great deal of herself, and on the other hand the individual is working alone in an area where feedback is often quite delayed. The delayed gratification may have been particularly difficult for Sexton because she manifested many strong social needs.

Biographers place great emphasis on Sexton's psychiatric treatment, which was significant as evidenced by the content of her poetry. And, it is possible, given her nonconformism, that Sexton suffered from a borderline personality disorder. There are reports of her schizophrenic language, for instance, as well as her tendency to enter some sort of trance at the end of her psychiatric treatment sessions. She apparently did not want to end the sessions, perhaps because of emotional and social needs.

Sexton's increased reputation as a poet seemed to cause a new kind of marital difficulty. There were reports that her husband did not appreciate her work, and additional suggestions that her schedule, required by her publishing and the promotion of her work, caused friction at home.

See also: SUICIDE INFLUENCES AND FACTORS: GENDER

Bibliography

Ludwig, Arnold. *The Price of Greatness: Resolving the Creativity and Madness Controversy.* New York: Guilford Press, 1995.

Middlebrook, Diane Wood. *Anne Sexton: A Biography.* Boston: Houghton Mifflin, 1991.

Sexton, Anne. *The Awful Rowing towards God.* Boston: Houghton Mifflin, 1975.

Sexton, Anne. *The Death Notebooks.* Boston: Houghton Mifflin, 1974.

MARK A. RUNCO

SHAKESPEARE, WILLIAM

For Shakespeare and his contemporaries, death—which modern society has sanitized and rendered largely invisible—was a brutally conspicuous presence. Early modern London, whose gates were decorated with the boiled heads of traitors and criminals, was a place in which public executions formed a regular staple of entertainment, where the corpses of condemned persons were available for public dissection, and where the fragility of life was repeatedly brought home by devastating epidemics of plague that swept away tens of thousands of citizens at a stroke. Magnificent pageantry might adorn the funeral processions of royalty and nobles; but every church in the kingdom contained a charnel house whose stench of putrefaction acted as a constant reminder of the grim facts of mortality. Under these circumstances it is hardly surprising that the drama of the period should be much possessed by death and preoccupied by the struggle to tame its apocalyptic menace.

"Death," Hamlet declares in the most famous of all his soliloquies, "is a *consummation* / Devoutly to be wished" (Hamlet, 3.1.62). He seeks to persuade himself that dying is no mere ending, but marks the fulfilment and perfection of mortal life. Behind his words lie centuries of consolatory writing, from the classical philosophy of the Stoics, for whom the encounter with death was the ultimate proving ground of wisdom and virtuous living, to the Christian *ars moriendi,* with its merciful translation to a better state. The prospect of mortality is seldom so reassuring for Shakespeare's characters, however; more typical than the calm resolve of Hamlet's final moments is the panorama of decay in the graveyard, with its parade of identically grinning skulls and the parables of levelling indifference they excite in the Prince's imagination: "Why may not imagination trace the noble dust of Alexander, till 'a find it stopping a bunghole?" (5.1.202–3).

In *Measure for Measure* it is the gross material realities of death, as much as its metaphysical uncertainties, that inspire Claudio's terror as he awaits execution:

> Aye, but to die, and go we know not where;
> To lie in cold obstruction and to rot;
> This sensible warm motion to become
> A kneaded clod. . . .
> To be imprisoned in the viewless winds
> And blown with restless violence round about
> The pendant world; or to be worse than worst
> Of those that lawless and incertain thought
> Imagine howling —'tis too horrible!
> (Measure for Measure, *3.1.117–27)*

This is what it means to be, like Cordelia in Lear's despairing phrase, "dead as earth" (*King Lear,* 5.6.262). Claudio's apparent imperviousness to the salvific promises of religion, and his existential vertigo at the prospect of annihilation, give his speech a distinctly modern feel; but underlying his horror, as it underlies the sardonic humor of Hamlet and the gravediggers, is a historically specific anxiety about the social menace of death, its arbitrary cancellation of the entire system of differences on which the profoundly hierarchical order of Renaissance society depended; for the dead in Claudio's vision are consigned to an utterly chaotic condition, as "lawless and incertain" as the restless imaginings it inspires.

Such anxieties are traceable everywhere in early modern culture. They are especially apparent in iconic representations of universal mortality, like the Dance of Death, whose grinning cadavers sweep off representatives of every rank to their common end; or the Triumph of Death, in which the corpses of monarch and peasant, merchant and pauper lie promiscuously heaped together beneath the chariot wheels of King Death. But they also motivated the lavish pomp of heraldic obsequies and the increasingly worldly extravagance of the memorials crowding the aisles of parish churches and cathedrals. "Never," marveled Francis Bacon, "was the like number of beautiful and costly tombs and monuments erected in sundry churches in honourable memory of the dead" (Bacon 1861, p. 158).

If this fantastic elaboration of funeral art can be explained as a defiant reaction to the leveling assaults of death—especially in the recurrent epidemics of plague whose cartloads of corpses were stripped of all individual dignity—it also offered a secular answer to a crisis in the management of mourning created by the Protestant denial of Purgatory. The consequent abolition of the vast medieval industry of intercession deprived the living of any power to assist the dead. Haunted like Hamlet by the Ghost's importunate "Remember me!" (*Hamlet,* 1.5.91), the bereaved had now to rely on the ambiguous consolations of memory and art—hence Hamlet's distress at the scanted mourning rituals allowed his father, or Laertes' rage at Ophelia's "maimed rites," and his bitter resentment of the "obscure funeral" and "hugger mugger" burial of Polonius, "No trophy, sword, or hatchment o'er his bones" (5.1.219; 4.5.84, 214–215); hence, too, Hamlet's dying insistence on the need for Horatio to remain behind, as a kind of "living monument" to "tell my story" (5.1.297; 5.2.349). The ending of *Hamlet,* with its self-conscious wordplay on "stage" and "audience" (5.2.378, 387, 396), itself constitutes an elaborate demonstration of the power of dramatic story and theatrical art to overcome the power of death.

The rivalry of art and death is, of course, a recurrent theme in the literature of the period—never more powerfully treated than in Shakespeare's Sonnets. At the heart of the sequence is a group of powerful lyrics in which the poet, performing his superb variations on a well-known trope from the Roman poet Horace (*"exegi monumentum aere perennius," Carmina,* 3.30), sets the monumental claims of poetry against the ravages of Death and his thieving ally, Time. Death is a leveling "churl" (Sonnet 32) or "wretch" (Sonnet 74) who renders his victims "base" (Sonnet 74) by consigning them to anonymous "dust" (Sonnet 32) and the degrading ministrations of "vilest worms" (Sonnet 71); while his "mortal rage" (Sonnet 64) reduces even the loftiest memorials to "unswept stone besmear'd with sluttish time" (Sonnet 55). Yet Shakespeare insists that his own "powerful rhyme," by its capacity to outlast death, can confer the immortality to which "the gilded monuments / Of princes" vainly aspire (Sonnet 55). It is this that enables the poet, despite his humble status, to assert a kind of parity with the beloved patron to whom his lyrics are addressed. The poet's mortal remains, consigned to the indifference of a common grave, may be "too base" to be remembered by his aristocratic "friend"; yet he can claim both immortality and a kind of equality by virtue of the "gentle verse" that memorializes his beloved's fame (Sonnets 74, 81).

The Sonnets create a kind of stage on which "the eyes of all posterity" can witness the spectacle of the patron's fame: "'Gainst death and all-oblivious enmity / Shall you pace forth" (55); and the touch of swagger in "pace" recalls the postures of heroic self-assertion with which so many protagonists of Renaissance tragedy confront their deaths. So Macbeth, defying the chaotic "wrack" of the apocalyptic storm that he himself has invoked, prepares to die "with harness on [his] back" (*Macbeth,* 5.5.50–51); or Othello reasserts his martial Venetian identity by transforming his suicide into a re-enacted triumph over the Turkish enemy; or Coriolanus calls on the Volscian mob to "cut me to pieces" with an insolent reminder of his conquest of Corioles ("Alone I did it. 'Boy'!" (*Coriolanus,* 5.6.115).

But even in the bleak world of King Lear, where the force of undifferentiation is so overwhelmingly felt as to allow no room for such egotistic self-assertion ("Why should a dog, a horse, a rat, have life, / And thou no breath at all?" 5.3.307–308), theatrical convention nevertheless contrives to impose a consolatory show of order upon the final panorama of desolation: The concluding stage direction, "Exeunt with a dead march," is a reminder of the extent to which Renaissance tragedy with its "industrious scenes and acts of death" (*King John,* 2.1.376) self-consciously mimicked the arts of funeral. The dressing of the tragic stage in black hangings, like those that adorned both churches and great houses in time of funeral; the use of black costumes; the display of hearses, tombs, and monuments as stage properties; and the convention of ending the play with a funeral procession—all these served as reminders that tragedy was conceived above all as the drama of death. But because the obsequies of the great, organized with lavish attention to the prerogatives of rank by the College of Heralds, were imagined (like coronations and royal progresses) as a species of "triumph," the incorporation of funeral pomps in tragedy also symbolized the power of art to challenge the universal monarchy of death.

The tragic catastrophe enacted the human confrontation with death's arbitrary cancellation of meaning; and through its displays of agony, despair, and ferocious self-assertion, early modern audiences were encouraged to rehearse vicariously their own encounter with death. Thus tragedy served, in a fashion that was inseparable alike from its didactic pretensions and its entertaining practice, both as an instrument for probing the painful mystery of ending and as a vehicle of resistance to the leveling assaults of death; for even as it paraded the emblems of undifferentiation, tragedy offered to contain the fear of mortality by staging

In the popular film adaptation of William Shakespeare's Romeo and Juliet *(1968), directed by Franco Zeffirelli, Juliet kills herself with Romeo's dagger when she discovers that he killed himself after he thought she drank the fatal poison.* CORBIS (BELLEVUE)

fantasies of ending in which the moment of dying was transformed by the arts of performance into a supreme demonstration of distinction. That is why Cleopatra carefully stages her death in a royal monument. Claiming her suicide as that which "shackles accidents and bolts up change" (*Antony and Cleopatra,* 5.2.6) through her double metamorphosis into spiritualized "fire and air" and eternizing "marble" (*Antony and Cleopatra,* 5.2.240, 289), the queen's language makes an exceptionally powerful connection between the bravura of her own performance and the dramatist's triumphant art.

Almost every tragedy of the period ends in a funeral procession of some kind, and this conventional expectation allowed playwrights to create striking theatrical effects by displacing the pageantry of death into other parts of the dramatic structure. Thus the national discord, which is the subject of *Henry VI,* is signaled as much by the disconcertingly abrupt obsequies of Henry V that open its action, as by the unpromising royal betrothal (a parody of comic ending) with which it concludes; while in *Titus Andronicus* the process of political and social disintegration is measured by the gap between the pompous interment of Titus's sons in the first act and the grotesque mock funeral of Tamora's sons, their heads encased in pastry "coffins," in Act 5.

Even more striking disruptions of convention could be achieved by transposing episodes of death and funeral into comedy—like the sober-faced travesty of burial rites which the repentant Claudio must perform at Hero's family monument in *Much Ado About Nothing,* or the mock deaths on which the plots of late romances like *Pericles, Cymbeline,* and *The Winter's Tale* depend. While the menace of death is always restrained by the expectation of a happy ending, such details are sufficient to remind the audience that the domains of folly and mortality are never quite as far apart as the symmetrically opposed masks of tragedy and comedy might at first suggest.

At one level, indeed, comedy—as the critic Marjorie Garber and others have shown—is deeply preoccupied with mortality, its action involving a symbolic expulsion of death from the stage world. But this comic victory is a fragile one, always vulnerable to some crack in the veneer of comic artifice. The concluding nuptials of *Love's Labours Lost* (a play that begins with a meditation on "brazen tombs" and the "disgrace of death") are suddenly arrested by the entrance of Marcade, like a black-clad summoner from the Dance of Death; Falstaff's parade of comic immortality never recovers from the moment when his mistress, Doll, "speaks like a death's head" (*Henry the Fourth, Part 2,* 2.4.31); and even *A Midsummer Night's Dream* follows the ludicrous mock deaths of Pyramus and Thisbe with the sinister frisson of Puck's chanting—"[Now] the screech-owl, screeching loud / Puts the wretch that lies in woe / In remembrance of a shroud" (5.1.376–378)—before Oberon and Titania reappear to summon the fairy dance of exorcism and blessing in which the play ends.

The latest of all Shakespeare's comic performances, the tragicomic *Two Noble Kinsmen,* written with John Fletcher, seems to concede the ultimate impotence of the comic triumph over death, ending as it does with a melancholy prospect of wedding overhung by funeral: "Journey's end in lovers meeting," Feste the clown had sung in *Twelfth Night* (2.3.43); but the lovers' reunion that resolves the accidents of plot in this final play only fulfills the prophecy of the mourning Queens in the "funeral solemnity" that concluded Act I: "This world's a city full of straying streets, / And death's the market-place where each one meets" (2.1.15–16).

See also: GREEK TRAGEDY; OPERATIC DEATH; THEATER AND DRAMA

Bibliography

Ariès, Philippe. *The Hour of Our Death,* translated by Helen Weaver. London: Allen Lane, 1981.

Bacon, Francis. "Certain Observations Made upon a Libel Published This Present Year 1592." In James Spedding ed., *The Letters and the Life of Francis Bacon,* Vol. 1. London: Longman, 1861.

Calderwood, James L. *Shakespeare and the Denial of Death.* Amherst: University of Massachusetts Press, 1987.

Evans, G. Blakemore, ed. *The Riverside Shakespeare,* 2nd edition. Boston: Houghton Mifflin, 1997.

Garber, Marjorie. " 'Wild Laughter in the Throat of Death': Darker Purposes in Shakespearean Comedy." *New York Literary Forum* nos. 5–6 (1980):121–126.

Gittings, Clare. *Death, Burial and the Individual in Early Modern England.* New York: Routledge, 1988.

Neill, Michael. *Issues of Death: Mortality and Identity in English Renaissance Tragedy.* Oxford: Clarendon Press, 1997.

Neill, Michael. " 'Feasts Put Down Funerals': Death and Ritual in Renaissance Comedy." In Linda Woodbridge and Edward Berry eds., *True Rites and Maimed Rites.* Urbana: University of Illinois Press, 1992.

Spinrad, Phoebe. *The Summons of Death on the Renaissance Stage.* Columbus: Ohio State University Press, 1986.

Watson, Robert. *The Rest Is Silence: Death As Annihilation in the Renaissance.* Berkeley: University of California Press, 1994.

MICHAEL NEILL

SHAMANISM

Shamanism is the world's oldest and most enduring religious, medical, and psychotherapeutic tradition. For tens of thousands of years and across the world, shamans have functioned as tribal general practitioners and have offered a means for understanding and dealing with death and the dead.

Shamanism is a family of traditions whose practitioners focus on voluntarily entering altered states of consciousness in which they experience themselves or their spirit(s) traveling to other realms at will and interacting with other entities from whom they gain knowledge and power in order to serve their community. Shamans often undergo a rigorous training program that may involve apprenticeship, solitude, asceticism, and spirit guides. When trained, they function as tribal physicians, counselors, priests, and spiritual practitioners.

Shamans' relationships to death and dying are multifaceted and involve both their training and their healing work. Shamans may sometimes be chosen because they unexpectedly cheat death by recovering from severe illness. During their training they may undergo one or more powerful death-rebirth experiences in which they experience themselves dying and being reborn, often finding themselves healed and strengthened by the process. In contemporary terms this can be understood as an early example of a profound, archetypal process that has been valued and sought in multiple cultures and religious traditions for its spiritually transformative potential. During training, the shaman is also expected to develop the capacity to see and relate to "spirits," some of whom are thought to be ancestors and ancient shamans, and some of whom may become helping guardian spirits that guide and empower the shaman.

Once shamans are trained, several of their practices relate to the dead. The spiritual entities that shamans interact with may be the spirits of the living or the dead. Sick individuals may lose their spirit—the term *dispirited* is still used—and face suffering and death unless the shaman can recover it. Spirits of the dead may be lost, troublesome, or malevolent, and the shaman must intervene by guiding, healing, or vanquishing them. Others might be troubled by spirits, but the shamans alone are masters of them and their realms.

Techniques such as fasting, solitude, drumming, dancing, and using psychedelics may be employed to induce altered states of consciousness in which spirit vision is enhanced for diagnostic and therapeutic purposes. These techniques may especially be preludes to, and inducers of, the shamanic journey: a controlled out-of-body experience to other realms where shamans may meet, mediate with, learn from, and heal spirit entities.

The tradition of shamanism has much to teach contemporary researchers and healers. It demonstrates an ancient form of medicine, spirituality, and thanatology; the power of disciplines such as solitude, asceticism, and spiritual practice; the responsible use of psychedelics; the potentials of altered states of consciousness and controlled out-of-body experiences; and the use of all these for dealing with death and serving one's community.

See also: COMMUNICATION WITH THE DEAD; GHOSTS

Bibliography

Eliade, Mircea. *Shamanism: Archaic Techniques of Ecstasy,* translated by Willard R. Trask. London: Arkana, 1989.

Harner, Michael. *The Way of the Shaman*. New York: Bantam, 1982.

Walsh, Roger. *The Spirit of Shamanism*. New York: Tarcher/Putnam, 1990.

ROGER N. WALSH

SHINTO

The term *Shinto,* which is translated as "the way of the gods," was not coined until the nineteenth century. Because Shinto, unlike Buddhism, has never been an organized religion or tradition and has no official doctrines or creed, its ideas concerning death can vary widely from one individual to the next. This entry makes references to *kami,* or native Japanese deities, as representative of the Shinto tradition and focuses on these deities as core to Shinto thought.

No moral notion of sin exists in Shinto. Death is not the "wages of sin," that is, the outcome of evil-doing. Rather, because purity is valued above all else, evil is defined as that which is "pollution." The primary pollutions are sickness, blood, and death. When kami are offended because of exposure to pollution, they can create disasters such as plagues and famines. Consequently, Shinto shrines usually do not conduct funerals. This tradition is evidenced in the familiar adage, "Shinto for weddings, Buddhism for funerals."

Nevertheless, historically, Shinto ideas have dealt with death. Practitioners believe that the spirits of the dead go to the mountains, above the sky, below the earth, or beyond the horizon. Kami and other supernatural beings also dwell in these places. Living beings from this world may visit those from the other worlds in border lands, which include cliffs, caves, and coastlines. The Japanese welcome

Asakusa's Sensoji Temple, said to be the oldest in Tokyo, was dedicated to the Goddess of Mercy, Kannon. Statues of the gods of wind and thunder are on either side of the Kaminarimon Gate. SUSAN D. ROCK

these souls back to their homes in August at the Obon festival. Usually, however, after thirty-three years deceased ancestors are no longer considered. There is no concept of an eternal soul in Shinto.

Two of Japan's oldest texts, the *Kojiki* (Record of ancient matters, 712) and the *Nihongi* (Chronicles of Japan, 720), tell the story of Izanami and Izanagi, the two kami who created Japan. After Izanami dies giving birth to the kami of fire, she goes to a place called the Land of Darkness (known as *Yomi no Kuni*). Her husband misses her so badly that he follows her, only to be shocked by Izanami's advanced state of decay. He flees the Land of Darkness, stopping at a river to cleanse himself on his way back to the land of the living. This early story emphasizes the Shinto understanding of death as pollution.

Occasionally deceased people have become kami, when the deceased were thought to be angry with the living or because of the circumstances surrounding their deaths. The most famous example of such a kami is Sugawara Michizane (845–903), who was exiled to Kyushu, a southern island of Japan, in 901 because he was viewed as a political threat by the scheming regent. Shortly after Michizane's death a number of disasters struck Japan, which were thought to be caused by his angry spirit. To pacify him, he was recognized as a kami and enshrined in Kitano Tenmangu Shrine in Kyoto in the middle of the tenth century.

In Japan's Meiji period (1868–1912), a time of extreme nationalism, leaders adapted Shinto ideas to fit their political agenda. Tokyo's Yasukuni Shrine, established in 1869, enshrines the spirits of all the Japanese war dead since that time. Nevertheless, most deceased persons in Japan are not regarded as kami, and most Japanese turn to Buddhism for answers to problems concerning death.

See also: BUDDHISM; CONFUCIUS; TAOISM

Bibliography

Aston, W. G., trans. *Nihongi: Chronicles of Japan from the Earliest Times to A.D. 67.* 1924. Reprint, New York: Paragon Press, 1956.

Ono, Sokyo. *Shinto: The Kami Way.* Rutland, VT: Charles E. Tuttle, 1962.

SARAH J. HORTON

SIKHISM

"We are destined to die, as death is an essential part of the life-cycle." These words of Guru Tegh Bahadur (reigned 1664–1675 C.E.), the ninth of the ten Indian Gurus who founded Sikhism, typify the approach to death of Sikhs. Death for this religion's 20 million members is an essential path in the journey of life and not to be feared. Death is followed by rebirth through transmigration—literally, metempsychosis, the passage of the soul of a human being or animal after death into a new body of the same or a different species, an understanding common to Sikhism, Buddhism, Jainism, and Hinduism—unless, through faith and divine favor, the deceased individual is endowed with the knowledge of God (*Brahm Gyani*) and released from the cycle of life, death, and rebirth (the laws of karma). Nevertheless, according to Guru Nanak (1469–1539 C.E.), the first Guru and founder of the line of Gurus, or inspired teachers, "rare are such men in the world whom after testing God has gathered unto his treasury."

At the deathbed of a Sikh, the relatives and friends console themselves and the departing soul by reading the religious hymns of the Sikh Gurus (*Gurbani*), especially *Sukhmani,* the Psalm of Peace, written by the fifth Guru, Arjan (reigned 1581–1606). When death occurs, no loud lamentations are allowed. Instead, the Sikhs chant *Wahiguru Wahiguru* ("Hail to the Guru," or "Wonderful Lord"). All dead bodies, whether those of children or of adults, are cremated, usually within twenty-four hours in the Indian subcontinent, but this may occur several days later in other countries where the body can be more easily preserved. Where cremation is not possible, it is permissible to throw the dead body into a sea or river.

The dead body is washed and dressed in new clothes (in the case of a male, complete with the five symbols of the Khalsa, the body of initiated Sikhs instituted in 1699 C.E.) before it is taken out on a bier to the cremation ground. The procession starts after a prayer, with the participants singing suitable hymns from the Sikh scriptures (*Guru Granth Sahib*) on the way. At the cremation ground, the body is placed on the pyre, the *Ardas* is recited, and the nearest relative (usually the eldest son) lights the pyre. When the fire is fully ablaze, *Sohila* is read and prayers are offered for the benefit of the dead. People then come away and leave the relatives of the deceased at their door, where they are thanked before departing.

The bereaved family, for the comfort of their own souls as well as for the peace of the departed, start a reading of the holy *Guru Granth Sahib* either at their own house or at a neighboring temple (*gurdwara*). Friends and relations take part. After a week or so they again come together when the reading is finished. The usual prayer is offered and the holy food or sacrament (*karah prasad*) is distributed. The charred bones of the dead, together with the ashes, are taken from the cremation ground three or four days later and, where this is permitted, thrown into the nearest canal or river (this is not allowed in the West, and therefore relatives often take the ashes to Punjab, India, to be disposed of there). It is forbidden to erect monuments over the remains of the dead, although a suitable monument in the person's honor at another place is permissible.

See also: CREMATION; GRIEF AND MOURNING IN CROSS-CULTURAL PERSPECTIVE; HINDUISM

Bibliography

McLeod, William Hewat. *Exploring Sikhism: Aspects of Sikh Identity, Culture, and Thought.* Oxford: Oxford University Press, 2000.

Oberoi, Harjot. *The Construction of Religious Boundaries: Culture, Identity, and Diversity in the Sikh Tradition.* Chicago: University of Chicago Press, 1994.

Singh, Harbans, ed. *The Encyclopaedia of Sikhism,* 2nd edition. Patiala, India: Punjabi University, 1995–1998.

RICHARD BONNEY

SIN EATER

For those who believed in an afterlife, death included the fear of punishment for misdeeds committed and unforgiven. For centuries, believers confessed their sins and sought forgiveness on their deathbeds. The souls of these who had not been forgiven were believed to wander where they had lived, bringing distress and ill fortune to their survivors. Over time, humankind developed various means to ease the passage of souls to a peaceful life in the hereafter. One method, whose origins can be traced to Egyptian and Greek civilizations, was embodied in the "sin eater," a person who was believed to possess the ability to symbolically ingest the sins of the deceased through eating and drinking over the recently deceased corpse. The sin eater, a secular person performing a quasi-spiritual role, was paid for this important service.

The central theme of this custom is the persistent, universal need to placate the souls of the deceased, to help the soul on its way and to be rid of it, lest it return and cause distress among the living. Eating in the presence of the corpse is customary in a number of cultures, as is token payment of a coin to those who assist in passage to the afterlife, such as the Greek mythological character Charon.

See also: GRIEF AND MOURNING IN CROSS-CULTURAL PERSPECTIVE

Bibliography

Habenstein, Robert W., and William M. Lamers. *The History of American Funeral Directing.* Milwaukee, WI: Bulfin Printers, 1955.

Lynch, Thomas. *Still Life in Milford: Poems.* New York: W. W. Norton, 1998.

Puckle, Bertram S. *Funeral Customs: Their Origin and Development.* Detroit: Omnigraphics, 1990.

WILLIAM M. LAMERS JR.

SOCIAL FUNCTIONS OF DEATH

When one reflects on the social upheavals and personal tragedies inflicted by deadly epidemics, terrorist attacks, droughts, and floods, it takes a change in thinking to reflect upon death's social functions. Further, one must consider from whose perspective death is perceived to be "functional." The bubonic plague, for instance, meant the death of roughly 25 million Europeans, but it also was the death knell for feudalism and, according to the historian William McNeill, laid the groundwork for capitalism. The death of a military tyrant may well be functional for his oppressed peoples, but dysfunctional for his nation's allies. Here we consider the positive effects for self and society as well as the ways societies attempt to harness death's power and minimize its disruptiveness.

Sociological Functions Served

As the old maxim goes, for there to be life there must be death. This holds true not only for biological systems but social systems as well. Just as programmed aging and death are evolution's requirements for species to gradually change over time, so social stability and change require the death of older generations so younger ones can take their turns on center stage.

Death checks population growth and avoids the Malthusian nightmare of overcrowding. As wildlife biologists know, once a species reproduces itself beyond the carrying capacity of its habitat, natural checks and balances come into play. Any species that breeds excessively will eventually experience a "die-back" or "population crash." The human species is not immune to this natural law, which is why the birth in 1999 of the planet's 6 billionth member received the mixed reception that it did: Human numbers had doubled since 1960 and tripled since 1927. Over the past 2,000 years the doubling time of the human population has accelerated roughly fortyfold, from sixteen centuries to forty years.

Paul Ehrlich, a Stanford professor of population studies and biological sciences, in *The Population Bomb* (1968), predicted that the population of the third world would double in the following quarter century and, unless a "birth rate solution" was made, one of three "death rate solution" scenarios would occur. These scenarios featured limited nuclear war, famine, social chaos, and deadly pollution. Humanity made it to the new millennium, of course, without the mass death Ehrlich had predicted. By the mid-1990s, fertility rates declined by at least one-half in seventeen countries. However, his grim prophecy may have only been postponed. Overfishing, overgrazing, and overcutting have become commonplace, as have shortages of fresh water suitable for human use.

Death constantly replenishes the vitality of the gene and meme (the cultural equivalent of DNA) pools, allowing for innovation and change. In his

Structure of Scientific Revolutions (1962), Thomas Kuhn describes how new scientific paradigms do not succeed by virtue of their truth but rather come to be accepted when proponents of old ones die off. Similarly, social progress in matters of gender and racial equality in the United States occurs when older generations die with their prejudices and beliefs. For instance, between 1972 and 1998, the percentage of white Americans who answered "yes" to the question, "Do you think there should be laws against marriages between blacks and whites?" decreased by two-thirds, from 39 percent to 13 percent. Approximately 40 percent of this decrease can be statistically explained by the deaths of older generations over the time frame.

In hierarchical organizations, death allows the upward mobility of younger generations, thereby securing their loyalty to the social order. Death of older generations allows younger ones to have their turn on life's central stages. Relatedly, death dilutes concentrations of power and wealth; consider, for instance, the Rockefeller family. Time has fragmented the wealth accumulated by John D. Rockefeller Sr. (1839–1937), whose Standard Oil at its peak controlled 90 percent of the American oil industry. In 1976 there were eighty-four descendants of John Sr.'s only son, John Jr.; a quarter century later they numbered in the hundreds.

Somewhat more abstractly, there is the power of death to bring people together, producing new social solidarities. Death commands human attention and its associated rituals, like human sacrifices and martyrdom, harness death's power to increase social solidarities and promote change. An example of how death can lead to new solidarities coalescing in the cause of greater social justice can be seen in the Triangle Shirtwaist Company fire. Before this disaster garment workers, largely fearful immigrant women, were unorganized. The broader public was generally indifferent or ignorant of the child labor being exploited, and was often opposed to unions. On one Saturday afternoon fire broke out in New York City's Triangle Shirtwaist Company, wherein 500 workers were crammed. Doors were locked to keep the young immigrant children within and labor organizers out. In the end 146 died, and were seen on the sidewalk in piles where they landed after nine-story jumps. The dead became martyrs for the International Ladies' Garment Workers' Union, which called for a day of mourning. With union pressure against unsafe working conditions, the New York State governor appointed the Factory Investigation Commission. Its hearings led to the passage of factory safety regulations.

Social groups often harness the power released by the deaths of their members to amplify the solidarities among the living. Consider, for instance, the November 1999 bonfire accident that killed eleven Texas A&M students and one alumnus. At 10:00 P.M. on the first Tuesday of the following month, the university community gathered in silence to observe Silver Taps, a century-old ritual for remembering fellow students who had died the month before. In this ceremony, silence is broken by three volleys of seven rifles followed by trumpeters playing taps. On April 21 the students' memories were reaffirmed on Texas Aggie Memorial Day. Honoring a tradition that has been in place since 1883, all around the world alumni of Texas A&M gather annually for a roll call (the Muster) of those who had died during the previous year.

Social-Psychological Functions

At a more social-psychological level, death poses the ultimate of "deadlines" and thereby forces prioritization and the setting of personal and collective goals. As is the case of all endings, death forces reflection and summary. Rarely does one give words to life's core meanings and goals, nor reflect on how life would have differed had not one existed, except within funerary observances. In addition, there is death's power to enhance appreciation of life. When ruminating on the leukemia death of his eighteen-year-old daughter, the baseball Hall of Famer Rod Carew shared the lessons he learned, such as appreciating what you have and the importance of giving one's child extra attention.

Several ingenious experiments have supported the social scientist Ernest Becker's Pulitzer Prize–winning thesis of how personal death anxieties intensify individuals' allegiance to moral codes. For example, in 1989 psychologist Abram Rosenblatt of the University of Arizona and his colleagues organized an experiment where eleven municipal judges were told to write about their own deaths, including what they thought would happen physically and what emotions were evoked when they thought about it. A control group of eleven other judges was spared the activity. When asked to set bond for a prostitute on the basis of a case brief, those who had thought about their deaths set an average bond of $455, while the average in the control group was $50. From this and other experiments researchers found that when awareness of death is increased, in-group solidarity is intensified, out-groups become more despised, and prejudice and religious extremism are increased.

How societies dampen death's disruptiveness. Despite its occasional social functions, death—even the "good," anticipated deaths of those who have lived full, complete lives—is invariably disruptive. To minimize the inevitable schism in the social fabric, a number of social shock absorbers have evolved to manage the problem of immortal social systems being populated by mortal members.

The most apparent of the social mechanisms for coping with death is the funerary ritual. Funerals evolved not only to dispose of the dead and to assist the surviving, but to harness death's power and direct it toward the reaffirmation of social solidarities. Consider the 1990 funeral of the business tycoon Malcolm Forbes, which attracted an assemblage of varied individuals, including such notables as Richard Nixon, Lee Iacocca, Barbara Walters, David Rockefeller, Ann Landers, and Mrs. Douglas MacArthur, as well as Hell's Angels motorcyclists.

Death's disruptiveness can be dampened by minimizing the social status of those most likely to die. For most of human history, for instance, children comprised the largest segment of societies' mortalities. Whereas in the twenty-first century a child cannot leave an American hospital until he or she is named, at least as late as the eighteenth century American children were often not called by name until they were about six years of age or older. The main reason that children "did not count" was their considerable likelihood of death; most couples could expect to lose two or three children before they reached the age of ten. In Puritan New England, parents often would send their children away to the home of relatives or friends. Ostensibly this was a method of discipline (Protestantism assisted the distancing by viewing children as sinful and corrupt) but in actuality this act served to prevent parents' emotional closeness to their children and thereby minimize their inevitable emotional pain if the children died. With social evolution, the old replaced the young as the cultural death lepers as they became those most likely to die. The Puritan custom of sending children away has been replaced by the American practice of sending the elderly to nursing homes to be cared for by others.

Social systems can also hide the dying and grieving processes, further minimizing the disruptions of dying and death. In contemporary American society, a reportedly "death-denying" culture, specialists are paid to impersonally manage the deaths of family members within institutional settings (where roughly seven out of ten now die) and then pay others to dispose of their physical remains.

The deaths of powerful leaders, particularly those of "founding fathers" and of charismatic individuals, pose severe crises of continuity for political, religious, and corporate systems alike. The power vacuum (and associated threats of disorder) becomes particularly acute when their deaths come suddenly and unexpectedly. Even rumors of their impending end of life can trigger power struggles from within and incite challenges from without. To address such crises of succession, social systems have devised explicit rules for the changing of the guard. In the United States, for instance, between 1841 and 1975 more than one-third of all the country's presidents have either died in office, quit, or become disabled, and seven vice presidents have either died or resigned. In response to this social phenomenon, the 1947 Presidential Succession Law specifies an order of presidential succession (comprised of sixteen role incumbents, beginning with the Speaker of the House, president pro tempore of the Senate, and secretary of state) should both the president and vice president die or be incapacitated simultaneously. In addition to the transference of power, social groups, particularly families, attempt to avoid conflict over the disposition of the deceased's possessions through rules of inheritance.

The changing nature of social roles has contributed to society's ability to dampen death's disruptive effects. Historically, there has been the shift from particularistic to universalistic roles, meaning that individuals are rarely known as entire selves but rather as role occupants. This creates an analytical distinction between individual and role, unlike the earlier situation where the two were so thoroughly fused that the death of the individual meant the death of the role. Instead, twenty-first-century roles can rarely be held indefinitely by their incumbents, but rather must be ritually surrendered. Roles have become more important than their interchangeable occupants. Within the bureaucratic structure of contemporary societies, such ritual surrenderings are part of the institutionalized rules of succession. In the case of the elderly and the institutionalization of retirement, older individuals are disengaged from many of their social roles to minimize the disruptions caused by their deaths. Further, given the accelerating pace of social change, many of these roles themselves have become obsolete before their occupants have grown old.

Finally, there are the successes of modern societies' war against premature death. By minimizing death risks—through environmental cleanups, warnings of the health dangers of cigarettes, gun control, improvements in sanitation, use of antibiotics to control infectious diseases, political control over the purity of food, and building safer vehicles—death is largely confined to the old. Rarely needed are the historical cultural consolations for the sudden, premature deaths, as death often comes to those who have completed their life projects and who, when suffering from the degenerative diseases of advanced age, often view death as preferable to a continued existence. And for the survivors of elderly victims of Huntington's chorea or Alzheimer's disease, their deaths may actually be viewed as a blessing.

See also: CAPITAL PUNISHMENT; DEATH SYSTEM; MALTHUS, THOMAS; POPULATION GROWTH; TECHNOLOGY AND DEATH; TRIANGLE SHIRTWAIST COMPANY FIRE

Bibliography

Becker, Ernest. *The Denial of Death*. New York: Free Press, 1973.

Blauner, Robert. "Death and Social Structure." *Psychiatry* 29 (1966):378–394.

Davis, James Allan, and Tom W. Smith. *General Social Surveys, 1972–1996*. Produced by the National Opinion Research Center, Chicago. Roper Public Opinion Research Center, 1998. Machine readable data tape.

Ehrlich, Paul. *The Population Bomb*. New York: Ballantine, 1968.

Greenberg, Jeff, Tom Pyszczynski, Sheldon Solomon, et al. "Evidence for Terror Management Theory II: The Effects of Mortality Salience on Reactions to Those Who Threaten or Bolster the Cultural Worldview." *Journal of Personality and Social Psychology* 58, (1990):308–318.

Kuhn, Thomas. *The Stucture of Scientific Revolutions*. Chicago: University of Chicago Press, 1962.

McNeill, William. *Plagues and Peoples*. Garden City, NY: Anchor Press/Doubleday, 1976.

Rosenblatt, Abram, Jeff Greenberg, Sheldon Solomon, et al. "Evidence for Terror Management Theory I: The Effects of Mortality Salience on Reactions to Those Who Violate or Uphold Cultural Values." *Journal of Personality and Social Psychology* 57 (1989):681–690.

Stannard, David. *Death in America*. Philadelphia: University of Pennsylvania Press, 1975.

MICHAEL C. KEARL

SOCRATES

Socrates is a name often relied upon when historians want to invoke a notable person from antiquity. There is good reason for the fame and durability of this name. In both his life and his death Socrates (469–399 B.C.E.) provided a model for wisdom and courage.

Socrates spent his life in Athens, the city of his birth (470 B.C.E.). Athens already had produced thinkers and artists of the highest order as well as an experiment in (limited) democracy that has continued to inspire and influence seekers of equality, freedom, and creativity through the centuries. The bust of Socrates in the Museo delle Terme in Rome displays the hearty features of a broad-faced, pug-nosed, thick-lipped, and generously bearded man. His friend Alcibiades teased Socrates by likening his face to that of a wild, sensuous satyr. Socrates not only accepted this comparison but added that he had better do more dancing to reduce his paunch. Humor came naturally to Socrates and, in fact, played a significant role in his philosophical method.

Specific information about Socrates' life is sparse. It is believed that he was the son of a sculptor and a midwife. He followed his father's footsteps, working as both a stonemason and a sculptor. He also claimed to be following his mother's line of work, "by helping others to deliver themselves of their conceptions" (Durant 1968,

p. 36). Socrates usually kept himself in good physical condition and earned a reputation as a soldier of exceptional stamina, as well as skill and courage. His marriage to Xanthippe produced a family but also her justified complaint that he spent more time gadding about and annoying people than with his wife and children. He enjoyed companionship, cared little about material possessions, and was considered the very model of a well-balanced person: moral, but too earthy to be revered as a saint.

The Athens of Socrates' time enjoyed exceptional intellectual vitality. Almost every facet of life was open for discussion. Here philosophical issues were fresh, live, and compelling—the same issues that would later become weighed down by centuries of further speculation and commentary. The political establishment, however, did not necessarily cherish this free exchange of ideas. Some of these ideas could be dangerous to the institutions that kept the establishment in power.

Socrates became the most adept and, therefore, the most fascinating and most dangerous asker of questions. The "Socratic method" is one of his enduring contributions to philosophical inquiry. He believed that everyone with a competent mind already knows the basic truths of life deep inside of one's being, even if unaware of possessing this knowledge. Socrates would educe knowledge through conversations guided by an unfolding series of questions. True education was educing—drawing something out of, rather than forcing something into—the mind. This dialect method was perfected rather than invented by Socrates. Zeno of Elea (born the same year as Socrates) had already introduced the art of questioning as a way to reach the truth. Socrates had the extra knack of making powerful people uncomfortable by undermining their assumptions with his deceptively simple questions. Bystanders found it amusing to see how people with exaggerated opinions of their knowledge became flustered as Socrates' casual, low-key questions eventually exposed their errors. The victims were not amused, however, and they did not forget.

Plato and Socrates

It is Plato's *Dialogues* that provide most of what has come down to readers through history about the life and thought of his mentor. There are no books written by Socrates, only his appearance as the main character in Plato's writings and, to a much lesser degree, in plays written during or after his life. There is no way of knowing for sure how much is "pure Socrates" and how much is Plato. The dialogues were not intended as fastidious reportage of actual events and conversations; they were imaginative riffs on ideas and people. *Symposium,* for example, takes readers to a banquet in which Socrates and his friends entertain and compete with each other to solve the mysteries of love. Plato's *Dialogues* offer episodes and scenes through which his philosophical points could be made through the characters themselves. His first generation of readers could separate fact from fancy, but this has become much more difficult for the following generations who lack insiders' knowledge of the political, historical, and philosophical milieu of Socrates' Athens.

Plato's account of Socrates offers a remarkable vision of a society superior to any previously known in one of the most influential of the dialogues, *The Republic.* A rational, managed, and futuristic society is portrayed where even genetic selection and psychological testing exist. The resonance of this imagined society can be felt in many spheres of life in the twenty-first century, including the ever-shifting boundaries between science and science fiction. One of the early masterpieces of philosophy, this dialogue ranges from vigorous discussions of the nature of justice to the recesses of a shadowy cave where readers are challenged to determine the definition of reality. Neither in his life nor in his *Dialogue* appearances does Socrates demand overthrow of the establishment or express disrespect to the gods. However, his relentless questions raised anxiety and created enemies.

The Death of Socrates

The faithful soldier, the relatively faithful husband, the good companion, and the subtle and witty philosopher all were now in their seventieth year of life and awaiting execution.

Socrates had inadvertently given his enemies an excuse for retaliation. The case against him was so insubstantial that it should have been immediately dismissed. He was accused of impiety, although he had never cursed the gods, and accused of corrupting the young, a charge so far-fetched that it was hard to keep from laughing out loud.

Socrates believed that a teacher should not besiege students with a barrage of words but instead help people to discover and articulate their own hidden knowledge. ARALDO DE LUCA/CORBIS

What gave the accusations their power was the undercurrent of annoyance at Socrates' habit of raising questions that set too many minds to thinking and could possibly destabilize the establishment. He was blamed for the current state of unrest against the establishment and even accused of being a traitor. These were "trumped-up" charges that Socrates expected the court to overturn. Even when convicted, he could have avoided a serious penalty by saying the right words and admitting some fault. This he would not do: Instead, he stood before them unrepentant and free-spirited. Few of his fellow citizens had expected the death penalty to be enacted. Something had gone wrong with the process of rebuking this distinguished gadfly, and now they would have to go through with the embarrassing act of taking his life.

It would not have been difficult for Socrates to escape. His friends were eager to spirit him away to a safe island, and the authorities seemed inclined to look the other way. Socrates would not accept such a plan, however, much to the distress of his friends. In *Phaedo,* he told his friend that there was nothing to fear. Death will turn out either to be a long sleep or, even better, the entry to a splendid new form of life. Socrates's ability to accept his death with equanimity became a model for wisdom and courage on the verge of death. He lived his philosophy to the last moment, treating the unfortunate jailer with kindness as he brought forward the cup of deadly hemlock. He bid an affectionate farewell to his friends. When Crito asked, "But how shall we bury you?" he replied:

> Any way you like—that is, if you can catch me and I don't slip through your fingers. . . . It is only my body you are burying; and you can bury it in whatever way you think is most proper. (Dialogues *1942, p. 150)*

Socrates quaffed the contents of the cup, described the changes occurring in his body—the rise of cold numbness upward from the feet—and died peacefully. At least that is the scene reported in *Phaedo.* Some doubt has been cast in late-twentieth-century scholarship. The medical historian William B. Ober notes, along with others, that Plato described an event he did not witness: He was too upset to see his friend's death. More significantly, perhaps, hemlock usually produces a variety of painful and distressing symptoms. Perhaps Plato sanitized the actual death to create a more acceptable memory-scene, or perhaps Greek physicians had mixed hemlock with a gentle sedative in the farewell cup for Socrates' journey to philosophical immortality.

See also: GOOD DEATH, THE; IMMORTALITY; JESUS; LAST WORDS; PHILOSOPHY, WESTERN; PLATO

Bibliography

Ahrensdorf, P. J. *The Death of Socrates and the Life of Philosophy.* Albany: State University of New York Press, 1995.

Brickhouse, Thomas C., and Nicholas D. Smith. *Plato's Socrates.* New York: Oxford University Press, 1994.

Durant, Will. *The Life of Greece.* New York: Simon & Schuster, 1968.

Ober, William, B. "Did Socrates Die of Hemlock Poisoning?" In *Boswell's Clap & Other Essays. Medical Analyses of Literary Men's Afflictions.* New York: Harper & Row, 1988.

Plato. *Apology, Crito, Phaedo, Symposium, Republic,* translated by B. Jowett and edited by Louise Ropes Loomis. New York: W. J. Black, 1942.

Stone. Irving, F. *The Trial of Socrates*. Boston: Little, Brown, 1988.

ROBERT KASTENBAUM

SOUL BIRDS

Belief in metempsychosis or the transmigration of souls into other living beings is ancient. In Western tradition, one of the most common sites for a formerly human soul to inhabit is that of a bird. Such birds are invariably also ominous, in its original sense of prophetic, the rationale being that the dead, as spirits, know both past and future. They are ominous also in its secondary meaning of "boding ill."

At sea, such soul birds include the storm petrel (*Hydrobates pelagicus*). Storm petrels, as their name suggests, were taken as a sign of approaching bad weather, so sailors saw them as helpful and considered it unlucky to shoot one. Moreover, into the nineteenth century, perhaps later, many seamen believed that petrels should be spared because they harbored dead sailors' souls.

Seagulls (*Laridae*), too, warned of approaching storm. An extension of this was the belief that they cried before a disaster. As with petrels, in West European fishing communities it was thought unlucky to kill a gull; and, as with petrels, some said they embodied the souls of fishermen and sailors, especially those who had drowned. Belief in gulls as soul-birds was still active in coastal districts of Great Britain and Ireland up to at least the late nineteenth century.

Other birds were also thought to house souls. Among East Anglian fishermen, the spirits of the drowned were believed to migrate to the gannet (*Morus bassanus*). From the eastern seaboard of the United States comes the story of a waterman on Chesapeake Bay who shot three ducks as they flew in to land. They fell into the marsh, and he could not find them. That night, a gale sprang up and blew for three days. When it was over, he returned to the marsh and in the water, where the ducks fell, lay three drowned sailors.

Sometimes the belief in transmigration has carried penitential implications. Aboard French ships

In the nineteenth century soul birds, such as petrels, gulls, and albatrosses, were considered useful because they were a sign of approaching bad weather and, as their name suggests, carried the souls of drowned fisherman and sailors. U.S. FISH AND WILDLIFE SERVICE

both storm petrels and shearwaters were known as *âmes damnées* ("souls of the damned"), the subtext being that, like some ghosts, part of their punishment after death was to continue to haunt the earth. Muslim seafarers in the nineteenth century similarly said that the Manx and Mediterranean shearwaters (*Puffinus puffinus* and *Puffinus yelkouan*) of the eastern Mediterranean were inhabited by damned souls, a belief possibly suggested by their dark plumage.

It is sometimes claimed that deep-sea sailors believed that the albatross brought bad weather and that killing one was unlucky because the souls of sailors reposed in them. However, these beliefs cannot be proved as existing before Samuel Taylor Coleridge's "The Rime of the Ancient Mariner" (1798):

At length did cross an Albatross,
Through the fog it came;
As if it had been a Christian soul,
We hailed it in God's name.

Coleridge is said to have based the mariner's shooting of the albatross—an act that brought doom on his ship—on an episode in Shelvocke's *Voyages* (1719). But in *Voyages* the bird was a black albatross, shot by someone who "imagin'd, from his colour, that it might be some ill omen."

Whether or not the superstition against shooting albatrosses generally began with Coleridge, it was never widespread: They were regularly shot at by ships' crews, who, among other things, made their webbed feet into tobacco pouches.

On land, the themes of ominousness and transmigration are attached to corvids, specifically crows and ravens, which were not always distinguished. From classical times to the present day, the raven (*Corvus corax*) and crow (*Corvus corone*) have been thought birds of ill omen. A document written in England between 680 and 714 C.E. reported that once, when King Edwin (585–633 C.E.) was on his way to church, a crow "sang with an evil omen." The king stopped to listen until Bishop Paulinus had a servant shoot the bird. He later showed it to the catechumens (converts before baptism) in the church to prove that heathen superstitions were worthless, since the bird did not know it was its own death that it was prophesying.

Elsewhere in Europe, the souls of the unbaptized were supposed to transmigrate into ravens; in Languedoc, France, it was wicked priests who turned into ravens when they died, something suggested, no doubt, by their black garments. In Britain, traditions of metempsychosis were attached to both the raven and the red-legged crow or chough (*Pyrrhocorax pyrrhocorax*) in connection with King Arthur. A belief that he had not died is expressed in medieval literature and later folklore in three different forms: that he had been taken to Avalon to be healed of his wounds; that he was sleeping in a cave, variously located in Britain; and that he had been enchanted into a crow or raven. This last was said by the Spanish writer Julian del Castillo in 1582 to have been common talk among the English. The incurably romantic Don Quixote had heard it and asked:

> Have you not read, sir, . . . the famous exploits of King Arthur . . . of whom there goes an old tradition . . . that this king did not die, but that by magic art he was turned into a raven; and that . . . he shall reign again . . . ; for which reason it cannot be proved, that, from that time to this, any Englishman has killed a raven? *(Cervantes 2001, 1:5:130)*

This taboo against killing ravens was still current in Cornwall at the end of the eighteenth century, when a young man walking on Marazion Green, near Penzance, with his "fowling-piece" on his shoulder, saw a raven and fired. An old man nearby immediately rebuked him, saying that he should not have shot at the raven because Arthur lived on in that form.

King Arthur is the archetypal protector of Britain, and there is probably a connection between this tradition of his transmigration and the custom of keeping six ravens at the Tower of London, instituted by King Charles II (1630–1685). The ravens are a palladium (national talisman); it being said that, so long as there are ravens at the Tower, Britain cannot be conquered. Some anxiety was caused during World War II by rumors that the ravens had fallen silent and had not croaked for five whole days.

See also: African Religions; Mind-Body Problem; Omens

Bibliography

Armstrong, Edward A. *The Folklore of Birds,* 2nd edition. New York: Dover, 1970.

Beck, Horace. *Folklore and the Sea.* Middletown, CT: Wesleyan University Press, 1973.

Cervantes, Miguel. *Don Quixote,* translated by Walter Starkie. New York: Signet Classic, 2001.

Collingwood, R.G., and J. N. L. Myres, eds. *English Historical Documents I: Roman Britain and the English Settlement,* 2nd edition. Oxford: Clarendon Press, 1937.

JENNIFER WESTWOOD

Spiritual Crisis

Humans typically assume the world to be a benevolent place; we regard ourselves with favorable self-esteem, and attempt to minimize chance in determining life events by believing in an abstract sense of justice, personal control, or a spiritual force that brings order to a potentially chaotic world. Illusory as these beliefs may be, as long as they go untested, they provide a stable cognitive framework for making sense of an individual's experiences and for providing meaning and purpose to his or her life. However, in facing a life crisis, such as confronting one's own death or the death of one dearly loved, these assumptions and beliefs may shatter, may be turned upside down, and might no longer be useful as a foundation to understanding the world or one's place in it.

For example, what happens to our beliefs in personal control of our world when confronted with our own death or when forced to respond to a loved one's painful illness, over which personal control is futile? Or how can a parent continue to assume that the world is just and fair, or that people get what they deserve, or that there is a loving God, after experiencing the death of a child by sudden infant death syndrome, random gunfire, or an automobile accident? Confused, depressed, and devoid of insights, answers, or coping skills, one can find oneself on the brink of a spiritual crisis.

Spiritual crisis or spiritual emergency is recognized by the American Psychiatric Association as a distinct psychological disorder that involves a person's relationship with a transcendent being or force; it might be accompanied by assumptions related to meaning or purpose in life. The disorder may be accompanied by any combination of the following symptoms, which include feelings of depression, despair, loneliness; loss of energy or chronic exhaustion not linked to a physical disorder; loss of control over one's personal and/or professional life; unusual sensitivity to light, sound, and other environmental factors; anger, frustration, lack of patience; loss of identity, purpose, and meaning; withdrawal from life's everyday routines; feelings of madness and insanity; a sense of abandonment by God; feelings of inadequacy; estrangement from family and friends; loss of attention span, self-confidence, and self-esteem; and frequent bouts of spontaneous crying and weeping.

As fundamental beliefs are brutally strained and the rules that previously guided our lives are nullified, distress builds, until we are challenged to deal with the crisis. In this effort some individuals will rely on long-held religious beliefs for guidance; some will embark on a spiritual quest in search of newer ways of finding meaning in life; some will reject religion and become bitter; and some will turn to philanthropic and other caregiving activities in the struggle to find solace and a renewed sense of purpose.

Spiritual Crisis and Loss: The Death of a Child

Parents mourning the death of their child are especially prone to spiritual crisis because the bond between parent and child is so powerful and unique. Most bonds between individuals are contractual—people enter the bonds based on an understood group of mutual obligations. The bond between spouses or friends, for instance, is contractual and, as such, may be abandoned if the interactions are no longer reciprocal and mutually satisfying. The bond between a caring parent and a helpless child is, obviously, not reciprocal. As with religious obligations or duty to God, to ancestors, or to an abstract principle, it is the sacred or spiritual nature of the parent-child relationship and its underlying assumptions that makes mourning the death of a child such a long, agonizing, and, at times, transformative process.

The parent's search for meaning in the child's death often results in the formulation of religious loss rationales. In their study of grieving parents, Cook and Wimberley isolated three parental loss rationales: reunion, reverence, and retribution. The most frequently used rationale was the notion that the child had gone to heaven, where parents and the dead child would eventually be reunited (reunion). Another frequent explanation was that the child's death served some religious purpose, for example, as an inspiration for parents to do good works (reverence). Finally, in some cases, the child's death was interpreted as a punishment for the sins of the parents (retribution).

In another study of bereaved parents participating in a chapter of Compassionate Friends, a support-group for parents-in-mourning, Dennis Klass found that nearly all the parents in the group rejected simple loss rationales, such as that their child's death was God's will, and instead confronted their spiritual crisis by creating new assumptions. Klass discovered that, in many cases, profound forms of psychospiritual transformation were an integral part of the healing process for bereaved parents. He states, "Many of these parents-in-mourning find solace in connections with that which transcended the physical and biological world, and with their perception of an underlying order in the world. These spiritual aspects of the resolution of the grief were central elements in the parents' rebuilding of their lives to be able to live in a changed world." Confronted with a profound and intense spiritual crisis, the bereaved parents in this study were forced to undertake a spiritual quest for individual meaning and solace and to "transcend the human limitations they find in the death of their child. They reveal what people in . . . 'the extreme situation' do and what all persons must do" (Klass 1995, p. 264).

Spiritual Crisis and the Search for Meaning

Other strategies for finding spiritual meaning exist for persons who cannot reconcile the "why" of their loss through traditional or modern religious doctrine. Some people may become involved in philanthropic, political, or caregiving work that relates to the illness or manner of death experienced by their loved one. By so doing—coping actively with the spiritual crisis rather than passively—the mourner may discover meaning in the loss, as if to say, "This death was not in vain."

The American businessman and philanthropist George Soros, for example, contributed more than $200 million to charitable projects, including the Project on Death in America, following his own spiritual crisis following the death of his parents. "I chose the culture of dying as one of the areas I wanted to address . . . because of my experiences with the death of my parents, both of whom I was very devoted and [to] loved dearly" (1995, p. 2). Soros was not present at his father's death:

> I let him die alone. The day after he died I went to my office. I didn't talk about his death. I certainly didn't participate in it. After reading Kübler-Ross, I learned that . . . I could have held his hand as he lay dying. . . . I just didn't know that it might have made a difference—for both of us. *(1995, p. 3)*

Years later, confronted with a second spiritual crisis involving his dying mother, Soros was present and participated in her dying: "I reassured her. Her dying was really a positive experience for all of us." The attempt to bring meaning to these experiences of loss prompted Soros to found the Project on Death in America with the goal of promoting "a better understanding of the experiences of dying and bereavement and by doing so help transform the culture surrounding death" (1995, p. 2).

These quests for meaning, whether they involve an affirmation of long-held religious beliefs, a search for new spiritual insights, or philanthropic work, often continue beyond the grieving process into the larger mourning process and include revising and restructuring one's assumptions regarding his or her own existence; integrating memories and meanings associated with the deceased into new ways of relating to the world; restoring one's self-esteem and sense of self-mastery; and exploring transformations in one's spiritual beliefs and practices.

Spiritual Crisis and the Experience of Dying

Because humans are essentially order-seeking creatures, the reality of dying presents a powerful cognitive upheaval to our sense of self and an intense challenge to our spiritual beliefs and assumptions. Perhaps we cannot imagine what it will be like to die, but we can easily imagine what it might be like to no longer cope, feel vulnerable and helpless, be dependent on others to meet our everyday physical needs, and to feel like we are no longer in charge of our own lives. We know what happens when we are admitted to hospitals. We are literally stripped of almost everything that is familiar—clothing, routine, personal objects—and we are told when to eat and sleep. Even when treated in a courteous manner, there is still an undeniable sense of dependency and vulnerability.

For the patient who is hospitalized for a short stay and a cure, the feeling of loss of control may be fleeting and masked by the visits of family and friends—and the good news of a successful treatment. The terminal patient, however, is in a much more vulnerable and tenuous position and much more likely to experience a spiritual crisis connected to the loss of integrity, control, and human connection. For many persons facing imminent death, coping strategies provide comfort and a sense of meaning within the context of traditionally held religious beliefs. For example, in a study of the role of spirituality in persons with AIDS, researchers found that it is not uncommon for AIDS victims to be drawn even closer to their traditional religious beliefs, including beliefs in a caring, higher power; the value of life; the importance of support from religious laypersons and close friends; living an ethical life; the importance of facing death; and the presence of an inner peace in identifying a meaning to their lives. Likewise, the greater religiosity of older persons, those most likely to die in modern societies, has been interpreted by some as evidence of such spiritual needs.

Another study of fifty hospitalized cancer patients also revealed that many found comfort and meaning in traditional religious beliefs, but over half had concerns involving spiritual issues connected with long-held religious beliefs; about one-third were actively struggling with a spiritual crisis. The crisis, according to respondents, involved conflicts between religious views, as when dying patients experience anger toward God or believe that their illness is somehow due to their sins; loss of religious support from their congregation or a particular minister; pressure to adopt a different religious position, as when a husband urges a dying wife to adopt his particular religious conviction; and, an all but obsessive preoccupation with religious/spiritual questions in an effort to understand what is happening to them in the process of dying.

Spirituality and Needs of the Dying

The psychologist Abraham Maslow viewed human motivation as consisting of needs ranging from those related to basic survival, such as needs for food and water, to "higher" psychological needs, such as the need for love, knowledge, order, self-fulfillment, spirituality. Maslow wrote of the need for "something bigger than we are to be awed by" (1971, p. 105). Exploring these higher reaches of human nature is always difficult, but is especially challenging in the midst of coping with one's own dying.

An important feature of Maslow's theory is the idea that some needs are more fundamental than others and need to be at least partly satisfied before other, higher needs become active. Thus, in living our dying, one must first satisfy his or her basic physiological needs (e.g., hunger, thirst, pain control) and safety needs (e.g., living in a secure, nurturing environment) before being motivated to satisfy needs higher up on the pyramid. Once physiological and safety needs are met, people begin striving to satisfy emotional needs (e.g., the need to receive affection from others and to feel part of a group) and self-esteem needs (e.g., the need to feel positively about oneself and to be esteemed by others). Finally, at the top of the pyramid, is the need for self-actualization—the desire to attain the full use of one's potential in acceptance of self, others, nature, and spiritual yearnings and insights. Based on his work with the dying, the German thanatologist David Aldridge contends that abandonment, suffering loss of hope and meaning, and the transitions from living to dying are essentially spiritual, not solely physiological, psychological, or social. He argues that in many instances, all of these contexts are interlinked in coping with a spiritual crisis.

Kenneth Doka has identified three principal spiritual tasks for those who are dying: First, the need to find the ultimate significance of life. Answers do not necessarily have to be found in religious beliefs, but an inability to find meaning can create a deep sense of spiritual pain. The dying person's belief system can give a sense of purpose in life and help sustain personal values. Second, the need to die an appropriate death. People who are dying need to accept their death within a framework that is congruent with their values and lifestyle. In some cases, individuals may need help in making decisions about the way in which they will die. Guidance from a special friend or from someone they recognize as a spiritual leader may be helpful in developing cognitive coping strategies. Third, is the need to transcend death; transcendence can be achieved through renewed assurance of immortality in religious doctrine, new spiritual insights, or the acknowledgement of future generations in recognizing that their deeds will live long after they die. To find meaning in the final moments of life, to die appropriately, consistent with one's own self-identity, and to find hope that extends beyond the grave may be among the most important cognitive transformations humans can experience during a crisis of spirit.

Spiritual Crisis and Hospice Care

Because many spiritual and existential aspects of human existence become magnified as death approaches, spiritual care has been an integral part of the hospice movement since its inception. For this reason, hospice clergy have been central to the work of the hospice team in caring for the dying. Clinical observations suggest that hospice clergy have two important roles to play in caring for the terminally ill—spiritual guide to the dying patient and teacher for family members and health care professionals about death and dying. All team members must attend to the physical, social, psychological, and spiritual needs of the patient and family members as death becomes imminent and questions and fears arise. But the chaplain, as a representative of faith and spirituality, must serve as a resource to the patient, family members, and staff.

Gentile and Fello believe that many of the patients to whom hospice chaplains minister have become estranged from formal religious beliefs and practices and hope to reconnect themselves with their spiritual roots. A chaplain with a caring and compassionate nature may, with sensitivity and discretion, facilitate the dying person's exploration of spiritual issues and thus allow the patient to die with greater dignity.

Spiritual Transformation, Faith, and Joy

For many persons, coping with and overcoming a profound crisis of spirit involves faith; that is, the willful suspension of humans' order-seeking, controlling behavior. People simply agree to accept that there is some greater order, purpose, structure, and meaning that is not self-evident in the seeming absurdity of events such as the premature death of a loved one. The exercise of faith and the acceptance of an order beyond one's control does not mean he or she concedes free will or relinquishes the desire to be in control. People achieve their greatest control over the living when they choose to exercise faith. When confronted by a grieving parent whose child has died and who asks, "Why has God done this to me?," there is no satisfactory answer. However, when the mourner has worked through the grieving/mourning process, there may be an emergence of faith and a willingness to accept one's suffering as a part of some greater pattern that escapes the cause-effect logic of his or her scientific worldview.

In fact, having met the challenges of a spiritual crisis, many mourners are able to identify positive, joyful, and triumphant aspects of their mourning experience. Kessler, for example, discovered that many of her subjects regarded the mourning process as liberating: Over half mentioned feeling freed from previously limiting ties. Many subjects in the study felt that they had become stronger and more confident people. Shuchter also found that after two years, the majority of widows and widowers studied were able to regard their spiritual crisis as "growth-promoting." Their experiences enabled them to reflect on their personal values, put things in a new perspective, and appreciate more important things in life. They perceived themselves to be more realistic, patient, sensitive, autonomous, assertive, open, and spiritual in their everyday lives.

In resolving the spiritual crisis, according to Klass, "The person feels his or her life is more authentic, more meaningful, the person's thinking is 'set straight' or true, and his or her actions toward others are right and true" (1995, p. 244). Such insights into leading a meaningful, spiritually based life have been codified in various religious traditions, as in the doctrine of Christianity, the dharma of Hinduism, the Tao of Chinese religion, and the notions of right living, action, and intention embedded in the Buddha's eightfold path to enlightenment.

Conclusion

Research reveals that during periods of profound loss, one's cognitive world may be turned upside down. The assumptions that guided one's life—that life is fair, that people get what they deserve, that God is benevolent, that the old die before the young, and so on—are strained and sometimes shattered. This collapse in beliefs and assumptions about the world and one's place in it has can lead to a spiritual crisis. Whether faced with our own imminent death or in coping with the death of a loved one, we confront the challenge of reconstructing our assumptions about the world.

People have much to learn about spiritual experience, cognitive upheaval, and psychospiritual transformation in the face of death; however, they do know that personal philosophies, religious belief systems, spiritual explorations, and the search for meaning are especially important at such times. Professional and voluntary caregivers are becoming more aware of these spiritual needs and the obstacles that prevent some individuals from fulfilling them.

This new research on dying, mourning, and spirituality suggests that the ways in which people rediscover meaning—such as belief in traditional religious doctrine, the afterlife, reincarnation, philanthropy, or a spiritual order to the universe—may be less important than the process itself. In other words, in the midst of dealing with profound loss in our lives, the ability to re-ascribe meaning to a changed world through spiritual transformation, religious conversion, or existential change may be more significant than the specific content by which that need is filled.

See also: ARS MORIENDI; DYING, PROCESS OF; GOOD DEATH, THE; GRIEF; HOSPICE OPTION; IMMORTALITY; IMMORTALITY, SYMBOLIC; KIERKEGAARD, SØREN

Bibliography

Balk, David. E. "Bereavement and Spiritual Change." *Death Studies* 23, no. 6 (1999):485–494.

Cook, Judith A., and D. A. Wimberley. "If I Should Die Before I Wake: Religious Commitment and Adjustment to the Death of a Child." *Journal for the Scientific Study of Religion* 22 (1983):222–238.

Dershimer, R. A. *Counseling the Bereaved.* New York: Pergamon Press, 1990.

Doka, Kenneth J. *Living with Life-Threatening Illness.* New York: Lexington Press, 1993.

Grof, S., and S. Grof. "Spiritual Emergency: The Understanding and Treatment of Transpersonal Crises." *Revision* 8, no. 2 (1986):7–20.

Horowitz, M. J. *Stress Response Syndromes,* 2nd edition. Northvale, NJ: Jason Aronson, 1986.

Janoff-Bulman, R. "Assumptive Worlds and the Stress of Traumatic Events: Application of the Schema Construct." *Social Cognition* 7 (1989):113–136.

Klass, Dennis. "Spiritual Aspects of the Resolution of Grief." In Hannelore Wass and Robert A. Niemeyer eds., *Dying: Facing the Facts.* Washington, DC: Taylor & Francis, 1995.

Klass, Dennis, and S. Marwit. "Toward a Model of Parental Grief." *Omega: The Journal of Death and Dying* 19, no. 1 (1988–89):31–50.

Mahoney, Michael J., and Gina M. Graci. "The Meanings and Correlates of Spirituality: Suggestions from an Exploratory Survey of Experts." *Death Studies* 23, no. 6 (1999):521–528.

Marrone, Robert. "Dying, Mourning and Spirituality." *Death Studies* 23, no. 6 (1999):495–520.

Marrone, Robert. "Grieving and Mourning: Distinctions in Process." *Illness, Crisis and Loss* 6, no. 2 (1998): 320–333.

Marrone, Robert. *Death, Mourning and Caring.* Pacific Grove, CA: Wadsworth/Thomson International, 1997.

Parkes, Colin M. "Bereavement As a Psychosocial Transition: Processes of Adaptation to Change." *Journal of Social Issues* 44, no. 3 (1988):53–65.

Rando, Therese A. "Grieving and Mourning: Accommodating to Loss." In Hannelore Wass and Robert A. Niemeyer eds., *Dying: Facing the Facts.* Washington, DC: Taylor & Francis, 1995.

Soros, George. "Reflections on Death in America." *Open Society News.* New York: The Soros Foundation, (1995):2–3.

Taylor, S. "Adjustment to Threatening Events: A Theory of Cognitive Adaptation." *American Psychologist* 38 (1983):1161–1173.

Turner, R. P., D. Lukoff, R. T. Barnhouse, and F. G. Lu. "Religion or Spiritual Problem: A Culturally Sensitive Diagnostic Category." *Journal of Nervous and Mental Disease* 183, no. 7 (1995):435–444.

Wheeler, Inese. "Parental Bereavement: The Crisis of Meaning." *Death Studies* 25, no. 1 (2001):51–66

ROBERT L. MARRONE

SPIRITUALISM MOVEMENT

Spiritualism is the belief that the living can communicate with the dead. The belief in a spirit world and the living's ability to correspond with the spiritual realm probably dates to antiquity. Spirit contact is facilitated when an individual is on his or her deathbed. James Crissman notes in his study of the dying process in Central Appalachia that several dying people had contacts, visual and/or auditory, with a friend or relative who had been deceased for many years. Some had encountered biblical characters.

The two greatest premodern spiritualism influences were Emanuel Swedenborg (1688–1722) in Sweden and Andrew Jackson Davis (1826–1910) in America. A well-known scientist and clairvoyant, Swedenborg reported being in constant communication with the spirit world throughout his life. Davis, a clairvoyant, while in a mesmeric (hypnotic) trance, could communicate with the spirit world and accurately diagnose medical disorders. While in a trance he supposedly foresaw the coming of the spiritualist movement.

The modern spiritualism movement began in March 1848 when Catherine and Margaretta Fox, after encountering numerous disturbances in their new home in Hydesville, New York, where they lived with their parents, devised a way of communicating with a spirit via the use of a tapping system. The sisters claimed to have discovered that the spirit causing the problem had been robbed, murdered, and buried in the house several years prior to the date that the Fox family moved into the home. Several neighbors were brought into the house to substantiate the fact that the Fox family had communicated with the dead. The press popularized the actions of the Fox sisters and the sisters capitalized on that popularity by turning their abilities to communicate with the dead into a stage act. They attracted the backing of the showman P. T. Barnum, who took them to New York and made them stars. The Fox sisters enjoyed several years of fame as mediums.

Following the events in Hydesville, spiritualism became a major international social movement. The Hydesville rappings demonstrated organized communication, the natural mediumistic abilities of certain people, and that communication could be enhanced through the use of a code. The major protagonist was a medium, someone capable of communicating with the dead, who served as the intermediary between the individual wishing to converse with the dead and the spirit of the deceased.

The most common form of communication with the spirit world became the séance, which typically took place in a darkened room with participants sitting in a circle holding hands. Occasionally, the medium would be tied to a chair with his or her legs secured, to prevent the use of the extremities to falsely produce ghostly phenomena. The environment of the séance might include sounds of various kinds, the appearance and disappearances of small physical objects, the medium talking in various voices, furniture moving about the room, and a spirit materializing in a temporary physical form.

Other séance effects utilized since 1848 are spirit bells and horns, electronic (flameless) candles, lightning and thunder, animated objects such as books or candles, and spirit photography. Methods of communicating with the spirit world, whether or not there is a séance, have included crystal balls, tarot cards, rapping or tapping a code, mental telepathy, a mesmeric or hypnotic trance, the Ouija board, and automatic writing.

The Hydesville incident led to the establishment of many independent churches and philosophical organizations whose main objective was to advance the ideas of spiritualism. A small group of spiritualists met in the Corinthian Hall in Rochester, New York, on November 14, 1849. As others realized they had psychic powers, the movement grew. The First Spiritual Temple was established by Marcellus Ayer in September 1885. According to Reverend Simeon Stefanidakis, a proponent of spiritualism and author of *About the First Spiritual Temple: Hydesville*: "The Church became an immediate success, with a membership of over 1,000 people" (2001, p. 3).

According to New Age spiritualists, crystals contain healing and energizing powers, in addition to promoting communication with spirits. PHIL SCHERMEISTER/CORBIS

The spiritualism movement made its way to England in 1852 via a Boston medium, Mrs. Hayden. It was very popular during the Victorian and Edwardian historical eras. The scholar Jenny Hazelgrove notes that it was also popular between the two world wars: "It continued to flourish in the interwar period, given a massive boost by the great war, which left many people desperately seeking to contact the spirits of loved ones killed in that conflict" (Hazelgrove 2000, p. ix). It was strengthened in this time period by support from several members of the Anglican Church. By 1900 the spiritualist movement was dying but enjoyed a minor revival during World War I, and by 1920 spiritualism finally lost its momentum, never again receiving the same level of notoriety—despite the fact that numerous well-known individuals such as *Sherlock Holmes* author Sir Arthur Conan Doyle and the well-known scientist Sir Oliver Lodge attempted to influence the spiritualist movement's popularity at the beginning of the twentieth century.

The spiritualist movement naturally drew many critics. First, there were those who did not believe in the continued existence of the spirit, and therefore scoffed at any notion of communicating with what did not exist. Second, many considered talking with spirits to be a form of mental disorder.

Criticisms were strong among members of the medical profession, especially those interested in explaining the human mind. The scholar Alex Owen stated that "the new specialists in insanity were swift to categorize a belief in spiritualism as symptomatic of a diseased mind" (Owen 1989, p. 139). Third, a number of charlatans, whose actions were revealed to be tricks, contributed to the movement's discrediting. This argument was strengthened in 1888 when, in an appearance in New York, Margaretta Fox said that spiritualism was a false science and that she and Catherine had been faking phenomena ever since they had been in practice. Fourth, some people have rejected the idea of communication with the dead because they fear the unknown, which may upset the stability, order, and understanding of the world in which they live. Fifth, numerous men and women rejected spiritualism because of a socialized fear of spirits. Through socialization, people in Western societies, particularly the United States, learn to fear ghosts, goblins, demons, witches, and other members of the spirit world. They avoid cemeteries because ghosts of the dead may prevail and generally believe that morgues and funeral homes are scary places because spirits may still be present.

While some Christians have been able to reconcile their religious convictions with a belief in spiritualism, the most vehement criticisms have come from organized Christian groups. While many of the criticisms mentioned have been expounded by organized religions, most opposition to communicating with the dead comes from passages in the Old and New Testaments of the Bible. Numerous passages—including Exodus 22:18, Leviticus 19:31, Leviticus 20:6, and Deuteronomy 18:10–12—provide warnings that communicating with the spirits of the deceased is wrong and condemned by God. The contention is that communication with the dead is to be done through Jesus Christ, not some self-professed medium. There are strong warnings of false prophecy, the existence of malevolent spirits, necromancy and demonic possession, and engaging in spiritualistic methods that make it easier for the devil (or demons) to gain control of one's mind and body. Several religious figures have argued that spiritualists place God in a secondary or nonexistent position. Finally, several religious groups, especially the Catholic Church, were critical of the important role of women in the spiritualist movement and its strong feminist theme. There was even a belief among some spiritualists in a female or perhaps an androgynous divinity.

There are several organized spiritualist groups in existence. In the United States in the 1990s there were about 600 congregations with a combined membership of more than 210,000 individuals. The largest organizations include the International General Assembly of Spiritualists, headquartered in Ashtabula, Ohio; the National Spiritual Alliance of the USA in Lake Pleasant, Massachusetts; and the National Spiritualists Association of Churches in Lily Dale, New York.

See also: COMMUNICATION WITH THE DEAD; DEATHBED VISIONS AND ESCORTS; GHOSTS

Bibliography

Campbell, John W. "Introduction." *14 Great Tales of ESP,* edited by Idella Purnell Stone. Greenwich, CT: Fawcett Publications, 1969.

Crissman, James K. *Death and Dying in Central Appalachia.* Urbana, Illinois: University of Illinois Press, 1994.

Doyle, Arthur Conan. *The New Revelation.* New York: George H. Doran Company, 1918.

Hazelgrove, Jenny. *Spiritualism and British Society between the Wars.* Manchester, England: Manchester University Press, 2000.

Kollar, Rene. *Searching for Raymond: Anglicanism, Spiritualism, and Bereavement between the Two World Wars.* Lanham, MD: Lexington Books, 2000.

Leming, Michael R., and George E. Dickenson. *Understanding Dying, Death and Bereavement,* 5th edition. Fort Worth, TX: Harcourt, 2002.

Lodge, Sir Oliver. *Why I Believe in Personal Immortality.* London: Cassell and Company, 1928.

Owen, Alex. *The Darkened Room: Women, Power and Spiritualism in Late Victorian England.* London: Virago Press, 1989.

Winter, J. M. "Spiritualism and the First World War." In R. W. Davis and R. J. Helmstadter eds., *Religion and Irreligion in Victorian Society: Essays in Honor of R. K. Webb.* London: Routledge, 2001.

Internet Resources

Setta, Susan M. "Spiritualism." In the World Book Online [web site]. Available from www.aolsvc.worldbook.aol.com/wbol/wbPage/na/ar/co/525640.

"Spiritualism." In the Anomalies [web site]. Available from www.sonic.net/~anomaly/articles/ga00005.shtml.

Stefanidakis, Simeon. "About the First Spiritual Temple: Hydesville." In the First Spiritual Temple [web site]. Available from www.fst.org/spirit4.htm.

"The Story of Spiritualism." In the Newage On-Line Australia [web site]. Available from www.newage.com.au/library/spiritualism.html.

JAMES K. CRISSMAN

STAGE THEORY

The stage theory of dying was first proposed by the Swiss-American psychiatrist, Elisabeth Kübler-Ross in her book, *On Death and Dying* (1969), is perhaps the single theoretical model that is best known to the general public in the entire field of studies about death and dying (thanatology). In its simplest form, this theory claims that dying people will proceed through five stages: denial, anger, bargaining, depression, and acceptance. More broadly, the theory maintains that other individuals who are drawn into a dying person's experiences, such as family members, friends, professional care providers, and volunteer helpers, may also experience similar "stages of adjustment."

Origins of the Theory

Kübler-Ross explained in her book that she was a new faculty member in psychiatry at a Chicago-area teaching hospital in the fall of 1965 when four theological students seeking assistance with a student project approached her. They had been assigned to write about a "crisis in human life" and had chosen to examine death as "the biggest crisis people had to face" (p. 21). In order to tackle this topic, she agreed to help them gain access to and interview some dying patients. According to Kübler-Ross, she encountered unexpected resistance from the physicians and others who were responsible for the patients whom she and her students wanted to interview: "These doctors were both very defensive when it came to talking about death and dying and also protective of their patients in order to avoid a traumatic experience with a yet unknown faculty member who had just joined their ranks. It suddenly seemed that there were no dying patients in this huge hospital" (p. 23).

Eventually, however, some suitable patients were found, and Kübler-Ross developed a procedure whereby she would approach likely candidates, secure their permission, and then interview them about their experiences, while the students and others who came to observe would do so from behind a one-way glass mirror. Following the interviews and the return of the patients to their rooms, the group would discuss the patients' responses and their own reactions.

On Death and Dying is based on interviews with approximately 200 adult patients during a period of less than three years. Examples from the interviews, along with the clinical impressions and the theoretical model that Kübler-Ross formed from these experiences, were subsequently reported in her book.

Stage Theory of Dying Examined

The theoretical model that Kübler-Ross developed from her interviews postulated that with adequate time and support, dying persons experience or work through five stages, including *denial,* often expressed as "No, not me, it cannot be true," is described as an individual's unwillingness to acknowledge or broad rejection of the fact that he or she is actually dying; *anger,* typically expressed as "Why me?," is a protest acknowledging at least in some degree that the individual is dying but simultaneously objecting or complaining that it is not fair or right that it should be happening; *bargaining,* often expressed as "Yes me, but . . . ," is less outraged and more resigned to death while focusing (whether realistically or unrealistically) on what might be done to postpone death or to have it occur at a time or in ways that are more acceptable to the individual; *depression,* which involves a great sense of loss and which can take the form of "reactive depression" (responding to losses the individual has already experienced) or "preparatory depression" (emphasizing impending losses, including the anticipated loss of all love objects); and *acceptance,* described as "almost void of feelings" (p. 113), a "final stage when the end is more promising or there is not enough strength left to live" (p. 176).

A valuable addition to this five-stage theory, which is often overlooked, is the observation that "the one thing that usually persists through all these stages is hope" (p. 138) and the comment that "it is this hope that should always be maintained whether we can agree with the form or not" (p. 265).

Understanding Stage Theory of Dying

Kübler-Ross sought to address a dehumanization and depersonalization that dominated the experiences of the dying persons with whom she came into contact. She believed that dying was often a lonely, impersonal experience for such persons, and thus an unnecessarily difficult burden for them to bear. In fact, Kübler-Ross found that most of her patients feared dying even more than death itself. For those who were isolated in their dying and who felt unable to help themselves or to find reasons to be hopeful, Kübler-Ross offered them a constructive opportunity by asking them to help teach others about their experiences. She was especially concerned that dying persons should share their experiences with and become teachers to their professional caregivers and their family members. At the same time, she asked others not to be judgmental about the reactions dying persons have to their experiences, but to try to enter into their perspectives and understand the origins of those reactions.

The theory that resulted was essentially an effort "to categorize crudely the many experiences that patients have when they are faced with the sudden awareness of their own finality" (p. 29). The "stages" within that theory were themselves understood by Kübler-Ross as "reactions," "defenses" or "defense mechanisms," "coping mechanisms," and "adaptations and defenses." At one point, Kübler-Ross wrote that these stages "will last for different periods of time and will replace each other or exist at times side by side" (p. 138), while in another place she stated, "these stages do not replace each other but can exist next to each other and overlap at times" (p. 263). The stages are, in other words, a fairly loose collection of psychosocial reactions to experiences associated with dying. As such, they remind us that dying is a human process, not merely a series of biological events. Also as such, they are not confined solely to dying persons, but may be experienced by others who enter into the worlds of those who are dying.

As initially proposed, the five stages in this theory were described in very broad terms. Denial and acceptance, for example, were presented as essentially mirror opposites, with the other three stages functioning mainly as transitional reactions experienced while moving from denial to acceptance. Both denial and acceptance were formulated in ways that permitted them to apply to a spectrum of reactions: from a complete rejection of one's status as an ill or seriously ill person to an unwillingness to admit that one is dying or that one's death is more or less imminent; and from acknowledgement, resignation, and acquiescence to welcoming.

Of denial, Kübler-Ross wrote, "Denial, at least partial denial, is used by almost all patients, not only during the first stages of illness or following confrontation, but also later on from time to time" (p. 39). More importantly, she added this further comment about denial: "I regard it [as] a healthy way of dealing with the uncomfortable and painful situation with which some of these patients have to live for a long time. Denial functions as a buffer after unexpected shocking news, allows the patient to collect himself and, with time, mobilize other, less radical defenses" (p. 39). Not everyone who took up this theory viewed denial in this constructive way.

Like denial and acceptance, anger, bargaining, and depression as the other stages in this theory were said to vary in their intensity, character, and focus. Individuals will differ, for example, in whether or not they experience anger, what arouses their anger, the object(s) on which it fixes, its degree, whether it is rational or irrational, and how it is expressed. One troubling feature of anger is that it is said to be "displaced in all directions and projected onto the environment at times almost at random" (p. 50).

As for bargaining, this reaction seems to reflect a view that one can postpone death or manipulate one's experiences of dying usually through more or less explicit promises involving a prize and some deadline: "I will faithfully follow the prescribed regimen you prescribe, if it will only ward off my death"; "I will pray each day, if you will preserve me from this awful fate"; "I need to stay alive until my son is married." Promises are usually addressed to presumed authorities, such as God or a physician, but Kübler-Ross noted, "none of our patients have 'kept their promise'" (p. 84).

Criticisms of the Stage Theory of Dying

There are essentially three distinct types of criticisms that have been raised against the stage theory of dying. First, some commentators have noted that empirical research has provided no support for this model. Kübler-Ross herself offered nothing beyond the authority of her clinical impressions and illustrations from selected examples to sustain this theory in its initial appearance. Since the publication of her book in 1969, she has advanced no further evidence on its behalf, although she has continued to speak of it enthusiastically and unhesitatingly as if its reliability were obvious. More significantly, there has been no independent confirmation of the validity or reliability of the theory, and the limited empirical research that is available does not confirm her model.

Second, the five sets of psychosocial reactions that are at the heart of this theory can be criticized as overly broad in their formulation, potentially misleading in at least one instance, insufficient to reflect the full range of human reactions to death and dying, and inadequately grounded for the broad ways in which they have been used. The expansive way in which these five reactions are formulated has already been noted. Kübler-Ross did not, of course, invent these five reaction patterns; her inspiration was to apply them individually to the human experiences of dying and facing death, and to link them together as part of a larger theoretical schema. Among its peers, the trait of depression seems most curious as an element in a healthy, normative process of reacting to dying—unless it really means "sadness"—since clinical depression is a psychiatric diagnosis of illness. Moreover, just as Kübler-Ross seems sometimes to acknowledge that a particular individual need not experience all five of these reactions, so one need not believe there are only five ways in which to react to dying and death. Finally, Kübler-Ross has applied this theory to children and to bereavement in ways that are not warranted by its original foundations in interviews with dying adults.

Third, the theory can be criticized for linking its five reaction patterns together as stages in a larger process. To a certain extent Kübler-Ross seems to have agreed with this point since she argued for fluidity, give and take, the possibility of experiencing more than one of these reactions simultaneously, and an ability to jump around from one "stage" to another. If that is true, then this is not really a theory of stages, which would require a linear progression and regression akin to the steps on a ladder or the calibrations on a thermometer or a hydraulic depth gauge. In short, the language of "stages" may simply be too restrictive and overly specific for what essentially appear to be a cluster of different psychodynamic reactions to a particular type of life experience.

This last point is particularly important because if this theory has been misused in some ways, its most unfortunate mishandling has come from those who tell dying persons that they have already experienced one of the five stages and should now "move on" to another, or from those who have become frustrated and complain about individuals whom they view as "stuck" in the dying process. When coupled with the limits of five categories of reaction to dying, this schematic approach tends to suppress the individuality of dying persons (and others) by coercing them into a rigid, preestablished framework in which they are expected to live out an agenda imposed on them at the end of their lives. That is particularly ironic and unfortunate since Kübler-Ross set out to argue that dying persons are mistreated when they are objectified and dealt with in stereotypical ways. As she insisted, "a patient has a right to die in peace and dignity. He should not be used to fulfill our own needs when his own wishes are in opposition to ours" (p. 177).

One serious evaluation of this stage theory of dying by Robert Kastenbaum raised the following points:

- The existence of these stages as such has not been demonstrated.
- No evidence has been presented that people actually do move from stage one through stage five.
- The limitations of the method have not been acknowledged.
- The line is blurred between description and prescription.
- The totality of the person's life is neglected in favor of the supposed stages of dying.
- The resources, pressures, and characteristics of the immediate environment, which can make a tremendous difference, are not taken into account.

As a result, what has appeared to be widespread acclaim for this theory in the popular arena and in certain professional quarters contrasts with sharp criticism from scholars and those who work with dying persons.

What Can Be Learned from Stage Theory of Dying?

Charles Corr has suggested that there are at least three important lessons to be learned from the stage theory of dying. The first lesson is that those who are coping with dying are living human beings who will react in their own individual ways to the unique challenges that confront them and who may have unfinished needs that they want to address. The second lesson is that others cannot be or become effective providers of care unless they listen actively to those who are coping with dying and work with them to determine the psychosocial processes and needs of such persons. And the third lesson, a point that Kübler-Ross always stressed, is that all individuals need to learn from those who are dying and coping with dying in order to come to know themselves better as limited, vulnerable, finite, and mortal, but also as resilient, adaptable, interdependent, and worthy of love.

Reflecting at least in part on the stage theory of dying, some writers have called for broader task-based or contextual theories of dying that would strive to offer more respect for the individuality and complexities of the many different ways in which persons live out their experiences of dying and of coping with dying. Various contributions have been made toward developing such broader theoretical frameworks, some emerging from lessons learned in reflecting on the stage theory of dying, but no final theory has yet been developed.

See also: DYING, PROCESS OF; KÜBLER-ROSS, ELISABETH; LESSONS FROM THE DYING

Bibliography

Coolican, Margaret B., June Stark, Kenneth J. Doka, and Charles A. Corr. "Education about Death, Dying, and Bereavement in Nursing Programs." *Nurse Educator* 19, no. 6 (1994):1–6.

Corr, Charles A. "Coping with Dying: Lessons That We Should and Should Not Learn from the Work of Elisabeth Kübler-Ross." *Death Studies* 17 (1993):69–83.

Corr, Charles A. "A Task-Based Approach to Coping with Dying." *Omega: The Journal of Death and Dying* 24 (1992):81–94.

Corr, Charles A., and Kenneth J. Doka. "Current Models of Death, Dying, and Bereavement." *Critical Care Nursing Clinics of North America* 6 (1994):545–552.

Corr, Charles A., Kenneth J. Doka, and Robert Kastenbaum. "Dying and Its Interpreters: A Review of Selected Literature and Some Comments on the State of the Field." *Omega: The Journal of Death and Dying* 39 (1999):239–259.

Doka, Kenneth J. *Living with Life-Threatening Illness.* Lexington, MA: Lexington Books, 1993.

Kastenbaum, Robert. *Death, Society, and Human Experience,* 6th edition. Boston: Allyn & Bacon, 1998.

Kastenbaum, Robert, and Sharon Thuell. "Cookies Baking, Coffee Brewing: Toward a Contextual Theory of Dying." *Omega: The Journal of Death and Dying* 31 (1995):175–187.

Klass, Dennis. "Elisabeth Kübler-Ross and the Tradition of the Private Sphere: An Analysis of Symbols." *Omega: The Journal of Death and Dying* 12 (1982):241–261.

Klass, Dennis, and Richard A. Hutch. "Elisabeth Kübler-Ross As a Religious Leader." *Omega: The Journal of Death and Dying* 16 (1985):89–109.

Kübler-Ross, Elisabeth. *The Wheel of Life: A Memoir of Living and Dying.* New York: Scribner, 1997.

Kübler-Ross, Elisabeth. *On Children and Death.* New York: Macmillan, 1983.

Kübler-Ross, Elisabeth. *On Death and Dying.* New York: Macmillan, 1969.

Metzger, Anne M. "A Q-Methodological Study of the Kübler-Ross Stage Theory." *Omega: The Journal of Death and Dying* 10 (1980):291–301.

Pattison, E. Mansell. *The Experience of Dying.* Englewood Cliffs, NJ: Prentice-Hall, 1977.

Schulz, Richard, and David Aderman. "Clinical Research and the Stages of Dying." *Omega: The Journal of Death and Dying* 5 (1974):137–143.

Shneidman, Edwin S. *Voices of Death.* New York: Harper and Row/Kodansha International, 1995.

Weisman, Avery D. *The Coping Capacity: On the Nature of Being Mortal.* New York: Human Sciences Press, 1984.

Weisman, Avery D. *On Dying and Denying: A Psychiatric Study of Terminality.* New York: Behavioral Publications, 1972.

CHARLES A. CORR
DONNA M. CORR

STROKE

As the third major cause of death and disability in America and the leading neurological disorder for morbidity, stroke is a major public health problem.

The incidence of strokes is predicted to become worse as the percentage of the aging population, which is predominantly affected, increases. Stroke (or "brain attack") is defined as an acute neurological dysfunction, usually focal in nature, which can be explained by either occlusion of a feeding artery to the brain or the rupture of such a vessel.

Ischemic strokes result from blood clots that originate from more proximal arteries to the brain such as the carotid bifurcation in the neck or even from the heart. The neurological deficits with ischemic strokes depend upon several factors—one being the size of the clot. With large clots, larger arteries with a larger area of brain to feed will be affected, leading to greater neurological impairment. Second, the specific vessel(s) is occluded. If the artery to the speech area is occluded, the patient will be unable to talk, so-called aphasia; or if the artery to the area controlling arm and leg movements is occluded, the patient will become paralyzed on the opposite side. Third is the rapidity of artery occlusion. The cause of clot or thrombus formation is most commonly due to atherosclerotic disease or hardening of the arteries, but other conditions exist that make the blood clot, such as abnormal conditions causing the blood to be very sticky, or what is termed prothrombotic states. With vessel rupture, the two most common conditions are aneurysms, which lie primarily in the subarachnoid space surrounding the brain, and intracerebal hemorrhages, which most commonly result from longstanding uncontrolled hypertension. Other conditions associated with vessel rupture include abnormal formation of arteries and veins.

Strokes, like heart attacks, are most commonly caused by atherosclerosis or hardening of the arteries. The major risk factors for atherosclerosis are high blood pressure (hypertension), smoking, diabetes mellitus, increased lipids (hypercholesterolemia and hypertriglyceridemia), stress, sedentary lifestyle, and obesity. These risk factors are mostly treatable, and therefore greater public health programs to educate the general public are generally viewed by health care practitioners as a partial solution to the problem. Risk factors for less common hereditary conditions predisposing to vascular, cardiac, and thrombotic disorders that result in strokes require preventive intervention as well, with the most common treatment being the thinning of blood (also known as "anticoagulation"). Use of DNA analytical techniques to identify as a yet unknown combination of gene defects leading to strokes as well as a large number of proteins, which also in combination can lead to strokes, an area called proteomics promise to identify stroke-risk predisposition more precisely and at an earlier age.

In addition to knowing one's stroke risk factors, individuals should be aware of stroke symptoms so that urgent workup and appropriate treatment can be instituted, possibly reversing neurological deficits. For example, use of the thrombolytic agent (clot buster) tissue plasminogen activator (tPA) has been proven to be the first statistically significant drug to reverse the effects of a thrombus or embolus causing stroke symptoms. But because this treatment must be instituted within three hours of stroke onset, this short timeframe means that the public, the emergency services, and treating physicians must develop a rapidly responding medical system that can triage and treat patients quickly. Other stroke syndromes that can benefit from therapeutic intervention include intracerebral hemorrhages (bleeding) with surgical evacuation of the clot, particularly cerebellar hemorrhages, and subarachnoid hemorrhages due to berry aneurysms with surgical or interventional ablation of the aneurysm. Embolic strokes, especially from cardiac sources, such as rhythm abnormalities, particularly atrial fibrillation, are prone to cause embolic strokes, and these can be prevented with anticoagulation.

See also: CAUSES OF DEATH

Bibliography

Barnett, Henry J. M., Jay P. Mohr, Bennett Stein, and Frank M. Yatsu eds. *Strokes: Pathophysiology, Diagnosis, and Management,* 3rd edition. Philadelphia: W. B. Saunders, 1998.

FRANK M. YATSU

SUDDEN INFANT DEATH SYNDROME

In typical cases of sudden infant death syndrome (SIDS), an infant between the ages of two to four months is found dead with no warning, frequently during a period of sleep. Because the typical victims are previously healthy infants with no record of any serious medical problems, their sudden death is all the more shocking and devastating. Some have said that this type of death is "a cosmic slap in the face" to parents, grandparents, other adults, and siblings who had previously delighted in the child's birth and growth, and plans for his or her future.

Definition

Sudden infant death syndrome—called "SIDS" by many professionals, but also termed "crib death" in the United States or "cot death" in some other English-speaking countries—is "the sudden death of an infant under one year of age which remains unexplained after a thorough case investigation, including performance of a complete autopsy, examination of the death scene, and review of the clinical history" (Willinger, James, and Catz 1991, p. 681).

Three aspects of this definition are worth noting. First, an accurate diagnosis of this syndrome requires a thorough investigation, including an autopsy (preferably performed by a medical examiner or forensic pathologist who is experienced in diagnosing infant deaths), along with a careful examination of the history and circumstances behind the death (including interviews of parents and others involved in the care of the infant, collection of items from the scene of death, and meticulous evaluation of all of the information obtained). Hasty or incomplete diagnoses can sometimes confuse SIDS with deaths resulting from child abuse or other causes. Such errors can compound burdens placed upon parents and other survivors of SIDS if they are wrongly accused of child abuse, just as they may cloak abusive situations under the more benign diagnosis of SIDS.

Second, a diagnosis of SIDS is essentially an exclusionary diagnosis, one that is made by ruling out all other possible causes and then recognizing the distinctive patterns of this cluster of events. A "syndrome" is precisely a familiar constellation of events arising from an unknown cause. Third, although no definitive diagnostic indicators unmistakably identify recognized abnormalities in SIDS that are sufficient to cause death, there nevertheless are some biological, clinical, and historical or circumstantial markers commonly found in this syndrome. These common but not universal markers include:

- tiny red or purple spots (minute hemorrhages or petechiae) on the surface of the infant's heart, in its lungs, and in its thymus;
- an increased number of star-shaped cells in its brain stem (brain-stem gliosis);
- clinical suggestions of apnea or pauses in breathing and an inability to return to normal breathing patterns; and/or
- circumstantial facts such as a peak incidence of SIDS at two to four months of age, which declines to almost nonoccurrence beyond one year of age.

Markers such as these, when identified by a competent, thorough, and experienced physician, justify recognizing SIDS as an official medical diagnosis of death.

Incidence

During most of the 1980s, SIDS accounted for the deaths of approximately 5,000 to 6,000 infants per year in the United States. From 1988 to 1999, however, SIDS rates fell by more than 52 percent in the United States, and the number of SIDS deaths declined to 2,648 in 1999.

In terms of the overall number of live births each year, SIDS is the leading cause of death in the United States among infants between one month and one year of age. For all infants less than one year of age, SIDS is the third-leading cause of death, following only congenital anomalies and short gestation/low birthweight.

Researchers have drawn attention to other aspects of the incidence of SIDS deaths, but those variables have not yet been sufficient to establish differential diagnoses, screening procedures, or preventive measures for SIDS. In fact, SIDS is a sudden and silent killer, often associated with sleep, but apparently involving no suffering. Characteristically, SIDS deaths show a pronounced peak during the colder months of the year: January through March in the United States or six months later in the southern hemisphere. Epidemiological studies suggest that SIDS is somehow associated with a detrimental prenatal environment, but infants who are at risk for SIDS cannot be distinguished from those who are at risk for many other health problems. In general, at-risk infants include those with low birthweight or low weight gain and those whose mothers are less than twenty years of age, were anemic, had poor prenatal care, smoked cigarettes or used illegal drugs during pregnancy, and had a history of sexually transmitted disease or urinary tract infection. But none of these factors is sufficient in predicting how, when, why, or if SIDS will occur.

In terms of social, racial, or other categories, SIDS appears in families from all social groups. Approximately 60 percent of all SIDS deaths are those of male infants. The largest number of SIDS deaths (approximately 70%) occurs in infants between two and four months of age, with most SIDS deaths (approximately 90%) taking place by six months of age.

The "Back to Sleep Campaign"

In the early 1990s research suggested that infants might be at less risk for SIDS if they were laid to sleep on their backs (supine) or sides rather than on their stomachs (prone). That idea ran contrary to familiar advice that favored infants sleeping prone in order to reduce the risk that they might regurgitate or spit up fluids, aspirate them into their airway, and suffocate. Some health care professionals and family members still seem to believe that prone sleeping is best for an infant, but the new research suggested that infants who sleep on their stomachs are at far greater risk of SIDS than they are of other problems.

Accordingly, in April 1992, the American Academy of Pediatrics (AAP) Task Force on Infant Sleep Position concluded it was likely that infants who sleep on their backs and sides are at least risk for SIDS when all other circumstances are favorable (e.g., when sleeping on a firm mattress without overheating, loose bed covers, or soft toys nearby). As a result, the AAP recommended that "healthy infants, when being put down for sleep, be positioned on their side or back."

In June 1994 a national "Back to Sleep Campaign" was initiated in the United States. A joint effort of the U.S. Public Health Service, the AAP, the SIDS Alliance, and the Association of SIDS and Infant Mortality Programs, the campaign seeks to employ literature, the media, and other avenues to raise professional and public awareness about the importance of sleep positioning as a way to reduce SIDS. SIDS Resources, Inc., in Missouri, provided one local example of how this campaign can be implemented in a simple but effective way by developing and distributing to new mothers tiny T-shirts for infants with the legend on the front of their shirt, "THIS SIDE UP . . . while sleeping."

Subsequently, the AAP revised and strengthened its recommendation by emphasizing that positioning infants on their backs is the preferred position for their sleep at night and during naps. The AAP acknowledged that it is acceptable to allow infants to sleep on their sides because that is significantly better for them than sleeping on their stomachs, but side sleeping without proper support is a less stable position for an infant and thus not as desirable as back sleeping.

Dramatic and sustained reductions in SIDS deaths in the United States and many other countries are associated with initiatives like the "Back to Sleep Campaign." Unfortunately, they have not applied equally to all racial and cultural groups in America. For example, it has been noted that African-American mothers are "still significantly more likely to place their infants prone" (Willinger, et al. 1998, p. 332). This reluctance to place infants on their backs for sleep appears to be directly correlated with less significant declines in SIDS death rates among African-American infants than among infants in other groups in American society.

Research

Research on SIDS is extraordinarily difficult, facing many problems that have long frustrated scientific investigators. For example, in SIDS there are no living patients to study because the first symptom of SIDS is a dead baby. In addition, risk factors for SIDS are not strong or specific enough to permit identification of high-risk groups as subsets of the general infant population in which the natural history of a disease can be followed with smaller numbers of subjects. And there are no naturally occurring animal models for SIDS. As a result, SIDS is currently unpredictable and unpreventable, although it is possible to modify some risk factors for SIDS deaths.

Most researchers now believe that babies who die of SIDS are born with one or more conditions

It's enough to make any parent lose sleep.
SUDDEN INFANT DEATH SYNDROME, or SIDS, claims the lives of nearly 6,000 infants in the United States every year. In fact, SIDS is the leading cause of death in infants one month to one year old.
But you can help reduce the risk of your baby's dying from SIDS simply by placing it on its back or side to sleep.
Talk to your doctor about SIDS and how you can help reduce the risk. For more information, write Back to Sleep, P.O. Box 29111, Washington, D.C. 20040, or call, toll-free:
1-800-505-CRIB
National Heart, Lung, and Blood Institute
National Institute of Child Health and Human Development
U.S. Public Health Service
American Academy of Pediatrics
SIDS Alliance
Association of SIDS Program Professionals

This poster informs the public about SIDS, the leading cause of death in the United States for infants between one month and one year of age, and offers information on its prevention. MICHAEL NEWMAN/PHOTOEDIT

that make them especially vulnerable to stresses that occur in the normal developmental life of an infant, including both internal and external influences. The leading hypothesis for study is delayed development of arousal, cardiorespiratory control, or cardiovascular control.

Meanwhile, research based on epidemiology and pathology has dispelled numerous misleading and harmful myths about SIDS (e.g., it is not contagious and does not run in families) and has also ruled out many factors that have been thought at various times to be the causes of SIDS. For instance, it is known that SIDS is not the result of child abuse. Likewise, SIDS is not caused by vomiting and choking, minor illnesses such as colds or infections, or immunizations such as those involved in DPT (diphtheria, pertussis, and tetanus) vaccines. Nor is SIDS the cause of every sudden infant death.

Bereavement

Any sudden, unexpected death threatens one's sense of safety and security because it forces one to confront one's own mortality. This is particularly true in an infant death because the death of a very young child seems an especially cruel disruption of the natural order: It seems inconceivable to most people, especially to new parents, that children should suddenly die for no apparent reason. The lack of a discernible cause, the suddenness of the tragedy, and the involvement of the legal system also help to make a SIDS death especially difficult for all those it touches, leaving a great sense of loss and a need for understanding.

As a result, in addition to tasks that all bereaved persons face in coping with grievous personal loss, those who have lost a child to SIDS face additional challenges. No postdeath intervention can be expected simply to dismiss such difficult challenges. However, classification of an infant's death as an instance of SIDS—naming it as an occurrence of a recognizable syndrome—may help provide some partial framework for understanding. This diagnosis can also go a long way toward easing the unwarranted guilt of survivors who might mistakenly imagine that they had somehow contributed to the death or that they could have done something to prevent it. SIDS survivors, especially parents and grandparents, are likely to require much information about the syndrome and extended support in their bereavement. Contact with others who have experienced a similar death may be particularly useful. Explaining the death to a surviving child or subsequent sibling will demand empathy and skill.

Education and Support

There is a great need at many levels in society for SIDS education and support. First responders (i.e., emergency medical personnel, dispatchers, police officers, and firefighters), day-care providers, funeral directors, and the clergy need to understand the differences between their clinical, legal, and human tasks. They must also recognize the different priorities that pertain to preventive tasks on the one hand and to emergency or follow-up tasks on the other. Counselors of all kinds must appreciate that those who are bereaved by SIDS are likely to have distinctive needs for information both about SIDS and about their own grief reactions and coping processes. For example, counselors will want to know how to validate the experiences of SIDS survivors, enable them to obtain access to medical resources, and introduce them to other SIDS survivors. Further, counselors will want to help those affected by SIDS to be patient with others experiencing their own unique bereavement from the same loss, and to assist them in moving on. Adult survivors may need help in explaining SIDS losses and grief reactions to siblings and other children, and in addressing questions related to a possible subsequent pregnancy. SIDS support groups and bereavement-support groups in other settings (e.g., a church or hospice program) may need guidance in meeting the special needs of those touched by SIDS.

See also: GRIEF: CHILD'S DEATH, FAMILY; MORTALITY, INFANT

Bibliography

American Academy of Pediatrics. Committee on Child Abuse and Neglect. "Distinguishing Sudden Infant Death Syndrome from Child Abuse Fatalities." *Pediatrics* 107 (2001):437–441.

American Academy of Pediatrics. Task Force on Infant Sleep Position and Sudden Infant Death Syndrome. "Changing Concepts of Sudden Infant Death Syndrome: Implications of Infant Sleeping Environment and Sleep Position." *Pediatrics* 105 (2000):650–656.

American Academy of Pediatrics. Task Force on Infant Positioning and SIDS. "Positioning and Sudden Infant Death Syndrome (SIDS): Update." *Pediatrics* 98 (1996):1216–1218.

American Academy of Pediatrics. Task Force on Infant Positioning and SIDS. "Positioning and SIDS." *Pediatrics* 89 (1992):1120–1126.

Carolan, Patrick L., and Kathleen L. Fernbach. "SIDS and Infant Sleep Positioning: What We Know, What Parents Need to Know." *Topics in Pediatrics* 12, no. 3 (1994):15–17.

Corr, Charles A., Helen Fuller, Carol A. Barnickol, and Donna M. Corr, eds. *Sudden Infant Death Syndrome: Who Can Help and How.* New York: Springer, 1991.

Dwyer, Terence, Anne-Louis Ponsonby, Leigh Blizzard, et al. "The Contribution of Changes in the Prevalence of Prone Sleeping Position to the Decline in Sudden Infant Death Syndrome in Tasmania." *Journal of the American Medical Association* 273 (1995):783–789.

Fuller, Helen, Carol A. Barnickol, and Teresa R. Mullins. "Guidelines for Counseling." In Charles A. Corr, Helen Fuller, Carol A. Barnickol, and Donna M. Corr, eds., *Sudden Infant Death Syndrome: Who Can Help and How.* New York: Springer, 1991.

Guist, Connie, and Judy E. Larsen. "Guidelines for Emergency Responders." In Charles A. Corr, Helen Fuller, Carol A. Barnickol, and Donna M. Corr, eds. *Sudden Infant Death Syndrome: Who Can Help and How.* New York: Springer, 1991.

Hillman, Laura S. "Theories and Research." In Charles A. Corr, Helen Fuller, Carol A. Barnickol, and Donna M. Corr, eds. *Sudden Infant Death Syndrome: Who Can Help and How.* New York: Springer, 1991.

Hoyert, Donna L., Elizabeth Arias, Betty L. Smith, et al. "Deaths: Final Data for 1999." *National Vital Statistics Reports* 49(8). Hyattsville, MD: National Center for Health Statistics, 2001.

Willinger, Marian. "Sleep Position and Sudden Infant Death Syndrome." *Journal of the American Medical Association* 273 (1995):818–819.

Willinger, Marian, Howard J. Hoffman, Kuo-Tsung Wu, et al. "Factors Associated with the Transition to Nonprone Sleep Positions of Infants in the United States: The National Infant Sleep Position Study." *Journal of the American Medical Association* 280 (1998):329–335.

Willinger, Marian, L. Stanley James, and Charlotte Catz. "Defining the Sudden Infant Death Syndrome (SIDS): Deliberations of an Expert Panel Convened by the National Institute of Child Health and Human Development." *Pediatric Pathology* 11 (1991):677–684.

CHARLES A. CORR
DONNA M. CORR

SUDDEN UNEXPECTED NOCTURNAL DEATH SYNDROME

Since 1977 more than a hundred Southeast Asian immigrants in the United States have died from the mysterious disorder known as sudden unexpected nocturnal death syndrome (SUNDS). SUNDS had an unusually high incidence among recently relocated Laotian Hmong refugees. All but one of the victims were men, the median age was thirty-three, all were apparently healthy, and all died during their sleep. Despite numerous studies of SUNDS, which have taken into account such varied factors as toxicology, heart disease, sleep apnea and other sleep disorders, genetics, metabolism, and nutrition, medical scientists have not been able to determine its exact cause. Medical opinion appears to favor an impairment of the electrical pathways and specialized muscle fibers that contract the heart. It is widely held, however, that some type of intense stressor is likely an additional risk factor.

The medical folklorist Shelley Adler postulates that a supernormal nocturnal experience that is part of Hmong traditional beliefs can trigger the fatal syndrome. The experience is referred to as a "nightmare," not in the modern sense of a bad dream, but rather in its original denotation as the nocturnal visit of an evil being that threatens to press the very life out of its terrified victim. Hmong refugees in the United States experience a culture-specific manifestation of the universal nightmare phenomenon. The Hmong Nightmare (known as *dab tsog*) causes cataclysmic psychological stress, which can trigger sudden death. Although the Dab Tsog attack in Laos is related to the worldwide nightmare tradition, the peculiar stresses of Hmong refugee experience transformed its outcome. The power of traditional belief in the nightmare—in the context of the trauma of war, migration, rapid acculturation, and inability to practice traditional healing and ritual—causes cataclysmic psychological stress to male Hmong refugees that can result in SUNDS.

See also: CAUSES OF DEATH

Bibliography

Adler, Shelley R. "Ethnomedical Pathogenesis and Hmong Immigrants' Sudden Nocturnal Deaths." *Culture, Medicine and Psychiatry* 18 (1994):23–59.

Hufford, David J. *The Terror That Comes in the Night.* Philadelphia: University of Pennsylvania Press, 1982.

Parrish, R. Gibson, Myra Tucker, Roy Ing, Carol Encarnacion, and Mark Eberhardt. "Sudden Unexplained Death Syndrome in Southeast Asian Refugees: A Review of CDC Surveillance." *Morbidity and Mortality Weekly Review* 36 (1987):43–53.

SHELLEY R. ADLER

SUICIDE

Suicide exists in all countries of the world and there are records of suicides dating back to the earliest historical records of humankind. In 2000 the World Health Organization estimated that approximately 1 million people commit suicide annually. Suicide is among the top ten causes of death and one of the three leading causes in the fifteen-to-thirty-five-years age group worldwide. In the United States, where suicide is the ninth leading cause of death (and where the number of victims is 50% higher than the number of homicides), the Surgeon General in 1999 issued a *Call to Action to Prevent Suicide,* labeling suicide "a significant public health problem."

Suicide is a tragic phenomenon that has preoccupied professionals from a variety of disciplines. Deaths by suicide have broad psychological and social impacts on families and societies throughout the world. On average, each suicide intimately affects at least six other people, and if the suicide occurs in the school or workplace it can significantly impact hundreds. Suicide's toll on the living has been estimated by the World Health Organization in terms of disability-adjusted life years, which indicates the number of healthy years of life lost to an illness or event. According to their calculations, the burden of suicide is equal to the burden of all wars and homicides throughout the world. Despite progress in controlling many other causes of death, suicide has been on the rise—becoming one of the leading causes of death.

The taking of one's own life is the result of a complex interaction of psychological, sociological, environmental, genetic, and biological risk factors. Suicide is neither a disease nor the result of a disease or illness, but rather a desperate act by people who feel that ending their life is the only way to stop their interminable and intolerable suffering.

Despite the magnitude of social damage caused by suicide, it is a fairly rare event. Suicide rates of between 15 to 25 deaths per 100,000 population each year may be considered high. Most people who are seriously suicidal, even those who attempt suicide, rarely have a fatal outcome (although, in the United States, 500,000 people annually require emergency room treatment because of their attempts). For each completed suicide (a suicide that results in death) there are at least six or seven suicide attempts that result in hospitalizations and, according to community surveys, for each completed suicide at least 100 people report that they attempted suicide without being hospitalized as a suicide attempter. Furthermore, if one asks in a community survey if people seriously considered suicide, about one person in twenty-five says that they have done so.

Research shows that the vast majority, at least 80 percent, of persons who died by suicide had been or could be diagnosed as suffering from a mental disorder, usually mood disorders and depression. People who suffer from the mental disorders of depression and manic depression, alcoholism, or schizophrenia have between a 4 percent and 15 percent lifetime risk of suicide. These mental disorders do not "cause" suicide, but people with mental disorders are at much greater risk of committing suicide. For this reason, the diagnosis and treatment of mood disorders, alcoholism, and schizophrenia may prevent suicides.

Besides mental disorders, there are numerous other risk factors that help identify who is at greater risk of suicide. The most important risk factor is gender, with men in Europe and the Americas committing suicide about five times more than women even though women are more likely to attempt suicide. People with some physical illnesses have greater suicide risks. In most countries, men over the age of seventy-five have the greatest risk of suicide of all age groups. Those who live alone or are separated are more vulnerable to suicide, including divorced, widowed, and single people. Also at higher risk are individuals who have lost a job.

Various situational factors also increase the risk of suicide. Individuals who are exposed to suicide in real life or through the media have a higher likelihood of suicidal behavior. Research on firearms and the availability of other means of suicide has shown that if a method is readily available a death by suicide is more likely to occur. For this reason control of firearms and reducing access to other preferred means of suicide, such as putting up barriers on bridges and getting rid of medications in the home of a suicidal adolescent, may help prevent suicides.

The crisis situation in which a person attempts or commits suicide is often precipitated by a stressful life event. Suicides are more likely to occur after an argument with family members or lovers following rejection or separation, financial loss and bereavement, job loss, retirement, or failure at school. Usually these events are "the last straw" for a suicidal person. They are generally not what caused the suicide but what resulted in an increased likelihood that the suicide would occur then.

People who consider suicide generally feel ambivalent about ending their own life. It is this ambivalence that leads desperately suicidal people to talk about their plans as they "cry for help." Telephone help lines, therapists, and friends strengthen the will to live of ambivalent people by helping them explore other options for changing their situation.

The psychoanalyst Edwin Shneidman described the mental state of suicidal individuals experiencing unendurable psychological pain and feelings of frustration. According to Shneidman, suicide is seen as the only solution to their problems, one that results in stopping intolerable feelings. Besides feeling ambivalent, suicide-prone individuals tend to have what he calls "constriction"—rigid and persistent preoccupations with suicide as the solution to their problems. These individuals believe that the drastic option of ending their own life by suicide is the only way out unless others help break this pattern of constricted thought.

Many countries, including the United States, have created national suicide prevention programs that utilize a variety of strategies. These programs involve a variety of actions. Some prevention methods begin very early, teaching young children ages five to seven how to better cope with everyday problems. Other programs focus on teaching high school students how to better recognize signs of suicide in friends and how to obtain help. Actions also focus upon educating "gatekeepers," such as physicians, counselors, and teachers, who may come into contact with suicidal persons. The World Health Organization publishes resources on preventing suicide in its web site (www.who.org), and Befrienders International has extensive information on suicide and its prevention available in several languages at www.befrienders.org.

See also: SUICIDE BASICS; SUICIDE INFLUENCES AND FACTORS; SUICIDE OVER THE LIFE SPAN; SUICIDE TYPES

Bibliography

Hawton, Keith, and Kees van Heeringen, eds. *The International Handbook of Suicide and Attempted Suicide.* New York: John Wiley and Sons, 2000.

Phillips, David P. "The Werther Effect: Suicide and Other Forms of Violence are Contagious." *Sciences* 25 (1985):32–39.

Shneidman, Edwin. *Suicide As Psychache: A Clinical Approach to Self-Destructive Behavior.* Northvale, NJ: Jason Aronson, 1993.

World Health Organization. *World Health Statistics Annual, 1995.* Geneva: Author, 1996.

BRIAN L. MISHARA

SUICIDE BASICS

EPIDEMIOLOGY *Danielle Saint-Laurent*

HISTORY *Norman L. Farberow*

PREVENTION *Brian L. Mishara*

WARNING SIGNS AND PREDICTIONS *Brian L. Mishara*

EPIDEMIOLOGY

Suicide, voluntarily taking one's own life, occurs in every country in the world. In Western societies, suicide is recognized as a leading cause of early death, a major public health problem, and a tragedy for individuals and families.

Epidemiology of Suicide

According to the World Health Organization (WHO) in 1999, suicide is among the top ten causes of death for all age groups in North America and the majority of northern and western European countries; it represents 1 to 2 percent of total mortality. Analysis of the mortality figures (see Tables 1 and 2) reveals important differences in the mortality rate between various countries and age groups.

The suicide rate in industrialized countries has increased since the beginning of the twentieth century and reached very high levels in many European countries and North America. The rise in suicides parallels the gradual increase in urbanization and education. It is also known that a major part of the increase in the suicide rate can be attributed to those people under forty years old.

Epidemiological knowledge about suicide in the world is limited to countries that report suicide statistics to WHO. The majority of countries in Africa, the central part of South America, and a number of Asian countries do not report data on suicides. What epidemiological data are available can often vary in quality. According to Ian Rockette and Thomas McKinley, the misclassification of suicide leads to underreporting. Classifying suicides as unintentional poisonings, drownings, or undetermined deaths is not unusual.

Underreporting and misclassification can be explained by social attitudes toward suicide, religious disapproval, and recording procedures. Some countries have a system whereby coroners can investigate unnatural deaths. In other countries a certificate is simply signed by the doctor. Autopsies also vary from one country to the next. For example, the autopsy rate is very high in Australia but very low in Germany. When there is no stigma associated with suicide, those close to the deceased are more likely to reveal information and characteristics about the deceased that would lead to a more accurate classification.

Suicide and Gender

In almost all countries for which statistics are available, suicide is more frequent among men than women (see Tables 1 and 2), a trend that prevails in most age groups. In a number of countries, a trend toward an increase in suicide has also been observed among men but not women. The gap in rates between men and women is smaller in Asian countries. Contrary to other countries, the suicide rate in China is higher among women than men in both rural and urban areas. However, the male-female suicide ratio is lower than in most countries.

Women's resistance to committing suicide may be explained by the strong role they play in family life, even if they work outside the home; their tasks prevent them from becoming socially and emotionally isolated. Women also seek medical treatment more often than men, increasing their chances of having any psychiatric problems detected and treated early. Conversely, men seem more vulnerable to losing their professional identity, a calamity often aggravated by solitude and loss of contact. Certain harmful behaviors linked to suicide, such as alcoholism and drug addiction, are especially common among men.

TABLE 1

Suicide rates per 100,000 inhabitants, men and women of various countries

Country	Year	Men	Women	Total
Argentina	1996	12.4	3.3	7.5
Canada	1997	20.0	5.1	12.4
Costa Rica	1995	11.8	2.3	7.0
Cuba	1996	28.2	12.9	20.3
Mexico	1995	7.3	1.0	4.0
United States of America	1997	19.7	4.5	11.7
Hong Kong	1996	16.7	9.2	12.9
Israel	1996	9.9	3.0	6.3
Singapore	1997	17.1	8.6	12.6
Austria	1997	30.1	18.6	9.0
Belarus	1997	66.8	10.2	36.0
Bulgaria	1997	24.5	9.4	16.4
Estonia	1996	68.9	13.0	38.4
Finland	1995	44.0	11.8	27.4
France	1996	29.0	9.8	18.8
Germany	1997	21.7	6.8	13.7
Greece	1997	5.9	0.1	3.4
Hungary	1995	53.6	15.0	32.5
Ireland	1996	20.4	3.7	11.9
Italy	1995	11.6	3.3	7.2
Kazakstan	1997	62.8	10.7	35.0
Kirgyzstan	1997	18.0	3.7	10.8
Netherlands	1995	13.2	6.4	9.7
Norway	1995	19.2	6.4	12.7
Poland	1996	26.1	4.7	14.9
Portugal	1997	10.2	2.5	5.9
Romania	1997	23.2	4.2	13.4
Russian Federation	1997	69.9	11.7	38.4
Spain	1995	12.4	3.3	7.5
Sweden	1996	19.5	7.9	13.6
Ukraine	1997	54.6	9.4	29.7
United Kingdom	1997	11.2	3.1	7.1
Australia	1995	19.7	5.2	12.3
New Zealand	1996	24.2	6.0	14.8

SOURCE: World Health Organization, 1999.

Suicide and Age

According to David Lester, the suicide rate increases with age among men and varies with age among women. In industrialized countries, the rate is higher for women in their middle ages. In poor countries, the suicide rate is higher among young women. In many industrialized countries and even in small communities, statistics show an increase in suicide among young people, especially among young men. In many areas, namely North America, suicide is the leading or second leading cause of death among young males. Suicide among children under the age of twelve is rare. The incidence of suicide rises sharply at puberty; the highest youth suicide rates occur during adolescence or early adulthood. The increase in suicide among youth dovetails with an overall rise in youthful depression. In addition, the earlier onset of puberty induces adult stresses and turmoil at an earlier age, including sexual activity and the abuse of alcohol, tobacco, and drugs.

Methods of Suicide

Methods of suicide vary greatly among different countries, depending on cultural traditions and social and political conditions. According to Canetto and Lester, the use of firearms in suicide deaths is definitely higher for both men and women in the United States than in Canada. This is mainly due to the large number of firearms in circulation and the absence of restrictions on access to them. In many countries, the use of firearms in suicide deaths is higher in rural areas than in urban ones because there are more hunters in rural areas.

Another interesting example of the link between methods and their availability is that of domestic gas in England used for exhaust poisoning. When England lowered the toxicity of domestic gas, suicide by this method was eliminated in the country and suicides decreased by one-third. Other countries such as Switzerland, Ireland, and Scotland have also reported changes in the suicide rate following the detoxification of gas.

There are also major differences in how men and women in Western countries commit suicide. Many men shoot and hang themselves while women tend to poison or hang themselves. In industrialized and developing nations, women most frequently use chemical products intended for agriculture.

Theories

Suicide has been the subject of many studies dating back to Émile Durkheim's *Le Suicide* (1897). At the dawn of the twenty-first century, however, no theory on suicide has been accepted by a majority of researchers.

Suicide may be associated with various pathologies. In Western societies, for example, suicide is considered to be a reflection of the social ills associated with crises such as unemployment, insecurity, weakness, or the loss of income, all of which contribute to the breakdown of family ties and the mental and physical isolation of individuals. Suicide often leads to various forms of exclusion in Western societies, in particular social isolation.

Although Durkheim's theory has been influential, it is has not gained universal acceptance as an

TABLE 2

Suicide rates per 100,000 inhabitants of various countries, men and women by age group

		Men (ages)				Women (ages)			
Country	Year	15–24	25–44	45–64	65 +	15–24	25–44	45–64	65 +
Argentina	1996	8.8	9.8	18.5	28.7	3.4	2.9	5.0	6.2
Canada	1997	22.4	25.0	25.5	23.0	4.5	6.6	7.6	4.5
Costa Rica	1995	11.8	16.3	15.2	9.2	4.0	2.9	3.1	0.0
Cuba	1996	14.2	25.3	33.8	83.8	13.1	12.9	15.3	26.6
Mexico	1995	7.6	8.4	8.0	1.8	2.0	1.1	1.1	1.1
United States of America	1997	18.9	23.8	22.5	33.9	3.5	6.0	6.5	4.9
Hong Kong	1996	11.8	17.9	20.1	34.1	7.5	8.3	9.0	27.4
Israel	1996	8.6	9.7	10.4	26.9	1.8	2.6	3.9	8.4
Singapore	1997	9.1	17.8	17.8	44.9	8.5	2.4	8.1	21.8
Austria	1997	24.3	30.9	35.8	68.2	4.8	8.7	12.8	20.8
Belarus	1997	32.9	79.3	116.5	81.3	6.7	9.8	16.4	17.8
Bulgaria	1997	14.1	18.5	33.4	63.5	4.8	7.3	12.1	29.0
Estonia	1996	34.9	72.6	120.8	84.2	7.8	9.9	22.5	28.8
Finland	1995	36.6	60.1	56.5	51.9	8.4	16.4	17.0	11.0
France	1996	12.8	35.6	36.8	58.5	4.2	10.5	16.3	17.4
Germany	1997	12.9	22.4	29.2	45.3	3.2	6.3	10.7	16.7
Greece	1997	2.8	7.0	7.6	9.7	0.8	0.8	1.4	2.0
Hungary	1995	19.2	56.6	77.6	112.8	3.8	13.1	23.1	41.2
Ireland	1996	25.4	32.0	19.7	15.8	4.5	5.3	5.4	1.3
Italy	1995	7.3	11.2	14.5	29.8	1.6	3.1	5.2	7.7
Kazakstan	1997	46.5	74.8	96.1	80.4	12.6	11.0	13.1	18.5
Kirgyzstan	1997	20.6	26.2	42.6	35.9	4.0	4.8	7.6	11.1
Netherlands	1995	9.2	16.9	16.7	20.9	4.4	7.6	8.8	10.3
Norway	1995	22.6	22.0	22.9	28.8	5.5	7.6	8.9	7.4
Poland	1996	17.2	31.8	41.6	30.8	2.9	4.7	8.4	7.0
Portugal	1997	4.3	9.3	11.0	32.2	1.2	2.3	3.7	6.4
Romania	1997	10.7	28.1	37.1	28.5	2.6	3.6	7.3	7.4
Russian Federation	1997	53.5	87.2	97.0	97.7	9.0	11.6	15.8	24.8
Spain	1995	8.7	12.1	14.4	32.3	2.1	2.8	5.1	8.5
Sweden	1996	12.0	22.6	29.1	32.8	4.6	8.0	14.0	12.6
Ukraine	1997	26.6	63.3	89.3	80.3	4.8	8.6	15.4	20.4
United Kingdom	1997	11.1	16.2	12.9	12.5	4.9	4.4	4.0	0.0
Australia	1995	23.1	27.9	21.6	21.4	6.1	6.7	7.0	5.1
New Zealand	1996	37.8	33.3	21.5	28.6	13.9	6.0	5.9	5.3

SOURCE: World Health Organization, 1999.

exhaustive framework. His theory contributes to the understanding of how social integration and cohesion influence suicide. Durkheim explained how individual pathology was a function of social dynamics and the underlying reason for suicide occurrence. The anomic suicide defined by Durkheim is associated with societal crises of economic or social nature. Suicide existed before the acculturation, exclusion, and complex changes characteristic of Western societies. In smaller communities, suicide is not associated with social alienation and urbanization, according to Tousignant. In some of these smaller communities, suicide is often a means of making amends or seeking redemption in the eyes of the community. In this context, suicide is a social regulator rather than an anomic gesture. People who commit suicide in these smaller communities appear not to live on the fringe of society, but are socially integrated in their society.

In addition to social factors, individual and biological factors are also associated with suicide, notably the presence of psychiatric problems. People who suffer from depression or other mental problems are statistically more at risk of suicide than the rest of the population. However, though mental disease is a risk factor that increases the probability of suicide, it does not itself explain the occurrence of suicide. Other individual syndromes associated with suicide are antisocial behavior and the abuse of drugs and alcohol. More recent studies have also linked genetic and biological factors to suicide, such as gender and serotonin production problems.

To counter the problem of suicide, many countries have set up prevention programs that focus on early detection of mental disease and more adequate treatment of potential victims. Other programs seek to purvey more accurate information about the problem through the media. Legislation restricting the use of firearms, the restriction and control of toxic substances, and the detoxification of domestic gas are the most common and successful preventive measures in advanced industrialized countries.

See also: DURKHEIM, ÉMILE; HOMICIDE, EPIDEMIOLOGY OF; SUICIDE; SUICIDE BASICS: PREVENTION; SUICIDE INFLUENCES AND FACTORS: ALCOHOL AND DRUG USE

Bibliography

Booth, Heather. "Pacific Island Suicide in Comparative Perspective." *Journal of Biosocial Science* 31 (1999):433–448.

Canetto, Silvia S., and David Lester. "Gender, Culture and Suicidal Behavior." *Transcultural Psychiatry* 35, no. 2 (1998):163–190.

Diekstra, Rene F., and Nadia Garnefski. "On the Nature, Magnitude, and Causality of Suicidal Behavior: An International Perspective." *Suicide and Life-Threatening Behaviors* 25, no. 1 (1995):36–57.

Durkheim, Émile. *Suicide: A Study in Sociology,* translated by J. A. Spaulding and G. Simpson. 1897. Reprint, Glencoe, IL : Free Press, 1951.

Fernquist, Rubert M., and Phillips Cutright. "Society Integration and Age-Standardized Suicide Rates in 21 Developed Countries." *Social Science Research* 27 (1998):109–127.

He, Zhao Xiung, and David Lester. "The Gender Difference in Chinese Suicide Rates." *Archives of Suicide Research* 3 (1997):81–89.

Kelleher, M. J., D. Chambers, P. Corcoran, E. Williamson, and H. S. Keely. "Religious Sanctions and Rates of Suicide Worlwide." *CRISIS* 19, no. 2 (1998):78–86.

Lester, David. "Suicide in an International Perspective." *Suicide and Life-Threatening Behavior* 27, no. 1 (1997):104–111.

Lester, David. "Effects of the Detoxification on Domestic Gas on Suicide Rates in Six Nations." *Psychological Reports* 77 (1995):294.

Mäkinen, Ilkka. "Are There Social Correlates to Suicide?" *Social Science Medicine* 44, no. 12 (1997):1919–1922.

Neeleman, Jan, and Glyn Lewis. "Suicide, Religion, and Socioeconomic Conditions." *Journal of Epidemiology Community Health* 53 (1999):204–210.

Neeleman, Jan, and Simon Wessely. "Ethnic Minority Suicide: A Small Area Geographical Study in South London." *Psychological Medicine* 29 (1999):429–436.

Rockett, Ian R., and Thomas B. McKinley. "Reliability and Sensitivity of Suicide Certification in Higher—Income Countries." *Suicide and Life-Threatening Behavior* 29, no. 2 (1999):141–149.

Sartorius, Normand. "Recent Changes in Suicide Rates in Selected Eastern European and other European Countries." In Jane L. Pearson and Yeates Conwell eds., *Suicide and Aging: International Perspectives.* New York: Springer, 1996.

Schmidlke, Armin. "Perspective: Suicide in Europe." *Suicide and Life-Threatening Behavior* 27, no. 1 (1997): 127–136.

Singh, B. S. "Suicide: The Public Health Crisis of Our Time." *Australian and New-Zealand Journal of Medicine* 28 (1998):295–300.

Tousignant, Michel. "Suicide in Small-Scale Societies." *Transcultural Psychiatry* 35, no. 2 (1998):291–306.

Wasserman, D., M. Dankowiez, A. Värnick, and L. Olsson. "Suicide Trends in Europe, 1984–1990." In Alexander J. Botis, Constantin R. Soldatos, and Costas Stefanis eds., *Suicide: Biopsychosocial Approaches.* Netherlands: Elsevier, 1997.

World Health Organization. *Injury: A Leading Cause of the Global Burden of Disease* Geneva: Author, 1999.

Zhang, Jie. "Suicide in the World: Toward a Population Increase Theory of Suicide." *Death Studies* 22 (1998):525–539.

DANIELLE SAINT-LAURENT

HISTORY

Although suicide has been recorded in both written and oral records in the history of man from primitive times on, no word existed for the phenomenon until the seventeenth century. According to the *Oxford English Dictionary,* the word *suicide* was first used in 1651, but Alfred Alvarez reported in 1972 that it appeared in Sir Thomas Browne's *Religio Medici* in 1642. The *Oxford English Dictionary* states that the word *suicidium* was actually derived by combining the Latin pronoun for "self" and the verb "to kill." The word sounds deceptively Latin, but Henry Romilly Fedden, in his 1938 book *Suicide,* stated that the Romans described the act using Latin phrases, such as *vim sibi inferre* (to cause violence to oneself), *sibi mortem consciscere* (to procure one's own death), and *sua manu cadere* (to fall by one's own hand). Early English also used phrases, such as self-murder, self-destruction, and self-killer, all of which reflect the early association of the act with murder.

Primitive and Traditional Societies

There is reliable evidence that suicide was present in most primitive tribes around the world, almost always associated with evil spirits, revenge, and unappeased anger. These attitudes in the form of superstitions and fears of magic found their way into Christianity as taboos that have persisted to this day. Attitudes toward suicide, however, have shown great variability depending on the culture and the part of the world. In primitive societies suicide was variously used as a means to exact vengeance, as a way of placing responsibility for the death on the person who had supposedly caused it, and as a way of embarrassing an adversary.

In other cultures suicide was not only tolerated but actually encouraged. The Goths and the Celts believed that to die naturally was shameful. Vikings unlucky enough not to die in battle fell on their own swords or jumped off cliffs in order to be able to enter Valhalla (the great hall of Odin for slain heroes in Norse mythology). And some Eskimo tribes believed it was better to kill oneself before growing feeble because people entered the next life in the same condition they left this one. In a number of societies tradition demanded that wives, retainers, servants, and ministers kill themselves so that they could continue to administer to the needs of their master after he died. Sometimes there was competition among the wives to be the first to follow the husband in death because that privilege identified his favorite. In Hindu India, the practice of *suttee,* the suicide of a widow by self-immolation on the funeral pyre of her husband, is reported to continue in some rural parts of the country, although it has long since been outlawed. Generally, however, the Hindu attitude toward suicide is ambiguous, condemning it but calling it justified in special cases, such as when a person has lived a full life or has achieved a special level as an ascetic.

In early Oriental sacred writings, suicide was viewed with contradictory attitudes that both encouraged and condemned it. In ancient China the ceremonial sacrifice of widows was almost as commonplace as it was in India; it was also reported to occur frequently because of the wretchedness of people's lives. In Japan, Buddhist tradition institutionalized suicide with several kinds of *seppuku,* a ritual form of disemboweling oneself that was used to admit failure, atone for a mistake, or avoid humiliation. Among the samurai, the professional warriors of feudal Japan, seppuku was incorporated into an ethical code known as *Bushido,* which required the warrior to follow his dead lord into the next life, to regain honor when revenge was not possible, and to avoid execution by the enemy in a lost battle. Brahmanism was sympathetic to suicide in that its philosophy incorporated denial of the body and the separation of the body from the soul in the intensive search for knowledge. Mohammedism condemned suicide with great severity, calling suicide a rejection of the divine will, which was expressed in many different ways and to which humans must submit themselves at all times.

The Jewish Tradition

Suicide among the Jews is generally infrequent, mostly because the value of life itself was so highly emphasized in the Torah. In the Old Testament of the Bible, a Jew is allowed to transgress every religious commandment in order to save his life except in cases of murder, incest, and the denial of God. Suicide was wrong, but was acceptable in instances of imminent capture and torture, apostasy, and shame or dishonor. Neither the Hebrew Bible nor the New Testament condemns nor condones suicide—nor does either contain the word *suicide.* The occasions of such deaths are described simply, briefly, and factually: Samson brought the temple of the Philistines down upon himself in order to kill his captors (Judg. 16:28–31); Saul, facing capture, disgrace, and torture in a defeat by the Philistines, fell on his own sword (1 Sam, 31:1–6); and Abimelech, not wanting the disgrace of being killed by a woman, killed himself (Judg. 9:54); Ahitophel chose to hang himself after he supported Absolam's unsuccessful revolt against King David (2 Samuel 17:23); Judas Iscariot simply "went and hanged himself" (Colt, 1991 p.153).

The Jews were involved in a number of mass suicides. In an early instance, Josephus, the Jewish general who later became a Roman historian, decided to surrender to the Romans when his army was defeated. His solders argued they should all kill themselves instead. They were able to overcome Josephus's arguments and proceeded to kill each other, but he was able to survive by persuading the last remaining soldier that the two of them should save themselves. The best-known occasion was the death in 74 C.E. of 960 Zealots who defended Masada through three years of siege by the Roman army and, facing capture, were persuaded by their leader, Eleazar Ben Zair, that death by their own hand was better than the slavery they faced when captured.

The Egyptians, Greeks, and Romans

The first recorded reference to suicide comes from ancient Egypt (about 4,000 years ago) in *The Dispute between a Man and His Ba,* in which a man describes the injustice and greed of his times to his *ba,* or soul, which has threatened to leave him if he kills himself, thus depriving him of an afterlife. There was no dishonor associated with the act of suicide itself, for death was seen as a mere passage from this life to the next and as a convenient way to avoid excessive pain or dishonor. The dead were considered coequals with the gods and to have the same physical and emotional needs as the living.

Suicide among the ancient Greeks and Roman varied widely with respect to tolerance and legal restrictions. The primitive attitudes of horror and condemnation for suicide were preserved in the lower classes, but the upper classes were more tolerant and accepting. Four motivations appeared most often: the preservation of honor, the avoidance of excessive pain and disgrace, bereavement, and patriotism. The major concern was honor, whatever the origin, such as patriotism, pride, or protecting one's virtue.

Among those opposing suicide, the Pythagoreans disapproved because it interfered with the regular orderly process of transmigration of souls on Earth, skewing the process. Socrates (c. 470–399 B.C.E.), possibly the most famous of Greek suicides, actually opposed suicide, reasoning that humans belonged to God, so suicide was destruction of God's property. Both Aristotle (384–322 B.C.E.) and Plato (c. 428–348? B.C.E.) condemned suicide but made exceptions, such as intolerable disgrace, unavoidable misfortune, or extraordinary sorrow. Aristotle felt that people belonged to the state, which made suicide a punishable act against the state. Plato considered a person to be a soldier of God, so the suicide deserted God, not the state. Suicide to avoid suffering was considered cowardice and weakness of character; suicide was acceptable, however, in cases of incurable illness or when God had summoned the soul. The Epicureans and Stoics, on the other hand, considered suicide an appropriate escape from the sufferings of physical illness and emotional frustration. For them neither life nor death was as important as one's right to decide about both. The manner of death was important, and suicide was often a carefully chosen validation of the principles by which one had lived.

Among the Romans, Pliny the Elder (23–79 C.E.) considered the existence of poisonous herbs as proof of a kindly Providence because they allowed a person to die painlessly and quickly. Suicide among the Romans became more and more economically oriented. The right to commit suicide was denied to a slave because it was considered a financial loss to the master. Likewise it was denied to a soldier because it weakened the armed forces. If a civilian committed suicide while under arrest, the state was deprived of taxes and services so punishment consisted of forfeiture of the estate. Suicide among the upper classes, however, was acceptable, in part because the attitude toward death had become so casual and public that death itself had little or no meaning. The records contain the names of many notables in Roman history who chose suicide to avoid defeat or dishonor or out of grief, including the poet Lucan (39–65 C.E.); the defeated general Cato (95–46 B.C.E.); Petronius (d. 66 C.E.), the gifted playwright and author; Paulina, the wife of Seneca (4 B.C.E.?–65 C.E.), who was allowed to kill himself when sentenced to death by the emperor Nero; and Nero (37–68 C.E.) himself.

Pre-Reformation Christianity

Christianity has contained markedly opposing attitudes toward suicide over time. The early era found suicide not only tolerated but also embraced by the church. Life was difficult, and the objective in life became to avoid sin and gain entrance before God and live there forever. Martyrdom was a quick way of achieving this eternal salvation. It guaranteed redemption for all sins incurred before death and was a way to provide for the members of the martyr's family, who were then taken care of by the church for the rest of their lives. As a result, martyrdom was eagerly sought, oftentimes by deliberately provoking the Roman authorities.

In the fourth century C.E., as Rome's influence declined, the attitude of the church underwent several changes. The church's attitude toward suicide became progressively more hostile, moving from tentative disapproval to severe denunciation. St. Augustine, writing in *The City of God* in the fourth century, declared that suicide was murder; that no private person could assume the right to kill anyone, including herself; that suffering is sent by God and is to be endured; and that suicide is the worst of sins because it precludes any possibility of absolution.

A series of church councils in the next several centuries progressively increased the condemnation and punishments with pronouncements denying funeral rights, forbidding burial within church cemeteries, and denying the saying of mass for the deceased. The penalties and the denial of burial rights suggest a reemergence of some of the early pagan horror of such deaths and were the basis for many of the practices that appeared later in many countries, such as desecrating the corpse of a person who committed suicide, mutilating the body, and burying it in a crossroad with a stake through the heart. In the thirteenth century, Thomas Aquinas summarized the position of the church in *Summa Theologica*. He stated that suicide was absolutely wrong because self-destruction was contrary to a person's natural inclinations; because a person has no right to deprive society of his presence; and because people are God's property so it is up to God, not people, to decide on life and death. Dante's *Inferno* (part of *The Divine Comedy,* which was completed in 1321) depicted the attitude of the time by showing the suicides condemned to eternal unrest in the woods of self-destruction.

Renaissance, Reformation, Enlightenment

With the Renaissance and the Reformation of the fifteenth through seventeenth centuries came a marked shift in the attitudes toward suicide. Values in religion began to change as German religious reformer Martin Luther's (1483–1546) arguments emphasized personal inquiry and responsibility and raised questions about the absolutism and obedience demanded by the church. Italy experienced a revival of learning, and a number of writings helped soften the absolute condemnation of suicide. Among these, English poet John Donne's *Biothanatos* (1644) is considered the first defense of suicide in English. Shakespeare incorporated fourteen suicides into his eight tragedies. Most of this change took place in the upper classes, with the lower classes remaining staunchly against suicide and continuing the custom of mutilation of the corpse all the way into the nineteenth century. The Industrial Revolution of the eighteenth century and the rise of commercialism resulted in a drastic change in the attitude of society toward the poor. Economic failure became a mark of sin, with the good being rewarded with prosperity and the poor becoming social and moral outcasts. In a 1732 incident, Richard and Bridget Smith killed their daughter and hanged themselves, leaving a bitter note blaming their fear of worsening poverty.

Writers and philosophers in this period through the eighteenth and nineteenth centuries (later known as the Enlightenment) wrote learned discourses on suicide. Some of these were sympathetic and focused on the rights of the individual. Such works included the English clergyman Robert Burton's *Anatomy of Melancholy* (1621) and the Scottish philosopher and historian David Hume's *An Essay on Suicide* (1783). Others held to the familiar arguments of duty to the state, the virtue of suffering, responsibility to the family, and the preservation of life as a primary law of nature. Among this group of writings was the German philosopher Immanuel Kant's *The Metaphysics of Ethics*.

The last half of the eighteenth century and the first half of the nineteenth became known as the Romantic Age because of the impact the Romantic poets of that era had on the concept of death. The suicide by poison of the English poet Thomas Chatterton (1752–1770) at age seventeen was taken as a model—premature death in blazing genius—in which youth, death, and poetry became synonymous. According to George Howe Colt, writing in his 1991 book *The Enigma of Suicide,* "The poetic sensibility was too good for this world; it was best to burn brightly and to die young, like a shooting star" (Colt 1991, p. 81).

The greatest change in the nineteenth century was the association of the word *disgrace,* a social value, with suicide. Survivors felt disgraced and the status of the family in the community sank. As suicide became more and more associated with mental illness, it was more often hidden, especially among the upper classes. The family thus often had the dismal choice of identifying their suicidal beloved one as either a weak sinner or a disturbed lunatic. Debates about social responsibilities versus individual rights and about the relationship between civilization and mental illness became common.

Studies appeared in two major domains—statistical (social) and medical (at first neurobiological and later psychological). Relationships between suicide and epidemiological factors, such as age, sex, marital status, socioeconomic class, occupation, and climate, were investigated. Some studies of suicide explored possible links of social factors with physiological symptoms (e.g., pulmonary conditions, cancer); others linked the social factors with behavioral and relational factors (e.g., trouble at home, intense worry, poverty, misery, alcoholism). French physician Jean-Étienne Esquirol, author of *Mental Maladies* (1838), maintained that suicide was almost always a symptom of insanity but was not a disease per se. Italian physician Henry Morselli, author of *Suicide: An Essay on Comparative Moral Statistics* (1881), held that suicide was primarily the result of the struggle for life and nature's evolutionary process. He concluded that suicide could be lessened only by reducing the number of people, and that could be accomplished only through birth control. Morselli blamed Protestantism, free discussion, and individualism for the increasing number of suicides.

Near the end of the nineteenth century, Émile Durkheim's *Suicide* (1897) established the field of sociology by offering the first comprehensive theory of suicide. Durkheim's theory postulated that two basic social forces exist and interact within any society—regulation and integration. Societies that were chaotic and confused produced "anomic" suicides; societies characterized by excessive constraints were likely to develop "fatalistic" suicides; societies in which the individual felt alienated and separate would have "egoistic" suicides; and in societies in which there was overidentification with the values or causes of a person's group, the suicides would be "altruistic." Durkheim's theory stimulated a continuing array of sociological-statistical investigations. It has been modified in innumerable ways, none of which seriously challenged his basic underlying theory.

Twentieth Century and Beyond

The early twentieth century was distinguished by the radical new innovations introduced into the field of psychiatry by psychoanalysis, especially in the study of the motivations and dynamics of suicide. The psychoanalytic approach of the Austrian neurologist Sigmund Freud delved into the individual searching for hidden conflicts, repressed memories, and complex defenses in a proposed new conceptual structuring of the personality into three layers: id, ego, and superego. Freud's first formulation of suicide, found in his essay "Mourning and Melancholia," developed from his studies of melancholia and depression. In this work, Freud contended that suicide resulted from rage originally directed against a loved one but now acted out on an image of that person that has been incorporated into the self. Not completely satisfied with this formulation, Freud later proposed, in his book *Beyond the Pleasure Principle* (1922), that suicide was an expression of the death instinct (Thanatos), which existed in continuous conflict with the life instinct (Eros), and which became more powerful in situations of extreme emotional distress.

The American psychiatrist Karl Menninger, in his 1938 book *Man against Himself,* extended Freud's concept of the death instinct and hypothesized that three elements exist in constantly shifting patterns in all self-destructive behavior—the wish to kill, the wish to be killed, and the wish to die. Other psychoanalysts formulated theories consistent with their own concepts of the important elements in personality development.

Investigations into the problems of suicide continued through the first half of the twentieth century with relatively little interest professionally or concern by the public, despite suicide as a mode of death appearing consistently in the list of the top ten causes of death in the United States. The establishment in 1958 of the Los Angeles Suicide Prevention Center, which provided a model for immediate consultation, guidance, and assistance to the suicidal person in the community by means of the telephone, initiated a belated reawakening of interest in the phenomenon. Since then, activity in the field has grown exponentially with the founding of various national professional associations, an international association, and several professional journals that publish articles primarily on suicide. Research is exploring various aspects of suicide with questions that sound strikingly similar to the questions raised in previous centuries. These questions are epidemiological, demographic, biological, constitutional, neurological, psychiatric, psychological, psychodynamic, and sociocultural in nature, and the questions explore such areas as mental illness, prevention, public health, individual rights, family obligations, treatment, and survivor relationships. The sinner/criminal suicide of yesterday is recognized today as a complex, multifaceted biopsychosociocultural phenomenon.

See also: SUICIDE; SUICIDE INFLUENCES AND FACTORS: CULTURE; SUICIDE TYPES: THEORIES OF SUICIDE; WIDOW-BURNING

Bibliography

Adler, Alfred. "Suicide." *Journal of Individual Psychology* 14 (1958):57–61.

Alvarez, Alfred. *The Savage God: A Study of Suicide.* New York: Random House, 1972.

Colt, George Howe. *The Enigma of Suicide.* New York: Summit, 1991.

Donne, John. *Biothanatos.* New York: Facsimile Text Society, 1930.

Durkheim, Émile. *Le Suicide,* translated by George Simpson. Glencoe, NY: Free Press, 1951.

Esquirol, Jean-Étienne. *Mental Maladies: A Treatise on Insanity,* translated by Ebenezer Kingsbury Hunt. New York: Hefner, 1965.

Fedden, Henry Romilly. *Suicide.* London: Peter Davies, 1938.

Hankoff, Leon D., ed. *Suicide: Theory and Clinical Aspects.* Littleton, MA: P. G. Publishing, 1979.

Menninger, Karl. *Man against Himself.* New York: Harcourt, Brace, 1938.

Morselli, Henry. *Suicide: An Essay on Comparative Moral Statistics.* New York: D. Appleton, 1975.

NORMAN L. FARBEROW

PREVENTION

Suicide prevention involves actions to intervene in an individual's suicidal pattern or mindset as well as a variety of public health measures to reduce the incidence of suicidal behavior in a community. There are many ways to prevent suicides. Suicides are the result of a combination of multiple risk factors, including mental disorders, personal characteristics, inadequate coping skills, and environmental variables, such as recent losses, lack of social support, and availability of lethal means. Any activities that help reduce risk factors, such as treating mental disorders and psychiatric difficulties, increase one's ability to cope with stressful situations and problems. Preventing or treating alcoholism and drug abuse and ensuring that people develop good social support systems have some effect in preventing suicides. National strategies that focus upon decreasing the number of deaths by suicide in a country generally take a combined approach, in which various types of complementary programs and services are provided in order to decrease the incidence of suicide.

Primary Prevention of Suicide

Suicide prevention may focus on primary prevention, which involves developing skills or reducing risk factors in order to prevent people from becoming suicidal. Primary prevention strategies can either focus on an entire population or specific high-risk groups. An example of a primary prevention program that focuses on the general population is National Suicide Prevention Week—a week of activities in which media reports and a publicity campaign focus on teaching the general population how to get help, give help, or identify suicide risk. Another example of primary prevention for a large population is a high school program, in which teachers, support staff, and students learn about suicide, particularly how to know when a student is at risk and how to find and use available resources for oneself and for others.

Some primary prevention strategies focus on suicide, such as in the previous example of a high school suicide prevention program. However, many primary prevention strategies do not focus directly on suicide but are concerned more with general risk factors, such as poor coping skills or stress related to school examinations. For example, research studies indicate that adolescents who attempt suicide have fewer coping strategies than adolescents who do not attempt suicide. The Reaching Young Europe program, called "Zippy and Friends," is offered by the Partnership for Children in different European countries. As a twenty-four-week program, it focuses upon teaching coping skills to young children. Although suicide is not mentioned in this program, it is assumed that children who can better cope with everyday problems will eventually be at lower risk of suicide because problematic situations will not become so severe that they will consider detrimental behavior or engage in behavior to end their own lives.

Primary prevention strategies that focus on high-risk groups try to identify people who are more likely to commit or attempt suicide. For example, high-risk groups include persons in custody, young gays and lesbians, persons who previously attempted suicide, and persons with mental health disorders, notably mood disorders such as depression, as well as schizophrenia, and alcoholism. Sometimes prevention programs for high-risk groups focus on all people in that risk group. For example, a program for Native people may focus upon the entire community and aim to develop better intergenerational cooperation and establish an identity using role models from traditional Native practices.

Public education programs generally focus on reducing the stigma associated with seeking treatment and providing social support for those who are depressed and suicidal. They may involve a popular spokesperson who is open and frank and whose discussions of suicide may encourage others to seek professional help and talk about their problems with friends and loved ones.

Secondary Prevention

Secondary prevention strategies involve interventions with people who are already suicidal or at high risk of suicide in order to reduce the probability that they will commit suicide. Suicide prevention hotlines and telephone crisis intervention services are regularly available in most developed countries and many less developed parts of the world. These centers vary from "active listening" services, where people can talk about any problem, to more specifically focused suicide prevention organizations that evaluate suicidal risk and urgency in all calls and focus their efforts on helping suicidal persons, friends and family members of suicidal persons, and sometimes persons bereaved by suicide. They are generally based upon the belief that suicide is a means of coping with a seemingly impossible and interminable situation or problem and suicidal people are ambivalent about using suicide as a solution.

Ambivalence in the suicide-prone is expressed in their desire to seek some other means of diminishing their anguish or problems. This leads them to contact a telephone help line. Suicide prevention help lines generally begin by assessing the urgency of the situation, that is, whether or not the person is likely to commit or attempt suicide in the near future. If the urgency is high, trained personnel may then focus upon seeking short-term solutions, such as sending an ambulance during an attempt or getting immediate help in a crisis situation. If the urgency is less high, they may focus upon exploring alternative means to resolve the caller's problems, or they may simply offer compassionate empathic listening. It is assumed that being able to talk about one's problems with a compassionate stranger helps the callers better understand what is going on, feel better about themselves, and encourages them to learn about other services that are available in their community. There is evidence that hotlines do help many callers. Although it is difficult to prove, studies indicate that help lines prevent suicide attempts and completed suicides.

There is substantial evidence that reducing the availability and lethality of means of suicide has a preventive effect. The risk of suicide in a home where there is a firearm is five or six times greater than in a home without guns. Countries that have adopted strict gun control regulations appear to have reduced suicide rates. Although someone who is determined to commit suicide can always find some means of completing the suicide, some people prefer certain methods and are less likely to kill themselves if those methods are not readily available. Furthermore, in a crisis situation, the availability of lethal means greatly increases the probability that a death by suicide will occur. Reducing the availability of means is not limited to gun control or making sure that firearms are taken out of the home of someone who is suicidal. Other prevention methods include constructing barriers on bridges to prevent people from jumping, constructing "suicide pits" beneath the rails of subway train lines so that people who jump in front of trains are less likely to be killed, and educating parents to dispose of potentially lethal medications in the homes of suicidal teenagers.

One of the most promising methods of suicide prevention is what is called "gatekeeper" training. Gatekeepers are people who may come into contact with suicidal individuals in their daily work, such as clergy, police officers, custodial personnel, teachers and school personnel, and physicians. Very often, these individuals receive little or no specific training in the identification of suicide risk and how to help suicidal individuals. Gatekeeper training involves not only information about assessing risk and intervening with suicidal people, but generally provides information on referral and help available from other services within their community, including treatment of depression, alcoholism, and drug abuse.

There has been much public health interest in training physicians to identify suicidal individuals and depression. This interest was enhanced by results from the Island of Gotland in Sweden, where a physician training program focusing upon the recognition and treatment of depression and suicide was evaluated. This training program resulted in increased identification and treatment of depression and a decrease in suicides on the island. Research has shown that as many as 50 percent of those who commit suicide consult a physician in the month before their deaths. For this reason, physician training is considered an important means of suicide prevention.

People who attempt suicide are at least a hundred times at greater risk of a future suicide attempt and dying by suicide than persons who have never attempted suicide. Suicide attempters who are treated in hospitals often do not appear for their first or second outpatient appointment after they leave the hospital. There are few follow-up programs that focus upon changing the circumstances that contribute to the increased risk of suicide before an attempt. One of the problems with the follow-up of those who have attempted suicide is lack of coordination and collaboration between different community services and agencies. In many suicide prevention centers, over 50 percent of callers also receive professional mental health services, but there is often little communication or collaboration between the different agencies. National strategies for suicide prevention often focus upon coordination of all services within a community and the development of protocols for collaboration to facilitate referrals between agencies.

Suicide Prevention in a Place Where a Suicide Has Occurred

When a suicide occurs in a school or at the workplace, there is an increased risk of another suicide or suicides occurring in the same environment. Public health officials have developed several programs to prevent the so-called contagion of suicide following such events. It is usually thought that the risk of more suicides increases because people who are bereaved by suicide are more vulnerable. Also, there is a tendency to identify with the suicide victim and fantasize about obtaining all the attention that the suicide provoked. For these reasons, several programs have been developed to prevent increased suicidal behavior in schools or workplaces where a suicide has occurred. These programs usually involve offering help to those who are troubled by the suicidal death and helping educate people about the nature of suicide and the resources for prevention. In any program following a suicide (often called "postvention programs") it is important to be aware that too much public attention to the event may help glorify the suicide in the eyes of vulnerable suicidal people. Successful programs do not have a fixed agenda about how to deal with a suicide event, but rather emphasize an understanding of the individual needs of people who were exposed to the suicide. They also focus on the need of family and friends to grieve in an appropriate manner.

Social Interventions

Suicide is an intentional behavior whose expression is greatly influenced by the cultural milieu. In some cultures suicides are common; in others they are rare. Although in Western cultures men commit suicide more often than women, there are areas of the world, such as China, where a significant portion of suicides are by women who do not want to be a financial burden to their families. In some cultures, including the United States and Canada, some people have killed themselves in a copycat manner following the publicized suicide of a rock star. The option of killing oneself under specific circumstances is acquired at a young age. In each culture, children learn when and how people kill themselves. In most Western countries children's first experiences with suicide are from exposure to television and other media depictions of fictional suicides and suicide threats, including suicides in popular cartoons. One may ask if it is possible to prevent suicides within a society by modifying the way the option of suicide is transmitted from generation to generation and changing attitudes and knowledge about suicide within the society.

A large body of research has shown that media depictions of suicides result in an increase in suicidal behavior by those who identify with the suicide victim. The emphasis in research on media

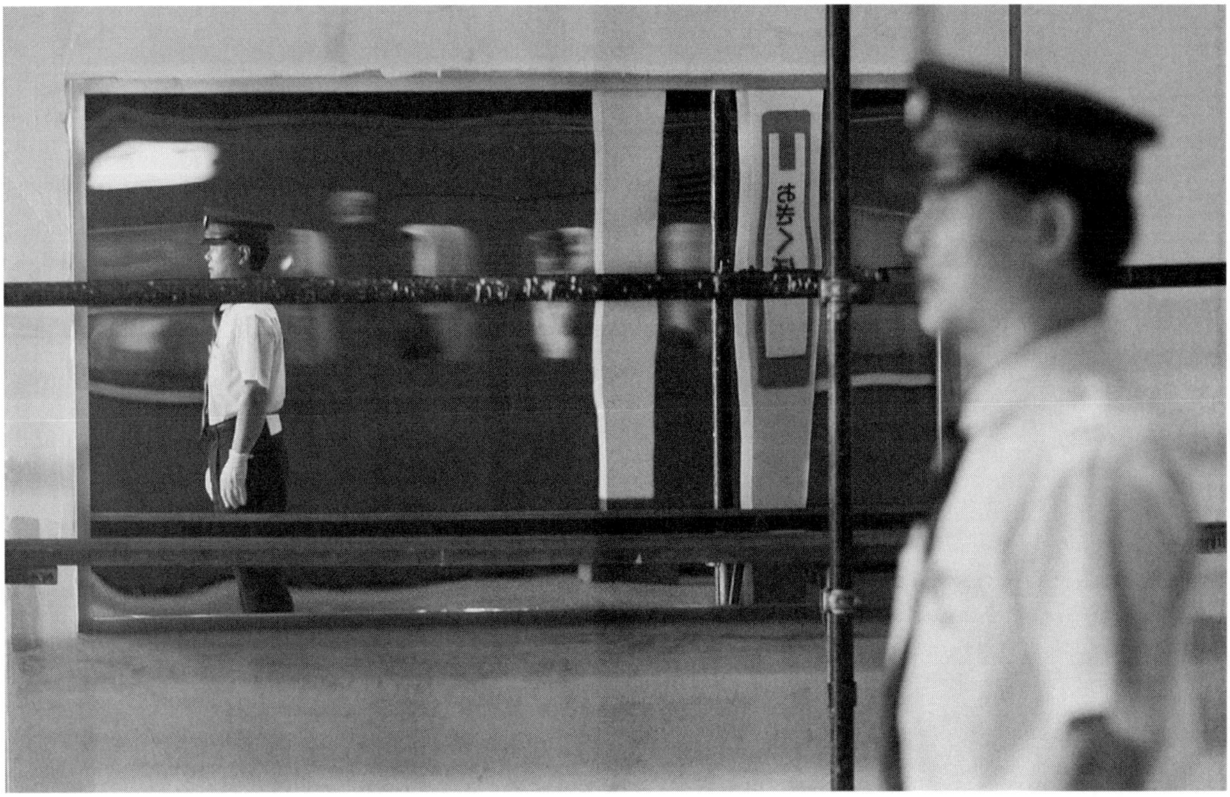

The East Japan Railway Company installed a large, stainless steel mirror in one of its Tokyo subway stations to prevent suicidal passengers from leaping onto the tracks. The purpose of this innovative method of prevention is to make people see their reflection in the mirror and think again about their suicidal behavior. AFP/CORBIS

and suicide has generally been negative: that is, it explores how media, such as television, newspapers, and the cinema, actually increase the incidence of suicide. There have been no studies of how the media may help prevent suicide. Researchers question if it is possible to reduce suicidal behavior in a society by developing media depictions and social campaigns that aim to change attitudes about the acceptability of suicide. These "positive" advertising campaigns are represented by National Suicide Prevention Days or Suicide Prevention Weeks, in which there is an objective of educating the population about the tragedy of suicide and how suicide may be prevented. Evaluations of the Quebec Suicide Prevention Week indicate that this national educational campaign's target population retained the positive messages the campaign conveyed. Although it is difficult to change attitudes and beliefs in a society, they can change over time. For example, the twentieth century has seen impressive changes in attitudes toward women's rights, women's participation in society, and sex role stereotypes. Similarly, one could imagine that attitudes toward suicide as an acceptable "way out" in certain circumstances could change if appropriate actions were taken to educate the population and influence how suicide is perceived.

See also: SUICIDE; VARAH, CHAD

Bibliography

Government of Quebec. *Help for Life: Quebec's Strategy for Preventing Suicide.* Quebec: Ministère de la Santé et des Services sociaux, 1998.

Hakanen, Jari, and Maila Upanne. "Evaluation Strategy for Finland's Suicide Prevention Project." *Crisis* 17, no. 4 (1996):167–174.

Mishara, Brian L. "The Prevention of Suicide in Adulthood." In Martin Bloom and Thomas Gullotta eds., *Encyclopedia of Primary Prevention and Health Promotion.* New York: Kluwer Academic/Plenum Publications, 2002.

Mishara, Brian L., and Marc Daigle. "Helplines and Crisis Intervention Services: Challenges for the Future." In

David Lester ed., *Suicide Prevention: Resources for the Millennium*. Philadelphia: Brunner/Mazel, 2000.

Mishara, Brian L., and Marc Daigle. "Effects of Different Telephone Intervention Styles with Suicidal Callers at Two Suicide Prevention Centers: An Empirical Investigation." *American Journal of Community Psychology* 25, no. 6 (1997):861–895.

Mishara, Brian L., and Mette Ystgaard. "Exploring the Potential of Primary Prevention: Evaluation of the Befrienders International Reaching Young Europe Pilot Programme in Denmark." *Crisis* 21, no. 1 (2000):4–7.

Murphy, George E. "The Physician's Responsibility for Suicide: Errors of Omission." *Annals of Internal Medicine* 82 (1975):305–309.

Shaffer, David, and Madelyn Gould. "Suicide Prevention in Schools." In Keith Hawton and Kees van Heeringen eds., *Suicide and Attempted Suicide*. New York: John Wiley and Sons, 2000.

Stack, Steven. "Media Impacts on Suicide: A Quantitative Review of 293 Findings." *Social Sciences Quarterly* 81, no. 4 (2000):975–988.

World Health Organization. *Preventing Suicide: A Resource for Primary Health Care Workers*. Geneva: Author, 2001.

BRIAN L. MISHARA

WARNING SIGNS AND PREDICTIONS

Suicide is a rare event. Most suicidal people find other solutions to their problems and do not attempt or commit suicide. Because of the large number of suicidal persons and small number of suicides, individual suicides are impossible to predict in a reliable manner. However, there are a number of warning signs that can help determine if a person is at risk. Many more people will always be identified as at risk than actually attempt or commit. Since the outcome is irreversible and tragic, it is best to take all indications of suicide risk seriously.

Who Is at Risk?

Although people with any characteristics can commit suicide, some people are more at risk of suicide than others. People who can be identified as having the following characteristics are more likely to be suicidal than those of the general population.

Persons with mental disorders or psychiatric problems are at great risk of suicide, particularly those suffering from clinical depression. Alcoholics and drug abusers are another category of individuals at great risk. Suicide risk may be greater for persons who discontinue medication they are taking for mental health problems. People who have previously attempted suicide are at greater risk of attempting suicide again than those persons who have never attempted suicide, primarily because the problems that led to the first attempt may not have been resolved.

People who have experienced a recent major loss, such as death of a close friend or relative, divorce, or separation or loss of a job, are at greater risk that the general populace. Also, people whose close friends have committed suicide or have a family history of suicide are at great risk, as are people who are in physical ill health.

Warning Signs

It is rare that a person who attempts or completes a suicide does not give prior indications of his or her suicidal intentions. This is because relatively few persons who commit suicide do so impulsively without having thought about ending their own lives beforehand for days, weeks, or months. Suicides rarely occur because of a sudden traumatic event. However, people at risk of suicide who experience a sudden traumatic event are at much greater risk of ending their lives at that time.

People who are suicidal are often seen as having changed their personality or humor recently. Changes include depression or apathy, pessimism, irritability, or "not seeming to be themselves." There may be changes in eating patterns (eating much more or stopping eating) and sleeping habits (sleeping much more or being unable to sleep, particularly waking up early and not being able to get back to sleep).

Suicidal people often feel lonely, misunderstood, helpless, hopeless, worthless or ashamed, guilty, and/or full of hate for themselves. These feelings are not normal, even for a person who has a mental disorder or psychiatric illness. They are indications that something is desperately wrong.

Any behavior that may be interpreted as "preparing" for death may be an indication of suicidal intent. For example, suicidal persons may put their personal affairs in order and update or write a will. Even more direct preparations include giving away important objects (particularly if the person makes statements like, "I won't need them anymore" or "I don't care about them anymore"). Sometimes people say good-bye or express feelings in a way they never did before (e.g., "I never really told you how much I care about you; I just wanted you to know").

Another danger sign of suicide is a preoccupation or interest in obtaining means for killing oneself. The purchase of a gun or getting hold of potentially lethal medications may be an indication of suicidal intent. Tying nooses in a rope or occupying dangerously high places are other possible indicators. Some people review web sites that provide information about how to kill oneself, or investigate what constitutes a lethal dose of medication. These and other dangerous behaviors are important indications that a suicide might be imminent. Some suicidal people write suicide notes that they may leave around where others might see them. Leaving a suicide note where it can be found beforehand or making "obvious" preparations may be interpreted as an expression of the suicidal person's ambivalence. Although the person intends to die, there is also some hope that someone will find the note or identify the risk and help find a solution to his or her problems before a suicide attempt.

Most suicidal persons express their suicidal intentions to others beforehand. These expressions may be in the form of direct suicide threats ("I can't stand it and I'm going to kill myself") or they may be much less direct ("Sometimes I think it's not worth going on"). Suicidal persons may be indirect in the communication of their intent because they are afraid of how a friend or family member will react. Depending upon the reaction, they may continue to confide their thoughts and plans or they may change the subject.

What To Do If There Are Warning Signs

Whenever a person gives some of the above indications that he or she may be suicidal, others may be of great help if they talk to the person about how he or she is feeling. Unfortunately, most people hesitate to ask questions or talk about suicide because they are afraid that they will say or do the wrong thing. Often they feel that they may make things worse or even cause someone who is vulnerable to get the idea to commit suicide. However, mental health practitioners maintain that this does not happen. Suicide is not something someone can suggest by asking questions about what a person is thinking and feeling and whether or not a person is thinking about suicide. Conversations about suicide serve the purpose of communicating to a person who is considering whether or not he or she should end life that someone else is interested in helping—despite the fact that the suicidal person is thinking of doing something that most people find unable to speak about. Most people feel quite relieved that they are able to talk openly about suicide and the problems they are having.

Discussions about suicide should focus on resources the person already has available. Does the person have a confident or friends with whom he/she can talk about the problem or get help? Is the suicidal individual seeing a mental health professional or other health care provider who can be of help? Conversations can be helpful if they explore alternative ways to help with the situation.

When confronted with a suicidal person, mental health practitioners uphold that it is important to stay calm and listen empathically to what the person is saying. Despite the possibility that the attempt may not be serious or the person may be manipulative, it is important to take the situation seriously and to ask questions to find out how serious the intentions really are. Friends and helpers should ask specific questions about risk factors such as previous attempts and mental health problems. Generally, people who know when and how they are going to commit suicide are at much greater risk than people whose plans are vague and uncertain. For this reason it is useful to ask if the person has considered how and when he or she plans to commit suicide. Asking such a direct question can do no harm and can provide important information. If the person knows how and has the means at hand, the risk is great and immediate help is needed. If a person has a means of suicide available, such as a firearm or lethal medication, it is important to remove the means from the home. Concerned parties should consult a suicide prevention service or agency or skilled health or mental health care provider who is knowledgeable about suicide. If a person is at high risk, that is, the person appears to be ready to take his or her own life soon, it is best to stay with the person or have someone else stay with the person during this crisis period.

It is not useful to get angry or panic. Nor is it useful to be falsely encouraging by saying things like, "I'm sure that everything will be all right." Also, it is best not to belittle or trivialize the problem by saying, for example, "I'm sure other people have been in much worse situations and they never thought of killing themselves." No matter how unimportant the problems may seem to an outsider, they may be sufficiently serious in the mind of the suicidal person for the person to consider taking his or her own life. A mature listener should not make promises he or she cannot keep or insist that things will change if he or she is not certain. One should not swear to keep secret a person's suicidal intentions. Saving a person's life is more important than betraying a confidence.

Not all suicides are preventable. However, people who give indications that they are suicidal usually experience great ambivalence about whether they should kill themselves or not. If a person wants to commit suicide without telling anyone or indicating what he or she intends to do, there is nothing anyone can do to prevent it. However, people who do give indications that they are suicidal, despite their insistence that they must complete this act, are generally experiencing ambivalence about whether or not this is the only way to stop their anguish or painful situation. In these circumstances it is important to talk with the person and offer help so that the ambivalence against committing suicide may be strengthened in the short term by the presence of a caring friend. However, in the long run suicidal persons need to take steps to resolve underlying problems. This may involve starting or continuing help from a mental health professional, trying to resolve a drinking or drug problem, or learning to expand coping skills. Identifying suicide risk and offering help is the first step in the process of helping suicidal individuals decrease their risk of suicidal behavior.

See also: SUICIDE BASICS: PREVENTION; SUICIDE OVER THE LIFE SPAN

Bibliography

Hawton, Keith, and Kees van Heeringen, eds. *The International Handbook of Suicide and Attempted Suicide.* Chichester, England: John Wiley & Sons, 2000.

Jacobs, Douglas G., ed. *The Harvard Medical School Guide to Suicide Assessment and Intervention.* San Francisco: Jossey-Bass Publishers, 1999.

Maris, Ronald W., Alan L. Berman, John T. Maltsberger, and Robert I. Yufit, eds. *Assessment and Prediction of Suicide.* New York: Guilford Press, 1992.

Maris, Ronald W., Alan L. Berman, and Morton M. Silverman, eds. *Comprehensive Textbook of Suicidology.* New York: Guilford Press, 2000.

BRIAN L. MISHARA

SUICIDE INFLUENCES AND FACTORS

ALCOHOL AND DRUG USE

Between 30 and 50 percent of persons who die by suicide have a dependence on alcohol or drugs or have shown a pattern of abuse of those substances. The data from four large studies in four different countries confirm this statistic. In a Finnish study led by Markus Henriksson covering all ages over the entire country, diagnoses of dependence and abuse were present in 43 percent of the cases, twice as often in men (39%) as in women (18%). In another study conducted in the United States (San Diego), alcohol abuse was found in 55 percent of cases. Alain Lesage's team in Quebec concluded that 30 percent of male suicide victims below thirty-five had alcohol-dependence problems and that a similar percentage suffered from drug dependence, with a combined dependence rate around 45 percent. Even in South India, where alcohol is difficult to find, Laskmi Rajkumar found in the city of Chennai (formerly Madras) that 35 percent of suicides showed signs of alcoholism.

Almost all the alcoholics who commit suicide also suffer from severe mental health problems. In the Finnish study, half of the suicides with alcohol dependence also had a depressive disorder and almost as many had a personality disorder that entailed difficulty in curbing impulsive behavior. In a large 1992 American study research of male alcoholic suicides, directed by George Murphy, researchers found that 72 percent had a depressive disorder and less than a quarter were free of any psychiatric disturbance. The probability that an alcoholic will die by suicide varies from 2 to 6 percent, which is far above that of the American population (1.3%) or the American population without any psychiatric problem (around 1 per 100,000 per year or less than 0.2%).

With respect to illegal drugs, a 1992 study done in New York City found that 15 percent of New York suicides tested positive for cocaine. In Norway Ingebor Rossow found that nearly 3 percent of a group of patients from both sexes treated for drug dependence had died by suicide after only ten years. Younger people from both sexes have a higher risk, and among them drug abuse leads to suicide more quickly than does alcohol abuse.

Attempted Suicide

Alcohol and drugs also have a major influence on attempted suicides. In a survey sponsored by the National Institute on Alcohol Abuse and Alcoholism in 1992, Deborah Dawson found that those who had frequently become inebriated were more likely to experience suicidal thoughts or to actually try to kill themselves. One out of seven persons who were frequently intoxicated reported suicidal thoughts or attempts compared to 4 percent for other current drinkers. The level rose to 20 percent for those who only used sedatives, tranquilizers, cocaine, or stimulants and to 25 percent in cases of multiple drug use. The link between marijuana and attempted suicide was well documented in a New Zealand study that found that one out of six persons who made serious attempts at suicide were seriously dependent on marijuana.

Slow Death and Overdoses

Many people wonder if the use of alcohol and drugs is a way of committing suicide by "slow death." Most persons who abuse these substances are taking them chiefly as a kind of self-medication to reduce their stress. This seems to be more the case with men than with women. A woman who takes to alcohol has often failed to find relief from drugs such as tranquilizers and is more likely to be desperate and vulnerable to suicide. Alcohol also leads to a greater risk of slow death from cirrhosis of the liver and of accidental deaths associated to risk-taking behaviors. Alcohol and drug abuse is also associated with a much higher risk of dying by homicide.

The problem of drug overdose is somewhat different. Young homeless adults often attempt suicide by overdosing on illegal drugs. A Norwegian survey by Ingeborg Rossow and Grethe Lauritzen (1999) has shown that nearly half of more than 2,000 drug addicts admitted for treatment reported having experienced at least one life-threatening overdose and that they were six times more likely to have made a suicide attempt than those who had not overdosed. Coroners are still reluctant to classify these deaths as suicides given the difficulty in distinguishing accidents from voluntary gestures.

Alcohol and Drugs As a Cause of Suicide

Do alcohol and drugs directly cause suicide by significantly diminishing the reasoning of the person at the time of the suicide? In the absence of personal data, it is difficult to know if those who drank before committing suicide did so to have the courage to commit suicide. There is evidence, however, to show that alcoholics who commit suicide usually don't act only on the spur of the moment. George Murphy has analyzed the issue of alcohol and impulsivity in a series of ten cases where the person had committed suicide within hours of a very stressful life event. In only two cases was there evidence of an unexpected impulsive act. In six other cases the person had communicated some time before the event his or her intent to die. However, even if the person had considered suicide before, we cannot rule out the possibility of the alcohol triggering an impulsive act. Long-term consumption of alcohol leads to depression, which in turn increases the probability of suicide, according to Murphy's study.

But it takes on average more than nineteen years of chronic alcoholism and seven years of depression before reaching this end, which leaves plenty of time for treatment and prevention.

If suicide is closely associated with alcohol, is there a direct link between an increase in alcohol consumption and the suicide rate in a population? Despite many attempts to prove this idea, an American study found that the sale of spirits, but not of beer or wine, correlated with increased suicide statistics. The fact that countries that were former members of the Soviet Union have both high rates of suicide and alcoholism supports the hypothesis of a direct link. But we have to wait for more information from China, which has a high incidence of alcoholism and low incidence of suicide, to have a more complete picture. If Islamic countries have both low rates of alcohol and suicides, there are countries such as Mexico or Jamaica where alcohol consumption is high and suicide rates relatively low. One likely explanation is that intoxication in these countries more often take place during religious or social rituals and that these contexts may lessen the adverse consequences of drinking.

The Psychosocial Context

As George Murphy and E. Robins warned physicians in 1967, "The physician should be aware of the critical periods of break in relationships (divorce, separation, mourning) in their alcoholic patients." Later studies comparing cases of alcohol and drug suicide with other suicides have since concluded that the breakup of a love relationship in the six weeks before suicide had more of a causal impact in the alcohol and drug group, perhaps because many alcoholics have suffered rejection and abandonment during childhood and might therefore be more vulnerable to the emotional trauma of separation. Another hypothesis is that the alcoholics progressively enter a process of social isolation, especially during the year before a suicide. Therefore, they may be more vulnerable to a key loss. A Finnish study by Heikkinen found that family discord (38%), financial problems (28%), and marital separations were the chief precipitants of suicides among alcoholics. Persons with an alcohol or drug problems who die by suicide have often alienated friends and family and therefore have little social support.

Murphy and his team studied the differences between alcoholics who committed suicide and other alcoholics living in the community. They found that two-thirds of the suicides had had at least four psychosocial risk factors as against only 1 percent in the community alcoholics. Those who committed suicide were twelve times more likely to suffer from a major depression (58% vs. 5%), three times more likely to be unemployed (54% vs. 18%), to live alone (45% vs. 17%), to lack social support (75% vs. 26%), or to have previously made suicide threats (79% vs. 23%). Almost all the suicides were very heavy drinkers (97%), twice as many as in the community alcoholic sample. Two-thirds of the suicide cases had four of these risk factors compared with only 1 percent in the community group of alcoholics. Young people with a drug problem who commit suicide are also much more likely to have had a brush with the law, to have a firearm available at home, or to suffer from depression.

Prevention and Intervention

If alcohol and drugs are closely related to suicidal behavior, we cannot conclude that all abusers are at risk. Those who also suffer from depression or a personality disorder are the ones in real danger. Consequently, the treatment of the addiction should also target the other psychological problems. One challenge is to communicate to adolescents that despite the immediate good feelings alcohol or drugs may facilitate, an unpleasant, depressive mood often accompanies abuse. We should recognize that both drugs and alcohol can sometimes alleviate suffering and despair. Limiting alcohol consumption to social rituals may help to minimize the damage in some societies. Furthermore, if alcoholics are working and are supported by their environment, the risk of committing suicide significantly decreases. Both professionals and family members should also realize that alcoholics, especially if middle-aged, are very vulnerable to loss and rejection and that they can benefit from increased social support.

The low suicide rate in Islamic countries that limit access to alcohol, contrasted with high rates in the alcohol-consuming West, suggests a direct link between suicide and alcohol abuse. The solution in most countries is not one of repression but rather publicizing the statistical association of suicide with alcohol and drug abuse.

See also: SUICIDE INFLUENCES AND FACTORS: GENDER, MENTAL ILLNESS; SUICIDE OVER THE LIFE SPAN: ADOLESCENTS AND YOUTHS, THE ELDERLY; SUICIDE TYPES: INDIRECT SUICIDE

Bibliography

Dawson, Deborah A. "Alcohol, Drugs, Fighting and Suicide Attempt/Ideation." *Addiction Research* 5, no. 6 (1997):451–472.

Henriksson, M. M., H. M. Aro, M. J. Marttunen, M. E. Heikkinen, et al. "Mental Disorders and Comorbidity in Suicide." *American Journal of Psychiatry* 150, no. 6 (1993):935–940.

Lesage, A. D., R. Boyer, F. Grunberg, F. C. Vanier, et al. "Suicide and Mental Disorders: A Case-Control Study of Young Men." *American Journal of Psychiatry* 151, no. 7(1994):1063–1068.

Marzuk, P. M., K. Tardiff, A. C. Leon, M. Stajic, E. B. Moorgan, and J. J. Mann. "Prevalence of Cocaine Use among Residents of New York City Who Committed Suicide during a One-Year Period." *American Journal of Psychiatry* 149 (1993):371–375.

Murphy, G. E. *Suicide in Alcoholism.* New York: Oxford University Press, 1992.

Murphy, G. E., R. D. Wetzel, E. Robins, and L. McEvoy. "Multiple Risk Factors Predict Suicide in Alcoholism." *Archives of General Psychiatry* 49 (1992):459–463.

Rajkumar, Vijayakumar L. "Are Risk Factors for Suicide Universal? A Case-Control Study in India." *Acta Psychiatrica Scandinavica* 99 (1999):407–411.

Rossow, Ingebor. "Suicide among Drug Addicts in Norway." *Addiction* 89 (1994):1667–1673.

Rossow, Ingeborg, and Grethe Lauritzen. "Balancing on the Edge of Death: Suicide Attempts and Life-Threatening Overdoses among Drug Addicts." *Addiction* 94, no. 2 (1999):209–219.

MICHEL TOUSIGNANT

BIOLOGY AND GENETICS

The possibility that biological and hereditary factors could be related to suicidal behavior has been written about for over 200 years. For example, in 1790 Charles Moore stated that the "propensity to suicide . . . by attacking successive generations of the same family proves itself to be hereditary"; in 1881 in the English translation of his Italian work, *Suicide: An Essay on Comparative Moral Statistics,* Henry Morselli wrote a chapter entitled "Influences Arising Out of the Biological and Social Condition of the Individual"; and in 1892 the physician Daniel Hack Tuke noted that "examples of hereditary suicides have occurred" (Goldney and Schioldann 2000, pp. 181, 184).

There has been considerable debate about the relative importance of biological and hereditary factors as opposed to sociological determinants, and this has led to a split between these two broad explanatory approaches to suicidal behavior. However, twenty-first-century scientists generally recognize that there is a far more subtle interplay between such factors than had previously been understood.

Despite the early descriptive work, it was not until the 1970s that biological and hereditary contributions to suicidal behavior were given a firm scientific basis. In 1976 the Swedish researchers Marie Asberg, Lil Traskman-Bendz, and Peter Thoren demonstrated a lowered level of five hydroxy indole acetic acid (5-HIAA) in the cerebrospinal fluid (CSF) of suicide attempters who had used violent methods, and suggested that it may be a biochemical suicide predictor. This was important as CSF 5-HIAA is a breakdown product of serotonin, one of the neurotransmitters associated with mood and behavior disturbances. In 2000 Traskman-Bendz and John Mann reviewed subsequent studies from a number of different centers, and found that there is general agreement within scholarship that those people with low CSF 5-HIAA have a higher likelihood of committing suicide. They also noted that other primate studies have shown a relationship between low CSF 5-HIAA and aggression.

The importance of serotonin transmission has also been demonstrated by postmortem studies, where in 1995 Victoria Arango, Mark Underwood, and John Mann reported reduced binding to serotonin transporter sites in the ventral prefrontal cortex of the brain of completed suicides compared to those who died from other causes.

The activity of another neurotransmitter, dopamine, has also been examined by measuring the growth hormone response to apomorphine in depressed persons, some of whom later suicided. In 2001 William Pitchot and his Belgian colleagues reported a significantly lower response in eight male depressed patients who suicided compared to eighteen depressed patients who had never attempted suicide, leading them to conclude that dopamine was involved in the biology of suicide in depression.

Further evidence of the importance of neurotransmitters and the hypothalamic-pituitary-adrenal axis has emerged from a fifteen-year follow-up study of depressed patients who had had the dexamethasone suppression test during their initial assessment. In a 2001 study conducted at the University of Iowa, William Coryell and Michael Schlesser reported that 7 of the 8 suicides out of 78 patients had been nonsuppressors of cortisol, a biological indicator of their depressive condition. They reported that nonsuppression increased the likelihood of future suicide fourteenfold.

The role of corticotropin-releasing factor (CRF) has also been examined in completed suicides. Researchers have reported a reduction of CRF binding sites in the frontal cortex of the brain. Although not all studies concur with this finding, the role of CRF may still be important, as studies reviewed in 1999 by Christine Heim and Charles Nemeroff have demonstrated that early life stress produces persistent elevated CRF activity, which is associated with increased reactivity to stress in adult life. They suggest that stress at critical stages of development in people with a genetic predisposition could result in neurobiologically vulnerable adults who were more likely to develop mental disorders following exposure to further stress.

The hereditary basis to suicide was first convincingly described by Fini Schulsinger and his colleagues in 1979 in a Danish adoption study, which examined individuals who were separated at birth from their biological relatives. Using a matched control design, more of the biological relatives of the adopted suicides committed suicide compared to the biological relatives of adopted controls. Subsequent research has suggested that the genetic factor could be related to impulse control independent of mental disorder. Since Schulsinger's early study, there have been important developments in genetic studies that have been reviewed by others. For example, in 2000 Alec Roy and colleagues reported that in 399 suicide twin pairs in the literature, there was 13.2 percent concordance for suicide in the 129 identical (monozygous) twins, compared to 0.7 percent concordance for suicide in the 270 nonidentical (dizygous) twin pairs.

The extent of the possible contribution of genetic factors to suicidal behavior has been illustrated well in a 1998 study of 5,995 Australian twins. In a sophisticated logistic regression analysis, which allowed for sociodemographic, personality, psychiatric, traumatic event, and family history variables, no less than 45 percent of the variance in suicidal thoughts and behavior was related to genetic factors. Furthermore, after controlling for those variables, a history of suicide attempt or persistent suicidal thoughts in a co-twin remained a significant predictor of suicidal thoughts and behavior in identical twins, but not in nonidentical twin pairs.

Other genetic studies have focused on possible associations between suicidal behavior and genetic variance in the serotonin system. In particular, the enzyme tryptophan hydroxylase (TPH), which is the rate-limiting enzyme in the synthesis of serotonin, has been examined in detail. In a 2001 review and further study, Gustavo Turecki and colleagues noted that most research has been carried out on those who had attempted suicide. They investigated 101 suicide completers and could not replicate previous research, although they found another genetic variation to be more frequent in suicides than in normal controls. They referred to "the substantial role that the gene that codes for TPH may play in the neurobiology of suicidal behavior," but it is not clear whether it is related to psychiatric disorders or to personality traits such as impulsivity (Turecki 2001, p. 98).

Biological and hereditary factors do not operate independently, and do not inevitably lead to suicide in any individual, even if there is a strong family history of suicide. Rather, they can only increase the susceptibility of some individuals to react more severely to stress. The relationship between stress and neurobiological reactions has been reviewed from an ethological perspective, and there are persuasive primate as well as human studies that have added weight to the theory of Robert Post in 1992 about the role of stress in producing depression, the psychiatric condition most frequently associated with suicide.

The finding of significant biological and genetic determinants of suicidal behavior does not negate the importance of the individual and his or her psychosocial environment. Therefore the results of any of the individual studies referred to need to be considered with caution, and integrated into science's existing psychosocial understanding of suicidal behavior.

See also: SUICIDE; SUICIDE INFLUENCES AND FACTORS: GENDER, MENTAL ILLNESS

Bibliography

Arango, Victoria, Mark D. Underwood, and J. John Mann. "Postmortem Findings in Suicide Victims: Implications for In Vivo Imaging Studies." *Annals of the New York Academy of Sciences* 836 (1997):269–287.

Asberg, Marie, Lil Traskman, and Peter Thoren. "5-HIAA in the Cerebrospinal Fluid: A Biochemical Suicide Predictor?" *Archives of General Psychiatry* 33 (1976):1193–1197.

Coryell, William, and Michael Schlesser. "The Dexamethasone Suppression Test and Suicide Prediction." *American Journal of Psychiatry* 158 (2001):748–753.

Goldney, Robert D. "Ethology and the Suicidal Process." In Kees van Heeringen ed., *Understanding Suicidal Behaviour.* Chichester, England: John Wiley and Sons, 2001.

Goldney, Robert, and Johann Schioldann. "Pre-Durkheim Suicidology." *Crisis* 21 (2000):181–186.

Heim, Christine, and Charles B. Nemeroff. "The Impact of Early Adverse Experiences on Brain Systems Involved in the Pathophysiology of Anxiety and Affective Disorders." *Biological Psychiatry* 46 (1999):1509–1522.

Hucks, David, et al. "Corticotropin-Releasing Factor Binding Sites in Cortex of Depressed Suicides." *Psychopharmacology* 134 (1997):174–178.

Kety, Seymour. "Genetic Factors in Suicide." In Alec Roy ed., *Suicide.* Baltimore, MD: Williams and Wilkins, 1986.

Nemeroff, Charles B., et al. "Reduced Corticotropin-Releasing Factor Binding Sites in the Frontal Cortex of Suicide Victims." *Archives of General Psychiatry* 45 (1988):577–579.

Pitchot, William, et al. "Reduced Dopaminergic Activity in Depressed Suicides." *Psychoneuroendocrinology* 26 (2001):331–335.

Post, Robert M. "Transduction of Psychosocial Stress into the Neurobiology of Recurrent Affective Disorder." *American Journal of Psychiatry* 149 (1992):999–1010.

Roy, Alec, et al. "The Genetics of Suicidal Behavior." In Keith Hawton and Kees van Heeringen eds., *The International Handbook of Suicide and Attempted Suicide.* London: John Wiley and Sons, 2000.

Schulsinger, Fini, et al. "A Family Study of Suicide." In Mogens Schou and Erik Stromgren eds., *Origin, Prevention and Treatment of Affective Disorders.* New York: Academic Press, 1979.

Statham, Dixie J., et al. "Suicidal Behavior: An Epidemiological and Genetic Study." *Psychological Medicine* 28 (1998):839–855.

Traskman-Bendz, Lil, and John J. Mann. "Biological Aspects of Suicidal Behavior." In Keith Hawton and Kees van Heeringen eds., *The International Handbook of Suicide and Attempted Suicide.* London: John Wiley and Sons, 2000.

Turecki, Gustavo, et al. "TPH and Suicidal Behavior: A Study in Suicide Completers." *Molecular Psychiatry* 6 (2001):98–102.

ROBERT D. GOLDNEY

CULTURE

Anthropology, comparative psychiatry, and psychology have contributed with their specific approaches to better analyze the cultural processes leading to suicide. This rich literature presents new ways of understanding the causes and the influences of suicide on the models of explanation and on specific ways of prevention.

Universality of Suicide

Suicide has been known to humanity since the beginning of time and can be found in the mythologies and legends of the great civilizations. There was a Mayan goddess named Ixtab who protected those who had died by suicide. In Virgil's *Aeneid,* Dido, queen of Carthage, took her life after Aeneas reluctantly left her to continue his mission. Several suicides are depicted in the Bible, but most characters profiled were trying to avoid a life-threatening and shameful situation like falling prey to the enemy.

Suicide was present in many cultures before any contact with the conquering Europeans. The Maoris of New Zealand were known to have had a high tolerance toward suicide. There was a famed cliff where people would jump and the port of Whangaroa presumably took its name from a word meaning suicide. The scholar Fredrick Maning believed that as early as 1843 suicide occurred every day among this people. A famous legend told of TeAohuruhuru, a young bride of great beauty, who had been dishonored by her husband when he unveiled her naked body to friends while she was sleeping. As revenge, she drowned herself in front of his boat.

In a 1985 overview of the Bimin-Kuskusmin and other groups of New Guinea, the anthropologist Fitz Poole found that their contemporary high rates of suicide had preceded acculturation and suicides were present during a period when intertribal warfare and cannibalism were not yet eradicated. Poole estimated that as much as 10 percent of deaths over the last six generations were by suicide. During a trip around 1970 he counted thirty suicides, which accounted for 57 percent of all deaths. The men who committed suicide were mostly in their early twenties and were trying to avoid making war; the women were stressed by the high number of male victims and by being forced to participate in cannibalism.

Cross-Cultural Picture of Suicide

Many countries report their suicidal rates to the World Health Organization (WHO). These rates are difficult to compare because the methods of recording vary between countries and even within geographical areas of a single country. For instance, the Indian sociologist Soltamin Aleem reported in 1994 that the rate was near 25 per 100,000 annually in the state of Kerala, a state of Southwestern India with a relatively high level of education and distribution of income, and below 1 per 100,000 in the state of Bihar, which is paradoxically one of the poorest states of India. For this reason, the anthropologist Robert Desjarlais concluded that the variations between nations were dependent upon the ability of local institutions to complete valid investigations. He quoted two field studies in North India that yielded rates three to five times the national rates.

The most recent rates reported to WHO in the year 2001 show that the highest ranking countries, with a rate above 16 suicides per 100,000 individuals per year, cover a large area, including the Baltic states, some countries of the former Eastern Europe, the federation of Russia, China, Japan, and Sri Lanka. In Western Europe, the rates are in the same range for Austria, France, and Switzerland. The rest of Western Europe, as well as the United States and Canada, was in the category of between 8 and 16 suicides per 100,000 per year, which also includes Australia and India. The countries from Latin America are in the lower range, with the exception of Cuba. The majority of the governments from the African continent did not report any data.

Rates of suicide also tend to vary little when members from a culture migrate to another country, as was found in Australia and the United States, at least during the first years of settlement, and they tend toward the rate of the host country as the years progress. The rates of suicide also vary within the ethnic groups of one country. For example, the rate for the large Hungarian community in Romania is more similar to that of Hungary than to that of the rest of Romania. The African-American population of the United States has a slightly lower rate than the national rate despite the group's lower average income. In the southwestern states, the rate is half for Latinos as compared to Anglos. However, a 1999 study on youth by the Centers for Disease Control showed that Latinos were more likely than African Americans or European Americans to have seriously considered attempting suicide. Consequently, the portrait of suicide and culture in the United States may change significantly in the upcoming decades of the twenty-first century.

Two reports from 1960 show that suicide was far from unknown in sub-Saharan Africa even before the end of colonization. Local reports from Uganda, Zambia, and South Africa illustrate a significant presence of suicide there, with a rate around 10 per 100,000. For example, the anthropologist Ellen Brown reported twelve cases among the Sara Nar of Chad, which corresponds to a rate of 20 per 100,000.

Suicide and the Mental Health of a Society

The rate of suicide is one of the many factors that reflect the mental health of a population. Suicide often indicates how a certain range of people with psychiatric or adaptation problems are excluded from social or family life rather than providing a good estimate of the happiness of a population. The rates of depression, alcoholism, or suicide attempts are more reliable indices of the mental state of a population. However, a suicide rate cannot be a good argument against a sociopolitical system. During his presidency, Dwight D. Eisenhower had been critical of the social democratic system in Sweden on the grounds that Sweden had a high suicide rate when, in fact, the Swedish rate had reached a peak during the country's period of capitalism.

Conceptions of Suicide across Cultures

The cultural attitudes of tolerance toward or repression against suicide probably influence individual choices about committing suicide. Sometimes a religion condones certain forms of sanctified suicides while condemning this mode of exit from life for the common people. The Hindu religion is a good example. In 1998 the anthropologist Karin Andriolo described how the Hindu society considered taking one's own life as a welcomed departure when a person had reached a state of perfection. In "The History of Suicide in India," Upendra Thakur documented many characters of high and low origin who committed suicide in narration of the religious texts. However, during the period of *Dharmasastras,* one of the sacred books, suicide was determined to be a sin and the suicide victim deprived from death rituals. In the modern period, suicide is viewed as shameful for the family.

In Bangalore, India, women are often accused of being the cause of suicide as shown in a 1998 survey conducted by Michel Tousignant, Shekhar Seshadri, and Anthony Raj. If women commit suicide, they are said to be ashamed of having transgressed a rule; if men commit suicide, they are thought to have been the victim of some form of abuse at the hands of a woman. This article also mentions that *sati,* the suicide by the self-immolation of a widow on her husband's pyre, is still romanticized by a wide section of the Indian population. There is a ban on sati and it has been determined that some modern cases of sati were not suicides but rather disguised homicides.

In Haiti public perception is that suicide is extremely rare. In this society, suicide is unacceptable among the poor because it is considered an example of letting down friends in their fight against the adversities of life. On the other hand, in 1998 the anthropologist Jeanne Marecek, working in Sri Lanka, found little tolerance of suicide despite the high rate in this country. The population attributes this gesture to the conditions of life, such as unemployment or romantic problems, and people are usually ready to give support to persons who have made an attempt.

In sub-Saharan countries many traditional religions view suicide as impure. In Uganda people avoid coming into contact with the corpse of a person deceased by suicide and in Rwanda survivors burn the person's possessions. A Senegal oral tradition requires that someone who comes across a person who died by suicide should make a sacrifice, and in Nigeria the body is buried on the spot, without any ritual.

Theories

The French sociologist Émile Durkheim's theory about suicide, which came into prominence at the end of the nineteenth century, was cultural. His argument claimed that regions with the highest rates of suicide were in a relative state of anomie; that is, situations where the rules guiding a society were either absent or weak. Similarly, societies with a relative absence of social integration were considered hardest hit by suicide. One of his points was that Jews and Catholics had low rates because they formed more cohesive groups, while Protestants had high rates because their relationship to God was more personal. This theory is still useful in understanding how rates are becoming higher in rapidly acculturating groups such as the Aboriginal peoples of Northern Canada, Greenland, Brazil, and the Melanesian islands. The rapid change from a nomadic to a sedentary life, the spread of alcoholism, the lack of access to modes of production, the changing patterns of family structure, abuse and incest, and racial discrimination from the dominant society are often the elements of the cultural breakdown.

However, the fact that people committing suicide are mostly young males calls for a less global explanation. The sociologist Francis Hezel has shown that suicide, as well as alcoholism in Melanesia, is a way of escaping social contradictions by young people with little faith in their future. The younger generation is often schooled to foreign values, far away from their families, and is later scorned by parents who have lost their moral authority over them. Not being able to adopt any model, these young people choose not to participate in life by committing suicide.

In China and in India where the rate of female suicide is very similar to that of males (in contrast to the ratio of one to four in many countries), women move to their in-laws' homes after marriage. One likely explanation of female suicides is that when repeated conflicts take place, not only is it shameful and in some cases impossible for the women to return to their families, they are threatened to be deprived of contact with their children.

In a form of ritual suicide, Buddhist monks in Saigon who protested the violence demonstrated by the Ngo Dinh Diem government during the Vietnam war died by self-immoliation in an open public square. BETTMANN/CORBIS

According to the Beijing-based journalist Shuhua Jia, women in rural areas rarely enjoy a marriage based on love and whole families are forced to live in one-room apartments.

In Western countries, men often commit suicide after the end of their marriage, sometimes after a long period of alcoholism when they have alienated their friends and relatives by their conduct. Here, they are the ones who are estranged from their children and who find themselves in a state of solitude and low social support.

Scholars confess the theoretical challenge in explaining why suicide is nearly absent in certain societies. In North Africa as well as in sub-Saharan Africa, many authors have identified the low prevalence of guilt and the habit of projecting aggression onto others rather than criticizing oneself, as well as the tendencies to express stress in bodily symptoms rather than by emotional means. These modes of expressing stress may eventually protect against depression and suicide.

The 2000 review of the sociologist Steven Stack on religion and suicide has contributed to a different perspective on some of Durkheim's ideas. First, there is mixed support in the United States for the hypothesis that Catholics are more protected from suicide than people from other religions and no support for this statistic is found in Canada. Reanalysis of data from 1905 to 1910 in the Netherlands suggests that Catholics may have been hiding some of their cases of suicide. However, a survey of seventy nations has shown that a high rate of Islamics in the country was associated with a lower suicide rate. There is some evidence that religious commitment may be a protective factor despite the fact that many studies have refuted this hypothesis. The connection between religion and suicide is weak and most studies indicate little about the religious status of those who have committed suicide, making it difficult to analyze the connection.

Prevention and Intervention

One of the most promising interventions has come from Sri Lanka in a project asking volunteers to travel to villages where suicide is spreading and to support families in which a member has died from suicide. In the United States, the Centers for Disease Control issued guidelines for Aboriginal communities that can be used with similar groups. Scholars maintain that prevention should be done both at the community level, to promote the sense of pride and efficacy of the group, and at the individual level, to follow up with those who are recognized as threatened, such as in schools and in emergency services. Because social scientists often find a situation of social rejection within certain ethnic groups, or the marginalization of certain persons within these groups, efforts to valorize these cultures is a first step toward preventing suicide.

In 1999 the researchers Michael Phillips, Huaqing Liu, and Yanping Zhang reported that there are more than 300,000 suicides a year in China. There is little recognition of depression and it is estimated than only 5 percent of the cases of clinical depression are currently treated. They proclaim that a wider access to treatment of depression and support would help prevent suicide. Since the rate is higher in rural areas where emergency medicine is not readily available, the researchers maintain that there should be a better control of pesticides, which is one of the most readily available and lethal ways of dying by suicide in that country.

Approximately 1 million people die from suicide each year around the world. Suicide is becoming an international public health concern on the same level as illnesses such as malaria. Researchers are in a position to verify that the experience of some cultures is being repeated elsewhere. For example, the suicide contagion experienced among rapidly acculturating Aboriginal peoples has started to appear in Brazil. Because of this prevalence, there is an urgency among social scientists to address suicide as soon as it appears among certain people groups, and to rapidly apply learned lessons in order to suggest methods of prevention.

See also: DURKHEIM, ÉMILE; SUICIDE; SUICIDE BASICS: HISTORY; SUICIDE INFLUENCES AND FACTORS: INDIGENOUS POPULATIONS

Bibliography

Andriolo, Karin R. "Gender and the Cultural Construction of Good and Bad Suicides." *Suicide and Life-Threatening Behavior* 28 (1998):37–49.

Desjarlais, Robert, Leon Eisenberg, Byron Good, and Arthur Kleinman. *World Mental Health: Problems and Priorities in Low-Income Countries.* New York: Oxford University Press, 1995.

Hezel, Francis X. "The Cultural Patterns in Trukese Suicide." *Ethnology* 23 (1984):193–206.

Marecek, Jeanne. "Culture, Gender, and Suicidal Behavior in Sri Lanka." *Suicide and Life-Threatening Behavior* 28 (1998):62–68.

Phillips, Michael R., Huaquing Liu, and Yanping Zhang. "Suicide and Social Change in China." *Medicine and Psychiatry* 23 (1999):25–50.

Poole, Fitz. "Among the Boughs of the Hanging Tree: Male Suicide among the Bimin-Kuskusmin of Papua New Guinea." In Francis Hezel, Donald Rubenstein, and Geoffrey White eds., *Culture, Youth and Suicide in the Pacific: Papers from the East-West Center Conference.* Honolulu: East-West Center, 1985.

Stack, Steven. "Suicide: A 15-Year Review of the Sociological Literature: Part II Modernization and Social Integration Perspectives." *Suicide and Life-Threatening Behavior* 30 (2000):163–176.

Thakur, Upendra. *The History of Suicide in India.* Delhi: Munshi Ram Manohar Lal, 1963.

Tousignant, Michel, Shekhar Seshadri, and Anthony Raj. "Gender and Suicide in India: A Multiperspective Approach." *Suicide and Life-Threatening Behavior* 28 (1998):50–61.

MICHEL TOUSIGNANT

GENDER

Consistent with current scholarship, gender, like race, is conceptualized as a social construct rather than as an attribute of individuals. It is what cultures make of the fact that a person is a woman or a man. Gender is also what cultures define as appropriate behavior for women and men across a variety of situations, including situations of distress. Finally, gender, like race, is a status variable determining a person's location in the social hierarchy, including the barriers and resources that a person will likely encounter.

Patterns of Suicidal Behavior by Culture

In the United States women and men tend to engage in different kinds of suicidal behavior. Women are more likely to engage in nonfatal suicidal behavior, while men are more likely to die as a result of a suicidal act. In 1998 the researchers Silvia Sara

Canetto and Isaac Sakinofsky called this phenomenon the gender paradox of suicidal behavior. United States gender patterns of suicidal behavior are similar to those found in other English-speaking countries, such as Canada and Australia. They are different, however, from those observed in a variety of other countries. For example, in Finland and in India, men have similar rates of nonfatal suicidal behavior as women. Furthermore, in China, it is women who typically die of suicide. China accounts for 21 percent of the world's population, 44 percent of the world's suicides, and 56 percent of the world's female suicides. Exceptions to the male predominance among those who die of suicides are also found within some ethnic communities in the United States. For example, according to a 1997 San Francisco study by Julia Shiang and colleagues, Asian-American women aged eighty-five and older have twice the rates of suicide mortality of same-aged Asian-American men.

Suicide methods are culturally specific. Common suicide methods in one culture may be unusual in another. Women and men tend to use the methods that are culturally permissible for them in their culture, not just those that are accessible. In some cultures, women and men use different suicide methods; in other cultures they use the same methods. Since the 1990s firearms have been the most common method of suicide in the United States with both women and men. However, they account for a greater proportion of men's than women's suicides (two-thirds vs. one-third). By contrast, in Canada women still prefer poisoning as a method of suicide, and men firearms. However, Canadian men's preference for firearms as a method of suicide is lower than that of U.S. women. In addition, among the Inuit of Canada, an Aboriginal hunting community, the most common method of suicide is hanging, despite the widespread availability of firearms.

Adolescent Suicidal Behavior in the United States

Gender patterns of suicidal behavior vary by age across the life span. In the United States adolescent girls are two to three times more likely to report being suicidal than adolescent boys. Suicidal ideation appears to be particularly common among Mexican-American youth. Adolescent girls are also more likely than adolescent boys to engage in nonfatal acts of suicidal behavior by an average ratio of three to one. Approximately one in ten adolescent girls reports having engaged in suicidal behavior. Gender differences in nonfatal suicidal behavior are not found in all ethnic groups in the United States. For example, among native Hawaiians and Native Americans, adolescent girls report similar rates of nonfatal suicidal behavior as adolescent boys. Rates of nonfatal suicidal behavior appear to be particularly high among Mexican-American girls. Nonfatal suicidal behavior is more common among adolescents from lower socioeconomic classes such as adolescents whose parents are not as well educated. Homosexual adolescent males have high rates of nonfatal suicidal behavior, relative to heterosexual males. Rates of nonfatal suicidal behavior decline after adolescence in women and men.

Suicide rates in U.S. adolescent males exceed those of their female peers by a ratio of five to one. The gender difference in mortality holds across ethnicity, although suicide rates vary greatly from group to group. Native-American boys have higher rates of suicide than Native-American girls, although the latter have higher rates of suicide than European-American boys. No definitive information is available on rates of death by suicide among homosexual males.

Adult Suicidal Behavior in the United States

For women, suicide rates remain low throughout the life span, with a small peak around forty-five years of age. For men, on the other hand, rates of suicide increase after sixty years of age. This is particularly true among males of European-American backgrounds. The female-to-male suicide ratio for those aged sixty-five and above hovers around one to six. There are ethnic variations in gender patterns of suicide mortality across the life span. For example, rates of suicide for Chinese-American women rise after the age of forty-five, and reach a peak in late adulthood.

Explanations for Gender Patterns of Suicidal Behavior

Most theories of gender and suicidal behavior have overlooked the local and international cultural variability in patterns of gender and suicidal behavior. Overgeneralizing from U.S. national trends, theorists have asked questions like, Why do women engage in more suicidal behavior and why do men die of suicide, instead of questions like,

Why are women in some cultures more likely than men to engage in suicidal behavior? or Why are men in some cultures more likely to kill themselves than women? As a result, most theories fail to account for the variations in gender patterns of suicidal behavior found both within and beyond the United States. For example, it has been argued that suicide in older adults is a response to the losses of aging (e.g., reduced financial resources, widowhood, and poor health). This theory does not take into account that in some cultures rates of suicide are low in both older women and older men. It also fails to explain why in many countries, including the United States, suicide is rare in older women, despite the fact that that older women experience more social, economic, and health problems than older men.

The theory of cultural scripts, which is based on the observation of a correspondence between cultural norms and behavior, addresses cultural variations in gender and suicidal behavior. According to this theory, individuals tend to engage in the behaviors (including suicidal behaviors) that are meaningful and permissible for people like them in their culture. Each culture has its own models and rules for suicidal behavior. There are specific conditions under which suicidal behavior is expected, and by whom. In other words, there are different scripts of suicidal behavior. These scripts define the scenario of the suicidal act (including the actor, the method, the precipitants, and the themes) as well as the consequences of the suicidal behavior. When suicidal behavior becomes a possibility, these scripts, transformed and individualized, provide a blueprint for action.

What are the cultural scripts of gender and suicidal behavior in the United States? Studies indicate that it is considered unmasculine to admit to suicidal thoughts. Nonfatal suicidal behavior is considered less masculine and less potent than fatal suicidal behavior. "Feminine" persons are expected to "attempt" suicide more than "masculine" persons. Males are particularly critical of other males who survive a suicidal act. Studies also show that killing oneself is seen as a masculine and relatively strong act: Male suicide is not judged as less wrong or less foolish than female suicide. Men who kill themselves are viewed as better adjusted than women who kill themselves, independent of the reasons for the suicide. Men are also more likely to agree with and accept a suicidal decision than women. These meanings and attitudes have been particularly well documented among adolescents and young adults.

Given these gendered messages about suicidal behavior, some scholars are not surprised by the fact that in the United States females are more likely to engage in nonfatal suicidal behavior but are less likely than males to kill themselves. The association of femininity and nonfatal suicidal behavior may be a factor in women's high rates of nonfatal suicidal behavior. At the same time, the association of suicide with masculinity may protect females against killing themselves. Research has also shown that identification with behaviors considered feminine, independent of sex, is associated with increased risk for nonfatal suicidal behavior. For example, homosexual and bisexual males who score high on a measure of conventional femininity are more likely to have a history of nonfatal suicidal behavior.

Prevention

The data on cultural scripts of gender and suicidal behavior suggest new directions for the prevention of suicidal behavior both in educational programs as well as in interventions with suicidal persons. Social scientists and health care professionals believe prevention programs and clinical interventions should educate about the epidemiology of gender and suicidal behavior across sexual orientation, social class, and culture. These prevention programs should assess beliefs about gender and suicidal behavior. Furthermore, they should challenge potential dysfunctional beliefs, such as the idea that nonfatal suicidal behavior is an acceptable way for young women to cope with problems, or the idea that killing oneself is powerful and masculine.

In terms of prevention, a promising finding is that androgynous persons tend to view the decision to kill oneself as foolish, independent of the reason for the suicidal wish. They also report less agreement, acceptance, and sympathy for such a decision. Researchers believe it may be that androgyny is associated with greater cognitive and behavioral resourcefulness and flexibility. This is not surprising given that androgynous persons are high in conventionally feminine traits, such as expressiveness, as well as in conventionally masculine traits like instrumentality. These findings suggest that suicide prevention programs may be more effective if they address the limitations that gender ideologies impose on coping, and if they encourage the development of androgynous behavior.

See also: GRIEF: GENDER; SUICIDE; SUICIDE BASICS: EPIDEMIOLOGY; SUICIDE INFLUENCES AND FACTORS: GENDER

Bibliography

Canetto, Silvia Sara. "Gender and Suicidal Behavior: Theories and Evidence." In Ronald W. Maris, Morton M. Silverman, and Silvia Sara Canetto eds., *Review of Suicidology.* New York: Guilford, 1997.

Canetto, Silvia Sara. "Meanings of Gender and Suicidal Behavior among Adolescents." *Suicide and Life-Threatening Behavior* 27 (1997):339–351.

Canetto, Silvia Sara, and David Lester. "Gender, Culture and Suicidal Behavior." *Transcultural Psychiatry* 35 (1998):163–191.

Canetto, Silvia Sara, and David Lester. "Gender and the Primary Prevention of Suicide Mortality." *Suicide and Life-Threatening Behavior* 25 (1995):58–69.

Canetto, Silvia Sara, and David Lester. *Women and Suicidal Behavior.* New York: Springer, 1995.

Canetto, Silvia Sara, and Isaac Sakinofsky. "The Gender Paradox in Suicide." *Suicide and Life-Threatening Behavior* 28 (1998):1–23.

Dahlen, Eric R., and Silvia Sara Canetto. "The Role of Gender and Suicide Precipitant in Attitudes toward Nonfatal Suicidal Behavior." *Death Studies* 26 (2001): 99–116.

Kral, Michael. "Suicide and the Internalization of Culture: Three Questions." *Transcultural Psychiatry* 35 (1998):221–233.

Lester, David. "Suicide among the Elderly in the World: Covariation with Psychological and Socioeconomic Factors." In Diego De Leo ed., *Suicide and Euthanasia in Older Adults.* Seattle, WA: Hogrefe & Huber, 2001.

Murray, Christopher J. L., and Alan D. Lopez. *The Global Burden of Disease.* Cambridge, MA: Harvard University Press, 1996.

Pritchard, Colin. "Suicide in the People's Republic of China Categorized by Age and Gender: Evidence of the Influence of Culture on Suicide." *Acta Psychiatrica Scandinavica* 93 (1996):362–367.

Remafedi, Gary. "Suicide and Sexual Orientation." *Archives of General Psychiatry* 56 (1999):885–886.

Shiang, Julia, Robert Blinn, Bruce Bongar, Boyd Stephens, Donna Allison, and Alan Schatzberg. "Suicide in San Francisco, CA: A Comparison of Caucasian and Asian Groups, 1987–1994." *Suicide and Life-Threatening Behavior* 27 (1997):80–91.

Yee, Darlene. "Issues and Trends Affecting Asian Americans, Women and Aging." In Jean M. Coyle ed., *Handbook on Women and Aging.* Westport, CT: Greenwood Press, 1997.

SILVIA SARA CANETTO

INDIGENOUS POPULATIONS

In the mid-1990s, during the course of a national commission into indigenous affairs, the Royal Commission on Aboriginal Peoples released a special report on Aboriginal suicide, stating:

> Collective despair, or collective lack of hope, will lead us to collective suicide. This type of suicide can take many forms, foreshadowed by many possible signs: identity crisis, loss of pride, every kind of dependence, denial of our customs and traditions, degradation of our environment, weakening of our language, abandonment of our struggle for our Aboriginal rights, our autonomy and our culture, uncaring acceptance of violence, passive acknowledgment of lack of work and unemployment, corruption of our morals, tolerance of drugs and idleness, parental surrendering of responsibilities, lack of respect for elders, envy of those who try to keep their heads up and who might succeed, and so on. *(Royal Commission on Aboriginal Peoples 1995, p. 38)*

Chief Jean-Charles Piétacho of the Mingan First Nation, whose submission is included in a special report from 1995 on Aboriginal suicide for the Canadian Royal Commission on Aboriginal Peoples, might have been speaking of indigenous suicide in any of the nations with histories of Anglo-settler colonialism. The indigenous peoples of Canada, the United States, Australia, and New Zealand were all exposed to colonization, dispossession, and depopulation through disease and violence. This was, arguably, most recent and devastating for Aboriginal Australians. Among the outcomes of these histories are levels of disease and ill health that are worse than for nonindigenous nationals. Using the crude proxy of the gap in life expectancy between indigenous and non-indigenous peoples in each nation, health inequality is also greatest for Aboriginal Australians, being shorter by nearly two decades. In all four countries, indigenous suicide has been recognized and systematically addressed as a major health issue in Australia only since the 1990s. Finally, indigenous suicide in all four countries occurs against a backdrop of increasing national rates of suicide for young men. For each of these countries, overall suicide rates for men between the ages of fifteen and twenty-four are high in comparison with most other industrialized nations, ranging between 20 and 40 per 100,000 in the early 1990s, with New Zealand followed by Australia being the highest of the four. While indigenous suicide in each of these four societies will be considered, for the reasons suggested above, particular attention will be given to Aboriginal suicide in Australia.

Patterns of Suicide Rates

Increasing rates of young male indigenous suicide in the United States have been documented from the 1950s, with rates varying across the nation from 8 to 120 per 100,000. Contemporary rates for young people are some three to four times higher than for the nation as a whole, with two-thirds of all indigenous suicides between the ages of fifteen and thirty-four being male. Violent means are the norm with firearms being responsible for over half of all indigenous suicides. A similar picture is found in Canada with a significant increase in suicide rates for indigenous young adult males in the 1970s. In 1987 the National Task Force on Suicide in Canada reported that suicides accounted for 15 to 20 percent of all violent deaths of native people in the early 1980s, with 60 percent of suicides occurring in those aged fifteen to twenty-four, at a male to female ratio of three to one. As in the United States violent means are common, but with a greater and increasing proportion of deaths as a result of hanging and with the proportion of deaths from firearms declining. As noted earlier, New Zealand as a nation has the highest suicide rate for young men of any of these four countries. Even so, Maori suicide rates were 50 percent higher for young men aged fifteen to nineteen years in the mid-1990s, with rates for males aged fifteen to twenty-four having peaked in 1989 at 49 per 100,000. Violent means, particularly hanging, are the norm and, as in Australia, attention has been brought to this issue as a result of deaths in custody.

In Australia indigenous suicide has been recognized as a major issue only since the late 1980s, having been brought to public attention by the Royal Commission into Aboriginal Deaths in Custody. Although the excess of indigenous suicide deaths in custody eventually was found to be a result of the massive overrepresentation of Aboriginals among those in police and prison custody, the attention and coverage of hanging was intense and supported the development of public perceptions and understandings of Aboriginal hanging that included a political dimension. It was a series of suicides in the custody of the State of Queensland in the mid-1980s that led to the formation of the Royal Commission, and in that state suicide in the wider Aboriginal population subsequently increased some fourfold between 1992 and 1996. For the period 1990 to 1995 that state had a suicide rate of 14.5 per 100,000, with the Aboriginal and Torres Strait Islander rate being 23.6. The elevated rate is entirely accounted for by the increased indigenous male suicides among those aged fifteen to twenty-four (112.5 per 100,000) and those aged twenty-five to thirty-four (72.5 per 100,000), with these figures being 3.6 and 2.2 times, respectively, the rates for the state as a whole. Australian indigenous suicide is not only increasing and concentrated among young adult males, it is also unevenly distributed geographically and temporally with "waves" of suicides affecting particular populations at different times. This suggests a condition of community risk mediated by individual vulnerability to harm (including accidents, homicide, and other alcohol-related problems), of which suicide is but one manifestation.

Explanations for the Higher Suicide Rates

While explanations for suicide rates in indigenous populations are diverse and complex, all of the studies of this phenomenon emphasize the impact of the breakdown of cultural structures, processes, and integrity. Almost all such interpretations link these influences on culture to colonization and its consequences for social and family functioning as was summarized by the Canadian Royal Commission:

> Commissioners have concluded that high rates of suicide and self-injury among Aboriginal people are the result of a complex mix of social, cultural, economic and psychological dislocations that flow from the past to the present. The root causes of

> these dislocations lie in the history of colonial relations between Aboriginal peoples and the authorities and settlers who went on to establish "Canada," and in the distortion of Aboriginal lives that resulted from that history. *(Royal Commission on Aboriginal Peoples 1995, p. 2)*

In Australia the historical context includes a period of enormous social change through the 1970s. Previously, indigenous lives and communities had been controlled through racist legislation, which began to lift only in the late 1960s. The next decade was characterized by political and social instability, the lifting of restricted access to alcohol, rapidly increasing rates of violence and accidents, high rates of incarceration, and many other manifestations of continuing turmoil and disadvantage, with serious consequences for the stability of family and community life. Aboriginal Australians who have taken their lives usually have been young men who grew to maturity during or since that period. They are members of the first generation to be exposed to the developmental consequences of widespread instability, much of which reflects the indirect effects of heavy alcohol use (particularly on paternal roles and, consequently, on male identity).

While such factors are critical to interpretation at a population level, they are mediated by effects on individuals. In a 1997 review of studies across these societies, Valerie Clarke, C. James Frankish, and Lawrence Green identified an association between suicide and factors relating to substance use and compromised mental health and self-esteem. The misuse of alcohol, particularly binge drinking, is a consistent association, as Anne Graham and her colleagues explained: "the script for 'drinking' in many indigenous communities includes binge drinking, anger over perceived past grievances and injustices, and suicidal ideation and injury" (Graham, et al. 2000, p. 13).

Most interpretations also highlight persistent social disadvantage. Studies in the early twenty-first century suggest, however, that the predisposition to suicide by vulnerable youth is influenced not only by absolute living standards but also by how they view their circumstances relative to those around them. Interpretations from Australia and Hawaii show that indigenous youth cite the widening gap between indigenous and Western cultures as an important factor in indigenous suicide.

A final consideration in explaining suicide rates in indigenous communities is that of "meaning." In indigenous settings, particularly in Aboriginal Australia, the occurrence of suicide and the circumstances of the indigenous communities mean that many people, including children, will have witnessed the aftermath of suicide. Clustering and the death by hanging of children, some as young as eleven years of age, in such communities suggests a powerful communicative and imitative dimension. At least in Australia, the communicative dimension of suicidal behavior has been influenced by events such as the Royal Commission into Aboriginal Deaths in Custody and by portrayals of hanging (as art, caricature, and graffiti) that associate hanging with political ends.

Intervention Programs

Intervention programs are necessarily informed by the service and policy frameworks in relation to suicide prevention and indigenous health across the four countries. These are significantly different. For instance, whereas there is a national Indian Health Service in the United States, in Australia indigenous health is largely the province of state health departments and, to a lesser extent, commonwealth-funded, community-controlled health services. Furthermore, initiatives related to indigenous suicide are encompassed within different national policy initiatives. For example, the Brighter Futures Program of Health Canada drives broad-based programs that address the social and cultural circumstances of young Native Canadians. In Australia there is as yet no nationally implemented indigenous health and well-being strategy, but partnerships with Aboriginal and Torres Strait Islander people form a key action area in the national framework for the prevention of suicide and self-harm.

Such differences aside, there has generally been a transition in each nation from crisis-oriented interventions targeting at-risk individuals toward broader, multileveled strategic approaches. This was exemplified by the recommendations of the Canadian Royal Commission: "A comprehensive approach must include plans and programs at three levels of intervention: 1) those that focus on building direct suicide crisis services; 2) those that focus on promoting broadly preventive action through community development; and 3) those that focus on the long-term needs of Aboriginal people for self-determination, self-sufficiency, healing and reconciliation within Canada" (Royal Commission on Aboriginal Peoples 1995, p. 75). The commission reported that to be effective, programs should be community driven, holistic, and situated in a broad problem-solving approach. They should also balance crisis management with social agendas, place priority on children and youth, train Aboriginal caregivers, and encourage community-wide involvement.

In Australia suicide continues to increase in Aboriginal communities and is functionally inseparable from the wider picture of higher rates of disease, premature mortality, and social disadvantage. Perhaps because suicide has most recently emerged in Australia, the responses have remained ad hoc and largely crisis oriented although veiled by the ambiguous or evasive title of "life promotion" programs. There is, however, increasing recognition in policy and service planning of the need for a strategic balance of targeted and functionally accessible services and broad social interventions. For the indigenous peoples of each of these nations, empowerment and investment in the long term is needed to ensure the security of the environment of indigenous children.

See also: CAUSES OF DEATH; SUICIDE

Bibliography

Barber, James G. "Relative Misery and Youth Suicide." *Australian and New Zealand Journal of Psychiatry* 35 (2001):49–57.

Baume, Pierre J. M., Chris Cantor, and Philippa McTaggart. *Suicides in Queensland: A Comprehensive Study, 1990–1995.* Brisbane: Australian Institute for Suicide Research and Prevention, 1997.

Clarke, Valerie A., James C. Frankish, and Lawrence W. Green. "Understanding Suicide among Indigenous Adolescents: A Review Using the PRECEDE Model." *Injury Prevention* 3 (1997):126–134.

Graham, Anne, Joseph Reser, Carl Scuderi, Stephen Zubrick, Meg Smith, and Bruce Turley. "Suicide: An Australian Psychological Discussion Paper." *Australian Psychologist* 35 (2000):1–28.

Hunter, Ernest, Joseph Reser, Mercy Baird, and Paul Reser. "An Analysis of Suicide in Indigenous Communities of North Queensland: The Historical, Cultural, and Symbolic Landscape." Report for the Commonwealth Department of Health and Aged Care, Canberra, Australia, 1999.

National Task Force on Suicide in Canada. *Suicide in Canada.* Ottawa: Mental Health Division, Health Services and Promotion Branch, Health and Welfare Canada, 1987.

Royal Commission on Aboriginal Peoples. *Choosing Life: Special Report on Suicide among Aboriginal People.* Ottawa: Royal Commission on Aboriginal Peoples, 1995.

Sakinofsky, Isaac, and Antoon Leenaars. "Suicide in Canada with Special Reference to the Difference between Canada and the United States." *Suicide and Life-Threatening Behavior* 27 (1997):112–126.

Shore, J. H., and S. Manson. "American Indian Psychiatric and Social Problems." *Transcultural Psychiatry Research Review* 20 (1983):159–180.

ERNEST HUNTER
DESLEY HARVEY

MEDIA EFFECTS

Widespread coverage of a suicide in the media has long been thought to be capable of triggering copycat suicides in the mass public. In fact, more than forty scientific papers have been published on the impact of suicide stories in the media on suicide in the real world. However, there have been some inconsistencies in the findings of this research. Some studies find significant increases in suicide after a widely publicized suicide story, while other research finds no effect. The following entry reviews the research evidence with four goals in mind. First, what hard evidence is there for a copycat effect? Do suicidal people actually imitate suicides in the media? Second, how can this association be interpreted? What are the major theories that have been used? Third, what scientific generalizations can social scientists construct from the existing studies through a comprehensive analysis?

Direct Evidence for a Media Impact

In 1774 the German poet Johann Wolfgang von Goethe's *The Sorrows of Young Man Werther,* a novel where the hero commits suicide due to a failed love affair, was banned in many European locations. It was perceived as responsible for imitative suicides in such places as Italy, Leipzig, and Copenhagen. Systematic scientific investigations on copycat suicide began with the work of the doctor David Phillips of the University of California in the

1970s. The largest possible copycat effect found was for Marilyn Monroe. During the month of her suicide in August 1962 there were an additional 303 suicides in the United States alone, an increase of 12 percent. In general, however, highly publicized stories increase the U.S. national suicide rate by only 2.51 percent in the month of media coverage.

Most of the evidence for a copycat suicide effect is very indirect and usually weak. That is, associations are drawn between the presence of a suicide story and a rise in the social suicide rate. This rise is often demonstrated to be independent of other social conditions such as season, year, holidays, and the state of the economy. However, it typically is not known to what extent the people committing suicide are aware of the suicide story and if it had anything to do with their suicides.

Nevertheless, there is some convincing evidence for a direct copycat effect. For example, in the book *Final Exit* (1993), a guide to suicide for terminally ill persons, asphyxiation is the recommended means of suicide. In the year that *Final Exit* was published, suicides by asphyxiation in New York City rose by 313 percent from 8 to 33 suicides. Further, a copy of *Final Exit* was found at the scene of 27 percent of these suicides. Michel Tousignant and his colleagues studied seventy-one coroner's reports on suicides in Quebec in the month following a publicized suicide and found direct evidence of probable copycat effects. They determined that at least 14 percent of the suicides in the month following a widely publicized suicide of a popular Quebec journalist were at least partially linked to the story. For example, a number of the suicides were found with a copy of the suicide story nearby. In some cases the victim stated explicitly to significant others that he or she was going to imitate the suicide of the hero. Ninety percent of the suicides used the same method (hanging) as the role model in the story.

Explanations of Media Impacts on Suicide

Explanations of media impacts on suicide have generally been framed in terms of social learning theory. The simplest rendition is the imitation explanation, which argues that suicide stories are advertisements for suicide. Simply put, one learns that there are troubled people who solve their problems (e.g., divorce, terminal illness, dishonor) through suicide. Mentally troubled persons in society may simply copy the behavior of troubled people in the suicide stories. The content and presentation of suicide stories may be secondary to the basic message conveyed about problem solving. Research using this model generally lumps all varieties of stories together, making no distinctions among subtypes by celebrity status, age, gender, occupation, or other characteristics.

A more complex set of explanations revolves around the learning process of differential identification. To the extent that people identify with a type of story, that type would be expected to have more of an impact. For example, men may be more apt to copycat the suicides of men than the suicides of women. If people tend to copycat the suicides of superior people, they would be expected to copy the ones of famous celebrities more than the suicides of ordinary people. Americans may identify more with the stories about American suicides than foreign suicides.

A third variety of explanation focuses not on story characteristics but on audience mood. Although this is the most understudied explanation for copycat suicide, the central thesis is that stories that appear when suicide-like conditions are high in society (e.g., high unemployment, high divorce, and low church attendance rates) have more of a copycat effect because more people are on the verge of suicide. Further, stories that appear in periods when suicidogenic conditions and moods are low will have less of an impact on copycat suicide.

Empirical Generalizations about Media Impacts on Suicidal Behavior

The researcher Steven Stack provides the only quantitative analysis of the findings of research studies to date. Stack's 2000 review is based on 293 findings contained in 42 scientific articles on the subject. There are essentially six solid generalizations that can be made about the conditions that maximize the relationship between the media coverage of suicide and suicidal behavior, including the characteristics of the suicide victim in the story (whether or not he or she is a celebrity), whether or not the suicide is real or fictional, the medium of coverage (newspapers or television), the dependent variable (suicide attempts or completions), the historical period of the analysis, and the amount of coverage of the suicide story. Two generalizations can be made on factors unrelated to the finding of a copycat effect: age range in the dependent variable and year of publication of the study.

Celebrity suicides. Studies that measured the presence of stories regarding well-known entertainment and political celebrities were 14.3 times more likely to uncover a copycat effect than studies that did not do so. Researchers argue that suicide stories about such well-known people (e.g., celebrities, U.S. senators, and U.S. cabinet members) spark a greater degree of identification than stories about the suicides of other persons. The entertainment celebrity, in particular, has the greatest impact on copycat suicide. According to a reference group approach, if a celebrity figure with all her fame and fortune cannot endure life, the suicidal person may ask, "Why should I?" Along these same lines, a 2001 study of a well-known and respected journalist in Quebec has been associated with a substantial rise in suicide.

Real vs. fictional. Stack's analysis found that studies based on real suicide stories are 4.03 times more likely to report copycat effects than studies based on fictional suicides. For example, the several works on the four television movies about teenage suicide that aired in 1984 generally found no imitative effect. People may identify with true-to-life suicides rather than make-believe suicides in movies or daytime television dramas.

Medium of coverage. Unlike televised suicide stories, newspaper suicide stories can be saved, reread, displayed on one's wall or mirror, and studied. Television-based stories on suicide typically last less than twenty seconds and can be quickly forgotten or even unnoticed. Detailed studies of suicides occurring during media coverage of suicide have often found copies of suicide news stories near the body of the victim. Stack's analysis found that research based on televised stories was 82 percent less likely to report a copycat effect than research based on newspaper stories.

Dependent variables. While the models in suicide stories are almost always completers, Stack's analysis found that studies based on completed suicides as the dependent variables were 94 percent less likely to find a copycat effect than studies based on suicide attempts as the dependent variable. Possibly those persons most susceptible to copycat effects are those who are less determined to die.

Period effects. Research has been based on three principal historical periods: 1910–1920, 1929–1939, and 1948–1996. Research based on the 1930s is 93 percent less likely than 2001 research to find a copycat effect. This may be due to the lack of television to echo the stories covered in the radio and print media. However, it may also be due to the presence of massive social movements for social and economic change (e.g., labor movement) that may have distracted otherwise suicidal people from thoughts about suicide.

Amount of suicide coverage. Generally speaking, research has found that the greater the coverage of a suicide story the greater the chances of finding a copycat effect. Stack's analysis distinguished between studies based on one network's (e.g., ABC, CBS, NBC) coverage of suicides versus studies based on two or three network stories. The former were 84 percent less likely to find a copycat effect.

Age-specific suicide rates. Hypothetically, certain audiences (e.g., the very young and impressionable or the high-suicide-risk group of elderly white males) may respond more to publicized suicide stories than their counterparts. Stack's analysis distinguished between studies based on a dependent variable measuring youth suicide risk (ages 10 to 34), middle-aged suicide risk (ages 35 to 64), and elderly suicide risk (aged 65 and over). Studies based on young people were no more likely than studies based on the elderly to find a copycat effect. Further, studies based on middle-aged people were also not any more likely to find a copycat effect. However, nearly all studies in this vein did not match the age of the suicide victims in the stories with the age of the victims in the suicide rate being analyzed. Further work will be needed in order to systematically assess the impact of age identification on age-specific suicide rates.

Year of story publication. Sometimes as statistical techniques advance and standards for publication increase, relationships between an X and a Y variable may emerge or disappear. Stack's analysis found, however, that year of publication of a study was unrelated to the presence of a copycat effect.

Suicide Prevention: Media Guidelines

Professional organizations, including the American Association of Suicidology, have often prepared guidelines for the media to follow in presenting suicide story content. For example, they often advise the media not to mention the method of suicide and to avoid presenting photos of the suicide victim. It is not clear to what extent these guidelines were ever empirically validated. However, there is only one systematic study on this issue.

One study that analyzes whether or not the guidelines are empirically validated was done by Phillips and his colleagues who studied characteristics of thirty-two televised suicide stories and their impact on teenage suicide in the United States. Twelve aspects of story content were measured, and included mention of the method of suicide, picture of the victim in normal life, picture of the victim's body or coffin, and whether or not the motive was specified. None of these characteristics of the stories was associated with significant increases or decreases in suicide risk. That is, for example, stories that mentioned the method of suicide were no more likely to be associated with increases in teenage suicide than ones that did not mention the method.

From the present review of empirical generalizations, social scientists believe that media guidelines should focus on the amount of coverage given to the story. The media might best control suicide by having fewer and shorter stories on the subject. Further, moving them to the inside pages of newspapers might also help reduce suicide risk. Because the suicides of celebrities are by far the most likely to trigger copycat effects, it has been suggested that perhaps the media should pay less attention to these "newsworthy" suicides. Researchers believe coverage in the print media should be reduced because it triggers more copycat suicides than the electronic media.

Finally, the mention of the negative consequences of suicide (e.g., pain and disfigurement) in suicide stories might reduce the imitative effect. These features of suicide are typically not included in suicide stories. One exception is the case of the late 1970s mass suicide at Jonestown where bloated and rotting bodies were shown in news stories and suicide declined. The Jonestown-triggered drop in suicide may not translate to suicide stories not dealing with cults; however, this one neglected aspect of the presentation of suicide stories may offset any copycat effect if it were enacted as part of a media policy.

See also: CHILDREN AND MEDIA VIOLENCE; SUICIDE

Bibliography

Lester, David. *Why People Kill Themselves,* 4th edition. Springfield, OH: Charles Thomas, 2000.

Maris, Ronald, Alan Berman, and Morton M. Silverman, eds. *Comprehensive Textbook of Suicidology*. New York: Guilford, 2000.

Phillips, David P., Lundie L. Carstensen, and Daniel Paight. "Effects of Mass Media News Stories on Suicide, with New Evidence on Story Content." In Cynthia Pfeiffer ed., *Suicide among Youth: Perspectives on Risk and Prevention*. Washington, DC: American Psychiatric Press, 1989.

Stack, Steven. "Media Impacts on Suicide: A Quantitative Review of 293 Findings." *Social Science Quarterly* 81 (2000):957–971.

STEVEN STACK

MENTAL ILLNESS

The term *mental illness* involves emotional suffering and/or with some degree of incapacity to perform a job or maintain fruitful social relationships. The illness most commonly associated with suicide is major depression, which is typically accompanied by chronic sadness, loss of energy, and an inability to tackle daily activities. Although none of these symptoms necessarily leads to suicide, most suicides experience one or more of them. Two other mental illnesses often associated with suicide are schizophrenia and manic depression or bipolar disorder, both of which can involve mental confusion and usually require hospitalization. Alcoholism and drug addiction, with their attendant loss of control over emotions and actions, are also associated with suicide. Personality disorders involving an inability to control anger and impulses have also been noted among suicidal patients.

Clearly mental illness does not always lead to suicide or even to suicidal thoughts. Some 30 to 40 percent of Americans experience some form of mental health problem during their lives, but only 1.5 percent of Americans die by suicide each year. Thus, the overwhelming majority of people with mental health problems do not take their own lives. Even if such people are given to suicidal ideas, the likelihood of their acting on those ideas is remote.

The majority of persons who commit suicide have experienced serious difficulties with their parents during childhood. More than half have been rejected, abandoned, or physically or psychologically abused. These early adversities may make them more likely to mistrust other people and less able to face difficulties such as marital separation or financial distress.

If most mental health problems do not lead to suicide, most suicidal persons do suffer from mental health problems. Studies from the United States, Canada, India, Taiwan, and Finland show that 90 percent of suicides have had a psychiatric problem during the year before their death. At least one-third were seen by a psychiatrist, and a majority of them had more than one problem (e.g., combination of drug abuse and depression).

Mental Health Problems Commonly Associated with Suicide

Almost half of suicides suffer from severe depression, and some researchers claim that as many as 10 percent of those suffering from a depression will eventually die from suicide. Yet depression alone will not trigger a suicide. For instance, twice as many women as men suffer from depression, but, in the Western world, men are three to four times more likely to die from suicide. People who suffer from melancholy, irritability, and lack of appetite—all well-known signs of depression—are not necessarily high risks for suicide. Those who suffer from more severe forms of depression, involving insomnia, memory difficulties, and unkemptness—are at greater risk for suicide. Errki Isometsä and her colleagues in Finland have found that only 3 percent of those who committed suicide and were suffering from depression had received adequate treatment with antidepressant medication.

The most salient indicator of suicide risk among depressives is the feeling of hopelessness. This feeling is not an essential element of depression, but it appears when friends and family members lose patience with the victim of depression. Having some form of family or community support is a key to preventing depression. Countries with a strong tradition of community support often have low rates of suicide even if they have experienced civil wars and generally high rates of depression.

Suicide results in 10 to 15 percent of the cases of those suffering from schizophrenia or manic depression. According to various studies, one quarter to one-half of persons with manic depression attempt suicide. One of the reasons why these patients are at such a high risk is because they often abuse drugs and alcohol to relieve the tensions resulting from their mental symptoms. The period of greatest risk is the five years following a hospital stay. Finally, those who are more depressive than manic are at a correspondingly greater risk of suicide.

Schizophrenics are more likely to commit suicide at a younger age, with only one-third taking place after age forty-five. Careful research does not support the widely held belief that persons with schizophrenia decide to kill themselves when they are feeling better, as a means of avoiding a relapse into their previous emotional agonies. On the other hand, four out of five commit suicide during periods of aggravated confusion and depression. It is also important to note that 40 percent of schizophrenic suicides were not taking their antipsychotic drugs as specified. Alcohol abuse is not common among schizophrenics, but they usually require less alcohol intake to experience inebriation. The most common feature of schizophrenic suicide is recent hospitalizations. Such hospital stays are typically repeated and brief and often coercive—many of them the result of previous suicide attempts.

Mental Illness and Stages of Life

Suicide increased among adolescents and young adults in Canada and many countries of Northern Europe in the latter part of the twentieth century. Many experts associate this increase with a rise in depression in this younger age group during the same period. Adolescents do indeed now suffer from depression as much as adults do (more, according to some studies), and half of adolescents who die by suicide suffer from depression. According to one study, adolescent depression may last for just a short period before the final act, leaving little time for intervention.

For older people, physical ailments are an important variable in suicide rates, but their frequency of psychiatric problems is just slightly less than in younger age groups. A serious handicap or illness is also a source of depression because it threatens self-esteem. In contrast to younger age groups, older people who die by suicide are more likely to suffer only from depression and seldom have multiple mental health problems. This circumstance renders their depression easier to treat.

The Role of Mental Illness in Suicide

Even if suicide is closely linked to mental illness, it does not follow that a rise in the rate of mental illness will bring about an increase in suicide since, as we have seen, the majority of people with some form of mental illness do not take their own lives. Furthermore, some countries with a low rate of suicide have a high rate of mental illness.

Can suicide, then, be attributed to new types of mental illness brought on by social change? For instance, psychiatrists have taken increasing note of the phenomenon known "borderline personality," a disease characterized by high impulsivity and a sense of emptiness, which now accounts for twenty percent of psychiatric inpatients. Drug abuse and social exclusion may contribute to the severity of this condition, which presents a correspondingly higher risk of suicide because of its association with impulsive behavior. For this very reason suicide can be highly unpredictable and thus difficult to prevent. With some impulsive persons, fewer than twenty-four hours elapse between a traumatic episode such as a separation and a suicide attempt. This trait of high impulsivity is not only an element of mental illness; it may result from experiences of abandonment and abuse suffered during childhood. In this regard, observations on social primates early maternal deprivation leads to self-injurious behavior later on in life. The chemistry of the brain is likely to have a role in the transmission of this reaction.

When impulsivity is a major symptom of mental illness, parents, especially single mothers, often have less success in intervening in the case. Increasingly permissive child-rearing methods seem to have aggravated this problem because many parents—not only those with mentally ill children—find it increasingly difficult to control and socialize children's aggressive behavior.

Society's attitudes of exclusion toward mentally ill persons can also make them more vulnerable to suicide. Once consigned to asylums, increasing numbers of the mentally ill now find themselves relegated to fending for themselves in the harsh milieu of metropolitan inner cities, perhaps interrupted by repeated short stays in hospitals in times of crisis. The health services other than hospitals are often insufficient to ensure that these patients have a decent quality of life. And among psychiatric patients, those who die by suicide tend to have been abandoned by their families.

Recent scholarship has identified a series of indicators for suicide risk in mental patients that have little to do with any specific psychiatric illness. The main characteristic is the state of hopelessness. The second is obsession with a single problem, a state referred to by suicidologists as "tunnel vision." The third indicator is social withdrawal, and the fourth is avoidance of activities.

Some genetic factors related to impulsivity have also been identified as a possible key to suicidal behavior, especially in cases of manic depression or bipolar disorder. But this genetic component cannot explain sudden changes in the rate of suicide in a population.

Finally, that the burden of psychiatric illness is aggravated by the onset of a physical illness in suicide. Some 40 percent of suicide victims suffer from a serious physical illness such as cancer or a neurological disorder.

Prevention and Intervention

Suggested preventive measures vary widely. An increase in antidepressant prescriptions in Sweden, Denmark, and Hungary has been accompanied by a decrease in suicide. However, during this period Scandinavian countries have also developed elaborate psychosocial suicide prevention programs. In contrast, in China, where the suicide rate is high, only 5 percent of those suffering from depression receive proper care. Antidepressant medication can become a factor in reducing suicide in the future, especially if accompanied by some form of psychotherapy and adequate social support.

As of 2002, more programs have been developed by psychiatric teams to follow up patients after a hospitalization for a suicide attempt. A plan to provide those persons with a green card giving priority to crisis intervention services in case of emergency has produced positive results in England.

About one-third of people who commit suicide are under psychiatric care. Many of them are not easy to treat, and they do not always take prescribed medications as indicated. More than three-quarters do not manifest any suicidal intent to their doctor, making screening very difficult. Yet new treatment methods for some of the most difficult suicidal cases, self-centered and impulsive alcoholic men, are bringing some hope. For example, the program implemented by Anthony Bateman and Peter Fonagy in England requires an extensive professional investment in group and individual therapy lasting over a year and a half, but this is less costly than the medical treatment of repeated suicide attempts.

See also: SUICIDE; SUICIDE BASICS: EPIDEMIOLOGY; SUICIDE INFLUENCES AND FACTORS: BIOLOGY AND GENETICS, CULTURE

Bibliography

Bateman, Anthony, and Peter Fonagy. "Effectiveness of Partial Hospitalization in the Treatment of Borderline Personality Disorder: A Randomized Controlled Trial." American Journal of Psychiatry 156 (1999): 1563–1569.

Brent, David A., et al. "Adolescent Psychiatric Inpatients' Risk of Suicide Attempt at 6-Month Follow-up." *Journal of American Academy of Child and Adolescent Psychiatry* 32 (1993):95–105.

Isometsä, Erkki T., et al. "Suicide in Major Depression." *American Journal of Psychiatry* 151 (1993):530–536.

Jamison, Kate Redfield. "Suicide and Bipolar Disorder." *Journal of Clinical Psychiatry* 61 (2000):47–51.

Roy, Alec. "Genetic and Biologic Risk Factors for Suicide in Depressive Disorders." *Psychiatric Quarterly* 64 (1993):345–358.

MICHEL TOUSIGNANT

PHYSICAL ILLNESS

According to a variety of studies suicide is more common among people suffering from physical illness. In addition, people with irreversible illnesses are much more likely to take their own lives than healthy individuals. Still, a minority of those who suffer from physical illnesses take their own lives, invariably well under 8 percent. Nevertheless, not all physical illnesses are related to increased suicide risk. Therefore it is important to understand why some individuals who are physically or terminally ill commit suicide while others do not.

Common Physical Illnesses Related to Suicide

In 1986 the researcher Francis Whitlock summarized the results from fifteen published research studies of suicide which include information on physical illnesses and found that when psychiatric and geriatric patients are excluded about one-third of persons who died by suicide had a physical illness at the time of their death. The studies varied, reporting 25 to 70 percent of patients as having a physical illness. Furthermore, the physical illness could be conceived as an important contributory cause of the person's death in between 11 percent and 51 percent of the cases. Almost a decade earlier, the researchers Donna Myers and Charles Neal reported that psychiatrically ill persons who committed suicide were, in almost 30 percent of the cases, also physically ill. Illnesses that are related to increased suicide risk include epilepsy, cerebral disease, Huntington's chorea, Parkinson's disease, cancer, gastrointestinal disease, renal disease, and AIDS (acquired immunodeficiency syndrome).

Epilepsy. A study conducted in England found that the risk of death by suicide among epileptics is 5.4 times greater than in the general population and about 5 percent of deaths by people suffering from epilepsy were suicides. The risk of suicide in females with epilepsy is twice that of males. There is little research indicating why those people suffering from epilepsy have a higher suicide risk.

Head injuries and cardiovascular disease. Major depression is associated with cerebral disease. Therefore, because of the significant link between depression and suicide, it is not surprising that there is a greater risk of suicide among persons who have sustained head injuries or who have had cardiovascular disease and also have symptoms of clinical depression. In a 1980 study conducted by Francis Whitlock and Mark Susskind, there was a six times greater prevalence of cardiovascular disease among suicide victims than the general population.

Huntington's chorea. When it was originally named in 1872 Huntington's chorea was described by George Huntington as a disease "with a tendency to insanity and suicide" (Adams 1994 p. 262). According to Whitlock, although about 7 percent of noninstitutionalized patients with Huntington's disease will eventually die by suicide, this is still a much greater proportion than in the general population. More than half of the suicides occur when individuals first showed signs of the early stages of the illness.

Parkinson's disease. In 1955 the researcher Peter Sainsbury found that the number of cases of Parkinson's disease among the suicides in England was 200 times greater than persons not suffering from Parkinson's disease. He interpreted the greater suicide risk as being associated to the higher rates of depression among Parkinson's sufferers.

Cancer. Studies indicate that there are fifteen to twenty times more people suffering from cancer who eventually commit suicide than those who do not suffer from cancer. Although one might expect that people with cancer would commit suicide fairly late in the development of the disease when they were more debilitated or experiencing more pain and suffering, studies show the opposite: The highest rate of suicide appears to be in the first year after the patient has received notification of the diagnosis. Most cancer patients are chronically depressed (80%), but so are suicide victims who are matched according to various epidemiological factors but do not have a cancer history (82%). In a 1995 review of studies indicating the prevalence of depression in cancer patients, the researcher Mary Lynch found that between 3.7 percent and 58 percent of cancer patients could be diagnosed as suffering from depression. However, only 5 percent of depressed cancer patients die by suicide.

Medical professionals know little about why some cancer patients who are depressed end their lives by suicide and others do not. Most researchers stop looking further once they determine that the person was depressed. When one considers the cause of depressive symptoms in cancer patients, one finds that depression is sometimes secondary to organic causes such as side effects of anti-cancer drugs and other pharmacological therapies. Depression may be a reaction to the crisis of having cancer or a reaction to pain and suffering that is not sufficiently controlled. In 1983 the researchers Letie Hansen and Charles McAler found that health care professionals were more likely to condone suicide in terminal cancer patients than in patients with other diagnoses. They found that the acceptance of suicide in their patients was more likely to occur if the practitioners had a high degree of death anxiety themselves.

Gastrointestinal disease. There are between two and one-half and eleven times higher rates of peptic ulcers among suicide victims than in the general population. Medical researchers interpret the high rate of peptic ulceration among suicide victims as being due to alcoholism, since gastritis and ulceration of the upper gastrointestinal tract are found in those people who have a history of alcoholism. Further, alcoholics have a high risk of suicide with or without gastrointestinal disorders.

Renal disease and hemodialysis patients. Depression is common among patients with end-stage renal disease and hemodialysis patients. There is an at least 100 times greater suicide risk among dialysis patients than nondialysis patients. These rates would be higher if those who stopped treatment or failed to follow the treatment program were included as suicides in these studies.

AIDS. In a 1999 review of all studies on AIDS and suicide published to date, Brian Mishara concluded that there is a high risk of premature death by suicide among AIDS patients. However, there appears to be an even greater risk among people who first learn they are HIV (human immunodeficiency virus) positive and do not have any symptoms. There are results from autopsy studies that suggest that persons who inaccurately thought they had AIDS have committed suicide.

Explanations of the increased suicide risk among AIDS patients have focused upon depression. However, alternative explanations include the possibility that those who become HIV positive are more often from groups with a high risk of suicide to begin with, including homosexual men and intravenous drug users. Other hypotheses have included the possibility that the symptoms and pain associated with AIDS are related to increased suicide risk, or that diminished meaning of life or coping abilities associated with AIDS are related to suicide risk. In a longitudinal investigation of persons with AIDS conducted from 1998 to 2001, Mishara found that although depression and several other factors were associated with greater suicidal contemplation, when all the factors were analyzed together, the only significant ones that remained were the ways people with AIDS cope with problems and meaning of life.

Other physical illnesses. Several physical illnesses that one might expect to be associated with greater suicide risk have not been proven to increase the risk of suicide. For example, people with multiple sclerosis appear to have a relatively low suicide risk. Persons suffering from senile dementia and Alzheimer's disease do not have an increased risk of suicide and in fact may have fewer suicides. In the case of senile dementia and Alzheimer's disease, the lower suicide risk may be related to an inability to complete a suicide in those who are disabled by the disease or, alternatively, it may be that persons with senile dementia are not necessarily suffering. It is not clear whether or not there is a higher prevalence of suicide among persons suffering from cardiovascular diseases or hypertension. There have been cases of suicides among people with cardiovascular disease and hypertension, and in these instances medical professionals have suggested that medications used for the treatment of hypertension and cardiac disease may induce depression in many cases and thus may increase the risk of suicide.

People with disabilities and chronic non-life-threatening illnesses are frequently diagnosed as having clinical depression. Some researchers feel that their diagnosis is an error because many of the symptoms of these diseases are also used to classify a person as depressed. Despite the frequent diagnosis of depression, there is no research evidence to confirm the hypothesis that persons with physical disabilities or chronic non-life-threatening illnesses are more likely to attempt or complete suicides than healthy individuals. A possible exception to this is people who suffer from asthma for whom there are clinical descriptions of deaths by suicide related to anxiety associated with the condition's symptoms. However, hard data on the number of persons suffering from asthma who commit suicide are not available.

Possible Explanations for the Link between Suicide and Illness

How can researchers, medical professionals, and social scientists explain the increased risk of suicide among people with serious or chronic physical illnesses? Most studies focus on the presence of depression and consider depression as if it were a "cause" of the suicide. However, depression is present among all suicide victims—those who are physically ill as well as those who are in good health. Furthermore, only a very small percentage of people who are depressed commit suicide and only a small percentage of people who are physically ill and depressed end their lives by suicide. For most people it seems logical to be depressed when a person suffers from a serious illness such as cancer or a physical disability. However, the depression may be a side effect of the illness itself or of medications used to treat the person. In some cases patients may be depressed because of their physical environment; for example, patients in a hospital are more depressed than patients who are terminally ill and treated in a hospice environment or in their own homes.

Researchers believe it would be worthwhile to identify depression among those who are physically ill and then identify the causes of the depression. Once the causes of the depression are determined, treatment would be indicated. In some instances treatment may include prescribing an antidepressant medication or changing or adjusting the dosage of medication the person is currently taking. In other instances counseling or psychotherapy can be helpful. However, professionals must not overlook the possibility that the quality of life in terms of daily experiences and interpersonal interactions may be related to the depression as well. Furthermore, side effects of the illness may be better treated or improved and this may have an important effect upon depressive reactions.

The second major explanation of increased suicide risk is that it is associated with direct consequences of the illness, usually pain and suffering. In the case of cancer, uncontrolled pain is related to suicidal behavior. There is a general consensus in the medical profession that if a physician administers adequate pain control a patient's desire to hasten death by suicide may significantly decrease. Despite the link between pain control and suicide in cancer patients, it is not obvious that there is a link with pain in other illnesses. For example, in people with AIDS pain and suffering do not appear to be related to suicidal intentions.

There has been little research completed on the relationship between suicide and how people cope with their illnesses. The few investigations that exist suggest that how people cope with their illnesses and the social support they receive may be important factors in determining whether or not those who are seriously, chronically, or terminally ill desire to continue living.

Conclusions

Physical illness is not invariably associated with greater suicide risk; however, many people with physical illnesses have a much higher risk of suicide than the general population. Many illnesses and physical disabilities may not be experienced as negatively as the general population believes. For example, in the case of people with physical handicaps and many chronic degenerative diseases, the time when there is a greater risk of suicide varies, depending upon the particular handicap or disease. In the case of AIDS and with some cancer victims, there appears to be a greater risk of killing oneself after learning about the diagnosis, rather than later when the illness results in serious symptoms and handicaps. The timing of the suicide suggests that it may not be the illness that results in increased suicide risk, but rather people's fears about the future and concerns about living with or dying from the illness. These fears may be alleviated or reduced by professional counseling and support from family and friends during the early stages when the person first learns of the diagnosis.

It appears that patients participating in hospice and palliative care programs are less likely to end their lives prematurely by suicide. If this fact were confirmed, it would suggest that greater availability of such palliative care may have an important preventive effect. However, hospice programs and palliative care are often only available to persons identified as "terminally ill" who have discontinued all treatments to prolong life. Many seriously ill persons do not benefit from the advantages of palliative care programs because they fail to meet criteria for being "terminally ill" or they have chosen to continue treatments despite the advances of their illness. Wider availability of hospice care programs as well as good palliative care services for those who are not yet terminally ill or for those have chosen to continue treatment may have a significant effect in preventing suicide with people who are physically ill.

It does not appear that the jurisprudence legislation in the Netherlands since the mid-1980s legalizing euthanasia has resulted in either a decrease or an increase in suicide among persons who are physically ill. Based on clinical knowledge, the best ways to prevent suicide among people who are physically ill are to develop protocols for identifying the potential sources of depression and to develop more effective means of treating depression. Furthermore, educators must change physicians' attitudes regarding suicide, since research shows that physicians are more likely to feel that a suicide is "justified" when a person is seriously or terminally ill. These attitudes may hinder appropriate identification and treatment of clinical depression. Besides treating depression it is important, particularly among cancer patients, to ensure that there is adequate pain management and control. Furthermore, any activities that improve the quality of life, social supports, and the amount of communication with family that are possible to employ would most likely result in preventing suicide.

See also: AIDS; COMMUNICATION WITH THE DYING; GOOD DEATH, THE; PAIN AND PAIN MANAGEMENT; SUICIDE; SUICIDE TYPES: PHYSICIAN-ASSISTED SUICIDE, RATIONAL SUICIDE; SYMPTOMS AND SYMPTOM MANAGEMENT

Bibliography

Adams, John Hume, and David I. Graham. *An Introduction to Neuropathology,* 2nd edition. Edinburgh: Churchill Livingstone, 1994.

Hansen, Letie C., and Charles A. McAleer. "Terminal Cancer and Suicide: The Health Care Professional's Dilemma." *Omega: The Journal of Death and Dying* 14, no. 3 (1983–1984):241–248.

Henriksson, Markus M., Erkki T. Isometsä, Päivi S. Hietanen, Hillevi M. Aro, and Jouko K. Lönnqvist. "Mental Disorders in Cancer Suicides." *Journal of Affective Disorders* 36 (1995):11–20.

Lynch, Mary E. "The Assessment and Prevalence of Affective Disorders in Advanced Cancer." *Journal of Palliative Care* 11, no. 1 (1996):10–18.

Matthews, Wendy S., and Gabor Barabas. "Suicide and Epilepsy: A Review of the Literature." *Psychosomatics* 22 (1981):515–524.

Mishara, Brian L. "Synthesis of Research and Evidence on Factors Affecting the Desire of Terminally Ill or Seriously Chronically Ill Persons to Hasten Death." *Omega: The Journal of Death and Dying* 39, no. 1 (1999):1–70.

Mishara, Brian L. "Suicide, Euthanasia and AIDS." *Crisis* 19, no. 2 (1998):87–96.

Myers, Donna H., and Charles D. Neal. "Suicide in Psychiatric Patients." *British Journal of Psychiatry* 133 (1978):38–44.

Sainsbury, Peter. *Suicide in London: An Ecological Study.* London: Chapman and Hall, 1955.

Whitlock, Francis A. "Suicide and Physical Illness." In Alec Roy ed., *Suicide.* Baltimore, MD: Williams & Wilkins, 1986.

Whitlock, Francis A., and Mark Susskind. "Depression As a Major Symptom of Multiple Sclerosis." *Journal of*

In one of several controversial lawsuits that blame rock music for a suicide death, Ozzy Osbourne, at a 1986 press conference in Los Angeles, denied all allegations that his song "Suicide Solution" was responsible for the death of a young boy who shot himself. BETTMANN/CORBIS

Neurology, Neurosurgery and Psychiatry 43 (1980): 861–865.

BRIAN L. MISHARA

ROCK MUSIC

Suicide as a rock music trope can have many meanings, including rebellion against established social norms, sometimes to the point of nihilism; criticism of authority figures, such as teachers, politicians, and parents; and evocation of emotional traumas. Often these songs use sarcasm to register disenchantment with society, family, interpersonal relationships, or life itself. In much the same way that Jonathan Swift's "A Modest Proposal" suggests that the starving Irish should eat their plentiful children, many rock songs suggest suicide, whether intentionally or unintentionally, as a response to the listeners' troubles.

Beginning in the 1980s, a series of wrongful death lawsuits focused public attention on the purported link between rock music and suicidal behavior. It seemed to many that rage-filled, overtly anti-establishment songs were actively encouraging adolescents to commit suicide. The rock group Judas Priest was alleged to use "subliminal" messages encouraging suicide. In the late 1990s concerns about the effects of music lyrics and controversial artists like Marilyn Manson resulted in a public hearing before the U.S. Senate. While no wrongful death suit has been prosecuted successfully against an artist and no empirical evidence exists that rock music in general, or any artist in particular, has directly caused any teen suicides, controversial music and musicians remain under scrutiny from scholars and officials who suspect a connection.

Although some may believe that only the most angry and nihilistic music includes suicidal themes, instead, it has been used by a wide variety of artists. Simon and Garfunkel, in their landmark 1966 album *The Sounds of Silence,* included two songs about suicide. One of them, "Richard Cory," is an adaptation of the well-known Edward Arlington Robinson poem that describes a community's shock when a rich and well-respected person commits suicide. Written in the turbulent 1960s, this song challenges the assumption that financial success is the measure of happiness. A very familiar song is "Suicide is Painless," the theme to the movie and television show *M.A.S.H.* While mainly known in its orchestral version, the lyrics describe the despair and hopelessness of suicidal depression. However, perhaps the most famous suicide song is decidedly non-mainstream Ozzy Osbourne's "Suicide Solution." The song lyrics, when taken out of context, can be interpreted as pro-suicide, but, in fact, the song as a whole is an ironic description of alcohol abuse as slow suicide: "Wine is fine, but whiskey's quicker / Suicide is slow with liquor."

Current research indicates that those most vulnerable to suicide often suffer from severe psychopathology, substance abuse, and/or extreme psychosocial stress. Hence, some analysts contend that music steeped in nihilism and social alienation may simply reinforce a suicidal predisposition stemming from other factors. Others point out that a vulnerable listener's extreme identification with a rock star whose behavior is suicidal or self-destructive can lead to imitation. A mitigating factor is the type of media coverage of celebrity deaths; since the 1994 suicide of Nirvana member Kurt Cobain, there have been confirmed reports of attempted or completed suicides by fans of his music and lifestyle, but not nearly the number feared. As long as there are rock stars whose music and lives romanticize the daring and rebellion of self-destructive behavior, their possible influence over the lives of their devoted followers will continue to raise questions and concerns.

See also: SUICIDE INFLUENCES AND FACTORS: MEDIA EFFECTS; SUICIDE OVER THE LIFE SPAN: ADOLESCENTS AND YOUTHS

Bibliography

Brown, E. F., and W. R. Hendee. "Adolescents and Their Music: Insights Into the Health of Adolescents." *Journal of the American Medical Association* 262 (1989): 1659–1663.

Gould, Madelyn S. "Suicide and the Media." *Annals of the New York Academy of Sciences* 932 (2001):200–224.

Jobes, D. A., A. L. Berman, P. W. O'Carroll, S. Eastgard, and S. Knickmeyer. "The Kurt Cobain Suicide Crisis: Perspectives from Research, Public Health, and the News Media." *Suicide and Life-Threatening Behavior* 26 (1996):260–269.

Litman, Robert E., and Norman L. Farberow. "Pop-Rock Music As Precipitating Cause in Youth Suicide." *Journal of Forensic Sciences* 39 (1994):494–499.

Phillips, D. P. "The Influence of Suggestion on Suicide: Substansive and Theoretical Implications of the Werther Effect." *American Sociological Review* 39 (1974):340–354.

Scheel, K. R., and J. S. Westefeld. "Heavy Metal Music and Adolescent Suicidality: An Empirical Investigation." *Adolescence* 34 (1999):253–273.

Stack, Steven. "Suicide: A 15-Year Review of the Sociological Literature. Part I: Cultural and Economic Factors." *Suicide and Life-Threatening Behavior* 30 (2000):145–162.

LAURA PROUD
KEITH CHENG

SUICIDE OVER THE LIFE SPAN

ADOLESCENTS AND YOUTHS

Suicides of the young, those who have most of life's highlights to experience, are profoundly challenging to cultural systems. Considerable soul searching was triggered in the United States when, between the mid-1960s and mid-1980s, the suicide rates of its ten- to fourteen-year-olds nearly tripled while doubling among those aged fifteen to nineteen. Although the suicide rates for adolescents in the United States and Canada are lower than for other age groups because adolescents die infrequently from physical illnesses, by the end of the twentieth century suicide was the second greatest cause of death in adolescence, after (mainly automobile-related) accidents.

The term *youth* is often considered to end several years after adolescence, with twenty-first-century tendencies setting the upper limit for "youth" at age twenty-five or older. In the United States, males aged fifteen to twenty-five commit suicide at least five times as often as females, although females are much more likely to attempt suicide. This difference has been explained in different ways, including male preferences for more violent and more lethal methods; male tendencies to keep problems to themselves and not confide in others nor use health and mental health services as frequently; increased male vulnerability to mental health problems; socialization into male stereotypes and "macho" role expectations. During the 1990s suicide rates began to decrease among those aged fifteen to nineteen except among African Americans. The decrease may be attributed to better identification and treatment of mental disorders in youth, increased awareness of suicide and access to suicide prevention resources, or other sociocultural changes in American society.

Risk Factors Related to Adolescent and Youth Suicide

Mental health professionals have identified those factors that pose the greatest risk to adolescents and youth suicides. Youths who attempt and commit suicide generally have several risk factors, which are combined with the ready availability of a lethal means and the lack of suitable sources of help.

Social and economic environments. The family is one of the earliest and most significant influences in a young person's development. There have been numerous studies of family troubles associated with youth suicidal behavior, including early parental loss, parental mental health problems, parental abuse and neglect, and a family history of suicide. In addition to chronic family troubles, there are usually precipitant events closer in time to a suicide attempt, many of which involve the family. These precipitants include serious conflicts with family members or divorce of parents, perceived rejection by one's family, and failure of family members to take an adolescent's talk about suicide seriously.

The school constitutes an important influence on youth. It is therefore not surprising that a history of school problems and the stress of disruptive transitions in school are potential risk conditions for youth suicidal risk behavior, as well as failure, expulsion, and overwhelming pressure to succeed.

The influence of peers on young people's behavior can sometimes be greater than that of family and school. There is a risk of copycat suicidal behavior in adolescents who have been exposed to a peer's suicide. This contagion effect is most pronounced for vulnerable youths who tend to identify strongly with someone who has committed suicide in their environments or in mass media. Common precipitating events in youth suicidal behavior include rejection from peers, the breakup of a significant relationship, or the loss of a confidant. Furthermore, adolescents and young people who fail to act when confronted with a suicidal peer, by dismissing it as insignificant or failing to inform an adult, can increase the risk of suicide.

Poverty in children and youth heightens the risk conditions for suicide, including school problems and failures, psychiatric disorders, low self-esteem, and substance abuse, all of which can increase vulnerability to suicide and suicidal behavior.

Physical environment. Having immediate and easy access to lethal means to kill oneself increases the risk that a suicide will occur. Firearms are common methods of male suicides in the United States, and young women are increasingly using guns to kill themselves. Having such an instantly lethal method available increases the risk that vulnerable young people may kill themselves impulsively.

Additional risk factors. The researcher Jerome Motto suggested that the increased use of alcohol and drugs might have been a significant factor related to the rise of youth suicide since the 1970s. According to David Brent, at least one-third of adolescents who kill themselves are intoxicated at the time of their suicide and many more are likely to be under the influence of drugs.

A history of previous suicide attempts and the presence of a psychiatric disorder are among the most important and well-established risk factors for youth suicidal behavior. As many as 10 percent of suicide attempters eventually die in a later suicide attempt. Depression is a major mental health problem associated with suicide. In addition, impulsive behavior, poor problem-solving and coping skills, alcoholism, and homosexual orientation also increase the likelihood of suicidal behavior.

Prevention

No single risk factor alone is sufficient to result in a suicide. Youths who attempt and commit suicide generally have several risk factors that are combined with the ready availability of a lethal means and the lack of suitable sources of help.

Primary prevention. Primary prevention consists of actions to prevent suicidal behavior before people develop a high-risk or a suicidal crisis. Most youth and adolescent suicide prevention programs have focused on school-based activities where adolescents receive training in identifying signs of suicide risks and how to best react to suicidal peers. Some programs also identify resources to help with suicide and encourage young people to talk with adults if they feel that they or their friends are feeling suicidal. Young people are specifically encouraged not to keep a "secret" confession of suicidal intentions to themselves. Controversy surrounds the usefulness and effects of school-based suicide prevention programs. Few programs have been the subject of rigorous evaluations and not all programs have had positive results. Research indicates that programs that provide a variety of resources within the school and community, including specially trained teachers, mental health services and counselors, and information and training for parents, may be of more benefit in preventing suicidal behavior.

In addition to school-based programs, many primary prevention approaches have focused on key persons who may come in contact with potentially suicidal youth. These persons, called "gatekeepers," include school staff, child welfare workers, community volunteers, coaches, police, family doctors, and clergy members. Training usually involves information on taking suicide threats seriously and asking specific questions to assess suicide risk, identifying behavior changes that may indicate increased suicide risk, better identification and treatment of depression and other mental health problems, and providing information about resources to help with suicide and other community youth problems.

Intervention

Given their higher risk of suicide, particular treatment should be given to persons who attempt suicide. Unfortunately, many young suicide attempters do not receive adequate follow-up after they are discharged from the hospital. Successful programs for young people who are hospitalized for suicide attempts involve treatment in the community by counseling, therapy, and/or medication after their discharge. The most effective programs treat more than just the suicidal individual but also involve the person's family in developing a long-term strategy to reduce the factors associated with suicidal behavior. Very often, young people do not want to continue with treatment after an attempt and they may tell others that they are better or that they want to move on in their life and ignore the "mistake" they have made. Despite this, it is important to ensure that there is regular long-term follow-up after any suicide attempt in order to treat the underlying problems and reduce the likelihood of a subsequent attempt.

After a suicide occurs in a school setting, it is important that the school react in an appropriate manner to the suicidal death in order to allow other students to grieve the death and prevent a contagion effect of others imitating the suicidal behavior. Many schools have established protocols for "postvention" which often use a "critical debriefing" model to mobilize members of the community following a tragic event, including a suicide by a student. These protocols define who will act as a spokesperson for the school, how to identify students and family members who are particularly vulnerable or traumatized by the event, and how best to help them, as well as general activities in the school to allow for appropriate mourning and discussions in order to understand what has occurred. Each suicidal event is unique and any general protocol must be adapted to the specific circumstances and the school environment. After a suicide schools should provide information and help facilitate access to skilled individuals who may help those troubled by the event. However, it is also important for those in authority not to glorify the suicide by having long extended commemorative activities that may communicate to some vulnerable suicidal students that committing suicide is an effective means of having the entire school understand their grief or problems. It is important that commemorative events emphasize that suicide is a tragic event, that no one is better off for this having happened, that help is readily available, and that most suicides can be prevented.

See also: SUICIDE INFLUENCES AND FACTORS: GENDER, MEDIA EFFECTS, ROCK MUSIC; SUICIDE OVER THE LIFE SPAN: CHILDREN; SUICIDE TYPES: SUICIDE PACTS

Bibliography

Brent, David. "Age and Sex-Related Risk Factors for Adolescent Suicides." *Journal of the American Academy of Child and Adolescent Psychiatry* 38, no. 12 (1999):1497–1505.

Brent, David, et al. "Psychiatric Sequelae to the Loss of an Adolescent Peer to Suicide." *Journal of the American Academy of Child and Adolescent Psychiatry* 32, no. 3 (1993):509–517.

Brent, David, et al. "Risk Factors for Adolescent Suicide." *Archives of General Psychiatry* 45 (1988):581–588.

Dyck, Ronald J., Brian L. Mishara, and Jennifer White. "Suicide in Children, Adolescents and Seniors: Key Findings and Policy Implications." In *National Forum on Health Determinants of Health,* Vol. 3: *Settings and Issues.* Ottawa: Health Canada, 1998.

Gould, Madeline, et al. "Suicide Clusters: An Examination of Age-Specific Effects." *American Journal of Public Health* 80, no. 2 (1990):211–212.

Groholt, Berit, et al. "Youth Suicide in Norway, 1990–1992: A Comparison between Children and Adolescents Completing Suicide and Age- and Gender-Matched Controls." *Suicide and Life-Threatening Behavior* 27, no. 3 (1997):250–263.

Motto, Jerome. "Suicide Risk Factors in Alcohol Abuse." *Suicide and Life-Threatening Behavior* 10 (1980):230–238.

Pfeffer, Cynthia, et al. "Suicidal Children Grow Up: Demographic and Clinical Risk Factors for Adolescent Suicide Attempts." *Journal of the American Academy of Child and Adolescent Psychiatry* 30, no. 4 (1991):609–616.

Shaffer, David, and Madeline Gould. "Suicide Prevention in Schools." In Keith Hawton and Kees van Heeringen eds., *The International Handbook of Suicide and Attempted Suicide.* Chichester: John Wiley & Sons, 2000.

Spirito, Anthony, et al. "Attempted Suicide in Adolescence: A Review and Critique of the Literature." *Clinical Psychology Review* 9 (1989):335–363.

BRIAN L. MISHARA

CHILDREN

Children develop an understanding of suicide at an early age and that follows their understanding of what it means to die and to be dead. Although children very rarely commit suicide before adolescence, they almost invariably witness suicide attempts and suicide threats on television. In addition, they talk about suicide with other children.

Children's Understanding of Suicide

Research indicates that by age seven or eight almost all children understand the concept of suicide. They can use the word *suicide* in conversations and name several common methods of committing suicide. Younger children, as young as ages five and six, are generally able to talk about "killing oneself," even if they do not know the meaning of suicide, and learn the unsettling effects of such talk on adults. By age seven or eight almost all children report that they have discussed suicide with others on at least one occasion, and these discussions are almost invariably with children their own age. In one 1999 study conducted by Brian Mishara, half of all children in first and second grade and all children above second grade said that they had seen at least one suicide on television. These suicides usually occur in cartoons and involve the "bad guy" who kills himself when he has lost an important battle with the "good guy." Children also experience suicide attempts and threats in soap operas and adult television programs. Surveys of parents have found that 4 percent of children have threatened to kill themselves at some time.

In Western cultures, children ages five to twelve rarely have positive attitudes toward suicide. At all age levels, children consider suicide an act that one should not do; few feel that people have a right to kill themselves. When there is a suicide in the family, children usually know about it, despite parents' attempts to hide the fact by explaining that the death was an accident. For example, in studies conducted in Quebec, Canada, by Mishara, 8 percent of children said that they knew someone who had committed suicide, but none of the children said they were told about the suicidal death by an adult.

Children's Understanding of Death

Although children understand death and suicide at a young age, their conceptions of death often differ from an adult understanding. Very young children do not see death as being final (once someone is dead, he or she may come back to life), universal (everyone does not necessarily die someday), unpredictable (death cannot just happen at any given time), nor inescapable (taking the right precautions or having a good doctor may allow someone to avoid dying). Furthermore, for the youngest children, once someone is dead he or she may have many characteristics that most adults reserve for the living, such as being able to see, hear, feel, and be aware of what living people are doing. These immature understandings of death change fairly rapidly, with children learning at a young age that death is a final state from which there is no return. Also, children learn at an early age that all people must die someday. However, as many as 20 percent of twelve-year-olds think that once a person has died, he or she is able to have feelings or perceptions that living people experience.

Children's View of Suicide

It is naive to think that young children do not know about suicide. However, the image that children get from television is different from what occurs in the vast majority of suicides in the real world. Those who commit suicide on television almost never suffer from severe depression or mental health problems, they are almost never ambivalent about whether or not they should kill themselves, and it is rare that children see suicidal persons receiving help or any form of prevention. This contrasts with the reality in which mental health problems are almost always present—where there is tremendous ambivalence and the fact that persons who consider suicide rarely do so, as most find other ways to solve their problems.

Prevention and Intervention Approaches

To counter such misconceptions and to reduce suicidal behavior later in life, several preventive strategies have been tried. One provides accurate information about suicide to children in order to correct erroneous conceptions that children may develop from their television experiences or discussions with other children. Another focuses upon children's coping abilities. Research on adolescents and young adults who attempt suicide indicates that they have fewer effective coping strategies to deal with everyday problems. Although it may take many years before programs begin teaching young children that there is a link between effective coping and long-term suicide prevention effects, this approach has had promising short-term effects in increasing children's abilities to find solutions to their problems and improve their social skills. For example, the Reaching Young Europe program, called "Zippy and Friends," is offered by the Partnership for Children in different European countries. Developed by the prevention organization Befrienders International (and now run by Partnership for Children), Zippy and Friends is a twenty-four-week, story-based program for children in kindergarten and first grade that teaches through games and role play on how to develop better coping skills. Short-term evaluation results indicate that, when compared to a control group of children who did not participate in the program, participants had more coping strategies, fewer problem behaviors, and greater social skills.

Research results suggest that it may not be appropriate to ignore self-injurious behavior in children and suicide threats because of the belief that children do not understand enough about death and suicide to engage in "true" suicidal behavior. According to official statistics, children almost never commit suicide. However, perhaps more children commit suicide than coroners and medical examiners indicate in reports. They may classify some deaths as accidental because of the belief that children are too young to know about death and suicide and are only "playing," or to spare parents the stigma of suicide. Nevertheless, there are numerous case histories and several investigations of factors related to suicidal behavior in children. Studies on the social environment generally focus on the greater likelihood of suicidal behavior in children from families where there is parental violence or sexual abuse, or have family histories of alcohol and drug abuse, depression, and suicidal behavior.

Depression in children appears to be a risk factor for suicide, although depressive symptoms in children are difficult to recognize and diagnose. Symptoms of depression in children include long-lasting sadness, which may be linked with frequent crying for little or no apparent reason, monotone voice, and seeming to be inexpressive and unemotional. Other possible symptoms include the development of inabilities to concentrate and do schoolwork, being tired and lacking energy, social withdrawal and isolation, refusing to continue to participate in games and group activities, not answering questions or having long delays before answering, and a variety of "somatic" complaints. These somatic complaints include sleep difficulties such as insomnia, frequent nightmares, and incontinence, anorexia, stomach pains, and complaints of physical difficulties that seem unfounded. Often depressed children seem anxious and may have multiple phobias or fears. Some children try to fight against depression by acting out or being angry a lot of the time. In these cases, the depressive symptoms are generally also present. If a child has several of the preceding symptoms, or symptoms are intense and long lasting, consultation with a professional is indicated. This is particularly true if a child threatens to commit suicide or becomes interested in suicide methods, such as tying nooses or playing suicide games with other children or with dolls.

It can also be beneficial to ask direct questions to a child who talks about suicide. Questions might include: "Are you thinking of killing yourself?" "Have you thought about how you would do it?" "Do you think you might really commit suicide?" Despite common adult beliefs that asking questions might "put ideas" in a child's head, if a child threatens suicide, the child almost always knows about suicide and it is impossible to suggest suicide behavior by talking about it. It is also important to ask suicidal children what they think will happen after a person dies. If the child gives the impression that one can return from the dead or being dead is like being alive, it may be useful to correct this impression or describe in some detail what it means to die and be dead.

One should seek advice from a mental health professional if a child has symptoms of depression and/or threatens suicide. It is also important to talk about what occurred when a child experiences a suicide in the family or in the family of friends or at school. Such discussions may begin by asking a child what he or she thinks about what occurred, including why the child thinks the person committed suicide and what the child thinks it is like to be dead. Often children have a good understanding of what has occurred, a fairly realistic notion of what happens when one dies, and a negative attitude toward suicidal behavior. However, in the event that a child glorifies or trivializes a death by suicide or feels that the suicide victim is "better off" now, it is important to continue the discussion to clarify the nature of what occurred and if necessary seek counseling or professional help. It is also important for children to be able to express their feelings about a loss by suicide (even if those feelings include "unacceptable" feelings such as anger at the person for having left). It is important for children to develop an understanding of the suicide as being a tragic avoidable death and not a situation with which the child can easily identify.

Although suicidal behavior in children is rare, one should not minimize suicidal threats and attempts in children, and it is important to be aware of persistent indications of depression in children.

See also: CHILDREN AND ADOLESCENTS' UNDERSTANDING OF DEATH; CHILDREN AND MEDIA VIOLENCE; LITERATURE FOR CHILDREN

Bibliography

Dyck, Ronald J, Brian L. Mishara, and Jennifer White. "Suicide in Children, Adolescents and Seniors: Key Findings and Policy Implications." In *National Forum on Health Determinants of Health,* Vol. 3: *Settings and Issues.* Ottawa: Health Canada, 1998.

Garfinkel, Barry D., Art Froese, and Jane Hood. "Suicide Attempts in Children and Adolescents." *American Journal of Psychiatry* 139 (1982):1257–1261.

Mishara, Brian L. "Conceptions of Death and Suicide in Children Aged 6 to 12 and Their Implications for Suicide Prevention." *Suicide and Life-Threatening Behavior* 29, no. 2 (1999):105–118.

Mishara, Brian L. "Childhood Conceptions of Death and Suicide: Empirical Investigations and Implications for Suicide Prevention." In Diego De Leo, Armi N. Schmidtke, and Rene F. W. Diekstra eds., *Suicide Prevention: A Holistic Approach.* Boston: Kluwer Academic Publishers, 1998.

Mishara, Brian L., and Mette Ystgaard. "Exploring the Potential of Primary Prevention: Evaluation of the Befrienders International *Reaching Young Europe Pilot Programme* in Denmark." *Crisis* 21, no. 1 (2000):4–7.

Normand, Claude, and Brian L. Mishara. "The Development of the Concept of Suicide in Children." *Omega: The Journal of Death and Dying* 25, no. 3 (1992): 183–203.

Pfeffer, Cynthia R. *The Suicidal Child.* New York: The Guilford Press, 1986.

BRIAN L. MISHARA

THE ELDERLY

Until the 1970s suicide was most common among the elderly, while in the twenty-first century younger people have the highest suicide rate in one-third of all countries. Reasons for such a change are unclear; however, many countries of different cultures have registered an increase in youth suicide that has been paralleled by a decline in elderly rates. Since the 1970s, the decline in elderly suicide has been particularly evident in Anglo-Saxon countries, and especially among white males in United States (around 50%). Proposed explanations have considered improved social services, development of elderly political and social activism, changing attitudes toward retirement, increased economic security, and better psychiatric care. By contrast, the lack of specific services for the elderly in Latin American countries may account for the increase in suicide rates in recent years. Moreover, the spontaneous support provided by traditional family structure has been progressively declining without being replaced by alternative sources of formal support or any better education on coping with age.

Despite tremendous cultural variability across nations, suicide rates in the elderly remain globally the highest for those countries that report mortality data to the World Health Organization (WHO), as shown in Figure 1. In general, rates among those seventy-five years and older are approximately three times higher than those of youth under twenty-five years of age. This trend is observed for both sexes, and it is steeper for males. Suicide rates actually present several distinct patterns in females. In some nations, female suicide rates rise with age, in others female rates peak in middle age while, particularly in developing nations and minority groups, female suicide rates peak in young adults. Based on 2001 data, half of all suicides reported in women worldwide occur in China.

Suicide is most prevalent among male subjects, and remarkably so at seventy-five and more years of age. Particularly in the Western world, this seems to contrast with the poor health and social status experienced by elderly women that results from more compromised psychophysical conditions secondary to greater longevity, poverty, widowhood, and abandonment. To explain this difference, social scientists have suggested that women might benefit from better established social networks, greater self-sufficiency in activities of daily living, and commitment to children and grandchildren.

General Characteristics of Suicide in the Elderly

There are characteristics that are particular to this age group. Older people are likely to suffer from a physical or mental illness, and in general tend to plan their suicides rather than act on impulsivity. The suicide methods chosen by elderly persons (including women) are generally violent with a high degree of lethality, expressing strong suicidal intention. The most common self-destructive methods are by hanging, firearms (particularly in the United States), jumping from high places (particularly in Asian metropolitan cities like Hong Kong and Singapore), self-poisoning (especially with medicine, benzodiazepines, and analgesics, among women), and drowning.

In most cases of elderly suicides, the act is performed at home alone. When suicide notes are left, they usually contain financial dispositions and burial instructions. The notes indicate a high degree of determination, accurate planning, and emotional detachment.

Underreporting of Suicidal Behavior in the Elderly

Suicide mortality data usually carry an underestimation of their real number, a phenomenon that is thought to be particularly frequent in the elderly. For a variety of reasons, there may be reluctance to call a death a suicide, particularly in those regions where religious and cultural attitudes condemn suicide. In general, a suicide may be voluntarily hidden to avoid public stigmatization for social convenience, for political reasons, to benefit from insurance, or because it was deliberately masked as an accident. Suicide can also be misclassified as an undetermined cause of death or as a natural cause (e.g., when people neglect to take life-sustaining medications).

Suicide can also go unrecognized when people overdose on drugs, starve themselves to death, or die some time after their suicide attempt (in these cases usually it is the clinical cause of death which is officially reported), or in cases of euthanasia or assisted suicide.

High-Risk Factors in Suicide among the Elderly

Although the majority of elderly persons may be suffering from psychiatric disorders at the time of suicide, the large majority of them who commit suicide do not have a history of previous suicidal behavior. In addition, researchers found that only a small percentage of psychologically healthy individuals have a "desire to die."

Psychopathology. Psychiatric pathology represents the most important risk factor for suicide in the elderly. Over three-fourths of elderly victims

FIGURE 1

Global suicide rates (per 100,000) by gender and age, selected countries, 1995

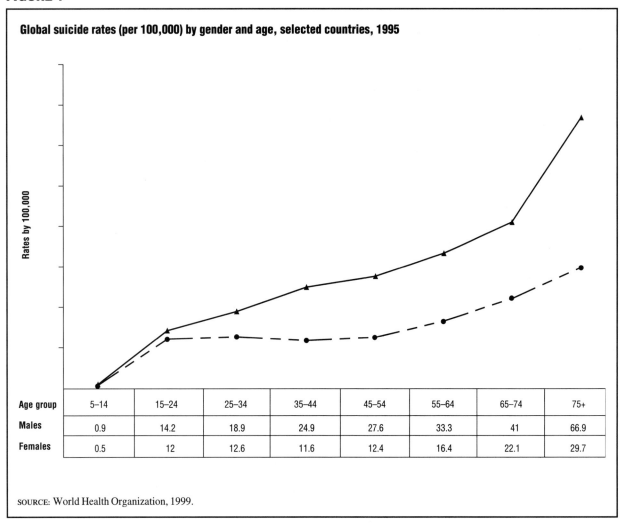

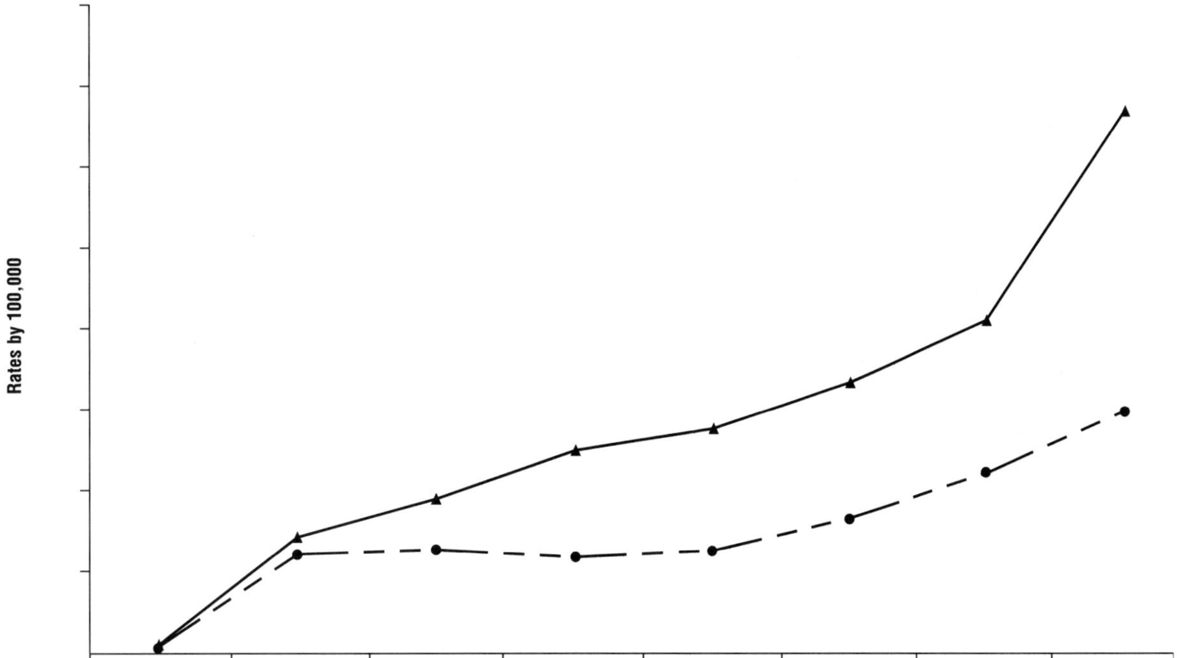

Age group	5–14	15–24	25–34	35–44	45–54	55–64	65–74	75+
Males	0.9	14.2	18.9	24.9	27.6	33.3	41	66.9
Females	0.5	12	12.6	11.6	12.4	16.4	22.1	29.7

SOURCE: World Health Organization, 1999.

are reported to suffer from some sort of psychiatric disorder at the time of their death. Mood disorders are highly associated with suicidal behavior at all ages but appear to play the most fundamental role in suicide in older adults. A study conducted by Harris and Barraclough in 1997 revealed that the mean suicide risk in subjects affected by major depressive disorder and dysthymia (a less severe form of mood disorder) was, respectively, twenty and twelve times higher than expected, in relation to the general population. An excess risk persists into old age, during which time the combined suicide risk is thirty-five times higher than expected. Most elderly victims suffered from major depression: 67 percent of suicides were aged fifty or over in a 1991 study by Yates Conwell and colleagues; 83 percent in those aged sixty-five and over in the 1993 study by Clark and Clark; and 44 percent of the over-sixty age group in the 1995 research by Markus Heriksson and colleagues.

The predominant role of mood disorders in increasing the risk of a serious suicide attempt suggests that elimination of these disorders could reduce the incidence of serious suicide attempts by up to 80 percent, particularly among older adults (sixty years and over), where the association between mood disorder and suicide attempts is stronger. However, the underrecognition and undertreatment of depression in older adults in the community is very common.

Older persons often do not present with the classic symptomatology. Nearly half of them lack a depressed mood (one of the most recognizable symptoms) in the clinical presentation. Furthermore, given the frequently simultaneous presence of a physical illness, often masking the symptoms of depression, older persons may deliberately deny symptoms such as suicidal ideation. The problem of underrecognition of elderly depression is exacerbated by very low rates of antidepressant treatment. Even if physicians recognize that the depression may need treatment, they are often concerned about adding to the already complex regimen of medications.

Similarly, identification of persons at risk of suicide is also particularly problematic in the elderly. The lack of forewarning of suicide attempts in elderly suicide leads to particular importance being placed on the detection of suicidal ideation. Recent research examining suicidal ideation in seventy-three completed suicides found that 38 percent had expressed their suicidal intent to their doctor prior to their death. However, when consulting with friends and confidants of the deceased they found that 85 percent had communicated their intent. Several patients had denied their intent to suicide to their doctor. These figures highlight the difficulty in detecting suicidal ideation in older patients in a primary care setting, as well as advocating consultation with close ones when suicidal ideation is suspected.

Alcohol abuse and dependence are present according to different studies in 3 to 44 percent of elderly suicide victims, which is higher than the general population of the same age, and are more common among those aged sixty-five to seventy-four. The combination of drinking and depression may produce a very high risk of suicide in the elderly, especially where drinking is a maladaptive coping mechanism. Only a small number of elderly suicides were suffering from schizophrenia or other psychotic conditions, and the same holds true for personality disorders. Suicides may generally be associated with the personality trait of "lower openness to experience," inability to form close relationships, tendency to be helpless and hopeless, inability to tolerate change, inability to express psychological pain verbally, loss of control, and feelings of loneliness, despair, and dependence on others.

Finally, the role of anxiety disorders seems to be relevant only as an added condition, especially in conjunction with depression. Likewise, dementia hardly features on the diagnostic list of suicides. It has been proposed that in the early stages of Alzheimer's disease there could frequently be suicidal ideation, but cognitive impairment may impede realization. Loss of insight from the very beginning of the disorders is more marked among subjects with deeper involvement of frontal lobes.

Physical illness. There is controversy as to the influence exerted by physical illness on suicidal behavior. In a study by McKenzie and Popkin (1990), 65 percent of older adults were afflicted by a severe, chronic physical pathology at the time of suicide and 27 percent suffered from persistent, severe illness. Because these conditions were likely to reduce autonomy and necessitate a change of lifestyle, they may induce symptoms of depression, helplessness, and hopelessness, particularly among men and those over seventy-five. Lack of trust in medical intervention and endless suffering were commonly found in depressed elderly suicides. However, the constant co-presence of a structured depressive disorder or other psychiatric pathology (e.g., substance abuse) suggests that physical illness alone does not bring about suicide outside of a psychopathological context. Researchers have suggested that most physical illnesses presenting an increased risk of suicide were associated with mental disorders, substance abuse, or both, and that these factors may be a link between medical disorder and suicide.

Recent studies reported increased suicide rates across cancer patients, especially in the first months after diagnosis and in men. However, among them a high prevalence of psychopathology has also been identified (e.g., severe depression, anxiety, and thought disturbances). An important aspect of suicide risk in relation to physical illness has to do with how patients feel about their illness and their unique fears. In most cases their fears are a manifestation of a deeper psychological problem.

Life conditions and events. Widowed, single, or divorced people are overrepresented among elderly suicide victims, particularly among men. The relatively low suicide rates for married people may reflect not only the companionship of marriage, but also its outlet for aggressiveness.

Up to 50 percent of elderly suicide victims, particularly women, are reported to live alone and to be lonely. Generally speaking, suicidal elderly have been found to have fewer resources and supports and to have less contact with relatives and friends than the younger. However, some researchers claim that apart from more frequent losses and the presence of physical illness in the elderly, there is no particular excess of social isolation and stressful life events, compared to youth. Suicide in the elderly could be related to a narcissistic crisis due to the inability to tolerate the accumulation of minor day-to-day failures. Suicidal behavior may then be precipitated by these events in conjunction to depression or alcohol abuse.

Retirement does not constitute an important suicide risk factor per se, unless it is abrupt and involuntary, particularly in the case of white men under seventy-five and in subjects who lack the flexibility to deal with role change or health and social support. Socioeconomic decline does not appear to be as important a risk factor for the elderly suicide as it is in younger populations. Conversely, bereavement very frequently represents a stressful life event in late life, and the death of a close relative or friend is a very important factor in precipitating suicide. Risk appears to be higher when it concerns the loss of a spouse, especially if it is sudden. Men seem to be more exposed than women.

Biological factors. The study of aging brain processes showed alterations of synaptic conduction and neurotransmitters systems, such as a reduction in dopamine and norepinephrine content in various areas of the brain of the elderly and an increase in monoamine-oxidases, the enzymes that eliminate those neuro-hormones. The hypothesized higher vulnerability of elderly people to depression and suicide could be related to a defective compensatory mechanism, which may favor onset and chronic course of psychopathological process. It has been suggested that impaired regulation of the hypothalamus-pituitary-adrenal axis and alterations in the circadian rhythm, both common in the elderly, may in turn play a part in inducing suicidal behavior.

Prevention and Intervention of Suicidal Behavior

Preventative initiatives include the introduction of social security programs, reduction in the percentage of elderly persons living below the poverty line, the development of flexible retirement schemes, and improved health care availability. Greater opportunities for relations with peers and better access to recreational facilities may provide support for urban elderly people and facilitate role transition typical of old age, including retirement and children leaving home. A systematic monitoring of physical health seems to be particularly important, in the light of its possible impact on suicidal behavior.

Identifying suicidal ideas and tendencies among the elderly is a first goal of fundamental importance. Abilities to detect mental suffering should be improved by appropriate training and educational programs, addressed particularly to general practitioners and other health professionals, such as nurses and social workers. Particular emphasis should be placed on recognition of early and atypical symptoms of psychopathology in the elderly (particularly depression in men) and on the need to eradicate passive therapeutic attitude and old-fashioned fears about psychotropic drugs to allow adequate treatment of potentially reversible mental illness. Some nonpharmacological approaches to the treatment of senile depression might also be considered, particularly cognitive therapy and interpersonal psychotherapy.

Suicide prevention programs and general mental health facilities are underutilized by elderly suicide victims. Reasons range from poor information available to the public, conviction that these services are costly, and the low credibility given by older adults to all types of agencies or institutions. An attempt to overcome elderly people's reticence to contact centers for collecting alarm signals has been through the use of active outreach programs. One such program is the "Tele-Help/Tele-Check Service" established in the Veneto region of Italy, where most disadvantaged elderly people (by loss of autonomy, social isolation, poverty, and/or poor mental health) are actively selected within the community by general practitioners and social workers. They are then assisted with at least two phone calls per week from well-trained personnel. This program is associated with a statistically significant decrease in the number of expected deaths among the elderly.

Ongoing strategies are more successful with female subjects. A possible explanation for success involves the generally more pronounced attitude of women to communicate their inner feelings and receive emotional support. Especially in Western cultures, men are less willing to express their emotions. Thus, it is more likely that males at risk are more often underdiagnosed and undertreated, especially by general practitioners, than their female counterparts. The most promising avenues include the development of crisis intervention techniques that are able to modify the male client attitude and environment in a way that promotes in them more adaptive strategies.

Individuals affected by the suicide of a relative or close friend experience emotional stress requiring special attention, as they too are at high risk for suicide. The most important differences in the grief experience of suicide survivors compared to survivors of accidental or natural deaths concern the associated stigma of the suicide and its ramifications: feelings of guilt, blame, embarrassment, shame, loneliness, and social isolation. Supportive interventions should therefore pay special attention to the elderly, be they survivors of peer suicides or younger individuals (children, grandchildren), bearing in mind that older adults rarely take advantage of formal crisis intervention and support facilities. A particularly important role in identifying needs and organizing the feasibility of such intervention could be assumed by general practitioners, who are often the only contact elderly people actively seek or request of health and social services.

See also: SUICIDE BASICS: EPIDEMIOLOGY; SUICIDE INFLUENCES AND FACTORS: GENDER, MENTAL ILLNESS; SUICIDE TYPES: THEORIES OF SUICIDE

Bibliography

Beautrais, Annette Louise, et al. "Prevalence and Comorbidity of Mental Disorders in Persons Making Serious Attempts: A Case-Control Study." *American Journal of Psychiatry* 153 (1996):1009–1014.

Canetto, Silvia Sara. "Gender and Suicide in the Elderly." *Suicide and Life-Threatening Behavior* 22 (1992):80–97.

Clark, David, and S. H. Clark. "Suicide among the Elderly." In Klaus Böhme, et al. eds., *Suicidal Behavior: The State of the Art: Proceedings of the XVI Congress of the International Association for Suicide Prevention.* Regensburg: S. Roderer Verlag, 1993.

Conwell, Yates. "Suicide in Elderly Patients." In Lon S. Schneider, et al. eds., *Diagnosis and Treatment of Depression in Late Life.* Washington, DC: American Psychiatric Press, 1994.

Conwell, Yates, et al. "Suicide in Later Life: Psychological Autopsy Findings." *International Psychogeriatrics* 3 (1991):59–66.

Copeland, J. R. M. "Depression in Older Age: Origins of the Study." *British Journal of Psychiatry* 174 (1999): 304–306.

Curran, David. *Adolescent Suicidal Behavior.* New York: Hemisphere, 1987.

De Leo, Diego, and René F. W. Diekstra, eds. *Depression and Suicide in Late Life.* Toronto: Hogrefe/Huber, 1990.

De Leo, Diego, G. Carollo, and M. Dello Buono. "Lower Suicides Rates Associated with Tele-Help/Tele-Check Service for the Elderly at Home." *American Journal of Psychiatry* 152 (1995):632–634.

De Leo, Diego, P. Scocco, and W. Padoani. "Physical Illness and Parasuicide: Evidence from the European Parasuicie Study Interview Schedule." *International Journal of Psychiatry in Medicine* 29 (1999):149–163.

De Leo, Diego, P. Hickey, and G. Meneghel. "Blindness, Fear of Blindness, and Suicide." *Psychosomatics* 40 (1999):339–344.

De Leo, Diego, W. Padoani, and P. Scocco. "Attempted and Completed Suicide in Older Subjects: Results from The WHO/EURO Multicentre Study of Suicidal Behaviour." *International Journal of Geriatric Psychiatry* 16 (2001):300–310.

Draper, Brian. "Suicidal Behaviour in the Elderly." *International Journal of Geriatric Psychiatry* 8 (1994): 655–661.

Forsell, Y., A. F. Jorm, and B. Winblad. "Suicidal Thoughts and Associated Factors in an Elderly Population." *Acta Psychiatrica Scandinavica* 95 (1997):108–111.

Frierson, Robert L. "Suicide Attempts by the Old and the Very Old." *Archives of Internal Medicine* 151 (1991): 141–144.

Girard, C. "Age, Gender, and Suicide." *American Sociological Review* 58 (1993):53–574.

Harris, E. C., and Brian Barraclough. "Suicide As an Outcome for Mental Disorders: A Meta-Analysis." *British Journal of Psychiatry* 170 (1997):205–228.

Harris, E. C., and Brian Barraclough. "Suicide As an Outcome for Medical Disorders." *Medicine* 73 (1994): 281–298.

Henriksson, Markus M., et al. "Mental Disorders in Elderly Suicide." *International Psychogeriatrics* 7 (1995): 275–286.

Ji, J. L., Arthur Kleinman, and A. E. Becker. "Suicide in Contemporary China: A Review of China's Distinctive

Suicide Demographics in Their Sociocultural Context." *Harvard Review of Psychiatry* 9 (2001):1–12.

Jorm, A. F., et al. "Factors Associated with the Wish to Die in Elderly People." *Age and Ageing* 24 (1995): 389–392.

Loebel, J. Pierre, et al. "Anticipation of Nursing Home Placement May Be a Precipitant of Suicide among Elderly." *Journal of American Geriatric Society* 39 (1991):407–408.

Lyness, J. M., Y. Conwell, and N. C. Nelson. "Suicide Attempts in Elderly Psychiatric Inpatients." *Journal of the American Geriatrics Society* 40 (1992):320–324.

McCall, P. L. "Adolescent and Elderly White Male Suicide Trends: Evidence of Changing Well-Being?" *Journal of Gerontology* 46 (1991):S43–51.

McKenzie, T. B., and Michael K. Popkin. "Medical Illness and Suicide." In Susan J. Blumenthal and David J. Kupfer eds., *Suicide over the Life Cycle: Risk Factors, Assessment, and Treatment of Suicidal Patients.* Washington, DC: American Psychiatric Press, 1990.

Neulinger, Kerrin, and Diego De Leo. "Suicide in Elderly and Youth Populations: How Do They Differ?" In Diego De Leo ed., *Suicide and Euthanasia in Older Adults: A Transcultural Journey.* Seattle, WA: Hogrefe/Huber, 2001.

Padoani, Walter, Massimo Marini, and Diego De Leo. "Cognitive Impairment, Insight, Depression, and Suicidal Ideation." *Archives of Gerontology and Geriatrics* Supp. 7 (2001):295–298.

Reynolds, Charles F., and David J. Kupfer. "Depression and Aging: A Look to the Future." *Psychiatric Services* 50 (1999):1167–1172.

Scocco, Paolo, P. Marietta, and W. Padoani. "Mood Disorders and Parasuicide." *Italian Journal of Psychiatry and Behavioural Sciences* 8 (1998):85–89.

Skoog, Ingmar, O. Aevarsson, and Jan Beskow. "Suicidal Feelings in a Population Sample of Non-Demented 85-Year-Olds." *American Journal of Psychiatry* 153 (1996):1015–1020.

Uncapher, H., and P. A. Arean. "Physicians Are Less Willing to Treat Suicidal Ideation in Older Patients." *Journal of American Geriatric Society* 48 (2000):188–192.

Vasilas, C. A., and H. G. Morgan. "Elderly Suicides' Contact with Their General Practitioner Before Death." *International Journal of Geriatric Psychiatry* 9 (1994):1008–1009.

Waern, Magda, Jan Beskow, Bo Runeson, and Ingmar Skoog. "Suicidal Feelings in the Last Year of Life in Elderly People Who Commit Suicide." *Lancet* 354 (1999):917.

World Health Organization. *Figures and Facts about Suicide.* Geneva: Author, 1999.

DIEGO DE LEO

SUICIDE TYPES

INDIRECT SUICIDE

Suicide, perhaps the most obvious type of avoidable death at any age, is an intentional act that quickly results in death. However, there is a wide range of indirect suicidal behaviors in which death results gradually rather than immediately, and in which the degree of intentionality is less obvious than in an overt suicide attempt.

Defining Indirect Suicidal Behavior

Robert Kastenbaum and Brian Mishara, in their discussion of the concept of premature death and its relationship to self-injurious behavior, suggested that behaviors that shorten life are varied in form and widespread. They recognized that in one sense all human behavior affects a person's life expectancy. Some obvious examples of potentially life-shortening behavior include smoking cigarettes, taking risks when driving, and ignoring doctors' orders. On the other hand, life span can be prolonged by exercising regularly, eating well, using care when crossing the street, and driving an automobile in good condition equipped with air bags while always wearing a seat belt.

Indirect suicidal behavior is thus a matter of probabilities rather than certainties. Not taking one's heart medication or crossing the street carelessly will certainly increase the probability of a premature death. However, the timing of the occurrence of a subsequent heart attack is unknown; some people cross recklessly and live a long life, while others are hit by a car and die the first time they are not careful. Similarly, smoking cigarettes is clearly associated with a reduction in life expectancy, and most people know this, including smokers. However, as many smokers will point out, there is usually a case of a person someone knows who has smoked for decades and lived to old age.

Suicides are often deemed indirect where there is no immediate and clearly identifiable intentionality. The pioneer suicidologist Edwin Shneidman spoke of "subintentioned death" and "indirect suicide" (1981, p. 234). He felt that orientations toward death, or "toward cessation," fall into four categories, which include intentioned, subintentioned, unintentioned, and contraintentioned. Suicide is by definition generally considered to be intentioned. Accidental deaths are unintentioned, and his category of "contraintention" includes people who feign death and threaten death. He specifies four groups of persons who have subintentional orientations. First, there is the "death-chancer" who gambles with death by doing things that leave death "up to chance." Suicidal behavior in which there appears to be a calculated expectation for intervention and rescue are examples of this form of subintentional suicidal behavior.

The "death-hasteners" are individuals who unconsciously aggravate a physiological disequilibrium to hasten death. Death-hasteners may engage in a dangerous lifestyle, such as abusing the body, using alcohol or drugs, exposing themselves to the elements, or not eating a proper diet.

The "death-capitulators," by virtue of some strong emotion, play a psychological role in hastening their own demise. These people give in to death or "scare themselves to death." Shneidman includes in this category voodoo deaths and other deaths in which psychosomatic illness and higher risk of complications (e.g., high blood pressure and anxiety) increase the probability of an early death.

Shneidman's fourth and final category is the "death-experimenter," who does not wish consciously to end his or her life but who appears to wish for a chronically altered or "befogged" state of existence. This includes alcoholics and barbiturate addicts.

Interpretations by Freud and His Followers

Although Freud did not discuss indirect suicide, he developed the concept of the death instinct later in his life. It was his student Karl Menninger who elaborated on the concept of a death instinct, Thanatos, which he viewed as being in constant conflict with the opposing force of the life instinct, or Eros. According to Menninger, there is an inherent tendency toward self-destruction that may, when not sufficiently counterbalanced by the life instincts, result in both direct and indirect self-destructive behavior.

Norman Farberow expanded upon Menninger's theory and developed a classification system for what he called "indirect self-destructive behavior." Farberow felt that direct and indirect self-destructive behaviors differ in many ways. The impact of indirect self-destructive behaviors is most often long-term and frequently permanent, so that only the results are clearly apparent. Unlike direct suicidal behavior, indirect self-destructive behavior is not linked to a specific precipitating stress; hence this behavior is not sudden or impulsive. Unlike completed suicides and suicide attempts, indirect self-destructive behavior does not entail a threat to end one's own life; nor does it involve clear messages that indicate a death wish. Indirect self-destructive people are generally self-concerned and unable to invest much of themselves in a relationship with significant others. They are often alone and have limited social support systems. In contrast, the suicide attempts of the direct self-destructive are often related to the loss of a significant other.

Studies of Other Species

Humans are the only species who engage in intentional self-destructive behavior. Philosophers generally limit the possibility of voluntary and intentional self-destruction to the human race. Nevertheless, self-initiated behaviors that result in harm and death do occur in other species. These behaviors, while obviously self-destructive, do not have the characteristic of conscious decision-making that is unique to humans. Nevertheless, they may ultimately result in injury or death. Researcher Jacqueline Crawley and her colleagues present a review of ethological observations of self-sacrificing deaths in some animal species—usually in defense of territory. Parental behavior may be at the core of many altruistic behaviors, with parents in many species performing some forms of self-sacrifice for the survival of their offspring.

When environmental conditions become stressful for animals, such as for those confined in zoos, self-mutilation and refusal to eat may result. Similarly, pets that are boarded at a kennel or have lost masters to whom they were very much attached may refuse to eat or may mutilate themselves. Crawley speculates that similar dynamics may explain the increased incidence of self-destructive behavior in humans who are imprisoned. More humane care in institutional settings can result in an elimination of self-destructive behaviors in animals. Crawley speculates that greater nurturing and caring behavior may similarly reverse many of the stress-related, self-injurious behaviors in humans.

Research Studies

Indirect suicidal behavior has been studied in several populations. For example, researchers Carol Garrison and colleagues conducted a survey of a community sample of 3,283 American youths in the range of twelve to fourteen years of age. They determined that 2.46 percent of males and 2.79 percent of females engaged in "nonsuicidal physically self-damaging acts" (Garrison 1993, p. 346). Those who engaged in these behaviors had more suicidal ideation, were more likely to have been suffering from a major depression, and had more frequently experienced recent misfortunes.

The researcher Yeates Conwell and his collaborators found that although suicide is rare in nursing homes, indirect self-destructive behaviors, such as refusing to eat or not taking life-sustaining medications, are commonplace. Reviews by McIntosh, Hubbard, and Lester suggest that more elderly persons may die from indirect suicide than from direct suicidal behavior.

Larry Gernsbacher, in his book *The Suicide Syndrome,* speaks of individuals who engage in what he calls "a suicidal lifestyle." He includes in this category alcoholics and drug addicts. These behaviors are considered to be expressions of unconscious suicidal motivations. Gernsbacher asks, "What better way for him to express his self-hatred than to destroy himself with alcohol? How could he more effectively express his vindictiveness than to inflict on those about him the consequences of his addiction? What better way to express his hopelessness than to drown his life in drink?" (1988, p. 175).

In *The Many Faces of Suicide: Indirect Self-Destructive Behavior,* Farberow presents chapters by different authors on a wide variety of indirect suicidal behavior. The contributors discuss physical illnesses "used against the self," including self-destructive behavior in diabetics, "uncooperative" patients, self-destructive behavior in hemodialysis patients, spinal cord injury, and coronary artery illness. Several chapters are concerned with drug and alcohol abuse and their relationship to indirect self-destructive dynamics. Hyperobesity and cigarette smoking are also analyzed as possible ways of increasing the probability of a shortened life. Similarly, gambling, criminal activities, and deviance are judged forms of indirect suicides. Criminals and delinquents often put themselves in situations where there is a high risk of a premature death. Finally, a variety of stress-seeking and high-risk sports activities draw on unconscious or subconscious motivations to risk death or to test one's ability to master death.

Conclusions

It may be that direct intentional acts that result in death (i.e., completed suicides) constitute only a small proportion of the various human behaviors that result in premature death. Perhaps these behaviors are, as Freud and Menninger hypothesized, the result of an intrinsic human proclivity to self-destruction that is locked in constant combat with an inherent motivation to preserve life at all costs. Perhaps indirect suicidal behavior is simply part of one's cultural baggage, with different societies encouraging or condoning certain forms of risky and dangerous activities, such as engaging in high-risk sports or having unprotected sex with a high-risk partner. Perhaps, as several research studies indicate, indirect suicidal behavior may be linked to treatable depression, stressful life events, and more obviously identifiable suicidal thoughts and intentions.

It is clear that indirect suicidal behaviors can decrease when the surrounding environment improves; for example, offering patients better treatment in a nursing home. Research in the twenty-first century indicates that it is important to be aware of indirect suicidal behavior and to understand it as a signal of treatable problems. Such vigilance cannot only improve lives, it can save them as well.

See also: FREUD, SIGMUND; MARTYRS; REVOLUTIONARIES AND "DEATH FOR THE CAUSE!"; SUICIDE

Bibliography

Conwell, Yeates, Jane Pearson, and Evan G. DeRenzo. "Indirect Self-Destructive Behavior among Elderly Patients in Nursing Homes: A Research Agenda." *American Journal of Geriatric Psychiatry* 4, no. 2 (1996):152–163.

Crawley, Jacqueline N., Mary E. Sutton, and David Pickar. "Animal Models of Self-Destructive Behavior and Suicide." *Psychiatric Clinics of North America* 8, no. 2 (1985):299–310.

Farberow, Norman L. *The Many Faces of Suicide: Indirect Self-Destructive Behavior.* New York: McGraw-Hill, 1980.

Freud, Sigmund. *Beyond the Pleasure Principle,* edited and translated by James Strachey. New York: Norton, 1975.

Garrison, Carol Z., Cheryl L. Addy, Robert E. McKeown, et al. "Nonsuicidal Physically Self-Damaging Acts in Adolescents." *Journal of Child and Family Studies* 2, no. 4 (1993):339–352.

Gernsbacher, Larry M. *The Suicide Syndrome: Origins, Manifestations and Alleviation of Human Self-Destructiveness.* New York: Human Sciences Press, 1988.

Kastenbaum, Robert, and Brian L. Mishara. "Premature Death and Self-Injurious Behavior in Old Age." *Geriatrics* 26 (1971):70–81.

Lester, David. *Why People Kill Themselves: A 1990s Summary of Research Findings on Suicidal Behavior,* 3rd edition. Springfield, IL: Charles C. Thomas, 1992.

Lester, David. "Genetics, Twins, and Suicide." In Ronald W. Maris ed., *Biology of Suicide.* New York: Guilford, 1986.

McIntosh, John L., Richard W. Hubbard, and John F. Santos. "Suicide among the Elderly: A Review of Issues with Case Studies." *Journal of Gerontological Social Work* 4, no. 1 (1981):63–74.

Mishara, Brian L., and Robert Kastenbaum. "Self-Injurious Behavior and Environmental Change in the Institutionalized Elderly." *Aging and Human Development* 4, no. 2 (1973):133–145.

Menninger, Karl A. *Man against Himself.* New York: Harcourt Brace Jovanovich, 1985.

Shneidman, Edwin S. "Orientations toward Death: Subintentioned Death and Indirect Suicide." *Suicide and Life-Threatening Behavior* 11, no. 4 (1981):232–253.

BRIAN L. MISHARA

MURDER-SUICIDE

The relationship between suicidal behavior and other forms of violence is not always clear. In the case of murder-suicide (or homicide-suicide), however, the two acts are directly associated. The typical definition of "murder-suicide" is "homicide followed within a week by the perpetrator's suicide."

In most cases, there is an intimate relationship between perpetrator and victim. Murder-suicide is uncommon, ranging in rate from 0.05 per 100,000 inhabitants in Scotland or New Zealand to 0.55 in Miami. According to the descriptive typology proposed by Nock and Marzuck, it falls into four main categories: spousal/consortial murder-suicide, filicide-suicide, familicide-suicide, and extrafamilial murder-suicide. Spousal/consortial murder-suicide is the most common type in Western countries. Committed primarily by males acting out of morbid jealousy and/or revenge, it usually occurs when the victim attempts to end the relationship, often in the context of verbal violence. In the United States, males perpetrate 57 percent of simple spousal homicides but 90 percent of spousal murder-suicides. The reason for this imbalance is that for women, spousal homicide is a desperate means of deliverance from an abusive relationship, whereas for men it is often a way to maintain control over their partner unto death. Compassion can sometimes motivate murder-suicide among spouses or cohabitants, especially in cases involving the frail and elderly. These "altruistic" mercy killings often assume the semblance of informal suicide pacts.

Filicide-suicide—killing one's own children before killing oneself—is the most common form of murder-suicide committed by women in Japan. Globally, women commit most filicides, but men are more likely to commit suicide after filicide. If a woman's victim is an infant who is less than six months old, the perpetrator usually suffers from serious postpartum depression or psychosis. Often such filicidal mothers view their infants as extensions of their own tortured psyches and hence claim the altruistic motive of rescuing their children from future emotional torments.

Even less common is familicide-suicide, in which the perpetrator kills all family members before committing suicide. In extrafamilial murder-suicide, the victims can be related to the perpetrator but not by consanguinity. It is the rarest form of murder-suicide but the one with the highest social toll per incident.

Most types of murder-suicide involve morbid forms of attachment between perpetrator and victim, especially when the relationship is threatened with dissolution, and/or impulsive personality traits. Depression, too, is a common factor in murder-suicide, as it is in simple suicide, although most depressives are not suicidal or homicidal. Murder-suicide is one of two special types of dyadic (paired) death, the other being the suicide pact. Alan Berman developed a more psychodynamic typology of murder-suicide that covers both types, classifying them according to four categories: erotic-aggressive, unrequited love, dependent-protective, and symbiotic.

Murder-suicide is hard to predict and prevent because of its rarity and apparent suddenness. Among various psychiatric treatments, the most successful preventive approach involves diffusing the intensity of the spousal relationship.

See also: HOMICIDE, DEFINITIONS AND CLASSIFICATIONS OF; HOMICIDE, EPIDEMIOLOGY OF; SUICIDE TYPES: SUICIDE PACTS, THEORIES OF SUICIDE

Bibliography

Berman, Alan L. "Dyadic Death: A Typology." *Suicide and Life-Threatening Behavior* 26 (1996):342–350.

Felthous, Alan R., and Anthony Hempel. "Combined Homicide-Suicides: A Review." *Journal of Forensic Sciences* 40 (1995):846–857.

Milroy, Chris M. "The Epidemiology of Homicide-Suicide (Dyadic Death)." *Forensic Science International* 71 (1995): 117–122.

Nock, Mathew K., and Peter M. Marzuk. "Murder-Suicide." In Douglas G. Jacobs ed., *The Harvard Medical School Guide to Suicide Assessment and Intervention.* San Francisco: Jossey-Bass, 1999.

MARC S. DAIGLE

PHYSICIAN-ASSISTED SUICIDE

Physician-assisted death did not begin with the 1993 government-sanctioned process in the Netherlands, nor with the first such acknowledged action by the pathologist Jack Kevorkian in the United States. The practice of ending the life of a suffering patient was so well established by the fifth century B.C.E. that opponents were motivated to mount a strenuous counterattack. The Hippocratic oath offered a landmark definition of the physician's responsibilities. Included was the key statement: "I will give no deadly medicine to anyone if asked, nor suggest any such counsel." In modern times, this controversial practice has become most commonly known as physician-assisted suicide. Some forensic experts and prosecuting attorneys, however, classify these deaths as homicides. The neutral term, physician-assisted death, leaves the question of whether the practice is actually homicide open for consideration.

History of Physician-Assisted Death/Suicide

There is no way of knowing how many physicians have abided by this stricture and how many have lent death a hand through the centuries. Concerned about possible consequences, physicians who have assisted death generally have not spoken openly of these actions. It is clear, however, that some physicians have been easing some patients toward death. These deaths have not necessarily occurred immediately after a medical intervention. Often the preference has been for a medication that reduces respiration or other vital functions in a gradual manner. If this technique functions as intended the patient drifts into a drowsy, painless state of mind until passing away.

In "mercy killings," as these actions have sometimes been described, it is usually assumed that the patient was (a) dying, (b) suffering severely, and (c) asking urgently for the relief. In practice, though, each of these conditions can be difficult to assess. For example, was this person of sound mind in making the request, or was judgment clouded and confused? Were there ways to relieve this person's suffering short of death? How accurate was the diagnosis and prognosis—was this person actually on a nonreversible terminal trajectory?

Furthermore, the medical interventions have not always proven effective. In twenty-first-century medical practice a patient is sometimes given medication to reduce agitation. There can be the unfortunate effect of a terminally ill person continuing to experience pain but now being unable to move or communicate. Even the passive form of euthanasia—withdrawing treatment rather than making a direct intervention—can fail. This was demonstrated, for example, in the landmark case of Karen Ann Quinlan, a young woman who never regained consciousness after lapsing into a coma in 1975. More than a year later a court ruled that she could be disconnected from the ventilator. It was assumed that she would then die almost immediately. However, the young woman remained in a persistent vegetative state for another ten years. Although this episode predated the emergence of the assisted death movement in the United States, it demonstrates that medical expertise in ending a life cannot be taken for granted.

Physician-assisted suicide entered the spotlight of public opinion in the 1980s as this practice was given a limited form of judicial acceptance in the Netherlands. Jack Kevorkian became the central figure in physician-assisted death in the United States in the 1990s. Many other nations have also been wrestling with this controversy. The Parliament of the Northern Territory of Australia, for example, approved assisted suicide in 1996, but a year later was overturned by the Australian Senate, which forbade all its territories from passing any such measures. Although significant cultural differences exist in response to the assisted death issue, the practice itself and the basic controversy can be identified by focusing on events in the Netherlands and the United States.

Physician-Assisted Death As an Alternative to Prolonged Suffering

Advances in health care have raised expectations. Many life-threatening conditions, such as smallpox, have been prevented by public health measures; others respond to skillful treatment. Nevertheless, dying people often have experienced uncontrolled pain and other distressing symptoms. A growing number of critics placed blame on the medical profession for isolating and neglecting the dying person, who reminded doctors of their still-limited ability to restore health. One major response was the development of the hospice or palliative care movement, in which relief of pain and provision of comfort were the top priorities. The other major response was the attitude conveyed by such phrases as "death on demand," "right to die," and "deliverance." The Hemlock Society and other organizations not only argued the case for suicide but provided information on how to proceed. Suicide and suicide attempts had already become decriminalized. Although religious and moral sanctions remained in place, there was increasing public toleration for a terminally ill person who sought to avoid further suffering by suicide.

Physician-assisted death came out of the shadows as some patients requested and some physicians proved willing to lend a hand. Why could not people who were resolved to end their lives do so for themselves? Two factors were certainly involved and another factor probable: (1) In some terminal conditions the individual did not have the physical ability to take his or her own life (e.g., an advanced stage of Lou Gehrig's disease); (2) some people were concerned that their suicide attempts would fail and only increase their suffering, and thus medical expertise was needed; and (3) case studies suggest that some people felt the need for approval and authorization from a physician, thereby releasing them from any moral hesitation. The basic need was for relief both from current suffering and from the prospect of additional suffering throughout the terminal phase of life. Many patients and family members expressed the opinion that when physicians could no longer restore health and prevent death, they should provide relief from suffering.

Arguments For and Against Physician-Assisted Death

The liberty interest was often presented as the legal and philosophical foundation for assisted death. The Fourteenth Amendment to the U.S. Constitution includes a due process clause whose provisions have been affirmed by the courts in many decisions over the years. The chief justice of the Supreme Court concluded in *Missouri* v. *Cruzan,* "the choice between life and death is a deeply personal decision of obvious and overwhelming finality" (Baird 1989, p. 184) and therefore protected by the Fourteenth Amendment. Citizens have a right to autonomy that the state cannot overcome without proving a compelling interest for so doing.

A few arguments against physician-assisted death state that (1) religion and the state consider life to be sacred (this does comprise a compelling interest that overrides individual choice); (2) legalizing assisted death even in the most appropriate cases would push society down the "slippery slope" to large-scale abuse of this practice; (3) physicians would lose public trust if they are seen as executioners as well as healers; and (4) palliative care can prevent or reduce terminal suffering, therefore assisted death is not necessary. There are counterarguments to all of these; for example, claims that life is considered sacred are contradicted by some actions of church and state; the argument that effective regulations can prevent abuse of the assisted death option; and the position that not all terminal conditions can be significantly eased by palliative care.

Another controversy centers around the most appropriate term for this practice. *Physician-assisted suicide,* the most frequently used term, implies that the decisive action is taken by the patient. Critics say that this is an attempt to gloss over the truth: The physician prepares the materials and places them at the disposal of the patient. It is, therefore, not any kind of suicide, but something closer either to euthanasia or murder. (The Michigan coroner who investigated the deaths involving Kevorkian classified them as homicides.)

The Netherlands Experience

The world has been observing developments in the Netherlands since physician-assisted death first received a limited kind of toleration in the 1980s. A physician was found guilty for ending her mother's life at her request. Her sentence was one week in prison. In 1984 the Dutch Supreme Court decided that physician-assisted death is acceptable if the following conditions are met: (1) The patient has been determined as incurably ill from a medical standpoint; (2) the patient's physical or spiritual suffering is unbearable or serious to the patient; and (3) the patient has indicated in writing that he or she desires to terminate life or that he or she wants to be delivered from his suffering.

This ruling had an uneasy coexistence with other provisions of Dutch law that had been established a century before; specifically, the statement: "He who deliberately incites another to suicide, then assists him therein or provides him with the means is punished, if the suicide follows, with a prison sentence of at most three years or a fine of the fourth category" (Henk 2001, p. 9). The semi-approved practice of assisted death also had a divided response within both the health care community and the general public. After years of study and debate, the Dutch Parliament voted to legalize assisted death. Additional criteria were established: (1) The patient's request must be determined to be voluntary, well-considered, and lasting (an advance directive or living will is acceptable); (2) a second physician must be consulted; (3) parental consent is required for people under the age of sixteen; and (4) the intervention itself must be in a medically approved manner. Physicians who function within the framework of these rules are free from criminal prosecution.

There remains heated controversy about the scope and manner in which physician-assisted death has been practiced in the Netherlands. About 2,000 cases of physician-assisted suicide are reported in the Netherlands, a small proportion of the approximately 135,000 total deaths. Advocates claim that there is no evidence that a slippery slope has developed because physicians are conscientiously following the guidelines. Opponents note that about half of the patients do not make an explicit request because they are no longer mentally competent or other reasons exist. Advocates reply that in these instances there is other basis for decision making (e.g., family request), and that the medical procedures shorten the patient's life by only a few hours or days. Opponents also argue that there are many more cases than reported and that it is in these cases that abuse of the law occurs.

Assisted Death in the United States

Kevorkian has been the most prominent person in the assisted death movement in the United States since 1987. A critic of the medical establishment's treatment of dying people, he promised to deliver them from their suffering and made himself available to all who might desire his services. In *Prescription: Medicide* (1991) Kevorkian listed the rules that he believed should be followed; they include calling for psychiatric consultation, calling for pain specialist consultation, allowing a twenty-four-hour waiting period after final request, conducting extensive patient counseling, and stopping the process if there is any sign that patient is ambivalent.

Surprisingly, perhaps, he expressed a strong emotional reaction against the specific act by which a person's life is ended: "Performance of that repulsive task should now be relegated exclusively to a device like the Mercitron, which the doomed subject must activate. What is most important is that the participation of doctors or other health professionals now becomes strictly optional. . . . A doctor no longer need perform the injection" (Kevorkian 1991, pp. 233–234). It seemed odd to speak of the dying person in both a melodramatic ("doomed") and distant ("subject") manner when his intent was to preserve human dignity. Critics also accused Kevorkian of trying to evade personal responsibility by replacing his own hand on the hypodermic needle with a device (also known as "the suicide machine") that provided first a muscular relaxant, then a drug to halt the action of the heart.

Many testimonials were given in appreciation of Kevorkian's services. He was described as a caring and sensitive person who had provided the blessing of pain relief. Public opinion was divided, but has moved toward increasing acceptance. In 1950 one-third of survey respondents agreed with the statement, "Physicians should be allowed to end the lives of patients with incurable diseases if they and their families requested it." In the 1990s the approval rate increased to two-thirds.

Numerous attempts were made to find Kevorkian guilty of criminal behavior, but none succeeded until he provided a television news program with a video in which he gave a lethal injection to a man in an advanced stage of Lou Gehrig's disease (amyotropic lateral sclerosis). The man and his family were grateful but, as Kevorkian had expected, he was found guilty of second-degree murder and sentenced to a term of ten to twenty-five years in prison. Kevorkian often said that he welcomed legal actions against him as a way of awakening the public and forcing a change in the system. Judge Jessica Cooper of Oakland County, Michigan, noted that Kevorkian was not licensed to practice medicine at the time he administered the lethal injection. It was also her opinion that the trial was more about Kevorkian's defiance of the legal system than it was about the moral and political issues associated with euthanasia.

Research Perspective on Kevorkian's Practice

Studies of Kevorkian's practice of assisted death produced critical findings. Most of the people whose deaths were assisted by Kevorkian were not terminally ill. Most were not in severe pain. A gender bias encouraged death: In the general population, women are much less likely than men to commit suicide; most of Kevorkian's patients were women who were depressed and dependent. This profile does not fit the population of terminally ill people, but it does fit the population of people who make nonfatal suicide attempts. The inference drawn was that Kevorkian attracted unhappy people who might otherwise have found other solutions to their problems. Kevorkian did not recognize or treat the depression that was experienced by many of the people who requested his services, nor was Kevorkian trained in palliative care and he provided little or no help in trying to reduce pain by methods other than death. Kevorkian functioned without adequate medical consultation. In fact, he violated all the rules that he himself proposed for assisted death in *Prescription: Medicide* (1991).

A 2000 study found that only one-fourth of Kevorkian's patients were terminally ill, as compared with 100 percent of those who requested physician-assisted suicide since this procedure became legally accepted in Oregon. The researchers conclude that Kevorkian's procedures did not provide adequate clinical safeguards to prevent the physician-assisted deaths of people who were not terminally ill.

Assisted suicide has often been criticized as an extreme and unnecessary measure that could be avoided in most instances by compassionate and informed care. Other physicians have perhaps criticized it most severely for presenting death as a treatment or therapy. The physician and scholar Thomas Szasz also observes, "a procedure that only a physician can perform expands the medicalization of everyday life, extends medical control over personal conduct, especially at the end of life, and diminishes patient autonomy" (Szasz 1999, p. 67).

Although Kevorkian's influence should not be underestimated, the assisted death movement has taken other forms that incorporate due process, extensive consultation, and compliance with existing laws and regulations. Whatever the future might hold for assisted death it is more likely to be worked out through the ballot, legislative acts, and consensus.

See also: EUTHANASIA; HIPPOCRATIC OATH; HOSPICE OPTION; KEVORKIAN, JACK; NATURAL DEATH ACTS; PAIN AND PAIN MANAGEMENT; SUICIDE INFLUENCES AND FACTORS: PHYSICAL ILLNESS

Bibliography

Battin, Margaret P., and Rosamond Rhodes, eds. *Physician Assisted Suicide.* Philadelphia: Brunner-Routledge, 1998.

Edelstein, Leo. *The Hippocratic Oath: Text, Translation, and Interpretation.* Baltimore, MD: Johns Hopkins University Press, 1943.

Cox, Donald W. *Hemlock's Cup.* Buffalo, NY: Prometheus Press, 1993.

Gomez, Leo. *Regulating Death.* New York: Free Press, 1991.

Hardwig, John, ed. *Is There a Duty to Die?* Philadelphia: Brunner-Routledge, 2000.

Kaplan, Kalman, J., ed. *Right to Die versus Sacredness of Life.* Amityville, NY: Baywood, 2000.

Kastenbaum, Robert. *Death, Society, and Human Experience,*7th edition. Boston: Allyn & Bacon, 2001.

Kevorkian, Jack. *Prescription: Medicide.* Buffalo, NY: Prometheus Press, 1991.

Lifton, Robert J. *The Nazi Doctors.* New York: Basic Books, 1986.

Minois, Georges. *History of Suicide: Voluntary Death in Western Culture.* Baltimore, MD: Johns Hopkins University Press, 1999.

Pernick, Martin S. *The Black Stork.* New York: Oxford University Press, 1996

Quill, Thomas E. *A Midwife through the Dying Process.* Baltimore, MD: Johns Hopkins University Press, 1996.

Roscoe, L. A., J. E. Malphurs, L. J. Dragovic, and D. Cohen. "A Comparison of Characteristics of Kevorkian Euthanasia Cases and Physician-Assisted Suicide in Oregon." *Gerontologist* 41 (2001):439–446.

Szasz, Thomas. *Fatal Freedom. The Ethics and Politics of Suicide.* Westport, CT: Praeger, 1999.

Worthen, Laura T., and Dale E. Yeatts. "Assisted Suicide: Factors Affecting Public Attitudes." *Omega: The Journal of Death and Dying* 42 (2000–2001):115–136.

ROBERT KASTENBAUM

RATIONAL SUICIDE

The question of whether or not suicide can sometimes be rational is a controversial topic that has been the subject of considerable debate among mental health practitioners, scholars, and laypeople alike. Some suicides are obviously irrational, for example, when a schizophrenic man kills himself because he hears voices commanding him to do so. However, the possibility that some suicides may be rational can be debated on both philosophical and scientific grounds.

In 1964 the philosopher Jacques Choron defined rational suicide as being when there is no psychiatric disorder, there is no impairment of the reasoning of the suicidal person, and the person's motives appear to be justifiable or at least understandable by the majority of contemporaries in the same culture or social group.

Choron's first requirement that there is no psychiatric disorder eliminates the majority of suicides, since most persons who die by suicide suffer from a mental disorder, such as clinical depression, alcoholism, or drug abuse. Given these data, rational suicide, if it exists, is a phenomenon that can only characterize a small minority of suicides. Even the most vocal proponents of rational suicide exclude persons suffering from mental disorders. In his defense of the Hemlock Society's support of rational suicide, the society director Derek Humphry stated in 1986 that there is another form of suicide called "emotional suicide or irrational self-murder." The Hemlock Society view on emotional suicide is to prevent it when you can. The Hemlock Society, which supports rational suicide, specifically does not encourage any form of suicide "for mental health or unhappy reasons" (1986, pp. 172–176).

Even when the suicide victim does not suffer from a serious mental disorder, some suicides may still be irrational by any standard; for example, when the suicide victim is in a temporary state of extreme agitation or depression or his or her views of reality are grossly distorted by drugs or alcohol, or a man whose wife has just left him, has a loaded gun in his house, and then consumes great quantities of alcohol that distorts his judgment may become highly suicidal even though he was not suffering from a previous mental disorder. There still remains the question of whether or not some suicides can be considered rational.

The psychiatrist Ronald Maris has argued that suicide derives from one's inability or refusal to accept the terms of the human condition. He argues that suicide may effectively solve people's problems when non-suicidal alternatives may not do so. Although no suicide is ever the best alternative to the common human condition, for some individuals suicide constitutes an individual's logical response to a common existential human condition.

The researcher and ethicist Margaret Battin, while admitting that no human acts are ever wholly rational, defines rational suicide in terms of the criteria of being able to reason, having a realistic worldview, possessing adequate information, and acting in accordance with a person's fundamental interests. Battin indicates that meeting the criterion of "ability to reason" may be very difficult to establish because of research and anecdotal information indicating that persons who commit suicide often leave messages that are illogical and tend to refer to themselves as being able to experience the effects of their suicide after their death as if they were to continue to be alive.

One of the basic criteria for being able to act rationally is the ability to use logical processes and to see the causal consequences of one's actions. It can be argued that many suicides do not accurately foresee the consequences of their actions. Furthermore, one can ask the philosophical question of whether or not it is possible to foresee the final consequence of suicide, which is to know what it is like to be dead. Battin suggests that when one imagines oneself dead, one generally imagines a view of one's own dead body surrounded by grieving relatives or located in the grave, which presupposes a subject being around to have those experiences. This may be an indication that one does not accurately imagine death. However, Battin points out that two classes of suicides are not necessarily irrational: first, those with religious or metaphysical beliefs that include the possibility that one goes on to have humanlike experiences after death; and second, persons whose reputation and honor are of primary importance, such as the case of the Japanese suicide of honor by a samurai who had been disgraced.

There is also the question of what is considered rational decision making. According to *Webster's New World Dictionary of American Language,* rationality is "exercising one's reason in a proper manner, having sound judgement, sensible, sane; not foolish, absurd or extravagant; implying the ability to reason logically, as by drawing conclusions from inferences, and often connoting the absence of emotion." This definition implies a degree of autonomy in the decision-making process, the presence of abilities to engage in logical and reasoned thought processes, and the absence of undue influence on the decision-making process by external factors. In a 1983 review of contemporary philosophical writings on suicide, the scholar David J. Mayo presented the definition that a rational suicide must realistically consider alternatives concerning the likelihood of realizing goals of fundamental interest to the person and then choose an alternative which will maximize the realization of those goals. More than a decade later Brian L. Mishara argued that the most important human decision making is more emotional than rational, including the most significant choices in life, such as whom a person marries and what career a person chooses. If important decisions have a predominantly emotional basis, what would lead one to expect that the paramount decision of ending one's life could then be different and more rational? Those who argue for rational suicide generally insist that the act must occur when a person is experiencing interminable suffering. Mishara argued that in the presence of severe suffering true rational decision making is even less likely to occur; the emotions associated with the suffering compromise one's ability to reason rationally.

Battin's second criterion for rational decision making is that the decision is based upon a realistic view of the world. She points out that there are multiple worldviews that vary depending upon cultural and religious beliefs; what appears to be irrational for some is considered quite rational in other cultural contexts. Her third criterion, adequacy of information, may be questioned because of the effect of one's emotional state on the ability to look for and see the full picture. Still the suicidal person's actions cannot be seen to be more inadequately informed or less rational than in any other important moral choices.

Battin's criterion of avoidance of harm is essentially the justification that organizations such as the Hemlock Society propose as their fundamental justification of rational suicide. They cite the cessation of the harm of unbearable suffering as the most common reason for suicide. The organization lists grave physical handicap that is so constricting that the individual cannot tolerate such a limited existence as a second reason. This justification goes against the Christian religious tradition that purports that pain and suffering may serve some constructive purpose of spiritual growth, has some meaning, or is part of God's plan.

The decision to end one's life when terminally ill is frequently construed as rational. The acceptance of ending life when extreme pain or handicap is experienced assumes that no relief for the pain is available and that the severe handicap may not be better tolerated. Derek Humphry defends people's "right" to refuse to experience even a "beneficent lingering" and to simply choose to not continue to live any longer when they are terminally ill.

Battin's final criterion of being in accordance with a person's fundamental interest raises the question of whether one can actually satisfy any kind of personal interest by being dead (and not around to be satisfied). Nevertheless, some individuals have long-standing moral beliefs in which the decision to foreshorten life under certain difficult circumstances is clearly condoned as in their interest.

The concept of rational suicide may sometimes be confused with the concept of "understandable" suicide. David Clarke's work suggests that the concepts of rationality and autonomy are less useful than the concepts of "understandability" and "respect" when considering the expressed wish to die. However, what an outsider considers to be understandable or respectful of a person's wishes is not necessarily congruent with the suicidal person's experience. In some situations, when outsiders often feel that a person would be "better off dead," persons who actually experience those circumstances feel differently. For example, despite popular beliefs, very few persons who are suffering from terminal and severely disabling chronic illnesses actually consider or engage in behavior to end life prematurely.

Debates concerning rational suicide usually center around society's obligations to provide easier access to suicide under certain circumstances. If one accepts the possibility of rational suicide, there is also an implicit moral acceptance of suicide under the circumstances in which rational suicides may occur. However, developing criteria for when a suicide can be considered rational is not an easy task. What constitutes unbearable suffering for one person may be an acceptable level of discomfort for another. Furthermore, individuals differ to the extent that rationality is an important component of their decision-making process. On what basis may one say that rational decision making is more justifiable than emotional decisions? Most suicidologists choose to try to prevent suicides that come to their attention, assuming that rational suicides, if they exist, are rare, difficult to identify, and merit interventions to challenge their reasoning.

See also: PHILOSOPHY, WESTERN; SUICIDE; SUICIDE INFLUENCES AND FACTORS: MENTAL ILLNESS

Bibliography

Battin, Margaret P. "The Concept of Rational Suicide." In Edwin S. Shneidman ed., *Death: Current Perspectives.* Palo Alto, CA: Mayfield Publishing Company, 1984.

Choron, Jacques. *Modern Man and Mortality.* New York: Macmillan, 1964.

Clarke, David M. "Autonomy, Rationality and the Wish to Die." *Journal of Medical Ethics* 25, no. 6 (1999): 457–462.

Humphry, Derek. "The Case for Rational Suicide." *Euthanasia Review* 1, no. 3 (1986):172–176.

Maris, Ronald. "Rational Suicide: An Impoverished Self-Transformation." *Suicide and Life-Threatening Behavior* 12, no. 1 (1982):4–16.

Mayo, David J. "Contemporary Philosophical Literature on Suicide: A Review. " *Suicide and Life-Threatening Behavior* 13, no. 4 (1983):313–345.

Mishara, Brian L. "Synthesis of Research and Evidence on Factors Affecting the Desire of Terminally Ill or Seriously Chronically Ill Persons to Hasten Death." *Omega: The Journal of Death and Dying,* 39, no. 1 (1999):1–70.

Mishara, Brian L. "The Right to Die and the Right to Live: Perspectives on Euthanasia and Assisted Suicide." In A. Leenaars, M. Kral, R. Dyck, and S. Wenckstern eds., *Suicide in Canada.* Toronto: University of Toronto Press, 1998.

BRIAN L. MISHARA

SUICIDE PACTS

A suicide pact is a mutual agreement between two or more people to die at the same time and usually at the same place. This is a rare phenomenon that occurs in less than 1 percent of suicides in the Western world. However, suicide pacts are a little more prevalent in the Eastern world where they represent approximately 2 to 3 percent of deaths committed

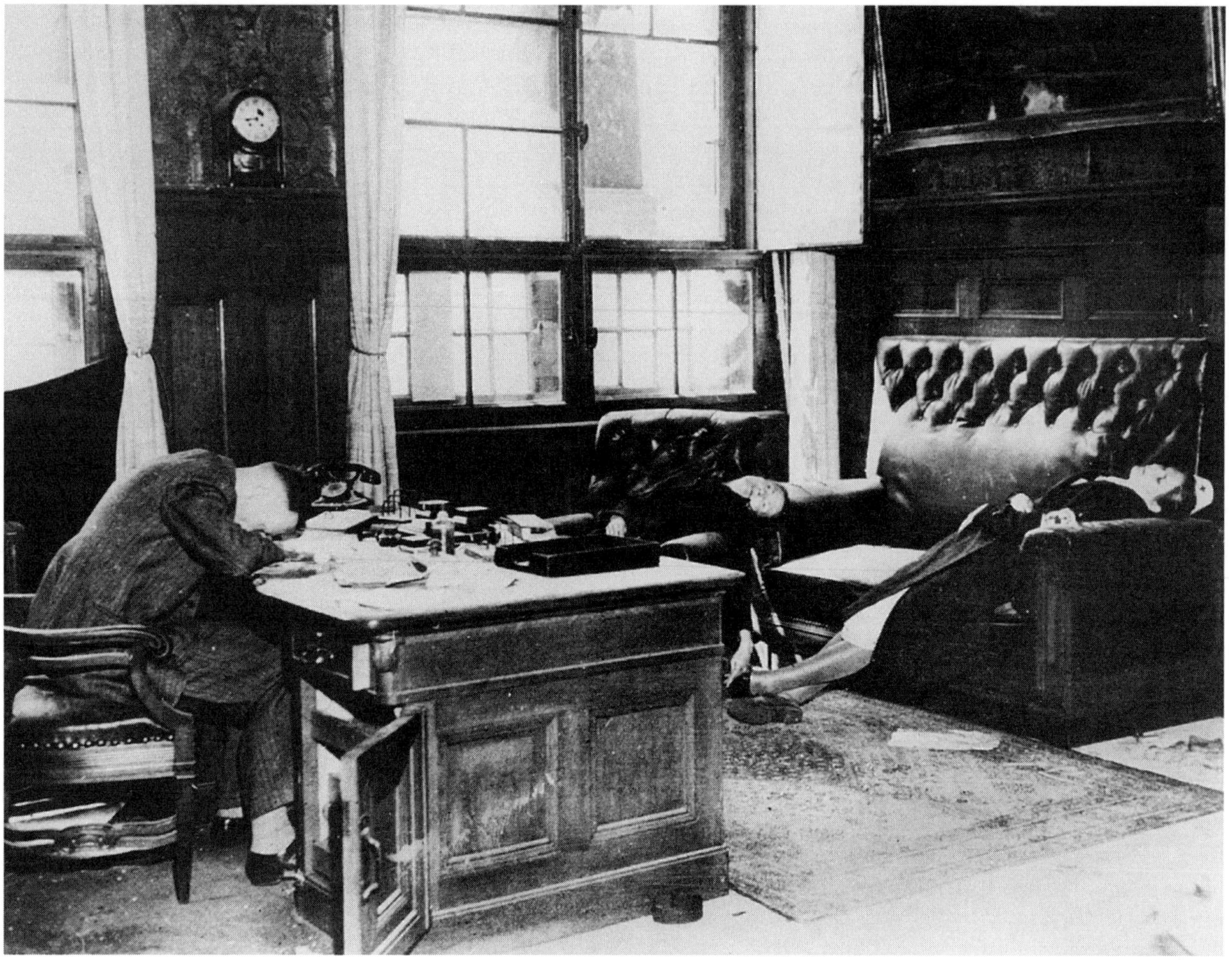

Nazi mayor Alfred Freyberg, his wife, and eighteen-year-old daughter (wearing Nazi armband) died by poison in a suicide pact before the Allies captured Leipzig, Germany, in 1945. BETTMANN/CORBIS

by suicide. Because suicide pacts are rare, they are difficult to study. Despite their rarity and the fact that suicide pact victims generally choose nonviolent suicide methods, suicide pacts are generally lethal and the chances of survival are low.

Suicide Pact Commonalities

Suicide pacts have some common characteristics. The suicidal persons have a close and exclusive relationship, often free of significant bonds to family or friends. The isolation can be caused or exacerbated by a recent retirement, loss of work, disease, or social rejection—for example, two lovers or two friends who are not permitted to be together. The suicide pact is often triggered by a threat of separation of the dyad, death of one of them, or social and familial restrictions on seeing each other. The fear of losing the relationship with the other person motivates the majority of suicide pacts.

The dyad is generally composed of a dominant person who initiates the suicide pact and convinces a more submissive person to agree to this plan. The dominant member is usually the most suicidal member and the dependent person is the most ambivalent. In most cases, the male plays the dominating role. However, there are no indications that someone can become suicidal only due to the suggestion of another person.

Most suicide pacts use poisoning. This nonviolent method allows the synchronization of the deaths and, at the same time, allows the pact members to change their minds. It appears that when the pact is aborted it is frequently because the passive member changes his or her mind and saves the instigator, sometimes against his or her will. However, some researchers claim that the dependent member may ask the dominant one to kill him or her in order to not survive and be left alone.

The prevalence of mental disorders is lower in suicide pacts than in individual suicides. However, researchers have found that at least one member of the dyad usually suffers from depression, borderline or antisocial personality traits, or substance abuse. Physical diseases are frequently observed, particularly in older suicide pact victims. Often, at least one pact member has attempted previously or has been exposed to the suicide of a close relative. This has led some researchers to suggest that suicide pacts are related to suicide clusters (a series of suicides in the same community) because there is a contagion effect. Besides these commonalities, some important differences exist. Three types of suicide pacts can be identified: the love pact, the spouse pact, and the friendship pact.

The love pact. Generally the love pact occurs between two young lovers who are faced with the threat of separation as imposed by their parents or society. There are some cases of love pacts in the Western world, but this type of pact is particularly frequent in the Eastern world where there are strict rules concerning dowry and marriage. For example, in India and Japan many young people are forced to break off a love relationship to marry the person that their parents have chosen for them. Some of these young lovers view suicide as the only way that they can stay together. Lover suicide pacts are often also seen as rebellion against parental authority and linked to the intense guilt of giving priority to one's own desires instead of respecting social conventions.

The spouse pact. Typically occidental, the spouse pact is the most prevalent. Generally it occurs between a husband and a wife, aged fifty or older, who are childless or not living with their children. At least one of them is likely to be physically ill. In most cases, there is interdependence and devotion to one another and the couple engages in a suicide pact because neither member wants to be separated by the other's death. However, the members are sometimes motivated by the fear of chronic pain or fear of losing their physical and mental integrity because of old age. Usually, a dominant/dependent relationship is present.

The friendship pact. The friendship pact has a lower prevalence. Usually it takes place between two or three adolescents of the same sex. This type of pact appears to be less planned and results in less lethality than adult suicide pacts. Attempters tend to share similar life stories; for example, they have been separated from their parents since childhood because of parental divorce or the death of a parent. As a result, adolescents see each other as a narcissistic double and this dynamic seems to be a mutual facilitator. In the days before the suicide members of the pact stay together almost all of the time, in isolation from the rest of society. This social withdrawal prevents them from seeking help. The dominant/dependent relationship seems to be less prevalent in the friendship pact.

Prevention of Suicide Pacts

Numerous risk factors associated with individual suicides are linked to suicide pacts. For this reason, it is important for health practitioners and loved ones to pay attention to general signs of suicide risk, such as major behavioral or emotional changes, sleeping or eating disorders, disposal of important possessions, loss of interest and energy, substance abuse, and hopelessness. One should also be watchful for signs of suicide pacts, such as the isolation of an older couple with a physical illness or emotionally unhealthy exclusive relationships in young friends. Moreover, the people who engage in suicide pacts often talk about their plans to family and friends.

Mental health practitioners suggest that one asks direct questions to verify suicide intentions and plans, such as, "Are you thinking of suicide?" "Did you plan your suicide (i.e., decide when, where, or how to do it)?" The more the suicide is planned, the more important it is to be direct and act quickly. One should be empathic and warm with a suicidal person, and try to find new solutions or alternatives to the person's problems, and encourage him or her to seek professional help if needed. Finally, despite the fact that suicide pacts share a lot of characteristics with individual suicides and are a rare phenomenon, health practitioners believe that education programs on suicide prevention should incorporate information on suicide pacts and guidelines for preventing suicide pact behavior.

See also: SUICIDE INFLUENCES AND FACTORS: PHYSICAL ILLNESS; SUICIDE OVER THE LIFE SPAN: ADOLESCENTS AND YOUTHS; SUICIDE TYPES: THEORIES OF SUICIDE

Bibliography

Brown, Martin, and Brian Barraclough. "Partners in Life and in Death: The Suicide Pact in England and Wales 1988–1992." *Psychological Medicine* 29 (1999): 1299–1306.

Cohen, John. "A Study of Suicide Pacts." *Medico-Legal Journal* 29 (1961):144–151.

Fishbain, David A., and Tim E. Aldrich. "Suicide Pacts: International Comparisons." *Journal of Clinical Psychiatry* 46, no. 1 (1985):11–15.

Fishbain, David A., Linda D'Achille, Steve Barsky, and Tim E. Aldrich. "A Controlled Study of Suicide Pacts." *Journal of Clinical Psychiatry* 45, no. 4 (1984):154–157.

Granboulan, Virginie, Alain Zivi, and Michel Basquin. "Double Suicide Attempt among Adolescents." *Journal of Adolescent Health* 21 (1997):128–130.

Noyes, Russel, Susan J. Frye, and Charles E. Hartford. "Conjugal Suicide Pact." *Journal of Nervous and Mental Disease* 165, no. 1 (1977):72–75.

Vijayakumar, Lakshmi, and Natararajan Thilothammal. "Suicide Pacts." *Crisis* 14, no. 1 (1993):43–46.

JANIE HOULE
ISABELLE MARCOUX

THEORIES OF SUICIDE

Theories of suicide have been formulated mainly by psychologists and psychiatrists. This analysis began a century ago with Sigmund Freud's psychoanalytic theory. Sociologists have since proposed theories, based upon the work of Émile Durkheim, that explain the variation in suicide rates over nations and over regions within those nations. These seminal theories are the foundation for more recent theories developed by suicidologists that account for both individual suicides and suicide rates within a society.

Early Theories of Individual Suicide

Suicide is an uncommon behavior, occurring in less than 50 out of every 100,000 people in nations with the highest suicide rate. Explaining and predicting such infrequent occurrences has proved to be very difficult. The major theories of personality and systems of psychotherapy have not addressed the etiology of suicide to any great extent, with the exception of Sigmund Freud's psychoanalytic theory. Freud never considered the psychodynamics underlying suicidal behavior to any great extent. Brief mentions of suicidal behavior can be found throughout his writings, however, and in 1967 the psychiatrist Robert Litman attempted to document and synthesize these dispersed thoughts.

By 1910 Freud had recognized many clinical features of suicidal behavior: guilt over death wishes toward others, identification with a suicidal parent, refusal to accept loss of gratification, suicide as an act of revenge, suicide as an escape from humiliation, suicide as a form of communication, and the connection between death and sexuality.

The more systematic views began with his discussion of melancholia. The essential feature of suicidal behavior is that the person loses a loved object, and the energy withdrawn from this lost loved object is relocated in the ego and used to recreate the loved one as a permanent feature of the self, an identification of the ego with the lost object. Litman called this process ego-splitting.

Freud's formulation is phrased in the more archaic version of his theory. In more modern terms, the person has already introjected some of the desires of the loved one. Children introject desires of their parents, and adults introject the desires of their lovers. In this way, it is as if part of one's mind is also symbolic of one's loved ones. Once this person is lost (e.g., by death or divorce), a person still possesses those introjected desires, and thus the lost loved one remains symbolically as part of the living person's own mind. This process can lead to suicide when the person also harbors hostile wishes toward the lost object, for now one can turn this anger toward that part of one's mind that is modeled upon and symbolizes the lost object.

A later development in Freud's thought was the postulate of the existence of a death instinct, an instinctual drive toward death that is balanced by the life instinct. The death instinct is primarily masochistic, and the individual tries to externalize the instinct as aggression or sadism. However, when there are cultural forces opposing sadism, the instinct is turned back onto the self. In 1961 the psychoanalyst Samuel Futterman stressed that neither the life instinct nor the death instinct could really function independently of each other, but that they were always fused in variable amounts.

Litman pointed out that this later development moves to a very general level of discourse and focuses on the universal elements of humankind's lot. Thus it is not clear how such a process can explain why some people kill themselves whereas others do not. At best, it provides a mere restatement of this fact. The earlier formulation was more heuristic in that it did propose a developmental process leading to suicide.

Freud's Influence on Theorists

Freud's postulate of a death instinct can be seen as a product of his era. Early in the twentieth century, every psychological theorist felt the need to explain why humans behaved at all. Therefore, they all proposed energy concepts in their theories. After Donald Hebb's classic book *The Organization of Behavior* (1949), psychological theorists no longer felt it necessary to explain why humans behaved. Rather, the motivational question focused on why humans do one action rather than another.

Freud's hypothesis of a death instinct had a great influence on thinking about suicide. For example, in 1938 the psychiatrist Karl Menninger suggested that suicidal motivation can be seen behind behaviors that at first glance are not obviously suicidal. Menninger noted that some people shorten their lives by choosing self-destructive lifestyles, such as alcohol or drug abuse, heavy cigarette smoking, and engaging in other destructive behaviors. He called such behaviors "chronic suicide." He noted that some people appear to focus their self-destructive impulses on specific parts of their bodies, leaving their minds unimpaired. For example, a person may blind himself or lose an arm in an industrial accident. Menninger saw the death instinct as behind such behaviors, and he called them "focal suicide."

The result of Menninger's ideas has resulted in some interest on the part of suicidologists in indirect self-destructive behavior, as in Norman Farberow's book *The Many Faces of Suicide* (1980), and other works on life-threatening behavior in general and the official journal of the American Association of Suicidology is called *Suicide and Life-Threatening Behavior,* indicating a broader focus than suicide per se.

Maurice Farber, a psychologist, proposed that the tendency to commit suicide is a function of the extent of the threat to acceptable life conditions experienced by the individual, the individual's sense of competence, and therefore the individual's degree of hope. Aaron Beck, a psychiatrist who has developed a system of counseling known as Cognitive-Behavioral Therapy for those suffering from depression and anxiety, and his associates later developed an inventory to measure hopelessness. Subsequent research has shown that hopelessness, which is one component of the syndrome of depression, is a much more powerful predictor of subsequent suicidal behavior than other components of the syndrome.

In 1996 Edwin Shneidman, the founder of the American Association of Suicidology, defined "lethality" as the likelihood of an individual committing suicide, while "perturbation" referred to the level of upset or distress that the individual was experiencing. Shneidman later called the subjective experience of perturbation "psychache." Shneidman suggested that the way to reduce the lethality of individuals was to reduce their perturbation. He also proposed that all suicides share ten common qualities, which include the:

1. common purpose of seeking a solution;
2. common goal of cessation of consciousness;
3. common stimulus of unbearable pain;
4. common stressor of frustrated psychological needs;
5. common emotion of hopelessness-helplessness;
6. common cognitive state of ambivalence;
7. common perceptual state of constriction;
8. common action of escape;
9. common interpersonal act of communication of intention; and
10. common pattern of consistency of lifelong styles.

These preliminary theories have not been subjected to extensive empirical testing. Instead most psychological research on suicidal behavior is based on the simple additive effect of a variety of psychological and experiential factors, such as loss of parents through death, experience of sexual and physical abuse, low self-esteem, and depression.

Explaining Societal Suicide Rates

In contrast to the unpredictability of individual suicides, societal suicide rates are remarkably stable from year to year, and this stability makes it easier to account for societal differences.

Composition theories. In 1990 Hungarian sociologist Ferenc Moksony noted that one simple explanation of differences in suicide rates between nations is that the national populations differ in the proportion of those at risk for suicide. For example, typically in developed nations, suicide rates are highest in men, the elderly, and the divorced. Therefore, nations with a higher proportion of men, elderly, and divorced people will have a higher suicide rate. Societies may differ also in physiological variables (i.e., serotonin levels) and psychological/psychiatric variables (i.e., levels of depression and anxiety).

Social causation theories. The most popular explanations of social suicide rates focus on social variables. These social variables may be viewed in two ways: as (1) direct causal agents of the suicidal behavior, or (2) indices of broader, more abstract, social characteristics which differ among nations.

The most important theory for choosing relevant variables is the one that the French sociologist Émile Durkheim proposed in 1897. Durkheim hypothesized that suicide rates were determined by the society's level of social integration (that is, the degree to which the people are bound together in social networks) and the level of social regulation (that is, the degree to which people's desires and emotions are regulated by societal norms and customs). Durkheim thought that this association was curvilinear, with very high levels of social integration and regulation leading to *altruistic* and *fatalistic* suicide, respectively, and very low levels of social integration and regulation leading to *egoistic* and *anomic* suicide, respectively.

The sociologist Barclay Johnson suggested that the association is linear in modern societies, with suicide increasing as social integration and regulation decrease. Studies of nations have found that suicide rates are associated with such variables as the birth rate, female participation in the labor force, immigration, and the divorce rate.

Some investigators see these associations as suggesting a direct link between divorce or immigration and suicidal behavior. For example, divorce may be associated with suicide at the aggregate level because divorced people have a higher suicide rate than those with other marital statuses. Other investigators see the associations as suggesting that divorce and immigration are measures of a broader and more basic social characteristic, perhaps social integration, which plays a causal role in the suicides of everyone in the society. In this latter case, societies with a higher rate of divorce, for example, should have a higher rate of suicide for those in all marital statuses, and this has been confirmed in the United States.

The other major social causation theory of suicide was proposed in 1954 by social scientists Andrew Henry and James Short, who assumed that the basic target of aggression for a frustrated person would be the frustrating object. What inhibits this outward expression of aggression and results in the aggression being turned inward upon the self?

At the societal level, Henry and Short argued that the primary factor was the extent of the external restraints on people's behavior. If these external restraints are strong, then frustrated individuals can blame others for their misery, and the outward expression of aggression (and, in the extreme, murder) is legitimized. On the other hand, if the external restraints on behavior are weak, then frustrated individuals can blame only themselves for their misery, and other directed aggression is not legitimized and must be inhibited, which increases the probability of the aggression being turned inward upon the self (and, in the extreme, resulting in suicide). Thus, in a multiethnic society such as America, the oppressed (namely, African Americans and Native Americans) may be expected to have higher rates of murder while the oppressors (European Americans) may be expected to have higher rates of suicide, a difference which is confirmed by crime and mortality rates.

Social stress. In 1969 the anthropologist Raoul Naroll proposed that suicide would be more common in members of a society who were socially disoriented; that is, in those who lack or lose basic social ties, such as those who are single or divorced. In this way Naroll's theory resembles Durkheim's theory. However, Naroll argued that because not all socially disoriented people commit suicide there must be a psychological factor that makes suicide a more likely choice when an individual is socially disoriented, and Naroll proposed that it was the individual's reaction to "thwarting disorientation contexts." These contexts involve a weakening of the individual's social ties as a result of the actions of other people or oneself (but not as a result of impersonal, natural, or cultural events).

Being divorced by a spouse or murdering one's spouse are examples of such contexts, while storm damage or losing a spouse to cancer are not. In thwarting disorientation contexts, some individuals commit *protest* suicide, which Naroll defined as voluntary suicide committed in such a way as to come to public notice. Societies differ in the extent to which they provide thwarting disorientation contexts, and so societies differ in their suicide rates.

Whereas Durkheim's theory refers to more steady-state characteristics of a society, Naroll's theory suggests the role of sudden and acute changes in a society: social stressors. Furthermore, Naroll's theory is phrased in a way that permits its applications to individuals as well as to societies.

The theories of societal suicide rates have been formulated more precisely and logically than the theories of individual suicide and have generated more successful predictions. Research findings from the 1990s to the present have not invalidated their assumptions, and the theories seem to predict suicide rather than psychiatric disorder in general. Henry and Short's theory has suggested that an appropriate comparison group for suicides would be murderers, a group that individual theories of suicide have ignored. The success of societal theories as compared to individual theories may be due in part to the relative stability (and therefore easier predictability) of social suicide rates as compared to the rarity and unpredictability of individual suicide.

See also: DEATH INSTINCT; DURKHEIM, ÉMILE; FREUD, SIGMUND; SUICIDE; SUICIDE BASICS: PREVENTION

Bibliography

Beck, Aaron T., Arlene Weissman, David Lester, and Larry Trexler. "The Measurement of Pessimism: The Hopelessness Scale." *Journal of Consulting and Clinical Psychology* 42 (1974):861–865.

Durkheim, Émile. *Suicide.* 1897. Reprint, New York: Free Press, 1951.

Farber, Maurice L. *Theory of Suicide.* New York: Funk & Wagnalls, 1968.

Farberow, Norman. *The Many Faces of Suicide.* New York: McGraw-Hill, 1980.

Futterman, Samuel. "Suicide." In Norman L. Farberow and Edwin S. Shneidman eds., *The Cry for Help.* New York: McGraw-Hill, 1961.

Hebb, Donald. *The Organization of Behavior.* New York: Wiley, 1949.

Henry, Andrew F., and James F. Short. *Suicide and Homicide.* New York: Free Press, 1954.

Johnson, Barclay D. "Durkheim's One Cause of Suicide." *American Sociological Review* 30 (1965):875–886.

Litman, Robert. "Sigmund Freud on Suicide." In Edwin Shneidman ed., *Essays in Self-Destruction.* New York: Science House, 1967.

Menninger, Karl. *Man against Himself.* New York: Harcourt, Brace & World, 1938.

Moksony, Ferenc. "Ecological Analysis of Suicide." In David Lester ed., *Current Concepts of Suicide.* Philadelphia: Charles Press, 1990.

Naroll, Raoul. "Cultural Determinants and the Concept of the Sick Society." In Stanley C. Plog and Robert B. Edgerton eds., *Changing Perspectives in Mental Illness.* New York: Holt, Rinehart & Winston, 1969.

Shneidman, Edwin S. *The Suicidal Mind.* New York: Oxford University Press, 1996.

Stack, Steven. "Domestic Integration and the Rate of Suicide." *Journal of Comparative Family Studies* 11 (1980):249–260.

DAVID LESTER

SUPPORT GROUPS

Support groups have become an important adjunct to the work of the medical and social support fields in addressing the needs of patients and families confronting the anguish of imminent death or the bereaved. Self-help groups provide a level of support that assists terminally ill individuals and their loved ones. Although some individuals need professional counseling and therapy, social support is a major element in coping effectively with life-threatening illness and bereavement.

The researchers Margaret and Wolfgang Stroebe suggest three areas in which support groups can be helpful. Groups can provide instrumental support; they offer help in dealing with practical matters such as funerals, household and personal needs, and even financial issues. They also can provide emotional support. In the case of the bereaved, they can encourage the work of grieving. They provide an appropriate place to retell the story as long as the griever needs to do so. Self-help groups give validation support; by participating in them, one discovers what is "normal" in grief and thus understands that one is dealing with the same issues that many others have dealt with in their grief.

Being part of a support group has social importance. It is a way for individuals to maintain social contact. Often bereaved individuals will avoid many of their friends and become socially isolated. Going to a support group meeting and interacting with other people is an important activity for them. In many cases, the groups develop into friendship networks that may continue long after the need for the support system is gone. Phyllis Silverman, who began the Widow-to-Widow program, considers the friendships formed as bridges between the past and the future. She believes that people with similar problems can help and learn from one another. Her program was the first of the peer-support groups for grievers and became the model for most other programs.

Psychologically the groups are helpful because they provide the outlet that grievers and individuals with life-threatening illness need, allowing people to freely express their feelings, fears, and dreams with others. The members of the group are ready and patient listeners. Seeing new members come into the group allows people to recognize the progress they have made. For new members, seeing others whose bereavement has been longer gives them an opportunity to see that one does move on in life.

Support groups take different forms. Some are time-limited, meeting only for a particular number of sessions. Others will go on indefinitely, with some people leaving the group and new people joining. Some support groups may have agendas that entail specific meetings in which a lawyer joins the group to talk about legal issues, a financial consultant talks about money management, and so on. Other groups rely solely on the participation of the group members. Groups are designed to be nonjudgmental and to not provide advice. Rather, they provide the opportunity for everyone to speak.

One of the early support groups for individuals facing life-threatening illness was Make Today Count, started by the journalist Orville Kelly in 1974. Many patients with life-threatening illnesses found themselves without people to talk to and share their feelings and experiences. Facilitators organize and get the meetings started, but the meeting itself belongs to the participants. Make Today Count chapters exist all over the United States.

In a similar fashion, numerous groups have developed to provide support to the bereaved. Perhaps the best known of these groups is Compassionate Friends. This organization assists families toward positive resolution of their grief following the death of a child. The organization has chapters nationally, most of which meet monthly.

Other well-known groups include Mothers Against Drunk Driving; Seasons, a suicide-survivor support group; and Parents of Murdered Children. In addition, most hospices provide support groups for both patients and families prior to a death and bereavement support groups after the death.

It is important to recognize that self-help support groups do not provide professional counseling. Rather, the support comes from the similarities between the experiences of the group members. Through the process of sharing, people can put their reactions into perspective. They have an opportunity to see how others have successfully dealt with many of the same issues they are facing.

See also: EMPATHY AND COMPASSION; GRIEF; SOCIAL FUNCTIONS OF DEATH

Bibliography

Corr, Charles A., Clyde M. Nabe, and Donna M. Corr. *Death and Dying, Life and Living,* 3rd edition. Belmont, CA: Brooks/Cole, 2000.

Kelly, Orville. *Make Today Count.* New York: Delacorte Press, 1975.

Silverman, Phyllis R. "The Widow-to-Widow Program: An Experiment in Preventive Intervention." *Mental Hygiene* 53 (1969):333–337.

Stroebe, Margaret S., and Wolfgang Stroebe. *Bereavement and Health.* New York: Cambridge University Press, 1987.

DANA G. CABLE

SUTTEE/SATI

See WIDOW-BURNING.

SUTTON HOO

The Sutton Hoo burial ground in East Anglia, England, provides vivid evidence for attitudes to death immediately before the conversion of an English community to Christianity in the seventh century C.E. Founded about 600 C.E., and lasting a hundred years, Sutton Hoo contained only about twenty burials, most of them rich and unusual, spread over four hectares. This contrasts with the "folk cemeteries" of the pagan period (fifth–sixth centuries C.E.), which typically feature large numbers of cremations contained in pots and inhumations laid in graves with standard sets of weapons and jewelry. Accordingly, Sutton Hoo is designated as a "princely" burial ground, a special cemetery reserved for the elite. The site was rediscovered in 1938, and has been the subject of major campaigns of excavation and research in 1965–1971 and 1983–2001. Because the majority of the burials had been plundered in the sixteenth century, detailed interpretation is difficult.

The Sutton Hoo burial ground consists of thirteen visible mounds on the left bank of the River Deben opposite Woodbridge in Suffolk, England. Four mounds were investigated by the landowner in 1938–1939; all are from the seventh century C.E., and one mound contains the richest grave ever discovered on British soil. Here, a ship ninety feet long had been buried in a trench with a wooden chamber amid other ships containing over 200 objects of gold, silver, bronze, and iron. The conditions of the soil mean that the body, timbers of ship and chamber, and most organic materials had rotted to invisibility, but the latest studies suggest that a man had been placed on a floor or in a coffin. At his head were a helmet, a shield, spears and items of regalia, a standard, and a scepter; at his feet were a pile of clothing and a great silver dish with three tubs or cauldrons. Gold buckles and shoulder clasps inlaid with garnet had connected a baldrick originally made of leather. Nearly every item was ornamented with lively abstract images similar to dragons or birds of prey. The buried man was thought to be Raedwald, an early king of East Anglia who had briefly converted to Christianity, reverted to paganism, and died around 624 or 625.

Investigations at Sutton Hoo were renewed in 1965 and 1983, and revealed considerably more about the burial ground and its context. In the seventh century, burial was confined to people of high rank, mainly men. In mounds five to seven, probably among the earliest, men were cremated with animals (i.e., cattle, horse, and deer) and the ashes were placed in a bronze bowl. In mound seventeen a young man was buried in a coffin, accompanied by his sword, shield, and, in an adjacent pit, his horse. In mound fourteen, a woman was buried in an underground chamber, perhaps on a bed accompanied by fine silver ornaments. A child was buried in a coffin along with a miniature spear (burial twelve). Mound two, like mound one, proved to have been a ship burial, but here the ship had been placed over an underground chamber in which a man had been buried.

Because the graves were plundered in the sixteenth century, interpretation is difficult. The latest Sutton Hoo researcher, Martin Carver, sees the burial ground as a whole as a pagan monument in which burial rites relatively new to England (under-mound cremation, horse burial, ship burial) are drawn from a common pagan heritage and enacted in defiance of pressure from Christian Europe. The major burials are "political statements" in which the person honored is equipped as an ambassador of the people, both at the public funeral and in the afterlife.

A second phase of burial at Sutton Hoo consisted of two groups of people (mainly men) who had been executed by hanging or decapitation. The remains of seventeen bodies were found around mound five, and twenty-three were found around a group of post-sockets (supposed to be gallows) at the eastern side of the burial mounds. These bodies were dated (by radiocarbon determinations) between the eighth and the tenth centuries, and reflect the authority of the Christian kings who supplanted those buried under the Sutton Hoo mounds in about 700 C.E.

See also: AFTERLIFE IN CROSS-CULTURAL PERSPECTIVE; BURIAL GROUNDS; CHRISTIAN DEATH RITES, HISTORY OF; CREMATION; QIN SHIH HUNG'S TOMB

Bibliography

Carver, Martin O. H. *Sutton Hoo: Burial Ground of Kings.* Philadelphia: University of Pennsylvania Press, 1998.

MARTIN CARVER

SYMPATHY CARDS

Acceptable expressions of sympathy vary across cultures from open and varied displays of compassion to the denial of any sympathy for even a society's most troubled members. While many people take sympathy for granted, its expression is more characteristic of some cultures and at some times in history than in others. Expressing sympathy requires energy, time, and sometimes money, and becomes problematic under conditions of extreme hardship when one's own misery is paramount. Sympathy is functional for society, however, because it provides a social connection among people; without it, life's emotional climate becomes colder and harsher. Each society's "sympathy logic," or when, where, how, and over what lost relationship sympathy is to be expressed, becomes a part of its social order. Norms develop about sympathy attitudes and behaviors and who is to express such concern for whom. Through expressions of sympathy, people can be linked in ways that affect the social interaction of families, work forces, and entire communities, as well as the individuals involved. Thus, expressing sympathy can increase social bonds while denying it helps unravel the social fabric.

The refusal to offer sympathy has profound effects on human relationships. This social emotion of compassionate affinity, of being personally affected by another's grief or suffering, can only take place in real or imagined social interaction. Sympathy is a complicated, multifaceted emotional process requiring elements of empathy, sympathy sentiment, and display. Genuinely sympathetic persons imagine taking the role of the other, have some feeling about recipients of the sympathy and their plights, and engage in nonverbal (a look), verbal ("I am so sorry"), tactile (a hug), gift-giving (providing money after a job loss), or aid behaviors (cleaning house during illness) as symbolic displays of their sympathy. Within these broad general categories of expression, most cultures have specific norms for the timing and displaying of sympathy to bereaved persons following a death. One form of showing concern for mourners is sending sympathy cards.

The Emergence of the Greeting Card

Most cultures view death as the most difficult type of loss humans experience, and expressions of sympathy in such traumatic circumstances can be difficult to convey. What does one say? How does one act when confronted with someone who is grieving? Matters surrounding death, once handled by family members and friends, have been given into the hands of professionals in modern societies. Increased standards of living, developments in medicine and science, urbanization, and affluence have allowed people in many nations to develop a degree of death denial not possible earlier in history, and people have become increasingly uncomfortable with and isolated from death. The introduction of sympathy cards in the nineteenth century offered an effective solution for maintaining social bonds in an increasingly technological and impersonal world.

In his *The Romance of Greeting Cards* (1956), Ernest Chase, a prominent figure in America's early greeting card industry, views the history of greeting cards as beginning with early human attempts to achieve or maintain relationships with others. Symbolic gestures of greeting, whether carvings on rocks, smoke signals, gloves, flowers, letters, or any others humans have devised, provided social connections in modern times in a manner elaborated upon and refined by greeting cards. As early as the 1600s, Valentine's cards were drawn, lettered, and sent, though not sold. The most popular holiday card, the Christmas card, originated in England in the 1800s and immediately captivated the public.

The Sympathy Card

Following a death, the surrounding emotion can be expressed in various ways, with each expression requiring a degree of investment and commitment. The sympathy card requires a minimum of both. In a sense, it is an expression of genuine concern without having to get involved. While other demonstrations of sympathy remain important, the pace of modern life, discomfort with death, widespread acquaintance, and mobility are among factors that encourage impersonal, minimally committed sympathy display.

Although the sending of greeting cards has become common, some societies have not developed the custom. In 1971 Richard Rhodes, a book editing manager of Hallmark cards and contributing editor for *Harper's,* reported that the English were sending few cards at that time, while the Europeans sent fewer still. By the year 2000, sympathy cards were common in Western societies, with the United States leading in their usage. However, even in countries where sending cards is popular, sympathy cards may not be included. Late-twentieth-century China experienced a greeting card deluge, with hundreds of millions of cards produced. New Year's cards, Christmas cards, and cards for other happy occasions were popular, but sympathy cards did not exist. Instead, people sent sympathy telegrams, which were deemed a more appropriate display of support during sad and difficult times. By the 1990s electronic and computer-generated greeting cards had appeared around the globe, and numerous online companies offered free cards for public usage. Even so, electronic sympathy cards were not as rapidly accepted as those for other occasions. Apparently many people still felt that paper cards, like sympathy telegrams, indicated more appropriate support to the bereaved following a death.

Just as the greeting card industry has expanded in modern societies, so have the "sympathy margins," or the situations in which sympathy is to be felt and expressed. These margins vary across cultures and according to demographic variables such as age, gender, ethnicity, religion, and others. For instance, women continue to buy the large majority of greeting cards and are culturally expected to offer sympathy for a larger range of incidents and more minor difficulties than are men. Women also tend to extend sympathy for a longer period of time. Women have always been the mainstay of the greeting card market and have been the primary purchasers and senders of sympathy cards. In an attempt to attract ethnic markets, companies in the United States began to offer cards aimed at African Americans and Hispanics. At the end of the twentieth century, age-specific markets were developed, as were specific religious markets.

Early sympathy cards were often announcements of death, with "in loving memory of" or "in affectionate remembrance of," followed by the name of the deceased. As with more modern cards, some were plain, whereas others used more elaborate drawings and imagery. Early cards sometimes featured tombstones with names and epitaphs. Sympathy cards from the mid– to late twentieth century used less overt imagery. These cards were sent to mourners to help soften the blow of death, and their colors, verbal content, and visual symbols became designed to reduce death's harshness for the bereaved. Their imagery has changed over time, with a movement from black and white to color and other alterations in content and presentation. Even into the twenty-first century, the words *death* and *dead* were virtually never mentioned. Modern views of tact and propriety led to a few standardized images.

Marsha McGee's 1980 groundbreaking content analysis of 110 American sympathy cards and a replication in 1998 by Charmaine Caldwell, Marsha McGee, and Charles Pryor of 137 cards found flowers to be the symbol most commonly used. Scenes depicting nature remained popular, while images such as seashells, rainbows, and butterflies generally increased over these two decades. Religious symbolism was used in only a small percentage of the cards analyzed in both studies. Dark colors and black were never used. Pastels were prominent, with bright colors increasing.

According to Hallmark's research division, by 2000 Americans alone were sending around 125 million sympathy cards each year. There were thousands of designs on the market, with card sending increasing each year. Sympathy margins had expanded, and cards were also designed for job loss, divorce, chronic illness and disability, and other experiences of loss for which sympathizers wished to show concern. Cards were aimed at grieving children as well as adults, and a huge array of sympathy cards for grieving pet owners continued to widen the market. Cards that expressed the message "thinking about you," in difficult times made up a rapidly growing market. Language had moved from poetry and verse to more conversational messages. Greeting cards are carefully designed to reflect what a society's people are thinking and feeling; Hallmark, like other companies working to keep ahead of market trends, developed and marketed cards appropriate for miscarriage, suicide, cancer, and other specific types of death when the public became receptive. Messages such as "When a special life ends in such an unexpected way, it can be totally overwhelming . . . ," and "Sorrow reaches even deeper when a loss comes so suddenly . . . ," were offered to cushion the shock of different types of loss.

Research samples show most Americans would appreciate receiving sympathy cards. While people report that personal letters are better to send, few do more than write a note along with a card. Mourners have reported that the expression of concern from others is more important during bereavement than its form or its content. Sympathy cards remain one prominent means of expressing this concern. As electronic communication and international markets continue to expand into the twenty-first century, more and more mourners across the globe may find comfort from such messages of condolence. As a simple gesture of support, sympathy cards provide meaning to both senders and receivers. At the least, the sending of sympathy cards links people together and "reinforces a sense of community and solidarity in the wake of the calamity of death" (Lippy 1983, p. 107).

See also: DEATH SYSTEM; GRIEF; GRIEF AND MOURNING IN CROSS-CULTURAL PERSPECTIVE; METAPHORS AND EUPHEMISMS; MOURNING

Bibliography

Caldwell, Charmaine, Marsha McGee, and Charles Pryor. "The Sympathy Card As Cultural Assessment of American Attitudes toward Death, Bereavement and Extending Sympathy: A Replicated Study." *Omega: The Journal of Death and Dying* 37 (1998):121–132.

Chase, Ernest. *The Romance of Greeting Cards: An Historical Account of the Origin, Evolution and Development of Christmas Cards, Valentines, and Other Forms of Engraved or Printed Greetings from the Earliest Day to the Present Time.* 1956. Reprint, Detroit, MI: Tower Books, 1971.

Clark, Candace. *Misery and Company: Sympathy in Everyday Life.* Chicago: University of Chicago Press, 1997.

Erbaugh, Mary. "Greeting Cards in China: Mixed Language of Connections and Affections." In Deborah Davis ed., *The Consumer Revolution in China.* Berkeley: University of California Press, 2000.

Hirshey, Gerri. "Happy ( ) to You." *New York Times Magazine,* 2 July 1995, 20–27.

Lippy, Charles. "Sympathy Cards and the Grief Process." *Journal of Popular Culture* 17, no. 3 (1983):98–108.

McGee, Marsha. "Faith, Fantasy, and Flowers: A Content Analysis of the American Sympathy Card." *Omega: The Journal of Death and Dying* 11 (1980):25–35.

Papson, Stephen. "From Symbolic Exchange to Bureaucratic Discourse: The Hallmark Greeting Card." *Theory, Culture and Society* 3, no. 2 (1986):99–111.

Rhodes, Richard. "Packaged Sentiment." *Harper's* 243 (December 1971):61–66.

Internet Resources

Greeting Card Association. "State of the Industry." In the Greeting Card Association [web site]. Available from www.greetingcard.org/gca/facts.htm.

MARSHA MCGEE

SYMPTOMS AND SYMPTOM MANAGEMENT

Many physical and psychological symptoms accompany the end of life. In one study, 1,000 cancer patients had a median of eleven symptoms during the terminal phase of illness, many of which affect the patient's quality of life. Assessment and management of common symptoms are thus integral to a balanced approach to end-of-life care. Because of the multidimensional nature of many symptoms, an interdisciplinary team approach to assessment and management is essential. Such an interdisciplinary team calls for the expertise of nurses, physicians, social workers, nursing assistants, spiritual care providers, and expressive therapists.

Prevalence and Relevance of Symptoms

Pharmacological and nonpharmacological efforts to alleviate the symptoms seek to accommodate the patient's desires. For example, if a patient has requested to be as alert as possible until death, and if the same patient needs an antiemetic agent to control nausea and vomiting, the common side effect of sedation represents an unacceptable tradeoff to the patient. If, on the other hand, the patient desires total control of the nausea and vomiting, even at the expense of alertness, such medication would be appropriate. The goal of symptom management is quality of life.

Fatigue. Fatigue is the most prevalent end-of-life symptom, second only to pain. In a study by

Conill, fatigue was present in 80 percent of 176 palliative care patients. There is not a universal definition of fatigue. Patients often speak of weakness, easy tiring, or inability to perform the activities of daily living. According to death experts Linda Tyler and Arthur Lipman, fatigue is a multifaceted symptom. Tyler and Lipman identify the following causes of fatigue: anemia, pain, depression, insomnia, dehydration, metabolic disease process, and side effects of drugs, especially opioids that cause central nervous system (CNS) depression.

Patients may be reluctant to report fatigue because they are unaware that there is treatment for this symptom. A thorough assessment, examining patterns of fatigue, activity, sleep, and interpersonal relationships, is essential in determining appropriate interventions. Healthcare professionals must ascertain the impact of fatigue on the patient's and family's quality of life.

Nonpharmacological interventions include educating patients and families about the disease process and reviewing their goals of care. Energy conservation or rest periods, along with good sleeping habits, enable patients to "bank" energy for more active times. Patients can also conserve energy by using devices such as walkers, bedside commodes, and wheelchairs.

Pharmacological interventions, which address the underlying cause of the fatigue (e.g., antidepressants or antihistamines for insomnia), may decrease the fatigue a patient is experiencing. CNS stimulants, such as methylphenidate (Ritalin), are especially helpful in treating fatigue caused by opioid sedation. According to Tyler and Lipman, corticosteroids (dexamethasone) may be effective in treating this symptom, even when the etiology is unknown.

Anorexia. Anorexia is a loss of the desire to eat or a loss of appetite accompanied by a decreased food intake. It is frequently associated with cachexia and progressive weight loss. The etiology of the cachexia/anorexia syndrome is unknown and may involve numerous physiologic mechanisms.

Causes of anorexia include oral or systemic infection, which may produce discomfort during eating; unresolved pain; depression; and gastrointestinal symptoms such as chronic nausea and vomiting, delayed gastric emptying, constipation, and/or diarrhea. As with other symptoms, treatment is based on the patient's goals. If eating is desirable, efforts to alleviate anorexia are initiated. Family and caregivers are taught about food preparation. If early satiety is a problem, serving smaller, frequent meals may be helpful. Under such circumstances it is important to eliminate strong odors while cooking.

Pharmacological interventions can stimulate appetite. Corticosteroids such as dexamethasone (Decadron) are cost-effective agents that enhance appetite and improve the sense of well-being. Appetite stimulants such as megestrol acetate (Megace) may be helpful. According to physician Walter Forman and educator Denice Sheehan, the cannabinoid dronabinal (Marinol) may also be effective, despite continuing controversy over its use for relief of gastrointestinal symptoms. Because eating is often a social event, the loss of appetite is emotionally trying for patients and caregivers.

Dehydration. Researcher Frederick Burge defines terminal dehydration as a clinical state in which dying patients are no longer able to consume adequate fluid volumes. According to nurse researcher Joyce Zerwekh, fluid deficits are common as a patient approaches death. Identifying the cause of the dehydration is not as important as identifying the goals of care of the patient and family. It is imperative that the patients and their caregivers be involved in all decisions related to food and fluids at the end of life. Artificial hydration should never become an end in itself.

Dehydration was once considered painful for dying patients. But there are many advantages to dying in a state of dehydration. As a patient becomes dehydrated, gastrointestinal fluids decrease, limiting nausea and vomiting. Lessened pulmonary secretions alleviate breathlessness and cough. Swelling of the hands and feet are less likely to occur because peripheral edema is reduced. Patients who are in a complete state of dehydration often experience the metabolic disturbance known as ketoacidosis, which seems to produce an analgesic effect that may improve a patient's sense of well being. Families are often more comfortable in an environment that limits the use of artificial hydration via tubes and machines. The relief of dry mouth is best achieved with ice chips. Families who want to be involved in caregiving appreciate the opportunity to moisten lips and offer ice chips.

Hospice and palliative care physician experts Fainsinger and Bruera report that hydration sometimes improves the quality of life of a dying patient, especially in cases of opioid toxicity or dehydration-induced confusion. Artificial hydration can be delivered by parenteral routes. Hypodermoclysis is the provision of fluids through a subcutaneous route (a small needle placed under the skin). Intravenous hydration provides fluids via the vascular system.

Constipation. Constipation, the abnormally infrequent evacuation of hard stool, occurs in 50 to 78 percent of adults (the average person has five to seven stools per week). Causes of constipation include side effects of medications, inactivity and weakness, intestinal obstruction from a tumor-compressed bowel, and fluid and electrolyte abnormalities such as dehydration, hypercalcemia, and hyperkalemia. In terminal patients constipation typically stems from multiple causes.

Nonpharmacological treatment may include altering food and fluid intake. Whenever possible, the patient should increase fluid intake and consumption of high-fiber foods. If the patient is close to death, pharmacological and/or mechanical treatments are preferable.

Medication-induced constipation can be treated with a stool softener/stimulant combination such as casanthranol with docusate (Pericolace) or senna (Senekot). A minimum goal is a bowel movement once every three days, regardless of intake. Constipation that is not secondary to a bowel obstruction calls for laxative therapy. About one-third of patients at the end of life require suppositories, enemas, and/or disimpaction to treat constipation despite the appropriate use of oral laxatives.

Constipation causes significant discomfort and embarrassment for patients. It can cause serious complications in the patient with advanced disease. Because it is such a common problem, prophylactic measures should be initiated in most patients. Prevention, aggressive assessment, and treatment are essential.

Nausea and vomiting. Nausea, with or without vomiting, occurs in 70 percent of terminally ill patients. Nausea is the unpleasant subjective sensation that results from stimulation of four major areas: the gastrointestinal lining, the chemoreceptor trigger zone in the fourth ventricle of the brain, the vestibular apparatus, and the cerebral cortex. Vomiting is a neuromuscular reflex that occurs as a result of a variety of mechanisms stimulating the vomiting center.

There are several causes of nausea, including gastrointestinal, such as gastric dysmotility, bowel obstruction, and constipation; treatment-induced, such as medications, chemotherapy, and radiation therapy; metabolic disturbances, such as hypercalcemia, uremia, and infection; and CNS causes, such as pain and increased intracranial pressure must be determined. Nonpharmacological treatments include guided imagery techniques, relaxation, music therapy, and hypnosis. Other nonpharmacological measures include decreasing food odors, serving meals at room temperature, and encouraging good oral hygiene.

Nurse researcher Cynthia King reported the use of nine classes of antiemetic drugs to treat nausea and vomiting in hospice/palliative-care patients. Medications are available to manage gastrointestinal causes, treatment-induced causes, metabolic disturbances, and central nervous system causes. For example, the prokinetic agents such as metoclopramide (Reglan) enhance gastric motility. Serotonin 5-HT3 receptor antagonists, such as ondansetron (Zofran), are used to block the neurotransmitter associated with treatment-induced causes. Phenothiazines and butyrophenones act primarily as dopamine antagonists and are most potent at the chemoreceptor trigger zone. Benzodiazepines work on the central nervous system, altering the perception of the nausea. Corticosteroids should be initiated in cases of increased intracranial pressure, hypercalcemia, or tumor-induced obstruction.

Patients may need more than one pharmacological agent to treat nausea and vomiting associated with multiple etiologies. For example, if the nausea is a result of tumor pressure on the gastrointestinal lining, pressure-reduction techniques are in order (e.g., coadministration of a corticosteroid to shrink the tumor burden along with a benzodiazepine to alter the perception of nausea).

Dyspnea. Dyspnea is a subjective symptom that involves a feeling of breathlessness or air hunger. The patient's perception of the degree of breathlessness is the only reliable indicator of the severity of the dyspnea, which occurred in 70 percent of terminal patients at time of admission to one study and 82 percent of patients one week before death. The causes of dyspnea vary; among them are anxiety, fear, airway obstruction, and infections such as pneumonia, thick pulmonary secretions, and fibrosis of lung tissue arising from radiation, chemotherapy, and fluid overload. Tyler recommends nonpharmacological interventions such as improving air circulation with fans, air cooling, repositioning, breathing exercises, and limiting strenuous activities.

Providing reassurance is essential in relieving the patient's distress. Anita Tarzian, nurse researcher, suggests that the fear of suffocation that accompanies dyspnea may be related to the concept that life begins with a breath and ends with the lack of breath. According to Tarzian, dyspnea symptoms may be the first time a patient and the caregivers acknowledge the reality of impending death. Her study of ten nurses who cared for air-hungry patients revealed that as patients experienced air hunger, the families panicked along with the patients. It is important, therefore, to provide patients and caregivers with clear explanations of the nature of the dyspnea and to reassure them that relief is possible.

Pharmacological management usually focuses on the cause of the dyspnea. Oxygen, although widely used as a treatment for dyspnea, is indicated only when there is underlying hypoxia. Antianxiety medications such as diazepam (Valium) or lorazepam (Ativan) are useful if the cause of dyspnea is restlessness. Kemp suggests the use of bronchodilators (albuterol or theophylline) or expectorants (guaifenesin) if dyspnea is related to bronchitis, emphysema, or a lung condition. Steroids (prednisone or dexamethasone) may be used in cancer patients to decrease tumor swelling, which can alleviate obstructive causes of dyspnea.

Morphine, the most widely used pharmacological agent in treating dyspnea, is effective in improving the quality of the breathing. Health care professionals should explain to patients why opioids are indicated because they may not be familiar with their use in the management of dyspnea.

Insomnia. The National Institutes of Health defines insomnia as the experience of inadequate or poor quality of sleep. It entails difficulty falling asleep, difficulty maintaining sleep, waking up too early, or experiencing a nonrefreshing sleep. In one study 61 percent of dying patients reported sleep disturbances on admission to the study, and 50 percent reported sleep disturbances one week before death.

There are numerous causes for insomnia. The most frequent cause among dying patients is nocturnal pain. Other causes include depression, decreases in daily activity or daily napping, and side effects of medications, especially steroids. Alcohol and caffeine may also contribute to insomnia because of their stimulant effects.

Nonpharmacological treatments include relaxation therapy, stimulus-control therapy to minimizing daytime napping, and moderate exercise. Encouraging a patient to verbalize concerns to a caregiver may decrease insomnia related to fear and anxiety.

Among pharmacological approaches, insomnia caused by nocturnal pain is best managed by treating pain effectively throughout a twenty-four-hour period with benzodiazepines such as lorazepam (Ativan). CNS stimulants taken in early daytime hours may decrease daytime naps, thus improving nighttime sleep.

Neuropsychiatric symptoms. Neuropsychiatric symptoms that occur at end of life are extremely disturbing to patients and families. Among the most common are anxiety, delirium, and depression.

According to physician and death expert Susan Block, these symptoms are distinct from the normal sadness, grief, and worry that accompany the terminal phase of life. When anxiety, delirium, and depression are identified and treated early in course of advancing disease, the patient's quality of life improves markedly.

Depression. Depression occurs in 25 to 77 percent of the terminally ill population. Feelings of hopelessness, helplessness, depression, and suicidal ideation are not normal at the end of life and should not be ignored. The most effective management of depression includes a combination of nonpharmacological and pharmacological approaches. Nonpharmacological management emphasizes supportive counseling and psychotherapy, including discussing short-term goals, identifying and reinforcing strengths, and employing successful coping techniques. All members of the interdisciplinary team need to be involved with the plan of care to address the physical, emotional, and spiritual issues associated with depression.

The choice of pharmacological management is guided by the expected life span of the patient. When time is limited and an immediate reversal of depression is desired, a rapid-acting psychostimulant, such as methylphenidate (Ritalin), is best. Selective serotonin reuptake inhibitors (SSRIs), such as paroxetine (Paxil) or sertaline (Zoloft), are highly effective but require two to four weeks to achieve a response. Therefore, the depressed, dying patient with less than three weeks to live should not be treated with an SSRI. Nor are tricyclic antidepressants, such as amitriptyline (Elavil), useful in such cases because of their delayed onset of therapeutic response and significant anticholinergic side effects such as constipation, dry mouth, and urinary retention.

Delirium. Delirium is "an etiologically nonspecific, global cerebral dysfunction characterized by concurrent disturbances of level of consciousness, attention, thinking, perception, memory, psychomotor behavior, emotion, and the sleep-wake cycle" (William Breitbart et al, 1998 p. 945). Often misdiagnosed as anxiety or depression, it occurs in up to 80 percent of dying patients. Early detection and treatment can lead to improved outcomes in the hospice/palliative-care setting.

There are multiple causes of delirium. Potentially reversible causes include metabolic abnormalities such as hypercalcemia, overwhelming systemic infection (sepsis), dehydration, or major organ failure. About 50 percent of patients have unknown etiologies and require empiric treatment. Nonpharmacological management is aimed at providing a comfortable environment. Measures to decrease anxiety and disorientation include encouraging the presence of family and familiar persons; a visible clock and calendar; a quiet, well-lit room; and the use of soothing music. Familiar sounds, smells, and textures offer comfort.

When a reversible cause for delirium is identified, pharmacological agents appropriate for the etiology should be initiated. Symptom management may be achieved through the use of butyrophenones such as haloperidol. Haloperidol, a blocking agent of the neurotransmitter dopamine, is usually effective in decreasing agitation, clearing sensorium, and improving cognition. However, there are circumstances, especially with terminal restlessness, when delirium can only be controlled with sedation. The use of pharmacological agents to sedate patients with terminal delirium requires serious consideration by the interdisciplinary team members, discussion with family about care goals, and careful monitoring. Sedation should only be considered after an exhaustive trial of evidenced-based pharmacological interventions.

It is important to distinguish delirium from episodes of awareness of imminent death. In the final days of life, patients may appear confused to caregivers and family, speaking of trips, wanting to "go home," talking of deceased family members, and reporting visions. Some health-care professionals believe that this confusion arises from physiological changes occurring during the dying process, while others consider it to be a spiritual experience. This imperfectly understood syndrome calls for sensitive exploration with the patient and family.

Anxiety. Patients often experience anxiety as their disease progresses and they face their final days. Anxiety may be evidenced by physical and/or cognitive symptoms such as shortness of breath, gastrointestinal distress, tachycardia, loss of appetite, irritability, and insomnia. A common cause of anxiety in the hospice/palliative care population is poorly controlled pain. Alleviating the pain often alleviates the anxiety, and no further treatment is necessary.

The most effective treatment is a combination of counseling therapy and pharmacological management. Goals of psychosocial intervention are to improve morale, self-esteem, and coping skills. Psychotherapy for patients at the end of life focuses on helping them deal with the anxiety of impending death. Fears and anxieties are best managed by the interdisciplinary team. All team members can address spiritual, practical, and emotional concerns.

In determining the need for pharmacological management of anxiety, the severity of the symptom is the most reliable factor. Patients with persistent apprehension and anxiety benefit from benzodiazepines, such as lorazepam (Ativan) and diazepam (Valium). Because many patients at the end of life are elderly, or have compromised renal and hepatic function, it is important to start with low doses of the benzodiazepines. Using lower doses also minimizes potential side effects.

Conclusion

Although symptoms in patients at the end of life increase in prevalence and severity with disease progression, they remain manageable with appropriate interventions. When patients' physical distress is well managed, it is possible for them to focus on their vision of a "good death." According to Lipman, end-of-life care that incorporates individualized, evidence-based medicine will lead to compassionate care. Health-care providers who are not familiar with end-of-life symptom management can consult the extensive literature, or they can access a local hospice/palliative care team for suggestions. The passage from life to death can be immeasurably eased by a team approach that focuses on giving the patient emotional reassurance and symptomatic relief in harmony with his or her care goals.

See also: DYING, PROCESS OF; HOSPICE IN HISTORICAL PERSPECTIVE; HOSPICE OPTION; PAIN AND PAIN MANAGEMENT; PSYCHOLOGY

Bibliography

American Academy of Hospice and Palliative Medicine. *Artificial Hydration and Nutrition in the Terminally Ill: A Review.* Baltimore, MD: Author, 1995.

Block, Susan. "Psychological Considerations, Growth, and Transcendence at the End of Life." *Journal of the American Medical Association* 285, no. 22 (2001): 2898–2904.

Breitbart, William, Harvey Chochinou and Steven Passik. "Psychiatric Aspects of Palliative Care." In Derek Doyle, Geoffrey W. C. Hanks, and Neil MacDonald eds., *Oxford Textbook of Palliative Medicine,* 2nd edition. Oxford: Oxford University, Press, 1998.

Burge, Frederick. "Dehydration Symptoms of Palliative Care Cancer Patients." *Journal of Pain and Symptom Management* 8 (1993):454–464.

Conill, C., E. Verger, and I. Henriquez. "Symptom Prevalence in the Last Week of Life." *Journal of Pain and Symptom Management* 14 (1997):328–331.

Donnelly, Sinead, and Declan Walsh. "The Symptoms of Advanced Cancer." *Seminars in Oncology* 22, no. 2 (1995):67–72.

Fainsinger, Robin, and Eduardo Bruera. "The Management of Dehydration in Terminally Ill Patients." *Journal of Palliative Care* 10, no. 3 (1994):55–59.

Ferrell, Betty Rolling. "The Family." In Derek Doyle, Geoffrey W. C. Hanks, and Neil MacDonald eds., *Oxford Textbook of Palliative Medicine.* Oxford: Oxford University Press, 1998.

Forman, Walter B., and Denice C. Sheehan, eds. "Symptom Management." *Hospice and Palliative Care: Concepts and Practice.* Sudbury, MA: Jones and Bartlett, 1996.

Grant, Marcia. "Nutritional Interventions: Increasing Oral Intake." *Seminars in Oncology Nursing* 2 (1986): 35–43.

Kemp, Charles. "Palliative Care for Respiratory Problems in Terminal Illness." *American Journal of Hospice and Palliative Care* (1997) 14:26–30.

King, Cynthia. "Nausea and Vomiting." In Betty Rolling Ferrell and Nessa Coyle eds., *Textbook of Palliative Nursing.* New York: Oxford University Press, 2000.

Kuebler, Kim K., Nancy English, and Debra A. Heidrich. "Delirium, Confusion, Agitation, and Restlessness." In Betty Rolling Ferrell and Nessa Coyle eds., *Textbook of Palliative Nursing.* New York: Oxford University Press, 2000.

Lipman, Arthur. "Evidence-Based Palliative Care." In Arthur Lipman, Kenneth Jackson, and Linda Tyler eds., *Evidence-Based Symptom Control in Palliative Care.* New York: Hawthorne Press, 2000.

Mannix, Kathryn A. "Palliation of Nausea and Vomiting." In Derek Doyle, Geoffrey W. C. Hanks, and Neil MacDonald eds., *Oxford Textbook of Palliative Medicine.* Oxford: Oxford University Press, 1998.

Roussea, Paul. "Antiemetic Therapy in Adults with Terminal Disease: A Brief Review." *American Journal of Hospice and Palliative Care* (1995) 12:13–18.

Tarzian, Anita. "Caring for Dying Patients Who Have Air Hunger." *Journal of Nursing Scholarship* 32 (2000): 137–143.

Twycross, Robert. *Symptom Management in Advanced Cancer,* 2nd edition. Oxon, England: Radcliffe Medical Press, 1997.

Tyler, Linda. "Dyspnea in Palliative Care Patients." In Arthur Lipman, Kenneth Jackson, and Linda Tyler eds., *Evidence-Based Symptom Control in Palliative Care.* New York: Hawthorne Press, 2000.

Tyler, Linda, and Arthur Lipman. "Fatigue in Palliative Care Patients." In Arthur Lipman, Kenneth Jackson, and Linda Tyler eds., *Evidence-Based Symptom Control in Palliative Care.* New York: Hawthorne Press, 2000.

Wilson, Keith G., Harvey Max Chochinov, Barbara J. de Faye, and William Breibart. "Diagnosis and Management of Depression in Palliative Care." In Harvey M. Chochinov and William Breitbart eds., *Handbook of Psychiatry in Palliative Medicine* New York: Oxford University Press, 2000.

Wroble, Rhonda, B. Nagle, L. Cataldi, and Mark Monane. "Insomnia in the Elderly: Assessment and Management in a Primary Care Setting." *Journal of Clinical Outcomes Management* 7, no. 3 (2000):50–57.

Zerwekh, Joyce. "Do Dying Patients Really Need IV Fluids?" *American Journal of Nursing* 97, no. 3 (1997): 26–31.

POLLY MAZANEC
JULIA BARTEL

T

TABOOS AND SOCIAL STIGMA

Death is the greatest mystery of life. Its inevitability has been a source of wonder, fear, hopefulness, and puzzlement throughout history. Humans, being the only species consciously aware of the inescapability of death, have sought from time immemorial to cope with this unique insight. In Western society the traditional patterns of death were shaped by an ancient attitude informed by simplicity, meaningful ceremony, and acceptance. The experience was public; that is to say, a caring community of family and neighbors ministered to the dying person. In the traditional context, death was conspicuously visible throughout society and people went to great lengths to remind themselves of how fragile life is. Reminders of mortality were everywhere, whether they be in literature, paintings, oral traditions, or the cemeteries and churches where the physical remains of death intersected with the daily activities of the community. In this convergence, death held sway over the imagination of individuals, and was a source of elaborate ritual known as the *ars moriendi.* In these ceremonies that characterized the traditional patterns of death, acceptance and openness were the most important qualities.

Traditional Views of Death Give Way to New Perceptions

Throughout the ages particular rituals, along with their participants and meanings, may have varied. Nonetheless, death, dying, and grieving in the traditional model were an important part of everyday cultural practices. And the rituals they spawned connected dying and grieving persons to a broader community and set of meanings. In this way, the ordeal of dying was never just personal, it was communal. These great ceremonies, along with their deep religious and social meanings, accompanied dying persons into their deaths. They provided a sense of strength for the broader community that was being threatened by the loss of one of its members. Additionally, these traditional rituals were a healing balm to dying persons and their intimates, offering strength and comfort to both.

In the twentieth century, the social and psychological landscape was transformed, redefining American cultural, social, and personal experiences of death. The result of this transformation is that dying, once an integral and meaningful part of social life, has become a source of terror and thus largely vanquished from public visibility. Herman Feifel has argued that this change has produced the American "taboo on death." Four major social trends are responsible: (1) the abdication of community to a pervasive sense of individualism; (2) the replacement of a predominantly religious worldview with one that is secular; (3) the sweeping power that materialism holds on the values, interests, and behaviors in modern society; and (4) the influential place of science and technology in daily life.

As individualism, secularism, materialism, and technicism have become driving forces in modern American culture, the experience of dying and its meanings have been dramatically recast. Specifically, as individualism replaces community in daily life, community presence and support is withdrawn from the dying and grieving processes. Secularism as a way of life offers many opportunities and great pleasures, but is ultimately unable to offer meaning and comfort at the end of life. Like secularism, materialism poorly equips individuals and societies to grapple with the mystery of death. In addition, technological achievement and dependence have enabled humanity to actively fight against dying, thus forestalling death for countless numbers of individuals. In this technological framework, dying is no longer a natural, necessary, and important part of life. Rather, it is as if it has become an enemy. Success lies in its control and defeat; failure becomes defined as the inability to turn it away.

The New Model of Death

These social changes have given rise to a new model of death, wherein dying and grieving are atomized and disconnected from everyday pathways of life, leading to their social isolation. As the historian Philippe Ariès astutely observes, in this context, dying has become deeply feared and a new image has replaced the traditional patterns of acceptance: the ugly and hidden death, hidden because it is ugly and dirty. As death has become frightening and meaningless, a culture of avoidance and denial has correspondingly emerged. Specifically, it has led to widespread pretense that suffering, dying, death, and grief do not exist. When individuals are forced to confront these inevitable experiences in their personal lives, they typically do so without social support and the comfort of participatory rituals or shared meanings. A pattern of death entirely unfamiliar in the traditional era has hence emerged. It is rooted in a sense of separation from the dominant culture and profound feelings of shame, both of which exacerbate the suffering inherent in the experience of dying and grieving.

As the legitimation and comfort of traditional ways of dying have given way to meaninglessness, isolation, and shame, stigma has become attached to suffering, dying, death, and grief. The stigmatization of death, wherein the experience of dying has become shameful, has helped to create an environment in which comfort at the end of life is scarce, and where suffering rages uncontrollably against dying individuals and their loved ones. As

Female children were once considered a social stigma in China where "one-child" policies existed, and infanticide was common if a woman gave birth to a baby girl. With the hopes of curtailing infanticide rates, billboard posters in the community still encouraged "one-child" policies, but said that it was acceptable to have daughters. OWEN FRANKEN/CORBIS

thanatologist David Moller documents, this stigma is far more than an abstract intellectual concept. It is a part of the actual experience of dying in the modern era, as embodied in the voices of persons facing the end of their lives. The following extract contains words expressed by different individuals who because of serious illness were forced to confront their own mortality. They are indeed testimonial to the profound suffering that accompanies dying in the individualistic, secular, materialistic, and technocratic organization of American life:

> Oh God the pain is so great. To go to sleep and
> feel normal, then to awake with such pain! Why

has God deserted me? I want to die. I can't live
with this newness. There are so many tubes in
my body. Every orifice. My hair is gone, my head
a giant bandage. Why can't I just die?
. . . illness creates in me a desire to withdraw from
society . . . I retreat to a resignation that most things
in life are empty-colorless-undesirable.

Because of all this, most days I try not to look in
the mirror, so I can still pretend that I look like
anything other than a cancer patient.

It seems that everything keeps going back to this cancer. It makes me feel so ugly, and it's just so depressing.
I'm not myself anymore. Oh, the way I used to be.
I can't even stand to look in the mirror anymore
(tears begin to stream from her eyes).
I'm no good to anybody. Why am I living? Why
doesn't God just let me die? I feel so useless, and
I'm a burden to everyone. This is no way to live.
The pain, oh why? I'm just no good.
Everything seems to lead me back to my cancer.
Cancer, cancer, that's it! That's all there is.
I'm just wasting my life away. There's absolutely
nothing positive happening. It's (having cancer)
all just so time consuming. It doesn't make me
feel well . . . feel good or happy. It's boring and
painful. Physically and emotionally, it's confusing
and depressing. There's nothing positive! All it
does is hurt. Everybody!
(Moller 2000, pp. 26, 33–35, 144–155)

The portrait that surfaces from these voices is one of agony and regret. It reflects an isolation and terror that was unheard of during the eras of traditional death. Also emerging is a silhouette of evil, whereby the body is being decimated by disease and the very foundation of cultural and social life is being attacked. The result is that dying people and their loved ones often live in a state of social exile, enduring their suffering in isolation. Simply, these people suffer deeply and unnecessarily, and they do so in a societal context where the very idea of death has become inconceivable and unbearable.

See also: CANNIBALISM; DEATH SYSTEM; INFANTICIDE

Bibliography

Ariès, Philippe. *The Hour of Our Death.* New York: Alfred Knopf, 1981.

Becker, Ernest. *Escape from Evil.* New York: The Free Press, 1975.

Becker, Ernest. *The Denial of Death.* New York: The Free Press, 1973.

Elias, Norman. *The Loneliness of the Dying.* New York: Basil Blackwell, 1985.

Feifel, Herman. *The Meaning of Death.* New York: McGraw Hill, 1959.

Gorer, Geoffrey. *Death, Grief, and Mourning.* New York: Doubleday, 1965.

Moller, David. *Life's End: Technocratic Dying in an Age of Spiritual Yearning.* New York: Bayword, 2000.

Moller, David. *Confronting Death: Values, Institutions, and Human Mortality.* New York: Oxford University Press, 1996.

Quill, Timothy. *Death and Dignity.* New York: Norton, 1993.

DAVID WENDELL MOLLER

TAOISM

In Chinese, the term *Tao,* or *Dao,* which means "way," can refer to phenomena as disparate as the proper mode of conduct in society to an abstract, transcendent order to the universe. Similarly, the Western term *Taoism* (or *Daoism*) refers to a number of distinct phenomena in China, all related in some sense to this concept of Tao. One of the more popular usages is as a reference to several philosophical works of the Warring States and early Han periods, especially the *Zhuangzi* (*Chuang-tzu*) and *Laozi* (*Lao-tzu,* also known as the *Daodejing* (*Tao-te ching*), or *Classic of the Way and Its Power*). The *Chuang-tzu* welcomes death as merely one more stage in a process of ongoing transformation that affects all and is directed by the Tao. It speaks of death as a returning home that humankind resists out of ignorance and sees the individual living on after death dissolved in the many creatures of the earth. The famous parable of the author dreaming that he was a butterfly, then waking to wonder if he were now a butterfly dreaming of being a human, is a metaphor for this sense that temporal life is but an illusion and death an awakening.

Prayer cards, photographs, and ritual offerings, including a tea kettle, vases, and flowers, characterize a Taoist courtyard altar at the Lung Shan Temple in Taiwan. G. JOHN RENARD

The *Laozi,* on the other hand, speaks of death as an inauspicious event to be avoided and mentions self-cultivation techniques intended to prolong physical life. This viewpoint is much closer than the *Zhuangzi (Chuang-tzu)* to mainstream ancient Chinese thought on death. Life does go on in a shadowy, subterranean realm, but it is not joyful, and much effort was expended from an early period to forestall its arrival. By the third century B.C.E., there were programs of exercise, diet, sexual practices, and meditation intended to nourish the life force while alive as well as jade burial suits and tomb guardians intended to preserve the deceased in the other realm. Alchemy, the belief that the human form could be made eternal through the ingestion of various mineral-based elixirs, developed through the Warring States era, Han Dynasty, and about fifth century B.C.E. to sixth century C.E. Practitioners were initially adepts of the occult arts without a clear sectarian identity, but eventually these practices would make their way into the ritual canon of religious Daoism.

The Confucian view of death, by contrast, forsakes all hope for extraordinary longevity and focuses on the secure installation of the dead in the other world, where they would be administered by a bureaucracy that mirrored that of the living and supplied with the necessities of continued life through ancestral sacrifice. The dead were recalled and, some argue, kept alive by meditative visualizations in which the dead person was called into the consciousness as if still alive. The Confucians also promoted a metaphorical interpretation of sacrifice that elided the question of personal survival and the ethical implications of a transactional relationship with the sacred.

Religious Taoism arose in the second century C.E., proclaiming a new pantheon of pure deities and a new, morality-based set of practices. The early Taoist church foresaw an imminent apocalypse in which the evil would perish and the faithful "seed people" would survive to repopulate a utopian world of Great Peace. Until then, ordained Taoists received celestial ranks that carried over into the world of the dead, assuring them a favored position of power and responsibility in the other world. Their offices might be in the cavern-heavens hidden within the world's sacred mountains or in one of the many celestial heavens. Nonbelievers went to a profane world of the dead, where they were subject to a variety of dangers, including lawsuits from those they had wronged in either realm. Living Taoist priests could intervene on their behalf, using their authority as celestial officials to have suits dismissed and punishments curtailed.

Popular conceptions of the afterlife came to focus on existence in hells where retribution was exacted for sins during life. Taoists, like Buddhists, developed ritual methods to save the deceased from these torments, submitting written petitions to celestial officials but also employing ritualized violence to force their way into the hells in order to lead the deceased out. Major Taoist rituals of renewal (*jiao*) typically end with a Rite of Universal Salvation intended to save the dispossessed souls.

Twenty-first-century priests of the Taoist church survive in Taiwan, Hong Kong, and diasporic Chinese communities and have been reestablished in China. There are some movements in the West that claim this mantle as well, but most do not maintain traditional ritual practice. The philosophical works of the Warring States era, on the other hand, enjoy a wide following in the West, though the disparity in the teachings of the *Laozi* and the *Zhuangzi* are seldom appreciated. The dominant Chinese approach to death remains that of Chinese popular religion, which eclectically mixes the beliefs of Buddhism and religious Taoism with traditional Chinese views of death, the afterlife, and the soul.

See also: CHINESE BELIEFS; SHINTO

Bibliography

Kohn, Livia, ed. *The Taoist Handbook.* Leiden, Netherlands: Brill, 2000.

Robinet, Isabelle. *Taoism: Growth of a Religion.* Stanford, CA: Stanford University Press, 1997.

TERRY F. KLEEMAN

TAYLOR, JEREMY

The Anglican bishop and writer Jeremy Taylor (1613–1667), one of the key exemplars of pastoral care and a gifted writer, was born and educated in Cambridge, England. He was ranked by the English poet Samuel Taylor Coleridge as the equal of Shakespeare and Milton. Taylor was probably ordained in 1633, the year in which he took his master's degree; he became a fellow of Gonville and Caius College and, two years later, a fellow at All Souls in Oxford. Shortly after being appointed the rector of Uppingham in 1638, he became the chaplain to the king of England on Laud's nomination; Laud also seems to have retained him as his own chaplain.

Taylor joined the Royalist army as chaplain when civil war broke out in 1642, and he was briefly imprisoned twice. In 1645 he became private chaplain to Lord Carbery at his Golden Grove estate. There, Taylor produced his greatest works, including *A Discourse of the Liberty of Prophesying* (1647), a call for Christian toleration that probably alienated Charles I; *The Golden Grove* (1655), a collection of daily prayers; and the *Unum Necessarium* (1655), a work on sin and repentance. His two famous books of devotion, *The Rule and Exercises of Holy Living* (1650) and *The Rule and Exercises of Holy Dying* (1651), were intended to act as guides for those not served by local Anglican clergy because of the ejection of priests during the interregnum. At the Restoration in 1660, Taylor published his comprehensive manual of moral theology, the *Ductor Dubitantium*. That same year he was appointed bishop of Down and Connor; in 1661 he was appointed bishop of Dromore, in Ireland; and later vice-chancellor of Trinity College, in Dublin.

Although he seemed conventional in his relations with the royal and Episcopal authorities, Taylor aroused controversy because of his defense of Christian toleration and his allegedly Pelagian views on original sin and justification, both of which were attacked by the Scottish Presbyterian Samuel Rutherford. *Holy Dying* was written in the circumstances of the death of his wife, Phoebe, but was directed at a general audience as a self-help manual: "The first entire Body of Directions for sick and dying People, that I remember to have been publish'd in the Church of England." The importance of the text was not only in the quality of its prose but in the serenity of its ecumenical verdict: "Let it be enough that we secure our Interest of Heaven," Taylor wrote, "for every good Man hopes to be saved as he is a Christian, and not as he is a Lutheran, or of another Division." Taylor advocated daily self-examination by the Christian to avoid divine judgment, and especially the "extremely sad" condition of many "Strangers and Enemies to Christ." Thus, he concluded, "He that would die holily and happily, must in this World love Tears, Humility, Solitude, and Repentance" (Taylor, 2:1:3).

See also: CHRISTIAN DEATH RITES, HISTORY OF; GOOD DEATH, THE; MOMENT OF DEATH

Bibliography

Askew, Reginald. *Muskets and Altars: Jeremy Taylor and the Last of the Anglicans.* London: Mowbray, 1997.

Hughes, H. Trevor. *The Piety of Jeremy Taylor.* London: Macmillan, 1960.

Taylor, Jeremy. *The Rule and Exercises of Holy Dying.* N.p., 1811.

RICHARD BONNEY

TECHNOLOGY AND DEATH

What is fantasy one day may be reality the next. The Human Genome Project and cloning are the twenty-first century's newest ventures into the relationship of technology and death. The mapping of genes looks for medical advances to prevent disease, cure patients, and extend human life. The goal of curing or preventing diseases linked to one's genes is a major incentive for researchers and investment capital to drive technological change for the greater good. Utilitarian arguments challenge traditional principles and values that seek to limit the number of deaths in the process of change.

Success in developing cures for various diseases has universally given rise to the expectation that it is just a matter of time until medical scientists will discover cures for cancer, HIV/AIDS (human immunodeficiency virus/acquired immunodeficiency syndrome), and other diseases. Supporters of change argue that society would benefit from more tax incentives, research grants, research centers, and educated researchers to meet these important challenges. Technology is not a concept set apart from society, as dramatically seen in medical, ethical, and political debates over human experimentation with somatic and stem cell cloning.

Technological Determinism, Cultural Lag, and Death

It is easy to recognize technology in society. It consists of devices, knowledge, and skills that can be used to control and utilize physical, social, and biological phenomena. A common intellectual error is to treat technology and society as distinct, independent entities. Technology, ideology, and social organization, while separate entities, are interrelated. This is particularly evident in the relationship of technology and death in modern and postmodern societies.

The argument that technology drives social change is not a new one. Great thinkers such as Karl Marx, Henri Saint-Simon, and William Ogburn made the argument that improvements in technology lead to social change in society. Ogburn further suggested that there is a social lag between inventions and adoption of the change in society. For Western societies, technological innovation is a major source of social change that impacts dying and death.

Consider the social and cultural impact that is involved in "brain death" laws that were enacted in most states by 1980. The impetus for redefining "death" to include "brain death" (the cessation of electrical activity in the brain and brain stem while circulation and breathing are sustained by machines) is due to medical research in human organ transplantation, particularly of kidneys, a major advance in medical technology.

Early success in human organ transplantation began in North America in the 1960s with the "harvesting" of kidneys, and other organs, from cadavers. The donors were healthy persons who had died in an accident where medical (machine) support was available to sustain breathing and circulation. The need to change legal definitions of death to include brain death came to the fore when prosecutors began to charge harvesting surgeons with murder under existing laws. For the sake of the greater good, states began to adapt by passing legislation that allowed for collection of human organs when a person was "breathing" and had "a pulse."

Still other social changes have taken place in the face of blood-borne pathogens and other contagious diseases. HIV/AIDS and other diseases have caused medical personnel and embalmers to adopt defensive measures including protective clothing, gloves, masks, and different chemicals to shield themselves from these diseases. The threat of terrorism in biochemical attacks challenges and changes both governments and everyday behavior in citizens regardless of the number and types of deaths that result.

Technology As an Interdependent Variable, Death As the Dependent Variable

Most changes in technology are slow to be accepted, causing a social and cultural lag between the development of the innovation and its adoption. Examples include the reluctance of China to acknowledge the spread of HIV/AIDS and of Japan to enact brain death legislation in support of organ transplantation.

While many technological developments languish for lack of support due to cultural belief, social values, or "the bottom line," others are seen as riding the tide of technological change. Medical information technology is accepted by some specialties as a way to be more efficient and accurate in treating patients and saving lives. High-tech medicine demands high-tech specialists to fight disease and challenge death.

The institutions of hospice and palliative medicine provide a holistic approach to caring for the dying person and support family and friends who are part of the support team. It is not uncommon for hospice observers to ask if one has to die to get that kind of quality care. Yet hospice provides care for only a small percentage of all patients who die in the United States and only in the last stages of dying.

Decisions by physicians, patients, and family members to reduce or stop aggressive medical treatments are not easy to make when high-tech medicine is standing by to try one more technique or treatment. Experimental protocols may be the only alternative treatment available, even though the study is being done to determine efficacy and side effects of the experimental drug.

Increasingly, aftercare grief support programs are available for family, friends, and others. These are provided in hospitals, churches, and funeral homes. With the widespread use of the Internet, cyber mourning has led to the development of web sites for those who are grieving. These include sites for those suffering from grief for the loss of a spouse, child, parent, friends, siblings, and even pets. Having the technology available does not mean that people will choose to use it, but as use of the Internet increases the use of such sites will also increase.

Technological and Values Congruence

Technological change may be supported or resisted by work, family, and politics. For example, some people believe that were it not for political considerations, public health problems such as HIV/AIDS or drug addiction could be solved or better managed. Others view traditional religious organizations as impediments to lifesaving medical inventions, such as cloning for medical cures.

Still other questions pose moral extremes: Should stem cell research be promoted or forbidden by legislation? Is abortion an evil to be avoided at all costs or a choice that respects the right of privacy? Is cloning research the hope of the future or an ethical error? Should experimental drugs be readily available to all patients even before their efficacy and side effects are demonstrated? Marked incongruence arises and persists between elements of technology and social organization.

Advances in medical technology have led to public discussion and the legalization of assisted suicide only in Oregon and active voluntary euthanasia in the Netherlands. While the desire to live long has led to the adoption of medical technologies to greatly extend life, there has not been an accompanying adoption of means to medically manage individuals who choose not to live with the increased pain and suffering that sometimes come with extending one's life.

Interestingly, physician-assisted suicide was less of an issue when the average life expectancy was under fifty years and medical science very limited compared to twenty-first-century methods. Until the ability to keep one's body alive long after the brain was functioning normally, little discussion of advance directives was put forth. Though the adoption of advance directives has been slow, its use is increasing in an era of high-tech medicine and frequent litigation that drives up the cost of American health care.

Technology and Mass Destruction

Technology has allowed each generation the ability to create evermore-destructive means of warfare, such as the use of laser-guided missiles and nuclear weapons. Governments and radicals use biochemical and nuclear threats to confront social, economic, and political vested interests. Violent actions increasingly result in targeted mass destruction and deaths. After the 1960s there was a resurgence of racial and ethnic rivalries, tension, and hostilities throughout the world and especially in the United States during the 1980s. During the 1990s prejudice, violence, conflict, and discrimination were found widely throughout the world between black and white in South Africa; between Islamic Arabs and black Christians in Sudan; between East Indians and blacks in Guyana; between Chinese and Malays in Malaysia; between Kurds and Iraqis in Iraq; between the Krahn, Gio, and Mano ethnic groups in Liberia; among other places. The collapse of the former Soviet Union brought forth conflicts between Armenians and

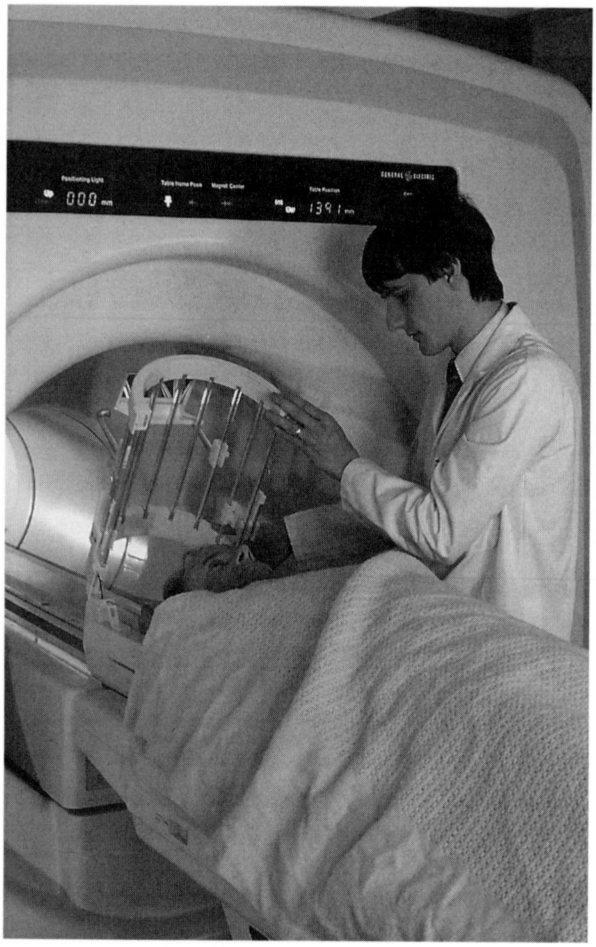

A radiographer prepares a patient for an MRI scan, a technology that revolutionized medical imaging by using magnets and magnetic fields. The results of a scan can save a patient's life by providing useful information in detecting serious health conditions. PHOTO RESEARCHERS

Azerbaijanis as well as Slavic nationalism in the former Yugoslavia.

The twenty-first century has brought changes in Northern Ireland and South Africa and terrorist attacks have modified the world scene. The world, and the United States suddenly seems to be a much less safe place to live. The news of the world and its violence are available twenty-four hours a day. Events are televised as they occur. The world may not actually be more violent, but it appears to be if one follows the news media. Fear of mass death has lead to fear of flying, public events, energy plants, and even one's work environment. Biological terrorism, nuclear destruction, smart bombs, and car bombings are part of conventional conversations. Technology has brought death from the battlefield to where people live and work.

Death

Those who experience illnesses are generally thankful that their illnesses did not occur ten or twenty years ago. Improvements in medical technology are occurring at a rate that is challenging even the most basic definitions of what it means to be human or to simply be alive.

In the midst of a population that is aging, increasing in diversity, and becoming more affluent, the available technology for combating illness and death is forcing an examination of social values and medical structures that deliver curative and rescue technologies. Should stem cell research be conducted on human embryos? Should abortion be used to eliminate fetuses with birth defects or genetic diseases? The ability to conduct fetal surgery has changed many of the issues. How much medical intervention and money should be spent in caring for low-birthweight babies when they are the most likely to die? In 2000 many more low-weight premature babies survived who would have died in 1970. Technology will continue to challenge assumptions on these and many other issues surrounding medical technology and the care of the ill and dying.

Policies and practices continue to change as technology opens new issues to be discussed and debated. Policies related to biomedical technologies are shaped by public demands and expectations. The mass media, interest groups, and the legal, political, and religious systems all have input in shaping policy decisions concerning biomedical technologies. For example, the distribution of medical resources is heavily skewed toward the more powerful, technologically sophisticated nations and to individuals in the upper social classes in those same nations. Individuals with money and social status are more likely to receive medical interventions—a practice labeled "concierge medicine."

Policy issues also include research and development. As of 2002 the U.S. government supports biomedical research. Strong efforts continue to attempt to block biomedical research for ethical and financial reasons. In 2001 Johns Hopkins had its biomedical research money temporarily rescinded because of public outcry over a death involving the use of human subjects. Questions concerning who does research, who should be funded, and who should receive the benefits of the research will continue to spark controversy.

Adequate policy decisions require that goals be clearly conceptualized, as no policy is fair for all people. Policies that maximize the greatest good for the greatest number tend to prevail because of historical roots of American utilitarianism. Alternative values, principles, and lifestyles are often protected and respected as an expression of individual choice. Yet, the ability to pay for high-tech services is not distributed equally. Some segments in U.S. society may have a "right" to health care, such as Medicare patients, but this is not the case for all Americans. Claims about the "sacredness" of individual autonomy, self-determination, and personal privacy confront issues of public concern and even those of vested interests (e.g., tertiary insurance providers). While not everyone believes that life should be prolonged at any cost, collectively, they have yet to determine at what point the "technological fix" is not in the best interest of the patient or society.

The Future of Technology and Death

Forecasting the future is at best an inexact science, but it will include an explosion of advanced technology. How will this technology impact dying, death, funeral rituals, and disposal of the dead? Biomedical advances will impact how and when people die and allow many diseases to be conquered. Genetic engineering may make many illnesses obsolete, allow organs to be regenerated when defective, and provide modification to one's genetic code to avoid disabilities and illnesses. Advances in technology might allow more precise definitions of when life begins and ends, which will facilitate ethical decision making.

Funeral rituals and grieving processes already include the use of technology via the Internet. One can chat online over grief, place memorials for pets, obtain information for aiding children and others who are grieving, and find information about funerals or related dying and death areas. The use of such technology can only increase in the future. Advances in technology have already made cremation a more reasonable alternative to burial and, for some, the deep-freezing of cryonics portends the way of the future. Tradition may slow the acceptance of technology, but it will not stop the impact of technological change on the future of death.

See also: Death System; Memorial, Virtual; Nuclear Destruction

Bibliography

Annas, George J., and Michael A. Grodin. *The Nazi Doctors and the Nuremberg Code: Human Rights in Human Experimentation.* New York: Oxford University Press, 1992.

Devries, Brian, ed. *End of Life Issues: Interdisciplinary and Multidimensional Perspectives.* New York: Springer Publishing, 1999.

DeVries, Raymond, and Janardan Subedi, eds. *Bioethics and Society: Constructing the Ethical Enterprise.* Upper Saddle River, NJ: Prentice Hall, 1998.

Gaylin, Willard, and Bruce Jennings. *The Perversion of Autonomy: The Proper Use of Coercion and Constraints in a Liberal Society.* New York: The Free Press, 1996.

Hoefler, James M. *Deathright: Culture, Medicine, Politics, and the Right to Die.* Boulder, CO: Westview Press, 1994.

Moller, David Wendell. *Life's End: Technocratic Dying in an Age of Spiritual Yearning.* Amityville, NY: Baywood Publishing, 2000.

Petrinovich, Lewis. *Living and Dying Well.* Cambridge, MA: MIT Press, 1996.

Schneider, Carl E. *The Practice of Autonomy: Patients, Doctors, and Medical Decisions.* New York: Oxford University Press, 1998.

Walters, Leroy, and Julie Gage Palmer. *The Ethics of Human Gene Therapy.* New York: Oxford University Press, 1997.

Zussman, Robert. *Intensive Care: Medical Ethics and the Medical Profession.* Chicago: University of Chicago Press, 1992.

GERRY R. COX
ROBERT A. BENDIKSEN

Terminal Illness

See Dying, Process of.

TERRORISM

Terrorism refers to the illegitimate use of violence or intimidation to advance a group's interests. Examples include detonating explosives in public places, taking hostages, or assassinating politicians. Central to the concept of terrorism is that its objective is primarily ideological. Terrorists typically do not employ violence to gain wealth but rather to bring attention to political causes.

Because the term *terrorism* hinges on a distinction between legitimate and illegitimate use of violence, controversy often accompanies its use. For example, governments routinely use force to advance their interests, but do not characterize their actions as instances of terrorism. The bombing of the Alfred P. Murrah Building in Oklahoma City is readily identified as a terrorist act because it was undertaken by a very small group of individuals and not an entire government. Yet much more violent attacks directed against large cities during World War II are not characterized as acts of terrorism. Within a single conflict use of the term "terrorist" in news reports can reveal the political sympathies of the broadcaster or the government that released information about the attack. For example, in the American press violent events undertaken by Palestinians are far more likely to be characterized as acts of terrorism than equally or more violent actions taken by the Israeli military. This political component became very clear in the United States during the Reagan administration, which aided the Contra rebels who were waging a campaign of violence against the Sandinista government in Nicaragua. Officials in the American government characterized the Contras as "freedom fighters" while supporters of the Sandinistas portrayed them as terrorists.

The use of violence by small groups to advance their interests is not a twenty-first-century development. The term *terrorism* first appeared during the French Revolution and the Jacobin Reign of Terror. Similarly, many other words associated with terrorism (i.e., *thug, assassin,* and *zealot*) derive from groups alleged to have used violence and death to advance their political objectives.

Historically terrorism is thought to have passed through several distinct stages, from its origin among religious groups fighting to defend or advance their organization's beliefs, to secular groups, whose objectives were clearly political. Traced by some historians to the French Revolution, this process of the secularization of terrorism continued throughout the twentieth century. Modern technology's ability to expand the audience for violent actions is thought by some analysts to have fueled terrorism's appeal, making nations with a free press particularly susceptible to the quest for media coverage. Twentieth- and twenty-first-century accounts of terrorism argue that it may have moved into a new period, as new technology allows small groups of individuals the ability to wield tremendous destructive power, and permits even faster coverage of that destruction to a wide audience, as evidenced by the terrorist attacks in the United States on September 11, 2001. Experts warn that such attacks are not limited to religiously motivated groups but can also include assaults stemming from personal grudges or psychopathological conditions.

In contrast to individual acts of violence, the use of terrorism by small political organizations is thought to serve several functions: (1) It makes the group committing the terrorist act appear large and powerful, thus intimidating outsiders and boosting morale of the terrorist group's members; (2) it reveals the vulnerability of the target, whose apparent strength is thereby placed in doubt and whose authority may become undermined; (3) it can eliminate opposition; (4) it may start a chain reaction of assaults undertaken by sympathetic political groups; and (5) it cements the terrorists to the organization because individuals who commit acts of terror cannot leave the organization very easily.

The impact of media coverage of terrorist acts is mixed. On the one hand, most Americans greatly overestimate the threat of terrorism, probably due to media coverage of the subject. In fact, the chances of being killed in an automobile accident are more than one hundred times higher than the chance of being killed by a terrorist action while overseas. On the other hand, sustained terrorist attacks can produce a backlash against the perpetrator's cause, as occurred in 1999 when bombings of Moscow apartment buildings increased the hostility of Russian citizens toward Chechens, who were thought to be responsible for the blasts.

Attempts to combat terrorism include use of metal detectors and dogs at locales thought to be likely targets for attack. While these methods are effective at reducing the frequency of terrorist acts, it appears impossible to protect targets completely against determined terrorists. Ironically, methods to offset terrorism exaggerate the public's perception of threat and thus advance one of terrorism's main objectives.

See also: DEATH SQUADS; TERRORIST ATTACKS ON AMERICA

Bibliography

Crenshaw, Martha. "The Logic of Terrorism." In Walter Reich ed., *Origins of Terrorism.* Cambridge: Cambridge University Press, 1990.

Fleming, Dan B., and Arnold Schuetz. "Terrorism, Assassination, and Political Torture." In Daniel Leviton ed., *Horrendous Death, Health, and Well-Being.* New York: Hemisphere Publishing, 1991.

Laqueur, Walter. *The New Terrorism: Fanaticism and the Arms of Mass Destruction.* New York: Oxford University Press, 1999.

Laqueur, Walter. *Terrorism.* Boston: Little, Brown, 1977.

Shurkin, Joel. "Modern Terrorists Are 'Anemic.'" *Stanford Observer,* 6 February 1988, 1ff.

Stern, Jessica. *The Ultimate Terrorists.* Cambridge, MA: Harvard University Press, 1999.

Stohl, Michael. *The Politics of Terrorism.* New York: Marcel Dekker, 1983.

JONATHAN F. LEWIS

TERRORIST ATTACKS ON AMERICA

On the morning of September 11, 2001, four commercial jets departed from three airports for their scheduled flights. Within two hours each of the planes had crashed. No passengers or crew members survived. Approximately 3,000 people on the ground had also perished. These catastrophic events soon became known as the terrorist attack on America. The impact was felt far beyond the families, friends, and colleagues who had known a victim of the disaster. Witnesses to the events, rescue personnel, and the media agreed that nothing of this kind had ever occurred and that life in the United States would never again be the same. Significant and widespread changes did occur. Heightened concern for security and prevention, economic turmoil, and altered behavior patterns (e.g., a sharp decline in air travel and tourism) were among these changes. This article provides an overview of the events and their consequences, but focuses on the response of individuals and societies to the sudden and unexpected deaths of many people.

The Events of September 11

At 7:59 A.M. American Airlines (AA) Flight 11 departed from Boston to Los Angeles with 81 passengers and 11 crew members. United Airlines (UAL) Flight 93 departed from Newark, New Jersey, just two minutes later; its 38 passengers and 7 crew members were heading to San Francisco. At 8:10 AA Flight 77 departed from Dulles Airport in Washington, D.C., with 58 passengers and 6 crew members en route to Los Angeles. Four minutes later UAL Flight 175 departed from Boston for Los Angeles with 56 passengers and 9 crew members. Within the space of fifteen minutes 266 people were about to meet their demise, with the four planes converted into lethal weapons by hijackers.

American Airlines Flight 11 struck the North Tower of the World Trade Center in New York City at 8:45 A.M. Sixteen minutes later UAL Flight 175 swept into the South Tower. AA Flight 77 crashed into a section of the Pentagon at 9:43 A.M. It was later determined that 184 Pentagon personnel were killed by the crash and ensuing fire. Officials would later say that its original target had been either the White House or the congressional building. UAL 93, the remaining flight, also crashed but did not cause any casualties on the ground. Several passengers, having become aware of the other crashes, resisted their hijackers. The plane came to crash about 80 miles southeast of Pittsburgh, Pennsylvania; its original target is still a matter of speculation.

The incredible sight of a passenger jet appearing out of the clear blue sky to strike the North Tower of the World Trade Center was at first taken to be a disastrous accident. It was obvious that the lives of many people were in jeopardy. First responders (firefighters, paramedics, police) rushed to the scene. The emergency rescue operation was already in action when the South Tower was also struck. The powerful impact hurled debris upon emergency personnel and their equipment. Onlookers had then realized that the expanding disaster was no accident: The World Trade Center, New York City, and the United States were under attack.

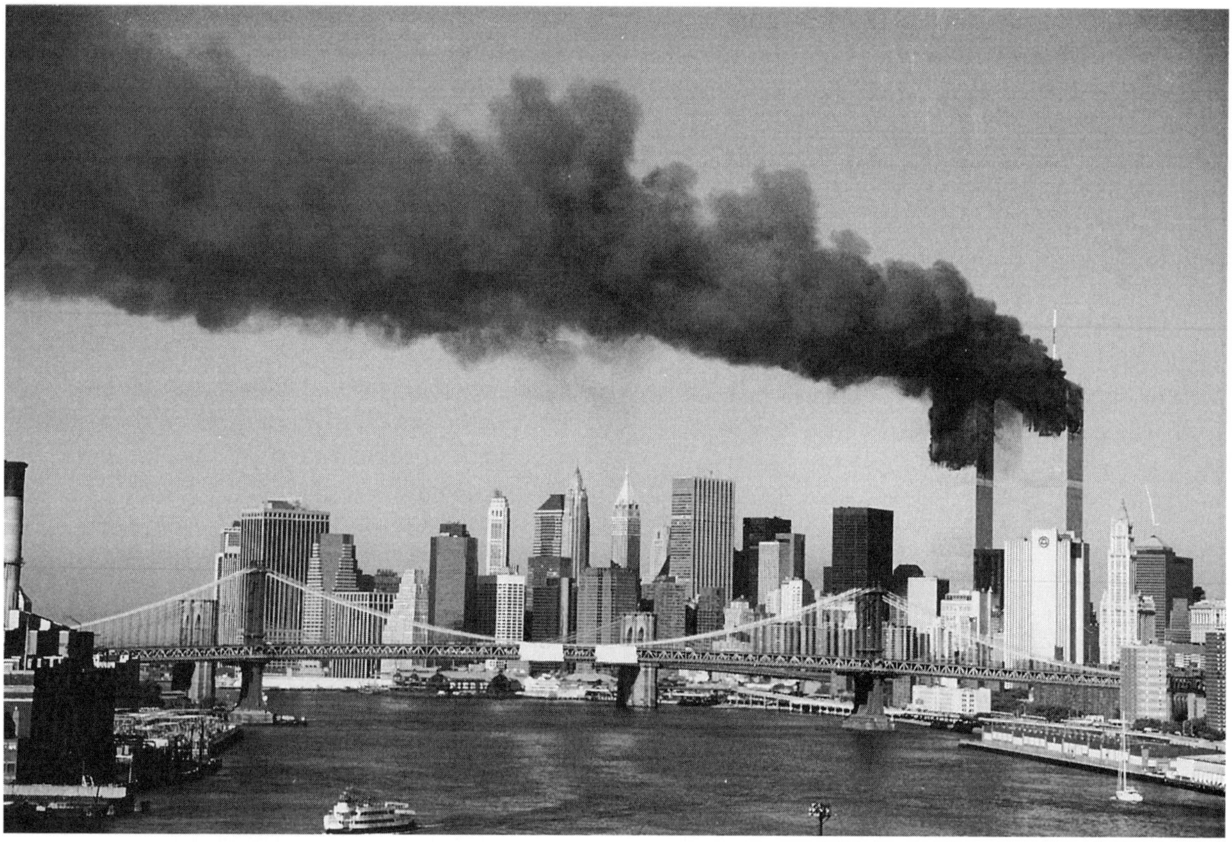

Smoke billowed from the World Trade Center towers after they were struck by two hijacked planes. The towers collapsed shortly thereafter and rescue efforts continued for weeks following the attack. REUTERS NEWMEDIA INC./CORBIS

The World Trade Center (WTC), one of the world's most important business districts, was devastated. The area would soon be known as "Ground Zero," often described as a scene from a nightmare with ruins stretching in every direction. Smoky clouds billowed along the streets. Buildings near the towers seemed in danger of collapsing upon the rescue teams and those who were trying to evacuate the area. Risking their own lives, the first responders, burdened by their equipment, ran up the staircases in the attempt to save those trapped in the buildings. Some survivors could be seen escaping from the towers either through their own efforts or with assistance from emergency personnel. However, witnesses were horrified to see people leaping to their deaths from the highest floors before major sections of the towers collapsed.

Millions of people throughout the nation and the world witnessed the tragedy and the chaos through television. Those who were on the scene would later report that no television camera could communicate the intensity and breadth of destruction; nevertheless, television viewers saw enough of the major developments and the individual responses to realize that this was a catastrophe unique in the history of the nation—and one that would have a profound effect on the future.

It was immediately evident that many people had perished at the WTC. Early estimates were as high as 15,000. For sometime thereafter the death toll was estimated at about 6,500. It would prove very difficult to determine both the number of fatalities and individual identities. There was no master list of people (including visitors) who might have been in the towers at the time. Many bodies had been covered by heaps of debris; others could only be identified by fingerprints or dental records; and still others had been so devastated by impact and fire that all forms of positive identification seemed unattainable. The work of recovering the remains of WTC victims would be long and arduous, requiring the use of heavy construction machinery cranes and the painstaking exploration of every possible site within the extensive Ground Zero area.

It was not until five months after the attack that New York City authorities could provide an official count of the deaths: 2,843. The evidence indicated that death had come quickly. No survivors were found after September 12, 2001 (despite some hasty news reports to the contrary). The city's health care facilities and providers had responded immediately and in force. Physicians and nurses made themselves available, ambulances stood at the ready, and blood supplies were increased. As the day drew into night it gradually became clear that there would not be an overwhelming wave of casualties in need of treatment. People who were caught in the attack either died quickly or were fortunate in escaping. Those waiting to provide emergency services reported feeling stunned and helpless as they realized that there were no lives they could save. Rescue workers at the site would continue their efforts vigorously for weeks even though they too realized that there was little hope for discovering survivors.

September 11 was also a day in which fear and uncertainty added to the shock and sorrow. It was generally understood that America had come under attack. An adversary capable of hijacking four jets and causing so much death and destruction in one morning might have other, perhaps even more catastrophic, plans in mind. The federal government acted quickly by grounding all other commercial airline flights, some for several days, and other security measures were put into place. What had happened within the span of two hours had taken many lives and, in the Manhattan towers, destroyed a symbol of American power—but it had also alarmed a nation that it might be in continuing peril from terrorist forces.

Loss, Sorrow, and Recovery

The impact of these deaths on family and friends could hardly have been more traumatic. There had been no expectation and therefore no preparation for the sudden loss of loved ones. It seemed beyond comprehension that a husband or wife would not be returning home from a day's work at the WTC. Even the families of firefighters and police, aware of the dangers of the profession, had to struggle with the fact that their worst fears had become real. "There is a big hole where my life used to be," was a feeling expressed by many family members. What researchers now call traumatic grief is especially intense and devastating. The hammer blow of a violent and unexpected death increases the difficulty of moving on with life. Even people with strong coping skills are likely to feel overwhelmed and isolated.

For many of the affected families the situation was even more stressful. They could not even be sure that their loved one had died. As already noted, the nature of the catastrophe made it very difficult to recover and identify the remains of the victims. Some would never be firmly identified, leaving families suspended between hope and despair. Determined efforts were made to find possible victims who were listed as missing. Photographs of missing WTC employees and first responders were posted on improvised street bulletin boards and circulated throughout the city. Desperate hope that their family members had somehow escaped the catastrophe kept many people in a state of high tension that limited their ability to deal with the ongoing needs of everyday life.

Furthermore, even acknowledgement of the death often was not sufficient to enable family members to direct their energies to the reconstruction of their own lives. There was a powerful need to conduct a proper funeral and memorialization. Paying last respects to the deceased would provide a sense of closure and the starting point for the long and difficult process of recovery. Unfortunately, many bodies were not recovered. The efforts of firefighters to recover the bodies of their comrades were demonstrated day after day as, along with others, they labored in the Ground Zero ruins. Their impassioned search for both their own friends and all victims made clear the strong impulse to honor the dead. When human remains were discovered from time to time the workers would conduct their own improvised memorial service: an American flag placed on the site, and a moment of silence.

Family members felt the same need for closure, especially as hope for a miraculous survival became increasingly dim. Practical needs also became increasingly pressing. It was difficult to conduct the business of family life with a member who has absent yet not officially considered deceased. Financial matters were particularly stressful; for example, no income, but also no insurance or other death benefits. After some time, the city of New York decided to issue death certificates upon request to families who had almost certainly lost a person in the WTC attack. One by one, next of kin had to make the painful decision to obtain a death certificate and thereby accept the loss but also have the legal and economic foundation to rebuild their futures.

The nation and much of the world shared in the grief experienced by families of the victims in New York City, the Pentagon, and Pennsylvania. The fact that they were not alone in their sorrow provided a measure of consolation although all had their private ordeals to endure. Numerous memorial services were held in local churches and national venues. Church attendance increased throughout the United States in the wake of the disaster as people sought meaning and comfort. There was also consolation in the heroism of the people who had braved the WTC inferno or resisted the hijackers over Pennsylvania. These demonstrations of character and courage became a model for many others.

The grief and the outpouring of compassion continued for weeks. The smoke still rising from Ground Zero was a constant reminder of the tragedy. There was also a subtle personal response on the part of many people. Perhaps Mayor Rudolph Giuliani of New York City was the most prominent person to express this response publicly when he mentioned that he had to face his own mortality issues while trying to do what he could in an official capacity.

America on the Attack

The national grief process was abruptly interrupted a month after the attacks. The government declared war on international terrorism, identified wealthy Saudi expatriate Osama bin Laden as instigator, and launched a military campaign against the al-Qaeda network and the Taliban regime in Afghanistan.

Media images of tearful families and memorial services were soon replaced with air strikes, Department of Defense press conferences, and speculations on the whereabouts of bin Laden. Energies bound up in shock and grief were released in the opportunity to go into action against an enemy who would slaughter innocent people. The Japanese attack on Pearl Harbor in 1941 was often mentioned as the only previous event that had been at all comparable in scope and casualties but that, at least, had targeted military forces. The nation overwhelmingly endorsed this response to the terrorist threat and a surge of patriotism supplanted the earlier renewal of interest in religion.

The national transformation of grief and passivity into purpose and action had an invigorating effect. It also, however, provided the opportunity to turn away from uncomfortable reflections on personal mortality.

Integrating September 11 into American Life

In a sense, September 11, 2001, is not over. It is in process of becoming part of the continuing and enduring story of American life. The destruction and eventual rebuilding of the World Trade Center will command attention. The first responders with their self-sacrificing heroism will take their place among the people most admired in American history. The issue of national security versus individual rights will almost certainly remain salient. The debate is already well under way: How far and in what ways should security measures intrude upon privacy and freedom? This issue has been of concern since the establishment of the republic, but has been given heightened prominence since the attacks of September 11.

The violence of September 11 was the most destructive but not the first terrorist attack on American personnel and interests. A bomb placed in the WTC garage in 1993 caused only limited damage but killed six people. American embassies and military resources were attacked in Saudi Arabia, Kenya, Tanzania, and Yemen. Attempting to prevent further attacks by diplomacy, covert operations, and military force could become a long-term priority for the nation. These efforts will be influenced by the way in which the United States perceives and is perceived by people who hold radically different views of life. Few of the numerous commentators could offer credible insights into the minds of terrorist leaders, their beliefs, and grievances. There was also little evidence that terrorists understood the American experience and perspective on life. Whether the gap in mutual understanding will be reduced or increased is likely to have a profound impact on terrorist and counter-terrorist activities in the future.

On the personal level it remains to be seen if American life will continue with resilience along its traditional path, shift into a more cautious and security-conscious pattern, or cultivate a broader and deeper sense of the human condition in all its mortal vulnerability and seldom-realized potential.

See also: DEATH CERTIFICATE; GRIEF: TRAUMATIC; GRIEF COUNSELING AND THERAPY; TERRORISM

Bibliography

Alexander, Yonah, and Michael S. Swetnam. *Usama bin Laden's al-Qaida: Profile of a Terrorist Network.* Ardsley, NY: Transnational Publishers, 2001.

Bergen, Peter. *Holy War, Inc.* New York: The Free Press, 2001.

Boyd, Jim, ed. *September 11, a Testimony.* New York: Reuters, 2002.

Dvorak, Petula. "New Crime Category May Cover Sept. 11." *Washington Post,* 22 December 2001, A02–03.

Fox, James Alan, and Jack Levin. *The Will to Kill.* Boston: Allyn & Bacon, 2001.

Goodson, Larry P. *Afghanistan's Endless War.* Seattle: University of Washington Press, 2001.

Magnum Photographers. *New York September 11.* New York: Powerhouse Books, 2002.

Miller, Judith. *God Has Ninety-Nine Names: Reporting from a Militant Middle East.* New York: Simon & Schuster, 1996.

Roy, Olivier. *Afghanistan: From Holy War to Civil War.* Princeton, NJ: Princeton University Press, 1995.

Salmon, Jacqueline L., and Lena H. Sun. "Victims at Risk Again." *Washington Post,* 19 December 2001, A01–02.

Vedantam, Shankar. "Legends of the Fall: Sept. 11 Myths Abound." *Washington Post,* 4 January 2002, A03–04

ROBERT KASTENBAUM

TERROR MANAGEMENT THEORY

While self-preservation is common to all species, the awareness of one's own mortality characterizes only human beings. This awareness presents a difficult problem for humans: how to manage the terror that accompanies this type of knowledge. According to proponents of terror management theory (TMT) the need for "terror management" is indeed a fundamental motivation of people as well as a main function of cultural systems. Building on the anthropologist Ernest Becker's writings, TMT explains a large variety of human behaviors, such as intolerance vis-à-vis others, by relating these behaviors to the basic motivation to protect oneself against mortality awareness.

Formulations

Terror management theory was developed by the researchers Jeff Greenberg, Sheldon Solomon, and Tom Pyszczynski based on Ernest Becker's writings, in which the universality of death terror and the need to protect against it play an essential role. Psychologically, the protective function is accomplished via a cultural anxiety buffer that has two components. One component consists of the individual's conception of the cultural worldview and the faith one has in this worldview. The second component involves a sense of personal worth or self-esteem that is attained by believing that one is living up to the cultural system's standards of values.

The need for defense is particularly high when one is reminded of his or her mortality (mortality salience is increased) and when one's cultural system is threatened. In those cases one can expect negative reactions against those who are considered to embody the threat, such as individuals who belong to a different group, known as "outgroupers," and positive reactions toward those who represent the cultural values, typically "ingroupers." This implication of TMT was labeled the mortality salience hypothesis. A second implication, the anxiety-buffer hypothesis, states that strengthening the anxiety-buffer, for example boosting a person's self-esteem, should reduce this person's death anxiety.

Experimental Work

Numerous studies have provided supportive evidence for the mortality salience hypothesis. Reminding people of their own mortality was shown to increase their inclination to respond favorably to people who bolster their worldviews and to respond negatively to people who are different from them—an effect that was found in adults and also in children as young as age eleven. In these various studies death salience was achieved in a variety of ways, by asking people to imagine their own death, filling out death anxiety scales, or having them visit a funeral home or watch a fatal car accident. Negative stimuli included violators of moral principles, such as prostitutes, out-groupers such as Jews and anti-American foreigners, or inappropriate use of cherished cultural symbols such as a flag or a crucifix. Generally, reminding people of their own mortality made them less tolerant vis-à-vis those stimuli. Liberally oriented respondents, however, became more tolerant toward a conservative target after being reminded of their own mortality. This apparent exception can be explained, however, based on the fact that tolerance is an important value for liberal individuals. They will tend, therefore, to emphasize this value more when death becomes more salient for them.

The work conducted as of 2002 on the anxiety-buffer hypothesis also supported TMT. In 1993, for example, the scholar Jeff Greenberg and colleagues found that positive personality feedback made people less inclined to deny the possibility that they may have a relatively short life expectancy.

Criticisms and Extensions of Terror Management Theory

Terror management theory was criticized for a variety of reasons. Experimental findings, such as increased intolerance toward out-groupers following reminders of death, can be explained using alternative theories. Thus the scholar C. R. Snyder suggests an interpretation based on the motivation to achieve control. Other criticisms were directed at the scope of TMT and at its claim to represent a general theory of motivation that provides an overarching explanation to a multitude of social motives. It was argued that either those human motives are not hierarchically arranged or that the hierarchy is not the one proposed by TMT—with terror management at the top. Even more drastically, some contended that death anxiety plays usually only a minor role in individual's behavior in everyday life.

An area of particular difficulty for TMT is the area of death anxiety in older age. Older adults appear to accept death more than younger adults, the opposite of what would be expected on the basis of considerations of death salience. Moreover, self-esteem may decline with increased age and, as a result, the use of it as a protective buffer may become more difficult. There is a need, therefore, to specify other protective mechanisms such as self-transcendence.

In addition, human creativity, growth, and genuine acceptance of death cannot be explained easily by TMT. For this reason TMT theorists have recently proposed a theory of growth that should complement TMT. The individual is striving not only to protect oneself against the terror associated with death awareness but, in addition, to develop and expand. Between the two motivations, to grow and to protect, there is a dynamic balance. Growth is also likely to engender awareness of one's limitations and, therefore, to make one more susceptible to death terror. On the other hand, the same growth, via creation of meaning, provides the means to deal with the terror.

Practical Implications and Evaluation

TMT connects fear of death to behaviors that appear to be conceptually very distant from death and dying, for example to prejudice and intolerance toward strangers. By doing this, the theory provides a useful tool for self-understanding. A good understanding of both the importance of death anxiety as a main motivation, and of the ways to protect against it, can allow one to achieve a double goal: defense against anxiety but not at the price of becoming intolerant toward others. From a theoretical viewpoint, it seems that TMT had to moderate somewhat its claims of being the fundamental theory of social motivation. This has been done both by recognizing the need to invoke other (expansive) motives, and by recognizing that mechanisms other than the one incorporated in the anxiety buffer may be used in dealing with one's awareness of mortality. Terror management theory can be viewed as a way to explain how the construction of meaning achieved by individuals within a culture fulfills the double function of protecting against fear of death and allowing, at the same time, creative expansion and development.

See also: ANXIETY AND FEAR; BECKER, ERNEST

Bibliography

Becker, Ernest. *The Denial of Death*. New York: Free Press, 1973.

Florian, Victor, and Mario Mikulincer. "Terror Management Theory in Childhood: Does Death Conceptualization Moderate the Effects of Mortality Salience on Acceptance of Similar and Different Others?" *Personality and Social Psychology Bulletin* 24 (1998):1104–1112.

Greenberg, Jeff, Tom Pyszczynski, and Sheldon Solomon. "Evidence of a Terror Management Function of Cultural Icons: The Effects of Mortality Salience on the Inappropriate Use of Cherished Cultural Symbols." *Personality and Social Psychology Bulletin* 21 (1995):1221–1228.

Greenberg, Jeff, Tom Pyszczynski, and Sheldon Solomon. "The Causes and Consequences of a Need for Self-Esteem: A Terror Management Theory." In Roy F. Baumeister ed., *Public Self and Private Self.* New York: Springer-Verlag, 1986.

Greenberg, Jeff, et al. "Towards a Dual Motive Depth Psychology of Self and Social Behavior." In Michael Kernis ed., *Self-Efficacy and Self-Regulation*. New York: Plenum, 1995.

Greenberg, Jeff, et al. "Effects of Self-Esteem on Vulnerability-Denying Defensive Distortions: Further Evidence of an Anxiety-Buffering Function of Self-Esteem." *Journal of Experimental Social Psychology* 29 (1993):229–251.

Greenberg, Jeff, et al. "Terror Management and Tolerance: Does Mortality Salience Always Intensify Negative Reactions to Others Who Threaten One's Worldview?" *Journal of Personality and Social Psychology* 63 (1992):212–220.

Greenberg, Jeff, et al. "Evidence for Terror Management Theory II: The Effects of Mortality Salience on Reactions to Those Who Threaten or Bolster the Cultural Worldview." *Journal of Personality and Social Psychology* 58 (1990):308–318.

McCoy, Shannon K., et al. "Transcending the Self: A Terror Management Perspective on Successful Aging." In Adrian Tomer ed., *Death Attitudes and the Older Adult.* Philadelphia: Taylor & Francis, 2000.

Muraven, Mark, and Roy F. Baumeister. "Suicide, Sex, Terror, Paralysis, and Other Pitfalls of Reductionist Self-Preservation Theory." *Psychological Inquiry* 8 (1997):36–40.

Pelham, Brett W. "Human Motivation Has Multiple Roots." *Psychological Inquiry* 8 (1997):44–47.

Pyszczynski, Tom, Jeff Greenberg, and Sheldon Solomon. "Why Do We Need What We Need? A Terror Management Perspective on the Roots of Human Social Motivation." *Psychological Inquiry* 8 (1997):1–20.

Rosenblatt, Abram, et al. "Evidence for Terror Management Theory I: The Effects of Mortality Salience on Reactions to Those Who Violate or Uphold Cultural Values." *Journal of Personality and Social Psychology* 57 (1989):681–690.

Snyder, C. R. "Control and Application of Occam's Razor to Terror Management Theory." *Psychological Inquiry* 8 (1997):48–49.

ADRIAN TOMER

THANATOLOGY

Thanatology is the study of dying, death, and grief. This study encompasses thoughts, feelings, attitudes, and events. Contributors to the growing knowledge of death-related phenomena include social, behavioral, and biomedical researchers as well as economists, health-care providers, historians, literary critics, philosophers, and theologians.

The word *thanatology* is derived from Greek mythology. Thanatos (death) and Hypnos (sleep) were twin deities. It was not until 1903 that distinguished scientist Elie Metchnikoff called for the establishment of a scientific discipline devoted to the study of death. He suggested that the life sciences would not be complete unless systematic attention was also given to death. Nevertheless, only a few scholars and educators followed his lead. Medical students had their obligatory encounters with cadavers but received almost no instruction in care for the dying, nor was death included in the curriculum for students of other professions and sciences.

The situation started to change following World War II, with its many casualties and haunted memories. Existential philosophers redirected attention to life-and-death issues. Researchers such as Herman Feifel challenged Western society's taboo on death, opening the way for improved communication. An international suicide-prevention effort responded to the anguish both of people contemplating self-destruction and their family and friends. The hospice movement introduced improved means of caring for dying people, and grief-support groups provided comfort to many who had been alone in their distress. Death education overcame early resistance to become a significant resource in both formal and informal settings. Thantological challenges in the twenty-first century include the emerging issues of physician-assisted death, children's rights, and lifestyle behaviors such as excessive drinking, use of tobacco products, and unsafe operation of motor vehicles that contribute to more than a million deaths a year in the United States.

See also: Anthropological Perspective; Cadaver Experiences; Children and Their Rights in Life and Death Situations; Death Education; Feifel, Herman; Hospice Option; Psychology; Saunders, Cicely; Suicide Types: Physician-Assisted Suicide

Bibliography

Feifel, Herman. *The Meaning of Death.* New York: McGraw-Hill, 1959.

McGinnis, J. M., and W. H. Foege. "Actual Causes of Death in the United States." *Journal of the American Medical Associations* 270 (1993):2207-2212.

Metchnikoff, Elie. *The Nature of Man.* New York: G. P. Putnam and Sons, 1959.

ROBERT KASTENBAUM

THANATOMIMESIS

Thanatomimesis is the simulation of death by a living creature. Perhaps the best-known example is "playing possum." Hunters and campers have observed that opossums sometimes feign death when threatened. This is accomplished by collapsing into a ball of inert fur. The head droops, the mouth hangs open and—most convincingly—the eyes are fixed in an empty stare. The most obvious explanation is self-protection: if a creature is already dead, why kill it? There is indirect support for this proposition from laboratory research in which opossums were shaken by an artificial dog jaw. The animals immediately took to shamming death, but their brain activity indicated a keen state of alertness, waiting for the danger to pass. At least some animals are capable of switching to a state of tonic immobility that contributes much to the appearance of death.

There has not been systematic research on thanatomimesis, but Charles Darwin observed thanatomimetic behavior in "seventeen different kinds of inspects belonging to different genres, both poor and first-rate shammers" (Carrington and Meader 1911, p. 51). Darwin compared these acts with the postures taken when either his subjects or others of their species were actually dead. He concluded, "the attitudes of the feigners and of the really dead were as unlike as they could possibly be" (Carrington and Meader 1911, p. 51).

Thanatomimesis has saved the lives of many people who escaped death on the battlefield or in other dangerous situations by pretending to be dead. The term itself is usually reserved for intentional efforts to escape harm. However, comatose or hypothermic people have also been misperceived as dead, especially prior to the development of improved methods of detecting physiological activity.

See also: Buried Alive; Cryonic Suspension; Definitions of Death

Bibliography

Carrington, Hereford, and James R. Meader. *Death: Its Causes and Phenomena.* London: Rider, 1911.

Kastenbaum, Robert, and Ruth Aisenberg. *The Psychology of Death.* New York: Springer, 1972.

Norton, Alan C., Arnold V. Beran, and George A. Misrahy. "Playing Possum in the Laboratory." *Scientific American* 211 (1964):64.

ROBERT KASTENBAUM

THANATOS

See Death Instinct; Gods and Goddesses of Life and Death.

THEATER AND DRAMA

It is no surprise that dramatists throughout history have drawn such creative inspiration from the subject of death and dying. Because of the difficulty of confronting this topic on a personal level, death as portrayed on the stage remains a powerful magnet for theater audiences. Aesthetic theory suggests that art is a major tool in humanity's quest for self-understanding. Humankind's perennial preoccupation with its mortality and identification with the characters who are metaphorically standing in for us in this once-removed space of the stage allow for the collective exploration of this most difficult of subjects.

The pop musical Rent *(1996) used the musical-theater version of* La Bohème *as its backbone, with similar themes of the AIDS epidemic, and artists, prostitutes, and homosexual characters living in New York's East Village. Sadly, Jonathan Larson,* Rent*'s creator, died of an aneurysm between the dress rehearsal and opening night.* ROBBIE JACK/CORBIS

Since Aristotle, the motif of death has permeated drama. The life and death of the hero of Greek drama was inextricably bound up with his or her sense of honor. This concept of dying for one's honor was carried through the Renaissance, particularly in Spain. In early medieval drama, liturgical plays ritualized death and dying with elaborate sets that depicted versions of the afterlife and the fires of hell. In these dramas, death was often seen as the great equalizer. In Greek and Elizabethan tragedies, the tragic flaw leading to the eventual demise of the hero was eagerly anticipated by audiences. There were the murders in *Oresteia* or *Oedipus,* and violent clashes in all of William Shakespeare's history plays.

In modern theater, there has often been a psychological as well as a real violence explored in dramatic literature. To Antonin Artaud, for instance, desire and death were a form of cruelty. His play *The Cenci* is about a girl who murdered her father to avenge her rape by him. Hélène Cixous claimed that "with even more violence than fiction, theater, which is built according to the dictates of male fantasy, repeats and intensifies the horror of the murder scene which is at the origin of all cultural productions" (1969, p.133). Modern drama has undoubtedly sustained this fascination with representations of death and dying on stage, where it exploits the components of both narrative and symbol.

Some scholars have suggested that death depicted on the modern stage was an attempt to transcend the fear of death and deny its finality by experiencing it fully or empathetically in the safety of the once-removed. The symbolic death in the theater acts as a double of our real lives and thus provides a cathartic experience. Even in some modern theatrical styles that seek to distance the audience from conventional identification with characters, there may be, nonetheless, a purgative experience for audiences. The plays and productions of Bertolt Brecht, for example, attempted to distance the audience from the narrative to enable viewers to maintain a critical perspective on the action on stage. But even in these distancing traditions, the audience is, in the end, at a sufficiently safe distance from the fiction of the play so that their actual lives triumph over the compressed and finite fiction of the stage. There may, therefore, still be a symbolic immortality possible through the semiotics of the stage.

Some suggest that the representations of death on stage offer one a kind of practice for one's own death, while others hold that the persistent theme of death on stage is a form of denial or avoidance. In her study of seventeenth-century drama, theater scholar Deborah Dogherty found that heroic characters enabled audiences to envision their own quest for immortality. Dramas of the Golden Age often involved a quest to overcome death a means of symbolic immortality, even if physical death was not overcome. This theatric development appears to be predicated upon Plato's insistence on a system of immortality wherein the soul exists before the body is born and is not, therefore, subject to death. Dogherty concludes, "As characters lived out their brief dramatic roles, the audience was reminded of the brevity of each individual's appearance in the ongoing drama of life, yet envisioned their own lives as somehow eternal" (1999, p. 2). In modern times, too, the conception of the immutability of the soul has persisted.

Although a character's death in theater may leave a void in the world, that absence is sometimes represented by a presence on stage. Since the ghost of Hamlet's father appeared to him, many plays have represented death with such ghostly apparitions. Isobel, in Judith Thompson's *Lion in the Streets* (1992), appears throughout the play and is visible to the audience although she is often invisible to other characters on stage. Raped and murdered before the story of the play begins, the prepubescent Isobel finally understands that she has died and become a ghost.

Even in children's theater, the convention of the ghostly apparition is common. Stage adaptations of Dickens's *A Christmas Carol* have featured characters from traditional white, ethereal garments to vaporous projections on a scrim. *Ghost Train,* written by Betty Quan and based on the book by Paul Yee, recognizes the hundreds of Chinese workers who died building the Canadian Pacific Railway; the play presents a fourteen-year-old peasant girl who gives an account of her own father's death. After the father is killed, he returns to his daughter Choon-Yi as a ghost. Theatrically, the father is realized by a shadow/silhouette projected onto the scrim upstage:

> CHOON-YI: What magic is this?
> FATHER: The magic is yours.
> CHOON-YI: (*running forward*) It is you!
> FATHER *holds his hands up, shakes his head, stopping* CHOON-YI.
> FATHER: No. You mustn't come closer.
> CHOON-YI: What is it? Are you ill? Where have you been? I searched all over Salt Lake City, looking for you.
> FATHER: I have left your world. I am no longer flesh and blood, but spirit.
> CHOON-YI: No. It can't be. Nooooo.
> *(2000, p. 38)*

Disease and dying have also become topics of contemporary theater, given the pandemic of modern diseases such as AIDS and cancer. Tony Kushner's *Angels in America* is one example of the terror of AIDS realized theatrically. Margaret Edson's award-winning *Wit* explores the complex of emotions yielded by a diagnosis of inoperable cancer. In this play, Vivian Bearing's journey is a redemptive one. Her experience of cancer and death leads her, paradoxically, to the light.

War and death in drama remain intricately entwined as well. Brecht's *Mother Courage and Her Children* is an example of life imitating art. This play about a canteen-woman serving with the Swedish Army during the Thirty Years' War (1618–1648) was written in 1939 but was not performed until 1949 because of Nazi suppression and thus came too late to serve as the warning Brecht had intended: In the course of the play, Mother Courage witnesses the deaths of all three of her children. Howard Barker's play *The Europeans,* another example of a war drama, is set in the aftermath of the climactic struggle between Christianity and Islam in the seventeenth century.

Many contemporary playwrights have explored the great massacres of the twentieth century. John McGrath's *Events While Guarding the Bofors Gun* concludes with a scene that has a soldier, caught in the futility of war, falling upon his own rifle and bayonet. John Murrell's *Waiting for the Parade* explores the lives of five women who attempt to survive World War II at home. Death is omnipresent.

Drama critic Martin Esslin asserts that drama has become one of the principal vehicles of information, one of the prevailing methods of thinking about life and its quandaries. He maintains that drama is a mirror of real life: "The theater is a simulacrum—at its highest level, ordered and elevated to the status of art—of the real world and real life" (1987, p. 176). If, as Esslin believes, humans crave the collective artistic experience that theater can provide, these works also compel one to face the inescapable certainty of his or her own mortality. Paradoxically, of course, theater also reminds people of their great potential as living, sentient beings.

See also: GREEK TRAGEDY; OPERATIC DEATH; SHAKESPEARE, WILLIAM

Bibliography

Artaud, Antonin. *The Cenci,* translated by Simon Watson-Taylor. London: Calder & Boyars, 1969.

Barker, Howard. "The Europeans." *Collected Plays,* Vol. 3. London: Calder Publications, 1996.

Brecht, Bertolt. *Mother Courage and Her Children,* translated by Stefan F. Brecht. London: Eyre Methuen, 1980.

Cixous, Helene. "Aller a la Mer." In Richard Drain ed., *Twentieth Century Theater: A Sourcebook.* London: Routledge, 1995.

Dogherty, Deborah. *Heroes: Death Denied in Selected Dramas of the Golden Age.* New Orleans: University Press of the South, 1999.

Edson, Margaret. *Wit: A Play.* New York: Faber and Faber, 1999.

Esslin, Martin. *The Field of Drama: How the Signs of Drama Create Meaning on Stage and Screen.* London: Methuen, 1987.

Kushner, Tony. *Angels in America: A Gay Fantasia on National Themes.* New York: Theater Communications Group, 1993.

McGrath, John. *Events While Guarding the Bofors Gun.* London: Methuen and Co., 1966.

Murrell, John. *Waiting for the Parade.* Vancouver, BC: Talonbooks, 1980.

Paller, Michael. *A Christmas Carol: Based on the Book by Charles Dickens.* New York: Samuel French, 1980.

Quan, Betty. *Ghost Train.* Toronto: Groundwood Books, 2000.

Thompson, Judith. *Lion in the Streets.* Toronto: Coach House Press, 1992.

KATHLEEN GALLAGHER

THEODOSIAN CODE

In 438 C.E. the Roman emperor Theodosius II (408–450 C.E.) published, in a single volume (*codex* in Latin), the general laws of his Christian predecessors beginning with Constantine I (306–337 C.E.). Roman law had always regulated the transfer of wealth from one generation to the next. The Theodosian Code reveals that, during the era when the empire was becoming Christian, emperors sought a greater share of that wealth for themselves and for the imperial Church through the control of wills and testaments. The law had also always punished violation of the tombs that lined the roads outside the city walls. The code's increasingly severe penalties for doing so suggest that the problem was getting worse. People were looting tombs for building materials and for marble to render into lime; and were digging up the bones of Christian martyrs. In 386 an imperial decree expressly prohibited the sale of these saints' relics.

Relics of the saints were a powerful symbol of Christian triumph over death. Their incorporation into urban churches first bridged the ancient borders between the cities of the living and the dead. In a similar way, the saints, who were present in their relics, bridged the communities of the living and the dead. Competition for their patronage at both earthly and heavenly courts created a market for their remains. The code's failure to restrict the cult of relics shows how helpless civil law could be against devotional practices supported by the populace and the Church.

See also: CHRISTIAN DEATH RITES, HISTORY OF

Bibliography

Harries, Jill. "Death and the Dead in the Late Roman West." In Steven Bassett ed., *Death in Towns: Urban Responses to the Dying and the Dead.* Leicester, England: Leicester University Press, 1992.

Harries, Jill, and Ian Wood, eds. *The Theodosian Code.* Ithaca, NY: Cornell University Press, 1993.

Pharr, Clyde, trans. *The Theodosian Code and Novels and the Sirmondian Constitutions*. Princeton, NJ: Princeton University Press, 1952.

FREDERICK S. PAXTON

THOU SHALT NOT KILL

The phrase "Thou shalt not kill" is well known throughout the world as one of the Ten Commandments. Originating in the Books of Exodus and Deuteronomy, this phrase was originally given to Moses and the Israelite people by God as one of the great commandments and is found in the holy scriptures of Jews, Christians, and Muslims. Seen as an admonition against murder, the sixth commandment often forms the philosophical foundation for arguments against suicide, capital punishment, abortion, euthanasia, war, and any other situation where one person might be inclined to take the life of another.

Translation of the Phrase

Traditional translations of this phrase into English have tended to use the word *kill*. Certain scholars have suggested that this is not the most accurate translation. The key phrase, often translated "to kill" (*rasah*), began in the twentieth century to be translated "Thou shalt not murder," is seen in newer translations of the Bible such as the New Revised Standard Version. The scholar Terence Fretheim notes, "In view of certain passages (e.g., 1 Kings 21:19) it has been suggested that the verb means murder" (1991, p. 232). He goes on to note that this phrase can refer to unintentional killing (Deut. 4:41–42) or the execution of a convicted murderer (Num. 35:30). A growing number of scholars now agree that this term for killing in Hebrew that is used in the Ten Commandments is never used in Hebrew Scripture to refer to the type of killing that takes place in a war.

Hebrew language scholars agree that killing in war is different and not covered by this use of the phrase "to kill." If one soldier is angry with another from his or her same army and shoots him or her, even in a battle, it would still be murder. However, to kill an enemy in the context of a "just" war is not directly covered in this passage. A majority of the world's religious traditions make this distinction, referring to "holy war" or "Jihad" as being acceptable. There are generally some criteria for this type of "just" war that, depending on the world tradition, generally reflects doing the work of God and/or serving the needs of justice in the world order. Historically this commandment is used as the foundation for an argument against going to war, by persons wishing not to serve in such a human conflict. However, to argue this point biblically requires other passages to support the argument.

The Ten Commandments were given to offer order in social relationships due to the understanding that, at the heart of all relationships, love is the model that is to be held up as ideal. Whether discussing God's love, or the love of Jesus Christ for Christians, God and God's prophets are the ideal of this message of love in the various faith traditions. Thus the various traditions understand Abraham, Jesus, and Mohammad, along with other key figures, as this type of model. Further, world religious traditions in general pray for world peace. The values of all three communities reflect the possibility of a world that is free of war and armed conflict. Finally, in each tradition there is a wide variance among interpreters of the various traditions as to what that criterion is. This is as true of Islam as it is of Christianity and Judaism. The complete criteria for a "holy" or "just war" are beyond the scope of what can be written in a book.

John Calvin, the Protestant reformer of the sixteenth century, summarized the meaning of this commandment by saying "that we should not unjustly do violence to anyone." The Book of Numbers clarifies that which constitutes murder as stabbing or hurting another in anger or enmity, or killing another person for personal gain. The primary foundation of this commandment, according to Calvin, reflects the understanding that "undoubtedly God would have the remains of His image, which still shines forth in men, to continue in some estimation, so that all might feel that every homicide is an offence against Him" (Calvin 1993, p. 20).

An Assault against God

The prohibition against murder should be understood in the context that in some way human beings were made in the image of God. Therefore to murder a person is to murder God. There are a variety of ways to explain this from the world traditions. God created the heavens and the earth. In doing so, God created humanity in God's image. Some Jewish and Christian scholars understand that with the Fall of Adam, or original sin, humanity was separated from God, yet something of God's image remains in each person. Some Islamic scholars suggest that the "essential sin is that of forgetfulness of God" (Renard 1998, p. 49). It is sin that separates human beings from the essential nature of humanity that is in the image of God.

To murder a fellow human being is to attack God. The implication is that it is a sin to assault God by killing any person. As such, the person will be judged accordingly by God. A more positive way to state the way human beings are to relate to one another comes from Matthew 7:12: "In everything do to others as you would have them do to you; for this is the law and the prophets." This is stated in Hebrew Scripture as Leviticus 19:18: "You shall not take vengeance or bear a grudge against any of your people, but you shall love your neighbor as yourself: I am the LORD." Muhammad said the same thing when he noted, "None among you is a believer until he wishes for his brothers and sisters what he wishes for himself" (Renard 1998, p. 49). Laws that are made by human beings do not offer the same type of universal agreement or sanctions if violated. For example, if human beings have created the law "Thou shalt not murder," then one should remember that in "Nazi Germany, and much of eastern Europe, it was acceptable to kill Jews, gypsies, homosexuals, the severely retarded, and any other group deemed inferior" (Renard 1998, p. 176). Laws made by human beings have sanctions that are of this world. Laws made by God have eternal sanctions. Believers find this latter prospect sufficient to serve as a deterrent to murder.

Not only is the person who commits murder subject to judgment by God, but, according to Hebrew Scripture, he or she is subject to judgment by human courts. Based on the first covenant between God and humanity with Noah, Noah suggests in Genesis 9:6: "Whoever sheds the blood of a human, by a human shall that person's blood be shed; for in his own image God made humankind." This admonition is made clear in the story of Cain and Abel when God says, "And the LORD said, 'What have you done? Listen; your brother's blood is crying out to me from the ground! And now you are cursed from the ground, which has opened its mouth to receive your brother's blood from your hand'" (Gen. 4:10–11). In response to this first murder, God curses the very ground.

Capital Punishment, Suicide, and Abortion

Jewish and Christian teaching is mixed on the application of these Hebrew scriptures. "For example Jewish law and tradition maintain that the death sentence in a capital case is prohibited if the conviction is on the basis of a strong presumption or circumstantial evidence, even though it appears conclusive" (Schlessinger and Vogel 1998, p. 180). Other persons of faith suggest that the termination of life by the state is the same as any other murder. Capital punishment can be said to be sanctioned by Hebrew Scripture, but these passages alone are not followed without question by all believers. This is particularly true of Roman Catholicism, which is generally against capital punishment. A significant issue for those against capital punishment is the fear that the innocent will pay this ultimate price. Clearly the problem is that capital punishment is employed by human beings who make mistakes. "The Midrash, a compilation of ancient rabbinic reflections, summed up the problem very concisely: Those who are merciful when they must be cruel, will, in the end, be cruel to those who deserve mercy" (Schlessinger and Vogel 1998, p. 182).

Suicide, or the murder of one's self, is the next common application of the commandment. It is understood that God has placed the soul within an earthen vessel that needs to be taken care of. This would suggest that the human body does not simply belong to the person, but rather that the soul which houses the body belongs to God. Catholicism prohibits any kind of mutilation of the body. In Judaism even tattoos that permanently alter the body are prohibited. It has been widely known that until recently Roman Catholics had the lowest incidence of suicide, based on the admonition not to commit such an act.

Abortion is possibly the most controversial of the ramifications of "Thou shalt not murder." Both those who are pro-life and pro-choice would agree that it is murder to take a life. However, the heart of the dialogue is the controversy as to when life begins. On this point the Bible is unclear. Ammunition for this dialogue, however, comes from the Book of Exodus: "When people who are fighting injure a pregnant woman so that there is a miscarriage, and yet no further harm follows, the one responsible shall be fined what the woman's husband demands, paying as much as the judges determine. If any harm follows, then you shall give life for life, eye for eye, tooth for tooth, hand for hand, foot for foot, burn for burn, wound for wound, stripe for stripe" (Exod. 21:22–25). The scholars Laura Schlessinger and Stewart Vogel note that the heart of the controversy is found in the implication as to who is hurt by the injury to the woman. In Judaism it is understood that this refers to the woman, while Christian interpretation often understands this to refer to the fetus. If it refers to the fetus, then the scripture suggests that any abortion is murder. If it refers to the woman, then it is less clear as to the abortion issue. Most arguments on this issue go on to discussion of the love of God for children. In Islam, "According to some religious scholars of the Hanafi legal school, abortion is permitted until the fetus is fully formed and ensoulment has occurred (about four months along, according to a Hadith)" (Renard 1998, p. 56).

The Ten Commandments have offered a set of rules that traditionally offer order to society. This order can become divisive when placed in public schools and buildings when it implies that the values of these religious traditions should be followed by all. The U.S. Constitution does not say that individuals cannot believe these rules in private, but it does say that the values and beliefs of one tradition should not be forced on all people through the First Amendment, which guarantees freedom of speech and freedom of religion. The sixth commandment offers a point of departure for ethical dialogue for all of those religions of Abraham. It is generally not taken out of context, but rather employed in the context of the entire scripture. As a part of the entire context of the messages as interpreted by Jews, Muslims, and Christians, the sixth commandment is an important rule for living.

See also: ABORTION; CAPITAL PUNISHMENT; HOMICIDE, DEFINITIONS AND CLASSIFICATIONS OF; MARTYRS; SUICIDE BASICS: HISTORY

Bibliography

Calvin, John. *Commentaries on The Four Last Books of Moses Arranged in the Form of a Harmony.* 1843. Reprint, Grand Rapids, MI: Baker Book House, 1993.

Fretheim, Terence E. *Exodus: Interpretation: A Bible Commentary for Teaching and Preaching.* Louisville, KY: John Knox Press, 1991.

National Council of Churches of Christ in the U.S.A. *The New Revised Standard Version of the Bible.* New York: Author, 1990.

Renard, John. *Responses to 101 Questions on Islam.* Mahwah, NJ: Paulist Press, 1998.

Schlessinger, Laura, and Stewart Vogel. *The Ten Commandments: The Significance of God's Laws in Everyday Life.* New York: Cliff Street, 1998.

JAMES W. ELLOR

THRILL-SEEKING

Americans dangle from hang gliders and parachutes; they race their cars, powerboats, snowmobiles, and dirt bikes; they stand on their hands upon skateboards, climb rocks without safety ropes, and pay to bungee-jump off towers. Less adventurous "adrenaline junkies" ride roller coasters with lethal-sounding names like Roaring Lightning or Big Death.

Why, despite the well-publicized lethality of such recreational risk-taking, do people continue to engage in such behaviors? Is there perhaps some need to flirt with death in order to feel "alive"? Scholars have discerned a blend of physiological, psychological, social psychological, and cultural causes.

Three-quarters of adolescent deaths are caused by accidents, homicide, and suicide, indicating a propensity for lethal risk-taking. Accidents alone account for 60 percent of this total. Though most recognize adolescence as a developmental period when risk-taking is a common form of testing one's identity and abilities, such behaviors need not be life threatening. As accidental deaths became the leading cause of death in this age group (which was the only one in which mortality had increased since 1960), in 1987 the federal government and various foundations financed research to study the reasons for the reckless behavior.

Psychological paradigms predominated, with explanations focusing on adolescents' lesser ability to evaluate risk and a life cycle, developmental need for excitement that blunts comprehension of

Experts have found that risk-taking, like bungee-jumping, can be linked to two types of mutant genes. Other theorists say that thrill-seeking is related to a person's quest for immortality. ROBERT HOLMES/CORBIS

risk. In addition, as suicide rates nearly tripled from the mid-1960s to the mid-1980s among boys and girls age ten to fourteen, and doubled among those fifteen to nineteen, suspicions arose that a portion of lethal accidents might actually be "subintentioned suicides." Similarly, increases in teenage smoking rates throughout much of the 1990s has coincided with teens' increasing suicide rates, particularly among blacks.

Analysts also noted the role of sensation- or thrill-seeking personality types. Even in adulthood, such risk-takers are more prone to high-risk undertakings like parachuting from planes, risky business deals, substance abuse, or even criminal activity. Such risky business might have a biological underpinning. A 1998 UCLA study reported the discovery of two types of mutant genes underlying compulsive novelty-seeking behaviors. The researchers claimed that 30 percent of the population is born with one of the thrill-seeking genes, and 20 percent with both. In addition, the neurotransmitter dopamine has been linked to sensation-seeking behavior and, at elevated levels, to drug abuse and schizophrenia. Richard Epstein and his fellow researchers found a link between novelty-seeking and a form of the D4 dopamine receptor gene.

Another psychological thesis is that a portion of such behavior stems from the quest for immortality. World-class athletes and those in the midst of a potentially lethal situation describe the sensation of transcendence while in "the zone," which they describe as a timeless and deathless realm where everything seems to stop and go silent.

Risk-taking is also a means of attracting attention and thus enhancing self-esteem, as when teenage girls were found demonstrating their toughness by having unprotected sex with HIV-infected gang members in San Antonio, Texas. Thrill-seeking behavior has long been a way that young adult males have attempted to win the admiration of their peer groups and to attract members of the opposite sex. War is one traditional social solution for harnessing such drives by putting them into the service of the state.

The argument for a cultural component to thrill-seeking is reinforced by the absence of reports of extreme sports and other thrill-seeking activities in developing nations. For instance, in the late 1990s the world's top-ranked male paragliders were from Austria, Japan, Switzerland, and Italy; the top women were from Denmark, Czech Republic, Japan, Great Britain, Germany, France, and Norway. Perhaps where death is a risk in everyday life, such contrived dangers are superfluous. In the past, society controlled the opportunities for such experiences: for example, in painful and challenging rites of passage and war, and in dangerous occupations as fishing, mining, and logging. Nature did her part with frequent bouts of lethal disease. Like animals in zoos, humans in modern societies do not face the environmental challenges for which they are hardwired.

A study comparing Indian males who had applied for Canadian immigration visas with a matched nonimmigrant group found that sensation-seeking and belief in an unpredictable world were two of the personality types that distinguished the two groups. Given the fact that the United States is basically populated with immigrants (the 2000 Census found 10.4% of the population to be foreign-born) and their descendents, it would seem reasonable to assume that among the developed nations, the United States has a disproportionate share of thrill- or sensation-seeking personality types, as psychologist Frank Farley claims.

Countering such risk-taking appetites has been the trend in modern countries to eradicate risk, such as through seatbelt regulations, Pure Food and Drug Act, bankruptcy laws, and the U.S. Consumer Product Safety Commission. Warning labels abound, with laws requiring their placement on five-gallon buckets (so children will not fall in them and drown) and step-ladders (30% the price of which goes to cover potential liabilities). On the packaging of one brand of electric iron appeared "Do not iron clothes on body"; on a child's Superman costume: "Wearing of this garment does not enable you to fly."

Out of this sanitized and risk-free cultural setting emerged during the end of the century extreme sports, featuring such activities as dirt-jumping on bicycles, sky surfing, inline skating, freestyle motocross (which combines motorcycles and ski-like jumping), ice cycling, snowboarding, and skateboarding on half pipes—reactions against what the extreme skier Kristin Ulmer, in *The Extreme Game,* calls a "scaredy-cat culture." Risk-taking became commodified leisure as the marketplace, seeking to profit from the new norm, generated extreme sports parks, new lines of clothing and footwear, nutritional additives, and televised X-games. The movement was significant enough that in 1999 the United States became the first country to honor extreme sports on its postage stamps.

See also: INJURY MORTALITY; SEX AND DEATH, CONNECTION OF; SUICIDE BASICS: EPIDEMIOLOGY; SUICIDE TYPES: INDIRECT SUICIDE

Bibliography

Cloninger, Robert C., Rolf Adolfsson, and Nenad M. Svrakic. "Mapping Genes for Human Personality." *Nature Genetics* 12, no. 1 (1996).

Farley, Frank. "The Type T Personality." In Lewis P. Lipsett and Leonard L. Mitnick eds., *Self-Regulatory Behavior and Risk Taking: Causes and Consequences.* Norwood, NJ: Ablex Publishers, 1991.

Noble, Ernest, Tulin Z. Ozkaragoz, Terry L. Ritchie, et al. "D-2 and D-4 Dopamine-Receptor Polymorphisms and Personality." *American Journal of Medical Genetics* 81, no. 3 (1998):257–267.

Ponton, Lynn E. *The Romance of Risk: Why Teenagers Do the Things They Do.* New York: Basic Books, 1998.

Wimmer, Dick, ed. *The Extreme Game: An Extreme Sports Anthology.* Short Hills, NJ: Burford Books, 2001.

Winchie, Diana B., and David W. Carment. "Intention to Migrate: A Psychological Analysis." *Journal of Applied Social Psychology* 18 (1988):727–736.

Zuckerman, Marvin. *Behavioral Expression and Biosocial Bases of Sensation Seeking.* New York: Cambridge University Press, 1994.

MICHAEL C. KEARL

TIBETAN BOOK OF THE DEAD

Since its first English translation in 1927, the Tibetan guide to spiritual and mental liberation called the *Bardo Thodol* has been known in the West as the Tibetan *Book of the Dead.* The book has reappeared in several English-language versions since then, some based only loosely on the original. The text has thus lived several lives in English alone, appearing to be reborn time and again before new audiences, often with varying titles and content. Yet these recent lives are part of a much older cycle of rebirths. The original is believed to have been composed in the eighth century C.E. by the great master Padma Sambhava, then hidden away by its author for the salvation of future generations. The text was rediscovered six centuries later by Karma Lingpa, believed by some to be an incarnation of Padma Sambhava himself. Since the fourteenth century C.E. the text has occupied a central place in Tibetan Buddhism, giving birth to a large number of parallel, supplementary, and derivative texts.

W. Y. Evans-Wentz coined the English title for the 1927 edition on the basis of analogies he perceived with the Egyptian funerary text *The Book of Coming Forth By Day,* known in the West as the Egyptian *Book of the Dead.* Both the Tibetan and Egyptian *Books* discuss death and its aftermath. Yet their views of death are sufficiently different from the Judeo-Christian tradition that the English titles are quite misleading.

This is particularly so in the case of the Tibetan *Book of the Dead*. The Tibetan title, *Bardo Thodol,* does not refer to death as such. *Thodol* means "liberation through understanding." *Bardo* means a "between state," an interval or transition between two mental states, whether experienced in life or after death. Hence the work's Tibetan title (which might be translated more literally as *Liberation through Understanding the Between*) alludes to bardo states that may be experienced at any point over the cycle of life, death and rebirth, yet the work itself overtly discusses only the bardo states experienced during death, offering explicit instruction on how to navigate them.

It is difficult to appreciate the significance of the work's overt content without a sense of its larger cultural context. The *Bardo Thodol* presupposes a cosmology of human experience in which existence is viewed as inherently fluid and impermanent, as involving a series of stages, of which death is merely one. The mind or soul continues to live after death, undergoing a series of experiences before rebirth. Human beings are believed to be able to guide themselves through the entire cycle by creating a more focused self-awareness through their powers of concentration, augmented, ideally, by means of meditation. The chief utility of meditation during life, or of the *Bardo Thodol* at the time of dying, lies in making the mind lucid enough to control its own passage over the cycle of life, death, and rebirth. The larger goal of these practices is to seek liberation from the suffering associated with this cycle, both for oneself and for others.

The Bardo States

Six main bardo experiences are distinguished in Tibetan Buddhism: Three are encountered during life and three are encountered after death. A single life span is itself a bardo state, a transitional zone in a larger cycle of rebirths. Dreams are bardo states that occur within the daily round, in the interval between falling asleep and waking; feelings of uncertainty, paranoia, and delusion are sometimes grouped with dreams on a looser interpretation of this second bardo state. A meditative trance is a third type of bardo state, an intermediate zone between ordinary consciousness and enlightened awareness. These are the main bardo states of life.

Death involves bardo states as well. On the Tibetan view, death is not an instantaneous event but a process taking several days, involving a successive dissociation of mind from body, which is manifested in characteristic outward signs. During this process, the conscious mind experiences three main bardo states.

The first of these, called the *Chikai Bardo,* is the experience of the death point, the moment at which the soul loses consciousness of objects and becomes aware only of itself. The experience is described as a vivid formless light emanating from all sides. At this moment, enlightenment lies close at hand, although one's capacity to attain it depends on the extent to which one has achieved lucidity and detachment in one's previous existence. For most individuals the vision of light can only be sustained for a brief interval, after which the soul, caught in desire and delusion, regresses toward lower levels of existence.

In the second state, called the *Chonyid Bardo,* the soul has visions involving a succession of deities: a series of beatific Buddhas in the first seven days, a series of terrifying deities in the next seven. The text describes these visions as projections of the mind's own consciousness, often involving a tension within the mind itself. For example, the dazzling visions of the beatific deities are accompanied by duller visions of other beings that distract from the splendor of the former. To be thus distracted is to give in to anger, terror, pride, egotism, jealousy, and other weaknesses. In contrast, to ignore the minor visions and to embrace the more awe-inspiring deities is to attain spiritual salvation through the very act.

A mind that fails to overcome these weaknesses encounters the darker, more horrific deities of the latter seven days. Many of these visions are merely aspects of the Buddhas encountered in the first seven days, now made terrifying by the mind's own weakness. Liberation is still possible here simply by recognizing these beings for who they are. Yet the act is also more difficult now because terror forces the mind to flee rather than to examine its experiences.

A mind that has failed to free itself by this point enters the *Sidpa Bardo,* the third, most desperate stage. Here the mind faces a host of hallucinations, including visions of pursuit by demons and furies, of being devoured and hacked to pieces. A mind may linger here for many weeks—up to the forty-ninth day after death—depending on the faculties of the particular individual.

These experiences culminate in rebirth in some sentient form. Whether one is reborn as human or animal, or is relegated for a time to one of the many Tibetan hells, or whether one achieves liberation from the entire cycle of life and rebirth, thus attaining Buddahood, depends on one's success in overcoming weakness over the course of the cycle.

Although the *Bardo Thodol* is a guide to the bardo states experienced after death, it can only be read by the living. It may be read in preparation for one's own death, or at the deathbed of another. Because the weaknesses attributed to the dead are all experienced by the living as well, a person learning to traverse the bardo states of death will learn to navigate better the bardo experiences of life as well. In this sense the book is a guide to liberation across the entire cycle of human existence as conceived in Tibetan Buddhism.

See also: DYING, PROCESS OF; EGYPTIAN BOOK OF THE DEAD; MOMENT OF DEATH; STAGE THEORY

Bibliography

Evans-Wentz, W. Y., ed. *The Tibetan Book of the Dead, or The After-Death Experiences on the Bardo Plane, according to Lama Kazi Dawa-Samdup's English Rendering*. 1927. Reprint, Oxford: Oxford University Press, 2000.

Fremantle, Francesca, and Chögyam Trungpa. *The Tibetan Book of the Dead: The Great Liberation Through Hearing in the Bardo, by Guru Rinpoche according to Karma Lingpa*. Berkeley, CA: Shambala Press, 1975.

Lauf, Detlef Ingo. *Secret Doctrines of the Tibetan Books of the Dead*. Boulder, CO: Shambala Press, 1977.

Leary, Timothy, Ralph Metzner, and Richard Alpert. *The Psychedelic Experience: A Manual Based on the Tibetan Book of the Dead*. Secaucus, NJ: The Citadel Press, 1976.

Rabjam, Longchen. *The Practice of Dzogchen,* edited by Harold Talbott and translated by Tulku Thondup. Ithaca, NY: Snow Lion Publications, 1996.

Rinbochay, Lati, and Jeffrey Hopkins. *Death, Intermediate State and Rebirth in Tibetan Buddhism*. Valois, NY: Snow Lion Publications, 1979.

Rinpoche, Sogyal. *The Tibetan Book of the Living and Dying*. San Francisco: Harper, 1992.

Thurman, Robert, tr. *The Tibetan Book of the Dead: Liberation through Understanding in the Between,* with a foreword by the Dalai Lama. New York: Bantam Books, 1994.

ASIF AGHA

TITANIC

When the supposedly unsinkable luxury liner *Titanic* hit an iceberg and sank in April 1912, killing 1,513 people, the disaster altered Western civilization's confidence in the very notion of progress. The *Titanic*'s doom has been exactingly recounted and re-created in countless books and documentaries, a Broadway musical, and three major motion pictures, the last of which, *Titanic* (1997), set records at the box office.

The early-twentieth-century equivalent of a space station or supercomputer, the *Titanic* was a vessel that inspired awe not only for its gargantuan dimensions and lavish accommodations but also for its claimed unsinkability, purportedly guaranteed by a double-bottomed hull with sixteen watertight compartments that would keep the ship afloat even if four were flooded, an unimaginable contingency.

Weighing 53,000 metric tons and measuring 882 1/2 feet long, the *Titanic* was the largest ocean liner of the era, and by far the most extravagant and splendid. It featured a theater, a variety of elegant restaurants, a reading and writing room, a gym, a barbershop, a swimming pool, a miniature golf course, ballrooms, and first-class cabins of unparalleled size and sumptuousness. The *Titanic* promised a dazzling voyage for those who could afford it—the top price for first-class passage was $4,350 (about $50,000 in twenty-first-century dollars). Its superabundance in nearly every particular was marred by one fatal deficiency: It carried lifeboats for only half of the ship's passenger capacity of 2,200.

Thus provisioned, on April 10, 1912, the *Titanic* set out from Southampton, England, on its much-heralded maiden voyage, bound for New York City. The ship's first-class passenger list was a roster of the elite of Anglo-American high society, politics, and industry, including the mining tycoon Benjamin Guggenheim; John Jacob Astor; Major

Archibald Butt; Isidor Straus, the head of Macy's department store, and his wife; Margaret Tobin Brown, the Colorado socialite later lionized as the "Unsinkable Molly Brown"; and the British aristocrats Sir Cosmo and Lady Duff Gordon.

Mindful that the *Titanic*'s management company, the White Star Line, hoped to set a speed record on its first crossing, the ship's captain, Edward J. Smith, maintained a brisk pace, averaging 550 miles per day. Second Officer Charles H. Lightoller reflected the high spirits during the journey in the following diary entry: "Each day, as the voyage went on, everybody's admiration of the ship increased; for the way she behaved, for the total absence of vibration, for her steadiness even with the ever-increasing speed, as she warmed up to her work" (Warren 1960, pp. 279–280).

All throughout the day on Sunday, April 14, the *Titanic* had begun to receive telegraph reports of approaching icebergs. At noon, it received this message: "Greek steamer *Athenai* reports passing icebergs and large quantities of field ice today." At 9:30 p.m. another such warning arrived from the *Mesaba*: "Much heavy pack ice and a great number of large icebergs." That last message was never sent to the bridge because the ship's chief radio operator, Jack Phillips, was overwhelmed with requests for personal messages to be sent on behalf of the ship's passengers.

Nevertheless, Smith had ample warning of the danger that lay ahead, yet he unaccountably failed to reduce the ship's speed or post additional lookouts. At 11:40 P.M., Seaman Frederick Fleet, peering out from his fifty-foot-high perch, noticed a hulking white object in the distance, and the *Titanic* was heading directly toward it. He rang out the warning bell and called the bridge to announce, "Iceberg ahead." Less than a minute later, a mild shudder rippled through the great ship's starboard side as it grazed the side of the ice floe.

The impact was so mild that it did not even rouse some of the sleeping passengers. Lady Duff Gordon recounted the moment in these words: "I was awakened by a long grinding sort of shock. It was not a tremendous crash, but more as though someone had drawn a giant finger all along the side of the boat" (Mowbray 1998, p. 216). Laurence Beesley, a science teacher in second class, portrayed it as "nothing more than what seemed to be an extra heave of the engines . . . no sound of a crash or anything else . . . no jar that felt like one heavy body meeting another" (Warren 1960, p. 27).

The ten-second encounter with the iceberg had left six seemingly slight gashes in the ship's steel hull, but they were sufficient to puncture and flood six watertight compartments and thus sink the fabled vessel. Later metallurgical tests revealed that the ship's steel was overly brittle and thus prone to fracture because of an excess of slag used in its manufacture.

The crew quickly became aware that the ship had, at most, a few hours left and began organizing the evacuation. Initially the first-class passengers greeted the news with bemused incredulity and seemed more concerned with extracting their valuables from the bursar than with leaving the warmth of a luxury liner for a tiny lifeboat adrift in the frigid open sea. When the first lifeboat was lowered at 12:45 A.M., it was less than half full. John Jacob Astor helped his wife into a lifeboat and graciously retreated when he was told that only women and children could enter it. Ida Straus decided that she would not avail herself of the safety of a lifeboat. She said to her husband, "Where you are, Papa, I shall be" (Mowbray 1998, pp. 205–206). She offered her coat to her maid, Ellen Bird, who proceeded to the lifeboat alone.

As the bow of the ship began to slip beneath the water at 1:00 A.M., the urgency of the situation became evident, and the pace of lifeboat launchings quickened accordingly. As that frantic hour wore on, Jack Phillips kept up his stream of SOS messages, adding, "Women and children on boats. Cannot last much longer." Benjamin Guggenheim stood on the deck with his valet, dressed in full evening attire. He told a woman waiting to board a lifeboat, "We've dressed up in our best, and are prepared to go down like gentlemen" (Biel 1996, p. 41).

At 2:20 A.M., the *Titanic*'s boilers exploded; the ship went into a vertical position and then disappeared into the icy waters. As the lifeboats splashed in the desolate darkness, none of the survivors knew if an SOS had been received or if they would ever be rescued. At about 4:00 A.M. the lights of the *Carpathia* appeared on the horizon, and its crew immediately set to work hoisting the 700 survivors from their lifeboats. Of the 2,223 passengers

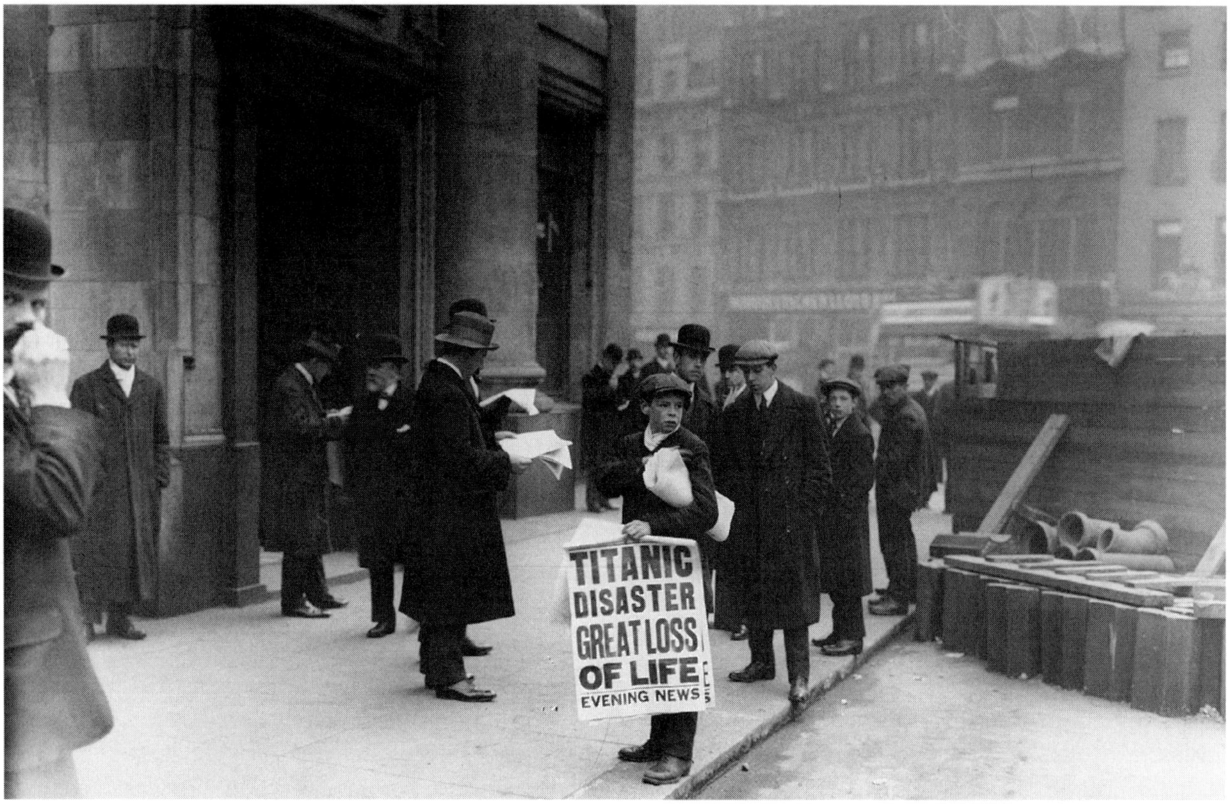

With approximately 1,500 people dead, London tabloids did not hesitate to let its citizens know about the sinking of the luxury liner, as printed in the April 15, 1912, edition of this newspaper. HULTON-DEUTSCH COLLECTION/CORBIS

and crew on board, 1,513 had perished. Many more lives might have been spared if another ship, the *Californian,* only ten miles from the *Titanic* at 11:40, had been alerted. But the *Californian*'s radio operator had shut off his receiver and retired for the night just before the moment of impact.

The inquiry following the disaster noted the insufficiency of lifeboats and the captain's heedlessness in maintaining full speed in the face of repeated iceberg warnings. To prevent another such catastrophe, an International Convention for Safety of Life at Sea was convened in London in 1913 and established binding regulations that included lifeboat space for all passengers; mandatory lifeboat drills; and 24-hour radio watches on all ships.

The wreck of the *Titanic* was found in 1985 and has since been thoroughly examined through the use of unmanned submersible vessels. The grand ship's tragic story has assumed the proportions of legend, most recently in the Hollywood spectacle *Titanic* (1997). The film's worldwide popularity helped to remind a new generation that the most advanced technology is easily humbled by the commanding powers of nature.

See also: DISASTERS; INJURY MORTALITY

Bibliography

Ballard, Robert D. *The Discovery of the* Titanic. New York: Warner Books, 1987.

Biel, Steven. *Down with the Old Canoe: A Cultural History of the* Titanic *Disaster.* New York: W. W. Norton, 1996.

Butler, Daniel Allen. *Unsinkable: The Full Story of the RMS* Titanic. Mechanicsburg, PA: Stackpole Books, 1998.

Eaton, John P. Titanic: *Triumph and Tragedy.* New York: Norton, 1986.

Hyslop, Donald, ed. Titanic *Voices: Memories from the Fateful Voyage.* New York: St. Martin's Press, 1997.

Lord, Walter. *A Night to Remember.* New York: Holt, 1955.

Mowbray, Jay Henry, ed. *Sinking of the* Titanic: *Eyewitness Accounts.* New York: Dover Publications, 1998.

Warren, Jack, ed. *The Story of the* Titanic *As Told by Its Survivors: Laurence Beesley, Archibald Gracie, Commander Lightoller, and Harold Bride.* New York: Dover Publications, 1960.

WILLIAM KAUFMAN

TOMBS

Death has inspired some of the world's most imposing and monumental architecture. Two of the seven wonders of the ancient world were tombs: the great pyramids of Egypt and the mausoleum of Halicarnassus. The latter was the tomb of Mausolus (hence the word *mausoleum*), the king of Caria (Asia Minor); it was constructed in the fourth century B.C.E. but no longer survives. The Egyptian pyramids have endured and are perhaps the most famous tombs of all time. Their sheer scale captures the power, wealth, and energy at the disposal of those who created them.

The word *tomb* derives from ancient Greek and was first employed by Homer to describe a tumulus or mound raised over a body. By transference, tomb has come to mean anything that is the last resting place of a corpse or cremated human remains. For this reason, the word *tomb* is often used interchangeably with *funerary memorial, funerary monument, mausoleum,* and even with *cenotaph* (an empty tomb), *gravestone* (a tomb marker), and *grave.* All can be said to perform some functions of a tomb.

A tomb is a structure built aboveground to house the remains of the dead. Many such structures are freestanding, but some exist within other buildings, most notably churches. Tombs often incorporate architectural features and sculpture into the design; many include identifying inscriptions and images; and some use extravagant decor and furnishings on the interior as well as the exterior.

Tombs come in a myriad of shapes, forms, and sizes: there are pyramids, obelisks, mounds, rotunda, rock-cut tombs, house tombs, and temple tombs, to name a few; these may house the remains of a single person or many. Some types of tombs are characteristic of specific peoples and places, but funerary architecture has an eclectic nature that often borrows forms from past societies to lend prestige to the present. Pyramid tombs may be associated with Egypt, but pyramids were also adopted in ancient Rome (e.g., that of Caius Cestius), in eighteenth-century England (e.g., that of the Earl of Buckinghamshire at Bickling, Norfolk), and in nineteenth-century America (e.g., the monument to Confederate soldiers in Richmond, Virginia). Most building types can be and have been adapted to house human remains and thus perform the function of a tomb.

The earliest impact of man upon the natural landscape was through funerary structures. The barrows and tumuli of the Neolithic period in Europe (c. 4000–3000 B.C.E.) or of the Mycenean period in Greece (c. 1600–1200 B.C.E.), for example, were large tombs that basically consisted of a stone chamber covered by a massive mound of earth. We can judge that these were highly visible statements expressing the ability of the constructors to deploy manpower and resources, even when little else is known of the prehistoric societies involved.

Tombs are a striking way of asserting desired power and stability. Monumental tombs are not a part of all cultures, religions, or political systems, but where they occur, they are often associated with times of transition in power, a transition frequently triggered by the death of a ruler. This is well illustrated by the pyramids of the Egyptian pharaohs or the mausoleums of the Roman emperors or the medieval papal tombs. The first Roman emperor, Augustus (ruled 31 B.C.E.–14 C.E.), asserted his claims to rule in Rome by building a large circular mausoleum, a dynastic tomb designed to hold the remains of Augustus and his successors. The message was clear: Augustus and his family were in charge and they intended to remain so. In the twentieth century similar principles underlay the construction and maintenance of the tomb of Lenin. Reverence for the dead, and tombs that house them, can be a unifying factor and thus those holding power can draw authority and legitimacy by association with the tomb. From the top of the tomb that housed Lenin's embalmed remains, Soviet dignitaries watched the May Day parades; Lenin was literally under their feet and symbolically holding up the regime.

Tombs may function as symbols of power, but one should not isolate them completely from a more personal world of emotion and sentiment.

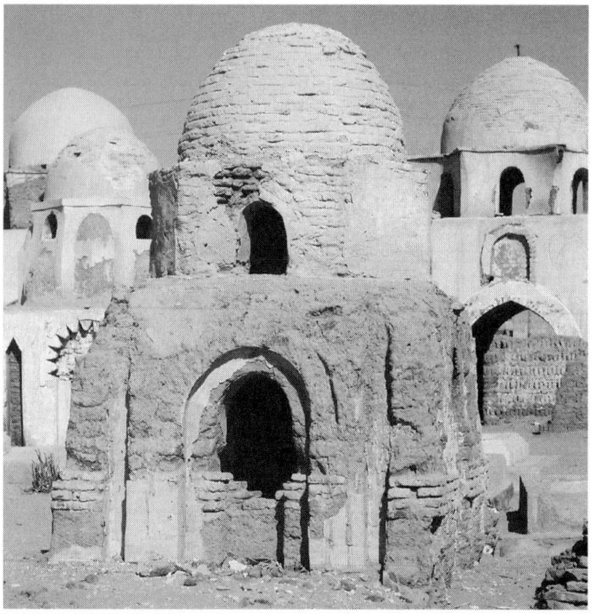

Although in Egypt, the Fatimid Tombs in this ancient Muslim cemetery are uncharacteristic of triangular pyramids usually found in that country. CORBIS

For past societies it can be difficult to reconstruct emotions. The Taj Mahal ("abode of the chosen one") in Agra, India, was built during the 1600s by Shah Jahan for his wife, Mumtaz Mahal, and could be interpreted as a beautiful token of love inspired by grief. This may have been so, but its wider political and physical impact cannot be ignored. The Taj Mahal was part of a massive building project that asserted Mogul rule onto the landscape of northern India. This tomb and its beautiful gardens may also represent heaven on earth, uniting this life with the afterlife. Indeed, spiritual and religious beliefs may strongly influence tomb design. On the one hand religion can seek to control and simplify, designating permanent monumental structures as inappropriate. On the other hand religion can inspire great funerary architecture and play a fundamental role in the design, form, and location of tombs. The secure construction and interior provisions of the Egyptian pyramids were dictated by beliefs about the afterlife; the filling of European churches with tombs had its origins in a desire to gain proximity to God. Religion, power, and sentiment could all play their part in tomb construction as epitomized by the Taj Mahal.

In the case of more modest tombs, it is sometimes possible to view them less as public symbols of power and claimed religious piety and more as personal statements of affection and familial duty. The tomb is a product of the human urge to remember; it is a focus for memory and a symbol of consolation to the bereaved. In nineteenth-century America and Europe, following cemetery reforms and the abandonment of overcrowded churchyards, there was a boom in tomb and gravestone construction because more people had the opportunity and ability to mark the graves of their loved ones. It was a fashion that did not last, since the same cemeteries came to be characterized by greater simplicity in the twentieth century.

Such changes in the significance and use of tombs reflect changes in society. But wherever and whenever they are constructed and on whatever scale, the public nature of a tomb must not be disregarded. A tomb may be commissioned from love and affection, but simultaneously its design, decor, and size are careful choices that convey important messages (even if indirectly) about the personal beliefs, wealth, status, and identity of the deceased and the survivors.

See also: BURIAL GROUNDS; CEMETERIES AND CEMETERY REFORM; CEMETERIES, MILITARY; CEMETERIES, WAR; CHARNEL HOUSES; GRAVESTONES AND OTHER MARKERS; MEMORIALIZATION, SPONTANEOUS; MEMORIALS, VIRTUAL; PYRAMIDS; QIN SHIH HUANG'S TOMB; VIETNAM VETERANS MEMORIAL

Bibliography

Colvin, Howard. *Architecture and the After-Life.* New Haven, CT: Yale University Press, 1991.

Curl, James. *A Celebration of Death: An Introduction to Some of the Buildings, Monuments, and Settings of Funerary Architecture in the Western European Tradition.* London: B.T. Batsford, 1993.

Davies, Penelope. *Death and the Emperor. Roman Imperial Funerary Monuments from Augustus to Marcus Aurelius.* Cambridge: Cambridge University Press, 2000.

Jupp, Peter, and Clare Gittings, eds. *Death in England: An Illustrated History.* Manchester: Manchester University Press, 1999.

Parker Pearson, Mike. *The Archaeology of Death and Burial.* Stroud, England: Sutton, 1999.

VALERIE M. HOPE

TRIANGLE SHIRTWAIST COMPANY FIRE

The fire that swept through the Triangle Shirtwaist Company on March 25, 1911, caused 146 deaths. Not only was it New York City's worst factory blaze ever, it was the second deadliest of any kind (after the General Slocum conflagration), and one of the worst disasters to afflict a group of workers since the advent of the Industrial Revolution.

Located in lower Manhattan, just east of Washington Square Park, the Triangle Shirtwaist Company was a typical American sweatshop of the early twentieth century, when the labor movement and government regulation of business had yet to take firm hold in the United States. The company employed 500 women—mostly Jewish and Italian immigrants between the ages of thirteen and thirty-three who worked long hours under unsanitary and unsafe conditions for an average of $6 a week. The Triangle Shirtwaist Company produced women's tailored shirts that were assembled on the top three floors of a ten-story building. Most of the exit doors were kept locked to enforce worker discipline, and fire protection was confined to twenty-seven buckets of water and a single fire escape.

At 4:45 P.M. on March 25, 1911, the sounding of the company bell signaled the end of another working day. As the workers assembled their belongings, someone yelled "Fire!" For reasons that remain obscure, flames had begun to sprout from a rag bin on the eighth floor, and several workers tried to douse them with the available buckets of water, but to no avail. Within minutes the entire eighth floor was engulfed in flames that fed on the abundant cotton fabrics. The 275 women on the floor bolted for the only exits: the two passenger elevators and the stairway.

The elevators, which only held ten people each, made enough trips to the eighth floor to vacate nearly all of its workers, many of whom staggered gasping onto the street, their clothing smoldering or partially burned. Most of the workers on the tenth floor managed to escape as well.

The workers on the ninth floor, however, were not as fortunate. The flames had raced upward and enveloped most of the ninth floor, where most of the additional 300 workers were struggling to escape from the rapidly igniting piles of cotton fabric. At first the women stampeded to the east stairway, but it was an impassable tower of flame. They then raced to get to the west-end stairway and passenger elevators, but the door was locked, and the elevator was slow in coming to their aid. The frantic women began to hurl themselves down the elevator shaft and out the ninth-floor windows, all of them falling to their death. In addition, those seeking to escape by the rear fire escape were

The high death toll of the Triangle Shirtwaist Company fire was a result of locked doors and inadequate fire escapes. New federal safety regulations were established to reduce the likelihood of other such disasters. UNDERWOOD & UNDERWOOD/CORBIS

killed when the structure collapsed under their collective weight.

By that time, fire rescue teams had arrived, but their life nets simply ripped apart when struck by the force of three or four bodies at once. Moreover, their ladders were useless, extending only to the sixth floor, and the stream of water from their hoses reached only the seventh floor.

The public revulsion over the abysmal working conditions at the factory prompted the governor to appoint an investigative panel within a month of the fire. New York Senator Robert F. Wagner, Alfred E. Smith, and Samuel Gompers, the president of the American Federation of Labor, headed the Factory Investigating Commission. Five years of hearings and fact-gathering led to the passage of important factory safety legislation. Several months after the blaze the New York City government established the Bureau of Fire Regulation, which enhanced the fire department's powers to enforce fire safety rules in factories. The tragedy proved to be a turning point in promoting the idea of government safety regulation of private enterprise in the United States.

See also: DEATH SYSTEM; GRIEF: TRAUMATIC; SOCIAL FUNCTIONS OF DEATH

Bibliography

New York State Factory Investigating Commission. *Preliminary Report of the Factory Investigating Commission.* Albany: The Argus Company, 1912.

Rosner, David, and Gerald Markowitz. *Deadly Dust. Silicosis and the Politics of Occupational Disease in Twentieth-Century America.* Princeton, NJ: Princeton University Press, 1991.

Stein, Leon. *The Triangle Fire.* Ithaca, NY: Cornell University Press, 2001.

ROBERT KASTENBAUM

V

VAMPIRES

Historians document that vampires have most often been reported as inhabitants of shallow graves in the Eastern European countryside. Bram Stoker portrayed *Dracula* (1897), most renown of all revenants, as master of a gloomy and forbidding castle. For contemporary novelist Anne Rice, the French Quarter of New Orleans has long been a favorite milieu for the undead.

Perhaps the best place to find vampires is in the darker recesses of the human imagination. There is something about the image of the vampire that has attracted and fascinated as well as frightened and repelled. Understanding the vampire, then, may be a way of understanding some of the mysteries of the human psyche. Nevertheless, the vampire has not been constructed entirely of moonbeams and fantasies. There is a practical, down-to-earth side of the vampire that deserves careful attention.

Definition and History of Vampires

The vampire seems to defy the firm, mutually exclusive categories of being dead or alive. A vampire's biography begins with death. Furthermore, much of the vampire's time is spent as a corpse or corpse-impersonator. But at night, when the living lie themselves down, up rises the apparent corpse with its dangerous cravings. In the twenty-first century new definitional issues related to brain death, life support systems, persistent vegetative states, and the freezing of both embryos and cadavers (cryonic suspension) have blurred the boundaries between life and death. It is also recognized that some structures, such as the mosaic tobacco virus, can exhibit the properties of either a living or nonliving structure depending upon their situation. For much of history, though, it was the vampire who most daringly crossed and recrossed the borders between the living and the dead.

Vampires are sometimes referred to as "the undead" and sometimes as revenants, reanimated corpses that drink the blood of the living to preserve their own existence. Scholars currently believe that the word *vampire* derives from the Slavic language spoken in Serbia. The consensus is that *vampire* derives from the Slavic verb "to drink." The term was known in England in the late seventeenth century and entered other European languages early in the eighteenth century. Perhaps surprisingly, this term did not make its way to the supposed homeland of vampires—Hungary and Transylvania—until some time afterward.

The vampire (by whatever name) may have been with humankind since earliest times. In his *The Great Mother: An Analysis of the Archetype* (1963), the analytical psychologist Erich Neumann suggests that early civilizations had an intensely conflicted attitude toward both the earth and femininity.

> In the myths and tales of all people, ages, and countries—and even in the nightmares of our own nights—witches and vampires, ghouls and specters, assail us, all terrifyingly alike. . . . This Terrible Mother is the hungry earth, which devours its own children. *(Neumann 1963, pp.148–149)*

Neumann offers many examples of rituals and artifacts to support his belief that the vampire is an ancient and universal symbol of the Great Mother swallowing up her own creations in order to recycle them in new form. However, this dramatic idea remains in need of more evidence for the supposed prevalence of vampirism in the ancient world and does not explain why males have been in the clear majority among vampire ranks (until the twentieth century). Scholars also reject the assumption that vampires are part of all world cultures. Native-American traditions, for example, have their own creatures of the night, such as the skinwalkers (restless spirits of the dead who sometimes make themselves visible), but these do not fit the precise profile of the vampire. A plausible case could be made for a widespread fear of the dead in many cultures, but not necessarily for belief in blood-sucking revenants.

It is clear that vampirism had a secure place in Slavic superstitions for many years before it became a household word with the publication of Bram Stoker's *Dracula* (1897). The author transformed these folk stories into a dark gothic romance. His leading character was inspired by a character he did not have to invent: Vlad Tepes, a fifteenth-century tyrant who slaughtered and sometimes tortured thousands of people. "Vlad the Impaler" was no vampire, though; he did his terrible deeds while alive and had a hearty appetite that did not include sucking blood. Stoker, using literary license, combined the historical Vlad with vampire legends and added a veneer of Victorian culture. Separating fact from fantasy became increasingly difficult as popular literary and theatrical vampires distanced themselves from their roots in anxiety-ridden folklore. Inquiring minds have therefore been following the trail of the vampire, classifying and explaining as best they can.

Folk and Literary Vampires

Classification and description are the first steps to shedding light on these dwellers in darkness. Of most interest to serious students of vampirism is the folk vampire. This is the creature who preceded the literary and commercial vampire. In general, the folk vampire is simpler, cruder, and less appealing than his citified cousin; therefore, folk vampires are seldom cunning or sexy. Many are just thirsty, and not always particular about their sources of nutrition. Rural vampires have been accused of rising from their graves to filch the blood of cows or other available livestock. Unlike the elegant Count Dracula, these revenants are foul-smelling and gross, as might be expected from those who, partially decomposed, spend much of their time in a grave.

Another common feature of folk vampires is that they are rarely, if ever, seen at work. The classic case for the existence of a local vampire is built upon (a) something bad that happened in the night and (b) discovering a corpse in its grave that did not appear sufficiently dead. The corpse might have flecks of blood on its face, especially the lips, and might seem to have changed position.

An important distinction can be made among folk vampires. Some are simple, brutish, and unfortunate creatures. Others, though, are corpses that have either been "vampirized" by evil forces or who have willed themselves to return and wreak vengeance on those they believe have wronged them. Not surprisingly, it is this more dangerous and evil form that has attracted the most attention. Vampire-finders, accompanied by the bravest of the brave and a representative of the church, sought and opened suspect graves and took measures to ensure that the inhabitants would henceforth remain in place. Decapitation and, of course, driving a stake through the heart, were among the specific remedies.

Literary and commercial vampires are generally more sophisticated and take better care of their appearances among the living. The sexual allure and prowess of vampires is almost entirely a literary embellishment, again owed chiefly to the Victorian imagination of Bram Stoker. There is little doubt that the popular success of vampires has been enhanced by their dangerous sexuality. These dark lovers were nearly perfect for a society that discouraged open expression of sexuality, especially for women. Vampires embodied both forbidden sexuality and escape from death but their wretched form of existence was punishment for their transgression.

Scientific and Philosophical Vampires

Another type of vampire has been created by those attempting to explain the creature on scientific grounds. The cultural historian Paul Barber has made a strong case for the vampire as a creature of

Friedrich Wilhelm Murnau's 1922 vampire film Nosferatu *starred Max Schreck, who played the uncannily realistic vampire. The title is Slavic for "plague carrier," linking a history of European plagues and unexplained deaths to the fascination with vampirism.* KOBAL COLLECTION

ignorance and circumstance. He notes that most people have little knowledge about the normal course of postmortem changes. Natural events may therefore be given supernatural explanations. Furthermore, bodies may emerge from the grave for a variety of simple if disquieting reasons. Because the most influential collection of vampire reports comes from rural areas of Eastern Europe, Barber offers the following alternative explanations to the folk belief in the reality of the undead.

- Animals dig up bodies from shallow graves.
- Flooding uncovers bodies from shallow graves.
- Grave robbers dig up corpses as they seek items or body parts for sale.
- People dig up corpses to move them to other places.
- Gases form in the corpse, sometimes causing postmortem movement.
- Some corpses decompose slowly for various reasons (e.g., cold temperature or death by poison).

It may be added that fears of being buried alive were widespread in the nineteenth and early twentieth centuries. Some of these fears were justified, for example, by an epileptic seizure or other loss of consciousness mistaken for death. Porphyria has been nominated repeatedly as a medical condition that produces pallor, giving the individual a somewhat bloodless appearance. The victims are highly sensitive to sunlight and therefore are likely to adopt lifestyles resembling the nocturnal vampire.

The philosophical (or inner) vampire has been created by those seeking to understand the meaning of vampirism in their own minds. Although the speculations have some grounding in fact, some are more appropriately offered as questions rather than answers. For example, is the vampire a sort of "middle man" who provides an image and focus point for all the organic recycling that occurs in nature through season after season and life after life? Is the vampire a concealed warning to humankind? Meaning, people should perhaps be content with one life and not grasp for more. Or, is it possible that within each person lurks an ancient and relentless archetype that seeks satisfaction in the most primitive ways despite one's learning, civilization, and moral development? However when one answers these questions, it is likely that the vampire will not be leaving its haunts in the human mind anytime soon.

See also: AIDS; BRAIN DEATH; BURIED ALIVE; CRYONIC SUSPENSION; DEATH INSTINCT; DEFINITIONS OF DEATH; GHOSTS; GODS AND GODDESSES OF LIFE AND DEATH; HORROR MOVIES; LIFE SUPPORT SYSTEM; PERSISTENT VEGETATIVE STATE; PERSONIFICATIONS OF DEATH; SEX AND DEATH, CONNECTION OF; THANATOMIMESIS; ZOMBIES

Bibliography

Barber, Paul. *Vampires, Burial, and Death: Folklore and Reality.* New Haven, CT: Yale University Press, 1990.

Dresser, Norine. *American Vampires.* New York: W. W. Norton, 1989.

Dundes, Alan, ed. *The Vampire: A Casebook.* Madison: University of Wisconsin Press, 1998.

Gladwell, Adele O., and James Havoc, eds. *Blood and Roses: The Vampire in Nineteenth-Century Literature.* London: Creation Press, 1992.

Heldreteth, Leonard G., and Mary Pharr, eds. *The Blood Is the Life: Vampires in Literature.* Bowling Green, OH: Bowling Green University Press, 1999.

McNally, Raymond T., and Radu Florescu. *In Search of Dracula.* Greenwich, CT: New York Graphic Society, 1972.

Neumann, Erich. *The Great Mother: An Analysis of the Archetype.* Princeton, NJ: Princeton University Press, 1963.

Perkowski, Jan L., ed. *Vampires of the Slavs.* Cambridge, MA: Slavica Publishers, 1976.

Rice, Anne. *The Vampire Lestat.* New York: Alfred A. Knopf, 1985.

Summers, Montague. *The Vampire and His Kith and Kin.* New York: E. P. Dutton, 1928.

Wolf, Leonard. *The Annotated Dracula.* New York: Clarkson N. Potter, 1975.

ROBERT KASTENBAUM

Reverend Chad Varah founded a worldwide movement of volunteers that offers emotional support to those who are suicidal and in despair. GETTY IMAGES

VARAH, CHAD

The eldest of nine children of an Anglican Church minister, Edward Chad Varah was born on November 12, 1911, in the small town of Barton upon Humber, County of Lincolnshire, England. He went on to read natural sciences at Keble College in Oxford, and later studied at the Lincoln Theological College, where he was ordained as a priest by the Church of England. In the culturally repressive atmosphere of the United Kingdom in the 1930s, Varah recognized the extent to which confusion and ignorance about many social issues, several still shrouded in taboo, contributed to the despair that often led to suicide.

One of Varah's duties as an assistant curate in 1935 spawned his lifelong commitment to suicide prevention. He officiated at the funeral of a thirteen-year-old girl who was so confused and isolated that she believed that the onset of menstruation was the sign of a mortal illness that would lead to a slow and painful death; the terrified girl killed herself. Deeply moved and upset by that suicide, Varah sought out other suicidal people in hospitals and within his parish, aware of the meager facilities for the suicidal and their frequent reluctance to see a psychiatrist. He believed suicidal people needed a way of being in touch with someone to whom they could talk at any time of day or night that was right for them.

The opportunity to help such people arrived when Varah was appointed rector to St. Stephen Walbrook, the London church where he founded The Samaritans, a volunteer organization dedicated to befriending those going through emotional distress. Remembering the young girl, and seeking to minister to the suicidal despair so common in a large city like London, in 1953 Varah advertised in the press and opened the first drop-in center where emotionally isolated and distressed people could go to find a sympathetic ear.

Varah originally envisioned the service as a counseling program, but within months he recognized three crucial points, which include:

- a significant number of suicidal people had nowhere or no one to turn to for emotional and psychological support;

- the number of people seeking help far exceeded his ability to satisfy the demand; and
- most of the visitors wanted to talk to someone who would give them time and space, who would listen in confidence with acceptance and compassion to their deepest, most anguished thoughts.

To meet the huge response, Varah organized volunteers to talk with those waiting to see him. He soon observed interaction between the many and varied callers coming to talk and the lay volunteers who listened empathetically and acceptingly. He called the listening therapy "befriending." One therapeutic model in the now-multifaceted approach to suicide prevention, it is a "response to an immediate emotional crisis by lay volunteers who are given professional support by appointed medical and psychiatric consultants" (Scott and Armson 2000, p. 703). At the end of the twentieth century there are thousands of volunteers around the world dedicated to befriending the suicidal in the manner first conceived in the 1930s by the visionary Varah.

See also: BEFRIENDING; SUICIDE BASICS: PREVENTION

Bibliography

Scott, Vanda. "Role of Volunteers in Preventing Suicide: A Befrienders International Perspective." Presentation at the symposium Towards an Evidence-Based Suicide Management: Linking Australia with the Rest of the World in Brisbane, Australia, 1999.

Scott, Vanda, and Simon Armson. "Volunteers and Suicide Prevention." In Keith Hawton and Kees Van Heeringhen eds., *International Handbook of Suicide and Attempted Suicide.* London: John Wiley, 2000

Varah, Chad. *Before I Die Again: The Autobiography of the Founder of Samaritans.* London: Constable, 1992.

Varah, Chad. *The Samaritans in the 80s.* London: Constable, 1980.

VANDA SCOTT

VENTILATOR

See BEFRIENDING; LIFE SUPPORT SYSTEM.

VIETNAM VETERANS MEMORIAL

The Vietnam Veterans Memorial is a tribute to the dead of the United States' longest, most unpopular, and least successful war. Like the war itself, this memorialization was highly controversial, but the site has become the most frequently visited memorial in Washington, D.C., drawing over 4 million visitors annually.

American casualties in Vietnam began in 1959 and ended with the evacuation of Saigon in 1975. Never officially designated a war, the Vietnam conflict became increasingly unpopular as casualties and news coverage of the fighting increased. Those people who served in Vietnam returned to an unsupportive nation and a media that emphasized the social problems of its veterans.

There were few attempts to honor Vietnam veterans until 1978, when an insignificant and ambiguous plaque was placed behind the Tomb of the Unknown Soldier. One year later, Jan Scruggs (a wounded Vietnam veteran) founded the Vietnam Veterans Memorial Fund (VVMF), which sought private funds from both war supporters and opponents to build a memorial honoring the veterans but not the conflict.

The VVMF held an open competition for a memorial design that would: "1. be reflective and contemplative in character, 2. harmonize with its surroundings, 3. contain the names of those who had died in the conflict or who were still missing, and 4. make no political statement about the war" (Fish 1987, p. 3). A panel of distinguished architects and artists reviewed over 14,000 submissions, and on May 1, 1981, announced its unanimous choice: the design by Maya Ying Lin, a twenty-one-year-old Chinese-American undergraduate at Yale University.

Lin's design was simple and elegant, consisting of two walls of polished granite (each 246 feet long) composed of seventy-four panels that gradually increase in height from eight inches to more than ten feet at the center, where they meet at a 125-degree angle. Shaped like an inverted V, the memorial is cut into a small hill sloping downward, invisible from most locations on the National Mall.

Although the design was supported by most veterans groups and won critical acclaim in the art

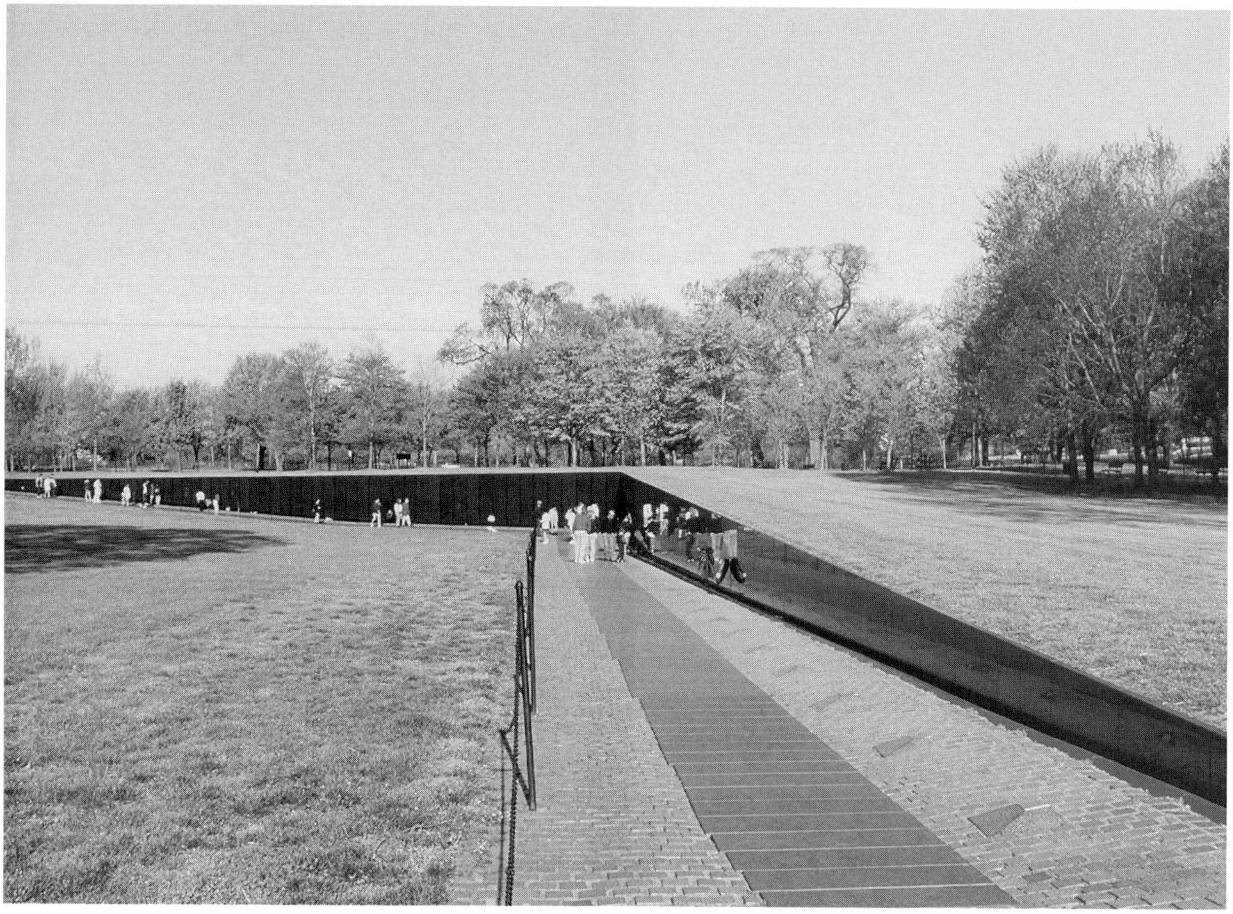

Maya Lin, a Chinese-American student at Yale University, designed the Vietnam Veterans Memorial Wall to be reflective—those stopping to read the names can see themselves reflected in the highly polished surface. In order of date of death, names of the over 58,000 American missing or dead are chiseled into the granite without reference to rank or branch of military service. CORBIS (BELLEVUE)

community, many veterans and conservative politicians were outraged at its selection. Critics targeted features that distinguished the design from other memorials, saying it was black instead of white, horizontal and in the ground instead of rising upward, abstract rather than a realistic depiction of soldiers or battle, and devoid of any patriotic symbols. The most influential of the critics was James Watt, Secretary of the Interior, who put construction on hold until the VVMF agreed to supplement the wall with more traditional patriotic symbols.

Lin's wall was dedicated on Veteran's Day in 1982; a flagpole with an inscription and emblems representing the branches of military service was added in 1983. A bronze sculpture by Frederick Hart entitled *Three Servicemen,* placed near the flagpole looking out toward the wall, was dedicated in 1984. The Vietnam Women's Memorial, a bronze sculpture created by Glenna Goodacre to honor the women who served and died in Vietnam, was added in 1993. In June 2001 plans for another addition were unveiled by the VVMF. The In Memory Plaque will honor individuals who died prematurely because of war-related illnesses, including Agent Orange poisoning and post-traumatic stress disorder (PTSD). Despite these additions, Lin's wall remains the focal point of the memorial.

The wall's unique design promotes interaction. Hidden quietly in its recessed hillside, it invites the visitor to approach and move along it. The names, chiseled in half-inch-high letters, promote intimacy; visitors get close to read them and are encouraged to touch and take rubbings of the names.

For some visitors, interaction includes leaving objects. According to legend, the brother of a man who died in Vietnam left the first object at the wall; during its construction, he tossed a Purple Heart into the wet concrete. Since then, over 500,000 nonperishable items left at the wall have been collected and are housed in the Vietnam Veterans Memorial Collection at the National Park Service Museum Resource Center.

Flags and flowers, the most frequent donations, are not collected, but all personal remembrances are carefully catalogued. Within the collection, military mementos are the most numerous, but more idiosyncratic gifts (e.g., a bicycle fender, a can of beer, a fishing pole) are common. Visitors and the objects they leave mirror the diversity of Vietnam experiences; war supporters and opponents as well those born after the conflict pay tribute at the wall. In this way, the memorial brings the nation together to a common place, but not a common understanding. While some see a memorial to fallen warriors, others see a challenge to war in the poignant demonstration of its costs.

Decades after its dedication, Americans continue to reflect on the conflicts of the Vietnam era at the wall. For the many psychologically wounded combatants, the wall is incorporated into their healing; therapeutic programs for veterans with PTSD often make visiting it part of their emotional healing. Efforts to extend the wall beyond its physical boundaries also demonstrate its significance. The Vietnam Veterans Memorial Fund began scheduling tours of the Movable Wall in late 1996 and to date more than 100 cities have been visited (as well as parts of Ireland). The Wall That Heals Traveling Museum and Information Center accompanies the half-scale replica on all of its stops and the Virtual Wall allows online visitors to see individual panels, click on names, leave e-mail notes, and request rubbings.

See also: CEMETERIES, MILITARY; CEMETERIES, WAR; LINCOLN IN THE NATIONAL MEMORY; MEMORIALIZATION, SPONTANEOUS; MUSEUMS OF DEATH

Bibliography

Fish, Lydia. *The Last Firebase: A Guide to the Vietnam Veterans Memorial.* Shippensburg, PA: White Mane, 1987.

Hass, Kristin Ann. *Carried to the Wall: American Memory and the Vietnam Veterans Memorial.* Berkeley: University of California Press, 1998.

Palmer, Laura. *Shrapnel in the Heart: Letters and Remembrances from the Vietnam Veterans Memorial.* New York: Vintage Books, 1988.

Wagner-Pacifici, Robin, and Barry Schwartz. "The Vietnam Veterans Memorial: Commemorating a Difficult Past." *American Journal of Sociology* 97, no. 2 (1991): 376–420.

PAMELA ROBERTS

VIKINGS

See SUTTON HOO.

VIRGIN MARY, THE

In Byzantine icons and Western medieval art, the most common deathbed scene is that of the Virgin Mary. In her study of Marian iconography, Gertrud Schiller reproduced more than 100 images of Mary reclining in bed surrounded by the apostles who grieve, pray, and in late medieval art perform the rites for the dying. In these images, Jesus either stands at the bedside or hovers above it, and holds Mary's soul in the form of a young child. This scene reflects the belief that Mary was the mother of Jesus, the incarnate Son of God, and therefore enjoyed the privilege of an especially holy death.

Yet the Bible says nothing about Mary's death. This silence, combined with growing devotion to Mary, allowed new material to flourish. The deathbed scene is derived from apocryphal narratives describing Mary's last days and dying, as well as her funeral, burial, resurrection, and assumption into heaven. Versions of this story survive in Syriac and Greek texts dating from the third to the fifth centuries. Emperor Maurice (582–602) set August 15 for the feast of Mary's Dormition (*Koimesis,* or "falling asleep") throughout the Byzantine church, and since the late seventh century the Roman church has celebrated Mary's Assumption on the same date. Once the feast was officially placed in church calendars, its narratives shaped preaching, doctrine, and art.

In the earliest surviving Greek sermon celebrating Mary's death, the bishop John of Thessalonica (610–649) claims to have edited the different accounts of her death and to tell "only what truly happened" (Daley 1998, p. 49). An angel told Mary that she would die in three days. She summoned

This thirteenth-century sculpture The Death of the Virgin, *at the Strasbourg Cathedral in France illustrates Christ accepting the Virgin Mary's soul into heaven. The most popular images in medieval art of Mary's death are the deathbed scene and the coronation in heaven.* GERALDINE DUCLOW

her relatives and friends to stay with her for two nights, and asked them to "sing praise instead of mourning." The apostle John arrived, followed by the other apostles who had been carried on clouds from all corners of the earth. During the second night Peter preached, urging all present to "take courage" from Mary and to live virtuously in preparation for their own deaths. The next day Mary lay down in her bed, and Jesus arrived with many angels. When he and the angel Michael entered Mary's room, "Mary brought the course of her life to its fulfillment, her face turned smilingly towards the Lord. And the Lord took her soul and placed it in the hands of Michael" (Daley 1998, p. 63). The funeral followed, but was delayed when an enraged chief priest attacked the bier; his hands stuck to the bier and were amputated until he repented, praised Mary in Hebrew, and was healed. Three days after the burial, the apostles opened Mary's sarcophagus, "but found only her grave-garments; for she had been taken away by Christ, the God who became flesh from her, to the place of her eternal, living inheritance" (Daley 1998, p. 67).

John of Thessalonica's entire sermon, even the disturbing anti-Semitic incident of the chief priest, highlights the importance and power of faith in Mary—specifically in her dying and final transcendence of death itself, for the sermon presents an idealized portrait of Mary dying surrounded by those she loves, supported by Christian rites, and finally reunited with her divine Son who escorts her to reign with him in heaven. And as Peter's preaching within the sermon makes clear, Mary's dormition provides "a model of Christian death" (Daley 1998, p. 69).

The Greek narratives entered the West in a Latin version attributed to Melito of Sardis. In the thirteenth century, Jacobus de Voragine combined several early sources in *The Golden Legend*'s account of Mary's assumption; as the *Legend* became the most popular collection of saints' lives of the later Middle Ages, the story of Mary's death assumed new prominence in art and drama. While medieval artworks occasionally illustrate all the major events surrounding Mary's death, they usually limit themselves to two images: the deathbed scene and the coronation in heaven. These images appear in sculpture, stained glass, and manuscript paintings of the private prayer books known as books of hours.

Moreover, in the late Middle Ages the treatment of Mary's death itself takes a more contemporary and realistic turn. Especially in altar paintings, Mary dies within elaborately furnished fifteenth-century rooms, and the apostles perform the prayers and sacramental rites for the dying with a new urgency. As Schiller notes, beginning around 1400 Mary is shown not as having just died, but in the process of dying; and Christ himself is sometimes not in the picture. Similar developments occur in the mystery plays or religious dramas. For example, the York cycle's "Death of the Virgin" presents the full story of Mary's dying, but adds new, concrete details: Mary suffers a painful illness that she hopes will soon end, and John and her attendants openly grieve and need to be quieted by Mary herself. While retaining the exemplary qualities of Mary's death, these images and dramas bring the dormition closer to the realities of late medieval dying.

Although the feast of Mary's Dormition remains a major celebration in Eastern Orthodox churches, Western Christianity has turned away from Mary's death since the Reformation. Protestant churches have generally downplayed devotion to Mary, and Roman Catholicism has increasingly focused on her bodily assumption into heaven, which Pope Pius XII declared official doctrine in 1950. Curiously, Pius's declaration made no mention of Mary's death, and thus bowed to the claim of some Catholic theologians that she was taken bodily to heaven without dying.

Yet in narratives, sermons, images, and plays, the Virgin Mary's death has long offered a powerful, consoling image of the Christian's good death. This was especially the case in the decades before the Reformation when, as Schiller comments, art highlighted Mary's "ability to help individuals who were about to die. Her death . . . was a model; the taking up of her soul by Christ gave consolation and hope: 'Pray for us sinners' was the daily prayer" (Schiller 1980, vol. 4, part 2, p. 133) to the Virgin Mary. For this reason, appeals to Mary also figured prominently in the fifteenth-century treatises on the *ars moriendi,* or art of dying. Like her exemplary life, Mary's dying has offered a model for Christian imitation and action.

See also: ARS MORIENDI; CHRISTIAN DEATH RITES, HISTORY OF; SAINTS, PRESERVED

Bibliography

Beadle, Richard, ed. *The York Plays.* London: Edward Arnold, 1982.

Daley, Brian E., tr. and ed.*On the Dormition of Mary: Early Patristic Homilies.* Crestwood, NY: St. Vladimir's Seminary Press, 1998.

Duclow, Donald F. "The Dormition in Fifteenth-Century Drama and Art." *Fifteenth-Century Studies* 21 (1994):55–84.

James, Montague Rhodes. *The Apocryphal New Testament,* Oxford: Clarendon Press, 1953.

Schiller, Gertrud. *Maria.* In *Ikonographie der christlichen Kunst,* Vol. 4, Part 2. Gütersloh: Gerd Mohn, 1980.

Voragine, Jacobus de. "The Assumption of the Blessed Virgin Mary." In William Granger Ryan tr., *The Golden Legend,* Vol. 2. Princeton, NJ: Princeton University Press, 1993.

Warner, Martina. *Alone of All Her Sex: The Myth and Cult of the Virgin Mary.* New York: Knopf, 1976.

DONALD F. DUCLOW

VISUAL ARTS

Death has always been a patron of the arts. How else would humankind know about the superb arts of King Tutankhamen's ancient Egyptian era if it were not for the exquisite glittering painted and sculpted masterpieces found in his tomb? Likewise, human culture would know little about early Asian sculpture and gilded adornments if it were not for the glowing artifacts found in the burial halls of the emperors of China. These art objects are symbolic translations of human thought and experience of past millennia and offer concrete evidence of those predecessors' beliefs about death and how they grieved.

Humankind has always turned to its earliest childhood memories when selecting a memorial for a loved one. As the visionary scholar Marshall McLuhan wrote in the 1960s, most people move into the future "looking through a rear-view mirror" (1997, p. 12). Artists, on the other hand, tap into a wavelength of the future. No illustration serves better to document the contrast than the creations of the Impressionist painters such as Paul Cézanne (1839), Claude Monet (1946), Berthe Morisot (1841), and Paul Renoir (1839), and the sculptors Augustus Saint-Gaudens (1848) and Auguste Rodin (1846). Although all of these artists were born in the early Victorian era, their compatriots were commissioning life-sized copies of sculptures and paintings created during the ancient Roman empire for their homes, public buildings, and memorials, as late as the early 1900s.

It takes a cataclysm to change the public's concept of appropriate new lifestyles as well as funerary art. Such a cataclysm rolled over Western consciousness in the aftermath of World War I, with its often futile destruction of a generation's most promising youth. It changed life irrevocably and forced public acceptance of a *Weltanschauung,* a new worldview, discovering the Impressionist art that had been there all the time.

The way humans face impending death and mourn losses induces the trauma that destroys thought. The poet W. H. Auden, grief-stricken by the death of the Irish playwright William Butler Yeats, compared his sense of desolation to the brutal weather: "He disappeared in the dead of winter / The brooks were frozen / and snow disfigured the public statues / the mercury sank in the mouth of the dying day / The day of his death was a dark, cold day" (1945, pp. 48–53). It is the artists who can give words and images to human devastation. Hopes, fears, and questions are invisible until they can be concretized into potent symbolic translations. Conferring posthumous fame on his friend and fellow artist, Auden is able to see beyond the physical decay and putrefaction of biological death: "Earth, receive an honored guest; / William Yeats is laid to rest; Let the Irish vessel lie / emptied of its poetry" (Bertman 1991, p. 35). It is through the transmission by artists into potent symbolic translations that humankind's inner realities can be communicated and understood.

Religious and Cultural Influences

Human expression of the symbols of death is influenced by the religious and cultural milieu of the times. The Old Testament provides evidence that marking gravesites is an age-old tradition, as Genesis 35:7 reads, "And Rachel died in childbirth. Joseph set up a pillar on her grave while on the way to Ephreth." In 2001 an illustrated article in *Biblical Archaeology Review,* titled "Standing Stones in the Desert," indicates the kind of "pillar" that might have graced Rachel's grave created by pre-Israelite nomadic tribes in the arid desert of the Sinai. The more artistically sophisticated ancient Egyptians created professionally sculpted markers, such as the example of a stela for Mani-Nakhtuf and son (c. 1200 B.C.E.), which tries to guarantee these ancestors eternal life by "Praising the Moon, Thoth, Bowing down to the stars of heaven . . ." The ancient Romans of the first century C.E. in Alexandria, influenced by Egyptian customs, painted sweet and accurate portraits of those they loved on the shroud wrappings in which they were buried.

In his historically comprehensive book *The Hour of Our Death* (1981), Philippe Ariès brings readers to the beginning of Western culture and the iconography with which they are more familiar. He writes, "the Christians of the first millennia believed that the end of time was that of the glorified Christ as he rose to heaven as he sat on a throne . . . with a rainbow around it" reminding his audience of these words made real in the magnificently reverent sculptures on Chartres Cathedral in France (Ariès 1981, p. 97). The same devotedly held faith is illustrated in *The Goodman on His Death,* a woodcut from the fifteenth century, reminding the pious that they need not fear damnation. It implies, as well, that righteous believers would be resurrected at the time of their Lord's Second Coming.

The more successful medieval families were positive that their souls would be immediately translated at the moment of that miraculous event because their position in life guaranteed a last resting place within the confines of a holy church. Just to make sure their rank was recognized, they reproduced their imposing status, in full regalia, in portraits sculpted in brass on their tombs. There were, of course, other concepts of sanctity. Puritans in England and in America saw death as a very grim reaper indeed. Their religion was full of warnings about the perils of hell, and very little about the blessings of heaven. The Americans commissioned their self-taught New World memorial carvers to recreate, on their tombstones, the ghastly skeletons rising from the biers that still frighten so many visitors of Great Britain's old cathedrals. They also had them inscribe on those old markers the frightening warning, "Death is a debt to nature due, which I have paid and so must you."

For a minimally educated population, a dictionary of images was etched into these stones. Images include down-pointed arrows (the dart of death), a descending dove, which represented the holy ghost, a snake with its tail in its mouth representing eternity, broken flowers representing a child's death, and a trumpeting angel, a more optimistic prediction of the resurrection of the soul. Co-existing with these grim conservatives, a milder, Protestant vision of life and death was portrayed by chubby angels who would surely carry the soul to heaven. This conception finally superseded its hell-ridden predecessors.

By the Victorian period, death had become an even more gentle visitor, demonstrated by marble creations of kinder, mostly female, angels who transported the soul to a divine paradise. And since, at that time, Americans decided that the republic duplicated the ancient Greek and Roman governments, sculptors were ordered to copy the urns and palls that graced the newly discovered Greco-Roman tombs. Only little children escaped these classical allusions—they were often represented as little lambs on little stones or full round figures of sleeping babies. Victorians also placed marble reproductions of these dormant infants in their parlors for remembrance. The practice of photographing deceased children, often as if they were sleeping and almost always surrounded by flowers, religious symbols, and special toys is as old as photography itself and suggests that remembrance photographs were important, valuable sources of solace for grieving families.

The Nineteenth and Twentieth Centuries As a Turning Point

When nineteenth-century excavators discovered the riches in Egyptian tombs, the fashion in home furnishings and memorials changed almost overnight. The Victorians duplicated the divans found in the pyramids for their parlors, and a forest of four-sided pointed structures arose in graveyards, nestled among the urns and palls of their predecessors. In the nineteenth century carvings of pet dogs, pairs of slippers, favorite chairs, books, and tools of the trades, such as fireman's hats and hoses, appeared on memorials.

Victorian artists did not discriminate against commissions for cemetery sculpture. Interested parties are just as likely to find a statue by Daniel Chester French in a cemetery as they are to stand in awe of his massive Lincoln in the capital in Washington. Though twenty-first-century fine artists rarely create memorials, they have continued to express their personal grief and cultural angst in their own work.

The wrenching images in Kathe Kollwitz's woodcut etchings express the conditions of German life after World War I. For an unforgettable demonstration of an artist's despair at humankind's inhumanity to fellow humans, one can stand, appalled before Picasso's *Guernica,* as a memorial to the martyred citizens of those victims of war. As Christina Schlesinger writes in *Grief and the Healing Arts* (1999), "Artists, poets, and painters are a natural resource for developing strategies of mourning. . . . [they] shape inarticulate feelings and bridge the gap between inner confusion and outer resolution" (p. 202).

In the twentieth century society has decided to curb ostentation and conspicuous displays of grief. Memorials no longer resemble the overblown sculptured pylons of the past, and instead, even for the most prominent, they resemble nothing so much as a bronze rectangular serving platter, containing only the name and death dates of the person remembered. There are notable exceptions—the stark Vietnam memorial in Washington, which has become a universally accepted icon of grief for a generation's lost youth, and the artists' cemetery at Green River in Long Island, New York, where the great painters, writers, and musicians of the 1930s are interred, such as Jackson Pollock, Joseph Liebman, and Lee Krasner. Harkening back to the *massebah* (sacred standing stones) mentioned in the Bible and in other ancient literature is the *Alphabet Garden, 2000,* a permanent memorial in Grafeneck, Germany, commemorating the victims of Hitler's 1940 "euthanasia experiments" that took place in that city. The sculptor Diane Samuels has inscribed in German a stone large enough to sit upon and reflect, "Please take my letters and form them into prayers." Other tiny stones nearby, are inscribed simply with letters X and A. Perhaps these representations of a bygone loss prove how much human beings have always needed a physical object only an artist can imagine into being. How similar are Joseph's millennia old pillar and the sinister ebony memorial to Holocaust victims displayed at the end of the film *Schindler's List* (1993).

On a road not imagined by McLuhan, grieving families and friends are setting up multipaged, illustrated dedicatory essays to the deceased on the Internet. An interest in death has also sprung up in the United States on web sites entitled Find-a-Grave, or mounted by historic cemeteries, such as Mt. Auburn in Boston and the National Trust for Historical Preservation. Working men and women have become proud enough of their livelihoods to commission stones that celebrate their labor as the carved ten-wheel vehicle commemorates the trucker Jackie Lowell Stanley (1949–1984), or the speaker's podium engraved with microphones and the logo of their first book *No Fear of Speaking* commemorates the work of the founders of the Speech Improvement Company. In less advantaged neighborhoods, grieving families are commissioning huge spray-painted murals on the walls of buildings to commemorate deceased family members. A remarkable album of these memorials, titled *R.I.P. Memorial Wall Art,* was produced in 1994 by Martha Cooper and Joseph Sciorra. Surely these spontaneous gestures indicate a hunger to break with the past and express a formerly shunned display of emotion.

Future Trends

Though dying, death, grief, and mourning are hallmarks of the human condition, their shapes and images have changed through the ages to a time when perhaps even the most acute observer cannot predict how they will be demonstrated next year. Humankind will continue to look to the visionaries—the artists—to document and update their thinking. The excesses of medical technology, the dangers of managed care, and the case for euthanasia or assisted death graphically depicted in twenty- and twenty-first-century treatments of Ars Moriendi would have been unimaginable terrors to the engraver who created the peaceful closure depicted on the woodcut, "The goodman on his deathbed" (Bertman 1991, p. 17). Cartoons of the grim reaper as "the closure fairy" or standing in front of a store window displaying gardening tools deciding whether to purchase the scythe or its more costly counterpart, the mower, or captioned "A Look Ahead," lecturing on the statistics of future deaths, demonstrates the way comic art continues to flirt with death through the use of traditional imagery. Whether mourners are represented striking their heads, tearing out their hair, beating their breasts, scratching their cheeks until they bleed as they are depicted in Greek objects dating back to the early fifth century, or sewing panels for the largest ongoing community arts project in the world, the AIDS Memorial Quilt, the visual arts have enabled society to both commemorate the lives of deceased loved ones and to support the human endeavor to conceptualize, endure, and make meaning of loss, suffering, and death.

See also: ARS MORIENDI; BURIAL GROUNDS; CHRISTIAN DEATH RITES, HISTORY OF; DANCE; QIN SHIH HUANG'S TOMB; TOMBS; VIETNAM VETERANS MEMORIAL

Bibliography

Ariès, Philippe. *The Hour of Our Death.* New York: Alfred A. Knopf, 1981.

Auden, W. H. *The Collected Poetry of W. H. Auden.* New York: Random House, 1945.

Bertman, Sandra L., ed. *Grief and the Healing Arts: Creativity As Therapy.* Amityville, NY: Baywood Publishing, 1999.

Bertman, Sandra L. "Ars Moriendi: Illuminations on 'The Good Death' from the Arts and Humanities." In Joan K. Harrold and Joanne Lynn eds., *A Good Dying: Shaping Health Care for the Last Months of Life.* New York: Haworth Press, 1998.

Bertman, Sandra L. *Facing Death: Images, Insights and Interventions.* New York: Hemisphere Publishing, 1991.

Cooper, Martha, and Joseph Sciorra. *R.I.P. Memorial Wall Art.* New York: Henry Holt and Co., 1994.

Forbes, Harriette Merrifield. *Gravestones of Early New England and the Men Who Made Them,* 3rd edition. Brooklyn, NY: Center for Thanatology, 1989.

Gamino, Louis. "A Study in Grief: The Life and Art of Kaethe Kollwitz." In Sandra Bertman ed., *Grief and the Healing Arts: Creativity As Therapy.* Amityville, NY: Baywood, 1999.

Halporn, Roberta. *Lessons from the Dead: The Graveyard As a Classroom for the Teaching of the Life Cycle.* Brooklyn, NY: Highly Specialized Promotions, 1979.

McLuhan, Marshall, and Quentin Fiore. *The Medium Is the Message.* New York: Random House, 1967.

Norfeet, Barbara. *Looking at Death.* Boston: David R. Godine, 1993.

Stillion, Judith. "Death and Grief Made Visible: The Life and Work of Edvard Munch." In Sandra Bertman ed., *Grief and the Healing Arts: Creativity As Therapy.* Amityville, NY: Baywood, 1999.

Internet Resources

"The AIDS Memorial Quilt. 1987–2001." In the Aids Memorial Quilt [web site]. Available from www.aidsquilt.org.

"Creative and Unique Memorials." In the Monument Builders [web site]. Available from www.monumentbuilders.org/crunmem6.html.

"Standing Stones in the Desert." In the *Biblical Archaeology Review* [web site]. Available from www.biblicalarchaeology.org/barmj01/bar2.html.

SANDRA L. BERTMAN

VOODOO

Voodoo is an animist religion that consecrates a cult to Loas (gods) and to the ancestors—the cult of ancestors constitutes a system of religious beliefs and rites which are used principally to reinforce the social system as well as the dependence of the family—and at the same time, voodoo spirits, guardians, deities, or forces of nature. Voodoo originated in Africa, specifically with the Fon, Yoruba, and Ewe tribes. Geographically, those ethnic groups can be found throughout Ghana, Togo, Benin, and Nigeria. More than a religion or a cult of death, voodoo plays a major role in everyday life through the symbolization of the African traditions for the Haitian people. Voodoo is far from a uniform worship, but evolved differently from one region to the next.

Voodooism is invested throughout Africa as evidenced by these voodoo dolls on display at a marketplace in Lome, Togo. CORBIS (BELLEVUE)

Voodoo is more than a synthesis of different African beliefs because it incorporates significant influences from Christianity. The word *voodoo* comes from the Fon language, spoken in Benin, meaning "a kind of power which is mysterious and, at the same time, fearsome." Voodoo is invested in all parts of Haitian life and has a considerable influence on each person and on each natural element. The voodoo pantheon consists of many Loas, which are generally associated with a Catholic saint. Despite the existence of these Loas, voodoo is essentially monotheist; in their conception, the Loas are neither more or less than the intermediaries between God and the human ones.

The cult of voodoo appeared in the New World with the African slave trade, which began in Haiti during the 1700s. The slaves brought with them these African traditions. There are also some variations of this cult in Brasilia and in Islands of Antigua. Voodoo involves a mix of different ethnic beliefs and it rapidly became an important element of cultural cohesion for the slaves, who came from different cultures and used different languages.

According to the tradition of voodoo, humans enter into communication with the Loas in a very ritualized manner. The Loas are capricious and they will only be of help if one comes into contact with them correctly through the elaboration of different rituals (according to the Loas one wishes to contact). The voodoo service takes place in the *oúfo* (voodoo temple) and this ritual must be officiated by a *hougan* (priest) or a *mambo* (priestess). Voodoo adherents attribute illnesses and deaths to the wrath of angry ancestors—hence, the considerable importance given to the ritual and appeasement ceremony. The voodoo ceremony embraces several elements, including music, dance, food offering, drumming, and animal sacrifices.

The ritual Rada, which is used in the initiation rite, involves the "Good Loas" who have come from Africa, and who represent the lost mystic world. Inside the voodoo ceremony, the Rada Loas are the first to be served; they represent the guardians of custom and tradition. The Rada Loas play an important function through the different healing processes and their principal characteristic is the fact that all of their actions are directed toward good. In opposition, the ritual Petro involves "Bad Loas," which originated in Haiti. The Petro Loas are considered to be the masters of magic. They embody a kind of relentless force. As the ethnologist Alfred Métraux describes, "the word Petro inescapably conjures up visions of implacable force of roughness and even ferocity" (1972).

The Rada and Petro rituals use both defensive and offensive magic, and can help to obtain justice for someone who has been wronged. The ritual of possession, which appears in the Petro ritual, constitutes the most important way to connect the spirits or ancestors with human beings. A possession crisis appears when the voodoo practitioner is in a situation of marriage with a Loa and becomes his "horse." The possessed person suffers from amnesia, which is explained by the fact that no one can be at the same time god and human. This possession crisis generally appears in a ceremony called *Manger-Loa* and constitutes the major happening in the voodoo ceremony.

The voodoo conceptualization of the world involves the belief in continuity between life and death. In voodoo, death is perceived as a regeneration of all society if the various death rituals and the burial services are well executed. Also, considerable importance is attributed to dead persons and the regular maintenance of the tomb. Thus the cult of voodoo succeeds in attaining a reconciliation between the world of the alive and the world of the dead.

See also: ZOMBIES

Bibliography

Davis, Wade. *The Serpent and the Rainbow.* New York: Simon & Schuster, 1985.

Derem, Maya. *Divine Horsemen: The Living Gods of Haiti.* 1953. Reprint, New Paltz, NY: McPherson, 1983.

Métraux, Alfred. *Voodoo in Haiti.* New York: Schrocken, 1972.

GENEVIÈVE GARNEAU

W

WACO

Public interest in the Branch Davidian movement reached unprecedented heights during the prolonged and ultimately violent standoff between federal authorities and the cult's members in the late winter and early spring of 1993. The Branch Davidian movement dates back to 1929, when Victor Houteff and his followers split off from the Seventh-Day Adventists. The Davidians moved to Mt. Carmel near Waco, Texas, in 1935. After Houteff died in 1955, a succession of leaders controlled the Davidian movement. In 1988 Vernon Howell, who later changed his name to David Koresh, became the movement's new leader.

Under Koresh's leadership, there was a heightened "sense of living in the end of time" (Bromley and Silver 1995, p. 56). Many researchers feel that Koresh saw the events in the New Testament book of Revelation as already unfolding. In Koresh's teachings, he became a central figure in humankind's future: He viewed the Branch Davidians as being responsible for the salvation of people living after Christ's crucifixion (Bromley and Silver 1995; Tabor 1994).

After years at Mt. Carmel, the Branch Davidians suddenly attracted the attention of law enforcement officials. Child-abuse allegations fueled interest in the group. As clinical child psychologist Lawrence Lilliston noted in 1994, it was easy for the public to believe the child-abuse allegations given society's dim view of people who join groups like the Davidians. Another motivation for such allegations involved child-custody disputes that arose when one parent either left the movement or was never a member, according to the sociologists Christopher Ellison and John Bartkowski. Stories in the media alleging abuse abounded; however, Ellison and Bartkowski report that the media made these charges based on anecdotal evidence. Lilliston noted that there was little substantive evidence; in fact, an investigation by Protective Services in Texas turned up no evidence of abuse. However, Bromley and Silver report that Koresh did have sexual relationships with minors; furthermore, Koresh allegedly "avoided recording paternity on some birth registration forms, apparently to deflect official inquiries about the group's sexual practices" (p. 64).

Notwithstanding the authenticity of the child-abuse charges, they were not grounds for involvement of the Bureau of Alcohol, Tobacco, and Firearms (ATF) because such investigations do not fall under federal jurisdiction. Nevertheless, the ATF chose to investigate these charges while also listing illegal weapons as a justification for their involvement; however, the legitimacy of the weapons charges were also disputed.

Federal agents raided Mt. Carmel on February 28, 1993. A year later, according to Moorman Oliver, a retired criminal investigator who specialized in gang and cult affairs, the scene was chaotic and left questions unanswered regarding the actions of both parties. Perhaps the biggest controversy involves who fired the first shot. The accounts from the federal agents and the Branch Davidians differ on this issue, with both sides maintaining their innocence. When it was over, the raid left four

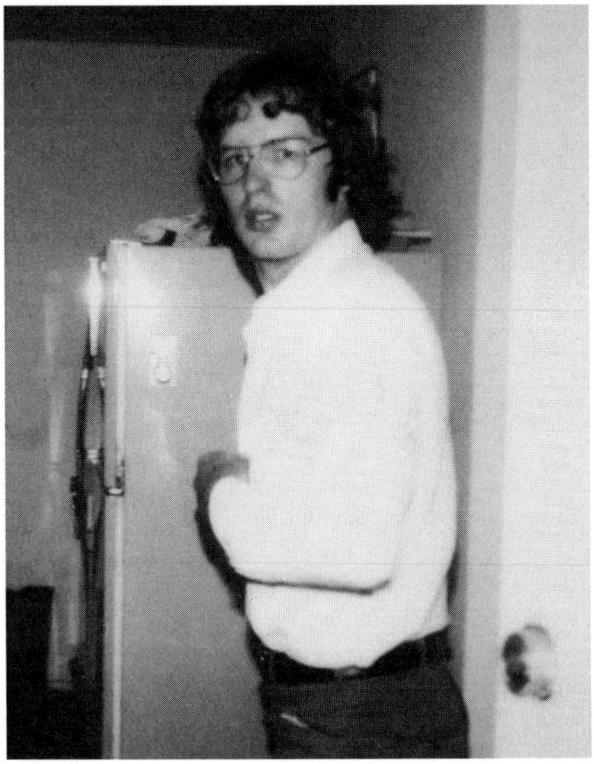

David Koresh joined the Branch Davidian cult in 1981 and became its official leader from 1988 until the federal raids in 1993. Claiming he received instruction from God, Koresh saw the events in Revelation as already unfolding during his leadership. AP/WIDE WORLD PHOTOS

federal agents and six compound residents dead, with Koresh suffering nonfatal injuries.

After the initial raid, a fifty-one-day standoff ensued. Federal agents made life difficult for compound residents—electrical service was shut off, medical care was denied, and grating noises were constantly broadcast over loudspeakers.

Nevertheless, the Branch Davidians remained in Mt. Carmel. James Tabor, a professor of religious studies who worked with federal agents during the standoff in an attempt to help them understand the belief system of the Branch Davidians, noted that the people inside the compound "were willing to die for what they believed, and they would not surrender under threat of force" (1994, p. 15). Tabor felt that Koresh believed he was living the events of Revelation. He felt that God had instructed them to wait inside until, at the end of the waiting period, they were to be killed by the federal agents. After continued pressure to end the standoff, Koresh informed agents that "he had been instructed by God to write an exposition expounding the secrets of the seven seals of Revelations" (Tabor 1994, p. 18). Upon completion, he promised to turn himself over to the authorities; however, agents thought Koresh was stalling.

On April 19, 1993, federal agents stormed Mt. Carmel, citing poor conditions within the compound as their motive. Tanks bashed holes in buildings in order to deliver tear gas. Eventually, the compound was engulfed in fire, though the cause of the fire has been debated. Federal agents felt certain that cult members started the fires in an attempt to commit mass suicide. Another possible source for the fires that has been proposed involves lanterns being overturned by the tanks during the delivery of the tear gas (Lewis 1994; Oliver 1994). An official arson investigation into the cause of the fires blamed the Branch Davidians; however, the government's decision to bulldoze the compound immediately after the investigation has been criticized by some because it prevented any further inquiries based on physical evidence into the cause of the fire (Lewis 1994). Former Senator John Danforth completed a fourteen-month investigation into the events at Waco in 2001. In his testimony before the Senate Judiciary Committee, he reported that the FBI was not responsible for the fires that ultimately killed seventy-four Branch Davidians, including twenty-one children.

Despite the findings of the arson investigation and the investigation by Danforth, some scholars do not agree with the conclusion that the Branch Davidians started the fires. Susan Palmer, an expert on religious suicides, feels that the mass-suicide explanation does not fit the evidence. Survivors of the fire "insist that there was no suicide pact" (p. 104). Furthermore, there were no suicide rehearsals, and there seemed to be no evidence of speeches by Koresh "exhorting martyrdom" (p. 107). Her analysis of the events points to mistakes made by federal agents as the likely cause of the Waco tragedy. A definitive answer regarding whether the fires resulted from mass suicide or from some form of ghastly accident may never be known.

See also: CULTS DEATHS; HEAVEN'S GATE; JONESTOWN

Bibliography

Bromley, David G., and Edward D. "The Davidian Tradition: From Patronal Clan to Prophetic Movement." In Stuart A. Wright ed., *Armageddon in Waco: Critical*

Perspectives on the Branch Davidian Conflict. Chicago: University of Chicago Press, 1995.

Ellison, Christopher G., and John P. Bartkowski. "Babies were Being Beaten: Exploring Child Abuse Allegations at Ranch Apocalypse." In Stuart A. Wright ed., *Armageddon in Waco: Critical Perspectives on the Branch Davidian Conflict.* Chicago: University of Chicago Press, 1995.

Lewis, James R., ed. "Fanning the Flames of Suspicion: The Case against Mass Suicide at Waco." *From the Ashes: Making Sense of Waco.* Lanham, MD: Rowman & Littlefield, 1994.

Lilliston, Lawrence. "Who Committed Child Abuse at Waco?" In James R. Lewis ed., *From the Ashes: Making Sense of Waco.* Lanham, MD: Rowman & Littlefield, 1994.

Oliver, Moorman, Jr. "Killed by Semantics: Or was It a Keystone Kop Kaleidoscope Kaper?" In James R. Lewis ed., *From the Ashes: Making Sense of Waco.* Lanham, MD: Rowman & Littlefield, 1994.

Palmer, Susan J. "Excavating Waco." In James R. Lewis ed., *From the Ashes: Making Sense of Waco.* Lanham, MD: Rowman & Littlefield, 1994.

Pitts, William L., Jr. "Davidians and Branch Davidians: 1929–1987." In Stuart A. Wright ed., *Armageddon in Waco: Critical Perspectives on the Branch Davidian Conflict.* Chicago: University of Chicago Press, 1995.

Tabor, James D. "The Waco Tragedy: An Autobiographical Account of One Attempt to Avert Disaster." In James R. Lewis ed., *From the Ashes: Making Sense of Waco.* Lanham, MD: Rowman & Littlefield, 1994.

Tabor, James D., and Eugene V. Gallagher. *Why Waco? Cults and the Battle for Religious Freedom in America.* Berkeley: University of California Press, 1995.

Wessinger, Catherine. *How the Millennium Comes Violently: From Jonestown to Heaven's Gate.* New York: Seven Bridges Press, 2000.

CHERYL B. STEWART
DENNIS D. STEWART

WAKE

The need to mark someone's death as an event affecting a whole group of people who knew, or knew of, him or her is as fundamental to human life as the necessity to provide opportunities for private grief. This kind of social gathering is usually referred to as a wake. It takes various forms in particular parts of the world. Because death is a potentially frightening subject and there are many taboos surrounding it, wakes are often low-key occasions. Their origins, however, are in behavior that is less inhibited, and it is this to which one must turn in order to understand their psychological and sociological importance.

Definitions of Wake and Their Implications

Broadly speaking, wakes are parties or social gatherings held in connection with funerals. These sometimes involve keeping watch beside the corpse and behaving in a demonstrative way, either by lamenting or merry-making. This implication of unruliness is widespread. According to *Brewer's Dictionary of Phrase and Fable* (1978), the wake is "a vigil celebrated with junketing and dancing." The word primarily means, of course, to prevent someone from sleeping, to wake the person up, to disturb the person's slumber and make it impossible for him or her to slip back into it. The "junketing and dancing" take place in order to wake the person up again. That is why, compared with ordinary social behavior, wakes stand out as wild and unrestrained: They have to be "fit to wake the dead."

From this point of view, then, "waking the dead" is carried out mainly for the benefit of the dead themselves, in order to restore them to wakefulness. To be the expression of a consciously focused intention on the part of the living is its ritual function. Not merely to give a dead person "a good send off," but to keep the dead properly moving in the right direction, instead of simply losing consciousness. In religious terms this means making sure that the person goes on living in the dimension of being he or she must now enter upon. In other words, the deceased must be awake among the dead, a state of affairs that is held to be beneficial to the deceased's survivors as well.

There is evidence of wake-related behavior in all parts of the world. The practice of "waking the dead" is ancient. For example, in Homer's *Iliad* both Hector and Patrodus are depicted as having had funeral feasts, which, if they resembled those of Achilles and Aeneas, included games and contests of skill. The practice of "funeral games" occurs as a common theme in accounts of funeral behavior throughout the world.

Everywhere the underlying intention of the wake is to honor the dead person. The Irish antiquarian Sean O'Suilleabhain believes that the intention was originally to avert the person's rage at having died: "It was an attempt to heal the wound of death and to do final justice to the deceased while he was still physically present. After the burial, the opportunity to do so would be absent" (O'Suilleahbain 1967, p.172). Thus, the practice is held to be an expression of a straightforward fear of dead people and what they are able to do to the living, in accordance with the world-famous anthropologist James Frazer's rationale of ancient funeral customs in his *Fear of the Dead in Primitive Religion* (1933) and the evolutionary doctrine of C. E. Vulliamy, who associates such ideas with a primitive mentality that most of the human race has now grown out of.

These definitions, however, fail notably to account for the "revelry" and "merry-making" that are essential parts of the word's definition. The wake is easier to define than to explain; along with fear and awe, thanksgiving and praise are easy to account for in religious ceremonies surrounding death and dying, but a determination to play games and invent ways of amusing the mourners seems rather more than out of place in such circumstances. Those who claim to understand such behavior at all tend to do so in terms of a reaction against sadness or a celebration of corporate optimism in the face of death—conviviality called upon to reinforce solidarity. One commentator speaks of "creating a space for 'irrational' grief to be acted out" (Toolis 1995, p. 18); another of "energy and activity" used to "anaesthetise the bereaved" (Clare 1995, p.7). From an anthropological point of view, however, the aim of the wake is not to disguise death or even to oppose it but to proclaim it: to proclaim the meaning of its presence for the social group in which it has occurred and to assert its human significance in the face of one's defensive attempts to play it down. The wake overcomes human defenses by demonstrating the provisional nature of life as individual women and men.

Wakes around the World

The wake appears as a holy time of uncharacteristic behavior that is symbolic of a world that has been reduced to disorder. The reversal of characteristic actions is often seen as a method of signifying to departing spirits that they must henceforth find a new life for themselves. In fact, however, these "funeral reversals" have two purposes: Not only are they intended to confuse ghosts and stop them from finding their way back to the land of the living, but they represent the formlessness that characterizes the heart of the funeral process. The chaos through which the dead person must pass is reproduced in the chaotic reversals of social practice that occur during the mourning period, mirroring the contradictory emotions and impulses of bereaved individuals as they rebound between their need to suffer and be comforted, to remember and forget, in the urgency of their search for an escape from the anguish of the present. Thus symbols adopted to express discontinuity with the past and the affirmation of a new status and direction also carry a strong implication of present personal and social chaos. Such symbols and others indicating chaos are widespread throughout the world. In Ireland, for example, the wake was a kind of exaltation of unruliness. In 1853 James A. Prim, a learned member of the Royal Society of Antiquarians of Ireland, complained, "it is difficult to obtain precise details about the wake games because of their apparent obscurity" (Evans 1957, p. 290). He is quick to point out, however, that the obscurity was not indulged in for its own sake:

> The peasantry had no idea of outraging propriety or religion in their performances, holding an unquestioned faith that such observances were right and proper at wakes, whilst under any other circumstances they would shrink with horror from such indelicate exhibitions. *(Evans 1957, p. 290)*

The obscurity and perversity belonged to the rite and were only to be regarded within the context of the rite as a whole. Prim described a game in which a mourner acts the role of a priest, the representative of all the forces of rationality and propriety, who enters into conflict with the master of the wake, a personage known as the Borekeen; the "priest" is first of all thoroughly discomfited and then finally expelled from the room. Again, in a game called Drawing the Ship out of the Mud, "the men actually presented themselves before the rest of the assembly, females as well as males, in a state of nudity" (Evans 1957, p. 291). In another favorite game, the women performers dressed up as men and "proceeded to conduct themselves in a very strange manner" (p. 291). Evans quotes descriptions of similar occurrences at African wakes, in which the female members of a tribe assume the dominant role in the proceedings and behave with unaccustomed lewdness, wearing men's clothing as part of the general reversal of normal behavior. In the same way, among the Ndembu, according to the scholar Victor Turner, "a multiplicity of conflict situations is correlated with a high frequency of ritual performance" (Turner 1974, p. 10). Turner describes how "instead of coming against one another in blind antagonisms of material interest . . . [opposing social principles] . . . are reinstituted against one another in the transcendent, conscious, recognisant unity of Ndembu society whose principles they are. And so, in a sense for a time, they actually *become a play* of forces instead of a bitter battle" (p. 71). The violence originates in frustration. It is the expression of a desire for obedience and conformity that cannot be satisfied.

In *Rituals of Rebellion in South-East Africa* (1954), Max Gluckman maintains that the purpose of such licensed outbreaks of violence and rejection is in fact to take nonconformity and dissent into the system by giving it the kind of social recognition afforded by all corporate rituals. "Such rituals of rebellion by canalising social tensions, perpetuate the established systems of political organisation" (p. 24). Thus, by its apparent exaltation of unruliness and perversity, the wake contrives to establish the primacy of that social order and stability which is sufficiently sure of itself to allow its opposite to be temporarily indulged. In itself, the very fact of public ritual asserts social order. Whatever the individual rite expresses is presented within the context of, and in relation to, the established fact of social belonging.

In Ireland, for example, up to the early years of the twenty-first century, the funeral wakes played a significant part in the social organization of Irish country life. The mere existence of such an institution was itself a symbol of anarchy. Wakes were officially deplored; however, they were secretly tolerated by the dominant Roman Catholic culture of the country. No doubt that the games described by O'Suilleahbain provided a welcome outlet for a variety of repressed feelings on the part of those who would have considered it inappropriate to express them while the deceased was still alive, even if they had been aware of harboring them at the time. The ceremonies with which a society greets the death of one of its members, though they may resemble unconscious patterns in the psychological life of individuals, are not to be simply identified with those patterns. What is expressed in the Irish wake is not merely an opportunity for individual mourners to find release for their feelings, but something more sociologically significant. This difference is not mainly one of quantity—many people finding relief from the unconscious pressure of the love-hate syndrome—but of quality. The ambivalence expressed in the wake is not a symptom, not even a symptom that special circumstances have revealed as outward signs of an unconscious malady, but a proclamation, a conscious message. It is not concerned with past feelings and attitudes but with the state of affairs in the present. The chaos of the wake is a public statement made about the present state, not of the individual but of the world. The wake is society's way of saying that, to a greater or lesser extent, according to the size of the social group involved and the importance of the dead person's role with that group, the world has been radically and permanently changed. For the mourners themselves the integrity of existence has been shattered, and the wake is the public image of an existential chaos. The revelers, pugilists, and buffoons described by O'Suilleahbain as being present at Irish wakes proclaim that, as of now, in the poet William Butler Yeats's words, "Things fall apart, the centre cannot hold" (Yeats 1989, p. 124). Even given the possibility that somehow the world may be remade, it will never be the same again. And for the present, the wake's explicit message is the proclamation of chaos and confusion in the place of order.

Ireland provides specific examples of the kind of funeral behavior observed in Europe, Asia, North and South America, Africa, Australia, and the Indian subcontinent. The scholar Kevin Toolis's 1995 article in the *Guardian Weekend* bears eloquent witness to the fact that genuinely expressive wake practices still exist in Ireland. Toolis has experience of what O'Suilleahbain calls "the old funeral movements" in traditional ways of dealing with death persisting even in the twenty-first century in districts and neighborhoods within Great Britain. Generally speaking, however, as the communal expression of personal feeling has become more privatized in those parts of the world influenced by contemporary Western attitudes, the practice of providing funeral wakes has become something of a rarity. From the point of view of bereaved individuals, families, and communities, this must be regarded as a deprivation, in that a powerful way of registering the significance of somebody's life, and the loss sustained by everyone as a result of that person's death, is no longer available to them. In its own way the "primitive" outrageousness of the wake was an expression of emotional honesty. In its absence, other ways must be found of coming clean about death.

Wakes in the United States

In his extensive study of the wake in the United States, particularly the Central Appalachian section, James Crissman found a variety of purposes for the death vigil in addition to "rousing the ghost," including friends and/or family staying up all night to keep insects, rodents, and cats away from the corpse. One example is given where "the cat got to the deceased and ate the fingers before it was discovered and removed" (Crissman 1994, p. 70). Among the more superstitious, there was a fear that members of the spirit world might carry the body away before it could be inhumed. In addition, some wakers guarded the corpse to deter "body snatchers" that might steal the body for medical purposes. Before embalming, the body had to be scrutinized continuously to make sure the person was actually dead. Another reason for the death vigil was that it was a time to pay one's respects to the departed and give comfort to the bereaved family. It also provided some people with a chance to socialize, and it gave family members a chance to adjust to the loss of their loved one before the corpse was placed in the ground. Finally, the wake sometimes served the purpose of guarding the body pending the arrival of a distant relative.

Psychologically speaking, funerals help human beings to die in the past so that they can live in the future. Wakes provide a crucial stimulus for the real personal changes on which personal growth depends. Certainly it would be profoundly valuable for the human understanding of funerals if the emotional effect of the wake could be studied and compared with the kind of funeral in which the expression of emotion is discouraged. In this vital area of human understanding of death, the field remains open for primary research; but wherever wakes survive, they act as powerful symbols of human reality as people struggle to express the reality of their experience of life and death.

See also: Buried Alive; Grief: Family; Grief and Mourning in Cross-Cultural Perspective

Bibliography

Bendann, Effie. *Death Customs: An Analytical Study of Burial Rites.* London: Kegan Paul, 1939.

Clare, Anthony. "Death and Dying." In Charles Kean ed., *Death and Dying.* Cork, Ireland: Mercier Press, 1995.

Crissman, James K. *Death and Dying in Central Appalachia: Changing Attitudes and Practices.* Urbana: University of Illinois Press, 1994.

Evans, Estyn. *Irish Folkways.* London: Routledge, 1957.

Frazer, James G. *The Fear of the Dead in Primitive Religion.* London: Macmillan, 1933.

Gluckman, Max. *Rituals of Rebellion in South-East Africa.* Oxford: Blackwell, 1954.

Grainger, Roger. "Let Death Be Death; Lessons from the Irish Wake." *Mortality* 3, no. 2 (1998):129–141.

Grainger, Roger. *The Social Symbolism of Grief and Mourning.* London: Kingsley, 1998.

Hockey, Jenny. "The Acceptable Face of Human Grieving? The Clergy's Role in Managing Emotional Expression in Funerals." In D. Clark ed., *The Sociology of Death.* Oxford: Blackwell, 1993.

Lysaght, Patricia. " '*Caoinseadh os Cionn Coisp*': The Lament for the Dead in Ireland." *Folklore* 108 (1997):65–82.

Malinowski, Bronislaw. *Magic, Science and Religion.* London: Souvenir Press, 1972.

O'Suilleabhain, Sean. *Irish Wake Amusements.* Cork, Ireland: Mercier Press, 1967.

Toolis, Kevin. "Death: An Irish Wake and Anglo-Saxon Attitudes." *Guardian Weekend,* 7 October 1995, 18.

Turner, Victor W. *The Ritual Process.* Harmondsworth, England: Penguin, 1974.

Vulliamy, C. E. *Immortal Man.* London: Methuen, 1926.

Yeats, William Butler. *The Collected Poems of W. B. Yeats,* edited by Richard J. Finneran. London: Macmillan, 1989.

ROGER GRAINGER

WAR

Most murders within the human species have been committed by soldiers in war. Though it remains a matter of debate whether the potential for warfare is lodged in genes, culture, or both, humans are the only creature that intentionally kills its own kind for reasons of religious, economic, or political ideology.

Although war has been a near constant in the human condition (estimates are that over the last 3,500 years there have been only 230 years of peace throughout the civilized world), it is the past 100 years that will undoubtedly be remembered as the military century. Of all war fatalities over the past half millennium, fully three-quarters occurred during the twentieth century—including roughly 26 million in World War I and 53 million in World War II.

War is certainly one of the primary driving forces behind cultural evolution. Its history features the increasing lethality of its instruments as well as shifts in acceptable target populations. Primitive warfare was highly ritualistic, often with checks to ensure the killing did not become too efficient and with casualties limited to the group's most expendable segment: young males. Such conflicts in hunting-and-gathering societies often entailed little more than demonstrations of courage and occasional expropriations of another group's food, women, and children.

With the evolution of social organization, the stakes increased, along with the potential for mass killing. Armies of trained warriors numbering in the thousands were fielded thousands of years before the birth of Christ. Whole peoples were slaughtered by the Assyrians, Scythians, and the Huns under Attila. In the thirteenth century, the Mongols brought a reign of terror to central and western Asia, where entire populations of conquered cities were systematically massacred. Genghis Khan led the slaughter of an estimated 40 million Chinese to open the northern part of that country to nomadic herding. With the advent of total war, genocide became a strategic goal. Nevertheless, the heroic individual could still emerge from the mass of slaughter, and there was still contact, however bloody, between warriors and their victims.

Over the past 500 years, international affairs have been largely shaped by European and American innovations in military technologies and strategies. From the sixteenth and seventeenth centuries on, wars of religion and territorial grabs were to be transformed into wars of nationality. To protect "national interests," each state had to maintain a military balance of power with other states. The Napoleonic era was notable for upsetting this balance through its exploitation of modern nationalism. The entire French civilian population was mobilized for war, producing a force so potent that it overran most of Europe. Never before had the world seen anything approaching the scale of mass war in 1812, when Napoleon entered Russia with a half a million soldiers and a thousand cannons. Yet, as Napoleon's failure in Russia showed, strategy combined with individual and collective valor still could overcome the numerical superiority of an enemy in an era that still featured cavalry attacks, infantry assaults, battle cries, and hand-to-hand combat.

Industrialization, technological innovation, and the strategy of mass war combined to relegate the heroic warrior to the annals of the past. During the U.S. Civil War, attempts to combine the Napoleonic tactics of charging in mass formations with the new factory-assembled instruments of death—specifically, breech-loading rifles (propelling bullets ten times farther than the muskets used by Napoleon's troops), land mines, and hand-cranked Gatling guns that fired 350 rounds a minute—led to the slaughter of more Americans than two world wars and the Korean and Vietnam conflicts combined. When Europeans turned their Maxim machine guns on each other in World War I, the individual soldier was reduced to an interchangeable, impersonal cog of massive industrialized killing machines. No Achilles or Hector could brave attacks originating from hundreds of feet beneath the sea or from thousands of feet in the air.

Before the outbreak of World War II, the bombing of civilians was generally regarded as a barbaric act. As the war continued, however, all sides abandoned previous restraints. War economies had to be created to support the millions on the front, employing women and the aged to replace the missing men. With so much of the population integrated within an elaborate wartime division of labor, distinctions between combatants and civilians were increasingly blurred. Aerial attacks on the great cities became standard strategy early in the conflict, carried out by bombers and later by Germany's unmanned V-1 and V-2 rockets. The war ended with the obliteration of Hiroshima and Nagasaki by atomic bombs; the crews brought about the death of over a third of a million Japanese civilians.

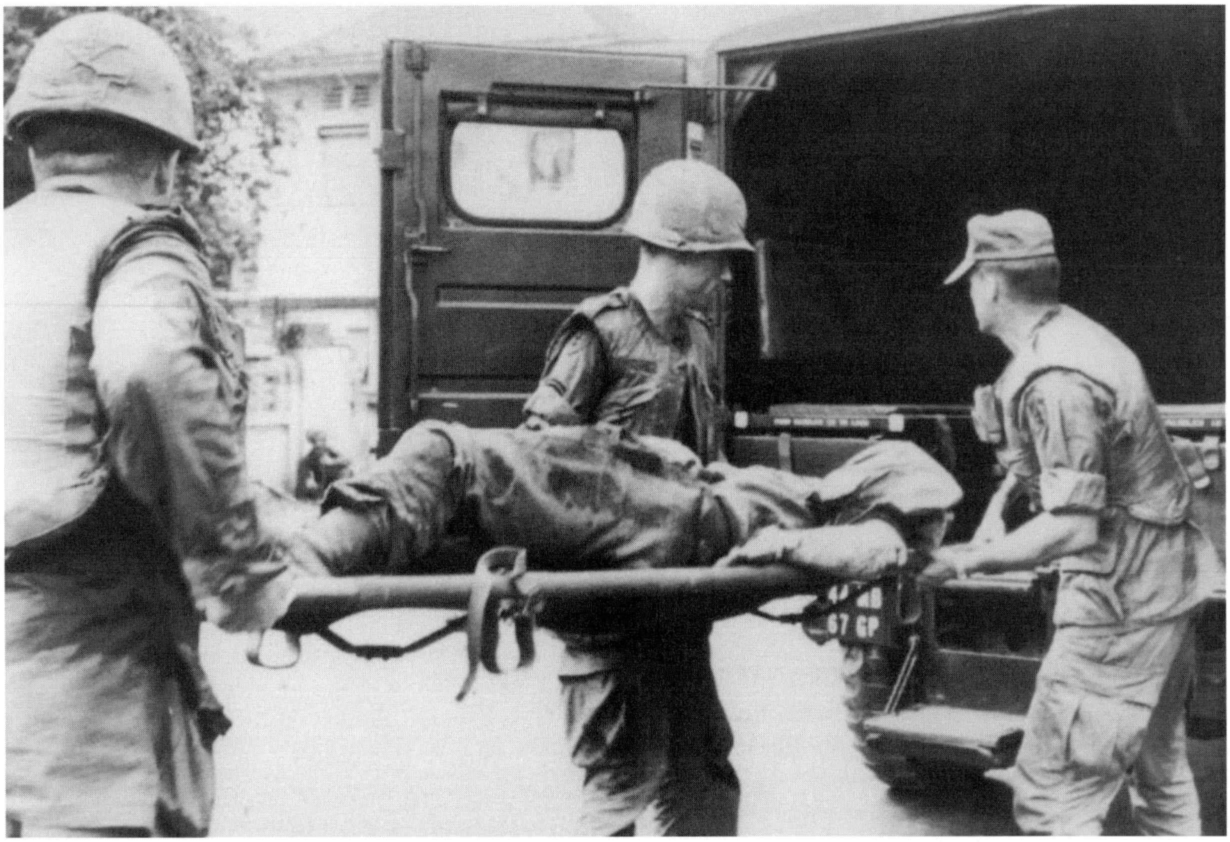

American soldiers move the body of a comrade who died in the 1968 bombing of the United States bachelor officers' quarters in Saigon during the Vietnam War. PUBLIC DOMAIN

Since World War II, the rule that soldiers should only kill other soldiers when in face-to-face combat also evaporated as civilians were increasingly drawn into the frays. In Vietnam, Americans killed unarmed women and children. Nearly 40 percent of the Panamanians killed in the 1989 U.S. Operation Just Cause invasion were civilians, as were three out of ten Croatians killed by Yugoslav Army and Serbian troops in 1991–1992, and over six out of ten casualties in Bosnia. The percentage of war-related deaths comprised of civilians increased from 14 percent in World War I to 67 percent in World War II to 75 percent in conflicts of the 1980s to 90 percent during the 1990s.

The twenty-first century began with the potential for nuclear, biological, and chemical holocausts. Despite the massive needs of the world community, governments continue to spend nearly a trillion dollars a year designing and perfecting the means by which to kill one another's citizens. The arms industry remains the world's largest manufacturing industry. Worldwide, for every dollar currently spent per pupil for education, twenty-five are spent per soldier.

Postmodern warfare also features a reversal of past trends toward total war and deindividualized warriors. With the end of the cold war, military conflicts are no longer the preserves of nation-states but rather increasingly involve terrorists such as al Qaeda's mastermind Osama Bin Laden, crude paramilitary forces, and cruel clashes between ethnic and religious groups. The early twenty-first century was an era when a single individual could produce a strain of lethal bacteria or a chemical weapon capable of decimating an entire city. Ironically, the modern West's high-tech culture has bred a complacency about risk that has combined with the dense interdependencies of society's parts to render the most advanced societies especially vulnerable to disruption by an attack on only one of its parts—as when a computer virus is unleashed, a water supply infected, a power grid disrupted, or office buildings obliterated in kamikaze attacks by hijacked commercial jumbo jets.

See also: CEMETERIES, MILITARY; CEMETERIES, WAR; DEHUMANIZATION; GENOCIDE

Bibliography

Crossette, Barbara. "UNICEF Report Sees Children as Major Victims of Wars." *New York Times,* 11 December 1995, A7.

Dyer, Gwynne. *War.* New York: Crown Publishers/Media Resources, 1985.

Keegan, John. *A History of Warfare.* New York: Knopf, 1993.

Moyers, Bill, David Gruben, and Ronald Blumen. "The Arming of the Earth." *A Walk through the 20th Century with Bill Moyers.* Washington, DC: PBS Video, 1983. Videorecording.

Toynbee, Arnold. *War and Civilization.* New York: Oxford University Press, 1950.

MICHAEL C. KEARL

WASHINGTON, GEORGE

George Washington died in his bed at Mount Vernon, Virginia, on December 14, 1799. As a Revolutionary War hero and the new nation's first president, Washington's life and death led to his glorification as a key iconic, mythological figure in United States history. The death of this founding father posed a threat to the emerging social identity that could only be resolved by massive, communal ceremonies celebrating his life, and his essential contributions to the birth of the new nation.

Born on February 22, 1732, in Westmoreland County, Virginia, Washington's early life included working on the family plantation and a short stint as a local surveyor. The French and Indian War (1754–1763) offered the Virginian a new career opportunity in the military, where the young Washington was quickly promoted to lieutenant colonel. In 1755, at only twenty-three years of age, Washington became a colonel and was appointed commander in chief of the Virginia militia. He left the army in 1758 and returned to Mount Vernon, when he married Martha Dandridge Custis and entered the political arena as a member of Virginia's House of Burgesses from 1759 to 1774. During this time Washington became a fierce opponent of British colonial policies, especially those relating to discrimination of colonial military officers and to western expansion.

Washington then served as a delegate to the First and Second Continental Congress (1774–1775), and in June 1775 Congress unanimously favored his appointment as commander in chief of the Continental forces. His leadership during the American Revolution, and his storied military exploits, including his crossing the Delaware River on Christmas 1776 for a surprise attack, contributed to his growing popularity as a both a warrior and civic leader. After the war Washington returned once again to Mount Vernon to work the land for a short time before leading the Virginia delegation to the Constitutional Convention and, eventually, assuming the office of presidency in 1789. Despite deep divisions in American political life during his first term, Washington was elected to a second term in 1792. After this term finished, he retired once again to Mount Vernon and remained there with Martha until his death in 1799, when he was entombed on the grounds.

Washington's death led to unprecedented levels of public mourning in the new nation. Rather than create debilitating social grief, his passing served as a critical source of cultural rejuvenation and optimism about the future of the young nation. In towns and villages throughout the land Americans celebrated his death with local ritual activities (which often included mock funerals) that produced deep and long-lasting forms of social solidarity uniting disparate regions in common cause to mark the occasion of his passing. Although these celebrations were tinged with sadness, they also provided significant opportunities for Americans to symbolize and celebrate both the mythic qualities associated with the man and the national virtues associated with the new republic.

Memorialization efforts began immediately, with the production of mourning art—which combined traditional genres of expression with innovative, more spontaneous expressions of sadness—playing a crucial popular role in efforts to publicly remember the national hero. The various symbolic motifs found in this art, ranging from ancient images of mourners in classical dress to Christian imagery invoking resurrection and redemption themes and common allegorical figures like

America, Columbia, and Father Time, gave citizens a shared frame of reference to imagine his life and continuing presence in American life after death. All of these motifs in mourning art produced at the time of his death reinforced the linkages between Washington, patriotism, and Christianity. The art also established a cultural link between death and the regeneration of national life that would prove to be so critical to the elaboration of a distinctly American form of civil religion, and that would be repeated throughout the course of American history with the passing of such critical political figures as Thomas Jefferson, Abraham Lincoln, and John F. Kennedy.

For artists, politicians, ministers, and other leaders, remembering the spirit of Washington translated into a spiritual practice that nourished nationalism and civic renewal. Rather than reaffirm social distance between classes, in death Washington added fuel to the fires of democracy and egalitarianism: His life not only taught Americans about virtues like hard work, love of country, and the value of home life, it conjured now-mythical stories about the birth of the nation and its future destiny. In addition to his central role in the political life of the nation, Washington could be understood as America's first celebrity. His death became a time for ardent fans to mourn collectively, and discover innovate rituals to worship his memory. The open forms of public display surrounding his death set the mold for later collective exhibitions of adoration, identification, and deification.

See also: BROWN, JOHN; CELEBRITY DEATHS; IMMORTALITY, SYMBOLIC; LINCOLN IN THE NATIONAL MEMORY; ROYALTY, BRITISH

Bibliography

Laderman, Gary. *The Sacred Remains: American Attitudes toward Death, 1799–1883*. New Haven, CT: Yale University Press, 1996.

Pike, Martha V., and Janice Gray Armstrong, eds. *A Time to Mourn: Expressions of Grief in Nineteenth-Century America*. Stony Brook, NY: The Museums of Stony Brook, 1980.

Randall, Willard Sterne. *George Washington: A Life*. New York: Henry Holt, 1997.

Schwartz, Barry. *George Washington: The Making of an American Symbol*. New York: Free Press, 1987.

GARY M. LADERMAN

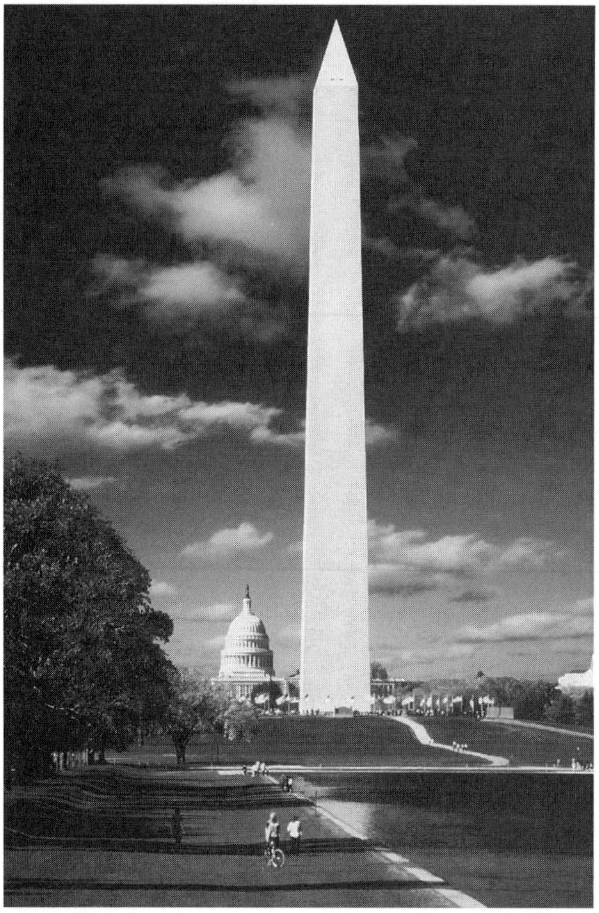

Construction of the Washington Monument began in 1848, although its design was significantly altered in 1876 to slightly resemble an Egyptian pyramid. The completed monument was opened to the public in October 1888; it stands just over 555 feet tall and an elevator takes visitors to the observation area in the pyramidian. CRAIG AURNESS/CORBIS

WEBER, MAX

Max Weber (1864–1920) is one of the most influential and prolific writers of sociological theory. In conceptualizing modernity, Weber focused on the rationalization of the world where a society becomes dominated by cultural norms of efficiency, calculability, predictability, and control resulting in dehumanizing rationalization where the average man is less important than the clock and the calculator. Just as the fast-food industry has become rationalized, so have the industries associated with dying and disposal of the dead.

Although Weber never actually dealt with the issue of death, many theorists using this definition of rationalization have shown that it can be extended to how society deals with death. As a society becomes more rational, efficiency in dealing with the dead becomes more important. There are funeral directors and other professionals who specialize in the systematic and routine caring for the deceased. Calculability is also evident in American society's view of death. Many actuarians and physicians focus on disease and death statistics in an attempt to better predict the causes and timing of death. The rationalization of society is evident in the demystification of death. Death is no longer "a journey to the next world" but simply an end to life. As a society moves toward rationality as its norm, death becomes a systematic and logical event, eliminating some of the most human aspects of dying.

See also: DEATH SYSTEM; SOCIAL FUNCTIONS OF DEATH

Bibliography

Ritzer, George. *The McDonaldization of Society.* Thousand Oaks, CA: Pine Forge Press, 1996.

Ritzer, George. *Sociological Theory.* New York: Alfred A. Knopf, 1983.

Weber, Max. *The Protestant Ethnic and the Spirit of Capitalism.* New York: Charles Scribner's Sons, 1958.

JOHNETTA M. WARD

WIDOW-BURNING

The burning of wives on the funeral pyres of their husbands, widow-burning, commonly known as *sati* ("suttee" in English), has been practiced in India since at least the fourth century B.C.E., when it was first recorded in Greek accounts. It was banned by British colonial law in 1829–1830 and survived in the native Indian states until the late 1880s, when it was effectively eradicated, although extremely rare cases persisted into the early twentieth century. Since India's independence in 1947—or more precisely since 1943—there has been a spectacular revival of the phenomenon in four Northern Indian states: Bihar, Uttar Pradesh, Madhya Pradesh, and especially Rajasthan, a former stronghold of sati. Although the number of women who have committed sati since that date likely does not exceed forty (with thirty in Rajasthan alone), an infinitesimal percentage of the female population, the reactivation of the practice has had considerable social and political impact, especially in the case of the "Deorala affair"—the burning of a young Rajput widow named Rup Kanwar in Rajasthan in September 1987. The nationwide trauma that followed this incident and the media coverage it received (in contrast to the relative indifference shown to the other cases) led the federal government to take legal action, issuing the Sati Commission (Prevention) Act a year later.

Sati was never a universal practice in India, even though the earliest statistics recorded by British officials in the late eighteenth and early nineteenth centuries were at times quite remarkable. Several reasons explain the high numbers logged in certain periods and regions of the subcontinent. For instance, a combination of external factors such as cholera epidemics and local customs, like the unbridled polygyny of Kulin Brahmans, might account for a portion of the 8,134 cases recorded in the Bengal Presidency alone between 1815 and 1828. Widow-burning is but one of a wide range of religious rituals implying self-mutilation and self-sacrifice observed by Indian men and women alike. Although death by fire has been the prevalent form of the ritual, cremation being the most common type of disposal of the dead among Hindus, sati could take the form of widow burial whenever the caste or community of the deceased called for it, as for example with the Jogi weavers of Bengal, or with the Jasnathis of Rajasthan, a lost branch of Ismaili Muslims who have reconverted to Hinduism.

The original meaning of the Sanskrit word *sati* was simply "faithful wife"; only later was the term applied specifically to the woman who immolated herself. In any case, it never referred to the rite or custom of widow-burning. It was the British who, at the close of the eighteenth century, officialized the confusion, expressed by many travelers before them, between the immolated woman and the sacrifice of widows. The Sanskrit language knows of no specific denomination for the practice and instead resorts to periphrastic and euphemistic expressions like "going with" and "dying with," when the widow is burned on the same funeral pyre as her husband, or "going after" and "dying after" when she is burnt on a separate pyre, these being the two major facets of the rite.

Also noteworthy is the fact that according to the Hindu belief system, the sati dies as a wife, eschewing the ill-fated, ominous, and impure state of widowhood: The "eye of faith," combined with the "belief effect" of the ritual, makes the joint cremation of husband and wife appear to onlookers (and as far as one can tell, to the sati herself) to be a reenactment of their marriage ceremony. Through her sacrifice, the sati preserves the bodily and spiritual unity of the couple, affording the Hindu sacrament of marriage its ultimate and truest expression.

Placed in a broader context, widow-burning is but one among a variety of forms of funerary ceremonial, found in many parts of the world, that involve the voluntary death of certain categories of survivors. These people sacrifice themselves (individually or en masse) in the course of the obsequies of a higher-ranking person—a ruler, master, or husband. The belief underlying this body of suicidal practices (termed *altruistic* by Émile Durkheim in his 1897 classical work *Le suicide*) is that the deceased will enjoy the same goods and services in the beyond as he had on earth. He will need his mount and his weapons to wage war, food to assuage his hunger, and finery to set off his beauty and glory. In like manner, he will need to be accompanied by his servants, his counselors, and, finally, his wives.

What seems to lie at the heart of the practice of "following in death" is the settling of a debt of obligation and love (the two go together) binding the various parties to a common master. In ancient China, for example, all the categories of survivors mentioned above were buried with kings or great warlords, together with horses, offerings, and artifacts. Such was also the case in Scythia. According to some authors, the custom would have been introduced into India when Scythians (locally known as Shakas) conquered parts of its territory in the first century B.C.E. It would then have been exported from India to the kingdoms of Southeast Asia—mainly Java, Lombok, and Bali—where Hinduism became the state religion during the first centuries of the common era.

An alternative thesis maintains that widow-burning was indigenous to India but belonged to the same pre-Aryan wild clans and tribes as those that had introduced human sacrifice to propitiate bloodthirsty deities, as well as other equally "loathsome" rituals, into the Hindu canon of practice. Following the same line of argumentation, the remarkable fact that neither the Vedas, the sacred revelation of ancient Brahmanism, nor such authoritative treatises on dharma as the *Laws of Manu* ever mention widow-burning, is taken as evidence for the repression of this barbaric custom by a civilized Aryan society, in which the widow was enjoined either to lead an ascetic life for the rest of her days or, if she had had no male issue, to cohabit with her husband's younger brother until she begot one. These reconstructions tell readers more about the fantasies and ideologies of the people who conceived them than they do about the history of the practice itself. The aboriginal versus Scythian origin theories seem, in fact, to serve the same purpose: to remove sati rituals from the pure land of the Aryans and exile them into its darkest inner or outer confines. In this way, not only is India's immaculate image as the golden land of spirituality and nonviolence preserved, but also the hard core of "barbarism" found in Hinduism is conveniently expelled and thereby repressed.

The latest version of this convenient scenario is the one used in the polemic following the 1987 burning of Rup Kanwar in Deorala. This was the last and most highly publicized of a series of widow immolations that took place in Shekhavati, a rural region of Rajasthan, one of India's most underdeveloped and conservative states. The "Deorala affair" has been interpreted in a variety of ways according to the different viewpoints of the various actors in the controversy of Himalayan proportions. The proponents of secularism and women's causes declared Rup's immolation to be a patent case of murder in a plot in which the rural illiterate masses had been fanaticized by obscurantist forces and demonic agents belonging to specific castes (mainly the Rajputs and Marwaris) who were backing the revival of an outdated, outlawed practice to further their own interests, whether political, economic, or symbolic.

Commenting on the case and its extraordinary impact on a theretofore indifferent public, the Indian social psychologist Ashis Nandy has offered the following interpretation: The burning of Rup Kanvar became a cause célèbre because of her social milieu. Kanvar was born in a semiurban, well-to-do family from Jaipur, the state capital of Rajasthan, and had received a quite respectable education. The English-speaking and Westernized elite that sought to protect itself from the backlash of acculturation by stigmatizing Hinduism and by conflating tradition with superstition, rural life with social backwardness, and belief with obscurantism—that same elite felt directly threatened by the sacrifice of a young woman whose level of education and social background linked her to an economically emerging social group. Kanvar's death could only trigger a defensive reaction because it demonstrated that the line of demarcation between barbarism and civilization, upon which the edifice of what Nandy has called "a new form of internal colonialism" (Hawley 1994) had been built, had proved very easy to cross.

Nearly nothing is known of sati's origin or of its spread across the Indian territory and social strata during the first millennium of the common era. The general opinion is that sati was originally only performed in Ksatriya milieus—by the women of kings, warriors, and persons who had died a heroic death—and that it was eventually adopted by other status groups of society in the course of the second millennium C.E. as the result of a change of soteriology; this is, for example, the position of the Indian historian Romila Thapar. Many invoke the well-known process of Sanskritization, as theorized by Indian anthropologist M. N. Srinivas in the 1950s, to account for this imitation of the royal model. It is true that the first accounts experts have—Greek sources from Alexander's time (Onesicritos and Aristobulos)—describe the competition between the wives of the warlord Keteus to burn themselves alive on their husband's funeral pyre. It is also true that widow-burning became, from the seventh century onward, a common feature and thus an emblematic caste-identity marker among the same Rajputs who claim to be the Ksatriyas, the "warrior caste," of modern India. However, this is hardly sufficient ground for claiming that this custom was originally the exclusive prerogative of the martial castes, especially when numerous early accounts, both textual and epigraphical, of other groups—from Brahmans at the top of the hierarchical scale down to middle, low, and even impure castes—practicing widow-burning.

This stone memorial in Jodhpur, Rajasthan, India, marks the location where several women committed sati. Leaving home for their funeral pyre, women dipped their hands in red pigment and left a symbolic mark of devotion and loyalty to their deceased husbands. BRIAN A. VIKANDER/ CORBIS

Another problematic issue is the prevalence of widow-burning in those regions of India in which "Shakta" Tantrism has been the dominant form of religious belief and practice since as early as the ninth century C.E. It is in an area comprising the modern states of Bengal, Orissa, Rajasthan, Gujarat, Madhya Pradesh, Karnataka, and Tamilnadu that are found at village boundaries memorial-hero and sati stones, sometimes stretching like vast funeral grounds as far as the eye can see. The presence of such memorials is actually the only means specialists have for approximately mapping sati, both geographically and historically. The overlap between Shakta devotionalism and the spread of widow sacrifice raises a particularly difficult question for Indologists insofar as Shakta Tantra—with its transgression and reversal of the fundamental values of orthodox Hinduism—gives primacy to the female aspect of the godhead, the well-known Shakti of which Tantric practitioners and believers are worshippers—whence the term *Shakta.* Because, according to this religious system, every woman is essentially the Goddess incarnate, and her female energy the source of life and salvation, it seems difficult at first to reconcile this worldview and ethos with the practice of widow-burning.

But the first question that arises with regard to widow-burning, a question that casts its long shadow across the entire field of its historiography, is that of knowing whether these immolations were voluntary acts or whether, on the contrary, women were forced to burn themselves—whether their immediate circle (family, priesthood, caste) and the dominant religious ideology they embraced did not force them, at the time of their declaration of intent and a fortiori in their hour of death, to mount the funeral pyre. This crucial element of the mystery of widow-burning is all the more intriguing inasmuch as the historical data provide as much evidence for the one hypothesis as for the other. According to the view one chooses to adopt, one will interpret widow-burning as a form of suicide, as a sacrifice, or as murder—a murder made all the more odious by the fact that it is also a matricide because it is the closest male relative of the deceased, the son, who lights the pyre on which his mother will be burned alive. When viewed as a murder, sati also takes on the dimensions of a collective homicide, being that thousands of men and women attend such events, and because the responsibility of the society as a whole is deeply implicated in it. At the opposite end of the spectrum, those Hindus who believe in "satihood" will view the ritual as a supreme act of selfless devotion and a manifestation of female sacredness, the sati literally becoming Shakti incarnate at her time of death and her burning a magical phenomenon of yogic self-combustion. In this perspective, her self-immolation is a sacrifice that, according to the Hindu belief system, entails no violence to the consenting victim.

Down to the present day, it is the dire fate of Indian widows in India that is invoked as the primary reason for existence of sati. Although widow remarriage has been authorized by law since as early as 1856, it was and still is rarely resorted to among higher or middle castes, or among groups that follow a strategy of embracing high-caste values and practices to collectively uplift themselves in the social hierarchy. An object of universal repugnance, the widow is required to lead a life of asceticism and self-mortification. In the higher castes, her head is shaved, and she is deprived of every finery, every pleasure, and every comfort. Because she is the bearer of misfortune and impurity, she is excluded from domestic festivities, and even from the wedding of her own children. Her existence is but a monotonous succession of fasts, religious observances, and devotional practices.

It can, however, become a veritable trial, given the fact that the hatred and resentment of her in-laws, legitimized by the belief that the widow has "eaten" her husband—caused his death through her misconduct in previous births or in this life—knows no limits. She is subject to humiliation, insult, and abuse. She can be thrown out into the streets and, if her own family refuses to take her back, have no other recourse than to join a widows' ashram at such holy sites as Vrindavan in Uttar Pradesh, or to make good on her reputation as a *whore*—a commonplace term of abuse for widows. The young widow is especially execrated, since it is judged that her unhappy fate is the result of abominable sins committed in a past life. Early widowhood was widespread in a society where life expectancy was notably low and where child marriage was common among certain castes and in certain regions until it was outlawed (the custom still persists in some rural areas of Rajasthan). So it is that a number of cases of women who committed sati before reaching puberty have come down to us, such as that reported in the late-seventeenth-century account of the French traveler François Bernier, who witnessed the burning of a twelve-year-old widow from Lahore who trembled and wept so vigorously that she had to be bound to finish the matter.

In sharp contrast to the miserable plight that would otherwise have befallen her, the bright prospect of the glory awaiting the woman who commits sati might have been a strong incentive to newly widowed Indian women; this was at least a widely shared idea. Not only was the sati ensured that her sacrifice—in which she would experience no pain—would bring her eternal bliss with her husband in the beyond, she was also persuaded that she would redeem the sins of seven generations in her father's, mother's, and in-laws' lineages, and never be born again into the "impure" female sex. In castes and milieus where sati had become the ultimate criterion of a woman's "wifely duty" and an icon of caste purity (and thereby, status), not only would family members, Brahman priests, and bards insist that the widow take the solemn vow to burn herself, but tradition at large—as represented by myths, literature, hagiography, and rituals in which satis were worshiped as deities—and, of late, propaganda and political and caste-based activism, left her little chance to escape her fate.

Once the sati declared her intention to follow her husband in death she had to burn herself, even if the Hindu legal treatises that sanctioned this highly controversial practice allowed her to retract. Very often, the would-be sati would have to prove her resolution by enduring a preliminary ordeal, such as burning her finger in a candle flame without showing any sign of pain. This would be taken as proof of her possession by "sat"—by the essence of her being in her role as the perfect wife, a sati—a supernatural power that enabled her to heal, protect, and foretell the future; to curse and bring misfortune on her community or in-laws; as well as to produce wonders and miracles, such as the lighting of her own pyre. The utterance of the deadly vow set in motion a process of mythification, and in certain cases of deification, that reached its climax in the burning itself, a sacred event for believers, granting merit to family, performers, and onlookers alike. One may further surmise, on the basis of a number of indications, that the sati no longer perceived herself as a flesh-and-blood woman but rather as some sort of deity at the very least, a Shakti in the making. In demonstrable cases in which no violence was used, this process of objectification within the sati herself might explain, at least in part, how burning oneself alive—an act which continues to be repressed in the recesses of the unthinkable—could actually form a part of human experience.

See also: CREMATION; GENDER AND DEATH; WIDOWS IN THIRD WORLD NATIONS

Bibliography

Bernier, François. *Voyages de F. Bernier (Angevin) contenant la description des Estats du Grand Mogol, de l'Indoustan, du royaume de Kachemire.* Amsterdam: D. P. Marret, 1699.

Courtright, Paul B. "*Sati,* Sacrifice and Marriage: The Modernity of Tradition." In Lindsey Harlan and Paul B. Courtright eds., *From the Margins of Hindu Marriage: Essays on Gender, Religion and Culture.* New York: Oxford University Press, 1995.

Durkheim, Émile. *Suicide: A Study in Sociology,* translated by John A. Spaulding and George Simpson. Glencoe, NY: Free Press, 1951.

Hawley, John Stratton. *Sati, the Blessing and the Curse: The Burning of Wives in India.* New York: Oxford University Press, 1994.

Nandy, Ashis. "Sati As Profit versus Sati As a Spectacle: The Public Debate on Roop Kanwar's Death." In J. S. Hawley ed., *Sati: The Blessing and the Curse.* New York: Oxford University Press, 1994.

Narasimhan, Sakuntala. *Sati: A Study of Widow Burning in India.* New Delhi: Viking, 1990.

Papers Relating to East India Affairs, viz. Hindoo Widows, and Voluntary Immolations. London: House of Commons, 1821–1830.

Sharma, Arvind. *Sati: Historical and Phenomenological Essays.* New Delhi: Motilal Banarsidass, 1988.

Thapar, Romila. *Interpreting Early India.* New Delhi: Oxford University Press, 1994.

Thompson, Edward. *Suttee: A Historical and Philosophical Enquiry into the Hindu Rite of Widow-Burning.* London: Allen and Unwin, 1928.

Trial by Fire: A Report on Roop Kanwar's Death. Bombay: Women and Media Committee, Bombay Union of Journalists, 1987.

Wadley, Susan. "No Longer a Wife: Widows in Rural North India." In Lindsey Harlan and Paul B. Courtright eds., *From the Margins of Hindu Marriage: Essays on Gender, Religion, and Culture.* New York: Oxford University Press, 1995.

Weinberger-Thomas, Catherine. *Ashes of Immortality: Widow-Burning in India,* translated by Jeffrey Mehlman and David Gordon White. Chicago: University of Chicago Press, 1999.

Weinberger-Thomas, Catherine. "*Cendres d'immortalité. La crémation des veuves en Inde.*" *Archives de Sciences Sociales des Religions* 67, no. 1 (1989):9–51.

CATHERINE WEINBERGER-THOMAS

WIDOWERS

Although the death of a spouse is more common for women than for men, a man's chance of becoming a widower increases as he ages. According to the U.S. Census Bureau in 2001, approximately 3 percent of the men capable of marriage are widowed compared to 12 percent of the women.

These proportions increase dramatically, however, among those sixty-five years of age and older (14% men versus 45% women) and even more so among those aged eighty-five and older where 43 percent of the men are widowers (compared to 80% of the women).

Often the widower experience is examined in light of similarities and differences between them and their female counterparts. Although there is a natural tendency to draw comparisons between widows and widowers, some features of "widowerhood" are unique and warrant special attention. It is also true that the course of bereavement among widowers is wrought with diversity and variability. The process of adaptation to the loss of their wives is rarely linear and is more aptly described as one of oscillation between good and bad days or even moments within a single day. Some cope more successfully than others who experience greater difficulty; however, there is a plethora of evidence that suggests that many ultimately demonstrate a high degree of resilience as time passes.

Oftentimes widowers' experiences are affected by a variety of factors, including their age, the relationship with their children, how well they are able to assume new responsibilities, and how much emotional and material support is available from others. Similarly, the loss of a wife can have adverse consequences on the widower's physical health. This too can vary depending on the widower's prior health, his lifestyle, and to what extent he possesses the skills he needs to take care of himself. Finally, while many widowers have the resources and skills that enable them to eventually cope and adapt on their own, a significant few turn to more formal sources of help. Widowers' motivation to seek assistance as well as the effectiveness of that help often is a product of their beliefs and expectations about how a man is to grieve and respond to loss.

What Widowers Experience

While women who lose their husbands often speak of feeling abandoned or deserted, widowers tend to express the loss as one of "dismemberment," as if they had lost something that kept them organized and whole. The Harvard Bereavement Study, a landmark investigation of spousal loss that took place in the Boston area during the late 1960s, reported that widowers often equated the death of their wives with the loss of their primary source of protection, support, and comfort. This went to the very core of their overall sense of well-being. It has been described as "being lost without a compass," usually due to their profound loneliness but also because widowers often depended on their wives for many things like managing the household, caring for their children, and being their only true confidant. This sense of being lost is more profound when widowers need help but have difficulty obtaining or even asking for it. They also can experience ambiguity about the emotions they are feeling and the uncertainty of how to express them.

Emotional response. Similar to widows, bereaved husbands experience an array of emotions, such as anger, shock (especially if the death is unexpected), numbness, denial, and profound sadness. Unlike widows, however, grieving men tend to control their emotions (with the possible exception of anger), for instance, by holding back and crying less openly. Widowers, more often than not, will channel their energy into active coping and problem-solving strategies like work, physical activity, or addressing disruptions in the household. At other times they may prefer to be alone with their thoughts, whether thinking about the circumstances surrounding their wife's death or reflecting on ways to cope with their new situation.

Widowers who experience the same emotions as widows but were raised with the belief that emotional control is a sign of strength often find themselves confronting an inner conflict about how to respond to a loss. The situation may instinctively call for a response that is emotional but the widower may not be socialized to express himself in that way. Adding to this confusion on the part of the widower is an assumption that there is only one way to grieve. Men usually express their feelings of grief in solitary ways, but this should not be construed as being any less intense than a widow's grief. At the same time, to a varying degree, some widowers express their emotions more openly than others, suggesting that while some responses may be more typical, any one widower's experience can be somewhat unique as well.

Mental health issues. Although not entirely conclusive, several studies suggest that widowers can be prone to depression after the death of their wives, especially when they are compared with their nonbereaved married counterparts. On average, married men are less likely than married women to be depressed. Most epidemiological studies report that marriage tends to be protective for men in terms of depression and other mental health problems, largely because a supportive marital relationship buffers them from the negative impact of the stress and strains of everyday life. Bereavement, therefore, is more depressing for many widowers because they, quite simply, have more to lose than widows. This is based on the assumption that a man's spouse is often his primary source of social support. Consequently, although a widower may have been more apt to express his thoughts and feelings to his wife when she was alive, he may be equally unlikely to be so open to others. Widows more frequently use alternative sources of support that can protect them more effectively from potentially adverse effects of the loss and other stressors.

In some studies, many widowers are more recently bereaved than the widows are, most often due to differences in life expectancy and remarriage rates between men and women. Men usually are widowed at a later age and are more likely to die before being bereaved for a long period of time. Younger widowers usually have more opportunities to remarry, whereas widowed women will have fewer options for remarriage and remain widowed longer. Because the most difficult time usually is early in the bereavement process, the widowers who participate in these studies will have had less time than the widows to adjust to the loss and more likely will report being depressed when they are interviewed. Not all research, however, supports the conclusion that widowers suffer more depression than widows. Many of the gender differences regarding depression and other mental health outcomes are largely unexplained and consequently are inconclusive.

The degree of difficulty that widowers face can be dependent on when in their own life the loss occurs. Although not necessarily true of everyone, many widowers whose wives die around the same time that they are retiring from their occupation (or soon thereafter) can be prone to more difficulty. Married couples often have expectations about how they intend to spend their retirement years together. Those expectations can be shattered as newly bereaved widowers suddenly find themselves facing retirement alone, which could be a source of depression or hopelessness. Conversely, men who are in their preretirement years might adapt more easily. They are typically still employed, could be more socially connected due to ties in the workplace, and might still have children in the home. Of course, these also can be potential sources of difficulty, particularly if relationships with children are strained or if assuming new responsibilities around the household interferes with the widower's effectiveness at work and elsewhere. Conversely, these life circumstances could represent a sense of feeling useful, involved, and being engaged in meaningful activity—all potential constructive coping mechanisms for the widower.

Health and Mortality among Widowers

Much of the research suggests that there is a greater prevalence of mortality and morbidity among the spousal bereaved compared to those who are currently married. Many of these same studies further report that the risk of becoming physically ill or dying soon after the loss of a spouse is greatest for widowers. The fact that men tend to be older when their spouses die could explain some of these findings. Although mortality is less common among younger widowers, the difference between their mortality rates and those of their married counterparts is greater than what is observed among older age groups, especially within the first six months of bereavement.

Why are some widowers at risk for illness and even death? One explanation is that married couples are exposed to the same environmental influences and often pursue similar lifestyles. If any of these have a negative impact on the health of one spouse, resulting in his or her death, a similar outcome could follow for the other. This explanation, however, fails to adequately explain the excess mortality observed among widowers compared to widows because the odds of illness and death would be similar for those whose health is similarly threatened. An alternative explanation involves the role of stress. Some believe that the degree of stress associated with spousal bereavement can suppress the immune system, rendering the bereaved more susceptible to disease and subsequent mortality unless they have adequate support to buffer the unhealthy effects of stress. Consequently, widowers who are unable to benefit from supportive relationships with others after their spouse's death can experience a potential negative impact on their health. Furthermore, some widowers respond to stress by engaging in unhealthy behaviors like smoking, excessive alcohol consumption, and poor nutrition practices.

The health of widowers can suffer because they lack many of the skills that are important in self-care. Many tasks of daily living that are essential to health and well-being could go unaddressed by widowers if any of them were primarily the responsibility of their deceased wife. These could include meal preparation, shopping for adequate food, housekeeping, doing laundry, among other daily chores, all of which if left unattended for a long period of time are added sources of stress that could have adverse health consequences.

The division of labor concerning these tasks and skills tends to be defined according to gender, particularly among the older generations, but younger widowers often do not fare much better. Although many women participate in the workforce, they still are largely responsible for household management, cooking, and other tasks of daily living important for the care of the entire family. Widowers unskilled in these areas not only could find their health compromised for the reasons stated earlier, but also might feel less confident to meet the daily challenges of widowed life, which detracts from their ability to cope. Alternatively, those who learn to master many of these new responsibilities often cope more effectively and are at lower risk for poor health because they become more autonomous and eventually take better care of themselves.

How Well Widowers Adapt

Although not without its common elements, the process of adaptation to spousal loss can vary from individual to individual. While the most difficult times can be within the first six months to a year, some adapt more quickly whereas a few do not manage well for an extended period of time. Some characteristics, however, are associated with more successful adaptation. These include positive self-esteem, keeping busy with meaningful activity, having adequate opportunity for support and to share one's feelings, and a sense of being in control and confident in one's ability to cope effectively.

These attributes are largely independent of gender. The Harvard Bereavement Study, however, did make a distinction between social and emotional recovery. The widowers in that study adapted emotionally to the loss at similar pace to the widows, although their strategies may have differed. Alternatively, the men tended to move more quickly toward social recovery—that aspect of adaptation that refers to the need to reorganize one's life. This often was driven by the necessity to balance their role in the workplace with those pertaining to managing a household and caring for children. This was a source of strain for some of them that adversely impacted their effectiveness on the job and they felt compelled to find a way to alleviate it.

This need to reorganize sometimes predisposes widowed men to remarry. Many use remarriage as a way to fulfill their need for companionship and to resume an active sex life. Some, especially those who are younger, also believe remarriage once again provides a partner to help them meet the multiple responsibilities of being a worker, father, and head of household. Whether or not widowers eventually remarry, however, is not necessarily an indicator of how well they coped with the death of their former spouse. It is true that some of those who remarry report lower stress levels and greater life satisfaction, but nearly half of these remarriages dissolve, especially if they occur more quickly after the prior loss. Widowers who do not remarry are equally capable of maintaining meaningful relationships and adapting successfully to their new life.

Like any life transition, becoming a widower is associated with its own set of challenges and tasks that need to be successfully met in order to adapt effectively. At first, this can be highly disruptive, but as widowers have opportunities to learn the skills to meet these new challenges (whether managing a household, tending to their children's needs, assuming new self-care responsibilities, or becoming more comfortable with how they express their emotions), they develop a greater sense of coping ability and feel more confident to meet future challenges. Many bereaved men over time demonstrate a high degree of resilience and some grow personally from the experience. While most manage to accomplish this on their own, however, others require some assistance along the way.

Support Systems

Most bereaved rely on their own personal resources as well as the support of others in their lives for the means to adapt and do not require more formal assistance. For those experiencing greater difficulty, however, interventions like support groups and one-on-one programs can be effective, especially if accessed early in bereavement. While a small proportion of bereaved spouses in general participate in these programs, widowers as a rule are typically less receptive to them and often shy away from helping situations, at least at first. Consistent with their need to appear in control, especially regarding the display of their emotions, most widowers try to make it on their own even when they can benefit from outside help.

This is not to say that all widowers avoid participating in traditional bereavement interventions like self-help groups. Many, however, are not drawn to what they believe to be counseling interventions because they often perceive them as services designed primarily for women. Widowers are typically uncomfortable with environments where the open expression of emotion is encouraged because it is not consistent with their preferred way to grieve. Instead, researchers and practitioners suggest that bereaved men are more suited to active coping mechanisms that may include being engaged in meaningful activities. Programs that primarily feature such activities could have more appeal to widowers. Group walks and outings, for example, can be just as beneficial as traditional support groups because men who participate are able to interact and support one another in these situations and can do so more comfortably. Because the focus is on activity, however, as opposed to support or counseling itself, it is more consistent with many widowers' coping styles and is consequently less threatening. Because widowers use strategies that tend to be more cognitive than emotional in nature, they do well with books and other educational resources that help them help themselves.

Because of the unique problems widowers have assuming new responsibilities, they can benefit from programs that focus on skill-building and self-care education to help them successfully manage those tasks of daily living important to health, functioning, and independence. Issues of greater concern for widowers might include meal planning and preparation, housekeeping, and doing laundry. These programs can focus as well on more general health promotion topics like stress management, health screenings, immunizations, medication management, and physical activity, to name a few, that are equally relevant to widows and widowers but often go ignored or neglected by them given their new situation.

Although most bereavement programs have differential appeal to widowers, the benefits of participating vary from widower to widower. Success rate usually depends on the level of difficulty they are experiencing, what resources they already have in place, their needs, and their own unique situation. Interventions are not a panacea and most eventually cope without them. Although the strategies they choose at times might differ, widowers are as likely as widows to cope and eventually adapt to their new lives.

See also: GENDER AND DEATH; GRIEF: ANTICIPATORY, TRAUMATIC; WIDOWS

Bibliography

Bonanno, George A., and Stacey Kaltman. "Toward an Integrative Perspective on Bereavement." *Psychological Bulletin* 125 (1990):760–776.

Campbell, Scott, and Phyllis R. Silverman. *Widower: When Men Are Left Alone.* Amityville, NY: Baywood Publishing, 1996.

Caserta, Michael S., Dale A. Lund, and Sarah Jane Rice. "Pathfinders: A Self-Care and Health Education Program for Older Widows and Widowers." *The Gerontologist* 39 (1999):615–620.

Gass, Kathleen A. "Health of Older Widowers: Role of Appraisal, Coping, Resources, and Type of Spouse's Death." In Dale A. Lund ed., *Older Bereaved Spouses: Research with Practical Applications.* New York: Taylor & Francis/Hemisphere, 1989.

Glick, Ira O., Robert S. Weiss, and Colin M. Parkes. *The First Year of Bereavement.* New York: John Wiley and Sons, 1974.

Hayslip, Bert, Susan E. Allen, and Laura McCoy-Roberts. "The Role of Gender in a Three-Year Longitudinal Study of Bereavement: A Test of the Experienced Competence Model." In Dale A. Lund ed., *Men Coping with Grief.* Amityville, NY: Baywood Publishing, 2001.

Lee, Gary R., Alfred DeMaris, Stefoni Bavin, and Rachel Sullivan. "Gender Differences in the Depressive Effect of Widowhood in Later Life." *Journal of Gerontology: Social Sciences* 56B (2001):S56–S61.

Lee, Gary R., Marion C. Willetts, and Karen Seccombe. "Widowhood and Depression: Gender Differences." *Research on Aging* 20 (1998):611–630.

Lieberman, Morton A. *Doors Close, Doors Open: Widows Grieving and Growing*. New York: G. P. Putnam's Sons, 1996.

Lund, Dale A., ed. *Men Coping with Grief*. Amityville, NY: Baywood Publishing, 2001.

Lund, Dale A., ed. "Conclusions about Bereavement in Later Life and Implications for Interventions and Future Research." *Older Bereaved Spouses: Research with Practical Applications*. New York: Hemisphere, 1989.

Lund, Dale A., and Michael S. Caserta. "When the Unexpected Happens: Husbands Coping with the Deaths of Their Wives." In Dale A. Lund ed., *Men Coping with Grief*. Amityville, NY: Baywood Publishing, 2001.

Lund, Dale A., Michael S. Caserta, and Margaret F. Dimond. "The Course of Spousal Bereavement in Later Life." In Margaret S. Stroebe, Wolfgang Stroebe, and Robert O. Hansson eds., *Handbook of Bereavement: Theory, Research, and Intervention*. New York: Cambridge University Press, 1993.

Lund, Dale A., Michael S. Caserta, Margaret F. Dimond, and Susan K. Shaffer. "Competencies, Tasks of Daily Living, and Adjustments to Spousal Bereavement in Later Life." In Dale A. Lund ed., *Older Bereaved Spouses: Research with Practical Applications*. New York: Hemisphere, 1989.

Martin, Terry L., and Kenneth A. Doka. *Men Don't Cry . . . Women Do*. Philadelphia: Brunner/Mazel, 2000.

Stroebe, Margaret S., and Wolfgang Stroebe. "The Mortality of Bereavement: A Review." In Margaret S. Stroebe, Wolfgang Stroebe, and Robert O. Hansson eds., *Handbook of Bereavement: Theory, Research, and Intervention*. New York: Cambridge University Press, 1993.

Stroebe, Wolfgang, and Margaret S. Stroebe. "The Impact of Spousal Bereavement on Older Widows and Widowers." In Margaret S. Stroebe, Wolfgang Stroebe, and Robert O. Hansson eds., *Handbook of Bereavement: Theory, Research, and Intervention*. New York: Cambridge University Press, 1993.

Thompson, Neil. "The Ontology of Masculinity—The Roots of Manhood." In Dale A. Lund ed., *Men Coping with Grief*. Amityville, NY: Baywood Publishing, 2001.

U. S. Bureau of the Census. *The Older Population in the United States*. Current Population Report Series P-20, no. 532. Washington, DC, 1999.

Wortman, Camille B., Roxane C. Silver, and Ronald C. Kessler. "The Meaning of Loss and Adjustment to Bereavement." In Margaret S. Stroebe, Wolfgang Stroebe, and Robert O. Hansson eds., *Handbook of Bereavement: Theory, Research, and Intervention*. New York: Cambridge University Press, 1993.

Internet Resources

U.S. Bureau of the Census. "Sex by Marital Status, 1990 Summary File Tape File 1 (STF1)." In the U.S. Bureau of the Census [web site]. Available from http://factfinder.census.gov/servlet.

MICHAEL S. CASERTA

WIDOWS

The features shared by all widows are that they are women who have been married and whose husbands have died. Beyond that, there is such a great heterogeneity among widows that there is no way of predicting the lifestyle, support systems, and identity of any one woman. Many factors affect these aspects of widowhood, such as the characteristics of the society and community in which she lives, the personal resources with which she and her husband built their lives, the circumstances of his death, and the personal resources with which she modifies, removes, or adds social roles and social relations to her lifestyle and support systems. What she is and how she lives are highly influenced by her self-concept and the identities she takes on or is given by others in social interaction.

The characteristics of a widowed woman's world that influence her throughout life include the presence or absence of resources for its members and whether and how these are available to women—particularly to women in different marital situations. The resources vary tremendously by society, and are influenced by forms and complexity of social development, by family systems, and by degrees of equality of opportunity to use or refuse resources.

Widowhood in America

In the United States there are great variations in the lives and identities of widowed women based on the geographical and social characteristics of the communities in which they reside, and the social, service, emotional, and economic support these communities provide. Some communities are active in outreach programs; others require initiative on the part of a member wishing to take advantage of them. An upper-class community provides very different opportunities to its members than a lower class or immigrant community. Ethnic and racial identities contribute their share of uniqueness to working within these support systems. Small towns offer different restrictions and opportunities than large cities for continuing and changing one's lifestyle. Personal resources include the ability to analyze a situation for what is needed or wanted and to reach these resources. Personal resources vary from woman to woman, but generally encompass economic support, personal ability to function, and approach to life, the status of the woman's health, and existing and future social and emotional support networks.

The Demographic Picture

According to the U.S. Census Bureau, there were 199.7 million persons aged 18 and over in the United States in 1999, up from 159.5 million in 1980. In 1999, 95.9 million were men and 103.9 were women, continuing the trend of many decades. Both the number of men and that of women increased by over 20 million between 1980 and 1999. Out of these, 2.5 million men and almost four times as many women were widowed. To a great extent the difficulties of remarriage by widows can be attributed to this disparity. In 1999 only 8.9 percent of the men and 10.5 percent of the women were widowed. Although both white and black widowed women formed around 10.8 percent of the total of women, only 10.8 of the whites but 37.9 percent of the black women never married. Only 6.5 percent of Hispanic women were listed as widows that year.

Only 2 percent of children under 18 years of age were living with a widowed mother in 1998. Eighty-one percent of female-headed households were headed by widows aged 65 or older. While the percentage of widowed men aged 65 and over remained between 13 and 14 percent from 1980 to 1999, the percent of women decreased from 51.2 to 44.9 percent, mainly due to the increase in the proportion of those who were divorced, from 3.4 to 6.8 percent. Divorced men also increased in percentage, but the vast majority remained married. The older age of widowed women is reflected in their lack of educational achievement. Thirty-seven percent of all widows, compared to 16.5 percent of the total American population, never finished high school and a smaller proportion of the total never finished college or pursued post-graduate education. Many had been full-time homemakers or held only minimum-wage jobs so that their income in widowhood is dependent upon the husband's Social Security. As widowed mothers or older widows, they have the income of a new husband if they remarry, and informal exchanges of goods and services occasionally offer work for pay. However, many studies indicate that widows are not as poor as expected. Most live in metropolitan areas, while farm women move to small towns and those in retirement communities return to hometowns to be close to their children.

Traditional, Transitional, and Modern America

The situation of American widowed women can best be understood through the prism of social change in this society. Many Americans were socialized into varying degrees of the patriarchal systems, in the family and at large. In fact, as the American society became more complex and industrialized, gender segregation became extended from the home to the whole society. The social world became divided into what has been called "separate spheres," the private sphere of the home under the management of women, and the public sphere, worked in and managed by men. The latter sphere included the economic, educational, religious, and political institutions. In order to ensure the separation, a whole ideology of separate gender personalities and abilities was created and incorporated into the socialization of children, occupational, and other areas of life. Men were defined as natural leaders, logical, and able to invent complex systems. Women were defined as compassionate, emotional, and natural caregivers. It was therefore a waste to educate them with the tools needed to function in the public sphere. The two-sphere ideology carried the genders throughout life and obviously influenced marital, parental, and other social roles.

The Role of Wife

The situation of any widow is heavily influenced by her life as a wife and the circumstances by which she becomes widowed. Even in modern America, and with some of the variations noted, social class accounts for main differences in the role of wife.

Lower or working class wives are often tied into family or racial and ethnic networks, affecting relations between husband and wife and affecting members of the social circle associated with that role. This statement is dependent upon a definition of "social role" as a set of mutually interdependent social relations between the person at the center of the role and the social circle of all those from whom he or she acquires rights and to whom he or she has obligations because of being the center of that role. It makes a great deal of difference if a wife's role includes active participation in her and her husband's immediate and extended families, her husband's coworkers and friends, neighbors, and the wider community. The husband's family may offer rights and demand obligations that can even exceed his mutual exchanges when he was living.

One of the changes between traditional American families and those striving for new, "modern" lifestyles has been the decrease in importance of the husband's extended family. This means that, although the family has lost much control over the woman's behavior as both a wife and a mother, it is also less available to provide support. One of the consequences has been an increase in the importance of the woman's family as a support system. In patriarchal, patrilineal, and patrilocal families the daughter moved away from her family of orientation upon marriage, and therefore the family was unable to both demand and supply support. In modern cases in which the mother-in-law is no longer close, the mother-daughter bond often increases in importance.

There are variations in working-class perceptions of the role of wife by social race. When asked how a wife influences her husband's job, white women in the Chicago area stated that a wife should avoid nagging her husband, because that can create problems in his behavior at work, but expressed resentment over the authoritarian attitude and abuse by the husband. Conversely, African-American women felt that nagging is necessary or the man will not work consistently or take responsibility for the family.

Middle-class wives of America living before the late nineteenth and early twentieth century, when women began to enter the workforce in large numbers, became highly dependent upon the husband—not only in the role of wife, but in all other social relationships. Men freed from educational and economic control of their family of orientation acquired the right to co-select their wives and move wherever they found it necessary. They then joined the "greedy institutions" of the occupational world (Coser 1974). This meant that the wife's residence, the amount of economic resources she had available to her, and the people with whom she was likely to associate all became influenced by the husband's job and its geographical and financial situation.

There was an interesting difference in how white and African-American middle-class women responded to the question as to the influence of a wife on her husband's job. The latter were very conscious of the discrimination faced by the man in the outside world and sought to support him at home. Some of the white women stated that they themselves had no influence but that "those women on the North Shore" are influential and that companies insist on interviewing the wife before hiring the man (Lopata 1971, pp. 94–104).

The wife's obligations to maintain, rather than raise, the family status is even more important in the case of the mid-century upper-class wife. Her background was often similar to her husband's but she had to make sure that the residence, the children, and her own activities ensured their status within the community. Her voluntary contributions formed a major part of her role of wife, which included making sure that the children went to proper schools and ensuring that her children's marriages did not pull down the family status. At the same time, all this activity could not interfere with the husband as a person, in his job, and in his own community action. Thus, as much as the middle-class wife, she took on the role of protecting the man from distracting family problems, assisting in status-maintaining behavior, such as the entertainment of important business associates, and sometimes even directly helping with his job in a subsidiary position.

Becoming Widowed

The extent to which the wife in the not-yet-modern times of the mid-twentieth century was dependent upon the husband for economic, locational, and social supports, the family's position in the community deeply affected what happened when the husband became ill or incapacitate and died. It was hard for a widowed woman to retain the status she gained vicariously from the husband or to continue activities that maintained her status. She was often dropped from his associations, and lost mutual friends if marriage to him had been the connecting link. Financial losses might require movement into another community, which was difficult for both her and the children. If she had been a homemaker without skills for obtaining a job, her social life may have narrowed. Although the husband's family was not likely to have been very important to her support systems, unless upper class inheritance was significant, their involvement in her network would not likely be expanded after his death. Membership in couple-companionate circles was made difficult by the asymmetry of membership, leaving her often out of the loop, or restricting contact to only wives during the daytime. All these changes affected her role as mother, as the social circle of her children decreased or changed due to all the consequences of the death of the husband/father.

Throughout the twentieth century, there was a great deal of scholarly debate whether sudden or prolonged death is more difficult for survivors. Sudden death leaves a lot of "unfinished business," in that all marriages go through periods of conflict or tension that remain unresolved, and can carry over into widowhood. On the other hand, prolonged death usually requires prolonged care by someone, usually the wife. Relatively few people die in hospitals or long-term care facilities, although most usually spend some time in these. The home caregiver experiences many problems, including heavy work, physical nursing, role conflict when there are children, having to support other relatives, or obligations to jobs. The patient can be very demanding and angry, causing tension in the emotional state of the wife. In addition, it is hard for someone to watch a significant other weaken, be in pain and deteriorate, physically and mentally. Prolonged care can also result in social isolation, as the social life becomes constricted and associates cease to visit and offer support. Estate problems or fear of family members can add conflict difficult to deal with in a time of stress.

Certain types of death and dying are especially difficult for survivors. Suicide is difficult because it is easy for the wife to blame herself for creating problems or not providing sufficient support. Others, especially the husband's family, are likely to blame her. AIDS patients provide additional strains, due to both the myths and facts of disease transmission. Some forms of dying provide danger to the caregivers or others in the household, resulting in a protective stance by the wife, antagonizing the patient and other family members. Age of both the dying person and the caregiver is allegedly an important factor, partially due to what the scholar Bernice Neugarten defined as "on" or "off" time. According to Neugarten, people live according to a culturally and privately constructed time schedule. One is supposed to be able to experience certain events at specified times. Death in the late twentieth and early twenty-first centuries is supposed to occur when people are older, not in youth or allegedly robust middle age. Each ethnic and other socioculturally socialized group has its own interpretation of what is proper death, reason, time, and circumstance, and these notions all affect the grieving process and the widow's life role.

The situation of the actual death can also create problems for survivors and related people, often associated with the type and form of information received by the others. There are definite norms as to the transmission of such knowledge, to be followed by medical personnel, the police, and family members. Often a male member of the family, such as a son, is first informed with the obligation to pass on the news to others. Some hospitals have a special room in which the family is told of the last minutes of life and any messages from the dying. A particular problem exists when the death is not definite, as in missing in action cases during wars or if the body is not found.

Each culture has its own norms for closing off life with ceremonies of mourning in religious or public centers, cemeteries, or funeral parlors. In fact, the taking over of the ceremonies by funeral directors and staff is a relatively new phenomenon; family and religious leaders have served that function in the past. According to Geoffrey Gorer, death has become almost a pornographic subject, hidden from public view and discussion as much as possible, the ceremonies in countries such as America and England shorn down to the minimum (1967).

However, part of every ceremony surrounding death involves protection of those expected to be most affected, such as the children, parents, or spouse of the deceased. In some cultures with strong extended family ties, mothers are always honored as the ones who suffer the most, even before the spouse or the children. Funeral cultures assume that the most affected cannot attend to all the arrangements for the funeral and burial, so that someone else takes over. The "role of widow," in which duties and rights surround the woman with the assistance of circle members, has been narrowed in modern societies into a temporary one. Once it is considered finished, circle members of that role return to their own lives, leaving the widowed woman to work out her "grief work" pretty much on her own. Eric Lindemann, the first psychologist and psychiatrist who devoted himself to an analysis of what the survivors must do to adjust to death, defined this grief work as "emancipation from the bond of the deceased, readjustment to the environment in which the deceased is missing, and the formation of new relationships" (Lindenman 1944). The death researcher Helena Lopata added a fourth necessary accomplishment: the reconstruction of the self-concept and the widow's various identities in relationships with others. All of these are complicated processes, worked through in varying ways and time frames.

An initial study of older widows of the 1960s and 1970s found that the more education a woman had and the more middle class a lifestyle she and the husband built while he was well, the more disorganized her life became after his death. This is true mainly because Americans of this social stratum tend to be emotionally and socially in their various social roles mutually interdependent; so, much of the wife's life depended on the husband as the center of her various roles. Thus, not only the role of wife, but other roles such as mother, member of both sides of extended families, friend, and neighbor experienced changes that had to be worked out in new ways. On the other hand, the more the woman had these multiple roles the more personal, especially individual, resources she had to reconstruct her whole self-concept, lifestyle, and social relations.

Husband Sanctification

One 1970s study of the role changes and support systems of widows dealt with the tendency of some widows to describe their husbands in highly idealistic terms. Certain parts of the interviews would reflect a marriage that was not perfect, often problematic, with which an idealized description did not match. In order to address this discrepancy, the research team developed a "sanctification scale" of two parts. The first asked the respondent for degrees of agreement with polar terms such as *warm-cold, superior-inferior, honest-dishonest,* and *friendly-unfriendly*. The second was a relational segment asking for agreement with such statements as, "Ours was an unusually happy home" and "My husband was an unusually good man." The final statement of this scale was, "My husband had no irritating habits." There was great variation in the scores on the sanctification scale. Women who had a hard time in life, especially those people uneducated and living in poverty, tended to answer with extremes. People belonging to ethnic groups that sanctioned "speaking no evil of the dead" scored high. Those who defined life as hard scored low. Highly educated women would not agree with the final statement, nor did most married women upon whom the scale was pretested.

The process of sanctification performs several important functions for the widow. It removes the dead husband from current life into the safety of sainthood, and thus from watchfulness and the ability to criticize. Besides, if such a saintly man was married to her, then she must not be as bad as her depressive moments indicate. On the other hand, it has some negative effects. It can antagonize friends with living husbands who definitely have irritating habits. It can also discourage potential male companions who cannot possibly compete with the memory of such a saintly man.

Modern Identities and Self-Concepts

The need to reconstruct the self-concept and the identities given off or imposed by others is a complicated process that often lasts a long time. These concepts must be defined. For the purpose of this entry, identities are seen as those images of the person as she presents the self or as others see her.

According to the scholar Morris Rosenberg, a self-concept is "the totality of the individual's thoughts and feelings having reference to himself [sic] as an object" (Rosenberg 1979, pp. 7–8). There is obviously a strong interconnection between identities, as used in social interaction and the self-concept. When life situations change, both of these aspects of the self must be reconstructed. Some identities are carried throughout life and influence one's roles. The self and others use comparisons of how that person behaves and is treated in that role in contrast to others. The person also evaluates the self and all these evaluations and interactions influence the self-concept.

Gender identities are pervasive throughout life, sex determined by others at birth and socialization is aimed at forming and maintaining appropriate gender. The same is true of social race as defined in American society. Other identities such as religion, ethnicity, occupation, community, and organization are acquired at different stages of life, voluntarily or by others. Finally, many identities arise out of special events, such as graduation or widowhood. Some of these are transformed into social roles, when the person acquires certain characteristics and a social circle from whom rights are granted and to whom obligations are met. In American society, gender—by this definition—is not a social role but a pervasive identity that enters, in more or less significant ways, into various social roles. The feminist and related movements have attempted to prevent gender identity from influencing important social roles, such as physician or astronaut. The traditional and transitional two-sphere ideology is difficult to change so the process of decreasing gender segregation is slow.

In the 1980s the scholar Lynn Lofland concluded that modern society makes the death of significant others, such as a spouse, more difficult than traditional societies, because it has narrowed down the number of persons with whom the self has multiple connecting blocks. Less than a decade later, the scholar Rose Coser argued that modern societies with multiple and complex social structures and relationships free the person, especially women, from dependence upon a small circle of associates who insist on obedience to norms and restrict opportunities to develop multidimensional life spaces. According to this perception of social change, American society is increasingly modern, in that opportunities for educational and occupational involvement have expanded, not for everyone, but definitely for many women. Although the basic responsibility for the home and children still falls on women, husbands and increasing segments of society are willing to open resources making women less dependent upon spouses for economic and social life spaces. This means that widowhood is no longer faced by women whose whole lives were limited to the home and children, but by women

Visiting the cemetery on Veterans' Day, a war widow polishes the marble of her husband's gravestone. JOSEPH SOHM, CHROMOSOHM INC./CORBIS

who have developed other abilities and broader social life spaces, enabling the reconstruction of self and life in new ways once the period of heavy grief has waned.

At the same time, if one follows Lofland's argument, individualization and the expansion of the variety of people available for interaction and social roles has been accompanied by the reduction of the number of persons with whom close, intimate building blocks and threads of connectedness of human attachment are developed. This increases the significance of each person who becomes close. Lofland concluded that grief is harder in the modern Western world when one of these few persons dies. This is particularly true if that person is a spouse. According to Peter Berger and Hansfried Kellner, marriage among middle-class couples involves a complex process of self, other, and world reconstruction, carried forth through constant conversation and other forms of interaction. Relations with others must be more or less transformed with couplehood. This means that the death of the partner necessitates another reconstruction, but the process has to be taken alone, with only partial support from others. The significant partner is not there to comment and either accept or critique the changes of the self and the world the widowed woman is trying to accomplish. The self as a wife exists only in memory and the future self planned before the illness and/or death is not possible. The present may be lonely and beset with other problems, such as shortage of finances, the grief of the children, and other challenges with which the widow may not be able to cope. Friends and relations may start making demands as soon as the role of widow has withered.

The various forms and components of loneliness expressed by women in several of Lopata's studies accentuate the problems of self and world reconstruction. The widow can miss that particular person with whom a unique relationship was formed, having and being a love object, a companion in front of television, a sexual partner, an escort to public events, a partner in couple-companion friendship, someone sharing the household for whom meals and routines are planned, and even just a presence. The widowed woman must also deal with the identities imposed upon her by others. Elizabeth Bankoff's 1990 study of friendship among widows concluded that old friends could become troublesome if they insisted on the widow remaining the same. Many women thoroughly dislike the label "widow," with its traditional implication of an old, helpless woman who is perpetually in weeping grief. They also find it self-demeaning when associates do not consider them worthy of continued interaction. Thus, as the woman tries to change, often in uncertain and conflicting ways, people around her keep thrusting on her identities she may dislike and refuse to accept. The absence of the late husband may necessitate the survivor learning new skills and areas for building self-confidence—from caring for the family automobile to managing her finances.

The process of change in the self-concept is inconsistent and, like grief, has no clear-cut ending, as new situations and roles affect what has been reconstructed and old images remain in live memory. However, many studies have found widows very resilient. They deal with the pain of caring for a dying husband, the shock of the death, the need to learn to live in a world without the deceased, and the need to change relationships and reconstruct a new self-concept and identities.

Family Roles in Widowhood

The role of mother is obviously changed by the death of the children's father, but many factors affect the form and direction of such changes, including the number, gender, and ages of the children, as well as their prior relationship to the father, and the contributions or problems in the support system from the social circle of that role. The woman may not have complete freedom in relating with her children. Even in the twenty-first century, in-laws may have definite ideas about how the children should be raised, especially if the family is prestigious and inheritance is involved. Ethnic and people of color groups may have definite ideas as to the rights of the husband's family over these children and their mother. The financial situation may influence what she can, or wants, to do with and for them. In the historical past of American society "charitable organizations" often interfered with the mother in the absence of father, sometimes even taking the children away from her, as happened to thousands of New York children sent to the Midwest at the turn of the twentieth century. It was not until 1905 that the society decided that children were best off with the mother and even passed a policy of "mother's pensions," which unfortunately were not available in many states. Amendments to the Social Security Act gave widows with minority children special funds, ending when the offspring reached adulthood. Neighbors, schools, even the police can impinge on the rights of mothers, allegedly guaranteeing safety and proper socialization.

Children can cause work for the mother, but they can also form a major source of support. As mentioned earlier, mother-daughter relationships tend to be closer in America than in some other societies and closer than the mother-son tie. This is particularly true in subcultures with strong gender-segregation norms. As the children and the mother age, role reversal can take place, with the children, and especially one child, taking over some of the household chores, contributing to the family finances, and caring for the parent. These modifications in relationships can be painful, or relatively easy, depending on the kind of bond between parent and child and the behavior and attitudes of others, especially other children. Children might cooperate by providing support, or withdraw, placing the burden on one offspring.

Lopata's studies found that widowed women received little support from their in-laws. One-fourth did not have such living relatives. Only one-third reported that they were helped by in-laws at the time of death, and only about one-third of the in-laws said that they visited the widow or invited her over. Although in-law contact with the children was more frequent, only one-half said that in-laws gave the children gifts or money. These figures may indicate difficulties in the relationship while the connecting link was still alive, or else that one side or both felt the contact need not be continued. Widows reported that the grandparents were not active in the family. Of course, most of the widows in Lopata's studies were fifty years or older and the children were not of a dependent age.

The two Lopata studies came to one conclusion concerning the contribution of siblings questioned by the scholars Anne Martin Matthews and Shirley O'Briant. Respondents in Lopata's support systems study were given three chances to report someone as contributing to 65 different economic, service, social, and emotional supports, for a total of 195 possible listings. Only 20 percent had no living sibling, but relatively few even mentioned a sister or brother. For example, the highest percent of listings, only 14 percent, was made in response to siblings as givers of food, and 10 percent to siblings who help with rent or with decision making, perform housekeeping or sickness care, function as companions in holiday celebrations, or act as the person to whom they would turn in times of crisis. Twenty percent indicated that they helped a sibling with work outdoors, the highest of service supports. If a sibling appears in one support she (it is usually a sister) appears in several. Martin Matthews studied widows in Guelph, Ontario, which has a low mobility rate and O'Briant in Columbus, Ohio, in which mainly one sibling was active. Chicago is a large city, with high mobility and family dispersal, which may account for the relative absence of siblings in those support systems.

Other relatives do not appear often, especially in the lives of older widows, mainly because of their unavailability. This varies among the studies of various populations. However, more African-American than white widowed grandmothers took care of and even mothered their grandchildren. "Black grandparents were much more likely to take on a parent-like role with their grandchildren. . . . These grandparents saw themselves as protectors of the family, bulwarks against the forces of separation, divorce, drugs, crime—all the ills low-income black youth can fall pray [sic] to" (Cherlin and Furstenberg 1986, pp. 127–128). Lopata and Jessyna McDonald, who studied African-American families in Detroit, Indianapolis, Los Angeles, and Washington, D.C., in 1987, found many widows living alone. One difference between white and African-American families was the fluidity of housing arrangements. African-American women may have children, grandchildren, even siblings and more distant relatives moving in and out, or she may move into their households more frequently than white women.

Women and Men Friends: Membership in the Community

Many widowed women, especially of the middle class, reported problems with married friends. Social events, whether at homes or in public places, tend to be built around friendships with couples. Respondents complained that they heard about dinner parties to which they were not invited. Some widows explained it in terms of jealousy of married friends who did not want an extra woman around their husband, or having a "fifth wheel" present (Lopata 1973, p. 151). More agreed that married friends were jealous of them than that the husbands actually propositioned. Such advances, if they happened, were met with anger. The widows often wanted male companionship, but not a sexual affair with a husband of a friend, endangering the other relationship. Also, many moved after the death of the husband and were located inconveniently to former friends. Bankoff reported that old friends were helpful only early in widowhood. New friends, on the other hand, accepted the widows as they were.

Close relations with men can become a problem for widowed women. Many simply do not want to enter into such interaction, and definitely not to remarry. They like freedom from prior constraints, do not want to take care of another sick man, and fear objections from children. Offspring often do not approve of such changes because of idealization of the father or inheritance concerns. In addition, of course, there is the ever-present knowledge of the statistical scarcity of available men the same age of most widows. Living men are either married or in poor health. Sexual relations themselves may be feared, with concern over physical appearance and experiencing emotions or difficulties of physical contact. Some widows do enter cohabitation arrangements, on either a part- or full-time basis, either in home or away. For the most part, widows who remarry desire such a relationship, lack inhibiting influences, are attracted to a specific individual, and feel that they can gain from the relationship, whether economically or from a parenting perspective. Walter McKaine's *Retirement Marriage* (1969) found conservative attitudes among "remarrieds," many of whom had ethnic backgrounds in which marriage rather than personal independence was very important. He notes that success in these marriages involves affection and respect.

American society has created many organizations whose membership is open to participants. Some of these are focused on providing resources, advice, companionship, or social events to the elderly, and some to the widowed. The American Association of Retired People (AARP) has developed the Widow to Widow program and many communities have variations on such themes. Other groups in which marital status is not a known characteristic attract people with special interests. In the past, widows felt like members of a minority group, with myths and prejudices against them, but active life in the twenty-first century appears to diminish these attitudes.

Becoming and being a wife, and then a widowed woman, involves complex processes of self and other reconstruction and changes in relations with different circle members. These are heavily influenced by many factors, such as the characteristics of the society and the communities in which a woman lives, and her personal resources. Becoming a wife involves relating to the husband but also to a whole social circle of the role, its composition, rights, and duties. An important aspect of American society is its patriarchal and related bases, modified by new forms of complex development, including opportunities and restrictions of resources available to all women, wives, and then widows. Personal resources include the ability to analyze and seek out resources at any stage of life. Although widows have gone through the trauma of an ill or suddenly dead husband, grief, loneliness, and the need to reconstruct the self-concept and identities, those who had a multidimensional social life space have been able to build independent, even satisfying lives. Others obtain support systems from families, friends, neighbors, and their community's organizations, with varying degrees of satisfaction. There are unknown numbers of widows in modern American society and its communities who live a very restricted life, but their frequency appears to be decreasing as societal resources become available not only in widowhood, but throughout life.

See also: CONTINUING BONDS; LOPATA, HELENA Z; WIDOWERS; WIDOWS IN THIRD WORLD NATIONS

Bibliography

Bankoff, Elizabeth. "Effects of Friendship Support on the Psychological Well-Being of Widows." In Helena Z. Lopata and David Maines eds., *Friendship in Context*. Greenwich, CT: JAI Press, 1990.

Berger, Peter, and Hansfried Kellner. "Marriage and the Construction of Reality: An Exercise in the Microsociology of Knowledge." In Hans Dreitzel ed., *Patterns of Communicative Behavior.* London: Collier-Macmillan, 1970.

Bernard, Jessie. "The Good Provider Role: Its Rise and Fall." In Arlene Skolnick and Jerome Skolnick eds., *Family in Transition*. Boston: Little, Brown, 1983.

Bernard, Jessie. *Remarriage*. New York: Holt, Rinehart and Winston, 1956.

Cherlin, Andrew. *Marriage, Divorce, Remarriage*. Cambridge, MA: Harvard University Press, 1992.

Cherlin, Andrew, and Frank Furstenberg. *The New American Grandparent*. New York: Basic Books, 1986.

Coser, Lewis. *Greedy Institutions*. New York: Free Press, 1974.

Coser, Rose. *In Defense of Modernity: Role Complexity and Individual Autonomy*. Stanford: University of California Press, 1991.

Daniels, Arlene. *Invisible Careers: Women Community Leaders in Voluntary Work*. Chicago: University of Chicago Press, 1988.

Finch, Janet. *Married to the Job: Wives' Incorporation in Men's Work*. Boston: Allen and Unwin, 1983.

Fowlkes, Martha. *Behind Every Successful Man*. New York: Columbia University Press, 1980.

Gorer, Geoffrey. *Death, Grief and Mourning*. Garden City, NY: Anchor Books, 1967.

Lindenman, Eric. "Symptomology and Management of Acute Grief." *American Journal of Psychiatry* 101 (1944):141–148.

Lofland, Lynn. "Personal Shaping of Emotion: The Care of Grief." *Symbolic Interaction* 8 (1985):171–190.

Lopata, Helena. "Widowhood: Reconstruction of Self-Concept and Identities." In Norman Denzin ed., *Studies in Symbolic Interaction,* Vol. 23. Stanford, CT: JAI Press, 2000.

Lopata, Helena. *Current Widowhood: Myths and Realities.* Newbury Park, CA: Sage, 1996.

Lopata, Helena. "The Interweave of Public and Private: Women's Challenge to American Society." *Journal of Marriage and the Family* 55 (1993):220–235.

Lopata, Helena. "Which Child? The Consequences of Social Development on the Support Systems of Widows." In Beth Hess and Elizabeth Markson eds., *Growing Old in America.* New Brunswick, NJ: Transaction, 1991.

Lopata, Helena. *Widows: North America.* Durham, NC: Duke University Press, 1987.

Lopata, Helena. *Women As Widows.* New York: Elsevier, 1979.

Lopata, Helena. *Widowhood in an American City.* Cambridge, MA: Schenkman, 1973.

Lopata, Helena. *Occupation: Housewife.* New York: Oxford University Press, 1971.

Lopata, Helena. "Loneliness: Forms and Components." *Social Problems* 17 (1969):248–260.

Lopata, Helena, and David Maines, eds. *Friendship in Context.* Greenwich, CT: JAI Press, 1990.

Matthews Martin, Anne. "Support Systems of Widows in Canada." In Helena Z. Lopata ed., *Widows: North America.* Durham, NC: Duke University Press, 1987.

McDonald, Jessyne. "Support System for American Black Wives and Widows." In Helena Z. Lopata ed., *Widows: North America.* Durham NC: Duke University Press, 1987: 139-157.

McKaine, Walter. *Retirement Marriage.* Chicago: University of Chicago Press, 1969.

Neugarten, Bernice. *Middle Age and Aging.* Chicago: University of Chicago Press, 1968.

O'Bryant, Shirley. "Sibling Support and Older Widows' Well-Being." *Journal of Marriage and the Family* 50 (1988):173–183.

Papanek, Hannah. "Family Status Production: The 'Work' and 'Nonwork' of Women." *Signs* 4 (1979):775–781.

Papanek, Hannah. "Men, Women and Work: Reflections on the Two-Person Career." *American Journal of Sociology* 78 (1973):852–872.

Rosenberg, Morris. *Conceiving the Self.* New York: Basic Books, 1979.

U.S. Census Bureau. *Statistical Abstracts of the United States: 2000.* Washington, DC: U.S. Government Printing Office, 2000.

HELENA ZNANIECKA LOPATA

WIDOWS IN THIRD WORLD NATIONS

In many traditional communities of developing countries (especially on the Indian subcontinent and in Africa), widowhood represents a "social death" for women. It is not merely that they have lost their husbands, the main breadwinner and supporter of their children, but widowhood robs them of their status and consigns them to the very margins of society where they suffer the most extreme forms of discrimination and stigma.

Widows in these regions are generally the poorest of the poor and least protected by the law because their lives are likely to be determined by local, patriarchal interpretations of tradition, custom, and religion. Unmarried women are the property and under the control of their fathers; married women belong to their husbands. Widows are in limbo and no longer have any protector.

Across cultures they become outcasts and are often vulnerable to physical, sexual, and mental abuse. It as if they are in some way responsible for their husband's death and must be made to suffer for this calamity for the remainder of their lives. Indeed, it is not uncommon for a widow—especially in the context of the AIDS pandemic—to be accused of having murdered her husband, for example, by using witchcraft.

The grief that many third world widows experience is not just the sadness of bereavement but the realization of the loss of their position in the family that, in many cases, results in their utter abandonment, destitution, and dishonor.

In some African cultures, death does not end a marriage, and a widow is expected to move into a "levirate" arrangement with her brother-in-law ("the levir") or other male relative or heir nominated by his family. The children conceived are conceived in the name of the dead man. In other ethnic groups she may be "inherited" by the heir. Many widows resist these practices, which are especially repugnant and also life threatening in the context of AIDS and polygamy. Refusal to comply may be answered with physical and sexual violence. While in earlier times such traditional practices effectively guaranteed the widow and her children protection, in recent decades, because of increasing poverty and the breakup of the extended family, widows discover that there is no protection or support, and, pregnant by the male relative, they find themselves deserted and thrown out of the family homestead for good.

Widowhood has a brutal and irrevocable impact on a widow's children, especially the girl child. Poverty may force widows to withdraw children from school, exposing them to exploitation in child labor, prostitution, early forced child marriage, trafficking, and sale. Often illiterate, ill-equipped for gainful employment, without access to land for food security or adequate shelter, widows and their children suffer ill health and malnutrition, lacking the means to obtain appropriate health care or other forms of support.

However, there is an astonishing ignorance about and lack of public concern for the suffering of widows and their families on the part of governments, the international community, and civil society, and even women's organizations. In spite of four UN World Women's Conferences (Mexico 1975, Copenhagen 1980, Nairobi 1985, and Beijing 1995) and the ratification by many countries of the 1979 UN Convention on the Elimination of All Forms of Discrimination against Women (CEDAW), widows are barely mentioned in the literature of gender and development, except in the context of aging. Yet the issues of widowhood cut across every one of the twelve critical areas of the 1995 Beijing Platform for Action, covering poverty, violence to women, the girl child, health, education, employment, women and armed conflict, institutional mechanisms, and human rights.

One explanation for the neglect of this vast category of abused women is the assumption that widows are mainly elderly women who are cared for and respected by their extended or joint families. In fact, of course, far from caring for and protecting widows, male relatives are likely to be the perpetrators of the worst forms of widow abuse. If they are young widows, it is imagined that they will be quickly remarried. In fact, millions of widows are very young when their husbands die but may be prevented by custom from remarrying, even if they wish to do so.

But in spite of the numbers involved, little research on widows' status exists (the Indian Census of 1991 revealed 35 million widows, but very little statistical data has been collected for other developing countries). Despite a mass of anecdotal and narrative information, public policies have not developed to protect widows' rights. Despite the poverty that widows and their children experience, organizations such as the World Bank have not yet focused on this hidden section in populations.

Laws, Customs, Tradition, and Religion

Across cultures, religions, regions, class, and caste, the treatment of widows in many developing countries, but especially in the South Asian subcontinent and in Africa, is harshly discriminatory.

Patriarchal kinship systems, patrilocal marriage (where the bride goes to the husband's location), and patrilineal inheritance (where succession devolves through the male line) shore up the concept that women are "chattels" who cannot inherit and may even be regarded as part of the husband's estate to be inherited themselves (widow inheritance). Where matrilineal kinship systems pertain, inheritance still devolves onto the males, through the widow's brother and his sons.

Disputes over inheritance and access to land for food security are common across the continents of South Asia and Africa. Widows across the spectrum of ethnic groups, faiths, regions, and educational and income position share the traumatic experience of eviction from the family home and the seizing not merely of household property but even intellectual assets such as pension and share certificates, wills, and accident insurance.

"Chasing-off" and "property-grabbing" from widows is the rule rather than the exception in many developing countries. These descriptive terms have been incorporated into the vernacular languages in many countries, and even (e.g., Malawi) used in the official language in new laws making such actions a crime.

The CEDAW or "Women's Convention" and the Beijing Global Platform for Action require governments to enact and enforce new equality inheritance laws. Some governments have indeed legislated to give widows their inheritance rights. But even where new laws exist, little has changed for the majority of widows living in the South Asian subcontinent and in Africa. A raft of cultural, fiscal, and geographical factors obstructs any real access to the justice system. Widows from many different regions are beginning to recount their experiences of beatings, burnings, rape, and torture by members of their husbands' families, but governments have been slow to respond, their silence and indifference, in a sense, condoning this abuse.

In India, many laws to protect women have been passed since independence. But it is the personal laws of each religious community that govern property rights and widowhood practices. The world knows of the practice of widow-burning (*sati*), but little of the horrors widows suffer within the confines of their relatives' homes, how they are treated by their communities, or their fate when abandoned to the temple towns to survive by begging and chanting prayers. There are approximately 20,000 widows in Vrindavan, the holy city; Varanasi; Mathura; and Haridwar.

Common to both regions are interpretations of religious laws, customs, and traditions at the local level that take precedence over any modern state or international law. Widows in any case, especially the millions of illiterate widows living in rural areas, are mostly ignorant of the legal rights they have.

Mourning and Burial Rites

All human societies have sought ways to make death acceptable and to provide opportunities for expressing grief and showing respect to the dead person. In societies where the status of women is low, the mourning and burial rituals are inherently gendered. Rituals are used to exalt the position of the dead man, and his widow is expected to grieve openly and demonstrate the intensity of her feelings in formalized ways. These rituals, prevalent in India as well as among many ethnic groups in Africa, aim at exalting the status of the deceased husband, and they often incorporate the most humiliating, degrading, and life-threatening practices, which effectively punish her for her husband's death.

For example, in Nigeria specifically (but similar customs exist in other parts of Africa), a widow may be forced to have sex with her husband's brothers, "the first stranger she meets on the road," or some other designated male. This "ritual cleansing by sex" is thought to exorcise the evil spirits associated with death, and if the widow resists this ordeal, it is believed that her children will suffer harm. In the context of AIDS and polygamy, this "ritual cleansing" is not merely repugnant but also dangerous. The widow may be forced to drink the water that the corpse has been washed in; be confined indoors for up to a year; be prohibited from washing, even if she is menstruating, for several months; be forced to sit naked on a mat and to ritually cry and scream at specific times of the day and night. Many customs causes serious health hazards. The lack of hygiene results in scabies and other skin diseases; those who are not allowed to wash their hands and who are made to eat from dirty, cracked plates may fall victim to gastroenteritis and typhoid. Widows who have to wait to be fed by others become malnourished because the food is poorly prepared.

In both India and Africa, there is much emphasis on dress and lifestyles. Higher-caste Hindu widows must not oil their hair, eat spicy food, or wear bangles, flowers, or the "kumkum" (the red disc on the forehead that is the badge of marriage). Across the cultures, widows are made to look unattractive and unkempt. The ban on spicy foods has its origins in the belief that hot flavors make a widow more lustful. Yet it is widows who are often victims of rape, and many of the vernacular words for "widow" in India and Bangladesh are pejorative and mean "prostitute," "witch," or "sorceress." The terrible stigma and shame of widowhood produces severe depression in millions of women, and sometimes suicide.

Widowhood in the Context of AIDS

AIDS has resulted in a huge increase in widows, especially in sub-Saharan Africa. For sociological and biological reasons, women are twice as likely to contract HIV through vaginal intercourse as men. In southern Africa, the rates of infection for young women between ten and twenty-four years old are up to five times higher than for young men. This is significant for widows for a number of reasons. In addition to the normal social practice of older men marrying far younger women that prevails in some communities, there is a belief, held by many men, that having sex with a young girl or virgin will cure men of their HIV infection or protect them from future exposure. Anecdotal evidence suggests that this myth has significantly increased the incidence of child marriage and child rape. Such early marriage does not bring security but serious risk and vulnerability to infection. Married thirteen- to nineteen-year-old women in Uganda are twice as likely to be HIV-positive as their single contemporaries. These child brides quickly become child widows bearing all the stigma of widowhood, the problems compounded by their youth and helplessness.

Widows whose husbands have died of AIDS are frequently blamed for their deaths because of promiscuity, whereas, in the majority of cases, it is the men who have enjoyed multiple sex partners but return home to be nursed when they fall ill. These widows may or may not be aware of their sero-positive (infected with the HIV/AIDS virus) status and may reject being tested, fearing the consequences of a positive result, which, with no access to modern drugs, can amount to a death sentence. Besides, the dying husband's health care will, in most cases, have used up all available financial resources so that the widow is unable to buy even the basic medicines or nutritious food needed to relieve her condition.

AIDS widows, accused of murder and witchcraft, may be hounded from their homes and subject to the most extreme forms of violence. A Help Age International Report from Tanzania revealed that some 500 older women, mostly widowed in the context of AIDS, were stoned to death or deliberately killed in 2000.

The poverty of AIDS widows, their isolation and marginalization, impels them to adopt high-risk coping strategies for survival, including prostitution, which spreads HIV. In the struggle against poverty, the abandonment of female children to early marriage, child sex work, or sale for domestic service is common because the girl, destined to marry "away" at some point in her life, has no economic value to her mother.

But widows are not exclusively victims—millions of surviving AIDS widows, especially the grandmothers, make exceptional but unacknowledged contributions to society through child care, care of orphans, agricultural work, and sustaining the community.

The international community, and especially the UN agencies such as WHO and UNAIDS, need to address the impact of AIDS on widowhood. So far, epidemiological studies have ignored them, and one can only rely on a few small localized studies, mainly from Africa, to understand the consequences and options for millions of women and their children.

Widows comprise the majority of the poor who beg on the streets of Afghanistan's capital, Kabul. AFP/CORBIS

Widowhood through Armed Conflict and Ethnic Cleansing

Sudden, cruel bereavement through war, armed conflict, and ethnic cleansing is the shared trauma of hundreds of thousands of women across the globe. Widowhood is always an ordeal for women, but for war widows the situation is infinitely worse. Widows from Afghanistan, Mozambique, Angola, Somalia, Cambodia, Vietnam, Uganda, Rwanda, Sierra Leone, Bosnia, Kosovo, Sri Lanka, East Timor, Guatemala—old women and young mothers—provide testimonies of brutalities, rapes, homelessness, terror, and severe psychological damage.

There are a few actual statistics for individual countries on numbers of widows, but it is estimated that, for example, in Rwanda, following the genocide of 1994, over 70 percent of adult women were widowed. In Mozambique, following the civil war, over 70 percent of children were thought to be dependent on widowed mothers. Widows of war are often uncounted and invisible. Many widows, survivors of ethnic cleansing, have been victims of gang rapes or witnessed the death of husbands, sons, parents, and siblings. They eke out a bleak existence as traumatized, internally displaced persons or languish in sordid refugee camps, having lost not just their bread winner and male protector but also their worldly possessions. In the postconflict period, they remain in danger. To add to their problems, widows who have survived terrible hardships are often abandoned or ostracized by their relatives who refuse to support them. The shame of rape, the competition for scarce resources such as the family land or the shared house, places conflict widows in intense need. They are unable to prove their title to property and typically have no documentation and little expert knowledge about their rights. They bear all the burden of caring for children, orphans, and other surviving elderly and frail relatives without any education or training to find paid work. Widows in third world nations have the potential to play a crucial role in the future of their societies and the development of peace, democracy, and justice, yet their basic needs and their valuable contributions are mostly ignored. Where progress has been made, it is due to widows working together in an association.

Widows' Coping Strategies

What do widows do in countries where there is no social security and no pensions, and where the traditional family networks have broken down? If they do not surrender to the demands of male relatives (e.g., "levirate," widow inheritance, remarriage, household slavery, and often degrading and harmful traditional burial rites) and they are illiterate and untrained and without land, their options are few. Often there is no alternative to begging except entering the most exploitative and unregulated areas of informal sector labor, such as domestic service and sex work. Withdrawing children from school, sending them to work as domestic servants or sacrificing them to other areas of exploitative child labor, selling female children to early marriages or abandoning them to the streets, are common survival strategies and will continue to be used until widows can access education and income-generating training for themselves and their dependents.

Looking to the Future: Progress and Change

When widows "band together," organize themselves, make their voices heard, and are represented on decision-making bodies locally, nationally, regionally, and internationally, change will occur. Progress will not be made until widows themselves are the agents of change. Widows' associations must be encouraged and "empowered" to undertake studies profiling their situation and needs. They must be involved in the design of projects and programs and instrumental in monitoring the implementation and effectiveness of new reform legislation to give them property, land, and inheritance rights; protect them from violence; and give them opportunities for training and employment.

Widows at last have an international advocacy organization. In 1996, following a workshop at the Beijing Fourth World Women's Conference, Empowering Widows in Development (EWD) was established. This nongovernmental international organization has ECOSOC consultative status with the United Nations and is a charity registered in the United Kingdom and the United States. It is an umbrella group for more than fifty grass-roots organizations of widows in South Asia, Africa, Eastern Europe, and East Asia and its membership is constantly growing. EWD is focusing on the plight of millions of widows in Afghanistan—Afghan widows in refugee camps. An offshoot of EWD, Widows For Peace and Reconstruction, was set up in August, 2001 to represent the special needs of war widows and to ensure that their voices are heard in post-conflict peace building.

In February 2001 EWD held its first international conference, "Widows Without Rights," in London; participants, widows' groups, and their lawyers came from some fifteen different countries. EWD represents widows at UN meetings, such as the UN Commission on the Status of Women, and is a consultant to various UN agencies on issues of widowhood. At last, widows are becoming visible, and their groups, both grass roots and national, are beginning to have some influence within their countries.

However, much more work is needed to build up the capacity of widows' groups and to educate the United Nations, civil society, governments, and institutions, including the judiciary and the legal profession, on the importance of protecting the human rights of widows and their children in all countries, whether they are at peace or in conflict.

See also: GENDER AND DEATH; WIDOWERS; WIDOWS

Bibliography

Chen, Marthy, and Jean Dreze. *Widows and Well-Being in Rural North India.* London: London School of Economics, 1992.

Dreze, Jean. *Widows in Rural India.* London: London School of Economics, 1990.

Owen, Margaret. "Human Rights of Widows in Developing Countries." In Kelly D. Askin and Dorean M. Koenig, eds., *Women and International Human Rights Law* New York: Transnational Publishers, 2001.

Owen, Margaret. *A World of Widows.* London: ZED Books, 1996.

Potash, Betty, ed. *Widows in African Societies: Choices and Constraints.* Stanford, CA: Stanford University Press, 1986.

Internet Resources

Division for the Advancement for Women. "Beijing Declaration and Platform for Action." In the United Nations [web site]. Available from www.un.org/womenwatch/daw/beijing/platform/index.html.

MARGARET OWEN

WILLS AND INHERITANCE

Wills are an important means of assuring that a deceased person's property, or estate, will pass to his or her intended recipients. In addition to distributing property, a will is also useful for leaving a public record of ownership of real estate, for appointing guardians of the deceased's minor children, and for designating a personal representative, or executor, to administer the management of the estate until the deceased's debts, taxes, and administrative expenses have been paid and the remaining property has been distributed to the appropriate parties. A person who leaves a valid will is said to die "testate." To the extent that a person dies without a valid will that effectively disposes of all the property owned at death, the person dies "intestate," and the law will determine the deceased's heirs for the purpose of distributing property.

In general, the laws of the state where the deceased lived at the time of death will govern disposition of personal property, although the state where real estate is located controls distribution of that property. Absent a will, state law also will govern the selection of a guardian for minor children and a personal representative of the intestate's estate. Both will and intestacy proceedings are supervised by a court in an administrative process known as probate; the tax consequences of testacy and intestacy are the same.

Although the intestacy statutes vary considerably among the states, there are some common features. In all states, a surviving spouse is an heir, and is entitled to a portion of the estate. If the deceased left children or other descendants, whether biological or adopted, in almost all states those descendants will share with the surviving spouse, or will take the entire estate if the deceased did not leave a surviving spouse. A number of states allocate the entire estate to the surviving spouse if the deceased did not leave surviving descendants, while others require the spouse to share the estate with the deceased's surviving parents and sometimes with the deceased's brothers and sisters and their descendants. When a person leaves no surviving spouse or descendants, the deceased's ancestors and their surviving relatives are designated as heirs. Relatives more closely related to the deceased are generally preferred to those who are more distant. In many states, heirship extends no further than the level of the deceased's grandparents and their descendants; if there are no relatives within those categories, the property is said to "escheat," or pass to the state.

The primary purpose of a will is to alter the intestate distribution of the deceased's property and allow the deceased, or testator, to designate who will take the estate. Through a will, a testator may leave gifts to charities or organizations and individuals (although not to animals), and is not limited to family members. Most states require that a testator be at least eighteen years old and of "sound mind." A will may be challenged, or contested, by those who would benefit if the will were invalid because of the testator's lack of mental capacity, fraud, influence by another party, or other circumstance indicating that the document does not represent the testator's true intentions.

Usually wills must be written and properly witnessed by at least two people, according to the individual state's formalities. While all states recognize properly executed formal wills, about half the states also allow "holographic wills," which require no witnesses but must be written entirely or in substantial part in the testator's own handwriting. Because the requirements for holographic wills also vary from one state to another, they pose risks that the handwritten will may be invalid.

Although a properly executed will is a valid legal document, it does not transfer any assets until the testator dies. If an intended recipient predeceases the testator, that gift will fail unless the state has a statute that preserves the gift for designated substitutes. Similarly, if the testator identified specific items of property to be given to a recipient, the gift generally fails if the testator no longer owned that asset at the time of death.

While a testator may change or revoke a will until death, including amendments made by "codicil," or a partial revision of a will, each change or revocation must be done in a manner that satisfies the statutory formalities. A will may be revoked by physical act as well as a subsequent formal writing, such as a later will, but burnings, mutilations, and other physical acts upon the will must be accompanied by an intention to revoke; otherwise, the will remains legally valid despite its physical destruction. Furthermore, certain changes in circumstances will result in all or a portion of a will being implicitly revoked. Most commonly, divorce revokes a gift to a former spouse.

The laws of most states protect certain family members from disinheritance. Usually these protections apply exclusively to a surviving spouse, but some cover the deceased's children as well. The vast majority of states designate a spousal "elective share" that guarantees a surviving spouse a specified fraction, typically one-third, of the deceased spouse's estate. A spouse who is given less than that share may elect to take the statutory portion, after which the remaining property is distributed to the other will recipients. Furthermore, if the testator's will was drafted prior to marriage to the surviving spouse, the omitted spouse may be entitled to a portion of the deceased's estate. Although a person is not required to leave children or other descendants anything if children are not specifically mentioned in the will, they may be regarded as unintentionally omitted and entitled to a statutory share. In many states, however, omitted children are not protected unless the last will was executed prior to the child's birth or adoption.

In order to avoid probate, which can be time-consuming and expensive, a person may transfer interests in property during life, while retaining considerable control over and benefit from the property. Such transactions are commonly regarded as "will substitutes," which frequently do not require the same degree of formality as a will but achieve a comparable result. Will substitutes include life insurance policies; payable-on-death designations in documents such as contracts, stock certificates, and bank accounts; joint tenancies with right of survivorship; and living trusts. While these types of instruments usually avoid probate, they typically do not result in tax savings and are frequently ineffective in avoiding a surviving spouse's elective share.

See also: END-OF-LIFE ISSUES; LIVING WILL

Bibliography

Andersen, Roger. *Understanding Trusts and Estates,* 2nd edition. New York: Matthew Bender and Company, 1999.

Averill, Lawrence. *Uniform Probate Code in a Nutshell,* 6th edition. St. Paul, MN: West Group, 2001.

Beyer, Gerry. *Wills, Trusts, and Estates: Examples and Explanations.* New York: Aspen, 1999.

Dukeminier, Jesse, and Stanley Johanson. *Wills, Trusts, and Estates,* 6th edition. Gaithersburg, NY: Aspen Law and Business, 2000.

Haskell, Paul. *Preface to Wills, Trusts, and Administration,* 2nd edition. Westbury, NY: Foundation Press, 1994.

Marsh, Lucy. *Wills, Trusts, and Estates: Practical Applications of the Law.* New York: Aspen Law and Business, 1998.

McGovern, William Jr., Sheldon Kurtz, and Jan E. Rein. *Wills, Trusts, and Estates.* St. Paul, MN: West, 1988.

Reutlinger, Mark. *Wills, Trusts, and Estates: Essential Terms and Concepts,* 2nd edition. New York: Aspen Law and Business, 1998.

SHERYL SCHEIBLE WOLF

Z

ZOMBIES

The phenomenon of zombies, the living dead, is one of the most popular aspects of Haitian voodoo that has created a morbid interest and has inspired myriads of movies. Voodoo is more than the sorcery or magic that is portrayed in movies or literature; voodoo is a religion, cult, healing process, and body of magical practice.

In voodoo practice, the *Bokor* is a sorcerer who uses evil forces to bewitch, and he can change a human being into a zombie. Essentially every *Hougan,* who is at the same time a voodoo priest, a doctor, and the intermediary between the community and the spirit world, is more or less a Bokor. In fact, the major difference between a Hougan and a Bokor is the nature of the bewitchment he or she performs.

To better understand the concept of zombies, one must first understand the Haitian conception of the duality of the soul. The *n'âmm* (soul) is principally divided into two distinctive parts: the *gro bonanj* ("big guardian angel") and the *ti bonanj* ("little guardian angel"). The gro bonanj, which represents the consciousness and the personality, is a spiritual substance connected with the world of living. When the individual passes away, the gro bonanj survives and joins the world of *lwa* (spirit) to eventually become a lwa himself. The second part of the soul, the ti bonanj, is the conscience or the spiritual energy of the person. This corresponds to the individuality of each human being and also corresponds to the individual will.

The most popular and well-documented hypothesis concerning how a person is changed into a zombie state is that of poison. The Bokor "work of the left hand" possesses the knowledge to constitute a powerful poison with a mixture of venom like tetradoxine, which is found in several puffer fishes. The victims sink into a state of catalepsy and passes for dead; however, it seems that the person is still aware of what occurs around him or her. The person is then buried alive.

At night the Bokor comes to help the person get out of the grave and captures the ti bonanj. He then administers an antidote that enslaves him. The Bokor can use the services of the zombie to carry out work in the fields or he can sell or rent his slave's services. This kind of zombie is the soulless body and the victim is "deprived of will, memory, and consciousness, speaks with a nasal voice and is recognized chiefly by dull, glazed eyes and an absent air" (Ackerman 1991, p. 474). The ethnobotanist Wade Davis suggests that zombie laborers were created to install order against antisocial individuals.

There exists a type of zombie of the soul, a disembodied soul of a dead person. In this case, the sorcerer uses the gro bonanj or the ti bonanj of the victims for magical purposes. The soul may belong to an individual who died in an accident or the sorcerer may use the soul of a sterile woman or even a soul that has been captured by a magical process and is enslaved. In any case, the soul must be stored in a bottle or jar and then the Bokor can either use it or sell it.

Whether myth or reality, zombies inspire an intense fear among the peasant Haitian population. The terror that is engendered by zombies is not the fear that they can be evil, but the fear that one might become one of them. In Haiti, a country that has known a long period of slavery with the Spanish and French colonizations until their independence in 1804, the fear of becoming enslaved has remained a part of their collective consciousness. The fear of being changed into a slave for the rest of one's life is a fear of being constrained to live without individuality, will, and conscience.

See also: Buried Alive; Persistent Vegetative State; Voodoo

Bibliography

Ackermann, Hans W., and Jeanine Gauthier. "The Ways and Nature of the Zombi." *Journal of American Folklore* 104 (1991):466–494.

Davis, Wade. *The Serpent and the Rainbow.* New York: Simon & Schuster, 1985.

GENEVIÈVE GARNEAU

ZOROASTRIANISM

The phenomenon of death, or nonlife as it is called in the Zoroastrian holy scripture the *Gathas,* is a concept accompanying the advent of creation. At the dawn of creation, twin primal spirits manifested themselves. They were spontaneously active and through encounter with each other established life and nonlife. So it shall be until the end of the world. These two primal spirits, Good (*Vahyo*) and Bad (*Akem*), are opposed in thought, word, and deed. No coexistence between them is possible. This constitutes the concepts of cosmic/moral dualism in Zoroastrianism. In his spiritual vision, Zarathushtra also conceived of two kinds of existence and consequently two worlds (*Ahva*): the spiritual (*Manhaya*) and corporeal (*Astavat*).

In the seventh century, after the Arab invasion of Iran and in order to avoid persecution, a significant number of Zoroastrians migrated to India where they became known as "Parsees." Although Iran and India continue to be the main strongholds of Zoroastrians, in the nineteenth and twentieth centuries many migrated and are scattered throughout North America, Europe, and Australia. These Zoroastrians continue to preserve and practice their religion; however, expediency has compelled them to adapt certain practices and rituals, particularly those related to death and disposal of the corpse, to the requirement of their adopted country of residence.

Zoroastrianism is based on seven main precepts: (1) theological monotheism; (2) moral/cosmic dualism; (3) prevalence of the eternal law of truth; (4) existence of the bounteous good spirit; (5) operation of the law of consequences; (6) immortality of the soul or afterlife; and (7) final triumph of good over evil.

Zarathushtra designates the universal supreme creator, who is transcendent, immanent, and a-personal, Ahura Mazda (literally, "the lord of life and wisdom"). Ahura Mazda is defined by six cardinal attributes: (1) sublime wisdom (*Vahishta Manah*); (2) truth, justice, and righteousness (*Asha Vahishta*); (3) boundless constructive power (*Khshatra Vairya*); (4) universal love, tranquility, and peace (*Spenta Armaity*); (5) wholeness and perfection (*Haurvatat*); and (6) immortality (*Ameretat*). Ahura Mazda is described in the *Gathas* as the giver (*Datar*) and the shaper (*Tasha*). Thus He (although in the *Gathas* the pronoun referring to Ahura Mazda is gender neutral) has not created the world, *ex nihilio,* but from His own existence. The Bounteous Good Spirit (*Spenta Mainyu*) that is in Ahura Mazda unfolds His immanence in its fullness, in His creation. Thus there is a unity of existence in Zoroastriansim. The teachings of Ahura Mazda, revealed to Zarathushtra, appear in the *Gathas* as holy hymns or mantra (*Manthra*), meaning thought-provoking words.

Immortality of the Soul

The *Gathas* describes the main constituents of a human being as body (*Tanu*) and soul (*Urvan*), which live for only a limited time in the world. At the time of death, the body transforms (or perishes) and the soul goes on to live its second existence. Death has always been an enigma. From extant unearthed records, the Egyptians were perhaps the first civilized people to conjecture that after death, human beings existed somewhere and somehow. However, there is consensus that Zarathushtra was the first to introduce the idea of an afterlife that was based on morality, with rewards for the good and suffering for the evil. In the biblical period the Jews believed that the dead would continue to exist in a shadowy form in *sheol,* the abyss of the earth. After their liberation from captivity by Cyrus the Great in Babylon and their contact with Zoroastrians, the Jews gradually adopted the eschatological divine plan of salvation. This concept eventually appeared in Christianity and Islam.

Eastern religions differ drastically from Zoroastrianism in their notion of life after death. They generally believe in rebirth as a corollary of *karma.* So long as the karmic force (ignorance, desire, and attachment), which is the root cause of life, exists, the life process continues. Cessation of the life stream constitutes the ideal, at which point the purified self is nirvanized and immortalized. Immortalization means the merger into cosmic *nirvana.* In this sense, nonlife is eternal.

According to Zoroastrianism, Ahura Mazda first created the spiritual world. In His wisdom, He then created the corporeal world to manifest the spiritual world. Ahura Mazda created the universe in His Sublime Mind, shaped it in His Conscience (*Daena*), manifested it through His Benevolent Spirit, and set it into motion in accordance with the Eternal Law of Asha. He created human beings in his own spiritual image as His coworkers and friends and sparked them with God-like attributes to assist them in achieving self-realization, perfection, and immortality. He also granted them with faculties to discern between right and wrong in order to work for the progress of humanity and the advancement of the world. These faculties are the mind (*Manah*) or the ability to reason and think logically, the conscience (*Daena*), and intuition (*Baoda*).

Ahura Mazda vouchsafed human beings with freedom of choice, His greatest and most significant gift. Hence individuals have the right to choose between Good and Bad. In his justice, Ahura Mazda forewarned individuals of the happiness or the suffering that results from their choices, all in accordance with the Law of Asha. Although human beings are endowed with the potential for goodness, in the end the decision between right and wrong and good and evil is the individual's alone. As a result of this right of freedom, the material world did not remain harmonious like the spiritual world.

When life manifested itself, by definition, so did its twin nonlife or death. Similarly, with light came darkness; with truth, dishonesty; with wisdom came ignorance; and so on. The good creations (i.e., truth, wisdom, health, and peace) are manifestations of the Benevolent Spirit of Ahura Mazda (*Spenta Mainyu*) while their twins are the display of opposition to the Benevolent Spirit. The opposing twins are collectively designated "Evil or Destructive Spirit" (*Angra Mainyu,* or later as *Ahriman*).

In Zarathusthra's vision, life and nonlife, truth and lies, light and darkness, all exist and are real, as with two kinds of time: boundless time (*Zrvan Akarana*) and limited time (*Zrvan Daregho Khvadhata*). In Zarathushtra's view, time and space condition existence in the world within the ambit of the Eternal Law of Asha. The outcome of the ethical struggle between Good and Bad is positive, evolutionary, and optimistic. The Zoroastrian doctrine envisages perpetuation of creation and creativity (the result of dynamism of the Benevolent Spirit) and progressive change (the result of dynamism of the Eternal Law of Asha).

Theodicy: The Origin of Evil

Theodicy, the explanation of the origin of evil without undermining the goodness and omnipotence of God, presents unsolvable problems in many religions. Doctrinal adversaries of the concept of theodicy, however, admit that the Zoroastrian doctrine offers the most rational explanation for the concept of evil. The appearance of evil is an inevitable phenomenon in the process in which the Benevolent Spirit of Goodness manifests itself. Nevertheless, the topic has aroused many debates, and consequently two opposing schools have emerged. One school, believing in moral dualism, considers evil as the creation of individuals who opt to oppose the Benevolent Spirit. In other words, evil is the negation of good and does not exist as an independent eternal force.

The other school, believing in cosmic dualism, maintains that both the Benevolent and the Evil Spirits are primordial. Accordingly, the evil acts of individuals are driven by an evil force and the conflict and clash continues up to the time when Good finally prevails. A subschool, a corollary of moral dualism, maintains that although Evil is no more than the negation of Good, it assumes an independent existence when it manifests itself alongside the Good and starts functioning independently (*Farhang Mehr*). Both cosmic and moral dualists hold that Good ultimately prevails over Evil and that at that time, the world is renovated or "refreshed" and characterized by peace and harmony. The two schools also agree that regardless of the origin of evil individuals ultimately decide whether to commit evil and as such will have to requite.

The Principle of Consequences and Divine Judgment

The *Gathas* does not speak of death, but rather of life (*Gaya*) and nonlife (*Aiyaiti*). The body, which is made of matter, may be alive or dead; the soul, however, never dies, experiencing one form of life in this corporeal world and another in the spiritual world. Zoroastrians believe in the survival of the soul after bodily death. The nature of the individual's other life is determined by the Law of Consequences, a corollary of the Law of Asha. The Law of Consequences is generally known as the principle of reward and punishment, whereby righteous acts in the world are rewarded with sustained happiness and evil acts, with misery.

In Zoroastrianism, the Eternal Law of Asha determines the consequences of an individual's acts and the fate of the soul after the individual's physical death. Asha is God's will. The individual's thoughts, words, and deeds in this world, through the exercise of one's free choice, set the consequences (*Mizhdem*) into motion and condition one's life and future according to the Law of Asha. Hence there is no predestined fate; the acts have predestined consequences.

Human beings seek happiness (*Ushta*) in life. Happiness originates in the Law of Asha, which prescribes a life of joy for the pious and eternal woe for the wicked. The *Gathas* warns individuals not to be deceived by ostensible or temporary victories that are illusory, nor to be disheartened by temporary defeats brought about by blows or condemnations from evil ears. In the end, the evil doers will pay for their arrogance and unjust acts.

The Nature of Consequences

The *Gathas* does not specify particulars on the nature of consequences nor does it mention specific rewards or punishment. Life in the hereafter is the continuation of life in the world. In this world, the righteous people (*Ashavan*) create the realm of righteousness (*Ashahya Gaeta*) that continues in the next existence. The concepts are indescribable in detailed terms, rather the terms refer to the best existence, defined as everlasting joy, tranquility, and peace as against the worst existence, defined as everlasting woe and anxiety.

According to the *Gathas,* the souls of the righteous people go in a state of perfect happiness, referred to as the Abode of the Song (*Garo Demana*), also called the Abode of the Good Mind (*Vangheush Demana Manangho*) or the Abode of Endless Light (*Anghra Raosha*). The souls of the evildoers go to the Abode of Wickedness (*Druji Demana*), also referred to as the Abode of the Worst Mind (*Aschishtahya Daena Manengho*) and Worst Existence (*Achishta Ahu*). These terms confirm that in Zoroastrianism heaven and hell are states of consciousness and not concrete geographical regions.

The Crossing Bridge: Chinavat

The *Gathas* alludes to a dividing line, a crossing boundary or bridge (*Chinavat*) between the two existences or the two worlds. No particulars about the shape or the locality of the bridge are provided. The term may have been used metaphorically indicating the end of one state of existence and the commencement of another or it may be a reference to a point of time when the final judgment is effected. According to the *Gathas,* the judgment takes place at death and before the deceased's true self or conscience (*Daena*) attempts to cross the bridge. On that occasion, the prophet will be present. This does not, however, imply the likelihood of any mediation on his part because there is no possibility of mediation or redemption by anyone. The predestined Law of Asha will run its course. The prophet's presence is simply a matter of good leadership; the soul of the pious will have an easy crossing and will be ushered into the next existence by his or her happy conscience as well as the prophet. The soul of the wicked will be led by his or her conscience to the worst existence.

The Intermediary Place between Heaven and Hell

It is not the *Gathas,* but the *Younger Avesta,* composed centuries after the prophet, which addresses the concept of human beings having a record with an equal number of good and evil acts; the *Younger Avesta* refers to an intermediary place

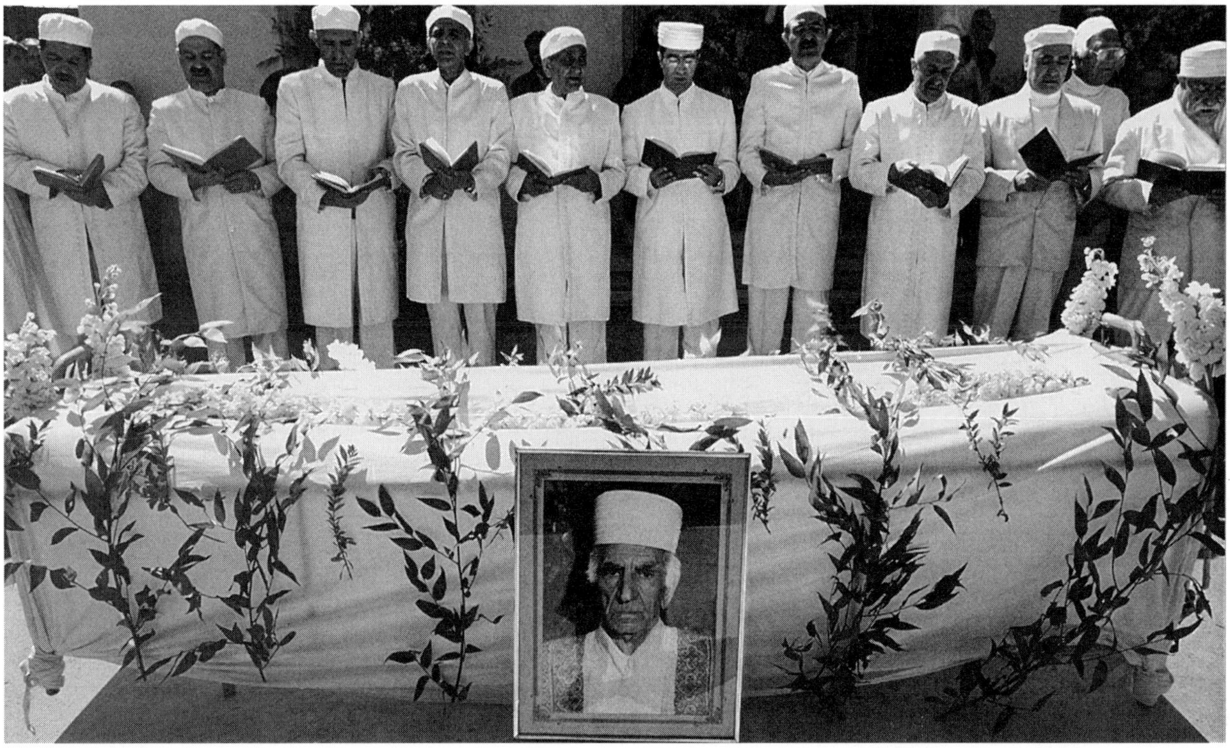

Zoroastrianism originated in ancient Iran sometime around 2000 B.C.E. In March 2000 at the Zoroastrian Qasr-e-Firoozeh cemetery in Teheran, Zoroastrian priests prayed at the funeral of the religious leader of the Iranian Zoroastrian community, Dastur Rostam Dinyar Shahzadi. AFP/CORBIS

called *Misvana Gatu,* where the souls of such persons reside. The reason the *Gathas* does not incorporate this concept is logically coherent. In Zoroastrianism each act has its own reward: potential happiness or suffering. The good and bad deeds are not added in the end of one's life to determine the level of reward or punishment. Recompense or retribution is not based on the excess of good deeds over bad deeds or the reverse. The concept of an intermediary place cannot be rationalized with the gathic doctrine.

Practices and Rituals Related to Death and the Dispoal of the Dead

The method of the disposal of the dead is a controversial subject among Zoroastrians in the twenty-first century. The methods used are the system of the *Dakhma* ("Tower of Silence" as it is called by Westerners), the burial system, and, less frequently, cremation.

Dakhma is a stone-surfaced tower, built on an elevated earth outside town, on which the corpse is exposed to be devoured by vultures. The heavy bones left behind are either buried or placed in a drain beneath the surface of the Dakhma where they are destroyed with chemicals. No Dakhma dating before the Arab conquest of Iran has been unearthed. Historians suggest that this practice started later in the Arab period to avoid desecration of the dead by the Muslims and that the low walls of the Dakhma increased during the period of the Turk and Mongol invasions. If the practice of using the Dakhma existed at all in the pre-Islamic period, as it is insisted by the Parsees in India, it must have been in order to preserve the environment, a concept Zoroastrians diligently observed; the Dakhma was used to prevent the pollution of soil and water and to avoid making land unusable for agriculture.

In 1937 the Zoroastrians in Iran started using the burial system along with the old system of Dakhma, but currently they use the latter almost to the exclusion of Dakhma. In contrast, the Zoroastrians of India still rely solely on the Dakhma. In the West, with some exceptions, the burial system and cremation are used.

Tradition requires the performance of certain rituals for the departure of the soul. According to traditional belief (not specified in the *Gathas*), the soul of a dead person lingers on earth for three days and nights following the death and stays near the place where the head of the dead was resting immediately before death, recounting all the acts the person had done in his or her life. The righteous soul chants the sacred hymns, experiencing great joy while the wicked soul recalls the evil acts, experiencing great sorrow. At the dawn of the fourth day, the soul starts its journey to the next existence or world. At the Chinavat bridge, it is met with his or her conscience (*Daena*) that accompanies the soul to its final destination.

Certain prayers and rites are performed during the three days and at the morning of the fourth day. Remembrance ceremonies are performed on the tenth day following the death, thereafter on each thirtieth day of the month for one year and finally annually for thirty years. Jews also believed that the soul fluttered in the neighborhood of his or her house for three days.

Renovation of the World: Frasho-Kereti

The *Gathas* refers to the end of time. The *Haptanhaiti,* the immediate sequel to the *Gathas,* composed by Zarathushtra's immediate disciples, speaks of boundless time (*Zrvan Akarana*) and limited time (*Zrvan Daregho Khvadhata*). Thus the reference to the "end of time" in the *Gathas* should be a reference to the latter—the end of the limited span of time one lives in this world and the transition into the other existence. That constitutes a turning point in life. For the righteous individuals this is the Great Turning Point that marks the attainment of their goal. Throughout their lives the righteous use their constructive power to advance the world, serve others, and work for the cause of peace. In doing so they seek to attain perfection (*Haurvatat*) and embrace eternity (*Ameratat*). At the Great Turning Point the righteous are ushered into the eternal spiritual existence. The righteous, through both individual and collective efforts, look to that event, which is the result of a long process of gradual progress toward perfection and immortalization. That event is called Refreshment of the World (*Frasho-Kereti*) and according to the Law of Asha this goal will be reached. That event will represent the final triumph of Good (*Spenta Mainyu*) over Evil (*Angra Mainyu*) and, as such, display the omnipotence of Ahura Mazda.

The Refreshment of the World is related to the concept of the Savior (*Saoshyant*). In the *Gathas,* the word *Saoshyant* is used in the generic sense, meaning "a group of saintly workers." They do not appear at set intervals but exist and operate at all times, in different capacities and with different effectiveness. Saoshyants are not of the same rank in righteousness or the role that they play in the perfection of the world. The Gathic Refreshment process is a gradual process resulting from the contributions of the righteous and the operation of the Law of Asha. Refreshment of the World is the apex of perfection of the existing world in its evolutionary process. The *Younger Avesta* has, however, changed the concept of Saoshyant, and thus Refreshment of the World, referring to three distinct saviors, who at given periods, arise and with big strides lead the world toward Refreshment. The last one is *Soshyos,* the Saoshyant proper, who gives the final touch to an almost-perfected world, heralding the final triumph of Good over Evil.

See also: AFRICAN RELIGIONS; AFTERLIFE IN CROSS-CULTURAL PERSPECTIVE; CHINESE BELIEFS

Bibliography

Boyce, Mary. *Zoroastrians: Their Religious Beliefs and Practices.* London: Routledge & Kegan Paul, 1979.

Dhalla, Maneckji Nusservanji. *History of Zoroastrianism.* New York: Oxford University Press, 1938.

Duchesne-Guillemin, Jacques. *The Western Response to Zoroaster.* Westport, CT: Greenwood Press, 1956.

Henning, W. B. *Zoroaster.* New York: Oxford University Press, 1951.

Irani, D. J. *The Gathas: The Hymns of Zarathushtra.* Boston: The Center for Ancient Iranian Studies, 1998.

Jackson, William. *Zoroaster: The Prophet of Ancient Iran* 1899. Reprint, New York: AMS Press, 1965.

Mehr, Farhang. *The Zoroastrian Tradition: An Introduction to the Ancient Wisdom of Zarathushtra.* Rockport, MA: Element Inc., 1991.

Pavry, Jal C. *The Zoroastrian Doctrine of Future Life from Death to the Individual Judgment.* New York: Columbia University Press, 1929.

Taraporewalla, Irach J. C. *The Divine Songs of Zarahushtra.* Bombay: Hukhta Foundation, 1993.

Zaehner, R. C. *The Dawn and Twilight of Zoroastrianism.* London: Winfield & Nicolson, 1961.

FARHANG MEHR

APPENDIX

INFORMATION ON ORGANIZATIONS IN THE FIELD OF DEATH AND DYING

Mary J. Carvlin

Alcor Life Extension Foundation

The Alcor Life Extension Foundation (ALEF) is a nonprofit corporation that offers interested people the option of being cryonically suspended after their death. Cryonics is the process of preserving clinically dead people at very low temperatures, maintained in liquid nitrogen, in hopes of returning them to life and health when medical science has become sophisticated enough to do so. Starting in the latter part of the twentieth century there has been a trend toward neural (head only) preservation with the expectation that it will eventually be possible to reconstitute the whole body. The ALEF believes that researchers will someday find a way to halt and even reverse the aging process, with the opportunity for people to extend their lives for centuries.

The ALEF was founded in 1972 and had forty members in suspension by 2001. The ALEF publishes *Cryonics,* a quarterly magazine that deals with the topic of life extension, as well as such booklets as *Cryonics and Christianity,* addressing the religious concerns of Christians who may wish to become members.

Alcor maintains a number of full-time salaried employees and also relies on many volunteers. The organization states that the majority of the money it receives from its members is spent on clinical procedures, administrative overhead, research, and the Patient Care Fund. The fund is designed for maintaining and eventually restoring people who are in suspension. The cost of cryonic suspension at Alcor ranges from $50,000 to $120,000.

The Alcor Life Extension Foundation is headquartered at 7895 E. Acoma Drive, Suite 110, Scottsdale, AZ 85260-6916. They can be reached by phone at 877-GO-ALCOR or by e-mail at info@alcor.org. Additional information can be obtained through the ALEF web site: www.alcor.org.

American Academy of Hospice and Palliative Medicine

The American Academy of Hospice and Palliative Medicine (AAHPM) is an organization whose members are physicians committed to the role of hospice and palliative care in medical practice, education, and research. In particular, they seek to firmly establish hospice and palliative care as a formal role of medical doctors.

The AAHPM states its mission as achieving excellence in palliative medicine, preventing and relieving suffering among patients and families, providing education, establishing clinical practice standards, fostering research, facilitating professional development, and advocating for public policy.

The AAHPM was originally organized as the Academy of Hospice Physicians in 1988. Although a number of organizations exist for those interested in issues of hospice, the AAHPM asserts that it is the only organization in the United States for physicians dedicated to the advancement of hospice/palliative medicine in practice, research, and education. The academy expresses its intention to begin an organized discipline devoted to the specialties of palliative care and the management of terminal illness. The academy states its belief that the role of the physician includes helping even those patients who cannot be cured.

The academy conducts continuing medical education courses for members and provides peer support services to hospice and palliative care physicians. It also encourages accreditation of physician training programs in hospice and palliative care. The AAHPM works to educate the public regarding the rights of the dying and other issues affecting hospice and palliative medicine.

The American Academy of Hospice and Palliative Medicine is headquartered at 4700 W. Lake Avenue, Glenview, IL 60025-1485. They can be reached by phone at 847-375-4712 or by e-mail at aahpm@aahpm.org. Additional information can be obtained through the AAHPM web site: www.aahpm.org.

American Association of Suicidology

The American Association of Suicidology (AAS) brings together individuals and groups who are interested in advancing the study of suicide prevention and life-threatening behavior. Its members include psychologists, psychiatrists, social workers, nurses, health educators, physicians, directors of suicide prevention centers, clergy, and others from various disciplines.

The AAS was founded in 1968 and has five regional groups and is affiliated with the International Association for Suicide Prevention (IASP). The AAS holds an annual meeting each spring.

The AAS works to recognize and encourage suicidology, which is the study of suicide, suicide prevention, and related aspects of self-destruction. The AAS promotes education, disseminates information through programs and publications, and cooperates with other organizations involved in suicidology.

The AAS has several publications that come with its membership, the most significant being *Suicide and Life-Threatening Behavior,* the official journal of the American Association of Suicidology. For three decades, the journal has provided a forum for professionals throughout the world to examine approaches to life-threatening behaviors. The journal investigates the complexity of suicidality and its treatment, addressing biological, statistical, psychological, and sociological approaches. The journal provides readers with the latest research on such topics as predictors and risk factors for suicidal behaviors. It also reviews important new resources in the field, including professional books, assessment scales, and international conference reports. Issues of the journal can be viewed on the Guilford Publications web site at www.guilford.com.

The American Association of Suicidology is headquartered at 4201 Connecticut Avenue NW, Suite 408, Washington, DC 20008. They can be reached by phone at 202-237-2280 or by fax at 202-237-2282. Additional information can be obtained at the AAS web site: www.suicidology.org

American Cancer Society

The American Cancer Society (ACS) is a voluntary health organization dedicated to controlling and eliminating cancer. The ACS seeks to prevent cancer and save lives through programs of research, education, patient service, advocacy, and rehabilitation.

The American Cancer Society was founded in 1913, and for more than eighty years has been the leader in cancer research. The ACS supports research through grants to individuals and institutions. The organization also supports service and rehabilitation programs for cancer patients and their families. It develops and directs educational programs for the public and for doctors and other health professionals. One of the primary goals of ACS is to provide the most accurate and current information on cancer. ACS promotes policies, laws, and regulations that benefit patients and families affected by cancer. The ACS publishes several annual reports and bimonthly journals that provide medical professionals with important research and statistical information on cancer.

A national board of 124 volunteer directors governs the ACS. Half the directors are laypersons and half are doctors and scientists. Most society funds are raised in its annual community crusade during April, designated as Cancer Control Month by the U.S. Congress in 1938.

The ACS is headquartered at 1599 Clifton Road NE, Atlanta, GA 30329. It has seventeen chartered divisions throughout the country and over 3,400 local offices. Local programs established by the ACS serve to educate the public about cancer prevention, early detection, treatment, survival, and quality of life. Additional information can be obtained through the ACS web site: www.cancer.org.

American Cryonics Society

The American Cryonics Society (ACS) is an organization for people who are interested in extending life through cryonics. Cryonics refers to the freezing of clinically dead humans in anticipation of reviving the person when the necessary scientific and medical technology becomes available. A person held in such a state is said to be in cryonic suspension. Maintenance of the body involves placing and keeping it in a container filled with liquid nitrogen. As a membership-only organization, the American Cryonics Society contracts with other organizations for the suspension and caretaking of suspended bodies.

The cryonics movement began in 1962, receiving a boost with the publication of *The Prospect of Immortality* by Robert C. W. Ettinger in 1964. The book explores the arguments and ideas that have given rise to cryonics and is a founding book of the movement. The ACS was founded in 1969 as the Bay Area Cryonics Society, changing its name in 1985.

The organization helps interested people arrange for their own cryonic suspension. It promotes and sponsors research, education, and information about cryonic suspension, life extension sciences, and low-temperature medicine. It conducts programs to freeze tissue samples from endangered species for possible future cloning.

The ACS publishes *American Cryonics,* a semiannual journal that gives readers a summary of research and national news regarding cryonics.

They also publish the monthly *Immortalist,* featuring articles on cryonics, health, aging research, and science.

The American Cryonics Society can be contacted at P.O. Box 1509, Cupertino, CA 95015. They can be reached by phone at 800-523-2001 or by e-mail at cryonics@jps.net.

American Heart Association

The American Heart Association (AHA) is a national voluntary health agency organized to fight diseases of the heart and blood vessels. The AHA seeks to reduce premature death and disability from cardiovascular disease and stroke by sponsoring research, community services, and professional and public education on heart disease. The association coordinates efforts of the medical profession in its fight against heart and circulatory disease.

The AHA was founded in 1924 and has fifty-six state offices and nearly 2,000 local offices. It has about 26,000 active members, including several thousand physicians and scientists. About 2.5 million volunteers also participate in the work of the association. The American Stroke Association is a division of the AHA.

The association gains all of its financial support from the general public through contributions, mainly from its Heart Campaign held each February and its Heart Fund.

The AHA publishes current research in the monthly medical journal *Arteriosclerosis, Thrombosis, and Vascular Biology*. The AHA also publishes several other publications regarding cardiac medicine.

The American Heart Association is headquartered at 7272 Greenville Avenue, Dallas, TX 75231-4596. People can contact and make donations to the AHA by calling 800-AHA-USA1, or visiting them on the web at www.pfk.com/aha/DonateOnlineGeneral.asp. Additional information can be obtained through the AHA web site: www.americanheart.org.

American Hospice Foundation

The American Hospice Foundation (AHF) is a charitable nonprofit corporation that seeks to aid those who face life-limiting illness and significant loss. The foundation advances the hospice concept of care; that is, a family centered concept of health care for people dying of an incurable illness. The hospice concept aims at easing the physical and psychological pain of the patient's illness so that the person can appreciate his or her remaining life. The hospice team includes the patient and his or her family, as well as physicians, nurses, social workers, members of the clergy, and volunteers. Hospice services may include nursing care and pain control, meal preparation, laundry, or shopping. This care may be provided at home, in a separate hospice medical center, or in a hospice unit of a hospital.

The AHF seeks to ensure the availability of hospice care for many who might otherwise not have such care available. The foundation aids programs that serve the needs of the terminally ill by supporting a range of community bereavement programs. The AHF promotes hospice benefits in health insurance and managed care programs, and fosters research on consumer needs. The American Hospice Foundation creates educational campaigns to aid bereaved employees and coworkers. It offers training and materials on grieving children for teachers and school counselors, and educational programs for clergy.

The American Hospice Foundation can be contacted at 2120 L Street NW, Suite 200, Washington, DC 20037. They can be reached by phone at 202-223-0204, by fax at 202-223-0208, or by e-mail at ahf@msn.com. Additional information can be obtained through the AHF web site: www.americanhospice.org.

American Lung Association

The American Lung Association (ALA) works to prevent lung disease and promote lung health. The association works to combat causes of lung problems, including smoking and environmental lung hazards such as air pollution.

The ALA was founded in 1904 to combat tuberculosis, and has become the oldest nationwide voluntary public health agency in the United States. The ALA has about 130 state and local affiliates.

The ALA provides public health education programs and materials on diseases such as lung cancer, emphysema, asthma, pneumonia, influenza, tuberculosis, and lung disorders in infants. It supports medical research and awards grants to medical professionals who specialize in lung health.

The work of the association is funded by public contributions, especially by its annual Christmas Seal Campaign. Additional funding comes from gifts and grants from corporations, foundations, and government agencies.

The ALA works to offer a variety of smoking control and prevention programs, some targeting adults and others intended for schools. ALA offers its Freedom from Smoking program, considered a top smoking cessation program.

In its work to fight lung disease caused by air pollution, the ALA led the fight for clean air, and became a key source of information on the hazards of air pollution. The association seeks to influence the laws and regulations related to lung health. It helped pass the federal Clean Air Act, as well as the law prohibiting smoking on airplanes.

Headquarters of the American Lung Association are in New York City. The ALA informs and educates the public about lung disease through its web site, public service announcements, news releases, and conferences. To reach a local American Lung Association office, call 800-LUNG-USA (800-586-4872). Additional information can be obtained through the ALA web site: www.lungusa.org.

Americans for Better Care of the Dying

Americans for Better Care of the Dying (ABCD) is a nonprofit organization committed to ensuring that all Americans receive adequate care at the end of life. The ABCD seeks to instill comfort, dignity, and meaning to the dying process for family members as well as their loved ones.

The organization was founded in 1997. Its goals are to reform current practices of caring for the dying, explore new systems for delivering care to the dying, and to shape public policy relating to end-of-life issues. It also seeks to improve standards of practice among professionals and greater reimbursement for end-of-life care.

ABCD aims to improve pain management, increase financial reimbursement, enhance care, support family caregivers, and change public policy. It helps organizations and individuals improve community care systems and assists health care organizations in implementing improvements. ABCD helps build networks of interested parties so they can share their expertise.

Americans for Better Care of the Dying is headquartered at 4125 Albemarle Street NW, Suite 210, Washington, DC 20016. They can be reached by phone at 202-895-9485, by fax at 202-895-9484, or by e-mail at info@abcd-caring.org. Additional information can be obtained through the ABCD web site: www.abcd-caring.org.

American SIDS Institute

The American Sudden Infant Death Syndrome Institute (ASIDSI), often called the American SIDS Institute, is a nonprofit organization of health care professionals, researchers, and laypeople concerned about sudden infant death syndrome (SIDS), the unexplained death of an apparently healthy baby under one year of age. Members include families who have lost babies to SIDS. The precise cause of these deaths is not known, and ASIDSI supports efforts to identify the cause and cure of SIDS.

The American SIDS Institute was founded in 1983. The institute seeks to advance infant health through clinical services, education, research, and support for SIDS families. Its sponsorship of research programs includes conducting research on siblings of babies lost to SIDS who are at higher risk. The ASIDSI conducts seminars for health care professionals and laypeople and maintains a speakers' bureau.

Because there is no known cure for SIDS, the institute works to inform the public of risk factors for SIDS in order to reduce those risks. Known risk factors include premature birth to extremely young mothers, lack of prenatal care, and exposure of the mother to cigarette smoke, alcohol, or narcotics during pregnancy. Poverty, poorly ventilated rooms, soft mattresses, and too much clothing or covers at bedtime also increase a baby's risk for SIDS. By promoting such information, the ASIDSI helped reduce the numbers of SIDS deaths in the early 1990s.

The American SIDS Institute's headquarters are at 2480 Windy Hill Road, Suite 380, Marietta, GA 30067. They can be reached by phone at 800-232-SIDS or by e-mail at prevent@sids.org. Additional information can be obtained through the ASIDSI web site: www.sids.org.

Association for Death Education and Counseling

The Association for Death Education and Counseling (ADEC) is a multidisciplinary professional nonprofit organization dedicated to creating high standards in death education, bereavement counseling, and care of the dying. ADEC's primary goal is to enhance the ability of professionals and laypeople to be better able to meet the needs of those with whom they work in death education and grief counseling. ADEC works to promote and share research, theories, and practice in dying, death, and bereavement. The association aims to provide an arena for professionals of various disciplines to advance awareness of issues in dying, death, and bereavement.

The ADEC began in 1976, with the Forum for Death Education and Counseling, organized by a group of educators and clinicians. The organization grew into the Association for Death Education and Counseling. ADEC is the oldest interdisciplinary organization in the field of dying, death, and bereavement. Members of ADEC include educators, counselors, nurses, physicians, mental health professionals, clergy, funeral directors, and social workers.

The ADEC hosts an annual conference and provides professional resources for its members. It also publishes a member directory, a newsletter, and an annual book from its conference.

The Association for Death Education and Counseling is located at 342 North Main Street, West Hartford, CT 06117-2507. They can be reached by phone at 860-586-7503 or by fax at 860-586-7550. Additional information can be obtained by e-mail at info@adec.org or through the ADEC web site: www.adec.org.

Befrienders International

Befrienders International is a charitable volunteer organization that works to prevent suicide with its network of 357 centers worldwide. These centers, run by trained volunteers, offer a free service of nonjudgmental and completely confidential telephone, mail, e-mail, or face-to-face contact. Befrienders try to prevent suicide by providing a listening ear for people who are lonely, despairing, or suicidal. They try not to judge suffering people or tell them what to do, but just listen. They believe that listening saves lives, and by listening to a suicidal person a befriender tries to help the person address a particular problem or pain.

Befrienders International was founded in 1974. By 2001 it had centers in forty-one countries. The organization supports and advises new and existing centers and offers its expertise and experience to other agencies. Befrienders International also initiates programs aimed at suicide prevention, including Reaching Young Europe, a program that teaches coping skills to young children.

Befrienders International is headquartered at 26-27 Market Place, Kingston upon Thames, Surrey KT1 1JH, England. They can be reached by e-mail at admin@befrienders.org. Additional information can be obtained through the Befrienders web site: www.befrienders.org. Through their web site, Befrienders International provides a comprehensive directory of emotional first aid help lines.

Brady Center to Prevent Gun Violence

The Brady Center to Prevent Gun Violence (BCPGV) is dedicated to reducing gun violence in the United States. The BCPGV began in 1974 when Dr. Mark Borinsky, a victim of gun violence, founded the National Council to Control Handguns (NCCH). In 1980 the NCCH was renamed Handgun Control, Inc. (HCI). After Jim Brady, the press secretary to President Ronald Reagan, was shot during an assassination attempt on the president in 1981, Brady's wife Sarah joined the cause. In 1983 the Center to Prevent Handgun Violence (CPHV) was founded as a sister organization to HCI.

The organization won several legislative battles, one of which led to the U.S. Congress banning bullets that can puncture police officers' bulletproof vests. Congress also banned handguns that cannot be detected by airport X-ray machines.

In 1993 the Brady Bill, requiring a five-day waiting period and background checks on handgun purchases, was signed into law. President Bill Clinton signed into law the Violent Crime and Control Act of 1994, which includes the ban on manufacture and importation of military-style assault weapons.

Also in 1994, the CPHV helped launch Steps to Prevent (STOP) Firearm Injury, training doctors to counsel patients and their families about the risks of guns in the home. In 1996 CPHV launched Project Lifeline, a national network of health professional committed to public education on gun violence prevention.

In 2001 the CPHV launched a nationwide initiative to encourage state officials to use their consumer protection authority to regulate gun design. Also that year the CPHV was renamed the Brady Center to Prevent Gun Violence.

The Brady Center to Prevent Gun Violence can be contacted at 1225 Eye Street NW, Suite 1100, Washington, DC 20005. They can be reached by phone at 202-289-7319 or by fax at 202-408-1851. Additional information can be obtained through the CPHV web site: www.gunlawsuits.org.

Canadian Association for Suicide Prevention

The Canadian Association for Suicide Prevention (CASP) aims to help reduce the suicide rate and minimize the harmful consequences of suicidal behavior. CASP's main purpose and function is to facilitate, advocate, support, and advise. CASP does not provide formal therapeutic services, and it is not a crisis center.

In 1985 a group of professionals incorporated CASP. They responded to a need they saw for greater information and resources among communities in order to reduce the suicide rate.

CASP promotes broad-based information sharing on suicide intervention and research. It holds annual national conferences, publishes a newsletter, and creates service and research networks and directories. CASP advocates for governmental policy development pertinent to suicide prevention. The association also develops guidelines for use in other institutions, such as schools.

CASP seeks to develop excellence in research and service in Canada by giving annual national awards for outstanding contributions in research and service. The association also develops and administers standards for crisis and research centers and develops funds for specific projects.

CASP News, the organization's newsletter, is published in English and French three times per year.

The CASP office can be contacted at Canadian Association for Suicide Prevention, The Support Network, #301, 11456 Jasper Avenue, Edmonton, Alberta T5K 0M1. They can be reached by phone at 780-482-0198; by fax at 780-488-1495; or by e-mail at casp@suicideprevention.ca. Additional information can be obtained through the CASP web site: www.thesupportnetwork.com/CASP.

Canadian Palliative Care Association

The Canadian Palliative Care Association (CPCA) is a nonprofit organization whose membership is made up of individuals and hospice/palliative care programs from all ten Canadian provinces and three territories. The CPCA is the leading national association in hospice/palliative care in Canada. The association states its goal as leading the pursuit of "excellence in care for people approaching death so that the burdens of suffering, loneliness, and grief are lessened."

The association describes palliative care as involving four main components: pain management; symptom management; social, psychological, emotional, and spiritual support; and caregiver support. The organization defines palliative care as aimed at relieving suffering and improving the quality of life for those who are living with or dying from advanced illness or who are bereaved.

CPCA declares "to achieve its mission through: collaboration and representation; increased awareness, knowledge and skills related to hospice palliative care of the public, health care providers and volunteers; development of national standards of practice for hospice palliative care in Canada; support of research on hospice palliative care; advocacy for improved hospice palliative care policy, resource allocation and supports for caregivers."

CPCA funding comes from membership fees, corporate and individual donations, project grants, and contributions from charitable organizations and foundations. The CPCA publishes many fact sheets with titles such as "Palliative Care: A Fact Sheet for Seniors."

The volunteer board of directors of CPCA includes representatives from each of the provincial associations and five elected members at large. Various committees carry out related activities. Questions regarding CPCA can be e-mailed to info@cpca.net. Additional information can be obtained through the CPCA web site: www.cpca.net.

Candlelighters Childhood Cancer Foundation

The Candlelighters Childhood Cancer Foundation (CCCF) seeks to educate, support, and advocate for families of children with cancer, survivors of childhood cancer, and the professionals who work with them. CCCF services include an information clearinghouse, resource database, peer support groups for parents of children with cancer, and a long-term survivor network. A group of concerned parents of children with cancer founded CCCF in 1970.

Using volunteers who are lawyers, doctors, teachers, and insurance experts, Candlelighters' Ombudsman Program helps families and survivors of childhood cancer who experience difficulties in areas of insurance appeals, medical opinions, employment discrimination, and disability rights.

A program called Candlelighters Survivors of Childhood Cancer Program aims to provide a forum for young adult survivors of childhood cancer in the United States. These people can educate themselves on issues related to being a survivor and can interact with other survivors.

Candlelighters works to influence public policy by maintaining a presence in Washington, D.C., working in particular to support federal funding of cancer research as well as legislation and benefits that impact children with cancer. Candlelighters collaborates with many other organizations to create a stronger force for children with cancer.

CCCF's publications include *Candlelighters Quarterly,* a publication for parents and professionals, as well as a number of pamphlets aimed at helping children with cancer understand their condition and treatment. Parents may call the CCCF national office at 1-800-366-CCCF (2223) for referral to the local group nearest them. Local Candlelighters groups provide much of the organization's direct services to families, such as support groups and parent hospital visitation programs.

Candlelighters Childhood Cancer Foundation is headquartered at 3910 Warner Street, Kensington, MD 20895. They can be reached by e-mail at info@candlelighters.org. Additional information can be obtained through the CCCF web site: www.candlelighters.org.

CDC National Prevention Information Network

The CDC National Prevention Information Network (NPIN) provides information about HIV/AIDS (human immunodeficiency virus/acquired immunodeficiency syndrome), sexually transmitted diseases (STDs), and tuberculosis (TB) to people and organizations working in prevention, health care, research, and support services. All of NPIN's services are designed to facilitate this sharing of information.

The Centers for Disease Control and Prevention (CDC), an agency of the Public Health Service, which is a division of the U.S. Department of Health and Human Services. The CDC works to protect public health by administering national programs for the prevention and control of disease and disability. The agency provides health information and statistics and conducts research to find the sources of epidemics. Established in 1946, CDC's headquarters and many of its laboratories are in Atlanta, Georgia.

NPIN staff serve a network of people who work in international, national, state, and local settings. All NPIN services are designed for reference, referral, and informational purposes only. NPIN does not provide medical advice or medical care.

Among the many topics on which the NPIN provides information is how HIV/AIDS, STDs, and TB affect groups such as African Americans, American Indians, Asians, Hispanics, incarcerated populations, people with disabilities, pregnant women, women, and young people. The agency provides information on statistics, trends, substance abuse, testing, counseling, travel, immigration, treatment, and support as they relate to these diseases.

The CDC National Prevention Information Network can be reached at P.O. Box 6003, Rockville, MD 20849-6003. They can be contacted by phone at 800-458-5231 or by e-mail at info@cdcnpin.org. Additional information can be obtained through the CDC NPIN web site: www.cdcnpin.org.

Center for Death Education and Bioethics

The Center for Death Education and Bioethics (CDEB) is a resource center that collects and archives academic materials concerned with the issue of death, dying, and bereavement in contemporary society.

The center was founded in 1969 as the Center for Death Education and Research at the University of Minnesota in Minneapolis. It was formed with the purpose of serving as a repository for materials concerning mortality. It was also intended as a center for the dissemination of literature and information to the academic and professional communities as well as to the public. The Center for Death Education later became affiliated with the Sociology/Archaeology Department of the University of Wisconsin in La Crosse.

The CDEB retains a large collection of journals, books, and articles concerned with death, dying, bereavement, terminal illness, hospice care, and related topics. Administrators of the center encourage users to visit the center and take advantage of its resources for their academic projects or personal interests. The center is open for certain hours of the week and by appointment at other times.

The CDEB sponsors *Illness, Crisis, and Loss,* a quarterly peer-reviewed journal published by Sage Publications. CDEB also sells brochures on grief and loss.

The Center for Death Education and Bioethics is located at 435NH, 1725 State Street, University of Wisconsin, La Crosse, WI 54601-3742. They can be reached by phone at 608-785-6784 or by e-mail at cdeb@uwlax.edu. Additional information can be obtained through the CDEB web site: www.uwlax.edu/sociology/cde&b/.

Children's Hospice International

Children's Hospice International (CHI) provides resources and referrals to children with life-threatening conditions and their families. The goal of CHI is to improve quality of life for the dying child and the ongoing, strengthened life of the family. It advocates on behalf of these children and families, helps to establish children's hospice programs, and provides education and training for health care providers.

Children's Hospice International was founded in 1983 as a nonprofit organization to provide a network of support and care for children with life-threatening conditions and their families. Very few hospice programs would accept children before the CHI worked to change that. Today almost all hospice programs in the United States are willing to consider accepting a child as a patient.

The hospice approach for children is a team effort that provides medical, psychological, social, and spiritual expertise. CHI recognizes the right and need for children and their families to choose health care and support whether in their own home, hospital, or hospice care facility. The organization works closely with medical professionals as a bank, providing technical assistance, research, and education.

The Children's Hospice International is headquartered at 901 N. Pitt Street, Suite 230, Alexandria, VA 22314. They can be reached by phone at 800-24CHILD or 703-684-0330, or by e-mail at chiorg@aol.com.

Concerns of Police Survivors

Concerns of Police Survivors (COPS) is a national nonprofit organization devoted to helping families and other survivors deal with the impact of police deaths. COPS acts as a support group for the survivors of law enforcement officers who have died suddenly and violently. Survivors include a police officer's squad partners and other such comrades and friends.

COPS was established in 1984 and grew to over thirty chapters by the end of the twentieth century. Grants from the U.S. Department of Justice help the organization continue and support some of its key efforts. COPS also receives funding from a number of organizations, including police unions, as well as from individuals.

COPS helps friends and families of slain officers through grief counseling programs. COPS aims to become a social network to help families recover from the shock and emptiness of death. Members are available to help one another in the immediate aftermath of an officer's death as well as for years to come.

The organization sponsors recreational camps, retreats, and other events for family members of all ages. Children aged six to fourteen can go to camps with their parents, and older children can participate in wilderness challenges designed to instill self-confidence and independence. COPS sponsors getaways for spouses of slain officers as well as outings for officers' parents. Many of these events are held at Lake of the Ozarks, Missouri. The national program raises money to provide for the camps, and local chapters cover transportation costs.

Official programs include national peer support, national counseling programs, national police survivors' seminars, scholarships, trial and parole support, and information on state death benefits. COPS also provides programs for agencies and raise public awareness.

The National Office of Concerns of Police Survivors offers information and accepts donations at P.O. Box 3199, S. Highway 5, Camdenton, MO 65020. They can be reached by phone at 573-346-4911 or by e-mail at cops@nationalcops.org. Additional information can be obtained through the COPS web site: www.nationalcops.org.

Council of Religious AIDS Networks

The Council of Religious AIDS Networks (CRAN) seeks to empower and mobilize faith communities to respond to the international HIV/AIDS (human immunodeficiency virus/acquired immunodeficiency syndrome) pandemic. Membership includes local, regional, and national faith-based, AIDS-specific ministries and organizations.

The council grew out of the AIDS National Interfaith Network (ANIN), a private, nonprofit organization founded in 1988. ANIN was created to secure compassionate and nonjudgmental support, care, and assistance for individuals with HIV and AIDS. The organization coordinated a network of nearly 2,000 ministries.

In 1993 representatives of ANIN met with the National Episcopal AIDS Coalition (NEAC), Disciples of Christ AIDS Network, Lutheran AIDS Network, and United Methodist AIDS Network to create a new organization. By their second meeting in 1993, the group had formally named itself the Council of National Religious AIDS Networks, a name that was later modified to the Council of Religious AIDS Networks.

Members of CRAN receive a newsletter that features information on AIDS legislation, upcoming events, and news from AIDS ministries nationwide. They also receive Action Alerts on time-sensitive issues of importance to AIDS ministries. The council hosts a web site that seeks to offer comprehensive and reliable information on HIV/AIDS and faith-based services, faith-based organizations, and communities of faith.

CRAN works closely with the United States Centers for Disease Control and Prevention in Atlanta, Georgia, and also seeks to coordinate efforts with AIDS organizations worldwide.

For further information, contact CRAN, c/o Dr. Jon A. Lacey, P.O. Box 4188, East Lansing, MI 48826-4188. Information can also be obtained by e-mail at info@aidsfaith.com or through the CRAN web site: www.aidsfaith.com.

Cremation Association of North America

The Cremation Association of North America (CANA) seeks to raise standards and ethics for cremation. Cremation, the practice of burning a dead body to ashes, has become increasingly common in the United States and Canada. Most funeral directors can arrange a cremation, which often includes a funeral service before or after the burning. CANA seeks to increase public awareness and knowledge of cremation and memorialization. Its membership is made up of owners of cemeteries and crematories, funeral directors, industry suppliers, and consultants.

CANA began in 1913 as the Cremation Association of America, changing its name in 1977. CANA conducts research, compiles statistics, holds certification programs, and hosts a trade show. CANA publishes a quarterly magazine, *The Cremationist.*

The CANA code of cremation practice states: "In the practice of cremation, we believe: in dignity and respect in the care of human remains, in compassion for the living who survive them, and in the memorialization of the dead; that a cremation authority should be responsible for creating and maintaining an atmosphere of respect at all times; that the greatest care should be taken in the appointment of crematory staff members, any whom must not, by conduct or demeanor, bring the crematory or cremation into disrepute; that cremation should be considered as preparation for memorialization; that the dead of our human society should be memorialized through a commemorative means suitable to the survivors."

The Cremation Association of North America is headquartered at 401 N. Michigan Avenue, Chicago, IL 60611-4267. They can be reached by phone at 312-644-6610, by fax at 312-321-4098, or by e-mail at cana@sba.com. Additional information can be obtained through the CANA web site: www.cremationassociation.org.

Death Studies

Death Studies is a peer-reviewed journal that publishes papers on research, scholarship, and clinical work in the areas of bereavement and loss, grief therapy, death attitudes, suicide, and death education. *Death Studies* is published eight times each year. Its readers are comprised of professionals in universities, hospitals, hospices, and counseling centers who are interested in the major topics in the field of death and dying. Death Studies online archives date back to January 1997.

Article titles published by *Death Studies* include "Grief Communication, Grief Reactions and

Marital Satisfaction in Bereaved Parents"; "No-Suicide Contracts among College Students"; "Survivors' Motives for Extravagant Funerals among the Yorubas of Western Nigeria"; "Exploration of the Relationship Between Physical and/or Sexual Abuse, Attitudes about Life and Death, and Suicidal Ideation in Young Women"; "Traumatic Stress and Death Anxiety among Community Residents Exposed to an Aircraft Crash"; "Firearms and Suicide: the American Experience, 1926–1996"; "Developing Beliefs That Are Compatible with Death"; "Israeli Children's Reactions to the Assassination of the Prime Minister"; and "Parental Bereavement: The Crisis of Meaning."

Death Studies is published by Taylor & Francis, a 200-year old international academic publisher. They have offices in London and other British cities as well as New York City, Philadelphia, Singapore, and Sydney. Prospective readers can visit the Taylor & Francis web site to browse the contents pages of *Death Studies* issues. Readers within institutions that subscribe to the journal can access the full text free of charge.

The editor in chief of *Death Studies* is Robert A. Neimeyer, Department of Psychology, University of Memphis, Memphis, TN 38152. Further information can be found at www.tandf.co.uk/journals.

Dougy Center for Grieving Children

The Dougy Center for Grieving Children is a nonprofit organization that provides families in Portland, Oregon, and the surrounding region, support for children, teens, and their families grieving a death. Through their National Center for Grieving Children & Families, they also provide support and training locally, nationally, and internationally to individuals and organizations seeking to assist children and teens in grief.

In 1982 the Center became the first in the United States to provide peer support groups for grieving children. The Center received national and international acclaim for pioneering a model for assisting children, teens, and families coping with the deaths of family members. Over 120 programs modeled on the Center have developed throughout the United States, Canada, Japan, England, Jamaica, Germany, and Rwanda.

The Dougy Center provides training nationally and internationally for companies and schools helping grieving children and teens coping with deaths from natural causes or from violence in a community. The Center also trains groups in starting children's grieving centers.

The Center publishes a guidebook series that grew out of their experience. Topics in the series include helping children and teens cope with death, children and funerals, helping the grieving student, and a guide for principals responding to deaths in school.

The Dougy Center is privately supported and does not charge a fee for services. The Dougy Center can be reached at 3909 SE 52nd Ave., Portland, OR 97286, by phone at 503-775-5683, by fax at 503-777-3097, or by e-mail at help@dougy.org. Additional information can be obtained through the Dougy Center web sites at www.dougy.org/about.html or www.grievingchild.org.

Elizabeth Glaser Pediatric AIDS Foundation

The Elizabeth Glaser Pediatric AIDS Foundation is a nonprofit organization dedicated to helping children with HIV/AIDS (human immunodeficiency virus/acquired immunodeficiency syndrome). The foundation's focus is on continuing research, especially on the effectiveness of drug treatments for children and decreasing their cost.

Elizabeth Glaser was a television actress who contracted HIV through a blood transfusion in 1981. By the time she was diagnosed, she had already passed the virus to her daughter Ariel through breast-feeding and to her son Jake during pregnancy. Ariel died in 1988, and Glaser herself died in 1994 at the age of forty-seven. She left behind her husband, Paul Michael, a Hollywood director and actor, and their son. Paul Michael was the only one in the family not infected. Jake remained HIV-positive but otherwise functioning.

After Ariel's death the Glaser couple and several friends founded the organization to raise funds for pediatric HIV/AIDS research. Elizabeth became a vocal AIDS activist and a critic of what she saw as governmental inaction toward the epidemic. Paul Michael became chairman of the foundation board.

In its first ten years, the foundation raised $75 million for pediatric AIDS research and treatment. The foundation supported a network of leading research institutions with an $8 million grant. The institutions, which included Harvard Medical School/Children's Hospital-Boston and Stanford School of

Medicine/Lucile Packard Children's Hospital, study treatments for serious pediatric illnesses. In addition, five Elizabeth Glaser Scientists are named each year by the foundation to receive up to $682,500 in a five-year research grant. The foundation also funds other grants and scholarships.

The foundation accepts donations by phone at 888-499-HOPE (4673) or by mail to Elizabeth Glaser Pediatric AIDS Foundation, 2950 31st Street, #125, Santa Monica, CA 90405. Additional information can be obtained through the foundation's web site: www.pedaids.org/index.html.

European Association for Palliative Care

The European Association for Palliative Care (EAPC) promotes palliative care in Europe and acts as a source for professionals who work or have an interest in this field.

From its foundation in 1988 the EAPC grew to reach a reported membership representing over 23,000 people by 2001. The EAPC head office is situated at the Division for Rehabilitation, Pain Therapy and Palliative Care within the National Cancer Institute in Milan, Italy.

The stated objectives of the EAPC include: "Increase the awareness and promote the development and dissemination of palliative care at scientific, clinical and social levels; promote the implementation of existing knowledge; train those who at any level are involved with the care of patients with incurable and advanced disease; promote study and research; bring together those who study and practice the disciplines involved in the care of patients with advanced disease; unify national palliative care organizations and establish an international network for the exchange of information and expertise; and address the ethical problems associated with the care of terminally ill patients."

The official publication of the EAPC is the *European Journal of Palliative Care.* Launched in 1994, it is published in English and French and aimed at palliative care professionals. In addition, the association's communication strategy includes its web site, which it considers crucial for informing members and sharing information among members.

The European Association for Palliative Care is also referred to by the acronym ONLUS, based on its foreign language title. The mailing address of the EAPC is National Cancer Instititute of Milan, Via Venezian 1, 20133 Milan, Italy. They can be reached by e-mail at eapc@istitutotumori.mi.it. Additional information can be obtained in French or English through the EAPC web site: www.eapcnet.org.

European Journal of Palliative Care

The *European Journal of Palliative Care* (*EJPC*) is the official journal of the European Association for Palliative Care (EAPC). The association promotes palliative care in Europe and acts as a source for people who work or have an interest in the field of palliative care. The *Journal* publishes authoritative articles covering a range of palliative care issues and acts as a resource for palliative care professionals throughout Europe and beyond.

The *Journal* is produced in English and French editions, and is available by subscription only. The *EJPC* is a review journal, therefore it does not publish original research. Commissioned review articles are aimed at covering all aspects of the care of patients with incurable diseases. Contributions are taken from members of every discipline involved in palliative care.

The EAPC launched the *EJPC* as a quarterly publication in 1994. Since 1997 it has been published six times a year.

The *Journal* aims to help advance the skills and expertise of professions that include palliative care specialists, general practitioners, nurses, oncologists, anesthetists, pain specialists, geriatricians, AIDS (acquired immunodeficiency syndrome) specialists, psychiatrists/psychologists, and social workers.

The *Journal* is published by Hayward Medical Communications, whose editorial offices are located in London, England. Additional information can be obtained through the Hayward web site: www.hayward.co.uk. The mailing address of the EAPC is National Cancer Institute of Milan, Via Venezian 1, 20133 Milan, Italy. Additional information can be obtained in French or English through the EAPC web site: www.eapcnet.org.

Funeral Consumers Alliance

The Funeral Consumers Alliance (FCA) is a nonprofit organization whose stated mission is to educate consumers and to establish, promote, and protect their rights in the planning and purchasing of funeral and memorial arrangements. The FCA monitors the funeral industry with the goal of protecting consumer interests.

Groups called "memorial societies" existed in the early 1900s, when people joined together to ensure an acceptable level of standards for burial. In 1963 several such societies formed the Continental Association of Funeral and Memorial Societies. After the Canadian societies dropped out, members changed the name to the Funeral and Memorial Societies of America in 1996. In 1999 the organization's board voted to consolidate its operations under the Funeral Consumers Alliance.

The FCA provides educational materials on funeral choice to increase public awareness of funeral options. It acts as a source of information for media coverage of issues on dying and death. The FCA lobbies as a consumer advocate for reforms at the national level and lends support for needed changes at the state or local level.

The Funeral Consumers Alliance publishes a quarterly newsletter that covers industry trends, legal issues, consumer information, and tips for local groups. The Funeral Consumers Alliance is supported by dues and donations from both local organizations and from individuals.

The Funeral Consumers Alliance is headquartered at P.O. Box 10, Hinesburg, VT 05461. They can be reached by phone at 800-765-0107. Additional information can be obtained through the FCA web site: www.funerals.org.

Hemlock Society

The Hemlock Society is a nonprofit organization devoted to helping people maintain choice and dignity at the end of their life. They believe that people suffering from irreversible illnesses must have access to peaceful means to hasten their death if they feel their suffering is unbearable. According to the Hemlock Society, "The primary means to accomplish this is with legally prescribed medication as part of the continuum of care between a patient and a doctor, although there are non-medical methods that are effective."

The Hemlock Society was founded in 1980 by Derek Humphry. It has since become the oldest and largest right-to-die organization in the United States with almost 25,000 members in seventy chapters across the country.

The Hemlock Foundation funds the educational and charitable parts of the Hemlock operation. The Patients' Rights Organization (PRO-USA) is Hemlock's legislative arm. Its funds go directly into legislative efforts to change the law. Hemlock seeks to change laws in order to protect patients and physicians involved in hastening a death.

The society does not distribute the means to a peaceful death, but they make available written materials on such matters. Their publications provide information on advance directives, pain management, hospice care, and all options for a death in which the patient retains choice and dignity. Their education efforts also occur through their web site and about 12,000 annual phone inquiries.

The Hemlock Society can be reached at P.O. Box 101810, Denver, CO 80250-1810. Interested people can call 800-247-7421 for the location of local chapters or other information. The society can be reached by e-mail at email@hemlock.org. Additional information can be obtained through the Hemlock Society web site: www.hemlock.org.

Hospice and Palliative Nurses Association

The Hospice and Palliative Nurses Association (HPNA) is an international professional association with the mission of promoting excellence in hospice and palliative nursing. Its stated purpose is to exchange information, experiences, and ideas; to promote understanding of the specialties of hospice and palliative nursing; and to study and promote hospice and palliative research.

The Hospice and Palliative Nurses Association began as the Hospice Nurses Association in 1986 at a meeting of the Southern California Hospice Association. The organization grew after 1993 in response to HPNA's formation of the National Board for the Certification of Hospice Nurses to develop a process to credential hospice nurses. The board became a separate organization, responsible for developing and overseeing the certification exam for hospice and palliative nurses. The national office of HPNA coordinates activities for the board.

The HPNA mission statement declares the organization's role of promoting excellence in hospice and palliative nursing, promoting the highest professional standards of hospice and palliative nursing, studying, researching, exchanging information, experiences, and ideas leading to improved nursing practice, encouraging nurses to specialize in the practice of hospice and palliative nursing, fostering the professional development of nurses, and promoting recognition of hospice and palliative care as an essential component throughout the health care system.

HPNA publishes the quarterly journal *JHPN.* The Hospice and Palliative Nurses Association is located at Penn Center W. One, Suite 209, Pittsburgh, PA 15276. They can be reached by phone at 412-787-9301 or by e-mail at hpna@hpna.org. Additional information can be obtained through the HPNA web site: www.hpna.org.

Hospice Association of America

The Hospice Association of America (HAA) is a national organization representing more than 2,800 hospices and many caregivers and volunteers who serve terminally ill patients and their families. Hospice is a family-centered concept of health care for people dying of incurable illnesses.

The hospice concept aims at easing the physical and psychological pain of the patient's illness so that the person can appreciate his or her remaining life. The hospice team includes the patient and his or her family, as well as physicians, nurses, social workers, members of the clergy, and volunteers. Hospice services may include nursing care and pain control, meal preparation, laundry, or shopping. This care may be provided at home, in a separate hospice medical center, or in a hospice unit of a hospital.

In 1996 the HAA's first special membership section, the Volunteer Hospice Network (VHN), was established to promote the growth, diversity, and development of volunteer organizations that serve people dealing with life-threatening illnesses and those who are grieving.

The HAA is the largest lobbying group for hospice in the United States, appealing to the U.S. Congress, the regulatory agencies, other national organizations, the courts, media, and the public.

HAA members can obtain expert advice from the HAA's legislative, regulatory, legal, research, and clinical specialists. A team of trained professionals works with the membership to advocate on behalf of hospices, caregivers, and those they serve.

HAA members receive a number of publications produced by the HAA. These publications include *Caring,* a monthly magazine covering all aspects of the hospice and home care field, and *Homecare News,* a widely circulated quarterly newspaper that reaches the entire hospice and home care community.

The Hospice Association of America is headquartered at 228 Seventh Street SE, Washington, DC 20003. They can be reached by phone at 202-546-4759. Additional information can be obtained through the HAA web site: www.nahc.org.

Hospice Association of South Africa

The Hospice Association of South Africa (HASA) is an international palliative care association that coordinates the development of hospices in the South Africa region by providing a centralized source of information, education, and training. The HASA represents forty-nine hospices in South Africa.

The association is among the very few care services for the terminally ill in South Africa. Hospices are funded mainly by private donations, some of which have been raised through benefit events. Only a small part of hospice income is from the government. However, hospice service is free and available to all, regardless of age, sex, race, color, or creed. The Most Reverend Desmond Tutu, Archbishop Emeritus, is patron of the Hospice Association of South Africa.

The Hospice Association of South Africa is headquartered at P.O. Box 38785, Pinelands 7439, Western Cape, South Africa.

Hospice Education Institute

The Hospice Education Institute is an independent, nonprofit organization that serves members of the public and health care professionals with information and education about caring for the dying and the bereaved. The institute defines hospice as a philosophy of caring that respects and values the dignity and worth of each person and good hospice care as the practical expression of that personal and professional commitment. Hospices aim to cherish and emphasize life by helping patients live each day to its fullest.

Founded in 1985, the institute seeks to educate the public about the history of hospice, which dates back to the Middle Ages. In modern times a resurgence of hospice care was seen in the latter part of the 1900s. From 1974 to 1978 hospices and palliative care units opened across North America. In the 1980s, hospice care, usually emphasizing home care, expanded throughout the United States, especially after Medicare added a hospice benefit in 1984 and after hospices began to care for people with advanced AIDS (acquired immunodeficiency syndrome).

From 1990 to 1999 almost 3,000 hospices and palliative care programs served the United States and soon there was well-established hospice and palliative care in Canada, Australia, New Zealand, and much of Asia and Western Europe.

The Hospice Education Institute is headquartered at 190 Westbrook Road, Essex, CT 06426-1510. Interested parties can telephone the institute at 800-331-1620 or 860-767-1620 to obtain information about good hospice and palliative care, to get referrals to hospices and palliative care organizations in the United States, or to discuss issues relating to caring for the dying and the bereaved. The e-mail address of the institute is hospiceall@aol.com. Additional information can be obtained through the Hospice Education Institute web site: www.hospiceworld.org.

Hospice Foundation of America

The Hospice Foundation of America (HFA) is a nonprofit organization that promotes hospice care and works to educate professionals and the families they serve in issues relating to caregiving, terminal illness, loss, and bereavement. The HFA provides leadership in the development and application of hospice and its philosophy of care. Through programs of professional development, research, public education, and information, the HFA assists those who cope either personally or professionally with terminal illness, death, and the process of grief. The Hospice Foundation of America seeks to enhance the role of hospice within the American health care system.

Hospice Foundation, Inc. was chartered in 1982 with the purpose of providing fundraising assistance to hospices operating in South Florida so that they could carry on their mission of providing compassionate care to dying patients. In 1990, with the help of a significant gift from Hospice Care, Inc., the foundation expanded its scope to a national level in order to provide leadership in the entire spectrum of end-of-life issues. The foundation board is made up of health policy experts. The HFA seeks to raise the visibility and credibility of hospice and advocate for principles of hospice that may enhance the medical system.

In 1992 the foundation opened a Washington, D.C., office for its policy and program work, and in 1994 the board changed the name of Hospice Foundation, Inc. to the Hospice Foundation of America. The Foundation is supported by contributions from individuals and corporations, grants from foundations, and gifts from associations.

The Hospice Foundation of America is headquartered at 2001 S. Street NW, #300, Washington, DC 20009. They can be reached by phone at 800-854-3402 or by fax at 202-638-5312. Additional information can be obtained through the HFA web site: www.hospicefoundation.org.

Hospice Information

Hospice Information acts as a worldwide link and resource for any health professional or member of the public concerned with palliative care. The service seeks to promote sharing of experience by spreading current information. They also seek to enable patients and caretakers to find and obtain needed palliative care support. Hospice Information estimates that there are over 6,500 hospice/palliative care centers in about ninety countries. The organization has links with services in over eighty of these countries.

The Hospice Information Service began in 1977, founded by Dame Cicely Saunders at the first teaching hospice, St. Christopher's Hospice in London. The Service grew in response to an increasing number of inquiries about hospice received by St. Christopher's. The Service shortened its name to the Hospice Information in 2002, and remained linked to the Department of Palliative Care and Policy, a joint venture between St. Christopher's and King's College London.

Hospice Information publishes a quarterly newsletter, *Hospice Bulletin,* which highlights the work of international palliative care centers and informs readers of new services, especially those in developing countries. It publishes a "Directory of Hospice and Palliative Care Services in the UK and Ireland," the "Hospice Worldwide" directory, and fact sheets with titles such as "Facts and Figures: Latest Palliative Care Statistics" or "Building a Hospice." The Hospice Information web site features a listing of hospices and palliative care services worldwide for both professionals and the public.

Hospice Information is located at St. Christopher's Hospice, 51 Lawrie Park Road, London SE26 6DZ and Hospice House, 34 Britannia Street, London WC1X 9JG. Hospice Information can be contacted by e-mail at info@hospiceinformation.info. Additional information can be obtained through the Hospice Information web site: www.hospiceinformation.info.

Illness, Crisis, and Loss

*Illness, Crisis, and Loss*is a quarterly journal based on the stated premise that significant progress in the fields of life-threatening illness and thanatology will be achieved by bringing together the expertise of many varied professionals. The journal attempts to explore all aspects of grief, death, and loss by publishing peer-reviewed articles, book reviews, and essays related to these issues.

The journal is sponsored by the Center for Death Education and Bioethics (CDEB), a resource center that collects and archives academic materials concerned with the issues of death, dying, and bereavement in contemporary society. The center was founded in 1969 as the Center for Death Education and Research at the University of Minnesota in Minneapolis. The center later became affiliated with the Sociology/Archaeology Department of the University of Wisconsin in La Crosse.

Robert Bendiksen is the editor of *Illness, Crisis, and Loss* and director of the CDEB. The journal is published by Sage Publications, headquartered in London, England.

The range of subjects covered by the journal includes HIV/AIDS (human immunodeficiency virus/acquired immunodeficiency syndrome), crisis intervention, death studies, ethical decision making, grief work, and palliative care of the dying. Specific sample topics include models of grieving, religion and spirituality, grief work with survivors of disasters, euthanasia, bioethics, and assisted dying.

Address correspondence to Dr. Robert Bendiksen, Editor, *Illness, Crisis, and Loss,* Center for Death Education and Bioethics, Soc/Arc Dept., 435 North Hall, University of Wisconsin, La Crosse, WI 54601-3742. The center can be reached by phone at 608-785-6781 or by e-mail at cdeb@uwlax.edu. Additional information can be obtained through the Sage Publications Ltd. web site: www.sagepub.co.uk.

International Association for Suicide Prevention

The International Association for Suicide Prevention (IASP), also called the Association Internationale pour la Prevention du Suicide (AIPS), is an organization for individuals and agencies of various disciplines and professions from different countries engaged in suicide prevention and research.

The goal of the association is to provide a common platform for the interchange of experience, literature, and information about suicide. It is also aimed at the wide dissemination of the fundamentals of suicide prevention in both professional and public circles. The IASP arranges for specialized training of selected people in suicide prevention. It encourages and facilitates research programs, especially ones that can be pursued through international cooperation.

The IASP was founded in 1960, and is financed by membership dues, voluntary contributions, and subsidies.

The IASP encourages the work of voluntary organizations, such as the network of suicide prevention telephone services. It also disseminates information on various other forms of crisis intervention, such as psychotherapy and drug treatment, aimed at suicide prevention. The IASP publishes a quarterly publication called *Crisis*.

World headquarters for the IASP are in Vienna, Austria. American headquarters are located at Rush Center for Suicide Prevention, 1725 W. Harrison Street, Suite 955, Chicago, IL 60612. They can be reached by phone at 312-942-7208, by fax at 312-942-2177, or by e-mail at iasp@aol.com. Additional information can be obtained through the IASP web site: www.who.int/ina-ngo/ngo/ngo027.htm.

International Association of Pet Cemeteries

The International Association of Pet Cemeteries (IAPC) is a nonprofit organization dedicated to the advancement of pet cemeteries everywhere. It pursues its goal mainly through public awareness programs.

There are more than 600 active pet cemeteries in the United States, most of which operate in conjunction with other pet-related business such as boarding kennels, grooming salons, training centers, and veterinarian hospitals. Some directors of human cemeteries have set aside a portion of their grounds for pet burials. Some pet cemeteries operate on a full-time basis, specifically dedicated to the burial or cremation of pets.

Pat Blosser founded the International Association of Pet Cemeteries in 1971 in West Chicago. Member pet cemeteries are expected to maintain the highest business and ethical standards. The IAPC operates on a budget that is supported only by dues and other contributions from members. The International Association of Pet Cemeteries has no paid employees—volunteers do all of the association's work.

Members of the International Association of Pet Cemeteries can receive continuous education management consultation, use of the IAPC logo, public relations services, promotional materials, and membership plaques. Members also receive a subscription to *News and Views.* They may attend the IAPC annual spring convention and the annual fall seminar.

The International Association of Pet Cemeteries can be reached at P.O. Box 163, 5055 Route 11, Ellenburg Depot, NY 12935, by phone at 518-594-3000, or by fax at 518-594-8801. Additional information can be obtained through the IAPC web site: www.iaopc.com.

International Cemetery and Funeral Association

The International Cemetery and Funeral Association (ICFA) is an international trade association representing the cemetery, funeral, and memorialization industry. The ICFA's stated mission is to serve and support its members in order to help them succeed in business.

The International Cemetery and Funeral Association was founded in 1887 as the American Cemetery Association, an organization of cemetery owners and operators who wanted to provide a means for accomplishing more together than they could as individuals. The organization gained its present name in 1997 when the American Cemetery Association merged with the National Association of Cemeteries.

In its mission statement, the ICFA includes its commitment to prefinanced funeral and cemetery services and to providing consumers with better value through open competition. It states its services to members as promoting high ethical standards, providing products and educational services, leading legislative, regulatory, and legal changes, encouraging members to promote the celebration of life, remembrance, and memorialization, and promoting cemeteries as guardians of a nation's heritage and as places of lasting tribute to the memory of the dead.

The ICFA reached a membership of more than 6,000 cemeteries, funeral homes, monument dealerships, crematories, and related businesses. The ICFA publishes a monthly journal, *International Cemetery and Funeral Management*. The ICFA offers members representation in the governmental arena, educational meetings, and other services and products to meet their needs.

The International Cemetery and Funeral Association is headquartered at 1895 Preston White Drive, Suite 220, Reston, VA 20191. They can be reached by phone at 800-645-7700 or by e-mail at gen4@icfa.org. Additional information can be obtained through the ICFA web site: www.icfa.org.

Journal of Loss and Trauma

The *Journal of Loss and Trauma* is published four times per year, bringing together scholarship on personal losses relating to family, health, and aging issues. The journal focuses on both psychological and physical health, as well as interpersonal losses within the contexts of extended family, community life, and society as a whole. In order to broaden the reader's perspective on loss and bereavement, and their pervasiveness in human life, the *Journal of Loss and Trauma* defines loss as a major reduction in a person's resources, whether personal, material, or symbolic, to which the person was emotionally attached. Types of loss covered include death and dying, dissolution and divorce, loss of employment, life-threatening diseases and long-term disability, loss of possessions, homelessness, recurring painful memories, disenfranchisement and stigmatization, losses resulting from war and violence, and aging.

The *Journal* highlights common as well as differing impacts of major losses while revealing commonalities of the various healing processes. Interdisciplinary in its approach, the quarterly publishes papers on experiments, case studies, discussions, theoretical analyses, and essays on therapeutic approaches. Book reviews are also regular features.

The *Journal* was formerly called the *Journal of Personal and Interpersonal Loss*. Readers of the journal include academics and practitioners in the fields of psychology, counseling, thanatology, gerontology, nursing, anthropology, family studies, psychiatry, sociology, oral history, and organizational management as it pertains to job loss.

The *Journal* is published by Taylor & Francis, which is headquartered in London at 11 New Fetter Lane, London EC4P 4EE. Additional information can be obtained through the Taylor & Francis web site: www.tandf.co.uk.

Journal of Near-Death Studies

The *Journal of Near-Death Studies* is a quarterly publication produced by a nonprofit organization called the International Association for Near-Death Studies (IANDS). The *Journal* features scholarly reports on near-death experiences and similar phenomena, and is included in membership dues for IANDS. The term *near-death experience* refers to what reported by some people who come very close to physical death or who survive a state of clinical death. IANDS calls a near-death experience one of the most powerful emotional and psychological events known. The organization seeks to provide reliable information about near-death experiences, as well as information and support for those who have been through it.

IANDS describes its mission as responding to the need for information and support concerning near-death and similar experiences, and to encourage recognition of the experiences as genuine and significant events. Its stated goals are to enrich understanding of human consciousness and its relationship to life and death. IANDS responds to people's needs to integrate the physical, mental, emotional, and spiritual aspects of the near-death experience. Founded in 1981, it provides information about near-death experiences to researchers, academia, the health care community, and the public, encouraging research and serving as a networking organization for near-death experiencers, their families, and caregivers.

IANDS hosts an annual three-day conference for experiencers, researchers, and health care professionals. The association coordinates peer-support groups across the United States and Canada to assist people who have experienced near death and need to reintegrate into daily life.

IANDS is headquartered at P.O. Box 502, East Windsor Hill, CT 06028. They can be reached by phone at 860-644-5216 or by email at office@iands.org or services@iands.org. Additional information can be obtained through the IANDS web site: www.iands.org.

Journal of Pain and Palliative Care in Pharmacotherapy

The *Journal of Pain and Palliative Care in Pharmacotherapy* is a professional quarterly journal that features information on end-of-life care. The publication includes original articles, reviews, editorials, commentaries, case reports, book and media reviews, news, and a meeting calendar.

The *Journal of Pain and Palliative Care in Pharmacotherapy* formed in 2002 from the merger of two other journals: the *Journal of Pharmaceutical Care in Pain and Symptom Control* and the *Hospice Journal*. The editors created the new title to reflect an increased focus on symptom control in end-of-life care. The international editorial board of the new journal includes over twenty experts in pain and palliative care from the fields of research, medicine, nursing, pharmacy, psychology, bioethics, and health policy.

The *Journal of Pharmaceutical Care in Pain and Symptom Control* was published quarterly beginning in 1993. It was a refereed journal concerned with issues of drug therapy in regard to its effectiveness, safety, cost, availability, delivery systems, ethics, health care policy, and other areas. These issues were addressed in relation to symptom control for both chronic and acute disorders. The *Hospice Journal,* which began in 1985, was the official journal of the National Hospice Organization. It addressed physical, psychosocial, and pastoral care of the dying.

The *Journal of Pain and Palliative Care in Pharmacotherapy* is published by The Haworth Press, 10 Alice Street, Binghamton, NY 13904-1580. Interested parties can obtain sample copies of the journal from that address. Single or multiple copies of all journal articles are available from the Haworth Document Delivery Service: 1-800-342-9678. The press can be reached by e-mail at getinfo@haworthpressinc.com. Additional information about the *Journal* can be obtained through the Haworth Press web site: www.haworthpressinc.com.

Junior Chamber Family AIDS Network

The Junior Chamber Family AIDS Network was founded by members of the Jaycees to provide help for children and families affected by HIV/AIDS (human immunodeficiency virus/acquired immunodeficiency syndrome). The organization allows young leaders to learn to mobilize community resources, build collaborative partnerships, provide volunteer support, and advocate for public policy change.

In 1995 members of the U.S. Junior Chamber of the Jaycees followed the Jaycee formula of national leadership and local solutions to address needs of children and families affected by HIV/AIDS. They formed a separate nonprofit organization called the Junior Chamber Family AIDS Network. Funding for the network comes from Jaycee chapters across the United States as well as private and corporate donations. The Jaycees stress individual development through leadership training and civic involvement. They learn to be leaders by working in community improvement programs.

The network maintains collaborative partnerships with three national organizations: Jaycees, Mothers' Voices, and Advocates for Youth. They also work with service providers in Missouri, Illinois, Michigan, Colorado, Oklahoma, and California.

Network services include providing child care, housing, case management, caregiver support, mental health treatment, and substance abuse treatment. Network volunteers help AIDS victims and families by hosting events, such as purchasing backpacks and school supplies for children, volunteering in direct service programs, creating residential facilities, and working to keep families together for as long as possible.

The Family AIDS Network is headquartered at 4 W. 21st Street, Tulsa, OK 74114. They can be reached by phone at 918-584-2481, by fax at 918-584-4422, or by e-mail at info@jcfamilyaidsnetwork.org. Additional information can be obtained through the Junior Chamber Family AIDS Network web site: www.jcfamilyaidsnetwork.org.

Last Acts

Last Acts is a campaign to improve care at the end of life. Its goal is to bring death-related issues into the open and help individuals and organizations pursue better ways to care for the dying. The organization believes in palliative care, which focuses on ways to ease pain and make life better for people who are dying and their loved ones. Palliative care means taking care of the whole person—body, mind, and spirit. It views death and dying as something natural and personal. The goal of palliative care is to provide the best quality of life until the very end of life.

Last Acts is a national effort to raise awareness about the need to improve care of the dying and to share issues and ideas at the national, state, and local levels. The honorary chair of Last Acts is the former first lady Rosalynn Carter. Last Acts' members comprise health care professionals, religious bodies, advocates, parents, educators, and health care institutions. They help partners find experts, schedule meeting speakers, and publicize their efforts.

Last Acts task forces address family needs, institutional change, professional education, palliative care, financing, and the workplace. Resource committees ensure that diversity, spirituality, public communication, standards development, and evaluation methods are incorporated in the work of each task force.

Last Acts works with policymakers and the news media to get and disseminate information about current policy issues. Last Acts sponsors national and regional conferences and publishes a quarterly print newsletter and special reports. Using electronic media, it conducts discussion groups on death and dying issues, distributes an e-mail newsletter, and publishes new information on its web site: www.lastacts.org.

Leukemia and Lymphoma Society

The Leukemia and Lymphoma Society is a national voluntary health agency dedicated to curing leukemia, lymphoma, Hodgkin's disease, and myeloma. The society is dedicated to improving the quality of life of patients with these diseases and their families.

Leukemia is a kind of cancer in which abnormal white blood cells multiply in an uncontrolled manner. It is a disease of the bone marrow and other blood-forming organs. Lymphoma is lymphatic cancer. A well-known form of lymphoma is Hodgkin's disease, a type of cancer in which the lymph nodes and other lymphoid tissues become swollen. The disease can be fatal and its cause is unknown. The most common lymphatic cancer is non-Hodgkin's lymphoma. Cases of non-Hodgkin's lymphoma have risen steadily since the mid-1900s, as many people with AIDS (acquired immunodeficiency syndrome) develop this type of cancer. Myeloma is a cancerous tumor of the bone marrow.

The society was founded as the de Villers Foundation in 1949 by two parents who lost their only son to leukemia and recognized the need for an organization dedicated to finding cures for the disease. In 2000 the society changed its name from the Leukemia Society of America to the Leukemia and Lymphoma Society to emphasize its commitment to fighting all blood-related cancers. The society has close to sixty chapters across the United States.

The Leukemia and Lymphoma Society can be reached at 1311 Mamaroneck Avenue, White Plains, NY 10605. They can be reached by phone at 800-955-4572. Additional information can be obtained through the Leukemia and Lymphoma Society web site: www.leukemia.org.

Living Bank International

Living Bank International is a nonprofit organization dedicated to the enhancement of organ and tissue donation and transplantation. The mission of the Living Bank is to motivate and facilitate the commitment of enough organ and tissue donors so that no one must die or suffer for lack of a donation. The board and staff of the Living Bank are dedicated to increasing the number of registered-informed donors.

Founded in 1971, the Living Bank is the oldest and largest donor education organization in the United States, and the only national one that keeps computerized records of donor data for future retrieval in an emergency. The Living Bank also cooperates with and supports any group or organization whose activities generate more committed donors or facilitates actual donation.

There is a large donor/transplant community in the United States consisting of organizations that seek to educate would-be donors, issue donor cards, and register donor information for efficient access and referral organ procurement organizations. The donor/transplant community also sends surgical teams into hospitals of the donors to take the donated organs and to transport the organs to hospitals where the chosen recipients wait. Transplant centers are located in authorized hospitals, where actual transplant operations take place.

Living Bank International is based in Houston, Texas. They can be reached by phone at 800-528-2971 or by e-mail at info@livingbank.org. Additional information can be obtained through the Living Bank International web site: www.livingbank.org.

Make-A-Wish Foundation of America

The Make-A-Wish Foundation of America exists to fulfill the wishes of children with life-threatening illnesses and to create moments of hope, strength, and joy for them. Although the foundation serves children diagnosed with life-threatening illnesses, many of these children survive their illnesses and go on to adulthood.

The foundation was created in 1980 by friends and relatives of a Phoenix, Arizona, boy named Chris Greicius who dreamed of becoming a police officer for a day. Officers of the Arizona highway patrol made his wish come true. Two of the officers, together with friends and Chris's mother, decided to offer that joy to other children with life-threatening illnesses. They formed the Make-A-Wish Foundation and the movement grew quickly throughout the United States and abroad. The foundation has international affiliates in Australia, Austria, Belgium, Canada, Chile, Costa Rica, Denmark, France, Greece, Hong Kong, India, Ireland, Israel, Japan, Mexico, Netherlands, New Zealand, Panama, Philippines, Taiwan, and the United Kingdom.

Since 1980 Make-A-Wish volunteers have granted more than 83,000 wishes worldwide. The foundation is funded primarily through corporate and private donations. Requests for wishes come from parents or guardians, from members of the medical community, and from children themselves.

For more information about the Make-A-Wish Foundation, call 800-722-WISH or visit their web site at www.wish.org. The web site provides a great deal of information and introduces ways to help, such as giving online, donating frequent flier miles, or volunteering for local chapters.

The Make-A-Wish Foundation of America is headquartered at 3550 N. Central Avenue, Suite 300, Phoenix, AZ 85012. Their e-mail address is mawfa@wish.org and the public relations e-mail address is comm@wish.org.

Mortality

The journal *Mortality,* an interdisciplinary peer-reviewed publication that focuses on the topic of human mortality, is of interest to academics in the fields of anthropology, art, classics, history, literature, medicine, music, sociolegal studies, social policy, sociology, philosophy, psychology, and religious studies. Death studies is an interdisciplinary medium. *Mortality* is also of interest to people professionally or voluntarily engaged in the health and caring professions, bereavement counseling, the funeral industries, and central and local government.

Mortality was started in 1996 and became of interest to international scholars and professional groups. Both new and established scholars in this field valued its interdisciplinary approach. *Mortality* aims to publish new material that is peer reviewed. The journal encourages debate and offers critiques of existing and classical work. The journal also promotes the development of theory and methodology. The journal seeks to develop substantive issues and research within an interdisciplinary context. It stimulates the growing awareness of the relevance of human mortality in personal and social life, in economic and institutional activity, and in systems of belief, ethics, and values. The journal editors pursue an international approach that invites articles addressing all historical periods and all subject areas.

Mortality is published by Taylor & Francis, which is headquartered at 11 New Fetter Lane, London EC4P 4EE. Additional information can be obtained through the Taylor & Francis web site: www.tandf.co.uk.

Mothers Against Drunk Driving

Mothers Against Drunk Driving (MADD) is a nonprofit voluntary organization whose focus is to look for effective solutions to problems of drunk driving and underage drinking, while supporting victims who have already experienced the pain of these crimes.

MADD was founded in 1980 by a small group of mothers and grew to one of the largest crime victim organizations in the world. With over 600 chapters, MADD is one of the most widely supported and publicly approved nonprofit organizations in America. MADD's funding comes from individual donors, grants, bequests, and MADD's corporate sponsors. MADD works with corporations to promote awareness campaigns and programs designed to stop drinking and driving.

MADD compiles statistics and facts from a number of reliable and credible sources, including the National Highway and Traffic Safety Administration. MADD also tracks laws having to do with drunk driving and underage drinking, including which states currently have these laws, and how the laws vary from state to state.

Drunk driving research supports MADD's positions on key issues surrounding drunk driving. Many of these journals and studies have formed the foundation for laws and policies in place today. Since MADD's start, more than 2,300 anti–drunk driving laws have been passed. A 1994 study found MADD to be the most popular nonprofit cause in the United States, well liked by 51 percent of Americans. It ranked second among the most strongly supported charities and third on the most credible list.

Mothers Against Drunk Driving is headquartered at P.O. Box 541688, Dallas, TX 75354-1688. They can be reached by phone at 800-GET-MADD (438-6233). Additional information can be obtained through the MADD web site: www.madd.org.

National Association of People with AIDS

The National Association of People with AIDS (NAPWA) advocates on behalf of all people living with HIV (human immunodeficiency virus) and AIDS (acquired immunodeficiency syndrome) in order to end the pandemic and the suffering it creates. The association's stated goal is to educate, inform, and empower all people living with HIV and AIDS.

NAPWA began in 1983 with the Patient Advisory Committee of the Second National AIDS Forum that was held in Denver, Colorado. One act of the committee was to adopt the term *people with AIDS* instead of *victim* or *patient,* which they saw as negative. The committee also created a set of recommendations for a more humane response to AIDS. The effort remained a loosely affiliated network.

NAPWA became incorporated in Washington, D.C., in 1987. From its place in Washington, the group sought to become an effective voice of people with AIDS at the center of national power.

NAPWA sponsors the National Call to Commitment Day, a grassroots action organized in collaboration with national, regional, and local organizations that serve the needs of people living with HIV and AIDS. Its goal is to increase federal funding to meet the needs of people living with and at risk for HIV.

The National Association of People with AIDS is headquartered at 1413 K Street NW, 7th Floor, Washington, DC 20005. They can be reached by phone at 202-898-0414, by fax at 202-898-0435, or by e-mail at napwa@napwa.org. Additional information can be obtained through the NAPWA web site: www.napwa.org.

National Center for Victims of Crime

The National Center for Victims of Crime (NCVC) is a leading advocate for crime victims in the United States. NCVC functions as a national resource center that seeks justice for crime victims. It does this by collaborating with local, state, and federal partners, and by pushing for passage of laws and public policies that create resources and win rights and protections for crime victims. The NCVC provides direct services and resources to victims, as well as training and technical assistance to victim service organizations, counselors, attorneys, criminal justice agencies, and other professionals. The National Center for Victims of Crime is a nonprofit organization supported by members, individual donors, corporations, foundations, and government grants.

The center was founded in 1985 and claims to have worked with more than 10,000 organizations and criminal justice agencies serving millions of crime victims by the early 2000s. The NCVC compiles statistics on crime and victimization and provides education through conferences, workshops, seminars, and videocassettes. The center also helps communities develop programs for victims of violent crimes. Among the center's most important services is providing crime victims and witnesses with direct assistance, such as social service referrals for crime victims.

The center maintains a database of over 10,000 organizations that link victims with key services, including crisis intervention, information, help through the criminal justice process, counseling, support groups, and legal counsel.

The National Center for Victims of Crime is headquartered at 2111 Wilson Boulevard, Suite 300, Arlington, VA 22201. People seeking an organization near them or any related referral can e-mail the service referral department at ddeskins@ncvc.org or call 800-FYI-CALL or 800-211-7996 (tty/tdd). The center also offers referrals for crime victims to attorneys for civil cases.

National Funeral Directors and Morticians Association

The National Funeral Directors and Morticians Association (NFDMA) is a nonprofit membership association of professional funeral directors and morticians.

The NFDMA began as the Independent National Funeral Directors Association in 1924. It was organized by a group of licensed funeral directors seeking to maintain high professional standards for the benefit of the public and their own business community. In 1926 the name was changed to the Progressive National Funeral Directors Association. In 1940 a merger with the National Colored Undertakers Association became the National Negro Funeral Directors Association. In 1957 NFDMA adopted its present name.

The stated objectives of the association are to foster research, conduct workshops and seminars, investigate funeral practices, develop and maintain standards of conduct designed to improve the business condition of its members, and maintain high standards of service for the benefit of the public. The association seeks to provide a continuing program of service and to develop and disseminate information beneficial to members and the public. The NFDMA promises to represent the common professional and business interests of its members before various federal, state, and local legislative, administrative, and judicial bodies throughout the United States.

The NFDMA awards an annual scholarship and they publish a quarterly magazine, *National Scope,* which is free to members.

The National Funeral Directors and Morticians Association is headquartered at 3951 Snapfinger Parkway, Suite 570, Omega World Center, Decatur, GA 30035. They can be reached by phone at 800-434-0958 or by e-mail at nfdma@nfdma.com. More information can be obtained through the NFDMA web site: www.nfdma.com.

National Heart, Lung, and Blood Institute

The National Heart, Lung, and Blood Institute (NHLBI) concerns itself with diseases of the heart, blood vessels, lungs, and blood, as well as with the blood supply in the United States. The NHLBI is one of the thirteen institutes of the National Institutes of Health (NIH), an agency of the U.S. federal government. The NIH is part of the Public Health Service of the U.S. Department of Health and Human Services. NIH conducts a broad range of biomedical research at its laboratories in Bethesda, Maryland, and provides funds for the training of research scientists. Elements of the NIH began in 1887, and it gained its present name in 1948.

The NHLBI is involved in many research efforts, including basic research, clinical investigations and trials, observational studies, and demonstration and education projects. The NHLBI is involved at the level of planning, conducting, and supporting such research programs. NHLBI research focuses on the causes, prevention, diagnosis, and treatment of heart, blood vessel, lung, and blood diseases and sleep disorders.

The NHLBI also conducts educational activities for health professionals, with an emphasis on prevention. The NHLBI seeks to spread information to the public, also emphasizing prevention.

The NHLBI coordinates its activities with other research institutes and federal health programs. It maintains relationships with institutions and professional associations, working with international, national, state, and local officials as well as voluntary agencies and organizations concerned with the heart, blood vessels, lung, and blood; blood resources; and sleep disorders.

People can direct health-related questions and requests for copies of publications to the NHLBI Information Center. They can be reached by e-mail at NHLBIinfo@rover.nhlbi.nih.gov. Additional information can be obtained through the NHLBI web site: www.nhlbi.nih.gov.

National Hemophilia Foundation

The National Hemophilia Foundation (NHF) acts as a leading resource on bleeding disorders information, also focusing attention on keeping the national blood supply safe. The NHF maintains that the number of people with hemophilia in the United States is 20,000. Hemophilia is a disease in which the blood does not clot normally, causing its victims, hemophiliacs, to bleed excessively if injured. The disease is hereditary and nearly all hemophiliacs are male. Because hemophiliacs often need blood transfusions, they are vulnerable to any disease that can be passed through the blood supply, such as HIV/AIDS (human immunodeficiency virus/acquired immunodeficiency syndrome).

The National Hemophilia Foundation was established in 1948 with the goal of generating awareness about the disease of hemophilia and calling for greater research. NHF works closely with the National Institutes of Health, the Food and Drug Administration, and the Centers for Disease Control and Prevention (CDC) to advocate for such issues as blood safety, medical insurance reform, and continued funding for hemophilia treatment centers and research.

The NHF also works with the CDC to spread information and awareness about von Willebrand disease and other female bleeding disorders. Von Willebrand disease is a hereditary disease, similar to hemophilia but occurring among women, in which the skin bleeds for an abnormally long period of time when injured.

The National Hemophilia Foundation is headquartered at 116 W. 32nd Street, 11th Floor, New York, NY 10001. They can be reached by phone at 800-42-HANDI or by e-mail at info@hemophilia.org. Additional information can be obtained through the NHF web site: www.hemophilia.org.

National Hospice and Palliative Care Organization

The National Hospice and Palliative Care Organization (NHPCO) is committed to improving end-of-life care. The organization seeks to expand access to hospice care with the goal of enhancing quality of life for dying people in America, as well as for their loved ones.

Hospice is a family centered concept of health care for people dying of an incurable illness. The hospice concept aims at easing the physical and psychological pain of the patient's illness, so that the person can appreciate his or her remaining life. The hospice team includes the patient and his or her family, as well as physicians, nurses, social workers, members of the clergy, and volunteers. Hospice services may include nursing care and pain control, meal preparation, laundry, or shopping. This care may be provided at home, in a separate hospice medical center, or in a hospice unit of a hospital.

In 1990 the World Health Organization defined palliative care, stating that it addresses not only physical pain, but emotional, social, and spiritual pain to achieve the best possible quality of life for patients and their families. Many hospice care programs have added palliative care to their names to reflect the greater range of care and services they provide.

The National Hospice and Palliative Care Organization was founded in 1978 as the National Hospice Organization and changed its name in 2000. The organization offers support for the terminally ill and their families and develops public and professional educational programs and materials to increase understanding of hospice and palliative care.

The National Hospice and Palliative Care Organization is headquartered at 1700 Diagonal Road, Suite 300, Alexandria, VA 22314. They can be reached by phone at 703-837-1500 or by e-mail at info@nhpco.org. Additional information can be obtained through the NHPCO web site: www.nhpco.org.

National Institute for Jewish Hospice

The National Institute for Jewish Hospice (NIJH) serves the needs of Jewish people who are terminally ill. The institute does this by providing free telephone counseling, making referrals, and training professionals in the needs of the terminally ill. The institute reaches out to families, businesses, and organizations concerned about seriously and terminally ill Jewish people.

NIJH was founded in 1985 to help alleviate suffering in terminal illness, death, and bereavement among Jewish people. Rabbi Maurice Lamm, a professor at Yeshiva University in New York City, is the founder and president of the National Institute for Jewish Hospice.

The institute serves as a resource center for terminal patients and their families, mainly providing information on traditional Jewish views on death, dying, and managing the loss of a loved one. The NIJH offers guidance and training to patients and interested hospice personnel, health care professionals, clergy, and family members who work with terminally ill Jewish people.

The NIJH provides materials to communities interested in setting up Jewish hospice care programs. The NIJH promotes its "Jewish Living Will and Durable Power of Attorney" document as covering the entire spectrum of Jewish thought regarding legal and medical ethics and offers it to anyone who wants a copy.

In addition to the Jewish living will, the NIJH publishes booklets and tapes that include: *Caring for the Jewish Terminally Ill, For Families of the Jewish Terminally Ill, Hemlock Is Poison for Society, How to Console, Introduction to Jewish Hospice, The Jewish Orphaned Adult, Realities of the Dying, Self-Healing and Hospice Care, The Spiritual Component Cannot Be Ignored, Strategies for Jewish Care,* and *The Undying Hope.*

The National Institute for Jewish Hospice is headquartered at Cedars-Sinai Medical Center, 444 S. San Vicente Boulevard, Suite 601, Los Angeles, CA 90048. They can be reached by phone at 213-HOSPICE or 800-446-4448.

National Institute of Diabetes and Digestive and Kidney Diseases

The National Institute of Diabetes and Digestive and Kidney Diseases (NIDDK) states that its mission is to conduct and support basic and clinical research on some of the most serious public health diseases. The institute supports much of the clinical research on the diseases of internal medicine as well as many basic science disciplines.

The NIDDK is one of the thirteen institutes of the National Institutes of Health (NIH), an agency of the U.S. federal government. The NIH is part of the Public Health Service of the U.S. Department of Health and Human Services. The NIH conducts a broad range of biomedical research at its laboratories in Bethesda, Maryland, and provides funds for the training of research scientists.

The diseases that the NIDDK concerns itself with are metabolic diseases such as diabetes, endocrine disorders, mineral metabolism, digestive diseases, nutrition, urology and renal disease, and hematology. Basic research studies of the NIDDK include biochemistry, nutrition, pathology, histochemistry, chemistry, physical, chemical, and molecular biology, pharmacology, and toxicology.

The institute supports research through grants, career development, and awards. The Institute contracts with various institutions and companies for research and development projects.

In 1950 President Harry S. Truman established the National Institute of Arthritis and Metabolic Diseases as part of the Public Health Service. In 1972 the institute's name was changed to National Institute of Arthritis, Metabolism, and Digestive Diseases. In 1981 the institute was renamed the National Institute of Arthritis, Diabetes, and Digestive and Kidney Diseases (NIADDK). In 1986 the NIADDK was renamed the National Institute of Diabetes and Digestive and Kidney Diseases (NIDDK).

The NIDDK is located at the NIH headquarters. The NIH is located at Building 31, Room 9A04 Center Drive, MSC 2560, Bethesda, MD 20892-2560.

National Kidney Foundation

The National Kidney Foundation (NKF) is a nonprofit foundation with the stated mission of preventing kidney and urinary tract diseases, improving the well-being of individuals affected by these diseases, and increasing the availability of organs for transplantation. The foundation states six goals: to educate the public, support research, expand patient services, provide educational opportunities for professionals, influence health policy, and raise funds.

The NKF was founded in 1950. Kidney diseases include kidney infection, the most common kidney disease, which can also involve infection of the urinary tract and can lead to kidney failure. Other diseases of the body, such as high blood pressure and diabetes, can damage the kidneys. Cysts, kidney stones, and tumors can damage the kidneys, and kidney disorders can also result from birth defects, injuries, poisoning, or from certain medications.

Some kidney patients have their diseased kidneys replaced by a transplant. Because people can function with one kidney, some patients receive a replacement organ from a close relative. However, most transplant organs come from victims of accidental death.

The NKF works to increase the number of organs available for transplant through such efforts as their sponsorship of the Olympic-style games for transplant recipients, distributing donor cards, and counseling donor families in their grief.

The NKF gives monetary grants to physicians and scientists involved in research of kidney disease. The foundation offers free health screenings, rehabilitation programs for recovering kidney patients, support for patients and families, summer camps for children with dialysis, and financial aid for patients.

The NKF publishes *Advances in Renal Replacement Therapy,* a quarterly journal, and the *American Journal of Kidney Diseases,* a monthly.

The National Kidney Foundation is headquartered at 30 E. 33rd Street, Suite 1100, New York, NY 10016. They can be reached by phone at 800-622-9010 or by e-mail at info@kidney.org. Additional information, including the addresses of branch offices, can be obtained through the NKF web site: www.kidney.org.

National Native American AIDS Prevention Center

The National Native American AIDS Prevention Center is a network of Native Americans with the stated mission of stopping the spread of HIV and related diseases among American Indians, Alaska Natives, and Native Hawaiians, and improving the quality of life for members of their communities who are affected by HIV/AIDS (human immunodeficiency virus/acquired immunodeficiency syndrome). The network works to eliminate sexually transmitted diseases and tuberculosis and seeks to improve Native American health status through empowerment and self-determination. The organization acts as a resource to native communities and supports community efforts by providing education and information services. The center also maintains a speakers' bureau and compiles statistics.

The National Native American AIDS Prevention Center was founded in 1987. Directors of the organization include people with HIV, tribal officials, public health professionals, health care providers, and substance abuse program administrators.

A primary goal of the National Native American AIDS Prevention Center is to establish working agreements with local service providers that help

HIV-infected Native Americans gain access to services. The network helps people find culturally familiar resources such as those using Native American spirituality and traditional healing. The network also offers cultural awareness training to service providers. The National Native American AIDS Prevention Center works in urban areas and on reservations.

The National Native American AIDS Prevention Center is headquartered at 436 14th Street, Suite 1020, Oakland, CA 94612. They can be reached by phone at 510-444-2051 or by e-mail at information@nnaapc.org. Additional information can be obtained through the National Native American AIDS Prevention Center's web site: www.nnaapc.org.

National Organization for Victim Assistance

The National Organization for Victim Assistance (NOVA) is a nonprofit organization that seeks to promote rights and services for victims of crime and crisis. Members include victim and witness assistance programs, criminal justice professionals, mental health professionals, researchers, former crime victims and survivors, and others committed to the concerns of victim rights and services.

NOVA was founded in 1975. In its role as advocate for victims, NOVA succeeded in such efforts as greatly expanding the number of victim compensation programs in the United States, so that by 1998 each state had such a program. In addition, NOVA helped write the Anti-Terrorism Act, enacted after the bombing of the Murrah Federal Building in Oklahoma City, which allowed the Office for Victims of Crime in the U.S. Department of Justice to use federal funds to help victims of terrorism and mass violence. NOVA also helped draft and pass the federal Victims of Crime Act of 1984. In its first twelve years, the Crime Victims Fund, based on the act, transferred about $2.2 billion in federal criminal fines to state compensation and local assistance programs. NOVA also helped pass the Violence Against Women Act.

NOVA provides direct services to victims through a twenty-four-hour toll-free crisis line and community crisis response teams. They assist professional colleagues through training and educational programs.

The organization's mailing address is 1730 Park Road NW, Washington, DC 20010. NOVA can be reached by phone at 202-232-6682 or 800-TRY-NOVA, or by e-mail at nova@try-nova.org. Additional information can be obtained through the NOVA web site: www.try-nova.org.

National SIDS/Infant Death Resource Center

The National SIDS/Infant Death Resource Center (NSIDRC) provides information and technical assistance on sudden infant death syndrome, also called SIDS or crib death, and related topics. Sudden infant death syndrome is the death of an apparently healthy baby under one year of age, the cause of which is unknown. In most cases, the baby is found dead a few hours after being put to bed. Even following an autopsy, a death scene investigation, and a thorough look at the baby's medical history, the cause of death cannot be found. In many countries SIDS is one of the leading causes of infant death.

The NSIDRC was founded in 1980 and was sponsored by the Maternal and Child Health Bureau (MCHB) of the U.S. Department of Health and Human Services.

NSIDRC seeks to promote understanding of SIDS and to provide comfort to those affected by SIDS. NSIDRC works with policymakers, parents, researchers, educators, medical and legal professionals, care providers, and counselors. NSIDRC's products and services include information sheets and other publications. NSIDRC also maintains a database of research and public awareness materials. NSIDRC distributes informational materials for the National Institute of Child Health and Human Development.

The National SIDS/Infant Death Resource Center is headquartered at 2070 Chain Bridge Road, Suite 450, Vienna, VA 22182. They can be reached by phone at 703-821-8955 or 703-821-2098, or by e-mail address at sids@circlesolutions.com. Additional information can be obtained through the NSIDRC web site: www.sidscenter.org.

National Stroke Association

The National Stroke Association (NSA) is a nonprofit organization dedicated to issues concerning strokes, including prevention, treatment, rehabilitation, and research.

Stroke is a leading cause of death in the United States. Strokes are usually caused by blood clots that block circulation to the brain. People at risk of stroke include those with high blood pressure, diabetes, high cholesterol levels, and a smoking habit. Depending on what area of the brain is affected, stroke victims may lose function of various parts of their bodies. Recovery usually includes professional rehabilitation services.

The National Stroke Association was founded in 1984. Soon after, the NSA produced a statement of guidelines for stroke prevention, published in the *Journal of the American Medical Association*.

The NSA acts as a resource for stroke victims and their families as well as health care professionals and health care institutions. The association works to prevent stroke through a number of programs, offering educational materials and assistance in the development of stroke support groups.

The National Stroke Association seeks to help create universal standards of care for stroke victims. The NSA promotes guidelines for American hospitals and works to keep health insurance reimbursement levels commensurate with increasing health care costs. The association works to place the problem of stroke on the national agenda as a top funding priority, collaborating with key organizations, institutions, and agencies throughout the United States on this and other goals.

The National Stroke Association is headquartered at 9707 E. Easter Lane, Englewood, CO 80112. They can be reached by phone at 800-STROKES. Additional information can be obtained through the NSA web site: www.stroke.org.

National Women's Health Resource Center

The National Women's Health Resource Center (NWHRC) is a nonprofit organization that aims to help women educate themselves about female health topics. The organization declares its dedication to helping women make informed decisions about their health and encouraging women to embrace healthy lifestyles to promote wellness and prevent disease. NWHRC works with leading health care experts and organizations to develop health materials specifically for women. The NWHRC began in 1988.

The center works to provide health care professionals with additional resources for their patients. NWHRC staff and its Women's Health Advisory Council, a group of health experts, seek to provide professional perspective and commentary on women's health issues.

Through partnerships with health care, education, and advocacy organizations and government agencies, the NWHRC tries to promote timely issues concerning women's health. The NWHRC also seeks partnerships with such commercial entities as pharmaceutical and managed care companies, hospitals and other health systems, corporations, and media establishments. The NWHRC sponsors national public education initiatives, such as campaigns to educate women about contraception, menopause, heart disease, and osteoporosis.

The NWHRC produces a number of publications on a variety of women's health topics, including *The Book of Women's Health,* a home reference source. Its newsletter, the "National Women's Health Report," presents an in-depth review of a featured health topic each issue. The NWHRC also seeks to supply media sources with credible health information. The center maintains a database of nationwide health resources as well as a web site intended to be a full resource for women's health.

The National Women's Health Resource Center is headquartered at 120 Albany Street, Suite 820, New Brunswick, NJ 08901. They can be reached by phone at 877-986-9472 or by e-mail at info@healthywomen.org. Additional information can be obtained through the NWHRC web site: www.healthywomen.org.

Omega: The Journal of Death and Dying

Omega: The Journal of Death and Dying is a peer-refereed journal that features articles about terminal illness, bereavement, mourning, the process of dying, funeral customs, and suicide. The journal accepts contributions from professionals in universities, hospitals, clinics, retirement homes, suicide prevention centers, funeral homes, and others concerned with thanatology, the study of death.

Omega is affiliated with the Association for Death Education Counseling (ADEC), a multidisciplinary, professional nonprofit organization dedicated to promoting excellence in death education, bereavement counseling, and care of the dying. ADEC works to promote and share research, theories, and practice in dying, death, and bereavement and to provide a forum for professionals to advance the body of knowledge and promote practical applications of theory in these areas.

The journal seeks to meet the needs of clinicians, social workers, and health professionals who must deal with problems in crisis management—for example, terminal illness, fatal accidents, catastrophe, suicide, and bereavement. *Omega* covers topics in the fields of psychology, sociology, medicine, anthropology, law, education, history, and literature.

Omega: The Journal of Death and Dying is published by the Baywood Publishing Company, located at 26 Austin Avenue, Box 337, Amityville, NY 11701. They can be reached by phone at 800-638-7819 or by e-mail at info@baywood.com. Additional information can be obtained through the Baywood Publishing Company web site: www.baywood.com.

Oncology Nursing Society

The Oncology Nursing Society (ONS) is an organization of registered nurses and other health care professionals dedicated to excellence in caring for cancer patients. ONS states its vision as leading the transformation of cancer care through initiating and actively supporting educational, legislative, and public awareness efforts to improve the treatment of people with cancer.

ONS's stated mission is to promote excellence in oncology nursing and quality cancer care. It seeks to do this by providing nurses and other health care professionals with access to the highest quality educational programs, cancer-care resources, research, and support networks. ONS works with many other nursing and health-related organizations throughout the world to educate professionals and promote information sharing among nurses. The society also seeks to make the issue of cancer care a priority on the legislative and policymaking agenda.

ONS began with the First National Cancer Nursing Conference in 1973. In 1974, after a group of nurses attended a nursing session at a major cancer conference, it gathered names of more interested nurses and initiated a newsletter, which later became the *Oncology Nursing Forum*. The society was officially incorporated in 1975. The society publishes two journals, *Oncology Nursing Forum,* the official journal of the ONS, and *Clinical Journal of Oncology Nursing*.

The Oncology Nursing Society is headquartered at 501 Holiday Drive, Pittsburgh, PA 15220-2749. They can be reached by phone at 412-921-7373 or by e-mail at customer.service@ons.org. Additional information can be obtained through the ONS web site: www.ons.org.

Palliative Care Australia

Palliative Care Australia is a key organization for palliative care in Australia, whose stated goal is to work toward the relief of pain and suffering of dying people and the provision of the care they need. Palliative Care Australia defines hospice and palliative care as "a concept of care which provides coordinated medical, nursing and allied services for people who are terminally ill, delivered where possible in the environment of the person's choice, and which provides physical, psychological, emotional and spiritual support for patients, and support for patients' families and friends."

Palliative Care Australia began in 1990 as the Australian Association for Hospice and Palliative Care, Inc. The organization sprung out of an affiliation of state palliative care associations who first came together at the Australian National Hospice Palliative Care Conference held in Adelaide in 1990.

Palliative Care Australia's aim is to provide a national forum for the exchange of ideas and information on matters relating to hospice and palliative care and to encourage the spread of information to the general community and to professional, paraprofessional, and volunteer caregivers through education and community awareness programs. It seeks to consult with government and health authorities on the needs of people with progressive and terminal illnesses and their families and caretakers. Palliative Care Australia advises hospice and palliative care organizations throughout Australia, assisting in the development of appropriate standards for hospice and palliative care in the country.

Additional information can be obtained through the Palliative Care Australia web site: www.pallcare.org.au.

Partnership for Caring: America's Voices for the Dying

Partnership for Caring: America's Voices for the Dying is a national nonprofit organization that brings together individuals and organizations in a collaborative effort to improve how people die in American society. Among other services, Partnership for Caring operates the only national crisis and informational hotline dealing with end-of-life issues. The organization also provides state-specific living wills and medical powers of attorney.

Partnership for Caring is devoted to raising consumer expectations for excellent end-of-life care and increasing demand for such care. It is the only end-of-life organization that puts individuals and organizations and consumers and professionals together to create a combined effort that insists that society improves how it cares for dying people and their loved ones.

In 2000 Choice In Dying, an organization dedicated to making advance directives available, became Partnership for Caring: America's Voices for the Dying, which broadened its scope.

Partnership for Caring promotes a society in which death and dying are respected as significant life-cycle events. High-quality, complete palliative care, including hospice, would be assured. Support for the tasks required to achieve a satisfying level of life completion and closure would be provided for dying people and their loved ones.

The Partnership for Caring hotline number is 800-989-9455. People can contact the Partnership for Caring office if they need assistance regarding a specific end-of-life situation, to speak with legal staff, to obtain information on living wills and medical power of attorney, or to speak with a representative about publications or becoming a partner.

Partnership for Caring is headquartered at 1620 Eye Street NW, Suite 202, Washington, DC 20007. They can be reached by e-mail at pfc@partnershipforcaring.org. Additional information can be obtained through the Partnership for Caring web site: www.partnershipforcaring.org.

Project on Death in America

The Project on Death in America (PDIA) works to promote a better understanding of dying and to transform the culture and experience of dying and bereavement in the United States through research, scholarship, the humanities, and the arts. Its claims to foster innovations in the provision of care, public education, professional education, and public policy. The PDIA seeks to help transform the culture surrounding death.

The PDIA is part of the Open Society Institute, which describes itself as "a private operating and grantmaking foundation that seeks to promote the development and maintenance of open societies around the world by supporting a range of programs in the areas of educational, social, and legal reform, and by encouraging alternative approaches to complex and often controversial issues." It was established in 1993 and is part of the Soros foundations network, a network of organizations created by the wealthy philanthropist George Soros. In 1994 Soros founded the Project on Death in America. He decided to give funds toward the problem of dying because of his own family experiences with death. The death of his parents "made me realize that there is a need to better understand the experience of dying," he said. The project seeks to encourage broader philanthropic support in the field of palliative care. The PDIA awards grants to academic professionals and others who are studying issues of death and dying.

Project on Death in America is headquartered at Open Society Institute, 400 W. 59th Street, New York, NY 10019. They can be reached by phone at 212-548-1334. Additional information can be obtained through the Soros/Project on Death in America web site: www.soros.org/death.

SHARE Pregnancy and Infant Loss Support

SHARE Pregnancy and Infant Loss Support is a nonprofit group with the stated mission of serving those whose lives have been touched by the tragic death of a baby through miscarriage, stillbirth, or newborn death.

The group's support includes emotional, physical, spiritual, and social healing. The secondary stated purpose of SHARE is to provide information, education, and resources pertaining to the needs and rights of bereaved parents and siblings. Its objective is to aid all of those in supportive roles, including family, friends, employers, church members, caregivers, and others.

SHARE began in 1977 at St. John's Hospital in Springfield, Illinois. The first support group met after one bereaved parent and several hospital staffers worked together. SHARE eventually grew to over 130 chapters internationally. SHARE helps form local groups whose activities include holding monthly support meetings, providing lists of resources, developing keepsake kits, and developing parent-to-parent support.

SHARE publishes a number of publications, including *Caring Notes,* a quarterly newsletter. All information packets, correspondence, and support is free of charge for bereaved parents.

A major SHARE fundraising effort is soliciting for "love gifts," which are monetary donations given in honor of someone or as a memorial to a baby, relative, or friend. People may send donations to National Share Office, 300 First Capitol Drive Street, Charles, MO 63301-2893. SHARE can also be reached by phone at 800-821-6819 or by e-mail at share@nationalshareoffice.com. Additional information can be obtained through the SHARE web site: www.nationalshareoffice.com.

Society of Military Widows

The Society of Military Widows is a national nonprofit organization whose stated purpose is to benefit widows of members of all branches of the uniformed services of the United States whose husbands died either during active service or following retirement. The society provides moral support, advice, and referrals to help the widows of career military members return to normal living. The organization seeks to educate the American public concerning the problems and needs of military widows. It works for fair legislation and survivor benefit programs, monitoring legislation and programs affecting military widows in the U.S. Congress, Department of Defense, and Veterans Administration.

The society was founded in 1968 by Theresa Alexander to serve the needs of women whose military husbands died. In 1984 the society affiliated with the National Association for Uniformed Services, which represents a broad spectrum of military-related interests, in order to create a strong, unified legislative force.

The society publishes a quarterly newsletter, the *National Association of Military Widows,* and hosts an annual convention for its members. Widows eligible for membership must possess a valid URW (un-remarried widow) military identification card.

The Society of Military Widows is headquartered at 5535 Hempstead Way, Springfield, VA 22151. For questions related to a spouse's death or about rights and benefits as a military survivor, the society can be reached by phone at 800-842-3451, ext. 3009 or by e-mail at benefits@militarywidows.org. Additional information can be obtained through the Society of Military Widows web site: www.militarywidows.org.

Suicide and Life-Threatening Behavior

Suicide and Life-Threatening Behavior is the official journal of the American Association of Suicidology (AAS), an organization of individuals and groups interested in the study of suicide prevention and life-threatening behavior. These members include psychologists, psychiatrists, social workers, nurses, health educators, physicians, directors of suicide prevention centers, clergy, and others from various disciplines.

The journal began in the early 1970s, and is published by Guilford Publications, known for its publications concerned with psychology, psychiatry, and the behavioral sciences. The journal is edited by Morton M. Silverman, M.D., from the University of Chicago, and includes scholarly research and clinical experience.

Suicide and Life-Threatening Behavior reaches professionals worldwide and employs an interdisciplinary approach, covering biological, statistical, psychological, and sociological approaches to suicidology. Article titles of the journal have included "Collaborating to Prevent Suicide: A Clinical-Research Perspective," "Suicide Among Adolescents and Young Adults: A Cross-National Comparison of 34 Countries," "Suicidality Patterns and Sexual Orientation-Related Factors among Lesbian, Gay, and Bisexual Youths," "Stressful Life Events and Impulsiveness in Failed Suicide," "Early Suicide Following Discharge from a Psychiatric Hospital," "Loneliness in Relation to Suicide Ideation and Parasuicide: A Population-Wide Study," "An Epidemiological Profile of Suicides in Beijing, China," and "Are UN Peacekeepers at Risk for Suicide?"

Guilford Publications is located at 72 Spring Street, New York, NY 10012. They can be reached by phone at 800-365-7006 or by e-mail at info@guilford.com. Issues of the journal can be viewed on the Guilford Publications web site: www.guilford.com. The AAS is headquartered at 4201 Connecticut Avenue NW, Suite 408, Washington,

DC 20008. Additional information can be obtained through the AAS web site: www.suicidology.org.

The Compassionate Friends

The Compassionate Friends (TCF) is a nonprofit, self-help support organization for bereaved parents. The stated mission of TCF is to help families resolve grief resulting from the death of a child of any age. The organization also provides information for friends and family of the bereaved. The group has no religious affiliation or membership dues. TCF does not participate in legislative or political controversy and operates primarily through local chapters.

The Compassionate Friends was founded in 1969 in Coventry, England, following the deaths of two young boys when a hospital chaplain introduced the two sets of parents. They invited other newly bereaved parents to join them and soon organized as a self-help group. The chaplain helped develop other chapters around the world. The Compassionate Friends was incorporated in the United States as a nonprofit organization in 1978. There are now TCF chapters in every state, totaling almost 600, and hundreds of chapters in Canada, Australia, Great Britain, and other countries.

TCF offers help to bereaved siblings. Since many areas do not have TCF groups, the Sibling Forum is available online for siblings from all over the world. Interested siblings need to request the password by e-mail from rep@compassionatefriends.org.

The Compassionate Friends publishes a national magazine, *We Need Not Walk Alone,* available by subscription. They also publish brochures such as "When a Child Dies . . . TCF Can Help," "Caring for Surviving Children," "Surviving Your Child's Suicide," "When a Brother or Sister Dies," and "The Death of an Adult Child." The organization hosts an annual national conference in the United States.

The Compassionate Friends can be reached at P.O. Box 3696, Oak Brook, IL 60522-3696. Chapter information can be obtained by phone at 630-990-0010 or 877-969-0010. Information about Canadian chapters can be obtained by e-mail at TCFCanada@aol.com. Additional information can be obtained through The Compassionate Friends web site: www.compassionatefriends.org.

The National Organization of Parents of Murdered Children

The National Organization of Parents of Murdered Children (POMC) is a self-help organization that seeks to assist families that have had a child who has been murdered. The issues that the group involves itself with include keeping murderers in prison, assisting families with unsolved cases, promoting murder prevention programs, providing emotional support for families, and providing information and advocacy for any survivor of a homicide victim.

Parents of Murdered Children was founded in 1978, and offers support and friendship to those who have experienced the violent death of a family member or friend. It seeks to help survivors return to physical and emotional health. POMC also works to increase public awareness of the problems faced by those who survive a homicide victim. It provides information about the grieving process as it pertains to murder as well as information about the criminal justice system as it pertains to survivors of a homicide victim.

POMC establishes self-help and support groups that meet regularly. It distributes literature and provides guest speakers for organizations. It has created prevention programs to help stop violence. In its newsletter, POMC includes a schedule of parole hearings for prisoners serving homicide sentences.

Parents of Murdered Children is headquartered at 100 E. 8th Street, B-41, Cincinnati, OH 45202. They can be reached by phone at 888-818-POMC or by e-mail at natlpomc@aol.com. Additional information can be obtained through the POMC web site: www.pomc.com.

United Network for Organ Sharing

The United Network for Organ Sharing (UNOS) is a nonprofit organization that maintains the organ transplant waiting list for the entire United States. This is mandated by law and under contract with the U.S. Department of Health and Human Services. UNOS matches organ donors to waiting recipients 24 hours a day, 365 days a year. Every transplant program, organ procurement organization, and tissue typing laboratory in the United States belongs to the UNOS network.

UNOS was founded in 1984 and is responsible for developing policies governing the transplant community. This work is done by its forty-member board of directors, comprised of medical professionals, transplant recipients, and donor family members.

UNOS is responsible for monitoring every organ match to ensure that it conforms to UNOS policy. UNOS members work together to develop equitable policies that give all patients a fair chance at receiving the organ they need. Recipients are not discriminated against on the basis of age, gender, race, lifestyle, or financial and social status.

All patients accepted onto a transplant program's waiting list are registered with UNOS, where a centralized computer network links all organ procurement organizations and transplant centers. UNOS maintains the database that contains all transplant data.

When an organ becomes available, UNOS coordinates the surgical teams that are involved. The computerized matching process locates best possible matches between donor organs and the patients who need them. The final decision rests with the patient's transplant team. If they decide the patient cannot use the organ for any number of medical reasons, the organ is offered to the next patient on the list.

The United Network for Organ Sharing is headquartered at 1100 Boulders Parkway, Suite 500, P.O. Box 13770, Richmond, VA 23225. Additional information can be obtained through the UNOS web site: www.unos.org.

World Health Organization

The World Health Organization (WHO) is an agency of the United Nations (UN) that assists nations throughout the world to build better health systems. WHO establishes standards for many goods including food and medicines. It also creates standards for some medical procedures and environmental health. A major goal of WHO is prevention of disease. Toward this end, the agency works with governments to provide safe drinking water, adequate sewage disposal, and immunization against childhood diseases. WHO identifies important research goals and organizes researchers all over the world to achieve these goals. It helps name and classify diseases.

WHO was founded in 1948, three years after the United Nations formed, and has its headquarters in Geneva, Switzerland. It also has six regional offices in various parts of the world. WHO has about 190 member nations. Its main branches are the World Health Assembly, the Executive Board, and the Secretariat. The World Health Assembly meets once a year and consists of delegates from all of the member nations. The Executive Board advises the World Health Assembly and implements its policies.

WHO has library services that provide users with access to international health, medical, and development information resources. These are available to WHO headquarters, regions, and country offices, ministries of health and other government offices, health workers in member states, other UN and international agencies, and diplomatic missions. WHO library programs help regions and developing countries achieve self-sufficiency in providing information services to the health sector.

Additional information can be obtained through the WHO web site: www.who.int.

INDEX

Page numbers in **boldface** indicate main article on subject.
Those in *italics* indicate illustrations.

B

C

D

E

F

G

H

I

J

K

L

M

N

P

Q

R

S

T

U

V

W

X

Y

Z

ISBN 0-02-865691-1
90000
9 780028 656915